Shavelings in Death Camps

Shavelings in Death Camps

A Polish Priest's Memoir of Imprisonment by the Nazis, 1939–1945

FR. HENRYK MARIA MALAK

Translated by Bożenna J. Tucker *and* Thomas R. Tucker

McFarland & Company, Inc., Publishers
Jefferson, North Carolina, and London

All drawings and photographs have been reproduced from the first and second editions of *Klechy w obozach Śmierci* by Fr. Henryk Maria Malak (Schwäbisch Gmünd, Germany: Press of Fr. Ignacy Rabsztyn, 1948; London: Veritas, 1961).

Frontispiece: Fr. Henryk Maria Malak.

LIBRARY OF CONGRESS CATALOGUING-IN-PUBLICATION DATA

Malak, Henry M.
[Klechy w obozach smierci. English]
Shavelings in death camps : a Polish priest's memoir of imprisonment by the Nazis, 1939–1945 / Fr. Henryk Maria Malak ; translated by Bożenna J. Tucker and Thomas R. Tucker.
      p.   cm.
Includes bibliographical references and index.

ISBN 978-0-7864-7057-0

softcover : acid free paper ∞

1. Malak, Henry M.   2. World War, 1939–1945 — Prisoners and prisons, German.   3. World War, 1939–1945 — Concentration camps — Germany.   4. Dachau (Concentration camp)   5. Stutthof (Concentration camp)   6. Sachsenhausen (Concentration camp)   7. World War, 1939–1945 — Personal narratives, Polish.   8. Concentration camp inmates — Germany — Biography.   9. Catholic Church — Poland — Clergy — Biography.   10. World War, 1939–1945 — Religious aspects — Catholic Church.   I. Title.
D805.G3M2913 2012   940.53'18092 — dc23   [B]   2012029281

BRITISH LIBRARY CATALOGUING DATA ARE AVAILABLE

©2012 Henryk Maria Malak. All rights reserved

No part of this book may be reproduced or transmitted in any form or by any means, electronic or mechanical, including photocopying or recording, or by any information storage and retrieval system, without permission in writing from the publisher.

Front cover: Fr. Maksymilian Kolbe (drawn by the author)

Manufactured in the United States of America

*McFarland & Company, Inc., Publishers
Box 611, Jefferson, North Carolina 28640
www.mcfarlandpub.com*

To my colleagues whose ashes were scattered about crematoriums by the wind, I dedicate this work. — Fr. Henryk Maria Malak

Table of Contents

Translators' Preface 1
Introduction to the 1961 Edition 3

1. The Merciless Summer of 1939 5
2. And That Day Arrived 8
3. "Invitation" to a Meeting 19
4. Górna Grupa 26
5. To Gdańsk 32
6. In the Hell of Stutthof 37
7. The Butchers of Stutthof 43
8. *Miserere* 49
9. A Hunger for Freedom 57
10. Holy Week 1940 61
11. Ethnic Germans 66
12. Grenzdorf 71
13. Here You Have to Work 76
14. Satan's Program 82
15. What Will Become of Us? 84
16. Sachsenhausen 88
17. The First Days 93
18. No Changes in Sachsenhausen .. 104
19. One-Eyed Fritz 108
20. In the Valley of Jehoshaphat ... 118
21. A Chapel in the Death Camp ... 122
22. The Stream of Time Was Flowing 129
23. Roll Call 136
24. The Last Days 142
25. A Holy Shipment 144
26. The Sanitarium in Dachau 148
27. Snow 158
28. The Year 1941 Approaches 164
29. When on Candlemas Day All Was Covered with Snow 169
30. Allow Us to Work 177
31. The Second Freiland 186
32. "Joyful Privileges" 197
33. The Reverend Bishop 206
34. September 15, 1941 211
35. The Fence Fell and with It the Privileges 216
36. A Memorable Transport 223
37. Zdzich's Hanka 228
38. Now You'll Rot in Dachau! 231
39. The Mountain Girl with Little Thérèse's Face 234
40. The Dismal Beginning of 1942 .. 245
41. Holy Week 1942 252
42. Polish Priests Build a Crematorium 259
43. Three Hundred Polish Priests to the Gas Chambers 263
44. Guinea Pigs 269
45. At the Turning Point of 1942 ... 276
46. My Mother's Brother 281
47. They Would Have Survived... .. 285
48. Autumn of 1942 291
49. Goebbels and the Catholic Nuns 296
50. The Year 1943 299

51. At the Turning Point of 1943 ... 305
52. Autumn of 1943 312
53. The Nazi Nero 322
54. Spring of 1944 327
55. The Fruitful Summer of 1944 ... 332
56. The Nun Barbara 340
57. A Diary 344
58. At the Dawn of 1945 351
59. The Last Month 357
60. The Last Sunday 376

Epilogue 389

Chapter Notes 395

Sources 401

Index 405

Translators' Preface

Shavelings in Death Camps (*Klechy w obozach śmierci*) by Fr. Henryk Maria Malak (1912–1987) is the story of Polish Catholic priests imprisoned during World War II. The author, who spent more than five years in these camps, begins his narrative before the war breaks out in 1939 and ends it with an epilogue about events right after liberation in 1945. Through his eyes we witness the German invasion and occupation of Poland, followed by the priests' arrest and brutal treatment in the Stutthof, Grenzdorf, Sachsenhausen and Dachau concentration camps.

Few people are aware of the suffering endured by these priests. Moreover, in comparison with what little is available on the topic, this memoir has the virtue of being a firsthand account written during and soon after the war. The final five chapters, in fact, are taken from a diary kept secretly by the author in the weeks before liberation. By 1948 he had published a first edition of *Klechy* in Germany. It would seem that an English-language version of Fr. Malak's book is long overdue.

Our translation is based on the second edition (London: Veritas, 1961), which retains the immediacy and vivid description of the earlier work. In this edition the author adds input from fellow prisoners, material from sources related to the war, and further reflection on all that happened. He skillfully frames the central narrative with events taking place outside the barbed-wire enclosure. But since much of the historical framework is already well known, we have chosen to omit two chapters and several shorter sections from our translation. Everything essential to the priests' story remains intact.

Fr. Malak wrote his memoir in order to keep alive the memory of his companions in suffering. That purpose was furthered on June 13, 1999, when Pope John Paul II beatified 108 Polish martyrs killed during World War II by the Nazis. At least a dozen of those martyrs were priests mentioned in this book. Again, on May 7, 2000, in a homily about the thousands of Catholic priests imprisoned by the Nazis, the Pope urged, "They must not be forgotten!" This book contains many names of Polish priests. When we come across a litany of their names, Fr. Malak wants us to remember them as real people, not just statistics.

It seems fitting here to add a few notes in memory of Fr. Malak himself. The following incident from 1940 is not mentioned in the memoir, but was witnessed by Fr. Dobromir Ziarniak, a fellow prisoner at the Sachsenhausen camp:

> For staining the wall of their barracks, the prisoners in Fr. Malak's block faced the threat of "sport," a punishment which for many would amount to a death sentence. At that point Fr. Malak offered himself, expressing his readiness to take the punishment for them all. Moved by this gesture, the capo spared the entire barracks from the brutal "sport."

After U.S. troops liberated Dachau, Fr. Malak volunteered to care for sick colleagues. He became ill himself and was diagnosed with typhus. Upon recovering, he undertook pastoral work at a succession of displaced person (DP) camps in Germany, most notably at Heilbronn, where he served as pastor from August 1947 until October 1950. He was a charismatic speaker with a deep and resonant voice. Every Sunday Mass that he celebrated was filled to overflowing. Thousands of his countrymen were inspired by his faith, patriotism, and concern for their welfare. Fr. Malak was a gifted artist. At Heilbronn he supervised the transformation of a horse stable into a chapel, carving many of the altarpieces himself. He also did the drawings for his first edition of *Klechy*, several of which are included in this English-language version.

Following disbandment of the Heilbronn DP camp, Fr. Malak accepted a position with the Franciscan Press at the Assumption of the Blessed Virgin Mary monastery in Pulaski, Wisconsin. He began working there in November 1950. Soon he was also writing and delivering religious broadcasts over radio. Through the years he conducted more than 300 retreats in the U.S. and Canada, regularly sending reports of his activity to Stefan Cardinal Wyszyński, the Polish Primate. In 1975 Cardinal Wyszyński named Fr. Malak an honorary counselor and paid him this tribute:

> The deeds of your life, marked by sacrifice and the cross of prison-camp torments and by uncommonly intense and diverse pastoral work, embody and reveal those most wonderful powers which the Heavenly Father calls forth in the human soul when that soul surrenders completely to the love of God's Work.

Fr. Malak never returned to Poland. He died on June 19, 1987, and was buried in Lemont, Illinois, in the cemetery of the Franciscan Sisters of Chicago.

We would like to acknowledge here those who helped us in so many ways. Our heartfelt thanks to Dr. John Pilch, Michael Glazier and Maria Nazarczuk for their support and advice; to Fr. Christopher Begg of Catholic University, who proofread the manuscript; to Professor Thaddeus Piotrowski, eminent author of works on Polish history; to Rachel Jenkins, who prepared our illustrations for publication; to our son, Mark Tucker, for his technical support; to Nancy Bagnasco, librarian at Madonna University, for access to a rare first edition of *Klechy*; to Brother Jude Lustyk, archivist of the Franciscan Friars in Wisconsin, for a photograph of Fr. Malak's carved crucifix and a photograph of seminarian Henryk Malak with Fr. Maksymilian Kolbe. We want also to thank Karen Hitcho, Deirdre Barcomb, and Mathew Fenton for their efforts on our behalf. Very special thanks go to Eva Behrens, who inspired us by her dedication to Fr. Malak and her faith in our work. We're deeply grateful to all of the above for help so generously given.

Note on Illustrations

All drawings and photographs have been reproduced from the first and second editions of *Klechy w obozach śmierci* by Fr. Henryk Maria Malak (Schwäbisch Gmünd, Germany: Press of Fr. Ignacy Rabsztyn, 1948; London: Veritas, 1961). Several of these images had a faded appearance in the original and, unfortunately, remain substandard despite efforts to improve their quality. We include them, nevertheless, for their potential interest to the reader.

Bożenna J. Tucker and Thomas R. Tucker

Introduction to the 1961 Edition

The first edition of *Shavelings* came into being in former Nazi barracks, on scraps of paper fished out of trash bins, during nights stolen between days of unique pastoral work in camps of the liberated. Printed by a German publisher in Schwäzbish Gmünd near Stuttgart in 1948 on newsprint, using a letter font without Polish diacritics, this very modest printing of several thousand copies went out among exile masses, reaching Poland together with repatriates. It had the merit, therefore, of being among the first works to describe experiences of Polish priests in German concentration camps.

The second edition of *Shavelings* appears today, in the fifteenth year following liberation from the Dachau camp. As it turned out, this work was acknowledged by the German justice system as a document bearing upon compensation issues, and it should retain this character. That is why I eliminate any kind of fictional plot from it. Since the work is to remain a document of those days, it presents only facts, contains only real names, and avoids drawing conclusions, which are left to the reader and researcher.

It would not be difficult today, following the publication of extensive writings and studies on the subject of concentration camps, to give this book the character of a scholarly work based on sources, but it would then lose precisely its character as a "living" document. Since I wish to retain this quality, I have also kept the second edition in the form of a diary, trying to recreate the most faithful picture possible of those times and experiences. This small volume, a handful of personal memories from one out of thousands of Polish priests and former prisoners, claims only to be one source, one little brick, in the monument to Polish martyrdom which will be erected someday by a historian called to the task.

I hope with this explanation to overcome the critical remarks of colleagues imprisoned with me who faulted the first edition for being limited to personal memories. For I consider this to be the most valuable aspect of my book since it is the most authentic and factual trait. I have no official assignment and no material resources to do a comprehensive study on the subject of Polish priests in concentration camps. Just as the first edition saw the light of day thanks to denying myself U.S. food rations, so the second goes to the reader thanks to personal savings of meager pennies. The only "capital" supporting this second effort is my fond memory of colleagues whose ashes were scattered about crematoriums by the wind. I therefore dedicate this work to them, without caring too much what else might be said about it ... by the living.

ks. Henryk Malak

Seminary of Christ the King in West Chicago, U.S.A.,
29 April 1960, the fifteenth anniversary of liberation from Dachau

1

The Merciless Summer of 1939

One always remembers his first love. At least that's what the old adage says. The first love of every priest is his first assignment in apostolic work. For me, this first love was and will remain old Września. It's the same town that recalled the days of the 1848 uprising, the same town that lived through the momentous days of the Września children's strikes. Royal Września, with its ancient parish church comfortably nestled in the town center, with the little old wooden Church of the Holy Cross dozing among ancient oaks on the Poznań road. The Września of the Stablewski, Prądzyński, and Krzyżagórski families, but also the Krauz and Szelągiewicz families: the Września beating with thousands of kind hearts.

It is a generally accepted belief that the first pastor to whom the bishop assigns a young priest following ordination often has more influence on his formation than years of seminary training. The pastor in Września at that time was a priest of unusual holiness, extremely kind and with a generous heart, Father Kazimierz Kinastowski.[1] Generations of vicars who passed through the Września parish church during the long years of his administration know well how this venerable priest continued our training in the radiant warmth of his exceptional heart.

As vicars we lived in the old rectory that formerly had been used by Fr. Stablewski, later the Archbishop of Gniezno, but most of the day was spent in the parish office located in the rectory proper across from the old parish church. My colleague was Fr. Henryk Warkoczewski.[2] At that time the parish had about 16,000 souls, a third of them living in villages that circled the town. Part of the time Reverend Professor Jernajczyk, the local high-school prefect, and also Fr. Feliks Staszak, the hospital chaplain, helped us in our work. Still, ministering to this large parish overwhelmed us. Aside from normal pastoral duties, we needed also to be mindful of the prison, the nursing home, the only "Higher Dairy School" in all of Poland, and the agricultural school; moreover, a lot of time was spent on organizational life, which was unusually active in the Września parish.

In addition, our pastoral duties included the infantry regiment stationed in town. We didn't realize that only a few months separated us from events that would link us in a special way with this particular part of our work.

Then came May 1939. The world was in a state of upheaval. But did a vicar, overworked from dawn to late at night, have the time to listen to the news? We sat in the confessional until midnight or later, baptized dozens of children on Sundays, blessed newlyweds, accompanied the dead to eternal rest almost daily, visited the sick, and prepared over 500 children for first Holy Communion; we sat in the parish office for hours attending to various matters, making notes in record books, writing reports, and issuing hundreds of documents. So a few months later, when as a prisoner I was repeatedly asked the question, always spoken with hatred: "How many Germans did you murder, you Polish dog?" ...I felt a bitter taste in my mouth and painful astonishment in my soul.

But that was to occur only after a few months. In the meantime, May was displaying its charms all around us. In lovely Września park, the pride of Wielkopolska parks, nightingales sang during humid nights; ancient chestnuts glowed with flower-candles; people hurried each morning to work; the old bell from its massive tower summoned the faithful to holy Mass; children's voices, mingled with happy laughter, bubbled around school buildings; bakers, butchers, barbers and other tradesmen opened the doors to shops fresh with coolness; heavily loaded railcars clattered at the railroad station; the sugar factory puffed out clouds of steam... Thus the daily life of a small Wielkopolska town flowed on quietly. Who at that time could sense that somewhere beyond the border new markers and roadsigns were already being made and that in a few months they would be posted around this ancient Polish city, their black letters proclaiming *Wreschen!*

The fragrance of flowering chestnuts drifts in through the open window of the parish office. From the street you can hear the chatter of children returning from school. A worn pen squeaks over rough paper. All of a sudden there's a knock at the door, the door handle moves, and a pale little face, surrounded by a swirl of copper curls, appears in the opening.

"Excuse me, Reverend Father," the big blue eyes of the child are filled with a happy smile, "Auntie is asking you to dinner." Her little finger is on her lips, her face is beaming. "We're having potato pancakes today," she exclaims in one breath.

Little Halinka, the pastor's niece, is highly initiated into what her vicar uncles like or do not like. Today we're having potato pancakes!

And there were potato pancakes for dinner with jam, and little Hala got some jam on her face, and the pastor's sister, Auntie Stasia, nagged in a kindly way, and there was talk of how we (both vicars) were late with first Holy Communion preparations for our group of over 500 children, and so on. Yet somehow no one thought or talked about war. The radio station predicted beautiful weather for the following day, Fr. Warkoczewski worried that on Sunday he would be unable to attend a KSM* meeting in Psary, the pastor reminded us about an afternoon funeral, and Auntie Stasia worried that her pancakes did not come out as they should; clearly, it was because the potatoes were old. And Halinka, taking advantage of her auntie's inattention, whispered in my ear: "Tomorrow there'll be pierogi."

The border town of Września knew nothing about any diplomatic steps and endeavors, nor did hundreds of Polish cities and towns, all unaware of the threat that was already rising like a wave over the quiet homes of millions. While Auntie Stasia in the Września rectory carried on a friendly debate with little Halinka about whether tomorrow's pierogi should be filled with farmer's cheese or plums, while the vicars and pastor discussed details of the upcoming first Holy Communion, and while organist Rosiński tried to figure out how to fix a hole in the bellows of the old organ, Hitler, accompanied by Minister of Foreign Affairs von Ribbentrop and Secretary Weizsaecker, was hosting the Vatican envoy. Apostolic Nuncio Monsignor Orsenigo took away the following assurance from Hitler's residence and conveyed it to Pius XII, the Pope of peace: "I do not believe in the possibility of war. Please convey my views to His Holiness, Pius XII, and express my most sincere thanks to him for his concerns regarding world peace."[3]

Translator's note: "KSM" stands for "Catholic Youth Association," established in 1934.

On 24 August, the day after the famous Ribbentrop-Molotov Pact was signed, Pius XII addressed the entire world over Vatican radio, calling for self-control to save humanity from the impending catastrophe: "If through peace we have everything to gain, so through war we can lose everything."[4]

I heard the call of the Vicar of Christ when I was already vicar at St. Joseph's parish in Inowrocław, where I had been transferred from Września by a decree of the Bishop's Curia. At that time, however, during the week preceding the first German bombs, not only Września, not only Inowrocław, not only Bydgoszcz — where I dropped in briefly to see my parents — but probably all Poland, while believing in the possibility of war, was still hoping deep down inside that perhaps, that after all, that...

2

And That Day Arrived

The pastor at the newly organized St. Joseph parish in Inowrocław was the former prefect of the seminary in Bydgoszcz, Fr. Grzegorz Handke. A huge new church, heralded as a marvel of architecture and technology, had just been covered with a roof and was still awaiting the completion of its interior. As a result, the new parish was temporarily assigned the oldest church in Inowrocław, Saint Mary's, popularly called The Ruin. This was a Romanesque stone shrine that reportedly dated back to the time of Poland's baptism. It was there, for the time being, that we celebrated holy Mass, heard confessions, and carried out all other pastoral duties of the parish.

On the last day of August, a Thursday preceding the first Friday of September, we sat down in the confessionals as usual. There were few penitents. First, because it was the summer vacation season and the day was unusually hot; and second, because uneasiness and concern were growing in the city. Military units were passing through the streets, supply columns were rumbling, and carts were advancing in long lines. There was probably not a family in the city that didn't already feel anxious because someone close had joined the ranks. Groups of people, agitated by the ominous news, were gathering in the streets to discuss radio bulletins.

Rays of the August sun entered the church through the small Romanesque windows that were narrow like loopholes. The heavy wrought-iron gate banged shut behind the last penitent.

"Reverend Father!"—this was the usual term used by Fr. Handke in addressing the vicars—"Let's go outside. We can recite the breviary."

We go outside. The wide tops of old trees cast deep shadows over the cemetery that encircles the church. In the distance, along streets bathed in the sun's heat, there flows an unbroken stream of humanity, wheels rumble, and soldiers' boots strike the pavement.

"Reverend Pastor, it already smells a lot like war."

"Ah, Reverend Father, Reverend Father, it smells like honey, not war." He points to the old linden trees. "Recite your breviary instead of thinking such dark thoughts." Signing himself broadly with the sign of the holy cross, he sets out with open breviary down the shady path into the cemetery.

I sit on the stone bench and rest my back against the moss-covered trunk of an ancient linden tree. Industrious bees are buzzing in the broad treetop. The fragrance of the linden flowers fills the cemetery. It really does smell like honey.

Faces and masks of some old Slavic gods, chiseled in granite, look down from the stone wall of the shrine. A son of this land, Jan Kasprowicz, admired them once and described them in a legend. They were placed mostly on the north wall of the shrine since, according to the Slavs, the North was the seat of evil spirits.

And now, from the evil North, a reign of evil powers threatens this ancient Slavic land. I open my breviary. The patron saint on this day is St. Raymond, redeemer of slaves. His love of the Immaculate Virgin led him to the highest sacrifice, a martyr's sacrifice of his own life... I try to think calmly. So what if hideous masks stare down from the wall of the old Slavic shrine?

At the altar above the tabernacle, the face of the Mother of God is full of sorrow. The industrious bees buzz in the tops of the lindens. Along the streets surrounding the cemetery, under the August sun, wave after wave of exhausted people move by.

Our rectory is a good 20-minute walk from the church. We return for supper. At every step we run into one of our parishioners. They ask questions. People are frightened. Uncertainty shows on their tired faces. At the rectory disturbing news overtakes us; the radio bulletins are full of contradictions.

Pastor Handke does not lose heart, however. His optimism begins to irritate me. After supper, I slip away to my room. I am tormented by an evil foreboding.

A humid August night has fallen. The window of my room looks out onto a small courtyard, separated from the street by a mesh-wire fence. The city is filled with a troubling din, the clatter of wheels, people's footsteps and shouts. After saying my prayers, I lie down to rest but cannot sleep for a long, long time. Finally, I fall into a restless sleep full of nightmares.

Rays of the rising sun have just begun to sparkle on the golden cupola of the Jewish synagogue across from my window when I jump to my feet. I have the first Mass. It's already time to get to church. From the street you can hear activity and noisy talk, unusual for that time of day. Just as I close the entry gate to the street, old Sikorzak comes up:

"Father, war! The radio announced that at 4:40 this morning German forces crossed the Polish border!"

"Crossed the Polish border? But," I object, "there was no declaration of war."

The old man raises his trembling hands and shrugs. "No, there wasn't. But on the radio..." A military unit of cyclists passes down the street at breakneck speed. War!

As I near the church, I meet more and more groups of frightened people. "War!" Scenes from that morning remain in my memory like the fragmented tape of a horror film: wringing hands, tear-stained faces, eyes filled with terror.

In the church, a handful of the faithful, fewer than ever. I come out to celebrate Mass. The organ is silent; the organist was drafted into the military several days ago.

"*Cogitationes Cordis ejus in generatione et generationem*. These are the intentions of His Heart through generations, to save their souls from death and feed them in time of famine," I start the words of the Introit for the First Friday's Mass. How hard it is for me to concentrate. There's rumbling coming from the streets. Yes, war, and right on the first Friday of the month, the very day of the Most Sacred Heart of Jesus.

The altar boy did not show up. Attending me is a gray-haired elderly man. How his hand trembles as he hands me the cruets!

"Orate, fratres."

In the dim light of the shrine a few bowed figures stand out. No, people have not forgotten God. Fear brought on by the sudden news has simply robbed them of self-control and confused them.

"Memento, Domine ... Remember, O Lord, your servants." On the borders of Poland blood flows, family homes burn, mothers' sobs and frightened children's cries resound, and soldiers die in the field... Pain grips my heart. Among them are my brother, many relatives, friends... Remember them, O Lord... Tears well up in my throat. The bell rings in the elderly server's trembling hand.

Jesus-Host trembles in my hands suddenly grown weak. The sad face of the Mother of God looks down from the painting; from her lips an agonizing complaint seems to emerge: "For such a long time I have held up God's arm poised in punishment over the world, but you didn't care at all..." In the silence of the Elevation, a woman's fitful sob suddenly echoes, and from the streets can be heard a rumbling that grows louder and more alarming.

Holy Communion. Tearful faces are raised toward Jesus offered to them.

"The Body of our Lord Jesus Christ preserve your soul unto life everlasting."

"Amen. Let it be so," whispers the elderly server, holding the paten. I shall not forget this holy Mass as long as I live.

Oh, how slowly this day drags on. The radio is broadcasting strange bulletins, that German motorized forces are penetrating Polish territory from all sides, that the German air force is bombing cities, villages, and even smaller hamlets, and that officials are calling upon people to stay off main roads so our troops can pass. In rapid succession several officers unknown to us appear at St. Joseph's rectory and try to persuade the pastor to leave with them. He refuses with characteristic humor, which now irritates me to the core.

There is confusion throughout the city. Local officials cannot give residents any decisive guidance. The only order given is for the preparation of bomb shelters. Regiments from Inowrocław went into the field weeks ago. In their place, masses of reservists keep pouring in. The barracks are filled to the hilt, and soldiers are housed in school buildings as well. They make a strange sight: entire units are dressed in military jackets and civilian pants, or vice versa. Some are not wearing military uniforms at all. It's even worse with respect to weapons.

"The warehouses near the barracks are full of uniforms and weapons," one sergeant explains to me, "but we're waiting for orders, for instructions."

Military units are passing through the city streets. Some march in one direction, others in the opposite direction, from which the first ones came. Supply transports move along, cyclists speed ahead, a communications unit installs lines along the streets.

Evening comes at last. Several priests from the city show up at our rectory. There is speculation, there are questions, and all of it taken together adds up to a new picture of confusion.

I notice within this group the tall and well-built figure of Rev. Professor Dębski. He says little, listening intently to what others are saying, and one can see concentration on his face. But when from time to time he says something, one senses that his point of view is correct. Even the two gray-haired canons respect his opinion. Without waiting for this unplanned conference to end, I leave quietly and go to my room. I have enormous childlike faith in the protection of the Immaculate Virgin.

Unable to fall asleep, I pick up the biography of St. Bernadette. I read... What terror gripped the soul of Sister Bernadette when she saw a victorious Prussian army march onto French soil in 1870! How her poor heart trembled. A feeling of shame comes over me. Was

2. And That Day Arrived

I, a man, going to be afraid the way this woman was afraid? But there's another reason for my feeling. She had deep faith in the protection of the Immaculate. Is it possible I don't have such faith?

Saturday, 2 September. First Saturday of the month, the Saturday of the Immaculate Heart of the Mother of God. Since early morning we've been sitting in the confessionals of St. Barbara's garrison church, hearing soldiers' confessions. A few priests from the city are helping us. There are such long lines, however, that we probably won't finish until tomorrow. Every few minutes I distribute Holy Communion. Tears well up in my eyes when I see the faces of people torn away from their families, their work, and their homes by the upheaval of war. I'm continually astonished at the shortage of uniforms. Entire units arrive wearing civilian shoes. And these poor souls are expected to march at any moment to the front?

At noon there's a two-hour break in confessions. Increasingly bad news awaits us at the rectory. The Germans are breaking through with one powerful spearhead toward Częstochowa. Another spearhead, coming out of East Prussia, approaches Warsaw. Here in Inowrocław it's quiet. Officials have left the city, taking cars full of documents, books, and equipment with them. What will happen to us?

At three o'clock we sit down again in the confessionals. Again the same beloved masses of soldiers, the same glaring shortage of uniforms.

Evening service. The church is filled to overflowing with troops. Jesus looks down from the monstrance on their bowed heads, "Holy God, holy, mighty, holy and eternal!" Hearts sob, tears flow. "From pestilence, famine, fire, and war, save us, o Lord! We sinners ask you, o God..."

Noise, shouts and cries come from the prison next to the church. " Mother, spare us, Mother, plead for us. Oh Mother! Mother! Mother! Intercede for us!" the humble prayer resounds throughout the church.

Toward evening, when the sun's disk is retreating behind high treetops in Solankowski Park, several aircraft appear over the city.

"Ours!" How much faith and hope and blessed relief is hidden in that cry.

"They're ours!"

"They're flying toward Berlin!"

"They'll give Hitler a thrashing!"

Alas, on 2 September 1939 we in Inowrocław still had a "super-power" mentality. "We won't give up an inch." With heads turned up toward the graying sky, these two thousand soldiers stood in civilian pants, bareheaded, without weapons. The aircraft, after circling the city, flew off ... to the east.

"You mean, not toward Berlin?"

And once again night fell. A dreadful night. I was a young priest. Two years ago I was still sitting at a seminary desk. How vividly I recalled some of the more significant lectures. One of them was a lecture by Rev. Prof. Gronkowski, explaining the vision of the prophet Ezekiel. I tried once to re-create it in a drawing. It turned out badly, but even so the vision stayed in my mind. Imagination filled in the rest. "...Then I heard the sound of their wings, like the voice of the Almighty. When they moved, the sound of the tumult was like the din of an army ... for this was the voice in the firmanent which was overhead..." In the vision of the prophet, terrifying in its grimness, enormous wheels rattled, powerful wings rustled, footsteps of apocalyptic figures rumbled, "and their voice was like the roaring of mighty waters, like the rush of a sudden wind." In those unforgettable September nights, the same apocalyptic sounds arose from Polish streets and roadways.

The hours of my nightmarish sleep pass by, bordering between dream hallucinations and images of a reality no less gloomy. At daybreak the clatter in the streets increased even more. It seemed entire columns of some huge army were passing through the city covered in darkness. I jumped out of bed in the gray dawn. Time to go to church. Crowds of soldiers are probably waiting there already.

Going outside, I stop as if nailed to the ground. As far as the eye can see, the street is blocked by carts piled high with people's belongings, by herds of cattle, and by pedestrians. All of this is pushing forward in an uninterrupted stream, pressing on in silence; weary human faces betray fear and dismay.

This was the first wave of those fleeing from the border area. The first. From then on they would come one after another, one after another, day and night! Driven by blind fear, torn to bloody tatters by bombs dropped from German aircraft, increasingly emaciated, increasingly hungry and exhausted.

"Hey, folks! Where are you from?"

"The border. The Germans are coming! They're killing people! We're trying to get away."

"Where to?" A puzzled shrug of their shoulders, helplessness in their sunken eyes.

The diversion sown by the Germans had accomplished its goal. Stirred by fear, crowds of people came out with their possessions into the roads, blocking them, preventing the army from passing, creating traffic-jams, obstructing travel, and creating an indescribable confusion. They were driven by terrible news. Where to? "Into the interior of Poland. It will be safer there." They still believed this.[1]

Despite the early hour, the garrison church is full of soldiers. I have the first Mass. The pastor and priests who came to help out have seated themselves again in the confessionals. This is the fourteenth Sunday after Pentecost. The pericope of the Sunday Gospel is about God's Providence. "Do not worry about that which..." I believe, my God, I believe, and yet I cannot throw "those" words out to this military group of husbands and sons who have left their homes, mothers, wives and children. I cannot appeal to them: "Do not be solicitous, you of little faith! Consider the lilies of the field..." The book of Gospels shakes in my hands. My heart pounds in my chest. Hundreds of eyes are fixed on my lips. Hundreds of tired hearts are waiting for words of consolation. How can I give them consolation when I myself am empty? Life-giving spring water will not burst forth from ashes. (Perhaps I was rather young? Perhaps I had too little faith?).

"Dearest Mother, protectress of people," the hymn breaks forth from my heart... The book of Gospels is placed on the altar.

"...May the cry of orphans move You to compassion..." is picked up by the soldiers crowded together in the shrine.

"*Credo in unum Deum,*" whisper trembling lips. Something whimpers in my soul. Something chokes with horrible cackling. Do you believe? Do you believe in what you're whispering? Do you believe in God's merciful fatherhood? "But when the angry Father lashes, happy is he who runs to Mother," the soldiers sing and cry.

2. And That Day Arrived

The Mass is coming to an end. The priest's Communion. Jesus enters into my weary body as into the tabernacle. This is probably how ashamed the doubting Thomas felt...

The sergeant who is serving at Mass signals with the bell. The group of soldiers moves toward the Eucharistic table.

"*Confiteor...*"

"May Almighty God have mercy on you... This is the Lamb of God..."

Heads bow. A sea of soldiers' heads. With rough hands they strike their chests.

"Lord, I am not worthy that you should come into my heart..."

Row after row they kneel at the Communion rail. Row after row they return to the crowd of soldiers, carrying the Lord in their heart... Maybe for the last time.

"Hail, oh Living Host, in which Jesus Christ conceals his divinity..."

The hymn flowed on, warming hearts absorbed in prayer. From a distance, above the melody rising up to the rafters of the shrine, you can hear the drone of aircraft engines.

"Ours!" the thought crosses my mind.

"Hail Jesus, Son of Mary," the song continues... And one more row and one more again... "*Corpus Domini nostri Jesu Christi*," trembling lips whisper over each soldier. The drone of engines grows louder, coming closer and closer...

"...You are the true God, In the Sacred Host!" Tears keep flowing down the soldiers' impassioned faces.

Suddenly a shrill whistling sound breaks the silence that had taken hold inside the church. The hand carrying the Lord is frozen motionless. For a moment all hearts stop beating. A terrible explosion shakes the walls of the church. The engines are now right above us. And again a whistling sound and another and another; in a powerful series, one explosion follows another! One after another! Plaster drops from the church ceiling onto our heads.

"Into the street!"

The shrine is in chaos. Crowds of soldiers rush toward the door. Bombs are falling closer and closer. The building no longer trembles but shakes perceptibly from the explosive blasts.

"Into the street!"

I take the Lord back to the tabernacle. My heart is weary. The sergeant-server has gone to his unit. I turn around for the "*Dominus vobiscum*" — the church is empty, but pastor Fr. Handke is kneeling at the Communion rail and turning pages of his breviary with the greatest composure. A moment later I'm in the sacristy.

"Reverend Father, please hurry because there could be another wave at any moment and then... In the meantime, I'll take out the Blessed Sacrament and preserve it in the fireproof safe."

At that moment for the first time I looked with amazement at this small modest man. I suddenly remembered the words he had often repeated:

"Reverend Father, once, when we were schoolboys, we rushed to attack with bayonets near Smogulec..."

He must have carried a rifle in his hands with the same composure as he now carries the ciborium containing the Blessed Sacrament.

Several minutes later, we stood on the church steps looking at the square in front of us and the streets radiating from it. And what we saw was staggering: a mass of people, horses, cattle, and carts, with personal belongings scattered everywhere. The frightened horses pull at their harnesses; the cattle, driven by fear, trample those who have fallen and overturn the carts. Screams, cries, wailing; the mooing of cows, the neighing of horses...

A new wave of attackers approaches from the west. The droning of their engines grows louder.

"Priests, against the wall!" a young officer yells. We fall to the ground. Soldiers are lying all around us. The planes are getting closer and closer. Again the terrifying whistling sounds. Bombs fall on the railroad station and surrounding houses. The planes are flying toward us. And now something happens that surpasses all our worst expectations. The aircraft crews open fire with machine guns on the frenzied mass of people. Dante could not have portrayed the picture of hell that broke loose over the crowded square and streets. Everything has been thrown into confusion at the same time. There is now but a single cry, and then a heart-rending moan. Oh, God, God! In one place, horses overturn a cart with someone's belongings; in another, a herd of cattle tramples an entire family. An old man is moaning, crushed under a trunk that fell from a cart; driven to madness, a mother is shaking her fist at the attackers. And again the cries and moans of the injured and the death-rattle of the dying; words of prayer and curses. Above this Dantesque frenzy, smoke from the explosions, clouds of dust, and the smell of burning. The blood-thirsty steel birds circle back again and again, striking each time straight into the crowd. One burst after another, and after each burst people fall to the ground: the old, women, mothers, children. A young non-commissioned officer next to us is crying, biting his clenched fists until they bleed.

"Why didn't they give us weapons? Why? Why?"

Not one shot was fired from the many soldiers who lay side by side. Soldiers without uniforms are, of course, without weapons. Not one anti-aircraft gun could be heard in the city. With impunity the pirates ravage unarmed masses.

This is the baptism of war that Inowrocław received. The harvest of death was monstrous. Following the air raid, scraps of human flesh had to be gathered up with shovels. In the cemetery long graves were dug, and into them were dumped the murdered, the unidentified, the unnamed.

For us, the priests, a "new" work had started: caring for the injured and blessing those laid to eternal rest. And once again I stood amazed as I looked at the small, humble figure of my pastor. It was not enough for him to take care of those who lay injured in the streets and on the square. When he heard moans, he walked into the ruins and slipped under the dangling beams and wall fragments, which threatened to fall down at any moment.

"There are souls out there who need our help," was his answer to all our admonitions to be careful.

"Reverend Pastor, you'll die under those falling ruins," an officer warned.

"And wouldn't you go to your wounded soldiers?" He looked over the bifocals sitting askew on his nose with what was for him a singular and unaccustomed dignity. "My parishioners are over there," he pointed to a house in ruins. "When I started work in this new parish, I needed them, and they gave me their help. Now they need me. Can I refuse them?" And he continued on in his cassock, soiled with dust and lime, with blood-stained hands. He went forward, moving aside beams, rubble and brick, just so he could reach an injured parishioner who needed help.

"Reverend Father, take care of the injured refugees in the streets, and leave my parishioners to me," he shooed me away from the ruins.

The raids by enemy aircraft were to be repeated many times that fateful first Sunday in September, but not one of them was as bloody as that early morning raid.

On the road between Bydgoszcz and Inowrocław the same thing was happening that happened in the city. Bombs were falling on thousands of people moving from Łobżenica,

At daybreak on 1 September 1939, Hitler's motorized armies began to advance in strong spearheads from all sides across the boundaries of Poland. The German Luftwaffe started bombing cities, towns, villages and hamlets (drawing by Władysław Krawiec).

Wyrzysko, Sadki, Nakło, from all points along the border, and even from Bydgoszcz itself. One after another, bombs fell upon those defenseless masses; even machine guns were fired at them to increase the bloody harvest. Bodies torn to pieces were hauled away to common graves.

And throngs of refugees swept through Inowrocław day and night, heading toward Kruszwica, Strzelno, Radziejów, not realizing that they were actually moving right into the fire.

One day I was called in to visit a sick man. Taking the Blessed Sacrament, I went to the given address. Upon entering the house, I came upon the following scene: a young policeman (wearing a uniform) was giving out revolvers to several boys. I overheard his last words to them: "Hit the Germans as hard as you can!"

After taking care of the sick man, as I was leaving the house, I noticed one of the boys. He was dressed in a boy scout uniform. He might have been fifteen years old.

"Hey, young man, who was the policeman giving you revolvers?" I asked.

The young man didn't know. While talking with him, I learned by chance that the mysterious "Polish" policeman had with him a huge German shepherd dog, to which he had said something in German. There was no doubt this was a German diversionist. There hadn't been any Polish police in Inowrocław for several days. Besides, what Polish policeman, knowing about the retreat of the military and the flight of the administrative officials, would be handing out weapons to children? Several days later, when a small group of young scouts opened fire on the Germans who were entering Inowrocław, it became even more clear that this was a provocation.

Masses of refugees were pouring out of Bydgoszcz. Many of them stopped in Inowrocław, spending the night in schools and other hastily prepared shelters. Too busy during the day, I usually searched among them in the evening for my parents, brothers, and other relatives. One evening I came across some acquaintances. My heart was pounding. I asked about my family. "No, your parents stayed home. Your father decided that if they had to die, they would die under their own roof."

The refugees bring terrible news about "a bloody Sunday" in Bydgoszcz. And the river of refugees keeps flowing. One day Fr. Henio Warkoczewski, my colleague from the parish in Września, arrives.

"I'm going straight to Warsaw. Will you come with me?"

I look at the tired horses.

"You know, don't you, that there's already fighting near Kutno, that the ring they're surrounding us with is tightening, that..."

"I'll still make it to Warsaw." He made it and ... died there as a chaplain at the military hospital.

On 6 September, Bydgoszcz and Kraków fall. Bits of news coming over the radio are increasingly terrifying. The barometer of our "power status" falls lower and lower. And ... "that" day arrived. The Germans entered Inowrocław!

The name *Inowrocław* was erased from the history of those days. "Hohensalza!" That foreign word once again was to stick for a number of years to this city dating back to the pre–Piast era. Hohensalza! On the granite wall of the ancient Piast-era shrine of the Virgin Mary the masks of evil Slavic gods sneered and laughed viciously.

Awful days of terror had begun for old Inowrocław. Evictions from homes, seizures, arrests; the roundup of all men into the sports stadium and their segregation — some to a life of slavery, some to death; the arrest of the Rev. Canon Kubski, the execution of the Rev. Dean Zabłocki by firing squad, the shooting death of Fr. Kozłowicz, mass executions: all this befell the residents day after day, blow after blow.

Rooms in our rectory were seized for use by officers. A small corner was left for us. My tiny room with the outdoor view survived. It was not fit to house an officer. The view from my window, as I mentioned earlier, looked out on the street leading to the prison. Concealed behind the curtain, I witnessed constant convoys of those arrested, including the most prominent residents of the city. One day they escorted the parish vicar of St. Mary's, Fr. Kazio Tyczka. He walked in his cassock in the middle of the road, his hands raised over his head. They led him from the prison toward Matwy. Since that day there has been no trace of him.

Nights were the most terrifying. The rectory was located near the prison. Not a night passed without hearing salvos from executions carried out there.

All the churches were closed! We were forbidden to celebrate holy Mass or perform any kind of priestly function. Every day I went with the pastor to the garrison church to recite the breviary and calm our nerves in the silence. Not a day would go by without our seeing fresh blood stains on the street that led from the prison gate toward anti-aircraft trenches that had been dug outside the prison walls. At daybreak the bodies of those murdered in the night were transported there and dropped into the trenches.

Parishioners would secretly call us to the sick and the dying. We were not allowed to be seen in the street dressed in clerical garb. But sacred duties called, so we went out on our ministry in civilian dress, carrying the Eucharistic Lord hidden under our clothing. The clothes of a laborer attracted the least attention. A mechanic's shirt and tool kit became a kind of identity card opening a way past all kinds of checkpoints. It was clear that the city had undergone much destruction from military operations, and it was important for the invaders to make repairs. The safest way to proceed with the last priestly ministry was in a mechanic's shirt with the Most Blessed Sacrament hidden among tools and oily rags.

On 17 September, Stalin invaded Poland ... and when the woeful news arrived about the capitulation of Warsaw, about the German victory parade held in its streets, there was no end to our tears.

October brought an increase in terror because the notorious Gestapo took control of the city. One October night you could hear gunfire coming from the prison, more sustained and louder than on other nights. The next day a frightened Rev. Prof. Szukalski, who lived across from the prison, arrived at the rectory. His face pale from emotion, he told us in a whisper what had occurred on that notorious "St. Bartholomew's night" in Inowrocław.

The Gestapo, led by German administrative officials and the district president, organized a day of pheasant hunting. In the evening, the hunters were given a lavish reception in one of the hotels. After washing down the roasted pheasants with liquor, they discovered it was really only then that they felt like going hunting.

"The game is in the prison!"

"But of course. It's a wonder this didn't occur to us sooner!"

Half an hour later the group of "hunters" took up positions in the prison hall. Prisoners were released. The hunt began. And at dawn the next day forty-seven dead prisoners were carried out to the anti-aircraft trenches!

As happens, however, Providence furnishes testimony about such crimes. One of the women prisoners, a teacher by profession and Rev. Prof. Szukalski's former student, after being shot in the arm, was pushed by a prison guard out into the courtyard and released into the street. She was bleeding but aware that it was strictly forbidden to go out at night and that she risked arrest by the next patrol. She remembered from her student days that her former prefect, a priest, lived in the house across from the prison. So she knocked at his door. It was from her, then, that Rev. Prof. Szukalski received an authentic account of the events of that dismal night.

The entire bloody story would have drowned in the flood of hundreds or thousands of similar cases taking place at that time on tortured Polish soil if the murdered group of top city and regional officials (among them the brother of the Rev. Bishop Laubitz from Gniezno) had not included Kiełbasiewicz, leader of the Inowrocław communists. The fact of his murder could hurt the friendship between Hitler and Stalin and become an "ugly blot" on the Ribbentrop-Molotov Pact.

But this "unfortunate indiscretion" on the part of our district official along with the Gestapo demanded punitive consequences. The district official was recalled from Inowrocław and transferred ... to a higher position, while the bloody Gestapo quieted down for a time. During the next few nights no sound of gunfire came from the prison.[2]

3

"Invitation" to a Meeting

Following "bloody St. Bartholomew's night," a new district governor arrived in Inowrocław. "You'll see, Father," Fr. Handke optimistically assured me, "you'll see that this new one will be completely different. After what happened that night, they'll try to blot out the unpleasant memories. They've surely sent us a man of character. A real human being!" he repeated with emphasis.

But somehow I couldn't forget the sentence whispered to me by a secretary in the records office as I handed her my identity card: "You priests should always dress warmly!" After whispering this, she ran to her desk, and, after a while, noticing that she wasn't attracting the attention of the other office workers, she winked meaningfully, with a nod of her head.[1]

"Eh, Father, you're young and handsome, like a redheaded David. It's no wonder that some German Abigail whispered something in your ear. Maybe you misunderstood, maybe..."

All Souls' Day came. After celebrating holy Masses in secret at the garrison church, Fr. Handke and I return to the rectory, which had been taken over by the military. The pastor's sister greets us with news that the district governor's office has sent an invitation to an upcoming meeting.

"Didn't I tell you, Father!" the pastor is exultant. "The new governor has arrived and intends to establish normal relations, and to do this he needs the priests. He realizes we have influence over the city residents. He's inviting us in order to..." During the morning we find out that the invitation to a meeting scheduled for 5 o'clock that afternoon was received by all priests not only from the city, but from the entire district.

"No, Father. One doesn't invite all the priests so openly in order to arrest them en masse. What a reaction that would create in the city and district! It would fuel the current public mood. They wouldn't dare do it. I know the Germans. They think and plan too logically."

This argument did not convince me. News regarding the arrest two weeks ago of all priests in the Szubin District, the awful campaign of terror against the clergy in the Wyrzysk District, and the execution of many of our colleagues by firing squad did not indicate at all that "they" were paying attention to what a terrorized public would say or how it would react to new arrests of the clergy.

Just after 4 o'clock we're ready to leave. In the street I notice groups of priests making their way to the district building. There are greetings, bows, an exchange of views. Somehow people always feel braver and more cheerful in a group. (Priests are not excluded from this psychological law.)

We walk in a group. The Rev. Prof. Dębski and the Rev. Prof. Wróblewski, my pastor's relative, are with us.

"My respects, Boleś!" shouts Fr. Handke to the other side of the street, where the Rev.

Canon Jaśkowski is walking with his vicars. Walking behind them is the Rev. Pastor Wierzbicki from Kościelec along with the Rev. Vicar Edward Skowroński. Behind them is Fr. Leoś Mencel and further back are the following priests: Ludwik Sobieszczyk, Ciemniak, Włodarczyk, Farulewski, Pomianowski, and others.

Near the district building we meet the huge Rev. Pastor Mieczysław Strehl with the Rev. Pastor Dobromir Ziarniak, who always accompanies him.

And again there are greetings, smiles, pleasantries. Of course. Inowrocław is the cultural capital of the Kujawy Region.

With carefree chatter, we walk up the steps toward the huge glass doors. The young priests yield to the older ones.

"No, please go ahead, please..." It's difficult to recall the next sequence of events. A push in the back, a brusque "*antreten* into ranks" transported me abruptly into a different, still unforeseen world. At that moment we stopped being free men for nearly six long years. Only three priests from the Inowrocław group were to make it out alive. From the whole administrative district — only about a dozen.

They line us up in the hall of the large district building. At the same time they kick us and hit us with rifle butts. As though through a fog, I see the pale faces of the priests: Farulewski, Pomianowski, Mąkowski, Ludwiczak, the Rev. Msgr. Schönborn. Lord, how the gray head of the old emeritus Fr. Niemir trembles. The hall doors open repeatedly. Well-aimed kicks push new victims in. The poses of those tumbling in are so comical they would elicit bursts of laughter if the situation had not been so tragic. I see the terrified faces of my colleagues: Miecio Siudziński, Józio Pućka, Janusz Komf, Edward Skowroński, Skoblewski, Skowron. Then Fathers Romek Budniak and Aloś Gotowicz tumble in, all out of breath. After them come others. Just after 5 o'clock our group is complete, all the priests from the city and the entire district.

"Put your hands up!"

The procession of prisoners flows through the open door, down the steps, and then into the street. We walk four abreast, with hands raised up. Armed guards, with rifles ready to fire, walk alongside. The early November evening of All Souls sets in. Yellowing leaves rustle under our steps. It's quiet all around. Not a living soul. The frightened residents are in hiding. Only here and there a curtain flutters in the window, and a pale face appears briefly. The blood-red setting sun casts its last rays on the rooftops.

The tight column of prisoners enters the prison courtyard. A high iron gate slams shut behind us.

Prison "receptions" have been and are still described so often that I will not recount here how "cordially" the Inowrocław prison greeted its clergy.

At last, they assign us to our cells. The prison is filled to capacity. Four of us priests and a local merchant named Cofta are packed into a tight, one-person cell. A bed of boards suspended from chains, a tiny table, one stool, and a smelly utensil taking the place of a toilet — that was the only "furniture." The older Rev. Canon Jaśkowski and Fr. Handke occupy places on the narrow bunk. Fr. Ksawery Krawczak, the merchant and I squat down against the wall. There is no room to extend our legs. I don't know what time it is when they turn out the light. The steps in the hallway never stop. Keys keep rattling...

"Isn't it amazing that we're all alumni of the Nakło high school?"

My pastor's humor, contrasting so painfully with our situation, irritates me intensely. In addition, there is that smelly, nauseating bucket next to the place I'm obliged to take (as the youngest).

They started mass arrests of the Polish intelligentsia, among whom they zealously searched out Catholic priests, so that in a short time hundreds of parishes were left without pastors (drawing by Władysław Krawiec).

"*Angelus Domini,*" the Rev. Canon Jaśkowski begins the prayer.
"*Ave, Maria, gratia plena,*" we whisper in the darkness.

Oh, how slowly the hours drag! The air becomes almost unbearable. Five people in a cell as tight as a cage and that smelly bucket; the steps in the corridors don't quiet down; my constricted legs are aching; Fr. Krawczak, sitting next to me, slumps on top of me with his entire weight and snores terribly. He's lucky to be able to sleep... And my head is spinning. I had seen and heard too much coming from the prison during nights while at the rectory;

after all, every day I saw fresh blood stains which led from the prison gate to the trenches mentioned earlier. Therefore, my restless imagination was recreating events of the "Bartholomew night." It had happened just behind these doors! It was there that they fired on the human game. Could that night possibly be repeated?

The night is still pitch-black outside the small window near the top of the cell when an electric light goes on with a bright glare. There is movement in the corridors. Doors slam, bolts click, keys rattle, footsteps clatter.

"Good morning, Boleś. How did you sleep? I slept splendidly."

My pastor's grim humor continues to grate on my nerves. How can this man joke at such a time? The bucket, filled to the brim, is overflowing with feces and urine. Steps. The grating sound of a key in the lock. The heavy door opens.

"You pigs! You don't even know how to relieve yourselves except on the ground. Take out this bucket!" A powerful kick is a most convincing incentive to hurry. But how do you carry out this awful utensil when it's spilling onto the floor? (A new series of kicks.)

"You'll lick this with your own mug, you filthy dog!"

They didn't mince any words. We finally found out "how to be well-mannered in a polite milieu!"

Days go by, nights go by. One night they called out the merchant Cofta. Awakened suddenly from sleep, he begins to get his shoes and socks.

"Leave them! You don't need those things where you're going!"

The heavy door bangs after him. The key grates. The four of us are left in a panic. Whose turn will it be tomorrow?

The nights are filled with nightmares. They are long, endless... Oh, how I understand Christ now, who spent the night before His execution in prison!

At such moments all that is human becomes so insignificant. From a person's every inner recess a frightened animal emerges, and everything revolves around the remaining scrap of life. Even prayer becomes something wooden. It's not the soul that talks with God, it's a numbed tongue that prattles...

We confess our sins. Just in case. Who among us knows when the end will come?

On 5 November, we hear movement in the corridors that is more disturbing than usual: the hollow sound of footsteps, the ominous rattling of keys, doors being opened, names being called. We strain to hear; the only names being called are those of our colleagues, priests.

"To execution?"

Our hearts beat loudly. The footsteps come ever closer. They're taking priests from nearby cells. The grating sound of a key in the door of our cell. We hold our breath. We stand in a row.

"Handke, Krawczak, Malak, *raus*! Jaśkowski stays!"

In a second, we're in the corridor. They lead us in small groups to the lower level. Execution?

"Put your hands up!"

They lead us along stone steps to the prison hall, and from there to some stairs. Backed up to them, a large bus awaits us, its windows painted over with black paint. This is the death bus, already known in Inowrocław. It takes the condemned to nearby woods, where executions are carried out by firing squad.

A giant dressed in a policeman's light-blue uniform rages by the open doors of the bus. He deals sharp blows either with his foot or the butt of his rifle. Where does all this hatred inside him come from?

"Gorilla!" I hear Fr. Handke's whisper, as he raises himself up from the bus floor and adjusts the eye-glasses hanging askew on his nose. "What bad manners. A real gorilla!"

Despite all the danger of the situation, I feel some satisfaction. For the first time I hear my pastor speaking seriously. We are packed into the bus like sardines in a barrel. Whispered information goes around about colleagues left behind in the prison. Who's winning? Are we or are they?

It's dark in the closed bus. Daylight doesn't penetrate the heavily painted windowpanes. We start out. The packed human mass sways and surrenders to the movement of the vehicle.

"Where are they taking us?"

The answer seems obvious, but no one dares say it out loud. Each of us knows they use this bus to transport those condemned to death. Which of us in the last few days and nights has not prepared for death at least once?

The bus starts to go faster. Romek Budniak has scratched a small hole in the paint covering the window. In a whisper, he passes along information about the landmarks.

"We've left the city; we're on the highway to Bydgoszcz."

To Bydgoszcz? My heart is pounding. Because my mother, father and siblings are there. They have no idea how near I am, and yet, at the same time, how much farther I am from them. Maybe there is no return from this trip?

The guards sitting near the driver pay no attention to us. There is no chance of escape. The doors are bolted shut. Besides, who would be able to jump out of such a fast-moving vehicle? Time passes and we continue to speed ahead; somehow we aren't turning into any of the woods bordering the road.

After a two-hour drive, we're sure they won't shoot us before Bydgoszcz. Maybe they're taking us to the local prison?

"Bydgoszcz suburb," relates Fr. Romek beside the scratched-out hole.

"May I look out? This is *my* Bydgoszcz."

We turn into Kujawska Street. Silhouettes of familiar houses flash before my eyes. The bus turns left, then right, avoiding rubble. Suddenly the blood rushes to my head. In the distance, over the rooftops, rise the church spires in Szwederowo. My family parish. We pass some streets. A new turn. A few meters farther and I would find myself in my family home, where my mother, father, and brothers wait. The bus leans into a turn. We're driving down toward the old town. The distance separating me from my family becomes greater with each revolution of the wheels. Could I have imagined then that the distance would extend across countries, continents, and oceans, that a quarter century would settle over it, that maybe, maybe the path of my life would never bring me to this place again?

"Where are we?" Fr. Romek's voice draws me away from a swarm of pressing thoughts.

"We're going up Gdańsk Street ."

This was my last view of Bydgoszcz, seen from a death bus through a hole scratched in the painted window.

"It seems most of the executions take place in the Gdańsk woods."

"Stop it! Don't wish evil on us. Would they take us this far just to kill us beyond Bydgoszcz?"

There is an indescribable stench in the bus. The packed mass of humanity reeks of body odor.

"We're going to suffocate before they get us to our destination."

"Well then we suffocate."

Apathy overcomes us after the hours of nervous tension. "In the name of the Father and the Son and the Holy Spirit," someone starts the Rosary. "In the first Sorrowful Mystery we meditate on how the Lord Jesus, while praying in the Garden of Olives, sweated blood. Our Father..."

"What day is it today? Probably Sunday? Yes, Sunday. You lose all track of time. It's Sunday..."

"Hail Mary, full of grace, the Lord is with thee..."

"Osielsko," Romek whispers quietly, continuing all the while to stand on watch.

"Where are they taking us? Not to Gdańsk?"

"Holy Mary, Mother of God, pray for us sinners..."

It was already well into evening when we rode into the first streets of some town.

"You can see the Vistula," Romek informs us. "We're in Świecie!"

The bus sways like a drunk, bouncing on the little town's cobblestones. The mass of humanity lurches forward when the vehicle moves along downhill streets, then shifts its entire weight toward the back when we drive uphill. One more turn, one more hill, and the vehicle slows down. Finally it stops.

"We're in a courtyard surrounded by some buildings," Romek gives us his last update.

Our guards jump out of the driver's cab. They pull back the bolts. A stream of fresh air pours in through the wide-open doors.

"*Raus*! How these sheep stink!" The guard moves away from the exit door, turning up his nose.

We stand in long lines. Count off. Report. We are transferred over to some kind of "pheasant" in an SA* uniform with a red arm-band on his sleeve. His bloodshot, drunken eyes look us over.

"So these are the damned Polish instigators and murderers who were shooting from behind fences? We'll cure you of that, we'll cure you!"

"Heil Hitler!"

Handed over by the Inowrocław guards, we become from that time the "object" of Gestapo officials in Świecie on the Vistula. Earlier they had moved patients from the local psychiatric hospital into the woods. Who cared about several hundred people suffering from nervous breakdowns? An unnecessary burden! The local prison was already packed. They needed a place for new loads of political prisoners. The vacated psychiatric hospital served this purpose perfectly.[2]

They put us up in rooms where hundreds of prisoners were already staying. After days and nights of squatting down in a confining prison cell, stretching your body on the bed of straw that covers the floor seems a luxury. Unfortunately, here for the first time we were to come into contact with lice, the companions of misery, which did not want to leave us

---

*Translator's note: "SA" refers to stormtroopers, called "brownshirts," a paramilitary organization of the Nazi Party.

through all our years of imprisonment. Here we were finally to learn from the guards what sort of felons and social outcasts we were. Here they made us realize that if they did not transport us right away to the woods to be shot, it was only due to compassion (?!?), but if that didn't happen to us right away, it could still happen at any moment, etc., etc.

One day they brought in a busload of priests from the provinces of Włocławek and Płock. Our group of priests was increasing. The latest arrivals brought with them tragic news... We were growing in number, but falling more and more into despair.

4

Górna Grupa

So this is the famous priest and author Fr. Liguda? As young seminarians we loved his modern homilies for youth. Could I have imagined then, as a student, that our meeting would come under such unusual circumstances? From Świecie, the Gestapo took us to the Society of the Divine Word (SVD) monastery in Górna Grupa. The monastery had already been taken over by occupation officials. Most of the housing was occupied by military units. They dumped us, about one hundred, into two monastery refectories. The rector of the monastery school—who was currently appointed by the guards as their liaison with our prisoner team—was the very same Fr. Alojzy Liguda, SVD.

We're sitting on a bed of straw that covers the floor of the huge refectory, and we're listening. Fr. Liguda is giving us a briefing. His huge, broad-shouldered figure almost reaches the low ceiling of the hall. The broad face of this Silesian miner's son bespeaks honesty.

"Reverend monsignors, dear reverend pastors, professors, vicars!" A smile appears on the speaker's face. "I'm beginning so formally, deceiving myself that I'm greeting you on the threshold of our monastery in days past, the days of freedom. Meanwhile, reality reminds us"—he motioned with his head toward the windows, beyond which soldiers were moving about in the monastery courtyard—"a sad reality reminds us that we are prisoners. The building has been occupied for two weeks. Several fathers and brothers remain in the monastery. They have held us here to keep the place in order. From now on, as long as Providence keeps us in this place, we are tasked with the following work: continue maintaining the monastery, provide fuel to the furnaces and heat to the soldiers' rooms, oversee the barns and pigsties, and also work with local farmers if they indicate to the guardhouse that they need our aid. As you Fathers can see, the monastery is guarded, but not to such an extent that escape is impossible. Especially through the park"—he moved his huge arm in the direction of the windows, where leafless trees were standing. "The Vistula is right over there, you can see it just behind the fence. But you have heard what they told you, that for each escapee ten would later be shot. And I assure you"—a deep sadness covers the face of the speaker—"I assure you this is not an empty threat. In our area we had"—he gestured with his big hand—"but that's for another time."

That very day—divided into groups—we went to work. One group, composed of the youngest priests under the leadership of Fr. Romek Budniak, a forestry official's son, who many times during his vacations had supervised the clearing of woods, took over the duty of felling trees in the monastery park and cutting them up for fuel. Another group started work in the farm buildings, which had the benefit that toward evening they could stop by the refectory windows with a cart of fresh straw. The third and largest group, made up of venerable monsignors, pastors, and professors under the "leadership" of brawny Fr. Mieczysław Strehl, was detailed to the kitchen, to peel potatoes and prepare vegetables for the soldiers. Some smaller groups worked in the bakery, the machine room, and other household areas of this huge building.

In the evening when each returning woodcutter took out a log smuggled inside his clothes, and when the crew of the "monsignor's" kitchen took out some smuggled food, the mood improved. "Maybe it won't be so bad after all in this Górna Grupa?" The fresh straw we put down is fragrant and induces sleep.

There is no shortage of tasks for us in the monastery. In addition to carrying out those mentioned above, we go when called upon — under guard — to the local German farmers, and since this is the season for the late harvest of beets and other produce, our hands are usually full of work. We're surprised that the farmers don't hesitate to drive priests in cassocks to do the dirtiest jobs, to throw manure out of a pigsty, but in the end we attribute this to the fact that maybe these are Protestants.

Sometimes a housewife would surreptitiously slip a chunk of bread into one of our pockets, and sometimes someone would offer a friendly word while looking around fearfully to see whether a guard had overhead. No, not all hearts are evil, not all are corrupt.

On Sundays — aside from having us do the most pressing jobs — they don't make us work. We prepare enough fuel and potatoes on Saturday to last for the holy day. Following a silent Mass, which they allow us to celebrate in the monastery chapel, they take us for physical exercises. These are led by young scamps from the auxiliary police, who chase us through the park and fields. This makes us younger priests even happy because we can run to our hearts' content in the fresh air, but it's worse for the elderly: monsignors, pastors, emeriti, including some who are almost eighty years old, like Fr. Wąsowicz and Fr. Niemir, for example. The latter return from those hours of exercise terribly worn out.

From time to time we greet new groups of priests, especially from Pomerania. Our number is growing. One day they bring in all the clergy from the Szubin District. Neighbors. There's a lot of joy, but there's also a lot of distressing news about horrible actions on the part of the invaders, executions and Gestapo violence.

One Sunday they call out my name and lead me to the guardhouse. As I walk in front of a guard, who walks behind me with a rifle, I feel shivers go down my back.

What can they want from me? I recall scenes from the prison.

At the entrance to the guardhouse I suddenly feel the blood rushing to my face. Before me stands my mother!

They allow us ten minutes for conversation. It turned out that the slip of paper with my parents' address, which I had secretly passed to a German nurse during our stay in Świecie, had reached my parents, revealing where we were. I had told my colleagues earlier about my attempt at giving a sign of life, but they hardly believed a German woman would want to take such a risk for us. The medal of the Immaculate, however, which I noticed on her blouse, had given me hope. "Catholic?" I asked. She nodded. "Please take this slip of paper. My parents are convinced that I've been shot and killed." She took it. She nodded her head, indicating she would deliver it. And she did.[1]

Is it possible to say much to each other in the course of ten minutes, after months of separation and painful experiences?

My mother was the first visitor to Górna Grupa. I whispered to her the names of colleagues imprisoned with me, and on the very next Sunday there stood at the guardhouse quite a large group of visitors. On Sundays thereafter, their number reached several dozen. The bribed guards permit our talks to last several hours and turn a blind eye to many things. From then on we do pretty well. Supplies of warm underwear and food have the desired effect. We could endure such "slavery" for years. With warm clothing and good food, the work is not too much of a burden. The guards that we've won over don't push the oldest to work and somehow forget about Sunday exercises. It's more "lucrative" to hang around the guardhouse on Sunday afternoons when visitors arrive. ...Yes, much more lucrative.

Imprisoned and isolated from the rest of the world, rather well supplied, we unfortunately forget somewhat about the tragedy in which the nation is plunged. It's so easy to forget and so easy to regard one's own lot as "heroic martyrdom!"

One day, and this was during the last days of November, they call us suddenly from our work stations and line us up in front of the monastery building. A large bus, its windows painted over with black paint, stands again at the entrance.

An officer, standing with a group of armed SS men in black uniforms, calls out fifteen names. All were priests and seminarians from Płock province, among them members of the Salesian Order. Those best known to me were the names of Fr. Walewski from Tomaszów and Rev. Dr. Kneblewski, the noted author.

The fifteen are quickly loaded into the bus. They are ordered not to take anything with them. Through the open door, one can see that the vehicle is already packed with men.

"Where are they taking them?" Fr. Liguda asks one of the non-commissioned officers.

"Silence on this is the best answer," he replies, walking toward the bus.

"The rest, back to work!" the order is given. We hurried off... But that day conversation falters among the woodcutters in the park, the domestic workers, and even among the talkative potato peelers. They sit quietly in the cellar and, with heads bent down, peel and peel. Even the tame stork Maciek, which they feed daily, cannot distract them from their dark thoughts by tapping on the window pane.

Providence reminded us painfully where we were and in whose hands.

"All of them were shot in a woods, near the garrison square in Dolna Grupa," Fr. Liguda explains to us that evening, whispering. He had received that information from the guards.[2]

"I ask that you be more careful," he continued, "and not endanger yourselves and others." (There was still a lot of kindness, after all, in those auxiliary policemen.)

From then on, every sound of an automobile outside made us shudder. Could this be the death bus again?

They continue to transport priests from Pomerania. They brought in the elderly: Rev. Counselor Konitzer from Świecie, Fr. Jan Brzuski and Fr. Michnowski, high-school prefect Fr. Bronek Szymański, and elementary school prefect Fr. Leoś Michałowski, Fr. Meger, Fr. Szczypiński. The youngest was 23-year-old Fr. Franek Krajewski from Brodnica, who had just been ordained, "still with the scent of holy oils on him."

"Why did they lock you up?"

"How do I know? They were locking up other priests, so they took me, too."

Grim news spreads about the murder of an entire chapter of clergy in Pelplin, about acts of extreme terror in Stare. It's hard to believe such atrocities are possible.

"Have you heard about the 'gas-works' vehicle?"

"Gas-works vehicle?"

"That's right. In the beginning people were taken into the woods and shot. Now they have specially built vehicles that are tightly sealed; they pack people into them, turn on the gas, travel a few kilometers, and ... it's done."

"Monstrous."

"And yet it's true."[3]

One day, they brought in Fr. Aloś Góranowicz, the pastor from Przechowo.

"Aloś," his colleagues greet him. "How did you get here? Because we had heard that..."

"What you heard is true. They took all my neighbors from the entire area. I was the only one left. I worried about this. Indeed, I couldn't sleep at night. I spoke out against the atrocities committed; it was reported to the officials, and here I am with you."

Oh, the unforgettable Fr. Góranowicz! What an angelic soul resided in that tall body. He was to survive with us all the way to Dachau, where he died of exhaustion. But during these days there was so much life and so much kindness in him!

"He's so tall that the bile in him was lost completely," they used to say.

December was approaching, white with frost and very cold.

"We haven't had such a winter in Pomerania in years," nodded the venerable Rev. Pastor Michnowski, a specialist in all kinds of forecasts. An extremely kind man!

The group of woodcutters has to be increased. And there are many to choose from! Quite a few young men have arrived: Fr. Zbigniew Młynik and Fr. Kazio Grzelak, both Franciscans and spiritual sons of Fr. Maksymilian Kolbe; and Franio Kmieć, a talker equal to none, and Fr. Zygmunt Kaczmarek with the following priests: Łój, Cześ Koczorowski and Szczepcio Weber from the Szubin District; Redemptorists Fr. Tadek Tybor and high-school rector Fr. Jan Szymaszek, who wants to stay in shape. The first one to take up the ax is pastor Fr. Seroka, older but very muscular. Ancient trees fall, saws grate, axes crack. In the cellars the potato peelers talk away. Of course, everybody knows this occupation is generally associated with chatter, no matter whether practiced by a woman or even a venerable pastor and monsignor.

The Rev. Dr. Ludwiczak, Director of the Public University in Dalekie, holds sway in that group. A frequent traveler to foreign countries, where he studied social issues, he has many tales, and it is only when he ventures too far in his storytelling and not everything seems to mesh with reality that objections are raised by Fr. Szczepcio Misiak. Having just returned from France, where he had worked many years, Fr. Misiak can put a check on the notions of Fr. Antoś, as we popularly call the Rev. Dr. Ludwiczak.

How often a disagreement would arise because of this. A stubborn disagreement. It was always subdued by powerful Fr. Miecio Strehl with his low bass voice:

"Give it a rest, gentlemen, give it a rest; we'd better say the Rosary instead."

Hail Marys flow forth, peels fall to the floor, peeled potatoes splash into buckets, and only from time to time can you hear the mumbling of kind-hearted Fr. Wąsowicz, whom we all call uncle (because of his venerable age). Uncle does not tolerate "shoddiness," as he calls it. It's all the same, whether we're peeling at the rectory for the bishop's reception or for German soldiers. The black spots have to be cut out. And kind-hearted uncle again takes the potatoes from the freezing water, patiently going over them and over them while trying to catch up with a missed Hail Mary.

"How do you know that?" we often asked when we heard some wild news, something hard to believe. "Could it possibly be from our dear potato peelers?"

Our potato peelers were indeed dear: monsignors, doctors, professors, pastors, priest-colonels, emeriti, people with darkened fingers. As you know, potatoes leave a stain.

"Staszek! If your patron, the countess, saw your dark nails now, she would hesitate to receive Holy Communion from you."

They joke... Sometimes they even tease each other.

"Give it a rest, give it a rest... Let's say the Rosary," the powerful Fr. Miecio, a giant with the heart of a dove, smooths over the disagreement.

Thus came Christmas 1939. The first spent in bondage. Our families brought us what they could afford, and, in gratitude for the potatoes we delivered, the military cooks stationed at the monastery prepared a batch of goulash; the monastery cook by some miracle set out modest Christmas Eve dishes, and the traditional *opłatek** was also found. The "host" of the occupied monastery, Fr. Liguda, spoke; tears flowed; our thoughts raced to our families.

I'm glad these sentimental formalities have ended. Burrowed in straw, I prefer to remain with my own thoughts. Besides, the artificially generated mood wasn't taking hold. Probably never, on any other evening, were the lights turned out so early as on that Christmas Eve.

January 1940 came. It's a cold January, exceptionally cold. One early morning, heavy military trucks arrive at the monastery.

"A transport? Maybe something worse?"

Fr. Liguda is extremely grave. More than that, he's really suffering. A painful grimace has settled on his usually calm face: "Forty younger priests will go for the day to the monastery library," he orders.

"Great. For months I haven't had a book in my hand."

We go. In the huge library several SS men, dressed in black, are already "working," pulling down books from the shelves to the floor.

"Open the windows and throw this trash into the trucks!"

Stupefaction.

"Get moving! Get moving, you swine-hounds!" (I don't know why "swine" exactly, but this insult was to be used very often in the next several years: "*Sau-Hunde!*")

So then? We throw them out. We load priceless ancient texts into the trucks, precious volumes of costly encyclopedias are dumped in, collections gathered with great effort over many decades are blown by the wind through the park. By evening the large and valuable library is already empty. All its books, collected over many years with monastic diligence, *were burned* in the furnaces of the Grudziądz sugar plant.

This was not just about destroying texts in the Polish language since, after all, more than half of the volumes were in other languages, including a great many in German. *It was about destroying everything that related to Catholicism and, in general, to faith in God,* according to the pagan doctrine of the Nazi "pope" Rosenberg. One of the guards watching us said so unequivocally. The senseless and hateful destruction of these valuable collections made an unpleasant impression even on them. One of them, looking over the pile of fallen books, hid a volume under his uniform. It was undoubtedly not in the Polish language.

The next day they summon us to disassemble the monastery print shop.

"We bought this wonderful printing press just recently," explains Fr. Liguda, "and now we have to disassemble it. But take it apart carefully and keep each part separate. Then we can pack it into boxes and..."

**Translator's note*: According to Polish custom, the "opłatek" is a wafer shared by family and guests before the Christmas Eve supper as a sign of love and peace.

The trucks arrive, the same ones that a day earlier had taken the library collections to the furnaces at the sugar plant. Amazement bordering on horror overtakes us when they order us to take shovels and throw precision parts of linotypes, machinery, and other print-shop equipment into the trucks.

"Everything is going for scrap anyway!" explains the SS man in charge.

In the same way, the valuable botany, physics, and chemistry laboratories of this old monastery school went, one after another, "for scrap." And in the same way, valuable geographic and missionary collections were sent to be burned.

"Away with this filth!" the SS men decided. "The monastery will be converted into barracks."

Consequently, our stay there was soon to end. As Fr. Liguda wrote in one of his publications: "World rulers, thinking they act as drivers of nations, are themselves 'driven' by God."

For the time being, however, "they" were still *doing the driving*.

5

To Gdańsk

It was understandable that only mothers and sisters came to visit us. Women found it easier to travel. Men were more subject to searches and arrests.

I experience fear mixed with joy when on the last Sunday in January my father visits me.

"You see, my boy, I have the feeling that we may never see each other again in this life, and that's why..."

"But they can arrest you, father, accuse you of..."

"It doesn't matter anymore," he gestured with his hand in resignation. "I was born under the partition, attended a German school, had to serve in their army, and where did I serve? Right in the Kaiser's guard near Berlin. But, my dear son, these"—his brows motioned toward the guard—"these are not the Germans from World War I. If you only knew how they behaved in Bydgoszcz! It was horrible. A horrible, bloody Sunday. It's a miracle that I came out alive."[1]

There was a moment of silence. Precious time passes.

"Józef is still imprisoned," my father changes the subject. "However, they're supposed to free prisoners. Maybe they'll release him, too. They picked him up in Warsaw. It's lucky that he didn't die there." (At that time neither my father nor I knew that my brother Józef was so close to us, just across the Vistula, in fact, in the Grudziądz forts.)

Old Town in Bydgoszcz. A moment before one of the bloody executions. Standing in the first row of the condemned are priests.

5. To Gdańsk

"Hey, old man! Your time's up!" The guard's voice rouses us from our quiet talk.

"Well, it's time. May the Mother of God watch over you, son." Father always felt very uneasy when we, his sons, kissed his hand. "Well, well," he mumbles, pressing me to his chest, "only take care of yourself, take care." The guard allows me to go with him to the steps.

He leaves without looking back even once. I know my dear old man too well not to see that just then he was very much moved. Bent over as if he carried a burden on his wide shoulders, he walks along the poplar-lined road which is covered by snow. He turns around at the bend. He stops for a moment. It seems that he's hesitating, that he intends to turn back. He takes control of himself, waves his hand, turns around and continues to walk without glancing back again.

Three years later, when news reaches me in Dachau about my father being tortured to death, I could still see his tall, broad-shouldered, bent figure walking on the snow-covered road...

On 5 February, heavy military vehicles arrive at the monastery.

"A transport!"

"Where to?"

"Who knows. They say it's to a place where we'll have better care and better conditions."

There's sudden excitement, bustling activity, the gathering into knapsacks of underwear, a little food, and some odds and ends.

All the SVD fathers are getting ready for the trip as well. They have to leave the monastery with us. Fr. Liguda tries to make the best of it, but you can see the anguish he feels.

They pack us in tightly. Maybe it's better this way because it will be warmer. The snow crunches underfoot. It's freezing cold. We leave at about 2 o'clock in the afternoon. Alone on the monastery steps stands the lame stork Maciek, watching us as we pull away.

We drive into the streets of Gdańsk at dusk. The drivers don't know which way to go next. They stop and ask for directions. From their questions we gather that they're taking us to Nowy Port (Neufahrwasser).

Unloading began during the cold night in Nowy Port. They hurry us into the huge hall of the port. There's a search. You need to show everything you have with you.

"Line up against the wall!" the order is given.

We stand there. Before us on the cement floor are our modest possessions, in the midst of which SS men are taking inventory.

They're taking inventory. One finds a breviary, another a Rosary, which they take into their hands and parody the prayers. Another, pulling a stole out from one of the suitcases, places it on his shoulders, sits on a box pretending he's a priest in a confessional, and urges his colleagues, with a gesture of his hand, to go to confession. There are peals of laughter, roars of laughter.

The SS men are all very young. They're the offspring of Gdańsk families. Most of them speak to us in Polish. In subsequent years of wandering from camp to camp, we would meet with various SS elements, but none was so aggressive, none so depraved, and none to the

They're moving us out of prison! Where?... Who knows! Earlier several priests had been executed in Inowrocław. We had news about shootings in the area. Is it our turn today...? (drawing by Władysław Krawiec).

same degree so brutal and savage as those young SS men from Gdańsk. This is what Hitler's propaganda accomplished after years of indoctrinating them.

After robbing us of our already meager possessions and trampling the rest, they herd us through the deep snow toward some huge granary, then drive us up some worn steps and finally push us into a kind of dark attic.

The dark vault of the enormous granary, with its huge beams, gives the impression of a gothic church. Under one of the beams swings a sooty barn lantern, which gives off a flickering glow. It's difficult to see anything in this light. We stand helpless.

"Lie down!" thunders a threatening voice from the door.

After the greeting we received earlier, we know it's no laughing matter to deal with someone who gives orders in that way. We lie right down on the spot. There's a strong musty smell of straw that's been worn to dust. Someone moans, someone curses, something moves on the straw matting. It seems that the hall is already partially occupied.

"Where are you coming from?" I suddenly hear a whisper nearby.

"From Górna Grupa."

"And where are you from?"

"From Gdańsk. I am, or rather was, a professor in the local Polish high school. My name is Wojnowski. I've been stuck here for six months now."

"Six months? *Here*? In this pigsty?"

A rhythmic breathing was the only answer. My neighbor is asleep. Resting on my elbow, I chase thoughts that spin in my head far into the night.

"Get up! Get up!"

It seemed to me I had just fallen asleep. In the doorway stands an SS man with a club in his hand.

"Get up, you mad dogs!"

Washing is out of the question. After shaking pieces of damp straw off our clothing, prodded by clubs and yells, we run down the rickety steps at breakneck speed. Someone is moaning, someone is rolling under foot... A minute later, an SS club "straightens" us into single files. The Rev. Dean Czaki is moaning, holding his abdomen. The old man is having a gall-bladder attack. Silver-haired Rev. Envoy Downar holds him upright.

"In step, march!"

We move ahead. It's still dark night. What time could it be? We go through courtyards, we pass some gates. The steel helmets of the guards glisten in the frosty darkness. Frozen snow crunches under our feet. Cold penetrates to the bone.

We finally stop in front of a building with clouds of steam escaping from its open doors. A kitchen. The smell of coffee says as much. Breakfast is served in the following way: they admit us single file into a narrow corridor, urging us along with clubs; in the passageway we receive a small piece of clay-like bread and a tin of coffee, which we consume on the march, and at the exit we drop our cup into a barrel of dish-water.

This first "schooling" was the most painful because it cost me several kicks and blows with a club. For many it ended with spilled coffee and a trampled ration of bread.

Following breakfast, they set us to work unloading trucks, which have brought furniture plundered from Polish residences, schools and offices all over Gdańsk. Here we receive our first beatings. And they beat us with everything that comes to hand, whether a broken chair leg or an iron fireplace poker, and they beat wherever they can: on the head, the back, or on hands carrying heavy loads.

"Brutes," I hear Fr. Handke's whisper, as he lugs an easy chair in front of him. It's the second time the "serious" tone of my pastor has pleased me.

"Do you know whose residence they robbed today?" Fr. Bruno Szymański, prefect of the high-school in Świecie, asks me in a whisper. "Fr. Górecki's."

"How do you know?"

"Look," he pointed to the pile. "Books with his signature, a stole, chasubles."

"Did Fr. Górecki live in Gdańsk?"

"Yes. He was a professor in the Polish high-school."

"Hey! You mad dogs!" the SS man comes yelling, swinging a rod. "I'll give you something to talk about!" The blows rain down. It's too bad. We're learning at a cost.

There would be enough material for an entire volume if one wanted just to summarize the experiences of these several horrible days spent in Nowy Port, including being herded to Westerplatte. For us this was a baptism of Nazi brutality, the first such "front-line fire" we had encountered. All of this seemed so terrible and inhumane then, we thought nothing worse could happen to us. During the long day, the clubs of the young SS men battered us; at night the lice devoured us. It was no longer despair that entered our hearts, but utter desperation.

"Will we get out of this hell?"

Out of hell?... The real hell was still ahead of us. Nowy Port with its persecutions was only the outskirts of hell.

6

In the Hell of Stutthof

The road from Gdańsk to distant Sztutowo, called in "those" days Stutthof, leads along the Baltic coast and then by ferries across the Vistula River and its tributaries. In deep woods near Vistula Bay, the Nazis established the first concentration camp on Polish territory. They must have searched out this location a long time before the start of the war. Years later I met many fellow prisoners who were in Stutthof, but in a Stutthof that had a sewage system, toilets, a camp hospital, a kitchen, a spoon and dinner-pail. As some of the first "citizens" of this death camp, we remember it from the days when there were still no such "luxuries."

Open SS trucks transported us to that Stutthof on a cold Sunday (11 February 1940); we climbed out of them covered with frost and chilled to the bone.

An enormous square was surrounded on the forest side by a high wire fence and to the right by low buildings of the "home for the aged." In front of us was a gate with barbed wire around it, and beyond that — as far as the eye could see — a street with low wooden barracks on both sides. Such was the Stutthof camp of that time.

They unloaded us from the trucks into deep snow that covered the square.

"Fall in! Straighten ranks! Stand up straight, you damned dogs!" They rage on, they kick.

Out of the commandant's barracks comes an impressive-looking older SS man, whose last name was Akold and who later turned out to be not completely heartless. The roll call takes quite a bit of time.

"You will not remain here long," offers Akold looking over a sheet of paper. "You have nothing but lucky numbers." (They registered us in the 9700s.)

"We're not going to stay here long. Did you hear?"

Oh, how little a prisoner needs to kindle hope in him or even unwavering faith.

The roll call is over. It's Sunday and the SS staff has the afternoon off. Akold himself leads us to the camp.

"You'll live with your colleagues."

"With priests?"

"Right. We've had a large group for several months."

We walk, looking around with curiosity. Finally, the priests' barracks.

"God! These are supposed to be priests?"

Covered in rags, the figures stiffen to attention.

"At ease!" Akold gives his kind permission. "I'm bringing you colleagues. Receive them cordially."

"Yes, sir!" The quarters leader, the Rev. Dean Piechowski, pastor from Lubiszewo, stiffens to attention. Smiling at us are faces darkened by frost and emaciated to the bone; yellowed teeth flash from under parched lips. The reception is somehow awkward. In their sunken eyes something like envy appears because we still look "like that," and our souls are filled with an undeserved shame because we're "like that," while they?... All around it smells like a cemetery.

"Wojtek!" Mirek Ziarniak's cry rouses me from my sad thoughts. "Wojtek! Dear Wojtek!" Mirek embraces his friend with a warm hug. How could he recognize this skeleton? "Allow me to introduce Fr. Wojciech Gajdus, director of Catholic youth in the Pelplin Diocese."

Tears well in my eyes. God! This sallow face, this bent-over back, these clammy, skeletal hands...

"Henryk!"

Before me stands a new skeleton, grinning with yellow teeth (this was supposed to be a smile) and holding out his hand in greeting. Feverishly I try to remember where I saw someone like this, then all at once I recognize him.

"Stach!" I couldn't find any other words.

This was Staszek Grabowski, a friend from my student days and later a master of novices in Potulice near Nakło, a member of the Society of Christ and one of the first co-workers of Fr. General Posadzy.

"They arrested me in Potulice back in October of last year. I spent several months in a prison in Bydgoszcz, then in Gdańsk, and since December I've been here. Here I am. Just look at me..."

No, I could not look.

"I'll introduce you, if only from a distance, to those who are here. The one over there, talking with such animation, that's Fr. Franek Bielicki, former chaplain from the ship *Batory*, who likes to brag a little about his acquaintance with Captain Borkowski. That poor fellow who's bent over is dear Fr. Alfons Muzalewski, a vicar from Gdańsk. They arrested him the day the war started, and ever since he's been sitting in Stutthof."

"An older man," I interject, "although he has a rather youthful face."

"Old? No. He's a young man, our age. He was twisted so terribly by illness. They slept here for weeks in the open air. Do you understand?"

I feel increasingly uneasy, increasingly ashamed. Increasingly I understand Fr. Aloś Góranowicz, who couldn't sleep because they took his colleagues but didn't want to arrest him.

"Oh, the one who's wrapped up in a sack is Józek Chmiel, a Bernardine from Skępe, and the one by the window is Fr. Bernard Czapliński, director of Caritas in Toruń. A lovable, honest soul. He's been in prison for a long time, but they brought him to Stutthof only a few days ago.[1] The one by the stove — that's Fr. Stef Frelichowski from Toruń, who leads us in joint prayers. A fireball. You'll get to know him better, and you'll form your own opinion. And that one, that's Msgr. Aloś Klinkosz from Tczew. Further over, Zygmunt Lewandowski from Kamień; next to him Kazio Litewski and Stach Manikowski. The little one is Jaś Osowski from Rybno. But I'm probably boring you? You'll get to know them soon anyway."

It's Sunday afternoon. Prisoners weren't forced to work today, so there's time to talk. And there's so much to say...

Next to the tiny windows, around the perimeter of straw, sit "the hunters." (This term was used to describe those who killed lice.)

6. In the Hell of Stutthof

"Do you have many?"

"Millions! You'll find out yourself during the night. They won't let you sleep, and whoever is a little weak, they literally eat him. Don't be surprised. There has been no change of clothes, no laundry, no bathing for a month. We simply lie down to sleep in our clothes, as we are, and then at night we freeze. There isn't even any water to wash in. Only one small pump for many thousands. It's just enough to quench your thirst sometimes, and even then not always."

The early winter evening declines. It's dark in the barracks. You can see the sunset's glow in the small windows.

"The sun is setting red. It's going to be freezing at night."

"Just so it doesn't snow."

"It would be warmer."

"But you don't know how much work is involved in that, how much drudgery. How many fall under the blows when you have to clear it away."

The evening roll call. My first in Stuffhof. The camp, which up to now has been quiet, suddenly comes to life. Movement, running, shouts, cries! Suddenly from the dark line of woods surrounding the camp the blinding light of huge watchtower floodlights brightly illuminates barracks, streets and residents, who have lined up in columns. The block leaders "establish order" in their units. Clouds of steam pour out of open doors.

"Good Lord! Stach! Over there, across from us, they're naked!"

"You'll see even worse scenes."

The block lining up across from us, on the other side of the street, consists almost

One small pump, which would freeze every day, was supposed to supply several thousand prisoners. Thus, washing was out of the question for months, since there was not even enough water to drink.

entirely of half-naked people. Only some kind of tattered rags hang on these human skeletons.

"That's our intelligentsia, arrested on the day the war broke out in Gdańsk. They are the remaining survivors. And these, too, will go soon. Not a day passes without them carrying out several dozen dead from their barracks. They're dying like flies. I bet not one will survive until spring!"

"*Achtung!*" The voice of the camp senior thunders from the gate down the entire length of the street.

The ranks stand motionless! Frozen bodies stiffen to attention. The naked shake in the cold. The camp commandant accompanied by an SS retinue is coming for the roll call. In the glare of the floodlights epaulettes sparkle, boots shine, and the guards' steel helmets glisten. Roll call lasts a long time... Finally, it's over. But the commandant does not leave. After asking the camp senior some questions, he walks toward us.

"So these are the dirty war instigators?!" Hate burns in his steel eyes. "We will break your habit of firing on innocent German people from behind fences. Fall down!" The sudden order goes out like the crack of a whip. We are standing so tightly rank upon rank that we fall in rows on top of one another.

"You accursed Polish dogs! You dirty shavelings!" Herr Kommandant tramples on heads, backs, and frozen hands! Herr Kommandant is angry! Herr Kommandant kicks, but woe if he dirties his shiny shoes. "We will re...edu...cate...you!" he spells out, as he strikes again and again with his heels into the living mass of bodies.

"Under Your protection," someone's whispered prayer can be heard.

"We will re...edu...cate...you!" The lips of the commandant twist in a hideous grimace. They're the same lips that probably whisper tenderly to his wife and children — about love...

That was our reception in Stuffhof.

"You know, this commandant is not even the worst one. You'll see his deputy tomorrow. His last name is Mathesius. He's the incarnation of all evil powers," Stach whispers in my ear when we're already lying down on our straw bedding.

We lie in our clothes, without any sort of covering, and so closely together that we can turn over only in unison when someone asks.

"Stach, are there holes in the roof? It's dripping on me."

"No, the roof is intact, but it's covered with frost on the inside. With so many warm bodies, the frost melts and then starts dripping. It's going to drip like that until morning."

"Until morning?"

Reveille is at 4 A.M.! We jump to our feet, shaking off the muck that's sticking to our clothes.

"*Antreten!*" We rush to the exit like a mad herd. Usually the SS men, who feel cold and want to warm up, wait by the windows to see whether they can detect any kind of delay in our leaving. Then they burst in with clubs and doomsday begins.

Breakfast consists of a tin of wishy-washy brew, called coffee, and a piece of clay-like sticky bread, hard as a rock.

"Form work units!"

We're herded through the camp to the huge snow-covered square mentioned earlier.

"Everything must be cleared away by evening!"

Our "capo," or work leader, is a fellow prisoner, a Pole from Gdańsk, whose last name is Gański. He's tall, bony, with a withered face and sharp features, giving the impression of a heartless man. That is not so, however.

"Priests," he explains. "I have no desire to murder you. Work with common sense. But when I start yelling at you, it will be a sign that one of the SS men is nearby, and then pick up the pace right away, or else in the evening you'll get ten on your rear."

Old Gański was kind. He had a good heart. But all this planning did not save either him or us from "catching" ten lashes on the...

"I don't know what's the matter with you," the old man would grumble later. "When I worked with groups of laymen, we never caught it so often."

"Because they weren't priests," Ignaś Wojewódka suggested.[2]

"Maybe that's true. Maybe that's it exactly, because you're priests."

And so it was. If the Pope spoke on the radio, they would let us have it, starting with the most senior monsignor, going through all the high dignitaries, and ending with the youngest vicar. This also happened at every major address by any sort of Church representative.

"They talk and talk, but we get the thrashing," you heard such complaints often, especially among the younger clergy. "They should have talked and yelled when it was the time for it!"

"Quiet now, quiet!" their shocked elders would calm them.

A psychologist would have interesting material for a study under such circumstances. Moralists could reach equally interesting conclusions. It's very easy years later to spin sentimental legends about torments, but right now, unfortunately, it's very hard... Let's put this issue aside, however. Life itself renders a verdict on it.

That's how the days passed in Stutthof: desperately warding off millions of lice, running like animals for a bowl of warm water with a large leaf of boiled cabbage in it, rushing to work from the dark of morning to the dark of evening.

The living conditions were horrible in the primitive Camp Stutthof of that time.

In the evenings we recited prayers together in secret, lying close like sardines in a barrel, covering our faces with our hands against moisture dripping from the ceiling, and tearing at skin mangy from lice bites. If anyone tries to spin sentimental legends about mystical flights under those conditions, I will challenge him! A human being crammed like an animal on a foul-smelling, rotten bed of straw can't pray! Unless he considers prayer to be the thoughtless chattering of numb lips. It often happens that such prayer-mills satisfy bodies rather than souls. It may be that the only real prayers a human being can summon under such conditions are short fervent prayers, sent like flaming arrows up to heaven.

We lived by them.

7

The Butchers of Stutthof

The sun's red disk is setting behind the tops of the old pine trees. The nearby woods are already slumbering. Long violet shadows lie down on the frozen earth. Increasingly severe cold sets in for the night. Thin streaks of gray smoke from the barracks chimneys float up into the sky. The camp is quiet, as if everything had died out. Only shadows flicker on the wet window panes. From time to time, a door creaks somewhere in the barracks, or wooden clogs tap against the frozen ground; a hunched-over silhouette floats quietly along the walls; again the creaking of a door and then a deeper quiet. Following the day's drudgery, the camp has come to a standstill awaiting evening roll call.

A sudden, shrill whistle pierces the air. Mayhem! Teeming with wretched humanity, the barracks reverberate. From the overcrowded interior pitiful human figures pour out through open doors amid a cloud of steam, which rises swiftly in tall columns toward the almost deep-blue dome of the sky. Floodlights glow from guard towers situated by the dark wall of the woods. In their light, the frost-covered roofs shine like silver. A scene as though from a fairy-tale. Romantic. Worthy of an artist's brush. If only the scene were not accompanied by a hellish din, shouts, cries, and curses mixed with someone's prayer; if only there were no helpless crowded mass of bodies, which the block leaders are trying to organize into units.

"Attention! ... Count off! ... Left flank forward! You so-and-so!"

Light streams from the windows of the commandant's quarters. Fear grips the soul. What will they devise for today? Maybe they'll keep us for several hours in the freezing cold?

Maybe...

"Shut your filthy mouths!"

It is said that the damned in hell, in addition to sensory punishment, will endure all the most vulgar expressions of meanness from depraved satanic souls.

We, too, endured them in Stutthof.

At last, the units are ready. The stronger among us support the half-dead. We stand. Minutes pass ... ten, twenty minutes... Our fingers stiffen. The "drops" hanging from noses turn into small icicles... The temperature falls well below zero... A cold wind bites at emaciated skeletons... I no longer feel my legs below the knees. They're like rubber... These long periods standing in anticipation of roll call had only one advantage, which was that lice, deterred by the cold, didn't bite. This was a phenomenon known to every prisoner. Burrowed into recesses and nooks and crannies, the lice sat there quietly.

We stand, freezing to the bone, whispering prayers. This tradition of praying during roll call, which started unconsciously in Stutthof, was to continue through the last days of slavery in Dachau. We stand... Oh, how slowly the minutes go by! A hungry stomach is demanding its rights. But then the thought occurs: How painfully must hunger torment those who have endured these conditions for months!?

"'God, Father of Abraham, you are power and goodness itself, look down from Heaven on this race, send...'"

But what if God Himself sent this suffering upon us as our just punishment? I recall the words of Fr. Kazio Grzelak, a spiritual son of Fr. Maksymilian Kolbe: "Henryk, what we are experiencing is our punishment for trampling on and not recognizing the greatest commandment, the commandment of love! This is what Fr. Maksymilian once explained to us, what he predicted."

Oh, how slowly the time passes... If we are feeling the cold, what must be the suffering of those who are naked in the block across from us? Many of them are covered only with the hanging shreds of sacks or decayed rags full of holes. In a few months, when our clothes also rot on us in these beds of straw, the same fate awaits us. For the time being, we're protected by the warm underwear we brought with us and the warmth of our own clothes.

"Why don't you take off your sweater and offer it, let's say, to the naked man across from you? St. Martin would have done that. And how many more saints would have..."

"Hail Mary, full of grace..."

"Hee ... hee ... hee!" Something snickers in my soul. "Do you think God will hear such prattling of the lips? Take off the warm clothing! Offer it to a freezing brother! That would be more wonderful than prayer! Why are you concerned about food and clothing? Look at the lilies of the field and the birds. They neither sow nor reap, and yet your Heavenly Father..."

Torment!

But maybe this is morbid delirium?

Ah, to eat my fill once more in life, and...

"Under Your protection..." Just once more in life to take a loaf of whole-wheat bread in my hands, to bite my teeth into it, to taste it and chew and chew and...

"*Aaaachtung!*" a voice suddenly shouts from the gate. Guards stiffen to attention, black helmets shine in the floodlights. Rifle barrels glisten.

"*Achtung!*" The camp senior's voice thunders along the camp street. Our ranks stiffen. Silence. Dead silence.

Officer Mathesius, the deputy commandant, accompanied by his retinue, walks over to receive the report. He is rather short in stature, thickset, broad-shouldered, with arms somewhat too long hanging at the sides of his corpulent body. A high cap bordered in silver is perched over his low brow. He walks with a quick step. His shining knee boots glisten. Mathesius, the butcher of Stutthof! Woe to the prisoner with whom he finds fault. The grimmest of stories abound about him. It's not without reason that he's been dubbed the butcher of Stutthof!

He's coming. Hearts stop beating. With one gesture he can send hundreds of innocent victims to death. And that has happened! It has happened many times.

Commands crack like whips! Block leaders give their reports. The Rev. Dean Piechowski stiffens in front of our unit. He's convinced that at the end he'll get a kicking anyway, but someone has to catch it. The role of senior in a clergy barracks is not easy.

Finally, the main report. The camp senior gives it to the report director, the latter — to Mathesius.

But what's this? There's no traditional "At ease!" Officer Mathesius is talking with his retinue. A thousand eyes rest upon the drunkard's bloated face. He has given some order that's inaudible to us. Two SS men stiffen to attention, turn around on their heels and with quick steps move toward the kitchen, located in the middle of the camp. We already know what they're heading for. There, under the eaves of the roof stands the notorious wooden saw-horse, which serves for meting out punishment.

It has been placed now in the middle of the street. Officer Mathesius slowly takes off his gloves and passes them to someone in his retinue.

"*Alle Pfaffen raus!* All shavelings step out!" (In disdainful, abusive language, "Pfaffe" is one of the accepted descriptions for a priest.)

"Faster! Faster, you accursed dogs!" barks the group of young SS men.

"For today's laziness at work each will get ten ... understand?"

"Yes, Sir!"

"On with it! First volunteer!" Mathesius takes the whip in his hand.

The first to step from the ranks is young Fr. Frelichowski. As always a fireball. He would certainly qualify for the arena of a Roman circus.

They've already stretched him out. One of the SS men holds his head, another his feet. Mathesius stands astride, makes several practice motions with the whip... A sharp hissing sound carries into the ranks. Mathesius had wasted his talent too long as a restaurant manager. It was finally the war that liberated in him "a man of worth..."

I realize that the present edition, like the first one, will reach the hands of Germans who know the Polish language, and that it will also get to the desks of German judges, and that, once again, I could face reviews like those I recently received from German officials: "Yes, of course, Father writes his *Shavelings* as a priest, but also very much as a Pole."[1] However, since I experienced these events, which, unfortunately, add up to hundreds upon hundreds of painful examples, how am I to treat them? I realize that the butcher Mathesius, who wore the epaulettes of a high-ranking officer, did not belong to the German officer ranks either by training, temperament, or culture. I also realize that Hitler, desiring to rely on soldiers who were dedicated to him for life and to the death, often drafted into officer ranks the most intellectually and morally impoverished element. I know that Mathesius, a restaurant manager from a local tavern, was not an officer by temperament. He was one by appointment, however, by his officer's insignia and epaulettes, and — what is most important — by the scope of authority vested in him as master of life and death for thousands of people. I'm trying to avoid sowing hatred. I'm far from having a sarcastic attitude toward the entire German nation. I have had and still have many close German friends. Real friends. Despite the traditional saying: "Never in this world will a German be brother to a Pole," I believe — at the risk of being called a Germanophile — that through good will on both sides we can and should be brothers, children of the same Father and the same Mother, the Immaculate Mary. In describing the painful events of years behind the barbed wire of Hitler's camps, if I take aim at anyone, it is at the bloody hydra of Hitlerism, at which every decent German takes aim. Therefore, I'm only availing myself of a right to which all decent journalists from your nation are entitled.[2]

Officer Mathesius, deputy commandant of the Stutthof camp, personally metes out punishment. He hits... hits... hits with the whip to exhaustion, in a frenzy. It may be that through this cruel beating he releases the animal instincts rankling his depraved nature.

Our entire unit of clergy has to count out loud:

"One ... two ... three ... ... nine ... ten!"

"Next!"

We proceed in order: young and old, vicars, pastors, professors, and monsignors. With the same zeal, the SS man's hand holds the blond hair of a church assistant or the white hair of old priest emeritus Fr. Niemir. (We still had hair then; they started to cut it short only later.)

We proceed more and more efficiently, with style. The block leader, Rev. Dean Piechowski, after getting his portion and then pulling up his pants, maintains order. What else would you expect?

There goes old Rev. Dean Czaki, and behind him the Rev. Counselor Konitzer, the Reverend Envoy Downar, the Rev. Canon Kiszkurno; there goes the giant Rev. Rector Liguda, then the Rev. Prof. Szukalski, famous throughout Poland as the author of marvelous cathechistic discourses; next seminary professors and those with doctorates, which were earned frequently in Regensburg and other German universities. But does Mathesius care? Has he ever heard of these learned institutions at all?

Officer Mathesius finally grew tired. He handed the whip to a nearby officer, the next in rank. He wipes the perspiration from his forehead. The whip now grasped by a rested hand cuts the air with a hiss; blows fall on an emaciated body. The victim moans...

"...Seven ... eight ... nine," chants the unit of clergy.

"...Nine ... ten," answers an echo from the dark woods, through the barbed wire fence.

"Next!"

"Sauber!"

"Next!" ... and the next after that.

Officer Mathesius watches, his hands on his hips. He stands in a wide stance, powerful like Jove.

"Give it to me!" he reaches out for the whip again. He cannot allow the torture to end without his active participation.

"One! ... Two! ... Three!" he now counts out loud himself. "You hit like this! Like this and this!"

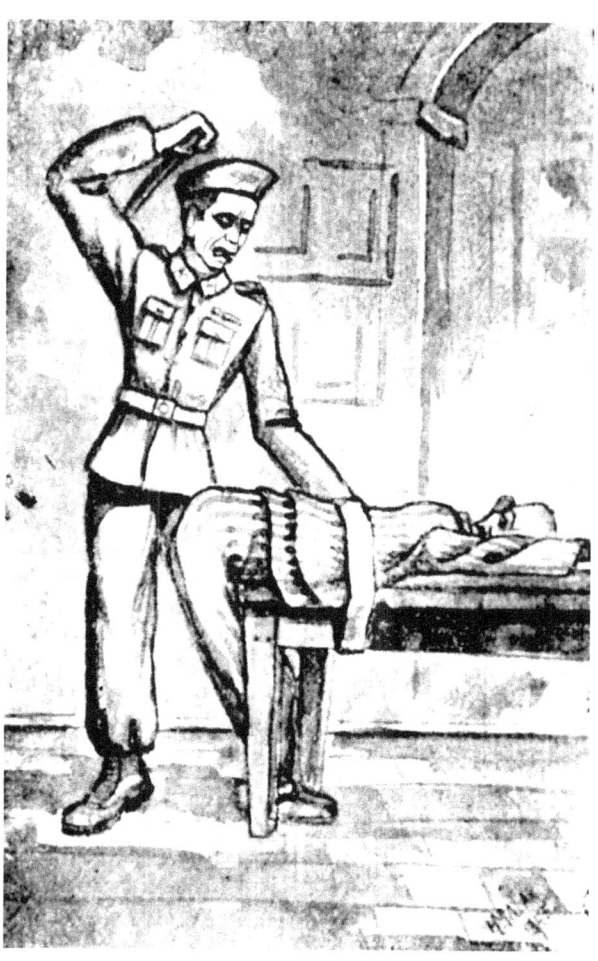

This is the "new order" in Europe! The SS men never deprived themselves of this praiseworthy task! (drawing by the author).

The end. The last of the monsignors pulls up his pants. Joyful sparks flicker in Mathesius' bleary eyes. Pride fills his wide chest. The eyes of the young Germans gaze at him with outright toadyism. Only decent Akold has an expression of disgust on his face. I believe there were more like him, and if they didn't show their disdain, it was because of fear. But, unfortunately, we also see that the group of young SS men from Gdańsk looks at the "leader" with real admiration.

A sigh of relief escapes from thousands of prisoners. The "masters" are content. The "masters" are sated. That's all for today. It doesn't matter that cut skin is burning and smarting. It could have been worse. Even a hundred times worse.

But what's this? (Terrified hearts sink again.) Butcher Mathesius walks up to our unit and suddenly gives the order:

"Fall down!!!"

We fall obediently as if cut down. We fall one upon another, with faces to the ground. No one dares to lift up his head. Naturally. That would mean death! No one wants to attract attention. And then — at a signal given by Mathesius — the group of SS men attacks us as we lie there. They tread over us, kick us, crush us with shod heels, and trample upon us, they *trample upon us*!

These are no longer people, these are animals!

There is moaning, whimpering, the hoarse gurgle of those trampled on the throat. Whips and rubber clubs are whistling, rifle butts are striking heads. Frozen puddles beneath us splatter mud mixed with blood. We have it in our mouths, our noses, our eyes.

Gentlemen of the German courts! God was looking down from heaven on these and many similar scenes, and He is the best witness. In any case, out of many hundreds, a dozen or so of us survived, survived perhaps to tell about it... To tell about it so that younger generations might be raised, after all, in a more humane spirit, so that the bloody, shameful hecatombs of "those" days might not be repeated!

Finally, the end.

"Get up!" the order whistles from the breathless chest of our heroic deputy commandant, officer Mathesius.

There are still a few who are strong enough to get up, oh Herr Mathesius. Don't bear any grudge, however, against those who still lie down, pressed into the mud, with crushed heads and broken limbs. And may you give a full reprieve to those who have passed on, beaten with rifle butts and trampled under the heels of your shining boots. Forgive their audacity, too, for splattering their blood on the spotless shine of your officer's boot-tops. Forgive the poor creatures. Tomorrow the hand of a humble slave will polish them again.

We get up... We pick up the injured and the beaten. The victors head toward the command center. That's all for today.

"Who knows?" someone among us plants a doubt. "If they get drunk enough now, they can barge in at night with a new torment."

And they often did barge in at night. Quite often. Then only the walls of the barracks, gray with frost, were witnesses to their inhuman, drunken pranks.

Gentlemen of the jury! So often you promote the expression that Polish priests suffered for their *national* beliefs! Why then was the following saying wide-spread among Polish prisoners: "How good it is not to be a priest!" Why did they especially hate and persecute us, the priests?

"Hail, Mary, full of grace," the prayer whispered in unison rises from the darkness when we finally lie closely packed together on the damp straw bedding.

"Holy Mary, Mother of God, pray for us ... for us sinners, now and at the hour ... at the hour of our death."

Death on this day had a fruitful harvest.

"Our Father, who art in heaven..."

The murmur of voices in the darkness sounds like sobbing.

"...forgive us our trespasses, as we forgive those who trespass against us..."

"Kazio," I hear a whisper, "even them? Mathesius, too?"

"Yes, Janusz, them, too, both Mathesius, and Hitler!" ...

"Amen."

"Sleep with God, Kazio."

"With God, Janusz."

I feel something warm fall on my frostbitten hand. It was a tear.

Poor Fr. Janusz Komf, heroic chaplain from Kutno, the very one who administered to the dying General Wład, and poor Fr. Kazio Grzelak, spiritual son of Fr. Kolbe and former assistant at the monastery in Gniezno, were soon to go before the throne of the Heavenly Father.

Streams of light beam from windows of the commandant's building, shouts and cheers resound, a drinking spree is in full swing. One must celebrate the "victory" of a strenuous day!

"Are they going to come tonight?"

"Don't think about it. Sleep. God watches over us."

"But what if ... what if God Himself is allowing us to be whipped?"

Such nights and others like them were perhaps the most fruitful retreats. Blessed are they who emerged from them ... *born anew*.

8

Miserere

The words defining Stutthof of that time as "real hell on earth" are as pale a reflection of reality as, for example, a faded (though valuable) Gobelin tapestry that attempts to represent the monstrosity of Dante's hell. The figures of Commandant Pohl, his deputies Mathesius and Just (rumored to be the Pole Gustowski) and their entire retinue, the report directors and guards of all ranks, were an incarnation of the "spirits" playing main roles in this grim tragedy.

Standing out in this group of non-commissioned officers was the director of camp operations, Neubauer, alias Neugebauer, who was known for liquidating several prisoners by shooting them in the woods while they were clearing land or by splitting open their heads with a shovel during construction work. That was part of his daily routine, like eating breakfast or smoking a cigarette. And the fellow was enormous, with fists like loaves of bread (supposedly a carpenter by trade), with wrestler's shoulders and a sullen, hateful gaze. We feared Mathesius, but we trembled at an encounter with Neubauer. Killing a prisoner on the street in broad daylight was an entertainment for him and a warm-up for work.

The cold was weakening us, hunger decimating us, work killing us, and millions of lice finishing us off. People were literally dropping like flies! Skeletons maddened by hunger dragged along the camp street, by the barracks, devouring the dirty snow. Death was a sweet release for which you whimpered each evening, begging that it come quietly, that it take you from the lice-infested bed of straw, so long as it wasn't under a bone-breaking club or in the agony of refined punishments, so long as it wasn't … a martyr's death! Perhaps a few individuals among us measured up to the martyrdom of Father Kolbe. Perhaps … The majority feared it with the panicky dread of an animal held at bay by hunters.

The Stutthof camp at that time did not have either a crematorium or a cemetery. Those who died or were killed had to be taken by vehicle once a week to Gdańsk. I don't know whether they were burned or buried there.

The camp "gravediggers," that is, those charged with taking the dead to the camp pigsty located near the headquarters building, were the priests.

"This is your occupation!" the leadership declared. "Earn your livelihood now while there are so many opportunities."

So we gathered the dead from near the barracks, from heaps thrown in backyards; we gathered them from their beds of straw because sometimes they were kept inside several days in order to get the tiny slice of hard bread that was due them. We carried them to the pigsty, throwing them into stalls that were empty of swine. A real plague in that building were rats, as big as small cats, which feasted on the dead. But who was shocked by this? The hardened SS men? We, who were systematically being stripped of our humanity and human feelings? Anyway, they say that rat meat is really not so bad! And if the rat had fed on dead bodies? ... It's so easy to feel disgust when you're full. You "reason" differently if you're starving and, unfortunately, sinking so very, very close to the level of an animal. Several years later, when we (Stutthof survivors) were already in Dachau, a transport of prisoners arrived there from Stutthof. After the cars were unloaded, it became evident that many bodies of the dead had "choice" parts cut out. Cannibalism! The most horrible cannibalism — eating human flesh! (Gentlemen of the jury, you know about this incident. It was investigated during the trial in Nuremburg!) People were eating people in the year 1943! Why shouldn't they have eaten rats fed on dead prisoners in the year 1940 in Stutthof?

So we gathered the dead, taking the greenish, slimy and malodorous bodies, placing them in a crude trough, and carrying them to that pigsty. On Saturday the dead were loaded into vehicles covered with linen hoods, and the transport went to Gdańsk. Before it had left camp territory, however, new stacks of the dead were already piling up behind the barracks.

It's Saturday, March 9, 1940, the Saturday before Passion Sunday. We worked through the morning, at noon we hunted lice, then, until four o'clock, we cleaned the camp and scrubbed the lavatory, and at last we were kindly given "free time" until supper.

We're sitting in the barracks on our straw. Here and there some are finishing "the hunt," one person is fixing his worn-down clogs, another is "darning" his ragged clothing (with fiber pulled out of a sack and threaded into a bent wire instead of a needle). One person dozes, another stares in front of him. We like these moments of silence. We like them even better than the prayers we murmur together. These are moments of meditation. The subjects don't matter. Perhaps they are not very much in the style of prepared manuals for meditation, and perhaps they don't stick to traditional points; it doesn't matter. They are surely meditations, however, and — most likely — they reach deeper into souls than meditations slept through in a seminary chapel (at least that is what a faction of young radical clergy maintains).

"Fratres," a quiet voice seeps from a dark corner near the stove, "today is the feast of the Mother of God ... the Mother of God, before tomorrow's Passion Sunday."

"It's starting to sound 'official' again," grumbles one of the young radicals. "Why are they forcing me to be a spiritual marionette, even here in the camp? Why don't they leave each of us with our own thoughts? Why these ready-made spiritual 'canned goods' again and again?"

"Placing ourselves in the presence of God, we ask, fratres, for..."

"Oh, merciful Jesus," the whisper is sharp, whistling, "I don't think I can stand it; I'm leaving."

"Easy, my friend, easy. Don't listen to him. Meditate alone."

"But I can't, I can't! I'm choking! Suffocating! For so many years they fed us this theoretical trivia, for so many years..."

Somebody's hand covers the agitated fellow's mouth.

The elders have settled around the stove. It's warmer there, and that place rightly belongs to the old and sickly. The young element of radical clergy is spread on the periphery, especially near doors and windows where it's drafty. And that's fine. One day we, too, will be old. We will? Will we live that long?

The division between the two generations, between the old and the young, is getting deeper and more pronounced. The former, conservatives, live with their memories; we — with a reality born in sweat, tears, and spilt blood. The former have behind them the dignity of age, positions, self-esteem. We? Nothing. Only these feverish heads full of turmoil and these hearts on fire. (At that moment a question, an issue, a problem occurs to me: to which of these two factions would Fr. Maksymilian Kolbe himself belong? Judging by statements made by Kazio Grzelak and Zbych Młynik, he would probably side with us, the young.)

"And so, fratres, the Mother of God was preparing in her heart for painful moments. Let this be the starting point of our meditation. The second point..."

Suddenly the doors open. An SS man rushes inside with a rubber club. Rosy-cheeked, well-fed, a frown on his forehead, the club raised over his head, he gives the impression of a Cherubim at the gates of paradise.

"Outside, you damned dogs!"

Chaos! The club bounces on a whirling human mass. There's a traffic jam at the doorway. People are being crushed!

"Hurry! Hurry! You mad dogs! Hurry!" The club is aided by kicks.

"Hurry! Hurry!" we urge ourselves on, just so we can get out.

Why is our exit going so slowly today? Other times it went more efficiently. "Hurry!" urge those in back, who are being beaten and kicked.

The reason becomes clear when we get outside. It's because another Cherubim stands at the exit with a fiery club, beating everyone who comes out. He pummels! Not only pummels, he thrashes! Standing with legs astride, he thrashes as if with a flail, slashing the knobby heads, the bald skulls, the angular and bony backs, the fingers... He thrashes, and on his wide face there's a smile... *Freude durch Kraft!* Through power to ... joy!

"Listen," a whisper reaches me, as we line up in ranks, "What was the topic of that second point of the medi..."

"Stop, you scoffer!" hisses another voice. "You're a cynic."

"Well, no, because you see ... I'm really..."

"Take your *Fleischkasten* (literally: meat crates) and go gather the rest of the corpses," comes the order. "Left face! In step, forward march!"

We go, dragging our heavy clogs through the freezing mud.

"Halt!" the order is given in front of one of the barracks. The crew with the trough disappears into the dim interior.

"And you," the SS man turns with a smile, "form a funeral procession."

Expressions of surprise.

"Form a procession! Do you hear me?!"

The rubber club helps get us into formation. The entire unit stretches out into two long lines. Even precedence is observed: the elders in back, the young toward the front.

The first pair of gravediggers is already emerging from the dim interior. Their gaunt fingers grab the door frame. Two feet wrapped in rags step over the high threshold. Above their bent heads emerges the top of the trough, from which protrude the bluish feet of a dead man. Bits of rotted straw are stuck between his toes. Following the first pair, bent under the trough, the next pair crosses the high threshhold. We can already see them when suddenly one of the bearers trips. The trough with the deceased sways and instantly slips forward. To find support, the bearers reach down with spread fingers to touch the ground,

And they proceeded that way — a living skeleton with a dead man clinging to him (drawing by the author).

and it seems the trough, together with the deceased, will smash into the mud, but the bearers regain control.

The club, however, is already bouncing on their heads.

"You almost dropped it, you dogs! Did they teach you to treat the dead like this?!"

And who knew exactly why they were being beaten? Was it because they almost dropped it or because they didn't drop it? In any case, who in the camp ever knew why they beat us?

"Now, pay attention! You'll walk in front of this stiff, and you'll sing your ... your..." he stammered trying to find the word. "Your hocus-pocus!" he finally blurted out, satisfied with himself.

"Forward, march!" comes the order. "Sing!"

We look at each other. We don't know what to do. If we start to sing, we could get a beating. If we don't sing, we'll get it for not following the order. And what are we to sing?

"Are you going to sing, you pig-hounds?!" Running down the long files, he hits left and right with his club. "Sing! Sing your hocus-pocus! Like you used to sing for the dead!"

Suddenly, there rings out from the front of the procession a dolorous *"Miserere mei, Deus..."*

"Yes, like that. That's good. Sing that!" The placated SS man is pleased. "But all of you sing, everyone sing!"

And suddenly from a hundred festering throats it bursts forth, like a wave that's been released, filled with tears of pain:

"Secundum magnam misericordiam tuam..."

"That's it, yes, good, good," the SS man approves in his broken Polish.

8. Miserere

"*Et secundum ... multitudinem ... miserationum ... tuarum ... dele ... iniquitatem ... meam,*" we wail out the Gregorian chant, with all its variations, as we did "long ago."

And the powerful song flows through the camp. It strikes against the walls of the barracks, it strikes the barbed wires. There's so much strength in it, so much pain... "Have pity on us, oh Lord, according to your great mercy."

"Louder! Louder!" the SS man urges.

"*Amplius ... lava me ...* Wash me of my guilt and of my sin purify me." ...

"You know, this sounds like the public confiteor of the Polish clergy!"

"You're a cynic! You can't even respect such a moment. Sing!"

"*Quoniam iniquitatem meam ego cognosco...* Because I acknowledge my iniquity and my sin stands ever before me," continues the repentant melody of the psalm.

Out from the shadows of the barracks crawl half-dead bodies. A grimace of surprise enlivens their pale, sunken faces. Eyelids that have lost their lashes blink, toothless mouths murmur: "*Miserere ... miserere...* Lord, have mercy on us."

Prisoners pushing wheelbarrows come to a halt. Shovels stop in mid-air. Even SS men supervising the work columns gape in astonishment. This has never happened in Stutthof before!

The unit of Polish prisoners of war, locked up with us and still wearing military uniforms, stands formally at attention. Sergeant Józek Kurzawa salutes. The rest of the prisoners follow the soldiers' example. Bent backs straighten. Mangy heads are bared. Crooked fingers, looking more like claws, are held along the seams of trouser legs. In eyes, in these eyes that haven't managed to cry for months, tears again are formed.

"*Tibi soli ... peccavi...* Against You alone have I sinned ... *et malum coram te feci...*"

The SS men have misjudged. They had wanted to create a spectacle deriding religion, but instead they met with a completely opposite effect. In those terrorized thousands of walking skeletons one thing continued to live with a flame: *faith*! The experiment was premature. Certainly they could have counted on some minimal effect — but only much later — in Sachsenhausen and an even greater one in Dachau, where our Polish element met with so many other nationalities and so many other faiths, not excluding non-believers and outright enemies of all religion. But in Stutthof? In Stutthof in 1940, when the thousands of those imprisoned consisted only of Poles?

"Shut your mugs, you rabid dogs! You damned shavelings! You..."

A veritable hell is unleashed. Clubs. Furious kicking. To help out, other guards also come running.

"At a run, march! Such damned dogs," explains the SS man who's escorting us. "They wanted to sing! And on top of it such a song?! This is open revolt. Revolution! I'll show you, you sickly dogs! I'm going to ... I'll order you to be shot!"

Beaten, kicked, pushed over, we break our ranks. We run like a confused, frightened herd. Driving us from all sides is a gang of SS men armed with clubs. Many of us fall. Many are trailing along with their last strength. Blood drips from the head of the gray-haired elder, Fr. Niemir.

"You're going to die today, dog!" bellows an eighteen-year-old SS maniac, beating the old man with a vengeance. Fr. Niemir falls. Steel-shod boots trample him.

We run in a disorderly pack. At the center, over our heads, is the trough with the deceased. It's just luck that they haven't dropped him and lost him. The pigsty is just ahead of us. That's why the blows and kicks are even more "wholehearted." People are falling. They're falling under the clubs into the black mud.

"*Miserere!* Oh Lord, have mercy! Have mercy!"

From the windows of the commandant's building, officers view this scene with amusement.

Well, these were first fruits of the "new order" brought to the world by pagan Nazism.

"What are you holding there? A book? A real book?" Amazement! We last saw books in Górna Grupa when we were dumping the monastery library to be burned, and now suddenly a book right here in Stutthof. An authentic book! Moreover, it's Polish.

"Where did you get this?"

Zdzich is in no hurry to answer.

"Well, tell us, tell us, where did you get it?" everyone around urges him.

Instead of giving an answer, he opens the first page and reads: "Fr. J. Schrijvers, Redemptorist, *The Message of Jesus to His Priest,* Retreat Readings, translated from the French by Fr. Stanisław Misiaszek. Published in Tuchów in 1935. From the editors. Dedication. This message is to…"

"Good Lord! Zdzich! Will you tell us where you got this? Tell us," they urge him.

"From old Goldman."

"From Goldman? From that red-headed Jew in the barracks across the way? Where did he get it?" Again Zdzich opens the first page. He reads: "Fr. Górecki, Polish High School, Gdańsk."

"Let's see!" Bronek Szymański reaches for the book. Zdzich doesn't let it out of his hands. He shows it from a distance.

"Yes, that's his signature," Bronek confirms.

"He's the one who's with Father Komorowski in the disciplinary unit?"

"That's the one."

"But how in God's name! By what miracle did this book get into the camp?"

"Remember how they were moving his furniture in Nowy Port?

"Well?"

"Yesterday they moved it to Stutthof. They're furnishing the commandant's building. They dumped the books to be burned. Our Jews were summoned to put things in order. This morning old Goldman comes to me and says, 'Well, Reverend Father, I think that I will make you happy. Let's go to the latrine, it will be safer there.' In the camp latrine this Old Testament man gave me the *Message* of our Master. Isn't that a sign of the times? Because you see…"[1]

"Zdzich, have pity! Let's do without the scathing sermon. Must you always and everywhere…"

"I won't say anything. I won't say anything," he waves his hand. "It seemed to me that at least I could convert you. You don't want to, oh you of the stiff neck and closed ears who resist the Holy Spirit, therefore…"

"How insufferable you are. You're starting it again."

"I'm done. I'm opening the book. Let the Master himself speak to you. You won't oppose Him. Or will you?"

He opens the book to a page at random and, without any preamble, reads:

"As I became food for souls, so you, priest, must agree that your faithful may take as their nourishment your time, your efforts, your talents, so that they may use and overuse your patience, health, possessions, with no advantage to you."

8. Miserere

The reader's sharp whisper penetrates minds, sinks into hearts, and kindles a hidden revolt in souls. More and more young heads bend toward him. Eyes, lowered toward the straw bedding, try to conceal inner thoughts...

"A fruitful vine must be pressed..." He moved the book more conveniently toward the faint light. "A fruitful vine must be *pressed*..." He enunciates the last word with emphasis. "Otherwise it won't produce the precious liquid! A priest is created in my image so that souls can crush him, squeeze him completely dry, depriving him of time, conveniences, and even life."

The elders sitting near the stove recite the Rosary in an undertone. From time to time they cast indignant glances toward the radicals' corner. Hidden from view by our heads, Zdzich reads on:

"What a disappointment for me if in the evening of your life, oh priest, I were to see the vine of your soul still intact and your chalice empty!"

"Amen," Zdzich closes the book and slips it under his dirty jacket.

"Is that the end of the chapter?"

"No, but it's the end of the thought," he answers as he puts his arms around his skinny knees. His gaunt face is flushed. His sunken eyes are shining. Around his thin, tightly pressed lips protrude the reddish hairs of an unshaved beard. I think this is how Savonarola must have looked. Silence sets in. A troublesome silence. We sit deep in thought. Suddenly Zdzich starts to talk quietly, very quietly, as if he were talking to himself, but loud enough so we can hear every word:

> "I shall never ever again tune the harp.
> Other roads are open before me.
> Vanish my songs! Arise my *deeds*!"

"What's that from?"

"From Krasiński. At the moment of his spriritual conversion."

"It was easy for him to compose moving verses. Beautiful Switzerland, sky-high Alps, cows with bells ringing out over babbling brooks, a bucolic atmosphere..."

"Does it matter when *He* strikes with his grace? Krasiński in beautiful Switzerland, Paul at the gates to Damascus, Nicodemus in bed at night, Teresa of Avila at the feet of Ecce Homo, us in Stutthof, and still others in..."

"Prophet!" someone hisses caustically from a dark corner.

"Prophet or not, but something's very clear to me, which is that the fruitful vine of my priestly soul was untouched. And the evening of my life would certainly have come with an empty chalice were it not for the Lord full of love."

"Did the Lord send you off to Stutthof?"

"Uh-huh."

"Then you consider imprisonment in the death camp a grace?"

"Yes, and a great one, a very great one!" he affirms. "We sang in life sentimentally plucking at the emotional strings of human souls. We talked big! Words, words, words, only words were uttered. We diligently cared for the plump fruit of our souls, and behold, the Lord of the vineyard came, noticed ... felt disappointed and..."

A shrill sound interrupts Zdzich's talk. Evening roll call. There's a commotion in the barracks.

"Reverend," my pastor says as we go out, "It's a pity you don't come to our corner to pray the Rosary together."

From the open doors of the barracks, columns of steam rise into a darkening sky. Shouting, the block leaders form their units. From the forest side, the terrifying eyes of floodlights look our way. Old trees rustle in the chill evening wind. A freeze is coming.

The omnipotent Mathesius comes from the gate with his retinue. He walks with his head held high, like a commander certain of victory.

"*Miserere*, Lord have mercy!" What will he think of today, after that incident with the funeral?

And he did think of something. He did not forgive the shavelings their revolt.

9

A Hunger for Freedom

A fine drizzle has been falling all morning, freezing into a glassy cover of ice. Since the snow had been shoveled, they marched us today to the edge of the forest behind the commandant's building to peel bark from felled pine trees. This work is neither hard nor unpleasant. On the contrary, planing resin bark would even bring joy were it not for the nagging hunger, the cold, and this wretched rain soaking us to the skin.

Slowly, terribly slowly, the hours pass. Thoroughly frozen, Gański makes his rounds from group to group. On his head he wears a paper bag that used to hold cement.

"Father, let me have the drawknife. I'll warm up a bit."

It's not easy to warm up when you're already soaking wet. A cold wind is blowing, biting the emaciated bodies. We work in silence. After all, somebody could be observing us from the commandant's building. Why risk it? The wind wafts the smell of roasted meat from the SS kitchen. Torment! The effect of these smells is that a hungry stomach makes even greater demands. Suddenly we hear the clanging of the camp plowshare, hung instead of a bell under the eaves of the kitchen roof. That's the much longed-for signal marking the end of work. Gański oversees the gathering of tools. We clean them conscientiously since negligence is cause for severe punishment, justified by suspicion of sabotage.

"Line up! ... Count off!" The number tallies. "In step, forward march!"

As we walk, we don't allow ourselves to forget, even for a moment, that someone could be watching us secretly at that moment, someone just looking for an excuse come evening to mete out punishment on the hated shavelings...

In front of the entrance to the camp, two SS men stop us. A new shipment of wood has arrived. It must be unloaded right away! We feel disheartened by this command. The SS men are furious. They, too, were denied an afternoon break. Who's to blame? Of course—the shavelings.

The unloading begins. We haul long pine timbers through the square, past the commandant's building, where a new building is to be erected. The route extends about 300 meters, and because it's covered with ice, it's slippery. At one point you need to cross a small stream, over which a rough footbridge has been thrown. Unfortunately, the bridge leads right into a wooden shed. In order to make a turn with a long beam, those holding the beam at the front end, having crossed the bridge, must head along the creek, so that those carrying the back end can get onto the bridge at all.

This is precisely the place one of the SS men selects for his "operations." He finally hits upon the idea that it would be more efficient if those carrying the back end of the beam, instead of crossing the foot-bridge (like those carrying its front end), would simply go into the creek. That way, the front of the beam could be raised above the roof of the shed, making it much easier to maneuver.

So we wade in the freezing water, driven forward, kicked, and beaten with clubs from the shore.

"Faster! Faster, you dogs! Dinner's getting cold." The pile of construction materials was growing behind the commandant's building...

When we finally return to the camp, the barracks have almost finished taking dinner. We need to hurry to get the coveted tin of what's known here as "soup."

The camp in Stutthof had a small kitchen that was intended for several hundred prisoners. In order to have enough meals for these thousands, they cooked dinner in three installments, pouring each of the cooked portions into an enormous wooden vat, which stood on an adjoining street. Around noon, the third installment was ready. It was mixed with the other portions, and distribution of dinner rations began.

The barracks leaders positioned their people in long lines on the camp street. Along the way (at a point more or less across from the camp toilets), you took an empty tin of sardines or some other canned food from a pile and moved ahead in two lines. At the vat with the soup stood two cooks, one on each side. The prisoner held out his tin, received a portion of the liquid, and, driven on by clubs of the SS men positioned along the route, slurped it from the tin as he turned with his line back in the direction from which he had come. Drawing even with the toilets, he had to throw the tin onto the pile, and ... dinner was over.

That was how we got our meals outdoors: whether it was fair weather or raining, whether snow was falling or a storm was raging. There were many who, after taking a tin of this liquid, would spill its contents when pushed and beaten by the SS men controlling traffic. You had to see their eyes as, with the despair of a hungry animal, they watched clogs trampling their meal in the dirt. No, it can't possibly be described!

It often happens that the SS man standing by the vat allows a prisoner to take food, but then gives the order "Bend over!" and beats him with a club! He beats and beats! Woe to the bent-over prisoner if he spills any of the liquid moving around in his tin. Then he has to pour the rest back into the vat and take another beating for "wasting" food.

This happens most often to the group of Jews. There was not a day when they were not mistreated, especially during the distribution of food rations. Often they were driven away without any food. Unfortunate ones! Unfortunate a hundredfold. Much worse off than we, the priests, although the SS men usually persecute us together: Juden und Pfaffen!

We barely have time to get our dinner when a shrill whistle sounds. It's the signal to form work units. And once again we go to the forest to debark pines. The drizzly rain doesn't let up. Our blunt drawknives slip on the wet trunks.

"Scrape them clean," Gański warns, "or else come evening you'll catch it on the..."

Suddenly, about four o'clock, shouts and cries rouse us from our dull numbness. A shot is fired, then another. After that it's quiet. Then there's some noise in the underbrush followed by a series of shots from a submachine gun. The SS men guarding us run up the forest slope, looking into the woods. They say something to each other, take aim and fire their rifles. The gunshots gradually move away from us, deep into the woods.

"Get to work, you dogs!"

And again drawknives scrape, chunks of bark fall to the ground, rain whips about, sadness overwhelms the soul; temptation stirs within us.

9. A Hunger for Freedom

The day was cold and raw. It was raining. We had been taken to rough-hew timbers behind the commandant's building, at the edge of the forest. Suddenly, off in the forest thicket, shots were fired! (drawing by the author).

"Run into the woods ... Run ... One well-aimed shot will end it all. So many others do. How fortunate they are! They no longer suffer. Drop this plane! Head into the woods! That fellow is just waiting for such an opportunity. You'll make him happy. He'll get a week's vacation with commendation for shooting an escapee. Head for the woods!"

Rivulets of rain flow down the bark. There's not one dry place for us. Your body shakes. Your teeth chatter. A finger cut by the drawknife burns and smarts.

They say that a man can endure more than an animal. That's true. But what is an animal's physical suffering when compared to the suffering of a tormented human being? I remember the quiet life at the rectory: warm slippers; the radio playing; as supper is prepared, a casual look through the most recent *World News* or some other newspaper.

The depression into which probably all of us fell brought horrible suffering.

"Hey, you! How old was your housekeeper?" an SS man again attacks. (This topic was one of their favorites. Nazi propaganda accomplished in their souls what it intended. For them every priest was a sexual pervert. They enjoyed these talks, which always ended with a beating, as punishment for ... "lying."')

Spiritual suffering was much more terrible, however, than physical suffering.

It's early evening. The drizzle won't stop. My purplish hands hold the tools with difficulty. I want just to fall into the mud and let them come, let them kill me, let them squash me like a worm! I don't have the strength to endure this suffering any longer...

Finally, the sound of the plow-share from the kitchen. The end of work.

"Fathers, Fathers, maintain a steady pace. They're watching us," Gański warns. "One, two, three, four ... your left! ... your left! Straighten the ranks!"

We enter the camp. Just outside the gates, on a wheel-barrow used to haul dirt, lies the bloody corpse of a prisoner, shot during an attempted escape. We're made to file past him in tight units. The whole camp goes.

"Such a fate awaits every one of you," explains Mathesius at the top of his voice.

And it was good that they got him. If he had succeeded in escaping, they would be shooting ten innocent prisoners right now. Nevertheless, prisoners did take the risk. Escapes, or rather attempts at escape, used to take place over and over again. Usually they ended with the escapee being shot, but sometimes ten others were also dispatched.

The sight of those last ten was horrible.

"My children! My wife!" wailed the inhuman voice of a badly wounded Jew, pushing himself up on his hands, imploring his executioners. Mathesius himself finished the man off with a shot from his revolver.

"My children! My wife!" Father Kolbe would willingly have taken his place!

"You've surely gone crazy! Would you like heroism from each of us? Go ahead! The road's clear!"

Torment in the soul. Disdain for oneself. The frightened little animal, holding onto a ragged scrap of life with all its might, still had the strength to spit on itself with contempt.

More and more a longing for death. "It's a cowardly desire to escape from suffering," something chuckles in your soul. "Coward!"

Evening roll call. Even the SS men don't want any tortures today in this freezing rain. Soaked to the skin, we throw ourselves down on our straw, lying closely next to one another. Our wet clothing begins to let off steam. The foul air is hard to bear. As our bodies warm up, the lice start to cut their wild capers... Behind our fogged-up windows stands the night. From the woods, the huge eyes of floodlights are watching. Intolerably frozen kidneys ache. There's painful stabbing in the lungs...

"God! Give this night a quiet ending."

10

Holy Week 1940

The day is 17 March 1940, Palm Sunday. After herding us to work for a week outside the camp, they push us today to clean up the camp. The sun is higher in the sky now, so the snow is melting, and the wide camp street turns into a river of mud. The camp leaders came up with the idea of hauling the mud into the woods. We are the first to go do this work, of course — we and the Jews.

Snow removal under clubs of the SS men stationed at intervals was a drudgery. How many victims it claimed! To carry the heavy mud, however, is murder! The SS men, infuriated because the work has spoiled their Sunday outing, are harassing us with even greater fury.

Backs are breaking under the weight. Muscles stretch to their limits. Feet, covered with mud, refuse to obey. Open mouths gasp for air.

"Faster! Faster, you damned dogs!" SS men positioned along the route urge us on. They beat. They kick. Some trip a prisoner carrying his load. The poor fellow falls into the mud. More kicking and beating.

"At a run, march!" Mathesius himself suddenly hits on the idea.

So we run. We run with fully loaded wheelbarrows. We run for new loads. We run until we lose all strength. Many already lie unconscious; covered with mud, looking more like logs than people.

Animals! Yes. Us! Like trapped animals we hang onto this wretched life. How long can we keep hanging on? Until tomorrow? For a week? ... A month? ... Not one of us will last a year.

"You'll all croak here!" Mathesius often repeats.

Older prisoners have already passed on: the Rev. Senator Bolt and the old man with silver hair and the heart of a dove, Fr. Niemir from Inowrocław. And not only the older ones: the young vicar from Gdańsk, Fr. Jasio Lesiński, who was shot on the camp street! And because the SS man fired a series of shots using an automatic from a high guard tower, the bullets also killed two others in the barracks. How many colleagues passed away? I can't determine the number. That would only be possible by questioning all who survived. (Considering the yearly harvest of death, however, I fear that before some historian takes this on, there won't be any witnesses left.)

They constantly bring in new priests, individually and in groups. They brought more priests from Płock Province, including Staszek Grabowski, Stefek Nowak, and brothers Franek and Staszek Sokołowski. From Pomorze they brought Fr. Marian Metler, Fr. Tadeusz Jasiński, Konrad Wedelstaedt, Alfons Kropidłowski, Aleksander Pronobis, and Aleksander Rutecki. Who could possibly remember all of them? Some were leaving, others were coming. The terrible Stutthof mill was grinding...

"Through this crushing a new man is born. It is God himself who stands at the press in His vineyard."

"Zdzich!"

He would gesture with his hand and sink into a quiet reverie. He talked to his colleagues less and less and became more and more introspective. The more he looked like a skeleton, the more his eyes shone. Strange eyes. I observe him at work. I look at him with admiration during the greatest ordeals. He is first everywhere, unruffled.

"Take care of yourself a little. You'll exhaust yourself. You'll die!"

He wouldn't answer. He would continue to push the wheelbarrow. In the evenings, he would burrow in a corner on the lice-infested straw and take his treasure from it, *The Message of Jesus to His Priest*, and without caring whether I listened to him, he would read under his breath: "If you follow me, if you give yourself to me completely, I will use you, priest, for my work and will give you strength. And if I send you trials and infirmities now, know that I have loving intentions in this."

I was silent. All kinds of thoughts were running through my head. He, too, was silent. After a while, as if he had awakened from sleep, he says:

"Remember our Żychliński? How often during our dogma lectures he would cite Father Mateo and his work, *Jesus, King of Love*."

"Yes."

"Do you remember how he fed our young souls with the words of that great disciple, that a priest should kill himself doing the work of Him who willingly let himself be killed for us?"

Holy Thursday, 21 March 1940

In the first edition of *Shavelings* I described this incident myself. After some years, I received a description of the same incident, written by Fr. Wojtek Gajdus, which was

Holy Mass in Stutthof, March 1940 (drawing by the author).

10. Holy Week 1940

included in the Kraków weekly *Tygodnik Powszechny*. It was one of Wojtek's last recollections prior to his death. I give him a voice, citing the account written by his hand, a hand already turning cold:

> ...It's Holy Thursday, the day of the institution of the Most Blessed Sacrament. The hour before dawn. Silence reigns in the barracks. Everyone lies in deepest silence on his straw. No one sleeps, no one even moves. If you were to listen carefully, you'd hear voices murmuring like the ocean, voices which in this pre-dawn hour cry out from two hundred hearts torn asunder. Only in one corner of the barracks is there movement and a stir. Someone's unseen hands place a curtain on nails in the wall, using an old blanket. It's a tent. All this takes place in silence. All details, such as how to build an altar, were discussed last night, and roles were assigned. Each knows what he must do and quietly builds a sanctuary where the Lord will come to observe Passover with his disciples.
>
> After a while everything is ready. A small box rests on the bed of straw, on decaying chaff. On the box is a white scarf—the altar cloth. The communion wafers are in a glass. Next to it is a smaller glass — that's the chalice. On the cloth is the host. Over the box-altar hangs a small wooden cross. That's the entire altar. The curtain is tight against the walls, and the front of it touches the backs of the celebrant and the acolytes. It's cramped under the curtain and hot as in a bath, so hot that the only thing illuminating this altar, a small candle-end held by Fr. Klinkosz, keeps going out every few minutes. It's necessary to raise the curtain from time to time to let in some air. Kneeling behind the curtain is an old man in dirty torn clothes. That's Fr. Bolesław Piechowski, who has shielded us so many times from blows. Fr. Frelichowski holds a small missal in his hands. Everything is ready.
>
> "Behind the curtain the conversation with God begins... It runs through the barracks: *Introibo ad altare Dei*... Someone next to me could not stand it ... he's sobbing like a small injured child. Another one hides his face in his hands ... someone sniffles, someone coughs ... whispers, sighs ... and behind the curtain a trio of voices already chants the Holy Thursday Credo...
>
> Offering ... *Oremus*... "The right hand of the Lord hath wrought strength, the right hand of the Lord hath exalted me. I shall not die, but live, and shall declare the works of the Lord." ... A terrible paradox. Around the altar on beds of straw lie two hundred priests, dirty and lice-infested... All around is barbed wire, slavery, fear ... and these words ... accept, Lord, accept, accept this offering of our wretched, emaciated bodies... Accept it for our friends here and beyond the barbed wire, for our enemies, that they may recover from hate, because only hate creates hell on earth. Accept it for those who are living and for those who, in a fit of despair, have run onto the wires at night... Accept it for our abandoned parishes, for our empty churches where perpetual lights in front of tabernacles have gone out... May our ashes attain our resurrection before Your Face... *Sanctus! Sanctus! Sanctus!*
>
> *Hoc est enim Corpus meum... Hic est enim Calix Sanguinis mei...*
>
> Our Lord and God has come to Stutthof. He became a prisoner in this concentration camp, in barracks Nr. 5. On Holy Thursday He observes Passover with his disciples, for in a few days He will again be given up to death in these same disciples, members of His mystical Body...

The doors to the barracks squeaked softly. Two shadows slip in quietly. Fr. Bronek Komorowski and Fr. Marian Górecki, both locked up in the disciplinary unit, have sneaked out furtively, in order to receive Holy Communion.

Dear madmen. It was a secret of the unforgettable Fr. Frelichowski and some who were closest to him how they almost miraculously obtained these several hosts and a tiny bit of wine for Mass. It was not in vain that for several days Fr. Frelichowski had conducted secret dealings with the Jews who went to work on farms outside the camp. Supposedly Fr. Józio

Mueller had a bit of wine on him in a tiny bottle; a missal was found in Fr. Górecki's things. The old Jew Goldman was simply invaluable. He was ready to deliver no matter what. The Old Testament was supporting the New. "Well, Reverend Father," the gray-haired Jew used to say, "In times of freedom, we used to make mutually beneficial deals, so why shouldn't we support each other now?" Moreover, some of our priests lived with the Jews in the same barracks, and contacts with them weren't difficult.

Good Friday, 22 March 1940

As on every other day, there's feverish bustling around, a meager breakfast, then morning roll call, and, finally, the formation of work units. Non-commissioned officer Neubauer appears. The bluish, alcohol-bloated mouth doesn't portend anything good. Where will he find a victim today?

"Jesus!" Neubauer is coming toward our unit! It's death walking in steel-shod boots! Now he's standing in front of us. We don't have the courage to look into those terrible eyes. Our hearts are pounding.

"Choose forty who are strong and young! They'll take shovels. Have them wait in front of the commandant's building!" he barked and ... went away.

Dozens let out a sigh of relief.

"But the day has just started. A day under the sign of the murderer Neubauer..."

They marched us into the woods. We clear the road, digging the still-deep snow. Along the route, between the pines, they've positioned guards close together. They're keeping a closer watch today than ever before. That's natural. The forest ... a temptation to escape.

We work like this for several hours. Finally a clearing opens up in front of us. In the distance, in the middle of the clearing, mounds of sand form yellow patches on the white snow. Could these possibly be holes where stumps were dug up? Or maybe the holes were dug for a special purpose?

At the edge of the clearing stand several armed SS men.

"Up to here! Not a step further!"

Bathed in sweat, we form a tight unit, and with shovels over our shoulders we march off. We're accompanied by the SS men who escorted us while we were clearing the road.

We walk. We may have walked a kilometer from the clearing when heavy covered vehicles suddenly appear on the road we had cleared of snow. One, a second, a third ... I don't know how many there were because at that moment came the command:

"Right turn! At a run into the woods!"

We run between the pines, breathlessly wading through the deep snow.

"Fall down!" sounds another command when we were already perhaps 100 meters from the road. We fall into the snow.

"Whoever lifts his head will get a bullet in it!"

The rifle bolts snap. We know well what this means. No one has the nerve to lift his head. We lie in nervous tension, while behind us on the cleared road heavily loaded trucks roll slowly by, their engines rumbling. They roll on...

"Stand up! March forward and don't look back!" comes the command.

Moving at an angle toward the road, we wade through the snow asking ourselves this one question: What were they transporting? Or maybe *whom*?

We return to the camp at high noon. We're greeted by news whispered with dread:

they had escorted the entire disciplinary unit out of the camp; it consisted of all the Polish intelligentsia from Gdańsk, and among them were Fathers Górecki and Komorowski.

In the afternoon they took all Jews from the camp.

? ... ? ... ? ...

But toward evening the Jews returned.

"We were folding clothes," old Goldman, Zdzich's friend, whispers cryptically and with fear in his eyes. "It seems to me, Reverend Father, that these were their clothes"— he points to the empty barracks of the disciplinary unit. "Among them were also the clothes of the two reverend fathers."

Everything was more than apparent to us. We had shoveled off the road to the clearing in which they executed today, this memorable Good Friday of 1940, the entire Polish intelligentsia from Gdańsk, including two priests, Fr. Górecki and Fr. Komorowski.[1]

"Fratres," a trembling voice comes from the area near the stove, the elders' corner, when in the evening we already lay on our beds of straw. "Fratres, let us pray for the souls that were murdered today..."

And they murmur quietly: Hail Marys... Our Father... and Grant them, Lord, eternal rest. But the windows of the commandant's building are ablaze with lights, loud talk comes from within, glasses clink ... songs ... toasts...

"And now, Henryk," Zdzich whispers, "let's pray for the murderers, that our Jesus may touch them with His grace."

"Ugh!" a voice of indignation is heard in the darkness. "May fire from heaven burn them!"

"Mother, refuge of sinners, look mercifully upon the sons of this nation who..." Zdzich whispers, not at all deterred.

Oh, how these tears burn and smart beneath our eyelids! How they burn...

"Amen."

All around can be heard the rhythmic breathing of those asleep. Moisture drips and drips from the ceiling. Streaming through fogged-up windows is the glow of floodlights that spy about the camp from the guard towers. Beyond the barbed wire the ancient forest whispers. It whispers "them" to sleep, shrouding all the while one more bloody crime.

11

Ethnic Germans

On the very feast of Easter, after hearing in secret the Mass of the Resurrection, which was celebrated this time by the youngest of our priests, God's fireball, the aforementioned Fr. Frelichowski, we were ordered together with the Jews to carry excrement out of the camp latrine.

Latrine in camp jargon means toilet. There was only one for the entire camp, situated at its center, and it was very primitive in construction. That is, just two rows of boards, under them a huge hole, and some sort of small roof over this... Chilled stomachs and intestines were subject to sickness, demanding relief many times during the day and at night. You would come out on the threshold of your barracks and call as loudly as possible toward the nearest guard tower:

"Sentry! Request permission to leave!" (Not too bad if the given barracks was located near the latrine. Worse if it was several hundred meters away.)

The guard would hear the call or not, or (and we often suspected this) he would pretend that he didn't hear. In the meantime, the sick organism, rebellious and ailing due to a bloody diarrhea, was moaning. For not holding back and soiling the camp, there awaited a terrible punishment, not excluding being tortured to death. The poor prisoner, assuming that the guard has heard him and given his permission, runs toward the latrine, when suddenly a series of automatic gunshots strikes him, and he falls dead on the camp street! For stopping an offender from "escaping," the guard would receive a week of leave to go see his mother, who's lonely for her dear boy.

So it was that on the very feast of Easter they made us and the Jews empty the latrine hole.

They treated the poor Jews even worse than us. Crammed into the hole, standing up to the waist in excrement, the Jews hand us full buckets and, in doing so, spill the contents on themselves. We pour out the contents into vats, located on vehicles, which are moved outside the camp.

Thus the New and Old Testament observe the holy day together. (And you, gentlemen of the jury, continue to insist that Polish priests were imprisoned purely for their nationalistic convictions. If all the Goldsteins and Apfelbaums who endured these torments in Stutthof together with us had not been murdered, they could provide you with much substantial testimony regarding the extent to which the SS men hated both their Yahweh and our Christ the Lord. It was not idle talk when Hitler predicted, "The Catholic Church will have nothing to laugh about when I gain power. I'm not a Protestant like Bismarck. I know how to bring it to its knees" (*Catholic Guide [Przewodnik Katolicki]*, 25 December 1938).

It's one of the warmer days after Easter. Not all of us were forced to work today. While some of us are scraping mud off the street, the rest have been allowed to stay in the barracks. Taking advantage of these few free moments, we take off our clothes and underwear and devote ourselves to a lice hunt. We have millions of them! The mood is unpleasant, according to Zdzich. The closer we get to spring, the more sadness in our souls and the greater the nostalgia. Young Fr. Kozubek, SVD, is moaning in a dark corner. He has pneumonia. He's strong: others die after several days of suffering, but he lingers on and on. His young system doesn't yield to the illness. Fr. Zygmunt Kaczmarek is taking care of him. But how and with what can he help since there isn't even a cup of water to drink?

Elderly Rev. Major Różycki dozes, his head resting on a box with his "treasures." The Inowrocław priests, confining themselves to one corner, recite the Rosary in a half-whisper. The handsome, sharp profile of old Rev. Msgr. Schönborn from Kruszwica stands out against the background of a fogged-up window. This is how St. Jerome the Hermit must have looked, emaciated to a sliver. His trembling lips indicate he's praying. We all know this is a profound, mystical soul and a man of prayer.

Another elder, Fr. Wąsowicz from Brudnia (it's amazing he has survived all the harassment this long) "hunts" while sitting undressed to the waist. Since his eyesight is poor, helpful Fr. Szczepcio Weber shows him the lice, which the old man "murders" himself. Quick as mercury in his movements, Rev. Director Ludwiczak gestures rapidly, explaining something to phlegmatic Fr. Ciemniak. The latter is the only one who still has patience to listen to him.

Suddenly there are loud footsteps, the door swings open. An SS man stands at attention in the doorway and bellows: "*Achtung!*"

We jump to our feet. Our hearts stand still. Mathesius? Or someone even worse?

Into the barracks comes the camp commandant himself, Oswald Pohl (later the right hand of Himmler, an inspector of concentration camps, condemned to death at the Nuremburg trials).

"*Weiter machen*! As you were!" he kindly gives his permission, gesturing with deerskin gloves. "It stinks in here!" he notes, pursing his lips.

Before he has even finished his sentence, obliging SS men are already opening the door and windows. The commandant walks through the barracks. He looks at us attentively.

"What's wrong with him?" he points to Fr. Kozubek, who's lying there.

"He's sick. He has pneumonia."

With a magnanimous gesture he restrains his retinue, their boots poised to kick. "It's not necessary. He'll die anyway," he gestures again with his gloves.

"And what are you up to?" pretending astonishment, he turns to old Fr. Włodarczyk. "Do you have lice?"

"Yes, sir!"

"You Poles have always been a lice-infested nation!"

"If he knew, Father, that you were such a close friend of General Sikorski, he would have taught you a lesson," his colleagues commented after the commandant had left. (Gen. Sikorski was Fr. Włodarczyk's parishioner, and they were close acquaintances.)

The commandant walks farther on. His retinue is behind him.

"Eh, you!" he turns to Fr. Ciemniak. "What's your name?"

"Ciemniak."

"Cii-em-nak ... Cii-em-nak," he repeats. "That is not a German name."

"No. It's a pure Polish name," he answers.

"*Mensch*! *Du bist kein Pole*! Man! You are not a Pole! Your appearance betrays you. There must be Germanic blood in you. You look like a native Tyrolese! Weren't any of your ancestors Germans?"

"No!"

"Maybe on your mother's side?"

"No."

"But I see it. There must be Germanic blood in you."

"No."

"What no?"

"There is no Germanic blood in me. I am a Pole." The black beard lifts up a bit higher. His clear eyes take on a steel luster.

"And wouldn't you want to be a German?"

"No, I wouldn't."

"Is that your final word?" The commandant's jaw twitches nervously. The SS men from his retinue clench their fists. Mathesius notes well in his mind what Fr. Ciemniak looks like.

"Be careful, be careful, you damned Polish dog!" Commandant Oswald Pohl cannot hide his rage.

"But you are a German," he suddenly addresses the giant Fr. Mieczysław Strehl. "What's your name?"

"Strehl, Mieczysław Strehl," the giant responds.

"So, so, Strehl, Strehl, a beautiful German last name; moreover, your build is Germanic, and the shape of the head is 'ours.'" He looks over the man in question as though he were a horse at a fair. "You, my good man, are a German by blood and name. You cannot deny it."

"I'm Polish to the core!" booms Rev. Pastor Strehl in his deep bass voice.

A good-natured smile plays on the commandant's face.

"Well, yes, I know, I understand, you were 'supposedly' a Pole, but certainly your parents and your grandparents..."

"My grandfather was a Polish deputy to the Prussian diet and defended the interests of partitioned Poland," Fr. Strehl interrupts the commandant's statement.

"Hold your tongue when the commandant is speaking!" Mathesius could not contain himself and was already raising his fist to strike.

"Leave him alone," the commandant pacifies Mathesius and then turns to Fr. Strehl: "You don't want to be a German? You speak German so beautifully..."

"No!"

This time, however, Commandant Oswald Pohl was determined.

"Herr Strehl" ("Herr"? This was something extraordinary!) "Herr Strehl," he addresses him a few days later. "I've looked over your papers. You attended German schools, you were nurtured in our German culture, you have such a beautiful German surname. Listen: Pohl ... Strehl ... Don't they sound like the names of two brothers? You could be released immediately. You were simply arrested by mistake together with these dumb Poles. You will return to freedom, you will immediately receive a position. Do you understand? Well, Herr Strehl? What nationality do you claim then?"

"Herr Kommandant! I am a Pole and will remain one!"

We witnessed these two meetings and conversations. For the third one they summoned Fr. Strehl to the commandant's office. Perhaps the commandant feared an ultimate public defeat, or perhaps he thought he could gain more from the prisoner in private.

"Well, what?" we ask Fr. Strehl when he returned to the barracks.

"Well," the giant says in his powerful bass voice, "he offered me a wonderful cigar, asked me to sit down, talked to me like an equal, tempted, promised, dangled hopes, and then threatened, and..."

"Then what? What happened?" we ask with interest.

"Nothing," the giant gestures with his hand, embarrassed like a child. "Then he kicked me and threw me out the door!"

"That was the 'stamp' certifying Fr. Strehl really doesn't have any Germanic blood in him," Zdzich scoffs. "You see, if he had renounced his lineage, he would be useful to them, like our deputy commandant Just-Gustowski and many, many other scoundrels." This time no one objected. Zdzich was right.

"Father Sroka, you will not deny that your mother was a native German and that she didn't know a word of Polish."

"Yes, sir. It's true."

"Further, you completed German schools; you were raised in the spirit of German culture; you speak perfect German. You ... Do you admit, then, that you're German?"

"No!"

"So who are you, Father?"

"I'm a Pole!"

At this, Commandant Colonel Oswald Pohl could not restrain himself. He jumped up toward the prisoner. He raised his fists... He strikes Father Sroka repeatedly with his fists and kicks him.

"You renegade! You turncoat! You chauvinist! You ... you damned Polish pig!"

The honorable Rev. Pastor Sroka did not get out of Stutthof.

"Prabukkki! ... Prabukkki! To the commandant's office!" the call resounds throughout the camp.

The three priests named Prabucki stand before the commandant.

"Which one of you is Prabukki? I only called Prabukki!" the colonel frowns.

"Our name is pronounced 'Prabootski,'" they declare as they stand at attention.

"All three of you have the same name?" Pohl is surprised.

"Yes, sir."

"Are you related?"

"We're brothers."

"Well, well, brothers, three brother priests? But which one of you was a captain in the German artillery?"

"I was."

"Your first name?"

"Paweł."

"Paweł ... Paweł," the commandant grinds his teeth. "Is that the same as Paul?"

"Yes, sir."

"So you were an officer in our artillery during World War I?"

"Yes, sir."

"You were highly decorated?"

"Yes, sir."

"Therefore, you entered our military to serve the German homeland."

"No! They drafted me by force, as a German subject."

"Therefore, you were a German!" the commandant declares.

"No! I was a Pole living under German occupation, in slavery, and I had to go."

"But you fought bravely. You were decorated. Therefore, you fought for Germany!"

"I fought on the Russian front in the belief that the German Kaiser would allow us to gain freedom for Poland."

"A free Poland, a free Poland," Herr Kommandant mutters with a smirk of pity, while striking the top of his boot with his riding whip. "Would you like to be released?" His vulture-like eyes stare through the prisoner. "Look, you have your two brothers here. Well? Would you like to be released?"

"Yes, I would."

"You can arrange this easily."

A questioning look.

"You and your brothers sign this document that you acknowledge belonging to the German nation, that you want to be Germans, that..."

"No!"

"No what?"

"I will never sign this, nor will either of my brothers!"

All three Prabucki brothers died in the camps. Not one saw the freedom with which they were so tempted.[1]

This, however, is only a handful of examples. How many were similarly tempted, deluded. It was enough just to sign, just to utter "I want to," and they would have been free, they would have saved their lives.

The method chosen was a bad one! In offering freedom, they demanded two renunciations: nationality and (what was more decisive) *the priesthood*! And this latter motive was strong, after all, stronger than anything. Out of thousands of Polish priests who suffered behind the barbed wire of camps, I didn't see *a single one* who, despite tempting promises, had renounced his priesthood and Polish nationality. The executioners did not even once manage to breach this unshakable fortress. This was stated, also, by Commandant Oswald Pohl, Himmler's right-hand man, as well as by others. But, as a result, they prepared a worse fate for the Polish priests. An irrevocable judgment was rendered: "These religious fanatics can be overcome by one thing only ... death!"

This judgment was rendered. We were ready for it.

12

Grenzdorf

Old ensign Jan Trembecki, while managing his knightly estate named Wieś Graniczna, did not dream in 1800 that the German *Drang nach Osten* surge would force him out of here, that it would seize this ancient Polish land, disinherit its rightful owners, name this place Grenzdorf, Germanize it, and declare it to be "centuries-old German land." And he could never have imagined that this place would someday become the slaughterhouse of Poles, his brothers.

I open a huge volume of the *Orthographic Dictionary of Polish Territories*, kept at the library of the City of Chicago (it wasn't enough to take the Górna Grupa library collection for burning in a sugar plant! It wouldn't even be enough to destroy all Polish libraries and archives. They would have had to reach far beyond the ocean in order to falsify historical truth). I open the volume and cite the following data from it:

> *Graniczna Wieś, Germanized into Grenzdorf, noble estates in the Gdańsk district, at the border with the Kościerski district, on the Czerwona River, which was Germanized into Rothfliess, Pragnowy parish, Czerniewo school, Skarszewy post office. Distance from Gdańsk 4 miles, from Skarszewy one mile, in possession of the knightly Trembecki family for centuries. The last owner was ensign Jan Trembecki. Later seized by the Germans ...* [idem, vol. ii, p. 795].

This place called Grenzdorf, the ancient Polish Wieś Graniczna, where in deep beech forests a stone quarry had been set up with a concentration camp established nearby, was one of the Stutthof units under the administration of Commandant Oswald Pohl.

Following failed attempts to break the priests' spirit, a verdict was passed to finish them off. We were chosen, about a hundred of the young ones, for the first transport.

"*Antreten*! Departure!"

Feverish goodbyes. Last minute instructions in case ... I even forgot my dear pastor's irritating optimism.

"Go, Reverend, go with God. I'll be praying for you, that you..."

"Have an easy death," finishes Zdzich quietly.

"Oh, you awful cynic! But let's have a hug even from you! I'll be praying for you, too."

They marched us into the square near the commandant's building and positioned us several meters from each other. Behind the fence, on top of the embankments stood SS men with machine guns ready to fire.

"Well, well, where is this leading to?"

Fear takes hold.

A group of SS men comes out of the commandant's building. They're unarmed. We breathe a sigh of relief. A search... On command we place all we have on the snow. They rob us completely. This had nothing to do with a real "robbery," which was usually accomplished by transports coming directly from the outside, often bringing in "goods of all kinds." In this case, it was simply a matter of harassment, of letting us go naked and stripped of everything to the place of torture.

Fr. Feliks Kamiński wears a warm coat that used to belong to Fr. Telesfor Kubicki, who was martyred a few days ago. Will they let him keep it? No. They tell him to take it off. Moreover, he catches hell. Fr. Bruno Wilczewski has an extra pair of wooden clogs. They take the clogs. It's good that they didn't punish him more severely, that it ended with just a few kicks. They found a couple of razor blades on Fr. Aloś Gotowicz... In a word, they take everything.

"Do not concern yourselves with what you will eat or drink," Zdzich murmurs quite audibly.

"Shut up, you..." The SS man is ready to jump, but then he spies a prize in Romek Budniak's bundle.

Finally, we're "ready." They pack us into open vehicles. It will be quite a ride in this cold air! We start. The engines roar. The overloaded vehicles climb with difficulty toward the main road. We're driving into the unknown. This was also one of the reasons for fear among prisoners, that they were never told where they were going.

One more glance at the barracks in the distance. A human being is a curious creature. He can come to love even a death camp, or at least get used to it. In the context of the mysterious unknown to which we're heading, even Stutthof leaves behind the feeling of a "home" that's been lost.

Finally we reach the main road and turn toward Gdańsk. Aha! That's probably where we're heading.

The vehicles, clambering out of the bumpy side road onto the good highway, pick up speed. A freezing wind stings our faces, penetrates our tattered clothing, bites like a hungry dog. We pass some hamlets. Puffs of smoke from chimneys rise into the blue of a cold March sky. The sight of children playing on their sleds tugs at the heart. Their joyful laughter jars or simply surprises us. So there are people in the world who feel happy, joyful, well-fed? The feelings we experience after so many months of confined life in the camp, in complete separation from the world of free people, are startling. Everything interests us, each observable detail. Even that man on the bicycle, pedaling slowly, and that woman returning from her neighbors with a basket, and the driver walking next to his loaded wagon, beating his arms for warmth, and the cat sitting in the window of a cozy room, looking greedily at the small flock of sparrows hopping under the window. Everything awakens thoughts and memories in us...

Twice we cross rivers on a ferry. First across the Vistula, then across its tributary. The ice is already breaking up. Chunks of ice push against the ferries, which clear their way through with difficulty.

And again we speed on. In front of us is the ribbon of highway; on either side are banks of snow; beyond them are fields, shrubs, buildings, and again fields and fields. The freezing wind chills to the marrow, and hunger gnaws.

"Look! It's the tower of St. Mary's Church," Bronek Szymański points to it.

In front of us rises ancient Gdańsk. I'm even ashamed to admit I didn't have a chance to get to know Gdańsk in the days of freedom. There was no time, there was no money.

"Do you see? Another spiritual benefit," Zdzich is clearly mocking now. "Look to the left. The Baltic! Our beautiful Polish Baltic! You've never seen it, either. But you used to sing your lungs out: 'The sea, our sea, we shall faithfully guard you...'"

"Stop annoying people."

"'Our orders are to guard you, or lie down on the bottom, on the bottom of the sea...'"

"Madman," someone behind us murmurs.

"It's true," Zdzich agrees. "If I weren't a madman, today I'd be..."

"For God's sake, be quiet, or else..."

We drive through the first section of houses in Gdańsk. The vehicles start to slow down. Only now, when the rush of the icy wind has subsided, do we feel how terribly frozen we are.

"I don't feel my feet," discovers Stach Gałecki, the pastor from Szubin.

"Don't rub your ears! They're completely white. You'll break them off," warns one of his neighbors.

We pass streets, cross bridges; we're extremely surprised to see people everywhere, especially men. We had imagined that by now everyone would be in uniform, that everyone would have been taken into the military, that... Passersby, curious about the transport, pause on the sidewalks. We must present quite a spectacle! Dressed in rags, covered with muck and bits of straw, unshaven and dirty, we probably look like a group of savages. We turn down one of the side streets. The vehicles stop in front of a restaurant. The drivers and guards jump out of the cabs. The cab doors bang shut.

"You're staying in the trucks!" the head transport officer decides. "If you attempt to escape, you'll get a bullet in the head and ten others will be shot!"

Two guards, armed with submachine guns ready to fire, remain standing on watch. The rest disappear inside. Through the huge windows one can see them sitting down at a table, with smiling waitresses coming toward them. Based on the relaxed attitude of both sides, one can conclude that this restaurant is an old "stopover" for SS men from Stutthof, that they take their meals here when they transport corpses to Gdańsk every Saturday, and also on other occasions. The fat restaurant owner goes up to the transport officer; they greet each other, slap each other on the back, gesture in our direction, laugh...

In the meantime, a rather large group of curious people gathers around our vehicles. The adults are standing somewhat at a distance, while the children run around the trucks.

"Who are you carrying?" asks a curious youngster.

We learn from the answer provided by our guard that we are a dangerous gang of Polish bandits; that we have on our conscience the murders of German mothers and innocent children; that we were caught in the act of firing from behind fences at innocent German people!

The children's faces, up to now curious, take on a seriousness that finally gives way to horror.

"Are they still dangerous, even now?" asks a child.

"Dangerous?" the SS man purses his lips while he strokes his submachine gun. "Just let them try!"

There is whispering in the children's group... Then, in a sudden move, a volley of stones, chunks of dirt and pieces of ice are falling on us...

"You Polish pigs! You Polish bandits! You murderers! You..."

"Do you understand now how the Nazis have 'nurtured' the residents of Gdańsk? You can see for yourself what propaganda can do," Bronek whispers, as we duck under the debris pelted at us.

"It's too bad the English and Americans can't see this example," someone adds.

"Do you really believe this would convince them?" Zdzich scoffs.

News about the transport of "blood-thirsty Polish bandits" reaches the adults standing nearby. The crowd becomes increasingly excited.

"They're going to lynch us."

Then the guards rise "bravely" in our defense. We want to laugh and cry at the same time. Pretense ... hypocrisy...

The SS man explains, "They must receive a 'just' punishment, imposed by the court."

"Of course! Of course," the adults nod, calling back the children.

"Unfortunate German children, ever so unfortunate!"

"Punish the hand, not the blind sword," Zdzich drawls. "Even these idiot SS men are not altogether guilty. Their propaganda molded them; they spread it further, believing in whatever..."

"Stop talking! You always have to..."

Two sated SS men relieve our guards. Through the windows you can see them eating heartily. Our stomachs demand their rights! We're terribly hungry. Since morning we haven't had anything in our mouths but a small piece of bread. On the other side of the street is a bakery, and the window is full of baked goods.

"Jump! Throw yourself with your entire body against that transparent obstacle. Grab a loaf of bread! Sink your teeth into it and chew! Chew! Chew ... Let them shoot! Let them kill! That's better than dying of hunger!"

"What are you munching on?" a whisper can be heard nearby.

Silence.

"Tell me, what are you munching on?" the voice of the questioner is insistent. His neighbors prick up their ears.

"A piece of belt from my pants," comes the reply.

"Is it good?" The Adam's apple of the questioner gurgles hungrily.

Again silence, fraught with temptations. The questioner pokes around his waistband. Then after a while he says:

"You, there, give me a piece. My belt is made of cloth."

The SS men, their stomachs full, come out of the restaurant. The waitresses are waving from the window.

"Until ... this ... evening!" the transport leader calls out to them. They understand. Joyful smiles. There will be more time in the evening. They'll have a good time. "Through joy to power!" Has this slogan been instilled for nothing?

The starters grind. The cold engines cough. We start ... Again we pass the streets of old Gdańsk, weave through side streets, and enter the suburbs. In minutes Gdańsk is already behind us. An hour passes, then another. Evening arrives and with it the cold. A cutting wind lashes our bluish faces. The body stops reacting. The SS men, having lost a lot of time in the warm restaurant, are making up for it. The trucks move at a crazy speed. It's hard to catch your breath.

"They're going to freeze us to death."

"Let's hope so!" This Zdzich is really impossible.

After two hours we turn off the main road into a narrow forest path that winds across

12. Grenzdorf

an old beech forest. At times we climb upward slowly, then we drive at break-neck speed down a hill. We roll so sharply on the turns that we have to hold on very tightly in order not to fall "overboard" (this again is Zdzich's expression).

A turn and ... we stop in front of a barbed-wire fence, with a similarly wired gate in the middle. Beyond the fence are several wooden barracks. Camp Grenzdorf. A slaughterhouse, which used to kill even the strongest within a few weeks!

The sun's red disk is sinking in the west. Dragging ourselves from the vehicles, we fall into line, standing at attention. Commandant Redig receives the transport...

"Heil Hitler!" The transport commander is happy he can go back.

"Heil Hitler! Have a good trip! And tell them in Stutthof that I'll take care of them," he points toward us.

"Jawohl!"

The vehicles start... We remain on the square. Commandant Redig, a high-ranking officer and a blacksmith by trade, a fellow with shoulders as broad as a barn door and the hands of a gorilla, reviews the transport. He assesses us with a sharp eye, like an old-time buyer of black slaves at a market.

And then the address. (How these SS men liked to hear themselves speak! Seldom did any of them pass up a chance to "have a talk." Maybe only Neubauer was an exception. Instead, he would "talk" with his fist and boot.)

"As a matter of fact, if it were up to me, I would prefer to have you shot even today! (These are his actual words, which those who heard them will corroborate.) Since I don't have enough people to work, however..." He gestures with his broad hand, does not finish his sentence, and points to a heavy machine gun that is mounted nearby. "This is always waiting for you! This isn't Stutthof, you damned dogs! This is a work camp! Here ... you either work and earn your food or you die! Understood?"

"Yes, sir!"

"And now, left turn and march to the barracks! Tomorrow morning you're going to the stone quarry!"

Food was out of the question. Hungry and frozen to the bone, we fell onto the bare wooden floor planks. As we were informed the following day by prisoners who were already there, Commandant Redig had made the momentous discovery that prisoners who sleep on a bare floor have fewer lice! From then on we slept in Grenzdorf on bare planks! The fact that a cold wind was blowing through the cracks was of no concern to Commandant Redig. At any moment he could have a new transport from Stutthof!

That evening we didn't pray together. It was too dangerous. Redig could be listening. First we had to look around and orient ourselves in our new situation.

But that evening ... we cried.

13

Here You Have to Work

It was three o'clock at night when a loud "*Aufstehen!*" (Get up!) makes us jump to our feet. It's still night behind the barred windows. We didn't rest much on the bare, cold planks.

"Get washed!" comes down the order.

This astounds us. Get washed? We never washed in Stutthof at all.

Indeed. There is a washroom in the wing of the barracks. A real washroom, with faucets and wash basins. The first thing is to quench our thirst. Since leaving Stutthof we haven't had a drop of water in our mouths. Drink ... drink ... drink ... to fool a stomach that's gnawing from hunger. Then washing. What a blissful sensation the cold water produces!

Breakfast, consisting of a cup of mealy soup and a small slice of bread, makes us quite well-disposed. We didn't have that in Stutthof either. We didn't realize yet that for those "luxuries" Grenzdorf had one unpleasant detail: a 12-hour day of torturous work in the stone quarry, which finishes off prisoners so quickly that new transports have to arrive here every few weeks.

"*Antreten!*" Assembly.

We stand in the square. It's still night; it's dark everywhere, and only the square and the barracks are lit by blinding floodlights. Commandant Redig himself divides us into groups. One group receives heavy hammers, another pick-axes, a third shovels, and the last one still other tools.

"Attention! In step, forward march!"

Surrounded by armed SS men, we go in darkness outside the camp fences. It's four o'clock in the morning. We'll be at the work site in half an hour. The SS men warn that we'll get a bullet in the head if we attempt to escape. We know. We take it into account. We move in a tight column along the middle of a forest path. The SS men are walking on the sides. There's deafening silence. You only hear clogs clacking on the path. All around is a beech forest. It was probably planted by ensign Jan Trembecki, and maybe he hunted in it... Our people in Stutthof are still asleep at this time. The weary mind runs toward the warm straw bedding. Never mind the lice, that it's wet, that it stinks of stable dung, we used to fall asleep, but here we have these awful bare planks...

What's happening in old Września at this time? What a question! Of course, they're still asleep. Little Halinka is dreaming about dolls and pierogi with preserves, Auntie Stasia is worried in her dream that she has such old potatoes for her potato pancakes, reverend pastor...

"Dress ranks, you mad dogs! Dress ranks!"

Blows are dealt out at random; someone moans loudly, and then only the dull tramping of clogs breaks the silence. Sometimes a shovel clangs against a marching neighbor's pickaxe; a new shower of abusive SS language erupts, and silence returns. In the silence my thoughts run doggedly to those close to me: to Bydgoszcz, to my mother and father, brothers, friends... Fr. Jasio Jakubowski, a friend from my student days, was killed together with a group of young scouts near the Jesuit church in Wełniany Rynek. Real legends are circulating regarding an imprint of his hand that had supposedly appeared on the church wall. They painted over it. Nothing helped. Finally they chipped out the plaster in that spot and...

"Straighten the ranks! Straighten the ranks!"

The first rays of dawn appear over the hill, through moss-covered beech trees. What time could it be?

"Left! Left! Three! Four! Left!"

How can you keep marching in step on this bumpy forest path full of roots and holes?

We keep going down lower and lower. It starts to get lighter. Slowly we begin to distinguish details in the scenery.

Half an hour later, as a rosy dawn peeks into the beech forest, the stone quarry is already reverberating with the blows of hammers, the ring of pickaxes, the grating of shovels, and the shouts of SS men.

The unit armed with heavy hammers and iron wedges takes its place up above, at the edge of the deep quarry. Hitting with hammers and breaking with wedges, they dump blocks of black basalt down below. Column after column of prisoners, beaten and herded

The commandant of the Grenzdorf camp and quarry would have shot us most eagerly — as he would assure us himself — but since he needed laborers, he "spread out" our death sentence over days ... and, at best, over weeks (drawing by the author).

forward, run toward the pile, hoist the blocks onto their shoulders, and take them to a far-removed area. Over there, another group of priests, equipped with smaller hammers and pickaxes, breaks up the blocks into smaller pieces, and throws them toward workers sitting on the ground, who try to "manufacture" valuable basalt paving stones from them.

The rest of our people are busy hauling away gravel and sand.

During the first hour, work doesn't go well either for those at the top, who are splitting the basalt rock, or those who are breaking up the blocks into smaller pieces; and those turning out the paving stones have the least expertise. The leaders (lay prisoners, whom we met in Grenzdorf) are serving as instructors. They are all Poles. They try to be understanding, and only when they feel SS men watching them do they pretend to be nasty, yelling and pushing. We understand them.

"I believe Father is from Bydgoszcz?" The skinny fellow working next to me looks at me inquiringly. "Because I'm also from Bydgoszcz. My name is Lorkowski. I used to have a barber shop in Szwederowo."

"In Szwederowo? God!"

"You know it, Father?"

"Of course, because that's our parish. My parents are there..."

We pound strenuously with our pickaxes because an SS man is looking at us with suspicion.

"They're going to murder us here," whispers Antoś Lorkowski after a while. "I've been here two months, and I'm probably the last one from my transport. Everybody's gone. Those men over there" — he pointed imperceptibly toward the leaders — "are old hands from former transports, and somehow they know instinctively..."

"Shut up!" a thrown stone flies just above our heads.

We pound furiously!

"*Arbeiten*! *Arbeiten*! Each of you must fulfill his work quota by evening. If you don't reach it, you won't get any food; instead, you'll get 'something else.'"

When the March sun finally rises over the hills and bare treetops and looks into the quarry hollow, we're already very tired. And it's such a long time until dinner!

Huge chunks of basalt are crashing from the top of the ridge down the precipice. Clouds of dust momentarily obscure the view, but columns of "porters" are already entering this cloud, and the metallic sound of pickaxes and hammers indicates that feverish work is going on there.

Commandant Redig himself spends most of his time at the top of the ridge, where the heavy hammers are pounding. He knows quite well that if those at the top provide the material, those at the bottom have to hurry. Therefore, he prods the ones at the top with his boots and club. Huge Fr. Liguda caught his eye and, after learning that the priest was rector of a college, he came down especially hard on him. The 30-pound hammer goes up and down without stopping, but after an hour of such work under the "supervision" of the commandant, Fr. Liguda feels totally exhausted. Kicks delivered from behind pose a danger of his being pushed down the precipice.

"My God! He's ready to throw him down!"

"Throwing prisoners down from the ledge into the precipice is his entertainment," explains Antoś Lorkowski. "You'll see a lot of this, Father."

And again an avalanche of basalt crashes down into the pit with a roar, breaking away chunks of the ledge, and again a cloud of dust and ... suddenly from out of the cloud we hear a cry, moans, calls for help!

"Someone got crushed," Antoś states apathetically.

They're dragging a human figure out of the dust cloud, lugging it toward one side of the pit...

"*Arbeiten!*" roars Redig from the edge of the ridge. "Leave that dog! Let him die!"

You can't lose even a minute, so hammers pound nonstop, pickaxes clang, shovels scrape against the gravel, wheels rumble on speeding wagons, porters lift up blocks again, artisans bend over the basalt paving stones ... Faster! Faster!

"It was Franek Bielicki who got crushed," whispers Fr. Leoś Michałowski, as he throws stones next to us.

"Did it kill him?"

"No. He's alive. It seems that his foot is crushed."

"*Arbeiten! Losss,*" the foreman urges us on.

The hollow is full of clatter and pounding. The work tempo is murderous. Several senior prisoners, specialists, are drilling holes in the wall and filling them with dynamite. When the charges are ready to be exploded, there's a command to leave our work sites and seek shelter behind the stone blocks. Little flames running along the fuses hiss quietly, moving toward the plugged openings. A moment of anticipation and then powerful detonations rip into the deep silence. One! A second! A fifth! Many. The echo reverberates through the beech forest. But even before the sound dies, before the clouds of floating dust have time to settle, you can already hear Redig yelling from the ridge:

"*Arbeiten!* To work, you damned dogs!"

So the hollow is pulsing with work. Stone blocks again crash down. Porters again rush forward, urged on with sticks, hammers pound, pickaxes clang, wheels on the little wagons rumble...

"Look, over there!"

Supporting himself on a shovel, hopping on one leg, the former chaplain of the ship *Batory*, Fr. Franek Bielicki comes toward us, goaded by an SS man's club.

"Ow, my foot!"

"You won't have to stand," explains the goading SS man. "You can chisel while you're sitting down. You'll earn your burning in the crematorium before you drop dead!"

So Fr. Bielicki chisels, shaping a basalt stone; he chisels despite broken bones in his foot.

"Grenzdorf is not Stutthof. Here you must work. Whoever doesn't work must die!"

And Fr. Franek wanted to live! At last, a shrill whistle. It's the signal for the noon break.

"Clean the tools! *Antreten!* Assembly!"

We fall into line.

"Each of you carry a stone on his back!" the command comes down. "Let anyone who dares take one that's too small!" Commandant Redig threatens. "The rest take the wheelbarrows with gravel!"

Loaded with tools and sizable stones and carrying poor Franek, we walk toward the camp. Truly, a Way of the Cross.

"They're finishing us off," whispers Stach Sokołowski. And Stach, the dear optimist, had never lost confidence up to now...

The half-hour dinner, or rather dinner break, goes by quickly. Too quickly, and we're standing again in tight units.

"March!"

They threw Fr. Franek into a damp cellar under the kitchen.

"He'll perish there!"

"He's not the first. How many has Redig finished off there!"

The path winds through hills covered with beech trees. Not a trace of buildings or people anywhere. Isolation. We have no idea where we are, what the nearest town is. That's that, we're lost people.

Once again the torturous work. The sun is high and warms as it shines into the quarry, but there's still a chill rising from the ground. Perspiration pours off those working with hammers or pickaxes, carrying stones or pushing the dirt in wagons, while those making the paving stones, who are forced to kneel or sit on the ground, are freezing.

It's back to hours of slave-driving because, following an afternoon nap, Commandant Redig reappears. He's raving, foaming at the mouth. Where does so much anger, hatred, and bestiality come from in a man? The more I observe him, the less I understand. Perhaps it's some sort of demonic possession?

The piles of stones grow; the mound of manufactured pavers grows. There are more bloody fingers. That's understandable. We don't have the experience, and the hammer often hits a finger instead of the stone. The broken skin on your finger from continuous handling of sharp stones becomes so sensitive that it starts to feel like you're grabbing them with raw flesh.

"It will go away in a few days," assures Antoś Lorkowski. "Then the skin will harden, corns will form, and you won't feel it anymore."

One of the young SS men finds fault with the group that's moving dirt in wagons. He's constantly chasing after them, beating their bent backs with a stick. The rails are laid directly on the ground without any ties; because the rails are uneven, the fast-moving little wagons jump the track, and then the club in the SS maniac's hand goes crazy.

Those on the ridge are working very hard, continuously pounding with heavy hammers, but those most tired are in the group carrying stones on their backs. The stones are so heavy and the terrain so full of bumps that it's easy to trip and fall with a stone, and then the SS men are right over the poor victim. Clubs batter, boots kick the emaciated body, blood flows... These persecutions are horrible. Isn't there any sensitivity in these young SS scamps? Because anyone with a heart doesn't even beat a dumb beast so inhumanely. Something in these young men has died. They are no longer human beings. They are some kind of degenerates.

Evening approaches slowly. The sun's disk goes down behind the bare tops of the beech trees. An ever deeper shadow covers the quarry, bringing an unpleasant chill.

There's a commotion among the SS men. Commandant Redig is scrutinizing the hollow from the ridge.

"Work faster! Faster, you dogs!" Blows, furious kicks fall one after another.

The commandant summons the unit leader. He tells him something in a raised voice while gesturing. The leader stiffens to attention. Finally, Redig leaves. Sighs of relief. But now the unit leader approaches and, halting the work with his whistle, announces the decision: "Since you did not complete the assigned quota, the commandant extends your work by two hours! Understood?"

"Yes, sir!"

"Then get to work, you dogs!"

All hell breaks loose. The SS men, furious that they, too, are losing two hours of free time that evening, give vent to their anger. An hour later, darkness covers the quarry. You can see almost nothing. How can you work? The leader, fearing that the onset of darkness might tempt one of the prisoners to escape, gives the order to assemble.

We clean the tools, tidy up the piles of stones. It's still a long way to the assigned quota. What will happen? Will they not feed us? Dusk gives way to full darkness. But the commandant has extended work by two hours, and we can't return to camp before that time. There's only one solution: wait out the hour in the quarry.

We stand, therefore, in close ranks. Armed guards surround us. We wait. The moon rises above the trees into the sky's deep-blue dome. The moon... Maybe at this moment my mother is looking at it; after all, it shines at this moment above the not-too-distant family roof, just as it shines above this valley of torture and death.

It gets much colder. It's still March, after all, and in addition, we're in a coastal area. The unpleasant dampness penetrates our tattered clothing. Many of us don't have shoes anymore. Our feet, wrapped in some rags that are soaked through and now freezing, feel wooden.

"Jesus! When will this suffering end?"

We finally move. When we pass a stack of wood, the order is given for each of us to take two logs to carry. The wood is wet and heavy, and each of us, of course, is already carrying his work tools. The march proceeds in silence. The path is full of roots and downed trees. People are falling down. The column is thrown into disarray. This is just what the SS men are waiting for. They're making up for lost time. They have to vent their feelings on somebody.

We finally come into camp after eight o'clock in the evening. Seven hours of work until dinner and seven until evening. The fourteen-hour "penalty" workday in Grenzdorf is coming to an end. There are still logs of wood to be stacked, still tools to be turned in, during which one or another of us gets a good-night beating (for improper cleaning). Then there's rushing into line for a small slice of bread and a cup of mealy soup, swallowing them with the voraciousness of a hungry animal, and going to sleep. But to sleep on bare planks! A terrible cold seeps through the cracks. It's blowing. We have no covers. We become stiff with the cold. Five hours of such sleep awaits us, and after that? After that another torturous day.

"Now do you believe that no one so far has survived more than two months in Grenzdorf?" whispers Antoś Lorkowski as a "good night." "I told you this is a slaughterhouse, and Redig is a murderer like few others."

14

Satan's Program[1]

March 1940. Poland lies defeated at the victor's feet. England and France, promising to aid her, prepare for military operations, but for now ... "there is no change in the West."

Hitler, possessing excellent intelligence on the state of affairs in France and England, makes plans for a surprise attack.

The multi-million Nazi army, among whose ranks SS units were the elite (according to Hitler's ideological principles), stood idle for the time being. It was a time when the first concentration camps had one SS man for every five prisoners. (This is confirmed by statistical data in depositions from the camp commandants themselves.)[2]

The author of the proceedings from the Nuremburg trials wrote, "The program of Hitler and his party was Satan's program..."[3]

And the young SS men of Grenzdorf were already its graduates. Here is one of Hitler's numerous program-related statements:

> My pedagogy is rigorous. Everything that is weak must be destroyed. In castles of my order (Hitler dreamed about organizing SS men into a kind of order, on the model of the Teutonic Knights) youth will grow up to become the terror of the world. I want young people who are impetuous, domineering, cruel, fearless! They cannot have any weak or gentle traits! Out of their eyes must shine a splendid predatory animal ... I want a young generation that is athletic. It is the first and most important thing in them... In this way I will obtain the purest material of a savage nature and can create with it —*something new*! I do not want intellectual training for the young. Knowledge will corrupt them for me.

Out of such youth he proposes raising "*Gottmenschen*— demi-gods!"[4]

On such ideological foundations Nazism educated new generations and instilled such horrible pagan principles in the nation's "aristocracy and elite"— the SS men! Inculcation of satanic principles about superior beings, a chosen race, and the special value of Germanic blood was to be accompanied by a belief in the historical calling of Germany to renew the world: Was this not truly Satan's plan? Could Satan possibly conceive anything more horrible?

Why then should we be astonished at blacksmith Redig, whose smithy's shirt was exchanged for an officer's uniform; why should we be astonished at those young SS maniacs, whose minds, souls, and hearts were poisoned with theories dictating the bloodiest practices, precisely in keeping with those satanic principles?

Those of us in Grenzdorf are growing weak at a terrible rate. Fr. Franek has been moaning in the cellar under the kitchen for several days. Overcome by pity, the cooks are secretly throwing him scraps of food. The cellar is terribly stuffy and humid. How long can he survive there?

"Maybe even longer than we," Zdzich notes. Even he has lost much of his previous spirit. He's also suffering. He suffers even more because it's done in silence. Such is his nature, that he must go through such spiritual conflicts alone.

Redemptorist Fr. Jan Szymaszek, high-school director from Toruń, is ill with bloody diarrhea. The afflicted stomach doesn't accept even mealy soup. Only a shadow remains of him, but he still has to go to work.

"You know," admits Fr. Bronek Szymański, "I'm on my last legs. Today I was sorely tempted to make a run at the guard chain (to run at the guard chain meant to choose death. They would shoot someone as though he were an escapee).

Every day the reveille makes us jump out of bed at three. Every day by five o'clock we are already at our torturous work. Every day in the evening we drop down half dead onto the bare planks. At this rate, not one of us can endure in the long run.

What's even worse, depression sets in. A black depression. In Stutthof things were bad, there was hard work, there were millions of lice, but, relatively speaking, there was enough sleep. Here, the lack of sleep, in particular, is finishing us off.

Then, suddenly, it is 6 April and they are calling us back from the quarry. Commandant Redig himself announces to those standing in ranks on the square that all the "Pfaffenshavelings" are returning to Stutthof.

God! Tears well up in our eyes! There's a spark of hope in our hearts. Grenzdorf is not going to finish us off! It doesn't matter what awaits us in Stutthof. Nothing worse than this slaughterhouse can be awaiting us.

We have nothing, so we're ready to get on the road right away.

An hour later vehicles drive up… And again we speed along, again Gdańsk, again crossings by ferry, but this time across a Vistula free of ice. We are so tired, hungry, and emaciated that we sleep while standing up. It's evening when we drive off the Gdańsk highway onto a side road leading to the camp. We're driving to a death camp, but with the feeling that we're coming back to "our place," coming "home." A human being is strange, strange indeed!

Gray streaks of smoke rise from barracks chimneys carrying the smell of burning pine resin.

Our reception is uneventful. We're even surprised as to why they're so, so … nice? Our colleagues in the barracks give us an explanation when, following joyful and tearful greetings, we sit down on the lice-infested straw.

"They're supposed to take us out of Stutthof. It's rumored that conditions will be better. It's rumored that the Vatican, that the nuncio from Berlin… There are rumors…"

We sleep again on smelly straw, but, even so, it's warm, and we sleep so soundly that even biting lice don't wake us up.

15

What Will Become of Us?

The next day they don't make us work. Following roll call, when other prisoners start out to their jobs, we're sent back to our barracks. What are they planning? What will they do with us? Where do these rumors about Vatican intervention come from? And what might this mean for today? April. This is already what month of the war? Is nothing changing for the better?

We're sitting in the barracks, hunting lice. The elders around the stove are reciting the Rosary. The younger generation, divided into small groups, talks without interrupting the "hunt."

"Don't you think that our Beck's policy* was unsound, that…"

"Of course it was unsound!" someone suddenly interrupts. "If we had been…"

And once again we're outdoing each other! Again, we're venting our anger. That's how people are. Only after years have passed, after we are released and have a chance to expand our horizons on the basis of sources, will we change our minds. But at that time, in Stutthof, in April of 1940? …

They're still bringing priests to Stutthof, while they're preparing us for a transport.

Tuesday, 9 April 1940. After the morning roll call, the order is given for all "Pfaffen-shavelings" to remain in place in tight units.

"What's going to happen?"

This was the most frequent and most disquieting of questions in the camp. The prisoner never knew what would become of him, what they would decide about him.

"A transport! All of us are going on a transport!"

There are over two hundred priests here. They add several dozen lay colleagues to our number, up to three hundred total, and they tell us to march.

"Where to?"

"Who knows."

The column, surrounded by armed SS men, passes the sinister border of the dark forest, where on Good Friday we were clearing snow off the road. We march toward the main road.

"Possibly to Gdańsk?"

"Certainly not. It's too far. Probably…"

"Shut your yapping mouths!"

After a while we turn onto the Gdańsk highway.

"So then it is to Gdańsk."

After walking perhaps two kilometers, we turn off the highway onto a side road leading

---

*Józef Beck, Polish foreign minister from 1932 to 1939

south. We're walking straight into the sun. Stutthof and its days are already behind us. Remaining there are colleagues so emaciated and ill that they were found incapable of going on the march. We realize we will never see them again in this life.

But what will become of us? Where are they taking us? Painful questions race through the mind... "The terrifying effect of transports lies in the disappearance without a trace of those hauled away, especially because no information is given as to where they will be or their fate."[1]

The marching column, heavily flanked by SS guards, slowly makes its way along the narrow road, like a gray caterpillar, through meadows already turning green. We present an awful and lamentable picture. Dressed in tattered clothing, wearing remnants of shoes or some kind of disgusting muddy rags wrapped around our feet, unshaven, with long shaggy hair, dirty, covered with bits of filth and straw, we make a horrible impression against the background of a sunny landscape.

For now, we walk in a tight column at a steady marching pace, maintained by shouts of the SS men.

Suddenly we hear part of a conversation between two guards walking nearby: "Tomorrow morning we should be in the capital, and..."

"In the capital? So they're taking us to Warsaw?"

"They're taking us to Warsaw! ... They're taking us to Warsaw," the whisper runs furtively from one group of four to another. In a few minutes, the entire column knows about it: they're taking us to Warsaw!

And joy enters our hearts! Worn heels tap livelier against the pavement, clogs laden heavily with mud don't fatigue us so much now. To ... War ... saw! We feel like singing! Warsaw is a symbol for us. Warsaw, the capital, is for us a promise of better days. (Isolated so many months from the world, what did we know then about the tragedy of Warsaw?) Suddenly, there comes from the head of the column a protracted: "Double ti-i-ime, march!"

Our steps resound.

"One, two, three, four ... one, two, three, four..." we run, with the SS men at our side. Several of them are on bicycles.

"Faster! Faster, you damned dogs!"

The caterpillar has revived. It's moving briskly along the narrow, winding road. The April sun is much higher now, and it's getting much warmer; sweat mixed with dirt streams down our faces and over our bodies, and it stings; the remnants of clogs are falling off feet, and many older prisoners already run bare-footed, while many others drop behind. Driven by clubs and rifle butts, they fall, skinning their knees and hands until they bleed. An SS man loads his rifle. A prisoner gets up with a last effort and tries to run...

Two hours later, wet with perspiration and out of breath, we arrive at the little town of Tiegenhof, formerly Nowy Dwór.

"Kee-e-e-p step!"

Some minutes later we're already near the train station, next to a train consisting of boxcars. We can't believe our eyes: on the ramp stand steaming kettles of soup! For us?

Of course! Since it's a farewell prior to our trip to ... the capital!

"Do you know where we are?" Fr. Bronek Szymański raises the question.

"I have no idea. It's the first time I've ever heard of this place."

"Tiegenhof is located practically in the center of the Malbork marshland, between the Vistula and the Nogat."

"Aha."

"Not too far to the south of here lies ancient Malbork. I was in that area with my father once as a boy..."

"Hey, you! Eat!" a passing SS man calls out with a smile.

"Look. They're even smiling."

"Naturally. They're taking us to the capital. They want to blot out our painful memories."

We're packed into cattle cars, fifty to a car. No, it isn't too crowded. In each car they put a "bucket" (a prisoner is accustomed to this utensil), then close the heavy sliding doors and bolt them.

Rays of the setting sun pass through a narrow little window near the top of the car. The train gives a start; cars knock together once, then again. We begin to move.

"He who entrusts his care," intones someone's quiet, tremulous voice... "to the Lord," the group rejoins half aloud. The wheels clatter, the car lurches sideways at each switch. "He can safely say, God is my protector, no harm will come to me..." The wheels clatter louder and louder. Tiegenhof is already behind us; before us lies the long road to Warsaw.

It's already evening when the train starts to slow down, rocks back and forth, and after a few minutes comes to a stop. We lift someone up to the window..

"What station is this?"

And suddenly there comes a surprised answer: "Chojnice?!"

"Chojnice? That's impossible! Because..."

"Chojnice," he repeats. "The name is printed on the sign: Konitz."

There's uneasiness in the car.

"So we're not going to Warsaw."

"Well, no."

"Then where are they taking us?"

"It seems somewhere in the direction of the Reich."

Silence.

The train stops a second time in the middle of the night. Most of us are in a deep sleep.

"Hey, see what station this is!"

For a moment you can hear impatient sounds, complaints of those awakened, someone being lifted up, and finally from the little window:

"Schneidemuehl."

"Schneidemuehl? But that's Piła! Is it possible?" the voice breaks off.

"It's clear. They're taking us to the capital, but not to Warsaw. To ... Berlin!"

"Berlin?!"

"You'll be there in the morning," we hear a fragment of conversation between the SS men and some railroad workers.

The train starts up. It's quiet in the car, but there's a storm in our hearts.

And so they're taking us to their lair, right to the den of the monster?

None of us knew it then, but on that night in Berlin no one gave a thought to the incoming prisoner transport of Polish priests. German armies were just entering Denmark and far-off Norway...

What's more, none of us realized that, at the same time, shots were resounding in Katyń Forest, the bodies of thousands of Polish officers were falling into huge graves, and...

"Ber! ... lin! ... Ber! ... lin!" the wheels cackle as they gain speed.

"Berlin! Berlin!" a voice in my heart cries out in fear.

Two hours of travel in the opposite direction, and you'd be in Bydgoszcz...

Snoring can be heard over the clatter of the speeding wheels. Weariness overcomes fear.

In Denmark and Norway there is at this very moment just such a clear, moonlit April night. The same moon gives the graves in Katyń a silvery hue. Like a shiny snake, the train that carries us glides toward Berlin.

What will tomorrow hold for us in ... Berlin?

16

Sachsenhausen

"Hey! You! Wake up now." Zdzich is tugging at my arm. "This is a historic moment. We're in Berlin!"

Semidarkness reigns in the boxcar. A small shaft of light comes through the little window near the top, which at this moment is covered by heads of the curious. The car sways, jolts, rocks.

"Berlin?" Somehow I can't gather my agitated thoughts.

"Berlin, brother, Berlin. Remember, how before the start of the war we wanted to go 'for coffee in Berlin'? Well, we're here. True, it's a somewhat different situation, but we're here." Zdzich's voice contains so much sarcasm.

"Why must you hurt yourself and others?"

"Eh, that's enough, we want a look, too," those doing the boosting remind those at the window.

"There's no sign of war," one of the observers seems surprised.

"He'd like to see signs of war in Berlin," Zdzich bursts out laughing again. "Berlin is not Warsaw."

"I thought that the English and the French…"

"Dreamer. People like you saw Americans landing in Gdynia on the second day of the war."

Then again total silence and depression reign in the boxcar. The crowded human pack is filled with uneasiness. Where are they taking us? What will they do with us? What awaits us?

The train did not stop in Berlin. It speeds on.

"We're going north," those at the window inform us. "We're passing through woods, sandy tracts, desolate places…"

"Of course. Because this is the Brandenburg area," someone explains.

"Could they be taking us to Hamburg?" someone worries. "There are supposed to be many concentration camps there."

Silence. People are too apathetic to take up the subject. It's terribly stuffy in the boxcar. It smells bad. The rim of the disgusting "bucket" is overflowing freely… What must it be like in cars packed with the old and sick?

"Let my lips start praising the holy Virgin," intones a voice.

"Begin to tell her marvelous honor," another picks up.

"Come to our aid, oh merciful Lady, and deliver us from the hands of our enemies…"

"Could it be the first time that the Little Office to the Immaculate is drifting across this Brandenburg land?"

"Far from it! Didn't a lot of our people who were taken into the military live in these parts?"

"That's right. Even my father ... I remember his prayer book. "See, my boy," he would say, "this prayer book was with me during my active duty near Berlin; it was on the Western Front, it was in the hell at Verdun.""

"Come, Queen of the world..."

After two hours the train slows down. An observer at the window announces:

"We're passing through some town ... Aha. O ... ranien ... burg. Oranienburg!"

We stop on a sidetrack, at a distance from the train station (only later do we learn that the sidetrack was specially set up, as at all the bigger concentration camps, to facilitate prisoner transports).

"A hundred SS men are standing by the railroad embankment!" comes a last bit of information from the small window.

We can hear voices, shouts, commands. After a while, someone moves the bolt on the doors of the boxcar. Our hearts are pounding. Suddenly the heavy doors open. Sunshine blinds our eyes, by now accustomed to the darkness, and then a voice roars: "*Raus*! Get out, you dogs!"

The train stands on a high gravel embankment at the bottom of which a group of SS men is waiting. The non-commissioned officers in charge run alongside the boxcars.

"*Raus*!"

The floor of the boxcar is high above the embankment. There are no steps or ladder. We jump down. It's so easy to twist an ankle or break a leg.

"*Raus*! *Raus*!" Clubs strike the heads of those jumping out. Bloody scenes are already taking place at the doors of the boxcars with older priests.

"Phew! How these dogs stink!" A kick. A prisoner rolls down the slope of the embankment.

The SS men are beginning to enjoy this "amusement." They push and kick again and again. We roll down over the sharp gravel. A group waiting below gives us "a reception."

"Line up! Line up!" Guards standing a bit farther away cock their rifles in case one of us tries to escape.

Thrown down from the boxcars standing above, one after another, are the bodies of those who grew weak on the trip, who suffocated, who have already died.

And at the bottom of the embankment, surrounded by SS men, the herd is trembling. The *herd*! It's so easy to write touching stories on topics such as this. If Sienkiewicz had spent just one week in a concentration camp, he wouldn't have described how groups of martyrs walked with such "blessed peace" across the arenas of Roman circuses. Poetry! Fantasy, dreamed up in a comfortable easy chair.

The herd of terrified priests stands at the bottom of the embankment, while all around barks a pack of the possessed. If we were dressed in cassocks and the monsignors were in their purple colors, maybe these paganized brats in SS uniforms wouldn't be making fun of us so brashly. But they see in front of them a group of half-shod and half-naked riffraff: dirty, unshaven, lice-infested, smelling of sweat and excrement, with wild-looking faces...

And so they amuse themselves, *they amuse themselves*!

Finally, the column is "in order."

"*Achtung*!" The handing over of the transport. At that moment, we cease to be the "property" of Stutthof and become "chattel" of the Sachsenhausen camp.

"Heil Hitler!" The commanders shake hands. The units salute, both the one in the black uniforms from Stutthof and the one in green from Sachsenhausen.

"Right turn! Double time, march!"

We start. SS men, holding their rifles at the small end of the stock, run alongside the unit.

"Faster! Faster!" Athletic, young, well-nourished, glowing with health, they consider this a morning walk. And we? ... For us, the young priests, who run in the first ranks of the column, it isn't that bad, but those poor old men barely dragging themselves on bare, swollen feet! The greatest "amusement," therefore, is at the back of the column!

It's only three kilometers from the station to the camp, but we'll never forget that road — those of us who have survived — until the day we die! That was our reception in Sachsenhausen.

At 9 o'clock we enter, sweating, many of us bleeding, through the camp gate.

The Sachsenhausen camp was created from an Olympic village, established there during the Berlin Olympics. Planned in the classical style of a Greek stadium, with an enormous assembly square from which radiate camp streets, with lawns, and with barracks painted green, it creates an aesthetic and pleasant impression. We were to find out very quickly that it's a slaughterhouse.

Next to the big camp is located the so-called small camp. It is there that incoming transports spend weeks in quarantine prior to being integrated into the big camp. That's where they take us, also, bringing us to a halt at a small assembly square.

We stand. We wait. They're herding in the poor elderly priests. They're still carrying in those who have fallen. We wait.

Finally, there's movement at the gate.

"*Achtung*!" We stand at attention.

Surrounded by a retinue of many non-commissioned officers, the deputy commandant makes his appearance to receive the transport.

The camp in Sachsenhausen, often called Camp Oranienburg, was located near Berlin and was one of the pearls of the butcher Heinrich Himmler (at right).

First an address. Such opportunities are never overlooked here.

"...During the quarantine, you will spend weeks retraining. Every sign of disobedience and insubordination will be severely punished. Every attempt to escape will be punished by death. Never forget where you are. There's no way out of this place! Unless it's there!"— he pointed toward the black chimney of a crematorium rising behind the barracks. "Unless it's that way" (chortling in the ranks of the retinue). "As offenders, you will be treated as you deserve to be treated! We, who give you the opportunity..."

Then a review of the ranks. The deputy commandant waddles on his duck's legs; his retinue follows behind. Among them is the infamous murderer Hoess (until 1 May of that year he was an adjutant to the camp commandant in Sachsenhausen; later, at an independent post in Auschwitz, he sentenced millions of people to death). There are also other minor officers, whom we would "get to know" that very evening and know even better in the days to come.

"Look, this is the Polish intelligentsia!" Such constant derisive comments were sometimes more painful than physical torments: "Polish intelligentsia! Lice-infested, dirty Polish pigs! Polish housekeeping! Poland ... Poland ... and Poland..." This is the outlet found by those whose ideological training was based on Hitler's principle: "Ich will keine intellektuelle Erziehung—I do not want any intellectual education. Knowledge will warp the youth for me."[1] In our ranks stand priests who are professors, people with doctorates, authors of works renowned throughout Europe, monsignors, people fluent in many languages, former deputies, scientists. But—and for the SS this was the only criterion—they are standing in rags, dirty and infested with lice.

"What's your name?"

"Franciszek Sokołowski."

"What's your occupation?"

"A Catholic priest."

"A priest?" "Duck" expresses surprise (that was the deputy commandant's nickname because of a deformity of his legs). "Were you a vicar?"

"No, a professor."

"A professor?" Duck is amazed. "Where did you lecture? What did you teach?"

"I was an assistant in archeology at the University of..."

"Hear that? Take a look! We have here a priest with a doctorate, a university professor!"

The SS group surrounds Rev. Professor Sokołowski. He stands small, bent over, in rags; they are looking at him as though he were an uncommon sight. Photo cameras are clicking, film cameras are hissing. "Well, well, how nice it must have been in your Poland if you had such professors at universities!" (Who among them knew that Rev. Professor Sokołowski was one of very few experts on the East in the entire world, or that even then, as a young scholar, he was known world-wide, not just in Europe?)

"And what are you?"

"A priest."

"Also a university professor?" Duck chokes on his own joke. The SS group chortles (also chortling is Hoess, who soon after would send thousands of similar people to death, among them Fr. Maksymilian Kolbe).

"No, I was not a teacher. I was an army chaplain."

"You were an army chaplain?" Duck is amazed.

"What rank?"

"The rank of major."

"Ha! ... Ha! ... Ha! ... Look at a major of the Polish military!" One of the obliging SS men pulls the Rev. Major Stryszyk out of the line. An amused mob surrounds him.

What a contrast! The lice-infested prisoner in rags coated with bits of filth next to those well-pressed uniforms with epaulettes, those shiny boots. There is no end to the questions: "Were you at the front?" "Where?" "Did we give you a thrashing?" "How many of your men died?" "What did you do then?" What? ... where? ... when? ... how?"—well, an entertainment.

But there are still long lines ahead of them. Duck moves on.

"Line up, you lice-infested Polish major!" A kick "helps" the victim. Suddenly, the SS man looks with dismay at his boot, which up to then was shiny.

"You damned dog! Your pants are full!"

Well, yes. Most of us were suffering from bloody diarrhea...

"You Polish swine! You..." A volley of blows with a club rains down on the gray-haired head of the priest-major; blood streams across his face...

This "review" lasted until dinner! The SS men, "emotionally" satisfied, go to get their physical nourishment.

We're herded into the washroom naked, since our lice-infested rags had to be thrown into a pile. After all, it's the quarantine.

In the washroom, in front of a clothing supply room, and in front of registration tables, the "Greens" are having fun with us. These are criminals, murderers and others, who have been sentenced to life in the camp for being incorrigible felons. In contrast to political prisoners, they wear a green triangle on their shirts, which is why they're called "Greens." We're handed over to these Green recidivist criminals. They become our direct superiors. It's not hard to imagine what the attitude of people in this category is toward the clergy. For each of them we're a reminder of what they trampled upon during their life of crime, that is, God's law. Many of them had met with words of condemnation from priests. Perhaps more than one had walked away from the confessional... People with a hate complex engraved on their hearts and souls toward representatives of God the Judge. And suddenly—we're delivered into hands stained with human blood! For example, One-Eyed Fritz, who had on his conscience the murder of his wife and children, and a Silesian known by the nickname "War," who allegedly committed murder seven times. The others were more or less of the same type.

These, then, were our *superiors*, leaders of the halls and blocks where we would be spending weeks in quarantine. Today in the washroom, in front of the clothing rooms, at registration we already had a taste of what awaited us from them. Beatings until blood flowed! The breaking of bones! Trampling and finishing off the dying! Oh, God!

This was our first afternoon in camp Sachsenhausen.

17

The First Days

Our dogma reminds us that *to all who are raised at the Last Judgment, God will reveal the most secret thoughts, intentions, plans, words, and deeds of every human being.* All the SS men will stand there, but *I, too, will be standing there!* I know this and — as I write, I remember it well. No, fear does not overcome me. *At the Last Judgment, God will reveal the horrors of the Nazi concentration camps to such an extent and will show them in such utter grimness that even the most faithful descriptions will pale.*

"Why on earth are you writing this?" Zdzich stops me cold. "We've survived, and 'all that' is lost in the past. Let it rest. Maybe," he looked at me with poorly concealed rancor, "maybe you intend to glorify yourself, those you name, and..."

"Zdzich! What motives, then, guided those who wrote about persecutions of the first Christians? No, Zdzich. I don't intend to glorify anyone or sow hatred of the Germans! I count many sincere friends among them, as many as you do. If there's anything I want to present in a true light, against a background of historical events, it's godless Nazism. Humanity must realize that all 'isms'— Nazism, Fascism, and Communism — which make *the state a deity* and trample the individual human being, God's work created in His image and likeness, will lead to the very results that Hitlerism produced."

When this conversation took place, quite a few years had already passed since 10 April 1940, when on the feast day of St. Joseph the Protector we received our "baptism" in the Sachsenhausen camp.

They placed us priests in two blocks standing opposite each other. Thus, we saw each other from that time at a distance. Mutual contact was rendered so difficult that we were afraid to exchange words during a fleeting encounter. That could threaten death.

I emphasize this because in my writing I must limit myself to facts that existed only in our group and in our block. While regarding the life of fellow-prisoners across the way, I will note only those events we witnessed.

The leader of our block was a Green, the murderer Bertold, and his aide was Ossi. The block leader for our colleagues across the way was Hugo. I don't remember the name of his aide.

The living conditions in Sachsenhausen were incomparably better than those in Stutthof: a washroom with several faucets, a piece of soap, a towel changed every Saturday, sleeping on a straw mattress, two blankets, a tin, a spoon, space in a cupboard, underwear changed once a week — all this was a real luxury for us now... We could regard even the short and patched denim trousers as a sign of a more bearable life if ... a sentence had not already been passed against us. And it had been passed under the influence of three motives: first, as priests, we were an entirely unnecessary element (*Für die Christliche Religion konnte hier kein Platz sein*—There could be no place here for the Christian religion)[1]; second, as hated Poles, we were subject to an order for the quickest possible destruction; third, because our group arrived in such lamentable physical condition, and almost everyone in it was infected with a bloody diarrhea, the Greens immediately received instructions that the quicker they finished us off, the better it would be for other prisoners in the camp. In fact, we were lucky they didn't take us straight away to the crematorium. The infamous, murderous law of euthanasia was already in effect: *Individuals incapable of working and a burden to the Reich had to die*! Hitler himself signed the law on 1 September 1939.[2] We were spared, but instead fell prey to "a new Nazi commandment," which is summarized (as a German document collection describes) in the following summons: "*Du sollst töten!*"—*You must kill!*[3]

And since along with this "new commandment" came an absolution that was given to SS men by Himmler: "...commanders and soldiers who participate in the liquidation of people do not in any case have personal moral responsibility, since it is borne by Himmler himself and our leader Adolf Hitler,"[4] it isn't hard to imagine with what zeal this liquidation began.

The first step in that direction was to establish a suitable daily program for the prisoners. And I quote again from German documents: "Nazism, attaining power through crime, began to consolidate its power, especially through concentration camps. So the first step toward this consolidation of power was a merciless persecution of opponents by means of murders and concentration camps."[5]

The entire program of the day was directed toward killing the greatest number of prisoners in the shortest possible time. Namely: getting us up very early, practically at night; beatings and harassment starting in the bathroom while we washed; driving us out into the street without regard for the weather an hour before roll call; food whose caloric value did not meet the most modest demands for sustaining life; work; bloody sports and other harassments, often carried out at night; inhumane punishments; beatings on the part of the Green personnel; lack of any medications or medical care in general.

In a nutshell, this was the daily bread of a prisoner in a Nazi camp, without even taking into consideration such extremes as Stutthof, Grenzdorf, and other camps that were still being organized.

Within the framework of this murderous program there appeared from time to time additional exceptionally drastic directives. Especially painful for our group was the merciless command that forbade those suffering from bloody diarrhea to sleep in the barracks on straw mattresses; they were ordered to lie down on stone floors in the toilets and washroom. During the day, the unfortunate were "nursed" in this manner: they had to stand all day in front of the barracks, where they were doused with cold water from time to time, or they were taken to the washroom where they were forced to sit up to their waist in freezing water. Already on one of our first days in the camp, I saw my pastor, Fr. Grzegorz Handke, sitting there. "Undergoing treatment" next to him was a colleague from school, dear Szczepcio Weber, and others as well, including elderly Uncle Wąsowicz from Brudnia and the honorable Fr. Farulewski, who suffered from bladder problems.

"Reverend Pastor!" Horror takes my breath away because I know they have been condemned.

"Eh, Reverend, somehow it's going to be all right. I'm in treatment, as you can see."

"There is no room in our system for the Christian religion!" No wonder that the SS men, raised on such "principles," were convinced that in murdering a priest they were rendering a service to their Führer and nation! (Printed in illustration at the bottom: "Love your enemies and pray for those who persecute you." Mt. 5:.44.) (Drawing by Władysław Krawiec.)

I hurry away. This grim humor of his, this humor even when he's already sitting with a death sentence...

"It's because you take everything too much to heart," Zdzich interrupts.

The SS men, into whose "care" our blocks have been entrusted, are three young non-commissioned officers: Schubert, Kaiser, and Seifert. Basically they're kids; I doubt any one of them is more than twenty-two years old. Our block is subject to Schubert. The smallest of the three, he looks like an eighteen-year-old boy with a pleasant swarthy face. He's well-built, elegant, and makes a good impression, but still he's the most terrible. Later we would find out that he is surpassed in ruthlessness only by "Iron Gustav," who rages exclusively in the greater camp and does not have access to the quarantine. Schubert, Kaiser, and Seifert are subordinate at this time to the reports director, the SS man Nowacki. It is he who "authorizes" the bloody acts of his subordinates. (Between 1958 and 1960, the German press covered in depth the crimes of Schubert and Iron Gustav, who were only then brought to trial.)[6]

Schubert gives out death sentences every day! Irrevocable sentences. Their executor is the leader of our block, the aforementioned felon Bertold. You would like to understand the psyche of an individual such as Schubert, and ... you cannot. In such criminals there always exists some kind of unexplained dualism. The French adage, that extremes are always adjacent, is justified in this case as well. While giving the impression of an innocent young man, looking more like a mama's boy and having many soft qualities in his nature (of which he even offers some proof), he is at the same time the personification of a criminal, maybe a sadist, who finds pleasure in committing murder.

Non-commissioned officer Schubert especially hates old people. Could he possibly have taken to heart the "Führer's" order about euthanasia, about the necessity of murdering, in particular, the old and the infirm?

The first in our group to be given a sentence by Schubert is old Rev. Pastor Wąsowicz, who was known to us all as Uncle. Dear Uncle! Small, shriveled, with his face covered in wrinkles like a drying apple, always cheerful, always friendly, always helpful, and the most beloved of anyone in our group of priests. Unfortunately, Uncle is suffering from bloody diarrhea and has been sleeping many nights now on the stone floor in the bathroom. It's heart-rending to see the ill old man lying there, especially since we cannot help him. During the day, on the other hand, he stands or sits crouching in front of the barracks. Every few minutes the "Green" Bertold pours water over him; the old man is shaking because it's only mid–April; mornings and evenings are still so cold that the patched denim freezes on him into a frozen shell. So the poor old man trembles as he unceasingly whispers prayers. Next to him are others, who are treated the same way. There is Fr. Lewański, Fr. Brząkała, Fr. Lenckowski; there are quite a few of them. It's the same in front of bloody Hugo's barracks. Over there I see Fr. Mąkowski and other acquaintances. A bit farther, in front of a barracks for lay prisoners, General Roja sits in a crouch along with many other personages. Farther still, in front of the Jewish blocks, entire groups of Jews are being mistreated.

It's already the sixth day that Uncle has been sitting crouched in front of the barracks. It's already the sixth day that Bertold has been dousing him with water. It's the sixth day he's been harassing him, beating him with a club, rolling the old man over the gravel-covered street; it's the sixth day that Ossi has been kicking him over and over again; it's the sixth day that Schubert, too, has been mistreating him, beating and kicking him, jerking him around and trampling him with steel-enforced boots; it's the sixth night that the old man has slept on the stone floor of the bathroom. He not only has no intention of passing to the next world, but, on the contrary, the bloody diarrhea stops and Uncle is of good cheer.

"I will soon return to you, back on the straw mattress," he whispers secretly as we pass him.

Poor fellow. He doesn't realize that whoever is sentenced to death by Schubert *cannot help but die.*

That day, since time drags on even for Bertold, he takes the old man to the washroom and puts him under the cold shower. Once, twice, three times. Then "exercises" in the street: kicking, beating, and rolling; and again he puts the perspiring prisoner in the shower. Usually the condemned dies very quickly then, since his heart cannot hold out. But the heart of this old man does hold out. Uncle lives.

The old man sits crouching in front of the barracks, dripping with water, with black-and-blue marks on his face, his eyes swollen from the beatings, and he's trembling like an aspen in the wind. On the ground next to him, Fr. Lewański lies dying. Uncle gives him absolution, traces the sign of the cross over him, whispers prayers; then, with his small old hand, he tries to warm him by rubbing his back.

At this moment, from behind a corner of the barracks, bloody Schubert appears. A shudder of fear runs through our ranks. Uncle, sitting in a crouch with his back toward Schubert, doesn't anticipate the approaching danger.

Like a blood-thirsty wildcat, the young SS maniac jumps toward him. He pushes him to the ground! He jumps on both of them lying there! He tramples them! He crushes them with his heels into the gravel...

A horrible sight. You can't look. This is a monster, not a man!

Fr. Lewański dies, but bleeding Uncle cannot — only a quiet moan comes from his lips, along with streams of blood.

Schubert, taking Bertold aside, whispers something to him. The latter stiffens at attention.

"Jawohl!" And when Schubert goes to the next barracks, Bertold gives us the order: "Left turn! Into the barracks in file, march, march!"

We run! Nearby, Uncle lies bleeding. Bertold's assistant aligns us in ranks (the straw mattresses were put in piles against the wall, so that the interior of the barracks would form a kind of exercise room). One of the last to come inside whispers that Uncle has revived, that he's trying to get up, that...

Ordinarily, if during the day they packed us inside the barracks, it would augur some kind of harassment which they were ashamed to disclose outside. Then Bertold would appear with a club, along with leaders from neighboring blocks, and judgment day would start.

But today it's different.

"Stand quietly," warns Ossi, Bertold's assistant. "The old man is in a bad mood today."

We know. We stand in ranks, whispering prayers in our hearts. About half an hour has gone by when Bertold — about whom it was said that he never smiles, but when he does smile, hell chuckles — enters, now *smiling.*

"That old man of yours," he begins, "you know, the one who used to sit in front of the barracks, he hanged himself!"

The small, little corpse of beloved Uncle, Fr. Wąsowicz from Brudnia, is hanging from the ceiling in the bathroom. (The rope was always kept in the storehouse near the washroom. Oh, how often it was used! And then a notification would go to the families that...)

In this manner, the priests "hanged themselves!" In this manner officers, professors, physicians, lawyers and other members of the Polish intelligentsia hanged themselves because, at that time, during the first year, they especially were arrested and sentenced for destruction in death camps.

Uncle was not the first nor the last one. Others passed before him, and others went after him. Most priests died of pneumonia. Thin denim overalls, and under them only shirts; morning assemblies on frost-covered ground, often even on ice; standing for long hours in the freezing wind; dousing with water after exercises that had caused profuse sweating: all that led to illness.

At present they're schooling us to become future "citizens" of the big camp. Therefore, we have hours of muster, exercises, marching, running, rolling on the ground; we have hours of singing, during which we must learn dreadful military songs; we spend hours learning the camp regulations by heart. Despite hygienic conditions, we still have lice! Twice a day we "hunt" them formally, with Bertold and Ossi nearby. Woe to him, however, on whom they find lice. He is then put outside naked in front of the barracks, he's doused with water, his clothing is sent to a delousing station while he waits and waits, shaking in the cold. This is again a reason for the many cases of pneumonia. It is how old Rev. Msgr. Ziemski from Toruń died, also Fr. Brząkała, and many others as well.

We're in a tight formation singing some kind of ugly song about degenerate sexual love, while behind us, on the ground, our fellow prisoners are dying. Bertold is walking around the unit with his club; he keeps watch well, and he beats even better. How is one to help those dying here? With what and how can one help those consumed with high fever? Often "moved by pity" when he sees the dying suffer, Ossi steps with his boot on their throat and ... the end.

It's worse when Bertold himself "helps" by striking heads with his club. Well, what's the point of going on and on? He murders in front of the entire unit. But a hundred times worse is bloody Hugo, leader of the clergy in the block across the way. It's well-known that he's a sadist who experiences sexual satisfaction while committing murders. Bertold murders horribly! Every morning, however, in front of the barracks across the way, there is a pile of bodies considerably bigger than in front of ours. We're panic-stricken before the sullen Bertold, but we thank God we weren't assigned to Hugo's block. Our colleagues over there are living through three hells, not one. Hugo is a monster in human flesh. There's talk that he has on his conscience several dozen murders of young girls. Looking at his bloody harvest, we believe it. And this kind of criminal is in charge, the lord of life and death for priests!

The following incident happened sometime in mid–April. Reveille. It's still dark outside the windows. We hurry to fold the blankets and stack the straw mattresses in high piles against the walls because Bertold isn't to be trifled with. If he comes in with his club and sees something still not in order, he'll use the club!

"What will we do with Mietek," asks Fr. Romek Budniak. "Look, he's lying down unconscious." (Oblate Fr. Mieczysław Skoblewski was arrested with us in Inowrocław, where he had close relatives and where he celebrated his first Mass.)

The prison rule is strict. The prisoner must show up for roll call, either alive and still standing on his feet or, if dead, lying on a heap with a number written on his chest.

With Zdzich's help, we carry the unconscious Mietek out into the camp street.

"*Antreten*! Assembly!"

"What are we going to do with Mietek?"

"We'll put him between us," Romek decides.

We form ranks. Mietek's completely emaciated body hangs down from our arms. At one point Rev. Counselor Konitzer calls to our attention that the poor fellow is dying. Sure enough. His eyes roll back, the death-rattle escapes from his throat, he foams at the mouth. After a quick absolution and hasty last prayers for the dying, we place Mietek on the ground in front of the barracks. Zdzich closes Mietek's eyes.

"Attention! Count off!" Bertold walks with his club along the strung-out ranks.

"What's wrong with this dog?" Bertold kicks the body lying there.

"He died."

"Good." And Bertold notes in a report book the number of the living and the number who died that night, those lying near the barracks.

We march to the assembly square...

On returning from roll call, we notice with amazement that Mietek is now standing at the barracks wall. His head is hanging on his chest; he doesn't have the energy to lift it. He stands with his legs wide apart, his mouth open, his skinny arms hanging at his side.

Bertold has already noticed him. He has stopped, also amazed. He probably has never had such an incident during his tenure as block leader, where someone reported dead suddenly comes to life. Bertold knows very well what consequences he could face. He utters a swear word. A prisoner reported to the commandant's office as being dead cannot come back to life. This one, however, dared to do it!

Several blows with the club—in front of the entire unit—and poor Fr. Miecio falls. Just to be sure, Bertold presses his boot down for a moment on his victim's throat... No, he no longer shows any sign of life. Profanities! (Spitting!) "This damned dog could have caused me some unpleasantness..."

That is how Fr. Mieczysław Skoblewski died, martyred in the prime of his priesthood as a "dangerous enemy" of Nazism. (?!?)

"I shall free humanity from the dirty, demeaning, and poisonous madness that is called morality and conscience!" the "Führer" cried out.[7] He liberated his SS men! And it wasn't even difficult to accomplish this horrible, godless plan. It was enough to select from among the people the morally and intellectually low element, inculcate in them the conviction that *they* have been called to be the *nation's elite*. It was enough for him to get the help of recidivist criminals as his agents, and the fruit of this sowing, the bloody fruit, grew ripe.

Sachsenhausen was a camp of terror. Under such conditions and with "such methods" Polish priests, other Poles, and Jews were finished off; even ethnic Germans were not spared if they were enemies of Nazism.

In this way, the Rev. Pastor Nowicki from Barcin was clubbed to death; in the presence of the residents of both clerical blocks, bloody Hugo clubbed the Rev. Pastor Mąkowski from Gniewkowo to death; the torturers broke the ribs of Fr. Sonsała, SVD, as he was dying; in this way the elderly priests Farulewski and Pomianowski died; also dying this way was Fr. Janusz Komf, chaplain from Kutno and a witness to the death of General Wład;

also finished off in this way were the Rev. Pastor Klein; the Rev. Dean Czacki; the young Fr. Kozubek, SVD; the Rev. Canon Charczewski; Fr. Wohlfeil; Fr. Gołąb ... In this way new victims died every day, passing from this world in truly a martyr's death. Truly, a martyr's death!

April 20 arrived, Hitler's birthday. Special persecutions hit the camp. The following day SS men brought in press articles and with real satanic malice showed a photograph of Nuncio Orsenigo, who, as head of the diplomatic corps, was conveying greetings to the "Führer." Oh, how we suffered, not understanding the motives behind this move...

"Fratres, fratres," the Rev. Prof. Dębski tried to calm us. "We don't know the profound reasons why the Apostolic See ... You see, fratres ... Oremus. Let us pray. (If someone were to say that on their way to death the Polish clergy did not remain faithful to the Apostolic See, he would be committing a colossal injustice! We were dying, suffering, and remaining faithful, even though ... we did not understand everything...)

On each of Hitler's birthdays, there was in the Reich an amnesty for a certain category of prisoners. Each year the Green felons in Sachsenhausen were sustained by new hope. This hope also sustained bloody Hugo: the closer it came to 20 April, the more he raged! Hugo, of course, had quiet instructions from the SS men, but he himself "sensed" how much it meant for them to have the priests finished off. He expected, therefore, that by "rendering service," he would perhaps get a favorable look and ... would be released. Every morning in front of his barracks lay a pile of the murdered. He murdered also during the day, in front of everyone. To kill a human being with a club, suffocate him with a stream of water (by thrusting a hose into his mouth), or choke him by stepping on his throat was for him not only a trifle, but even a sadistic pleasure. Death walked in front of him and behind him. Whenever the sound of a death cry came from a terrified victim, it was well undertood that bloody Hugo was "operating" there.

April 20 arrived, sending a group of prisoners to freedom, but Hugo was not among "the deserving."

What Block 20 experienced after that date is difficult to describe. Things that took place there were appallingly monstrous because, although bloody Hugo was not included in the amnesty that year, he could perhaps be included the following year! He needed to make "a deserving reputation" for himself with even greater zeal. The place of his most monstrous crimes was the washroom. Woe to the prisoner whom he took there, closing the door. Only the victim and God himself witnessed what happened there. A shrill cry, moans, and death rattles said enough, but certainly did not tell all. After such an "operation," Hugo would always come out in a good mood, with eyes shining like a morphine addict...

And Schubert, although he was very sorry that the amnesty did not include Hugo, nevertheless — looking every day at the pile of those murdered — smiled at the murderer more and more sincerely. This stirred up jealousy in our Bertold. Go to it, then! He's not any worse than Hugo...

It is Thursday, 25 April. Hugo is devising all kinds of new tortures. The rainy day is cold; a strong wind is blowing from the north. We already got soaked to the skin during

The punishments in camp Sachsenhausen were horrible! All kinds of them. Sophisticated... One of them consisted of pushing a prisoner's head down into a barrel half-filled with water, then beating him ... and beating ... and beating... Doing this was no problem for Hugo (drawing by the author).

the long roll call, but then, right after returning from the square, both Hugo and our Bertold begin the so-called "sport." In our camp this word stirs up more fear than the word death. Contrary to its true meaning, "sport" in camp language means a punishment, and it is one of the most dreadful; it consists of running for many hours; rolling on the ground; jumping, that is, practicing so-called "leapfrog"; falling and crawling; and prisoners all the while are beaten with heavy clubs and whips. SS men tread upon backs and heads, breaking bones, and blood flows. Several hours of this kind of sport always end with many victims: those who are killed off or trampled, and those whose hearts could not endure.

"Forward! Forward! You damned dogs!" They scream and beat us with clubs!

We run, our hearts pounding, unable to catch our breath! Pain and the blind fear of death at our heels turn us into a herd of frantic animals!

Finally, both Greens also feel tired.

"Halt! Fall down!"

We crash to the ground. A brief respite after so many hours of suffering. Even though they tread on us and beat us, it doesn't take the joy away from this moment of rest.

But then Hugo gets an idea. He grabs someone at random; it happens to be Fr. Czesio Koczorowski.

"Bless them!" he orders.

"Bless!" he repeats the order to the surprised priest, encouraging him with a kick.

"*Bene ... Benedicat vos*!" Czesio's voice trembles as his thin hand traces the sign of the cross in benediction over the group of priests lying there. But the moment he finishes, he receives such a strong blow to the abdomen that he falls with a moan to the ground.

"Next!"

And again, at the end, a blow to the abdomen and again a victim's cry.

"Next! ... and next! ... and next!..." Finally the criminal has had enough fun.

"Sit up! Hands up!" Hugo enters the barracks, sits at the table, and eats breakfast while looking at the unit through the window.

That day, when it was certain that Hugo, "worn out" from the murders, had fallen asleep in his private cell, our whole group began a novena to the Mother of God, Queen of Poland, whose feast on 3 May was approaching.

The next days were difficult, the liturgical Rogation Days (prior to Ascension), but they were real days of the Cross for the group of priests. It's as if an evil spirit possessed Hugo! He raged more every day, and on 2 May, the Feast of the Ascension, all hell broke loose in Block 20! ...

On the following day, the sunny morning of 3 May, that is, the Polish national day and the feast day of our Heavenly Lady, several SS men hurry along the camp streets in the direction of Block 20. Fear seizes the prisoners. For it was during those feast days of the Blessed Mother, so dear to our hearts, that we would always suffer the greatest harassment. This fact was so well known among us that, like it or not, we would tremble when they approached.

But, how strange! The SS men pay no attention at all to us, but hurry on further. One of them carries metal handcuffs.

They burst like a storm into Block 20.

"They're arresting Hugo!"

"Hugo?"

After a while, bloody Hugo emerges from the barracks, driven out by SS men's kicks, with his hands bound in handcuffs, bleeding. The SS men are behind him...

It appears they caught him at night committing some offense, but none of us knows what it was. Beaten, kicked, and pushed, the bloody torturer leaves the barracks as a prisoner, in the rays of the morning sun, on the feast day of the Virgin Mary!

We line up for morning roll call...

"Tell me, didn't Mary answer our plea?"

Zdzich doesn't respond. Maybe he didn't hear? He stands in the ranks, and the movement of his lips shows that he's praying.

"Zdzich! Who are you praying for so fervently?"

He gives me a rather strange look. There's so much expression in those clear but steely eyes.

"For Hugo! For Hugo," he repeats, as he watches him being taken away. "Because it was precisely for such people that Jesus suffered on the Cross."

"Zdzich!"

"Hey, stop it. We're priests, and yet we're like pagans. If Jesus were in our ranks, He would lie crying at Hugo's feet, begging him to believe in His boundless mercy."

Zdzich's words spin around in my head! ... Jesus would beg bloody Hugo for the favor of receiving His forgiving mercy? I start to observe this eccentric Zdzich with greater curiosity. And although his words sometimes cut like knives, nevertheless ... nevertheless, I sense that he's closer to me, more and more indispensable.

"Zdzich!"

"What?"

"Let's pray ... Let's pray for ... Hugo."

I feel his hand suddenly take hold of mine. This brief handclasp says more to me than a long declaration.

On this feast day of Mary a precious grace was given to me. I found a friend!

"*Achtung*! Attention! Unit, quick time, march!" We march to roll call.

And that afternoon, the body of bloody Hugo hung on the window bars of the camp prison.

Did he administer his own justice? ... Did SS men administer it for him? But Zdzich has a problem:

"You know, all the same, I wonder how it was for him... Do you understand? At the last second of his life... Because, you see, today is the feast of the Blessed Mother, and, after all, she's the Mother of Mercy ... and Hugo, too, is her child!"

18

No Changes in Sachsenhausen

Although there are fewer of us every day, our ranks fill immediately with priests from new transports. At the time Hitler is delivering a triumphant speech to honor the victory of German troops in Norway, a transport from the Działdowo camp comes to us, which includes priests from the Łomża Diocese. Other transports follow that one, and each has a group of priests. The arrivals include Fr. Mietek Filipowicz, Fr. Antoś Złotożyński, Fr. Bolek Szkiłądź, Fr. Stach Borowczyk, Fr. Jaś Tymiński, Fr. Śledziński, Fr. Kazik Równy, the Rev. Dr. Józef Przekop; also with them is Fr. Walery Przekop of the Society of Christ and others. They passed through the hell of Działdowo, and another hell awaits them in Sachsenhausen.

The days of torture drag on, each of them an eternity. We lose track of time; we lose track of who among us has already passed away, who is close to the end, and who is still living. In neighboring blocks they're killing off great numbers of Jews! About two hundred young Polish boys, between the ages of six and fourteen, are brought to one of the currently empty barracks. Two priests (I don't remember their names), caught encouraging the youngsters to persevere and not break down, have been tortured to death. In front of Barracks 15, which is a temporary hospital for quarantine and a place where they finish off the sick, there stands each day a new stack of black coffins. Each day they carry off piles of bodies to the crematorium. And we live from mess-tin to mess-tin, thinking about food, dreaming of it, wishing for it. At night, Schubert drives us out into the street, orders us to fall into the cinder dust, douses us with water from a hose, chases us until we break into a sweat, orders us to fall down again, douses us again, and orders:

"Into the barracks march, march!"

From time to time, entire groups of young SS men appear in the camp. (The former commandant of Sachsenhausen testified later in court that under his command he had 4,700 SS men for "servicing" the camp![1] I don't exaggerate, therefore, when I say that for every four prisoners there was one SS guard.) These young people need to have something to do, they want to blow off steam.

And—*they do blow off steam.*

In the international arena, there is silence. Since the occupation of Poland, German armies stand with their weapons in readiness, turned against France and England. Instead of attacking, Hitler is conducting a war of nerves, making peace proposals to England and France.

Then 10 May arrives. German armies, with the aid of the powerful Luftwaffe, violate the neutrality of Holland, Belgium, and Luxemburg!

Radio loud speakers, located throughout the camp, have been booming out marching melodies since morning. To the point of painful boredom, one of them keeps coming back with the words:

"*Denn wir fahren* ... For we're going, for we're going, for we're going against England..."

Bloody terror increases now in the camp. It stands to reason. If their colleagues at the front can gain new lands for the fatherland, the SS men here — wanting to serve their country — must destroy the domestic enemy even more relentlessly!

And ... *they do destroy*!

The violent German offensive on the Western Front moves farther and farther, like a crushing steamroller. Each day brings the Germans new victories, and we feel each of them in the camp. Schubert and other camp tormentors are bursting with tremendous pride.

On 15 May, Holland capitulates.

The SS men in Sachsenhausen vent their joy their own way. The drunken horde tries to outdo itself in atrocities. Each morning the piles of bodies near the barracks grow higher and higher!

"Has God forgotten about us?"

"Oh, no!" Zdzich quickly denies it. "It's precisely when He scourges us that He most remembers."

Triumphant melodies of victory blare from the loudspeakers, and for us it's becoming harder to defend ourselves against despair. Cases of "going onto the wires" are multiplying ("to go onto the wires" meant feigning an escape attempt, so that a merciful burst of shots from the guard tower would put an end to your suffering...). So far, not one of our group has gone, but ... will one go soon?

While visiting the barracks, Schubert takes out a revolver from his pocket, makes threats with it, forces prisoners to look down the barrel.

"See the bullet? ... This one could be for you."

Up to now, however, he hasn't dared openly to shoot any of the priests, but sometimes shots are heard coming from the Jewish barracks...

On 17 May, an official communiqué from the High Command of the Armed Forces (O.K.W.) announces via the blare of loudspeakers that the Allied armies are retreating from Belgium, that Rommel's invincible motorized units are forging ahead like a hurricane! And again the resounding: "For we're going, for we're going, for we're going against England!"

On 21 May, German units reach the English Channel. The SS men are walking in glory! And we? Our hearts are increasingly heavy.

"You're going to be sent to mines in Belgium," Schubert declares. "You'll rot there!"

"Yes, sir!"

On 28 May, we learn the terrible news about the capitulation of Belgium.

"Jesus!"

On the following day, the loudspeakers are blaring about the imprisonment of King Leopold III.

On 30 May, the SS men chase us into the assembly square. A medical committee arrives. Selection begins for a transport to the Gusen quarry.

"To Gusen?" We're overcome with fear.

But they're picking only the strong and those who look good. After months in Stutthof, after bloody diarrhea and almost two months of "quarantine" here, we do not constitute tempting morsels for the committee. Among those chosen is my professor from high school in Nakło, Franciszek Marciniak; my friend, the Polish record-holding athlete Kliniakowski; my cousin, the teacher Jasio Latos, and many, many acquaintances, including Fr. Przekop of the Society of Christ.

An official German communiqué from France announces that Dunkirk is burning, that ships in which the English are evacuating their armies are sinking, that there's general panic.

Later, in the post-war years, a French historian would write: "We had eight months of time after the occupation of Poland, and what had we done for our defense? When Hitler attacked us in May, we had barely 54 bombers (!?!), and when it came to fighter aircraft, our infantrymen and artillerymen scoured the sky for them in vain..."[2]

And we had counted so much on France, on England, on the United States...

The English have hidden on their island.

The French retreat in haste.

The United States keeps "giving assurances" of its unwavering policy of isolation.

And as for us? ... Preyed upon by despair, we fight for a wretched shred of life!

Weeks of bloody quarantine in Sachsenhausen were decimating us even more than the camp in Stutthof.

On 10 June, Mussolini enters the military arena, declaring war on France!

On 14 June, when they chase us once again into the assembly square, we hear through the loudspeakers not only triumphant marches, but also the boots of thousands of German soldiers striking the cobblestones ... of Paris! It seems to us that on this warm sunny day in June the lid of a dark coffin is closing over us... For us, France's capitulation means extinction of the last ray of hope. The louder the loudspeakers howl, the more the tears stream down our emaciated faces.

A transport from Lublin province arrives on 20 June, bringing several thousand Poles. Among them is a sizable group of priests, mostly Capuchin Fathers and Jesuit seminary students. There is the elderly Fr. Viator Mojówka; there is the superior from Lubartowo, Fr. Efrem; there is Fr. Bonawentura, and there are many others.

They're new, and so for them inhuman torments will begin. Already SS men are "operating" among them, as well as the criminals charged with maintaining "order" in this group of many thousands.

Among the Greens, one especially stands out for viciousness. Short, stocky, with wide shoulders like a barn door, he speaks with a Silesian dialect. He utters curses that make your skin crawl, and he blasphemes like Lucifer himself. His nickname is "War." None of us knows why. He thinks nothing of picking someone up by the waist, turning him upside down in an instant, and striking his head on the ground so that his brain splatters all around.

The new arrivals, watching this, grow pale and cringe. And we? ...

There are hardly any survivors left from our Stutthof transport. Those of us who have survived are already "older" prisoners. Even the Greens, recognizing seniority by the numbers we wear on our shirts, persecute us less. Objects of their bloody interest are the new arrivals.

19

One-Eyed Fritz

At the entrance to the small camp, that is, to the "quarantine," stands a barracks designated as a clothing storehouse. Prisoners' civilian clothes are deposited and stored there. It is Thursday, 30 May, the octave of Corpus Christi. That day happened to be when the storehouse was to be straightened up. This is done by the Greens, under supervision of one of the young SS men.

A quiet May evening slowly comes to a close. The sun is sinking toward the forest that surrounds the camp. A young SS man, sprawled in a chair, is observing the Greens as they work. He knows them well enough to know that, given one moment of inattention, they will steal whatever they may have already chosen. The young SS man is in an exceptionally bad mood today. Well, why not? The day was so beautiful, and he had to spend it in this stuffy storehouse. Suddenly he notices that one of the Greens picks something up from the floor and is looking at it.

"Show me what you have."

The Green approaches and shows a Rosary in his hand.

"Where did you get it?"

"It fell out of one of the bundles."

"What is it?"

"I don't know," the Green pretends, shrugging his shoulders; "it's from a bundle left by one of the shavelings. It's probably some of their 'hocus-pocus.'"

Our unit was just then passing along the street near the open door to the storehouse.

"Oh," the Green notices, "the shavelings are just going by. They ... "

"Bring one of them here."

Soon we're standing in long ranks in front of the entrance to the storehouse. The SS man asks the first one in the row to come forward. He is the Rev. Professor Dębski from Inowrocław.

Tall and so emaciated that he gives the impression of a skeleton, holding a cap in his hands, he stands at attention before the young SS man. The latter puts the Rosary on the tip of his club and swinging it asks:

"What is this?"

"It is a Rosary."

"What's it used for?"

"For reciting prayers." And Rev. Professor Dębski gives an explanation. When he finishes, the SS man continues to ask with a smile:

"Is this something very holy for you?"

"Yes," answers the priest. "The Rosary is a very holy thing for every Catholic."

Then evil enters the SS man. His smooth face is suddenly contorted with an ugly grimace, there are satanic fires in his squinting eyes, a whistling hiss comes out of his lips:

"You damned dog! You shaveling! If this is such a very sacred thing for you, then kneel and kiss it!" He throws the Rosary into a pile of rubbish from which rusty cans, pieces of broken glass, broken bottles and jars are sticking out. "Kneel and kiss it!"

The Rev. Professor Dębski kneels down. He realizes that in order to reach the Rosary with his lips and not cut his face with the sharp metal and glass, he must be very careful. He bends down carefully, therefore, lower and lower. Suddenly, the SS man raises his foot above the bent head of the prisoner and with his boot pushes his face into the broken pieces of bottles and jars.

When the priest finally lifts his head up, blood is streaming profusely down his face. And it seems as though an evil spirit really has entered into the SS man. He growls with foam on his lips: "Kiss it once more!"

The prisoner bends down again, and again the SS man's boot presses the bleeding face into the broken glass.

"Kiss it again! Again! Again!" And when the priest falls down motionless by the rubbish pile, the enraged SS man kicks him in the head, chest, abdomen, back; and when quiet moans come out of the tortured victim's chest, the SS man jumps on top of him and stomps down, while flames of hatred shoot out of his eyes: "You dog! You carrion! You ... You ... "

Fr. Dębski lies unconscious and only bleeds and bleeds.

"Take this mad dog away!" the SS man tosses the order in our direction, again kicking the battered victim.

We go back to the barracks. Several colleagues carry Fr. Dębski.

"Lay him down in the bathroom. Let him rot there!" the block leader decides.

"Unit, turn left! On the double, march!"

The bloody sport begins.

Nevertheless, my pastor, Fr. Handke, managed to slip into the bathroom without being noticed. He risked a lot, namely, his own life. In the evening, he tells us: "Fr. Dębski regained consciousness. Kneeling next to him, I gave him the last rites. We said goodbye. 'Grześ!' he asks me in a whisper, 'What day is it today?' 'The octave of Corpus Christi,' I say. 'Octave of Corpus Christi,' he repeats quietly, and on his bruised and cut face there's a smile. 'Grześ!' (The whisper is now more difficult; the voice breaks off, makes a whistling sound...) 'Grześ! Every year I celebrated the Eucharistic procession in your parish ... in the evening ... on the octave of Corpus Christi. Re ... Remember?' 'I remember,' I answer. 'Grześ,' it's hard for him now to catch his breath, 'if we were in ... Ino ... Inowrocław, then ... then I'd now ... be cele ... celebrating ... the proces...' He didn't finish, he just breathed a sigh and died."

Fr. Handke is silent for a moment. Then he speaks again: "Reverend Father, you know I'm a tough person, but I cried like a child, and I didn't care if the block leader caught me and attacked me. Reverend Father! Fr. Dębski was my, was my..." Now it's the pastor stammering. "He was my friend. Reverend Father, this truly was a holy priest! Truly a saint!"

"I know. He was my confessor."

"Well, then you know. A saint has left us, and tomorrow they're going to burn him in the crematorium."

Throat clearing and sniffling in the darkness... For the first time I discover that my spirited and good-tempered pastor also knows how to cry.

There's another big transport of Poles from the "General Gubernia,"* which includes priests from the Lublin area: the Rev. Dr. Franciszek Trochonowicz, Fr. Franek Zawisza, Fr. Jan Orzeł, Fr. Stach Stachowicz, Fr. Dominik Maj, Fr. Władzio Kłos, the Rev. Prof. Wacław Staniszewski, Fr. Jan Samolej, Fr. Miszczuk, Fr. Olek Murat, Fr. Ludwik Liwerski, Fr. Jaś Kozak, and many others.

"You know," says the newly arrived Fr. Trochonowicz, "several of our colleagues have been here since 1939. Most of them were clerks in our Curia."

"They're not among us."

"They're in the big camp. I already found out. Maybe we'll meet them sometime."

Near the end of July there's a transport from Śląsk, which includes Fr. Przybyła and Fr. Sylwester Baksik.

One day they drop a bombshell on us: "Starting today, you are going to be transferred to Block 56, to One-Eyed Fritz."

"To Fritz? Oh, God!"

The one-eyed criminal Fritz, murderer of his own wife and children, was the terror of the entire "quarantine." With regard to atrocity, he was second only to bloody Hugo and maybe the notorious "War."

Following the afternoon meal, which consists of a daily bowl of warm water with or without a cabbage leaf floating in it, we stand in tight formation. Ossi, Bertold's aide, escorts us to Block 56.

"Haaalt!" We stand at attention. Ossi disappears inside the barracks. After a while he comes out with — One-Eyed Fritz.

"Keep well, you guys!" Ossi wishes us as he leaves.

Fritz, wearing only a shirt and trousers, stands on the threshold, looks us up and down with his one blood-shot eye, and rolls up his sleeves. He looks like a bandit who is getting ready for a fight. Bluish-red scars cross his bony face. He inspires fear and dread just with his appearance. Besides, we've already seen him tormenting prisoners every day during preparations for roll call... We know what to expect from him. Consequently, we stand there filled with fear. And he gives orders in a hoarse bass voice:

"Crouch ... down! Hands up!" Then glancing again over the ranks sitting in a crouch, he goes back inside.

While Fritz is peacefully eating his dinner under the roof, the sun at high-noon is burning our shaved heads; heat is rising from the surface of the street, our upraised arms are becoming weak, we're getting cramps in our bended knees. How long are they going to make us stay in this position? Through the windows you can see the inside of the barracks. Fritz is not in a hurry. What thoughts could be going around in the head of this murderer of his own wife and children? What are the feelings of such a monster? How much of man is there in him, and how much of animal?

From neighboring barracks, Greens and block leaders are coming down together and going inside. We see them talking cheerfully with Fritz; we can hear the peals of their chortling laughter. Their bloated faces are smiling; their shaved heads, covered with scars, are shining; their strong, gnarled hands are gesturing. Terrible "War" is in charge. This assemblage makes us uneasy. Why are they gathering here?

There is among them one, very likely the youngest, tall, thin, well-built, handsome, with a very pleasant face and blue eyes. He doesn't take part in the talks. He stands leaning

---

Translator's note: a province in German-occupied Poland, 1939–1945.

against the wall and looks at us with some kind of strange look; could it possibly be with compassion?

"Oh, if only that fellow were the leader of our room," the wish runs through my mind.

In the meantime, the sun is burning more and more, our legs cannot hold our bodies in a crouch any longer, so we slowly start lowering ourselves to sit back on our heels, although we know what kind of punishment and tortures we can expect for that. Luckily, those behind the windows are paying no attention to us. We can no longer hold our arms up. They fall on our heads against our will. Again, an insubordination that is severely punishable. Anyway, what don't they punish us for?

"*Achtung*!" The camp senior's sudden command from off to the side terrifies us. Schubert, Kaiser, and Seifert are coming toward us.

Fritz runs out of the block, quickly buttoning his uniform. Behind him are the other Greens.

"Block 56!" reports One-Eyed, standing at attention. "The detachment..."

Schubert waves his gloves, interrupting the report.

"Begin!"

"*Achtung*!" Terrible Fritz stands before us with a severe expression. "Left turn! On the double, march!"

Our tendons, numb from crouching so long, are very painful, but we run. The three SS men are standing in the shade of the barracks. Nearby are groups of Greens.

"Faster! Faster, dogs! *Eins, zwei, drei ... eins, zwei, drei,*" Fritz urges us on.

Schubert says something to the group of Greens. They rush inside the blocks... Soon they're next to us, armed with sticks and clubs. They position themselves along both sides of the street, and they beat us. They beat without mercy, hit or miss, on the skinny skeletons, on the shaved heads, on the hands covering our faces from the blows.

"About face! March!"

Again the blows fall. And the sun is scorching hot. Cinder dust rises in a black cloud, covering our perspiring faces and our denims, which are soaked through with sweat. We're as black as Negroes, and all that glistens are the whites of our eyes, opened wide in fear, and our teeth, bared in exertion.

If I had not been in the concentration camp and had not experienced this myself, and if someone were telling me he had taken part in sport five full days in a row, running, jumping, rolling and crawling (without interruption) from early morning to dinner and from dinner to evening, it would be hard for me to believe. It will likewise be hard for the reader to believe that this kind of sport, ordered from the commandant's office, could last for five days. It did last, however. No pen, no narrative, no film can recreate all the details of this grim SS "amusement."

Each day the Greens arrive in the morning with clubs, and each morning the command is issued: "On the double, march!" And beating! And pushing! And kicking! Then, for a change, two hours of "leapfrog." That exercise is so terribly tiring that we tremble at the very command: "Leapfrog!"

It's the older and most emaciated priests, in particular, who fall. Many of the runners trip over their bodies. The young try to jump over them, but then a Green with a club stands next to the fallen and, by beating, forces the runners to trample them. Yes, to trample them! These aren't priests who are jumping, leaping, rolling, and running this way. It's a herd of animals crazed by torture and fear (this is how they kill the humanity in us, which is probably worse than anything).

Then, for a change: "Crawl!"

Already black from coal dust, we fall down again; we crawl while the torturers stomp on our backs, beating us with clubs, kicking and pushing us, crushing us into the dust.

"Stand up! On the double, march, you damned shavelings!"

With one swing of his club, a Green breaks Father Strehl's arm. The priest cries out in pain, but he has to run. One person's eyes are covered by blood that streams from a cut forehead; another has a split head with blood flowing down the back of his sweaty, emaciated neck.

"On the double! On the double!"

Fallen bodies cover the street.

"Trample them! Let them rot!"

Standing at the end of the street, which is blocked off by a fence, at the place where our unit turns around, is the Green with the face of an archangel, the handsome one, whom we had wanted to be our room leader. He's holding a blood-stained club and beating someone with it. Oh, God, how he beats! He's the very Satan incarnate! His blue eyes are bloodshot; on his face you see implacable cruelty. In front of him lies the greatest number of beaten bodies.

Fritz takes off his jacket, rolls up his shirt sleeves, spits into his gnarled hand, and ... let's get the shavelings! They must be finished off once and for all. "War" is laying waste like a hurricane, others are trying to keep up with those three.

And the sun bakes unmercifully; sweat pours from our bodies; thirst burns our insides! Only at dinner can you get a drink. Nor can you leave the file to go to the bathroom. It's not allowed! So the unfortunate relieve themselves in their pants. Upon noticing this, the Greens start beating again without pity.

"You Polish swine!"

Each day before evening roll call, Schubert appears. He inspects the ranks of those still living, complains, shakes his head in disapproval:

"Too few of these dogs are dying! Too few! Eh, Fritz! Do you hear, you dog? Too few! There must be more tomorrow!"

"*Jawohl*!" bloody Fritz assures him, leering with his terrible eye.

So the next day is even worse. Fritz tries as hard as he can to make it worse. More and more priests are finished off. Among them is the Rev. Professor Szukalski from Inowrocław, author of the famous religious instruction books. Also falling are the unforgettable Rev. Prefect Bruno Szymański from Świecie, the young Fr. Franciszek Hinc, as well as Fr. Wohlfeil and Fr. Gburczyk. Is it possible to remember all the names of the many who were murdered during those five sinister days?

This is what happened on one day of those deadly "exercises." Battered, we drag ourselves to evening roll call.

"Attention! Schubert!" the warning runs through the ranks.

We straighten up. We stiffen. Of course. Just don't draw his attention to yourself in any way, for that would mean a death sentence. When Schubert looks at someone, it's as if death looked him in the eyes.

"Halt!"

Before the unit could come to a standstill, Schubert charges into the ranks like a rapacious hawk, pushes some off their feet, pushes others aside, and reaches the young Fr. Śledziński from Łomża. A powerful kick of his boot to the abdomen, and the prisoner crashes to the ground with a groan. Schubert stands over him. He kicks, stomps, jumps on

One of the bloodiest butchers at the Sachsenhausen camp was the young non-commissioned SS officer Schubert, later decorated (as the authentic clip from the German press informs) with the highest cross of merit for ... *murdering* prisoners!

the living human flesh. He stops only at the signal for the start of roll call. Blood flows from the mouth of the priest.

"Until tomorrow!" Schubert tells Fritz with a meaningful wink.

"*Jawohl*!"

A whispered explanation goes round the ranks that poor Fr. Śledziński had found a piece of caraway stem, and what would a starving prisoner not take into his mouth? So Fr. Śledziński took the tiny stem and was chewing on it. Schubert noticed this and ... the verdict was passed.

We return in tight formation from the roll call to the front of the block. Fritz leaves us crouching, and then turns to Fr. Śledziński:

"Well, come here, dog!"

The doors to the bathroom close behind them. We know too well what's going on at that moment. Fritz is drowning the poor priest, carrying out the sentence handed down by Schubert.

When we go inside the barracks fifteen minutes later, we look through the open door to the bathroom and see Fr. Śledziński lying by the wall. He's already "resting from the work and torment" that we still have ahead of us. A steaming bowl, however, soon makes us forget not only about the drowned man, but also about the fact that it could be our turn tomorrow ... (A psychologist might find rich material here for a study, and he might ponder at times to what extent inhumane conditions can influence people, even people with high spiritual standards.)

"You say only a psychologist might have a mine of material? It seems to me that if St. Alphonsus were to experience with us what we're experiencing, he would certainly change a lot in his manual on moral theology," Zdzich says.

"What are you trying to say?"

"Oh, nothing," he waves his hand. "Anyway, you wouldn't understand me."

In the evening, when we're already lying down on our straw beds, the beast with the innocent face of an archangel suddenly comes in; it's the room leader whom we had wanted for a supervisor, but who had struck so ferociously with his club during the hours of sport. His name is Helmut. He enters holding a guitar, sits down, and (good Lord!) ... starts to sing. And what he sings! All kinds of melancholy songs: about his mother, about his family home, about days of homesickness spent behind prison bars. We lift our heads and listen in astonishment. It seems to us impossible that a man who during the day is one of the most merciless and bloody butchers could in the evening of that same day reveal such sensitive strings of his heart. How can you explain it? It is, after all, an astonishing case!

"Didn't I tell you a psychologist would have extremely rich opportunities for research?"

"Well, yes. These are, indeed, unexpected phenomena."

And the murderer Helmut continues to sing to the accompaniment of soft guitar chords, and his voice is so poignant, so boyish...

"Look," whispers Zdzich, "look: Helmut *is crying.*"

What's going on in that murderer's soul? (Helmut was also a recidivistic murderer. I don't know how many human lives he had on his conscience.) Helmut is crying! Was it possible Fritz, too, could cry?

In the bathroom, by the wall, lies the body of Fr. Śledziński. Tomorrow morning there will be a pile of them! And tomorrow evening, after a day of deadly sport, Helmut will wash his blood-covered hands so as not to stain his beloved guitar, and ... with the look of a child, he will again sing tenderly...

"You know what? Sometimes I have the feeling this entire camp is a gathering of the possessed and demented."

"Oh, God, my God! I pray so hard that God will take me quietly, in the night, so that in the morning I don't have to get up from the straw mat; I feel such fear, I'm so afraid of dying under the clubs of these executioners," whispers the Rev. Pastor Wierzbicki from Kościelec.

In the morning, Fr. Edward Skowroński, who was sleeping next to him, shakes the pastor by the arm in vain. Fr. Wierzbicki had died that night. He did not perish under the club.

Fr. Lenckowski has been sitting for several days now in front of the barracks with a trash can on his head. As they pass by, the Greens hit, kick, trample, and pour water over him, but dear Lencek lives, endures. A strong Kashubian constitution.

Terrible things are going on in the blocks of Polish Jews. Not a night goes by without SS men creating absolute havoc over there! We can hear sounds of blows, shots, inhuman yelps of the tortured victims, the gagging sounds of those choking; the wild, blood-curdling squeal of those being battered, and in the morning piles of corpses lie in front of the barracks. They don't treat the Polish intelligentsia, isolated in another barracks, any better. They finished off General Roja yesterday on the street in front of the barracks. A young SS man suffocated him by stepping on his throat.

"See! This is how a Polish general dies!"

Degenerate, snotty kid! A bastard of the depraved Nazi ideology.[1] And Hitler called such people the nation's elite, a spiritual aristocracy. He made them demi-gods. With such as these, he intended to establish his "new order of knights!"[2]

On the fourth day of that terrible sport, right after dinner, in the hottest part of the day, they force us to go into the barracks. It's so hot and stuffy inside that it's hard to catch your breath. There's no ceiling. Heat pours down from the roof, burning-hot as though from the top of a baker's oven. We stand in tight formation. There are about three hundred of us.

"What have they dreamed up for us today?"

"Fall down!" screams Fritz.

We fall down one on top of another. They've closed the windows, and the heat is unbearable.

"*Rrrrollen*! Get started!" and the gang of thugs is ready to stomp on us, striking at random and kicking.

Moans, yelps, cries, sobs, whimpers. The room looks like a pot full of bugs, a heap of bugs climbing over each other, pushing each other off, choking... This lasts a long time, that much I know, but I don't know how long because at such moments time stands still.

"*Rrrrollen*! Faster! Hurry up! You ... you damned shavelings! You spongers off the people! You black internationalists! You..."

Finally, even the butchers are sweating, tired, and having a hard time catching their breath.

"Crouch!" comes Fritz's hoarse command.

They finally open the windows. The heat that enters from the outside feels like refreshing coolness. We crouch with our hands raised high over our heads, waiting for the sequel. The gang of Greens looks at us, scoffing. Suddenly Fritz pulls out Fr. Romek Budniak, Fr. Władek Rolbiecki, Fr. Meger, Fr. Szczepański, and then others. He stands them in pairs and gives the order:

"Hit each other's mangy mugs!"

The priests standing there look surprised. This is something new. We haven't experienced this kind of harassment yet.

"Hit each other in the mug!" Fritz urges, glancing with his blood-shot eye. "Oh, like this!" he demonstrates, hitting one of the priests in the face.

"Hit!" His club is raised over the head of the victim. "What? You don't want to?" A powerful blow to the abdomen and the victim crashes to the floor with a moan. "War" and the rest of the Greens, encouraged by Fritz's example, are beating, flailing!

After some time, all the priests who were called forward lie battered on the floor.

"Outside, march!" comes the order.

We jump to our feet. We know that any semblance of delay will provoke new harassments. But there is only one narrow door in the room, leading only to the adjoining room, from which you can only go outside.

"Faster! Faster!" Clubs of the gang members are striking backs and shaved heads. The wooden wall shakes under the pressure of bodies, it creaks, it's liable to crack. The terrified crowd moving into the next room overturns the block "master's" cupboard. Out of it fall "appropriated" treasures. Cyclop Fritz goes berserk. Roaring like a wild animal, he grabs the first person at hand. Oh, God, it's Zdzich!

While we try to get outside as fast as possible, overcome by panic, the Greens are stretching Zdzich on the table. Four of them hold him by the feet and hands while the others beat him... Zdzich is paying for everyone and everything. And ... for nothing!

"Crouch!" Fritz yells through the window.

We crouch, raising our hands above our heads. Others inside are now doing the beating. Zdzich is a strong man, yet he's beginning to moan.

"*Raus!*" We see them push him off the table, then kick him. After a while, he goes outside, beaten, bloodied, with a pale face. He crouches nearby and ... and I know for sure that he's ... praying for them.

And again hours of "sport," again bones crack, again blood drips into the gravel of the street, again colleagues fall, but God seems not to see, although just now He is closer than ever.

"Henryk! Are you asleep?" Zdzich asks in a whisper when we're already lying down on our straw mats.

"No, why?"

"Look at my back. It's really burning!"

It's nine o'clock and still light enough to see.

"Oh, God, Zdzich! Your back and buttocks are cut to the raw!"

"I thought so."

"Wait," interjects Romek Budniak, who lies nearby. "I have a wet towel, we'll put it on."

One day they bring to our barracks all the priests from the big camp, who have been held in Sachsenhausen since 1939. Among them are several German priests, as well as Poles: the Rev. Dr. Salamucha, a professor at the Jagiellonian University; the Rev. Dr. Zawistowski, a professor at Lublin University; the Rev. Dr. Ochalski, chancellor of the Lublin Curia; the Rev. Dr. Olech, notary of the Lublin Curia; the Rev. Dr. Krynicki, episcopal court auditor from Lublin; Fr. Styp-Rekowski, director of Polish schools in the Reich; and several others. It appears that most of the lay university professors were released (except for those, of course, whom they managed to torture to death), whereas they detained all the priests who were professors.

The end of our punishment is for many ... the end (drawing by the author).

"Today your quarantine ends," Fritz tells us. "From now on you'll be taken to work, and from now on you'll go for roll calls in the big camp. Understood?"

"Yes sir!"

"You know," whispers Mirek Ziarniak in the evening, "they thought they could finish us off in two months of quarantine, but since they couldn't, they staged these days of torturous sport for us, so that many more might pass away, and now? Now they'll force us to work like slaves."

20

In the Valley of Jehoshaphat

The following day they split us up into work units. They take some of us to the canal to unload coal and cement off boats; another group goes to the forest to carry logs; they send the rest to the so-called industrial yard—Industriehof. This is an enormous area, surrounded by a high wall that encloses all kinds of industrial plants, smaller factories, workshops, warehouses, depots, a crematorium, and an infamous place of terror, namely the large pit of gravel and sand where (by one of the sandy mounds) firing-squad posts stand imbedded in the ground. We call this macabre place the Valley of Jehoshaphat. Hundreds of prisoners who don't have a work assignment at a given moment are rounded up into this place. From time to time either the Greens or even the SS men themselves come here as work foremen, and they select groups for special tasks. It gives the impression of some kind of Eastern slave market. And the miserable humanity they round up here is truly dreadful. *Muselmann*—Mussulman, i.e. Moslem—is the generally accepted term to describe these camp wretches. This nickname originated because the prisoners brought here are half-naked and wrap their heads with dirty shirts to protect themselves from the sun. Looking at these groups with improvised turbans on their heads, at their emaciated, sunburned skeletons, you get the impression that this really is a tribe of Bedouins or Mussulmans, leading a nomadic life in the desert. Trash of all kinds is burned in the valley, including bandages from the camp hospital that smell terribly of pus (the opinionated allege that one can often find amputated body parts there. It could be that instead of being sent to the nearby crematorium, some do, indeed, find their way to the valley ... of Jehoshaphat.) The continual smell of the burning trash and the smoke streaming over it gave it the name Valley of Jehoshaphat (where the Last Judgment is to take place). Moreover, the look of the valley at the Industriehof in Sachsenhausen, with firing-squad posts standing in it, really brings to mind an image of the Last Judgment.

"You know," admits Romek, who is assigned to unload barges on the canal, "it's terrible there! A barge arrives, they put down narrow wooden planks from the landing-place, and we haul coal in wheelbarrows over the planks. The SS men and Greens, positioned along the route, urge us on with clubs! They beat us! They push us into the canal!"

"It's even worse hauling cement," says Szczepek Weber. "Each of us has to carry 150 hundred-pound bags every day. Oh, how they drive us there!"

In the evening we return to the camp dead tired. We know that tomorrow, from early morning, torturous work again awaits us, and yet we would rather do even this work than remain in camp, where we're subjected to new harassments.

"Today you're all going to carry bricks!"

The brickyard is located almost three kilometers from the camp. A penal company and Jews work in it. The work there is considered the hardest in Sachsenhausen and the fastest at killing people off. The threat: "You'll go work in the brickyard!" makes one shudder in fear.

Fortunately, they take us only to carry bricks from the brickyard to a new construction site nearby. Our foreman is a Green whose name is Max. He's an older man with a wide, puffy face. Probably some type of petty thief and not a murderer. Max is not a bad man, but he's terribly limited. He's deathly afraid of the SS men. When he notices that none are nearby, he leaves us alone, but as soon as he sees a green uniform, blood rushes to his head, and ... Max goes crazy. Afterwards, stuttering, he explains:

"You see, I have to, because..."

Max, we understand you. You'd be less brutish — even when an SS man approaches — if you weren't so limited. For someone like that, a lot is forgiven.

We each carry four bricks. Each brick weighs about ten pounds; that is, we carry forty pounds altogether. It isn't much, but taking into consideration our weakness, the uncomfortable wooden (Dutch) shoes that make our bare feet bleed, as well as the distance — the effort is very great. We have to make ten trips daily, that is, traverse three kilometers twenty times. On the whole — for us — it's an awful lot, so we return in the evening for roll call barely dragging our sore and blister-covered feet.

One day we take a different route: we carry bricks not to the construction site behind the camp, but to the prison, which is located inside the camp, isolated from it by a high wall. Various stories circulating about this prison make your flesh creep. It is said that horrible things happen there. Rumor has it that sitting in the prison are Bishop Goral, General Rowecki, and other distinguished prisoners. One of the more friendly Greens once whispers, "People, if you knew what goes on there at night!" It's there that Schubert most frequently operates with Iron Gustav!

We carry bricks inside the prison yard. The SS men stationed at intervals warn us not to come too close to the windows.

Carrying bricks (drawing by the author).

"Hurry up! Hurry up!" Max urges us. "It's almost time for noon roll call. If we don't make it, there'll be punishment."

We quicken our pace. The sun is scorching our bare heads. The bricks weigh heavily on our shoulders. When we enter through the camp gate, the clock on the tower indicates five minutes to twelve. The units are already on the square. The SS men are impatient.

"On the double! On the double, you dogs!" Schubert greets us at the gate.

"On the double, march!" We rush toward the distant prison. In the yard, they're already waiting for us! A veritable judgment day ensues. There's no time to stack the bricks as has been done so far. We simply have to toss them. But to break a brick is *sabotage*. Sabotage is punishable by a severe penalty, including the death penalty.

"Oh, you damned dogs! Is this how you take care of our property?"

The mayhem grows worse. Under the press of bodies, stacks piled up since morning are falling over. The SS men become more infuriated. This makes the frightened herd of prisoners run even more desperately around the small yard.

Over there they've cut open the head of the saintly old Rev. Msgr. Schönborn, pastor in Kruszwica, and elsewhere several others have fallen.

But we made it on time for noon roll call. The colleagues we dragged to the square also made it on time.

The sun, motionless above our heads, irritates the dying men's eyes, now clouding over. Large green flies can already sense the malodorous corpses.

An exaggeration? No! In many cases we considered these green flies as good doctors.

A serious epidemic of huge abscesses is a scourge that afflicted us after the torment of bloody diarrhea. Some colleagues have several of them, others have several dozen. Some are the size of a large drinking cup. Embedded in them are cores of a disgusting green color, thick as a thumb or thicker. There are no medications. So we catch a green fly, set it on top of an open abscess until maggots hatch that will gnaw out the rotting flesh. This is apparently a very effective way to get rid of gangrene.

They say that those who have leprosy have a disgustingly foul smell. Those among us with abscesses smell so bad that it's hard to bear. Is it any wonder? After all, flesh decaying in the heat of the day isn't fragrant...

"My boy," saintly old Rev. Professor Detkens, rector and academic pastor from Warsaw (what a wonderful priestly figure he was, full of goodness and serenity!), asks one day, "would you take a look at the abscess on my back?"

"I'll be glad to."

We go into the washroom. The Reverend Rector takes off his shirt and ... tears come to my eyes. There, on the poor fellow's skinny, stooped back is an abscess the size of a cup! (If I had to testify about this under oath, I would do it again.) The huge abscess, full of green pus, was surrounded by horrible inflammation. Where do I start? What can I clean it with? I feel helpless.

"Allow me." Zdzich is nearby. "I have experience in this. This will hurt a bit, Reverend Rector," he warns, "but it will help."

There was, admittedly, a prison hospital in the big camp, supposedly rather well equipped, but while all other prisoners were managing to get in, Jews and priests stood at the end of the line. Sometimes out of pity a Green would send one of us to get a dressing, though only in very serious cases, but so what, since after a long wait in line it would turn out that for Jews and shavelings, there wasn't enough time! After dinner, prisoners of other nationalities again had priority, and again there wasn't time for priests. Once, after being sent to the hospital by a Green (the block leader) due to wounds on my legs, I waited there three days ... without success. Was it worthwhile to go? Standing in the heat with an uncovered head resulted in heat strokes. Someone waiting in line, instead of getting to a first-aid station, would find himself in a cellar where dead bodies were stacked before being taken to the crematorium.

The crematorium, meanwhile, emits smoke day and night! Several times a week they take groups of prisoners to be shot. Often they bring some kind of secret transports from outside the camp. Stories then circulate that officers or some other distinguished personages have been brought in.

Executions are carried out toward the evening, specifically in the Valley of Jehoshaphat when there are no longer prisoners in Industriehof. On those occasions they deliberately keep us for a long time at the assembly square; from the valley come bursts of machine-gun fire, followed by individual revolver shots. That's when they're finishing off the wounded. The following day there are dark rusty stains of blood around the posts, while bivouacking all about are ... the "Mussulmans." Who's shocked? Yesterday, it was them, today us, tomorrow others... It's all the same.

One day they shoot two hundred young Germans who were called into the military but — as Jehovah's Witnesses — refused to bear arms. Out of the two hundred, there were only one or two who, at the sight of rifle barrels, broke down and agreed to put on uniforms. The rest were mowed down. That's how the horrible Nazi hydra devours even its own children, the flower of German youth.

This was already the time when Hitler's inhuman order on the necessity of murdering the handicapped, the old, and the mentally ill was widely put into effect, when special medical boards, at the service of the Nazis, traveled from one German institution to another, using syringes and later gas to do away with tens of thousands of native Germans, a sum total of about 300,000.[1]

Day after day, crime after crime, behind the barbed wires of concentration camps mass murders are committed by the Gestapo and the Security Service (SD) in Poland, France, Holland, and Belgium, while Hitler again proposes peace to England ("*Appell an die Vernunft in England*"), promising that if England only allows Hitler to institute a "new order" in Europe, he will give it complete freedom in its insular and maritime policy. "*Und der Herr Churchill sollte mir dieses Mal vielleicht ausnahmsweise glauben...* And Mr. Churchill should believe me this time, perhaps by way of an exception..." This speech took place on July 19, 1940.[2]

Churchill, however, didn't believe in the "new order" of the Nazis. Did Churchill already know what was happening in Nazi death camps?

21

A Chapel in the Death Camp

We are carrying heavy kettles of coffee from the camp kitchen. How much does such a kettle weigh? Maybe a hundred and twenty pounds, maybe more. For prisoners starving and staggering from weakness, that's a great effort. Dawn is breaking behind the pine forest, and with it a new day of suffering. The fogged-up barracks windows reflect a cadaverous glow from light bulbs, in faint contrast to dawn's lively colors flowing onto the dome of the sky.

"It will be a hot day."

Zdzich doesn't respond. Perhaps he didn't hear?

"Maybe you should be more careful! Don't get in the way!" barks one of the two puffing "bearers" behind us. His voice is impatient, irritated, trying to pick a quarrel. It's no wonder. In each of us there are the same pent-up emotions ready to explode at any moment. How easy it is from a distance, while in a good mood, to spin legends about martyred heroes and heroism, and how different all this looks from personal experience, when you have to keep your teeth clenched in daily gnawing torment. How different it is to "read up" on the heroism of little St. Thérèse, and how completely different these small heroic acts must have seemed when the nun working at the same tub across from her would splash her face with water used to launder dirty handkerchiefs. Each day that we priests live together presents us with just such quiet acts of heroic suffering. How many occasions for mutually painful irritation! How many emotional wounds!

"You see," explains Zdzich on such occasions, "great principles of theology and other supernatural teachings have been inculcated in us, but the fundamental principle that "grace demands a human nature acquired by effort" has been forgotten. Where, prior to recommendations of asceticism and mysticism, there's a lack of training according to the most basic manual of proper conduct, where natural virtues have not been instilled, there supernatural virtues..."

"Zdzich!"

"Do you think I don't notice the way empty space forms around me, the way you all avoid me, steer clear of me, think of me as a heretic, a revolutionary on the order of Savonarola? I see it. Yet few of you know that I'm hurting myself more than my colleagues."

The procession of those carrying kettles is nearing the "quarantine" gate. We stop every dozen steps or so, set the heavy kettles down and, panting, try to catch our breath.

"Attention! Let's pick 'em up! March! One, two, three ... one, two, three." Just maintain a steady pace and don't tip the kettle to one side because then the boiling acorn brew, called coffee, can burn our hands. One, two, three... Just a few more steps...

"Look! No, not there. Over there. A few more have gone onto the wires."

"To go onto the wires" in camp jargon meant this: finally to find a merciful death.

Such a death was sought in the daytime as well, but especially at night. Some poor wretch would run out of the barracks and head right for the camp's wire fence, which was charged with high voltage. Most often, before he managed to reach the fence, a series of shots from a machine gun in the guard tower would catch him. There wasn't a day in Sachsenhausen when corpses didn't hang from the coiled barbed wire of the camp fence.

"They're already free," Zdzich says as we pass by with the kettles.

They are already free... Again this shock inside me! I know. It's the fault of my temperament that I'm affected by such events more deeply than others are. In addition, there's my hypersensitive imagination... I already see the mothers of these unfortunates waiting somewhere back in Poland, or maybe their wives, their small children... The despair must have been terrible if it crushed even a desire to return to their loved ones... In the faint light of the new day, scraps of human flesh, riddled by bullets, hang on the barbed wires. Here, where they fell, was the place of their judgment. Here sentences were passed about their eternal life. Judgments. Was God, who saw the depth of their despair, merciful to them? Oh, kind Jesus, our Lord, grant them eternal rest! Even today their bodies will be burned in the crematorium. Tomorrow, or the next day, a perfumed young secretary in the records office will type out a notice for the family that ... and again suffering fills my soul. My imagination paints pictures of family homes, mothers, wives, children. Tears. A sea of tears.

"Zdzich, why is it like this?"

He doesn't answer. The coffee splashes in the kettles. Through the fogged-up windowpanes we can see our colleagues bustling around.

"*Coffee*!"

Their tins are steaming with the acorn infusion. This is the only "meal" until dinner.

"You there, drink, and don't blubber!"

This Zdzich can be so brusque, and yet it's precisely from his brusqueness that real goodness speaks. There are people who vent their feelings of friendship only in this way. Unfailingly, they're steadfast friends.

"You know what? They're supposed to open a chapel for us!"

"A *cha ... pel*? ... Here? In the camp?"

The news is too wild to be believed. It's simply camp *parola*, like so much else. (The word "parola" refers to camp gossip.)

After the morning roll call, they rush us to work as usual. Again, as every day, the hours of lingering death drag slowly on. (This word "death" may seem an exaggeration. Unfortunately, each day in the Sachsenhausen death camp substantiated this word only too well. Each hour in that horrible death mill was an act of dying!) The sun burns backs that are bent over; shaved heads again swell from the heat; again so many of us fall from sunstroke and exhaustion, and those who are weaker fall under the clubs. Oh, how slowly the sun's scorching globe drags across the ashen dome of the sky! In the evening we'll carry dead colleagues on our shoulders. But maybe someone will be carrying us as well? And tomorrow at dawn, scraps of human flesh, cut to bits by bullets, will again hang on the wires. And then new, but always the same, days of suffering. How much longer, oh Lord?

In the evening after roll call and supper, the rumor about a chapel goes around again, this time allegedly coming right from Schubert...

At the end of July they assign some German priests to our clerical block, and among them are also several Polish priests who arrived in Sachsenhausen before us and have been in the big camp all this time. They also confirm the news about a chapel.

One day the camp officials begin to tear down the small hospital within the so-called quarantine. It had seen the death of many of our colleagues, and we always passed it with trepidation, as though passing some grim symbol of death.

"We're transforming it into a chapel for you," prisoner carpenters and woodworkers, brought from the big camp for this work, inform us. "The altar is now ready!" They point to an enormous, heavy table.

This is the table that was used for performing autopsies and heinous experimental operations. Truly a sacrificial table! A veritable altar of blood. And it is on this table (if the rumor about the chapel is real and not some horrible new harassment) that Jesus is to rest?

On 2 August, Schubert appears in our barracks.

"Prabuki! Where's Prabuki"

Fr. Paweł Prabucki, former army captain, stands at attention before the SS maniac.

"Paul," for the first time, a somewhat more human sound comes from the lips of this murderer. "You will take command of this shack." Schubert waves his gloves toward the barracks chapel. "Only you will conduct your hocus-pocus in it each day, but woe to you if some kind of disorder occurs there. You'll be the first to get fifty on your behind, or ... " Here the young SS man hits his revolver case with his gloves. "Understand?"

"Yes, sir!"

"And now," Schubert moves his clear child's eyes over the group of priests standing at attention. "Fall down! You damned dogs! You Roman swine!"

So the group of priests falls down, one beside another. Fr. Prabucki is right next to the steel-reinforced boots of the young SS man.

"If you think, you crazy dogs, you swine, that just because we're giving you a chapel, you can..." He didn't finish. He only managed to let out an awful sputter from his saliva-covered lips...

That was how the Lord gave us his sanctuary. We receive it not from the hands of a consecrated bishop, but lying in the dust, downtrodden, at the feet of an SS man.

"Isn't this a painful symbol?" whispers Zdzich.

Perhaps it is a symbol. Jesus told Sister Faustyna Kowalska that He would hand the churches and monasteries of "this world" over for annihilation because they betrayed His most important commandment, the commandment of love.

None of us knew then that the chapel given to priests in the death camp was the fruit of intensive diplomatic interventions by the Holy See. That fact was just as incomprehensible for us then as was our entire life in the camp, in all its painful aspects.

But the chapel was not the only reason for our astonishment at this time. The next day it was announced that from now on, "Having *complete freedom* to practice religion (!?), we were also excused from all physical work, unless one of us wanted voluntarily to do some work for recreation or to kill time, in which case camp authorities were ready to consider such a request favorably and provide a recreational task." (!?)

If the Holy See had realized what painful new harassments it had unwittingly and with the best intentions prepared for its priests precisely by having obtained these "privileges," it would never have sought them. During those years of suffering, we wanted more than anything — without damaging our priestly dignity — to lose ourselves as completely as possible within the ranks of lay prisoners. Because, unfortunately, during that time there were two categories of prisoners whom no one envied: Catholic priests and Jews! Those two categories bore a stigma. The worst recidivist murderer had more rights in the concentration camps than a priest. In the eyes of every SS man, the priesthood was an unpardonable offense and crime.

This, then, is how religious life on command started at camp Sachsenhausen, introduced as one of the items in the "program of torture." Let no author who has not experienced these moments, and no preacher carried away with pathos, spin legends on this topic; let them not draw shallow conclusions nor prompt tears with sentimental examples! If in the writings of St. John of the Cross or other mystics we read about mystical *nights* filled with spiritual suffering, then just such a night of the soul became the lot of the entire group of priests in striped camp clothing. It's true that every day Jesus with His humanity descended upon the altar — a table stained earlier with the blood of so many priests cut to bits on it; it's true that faith and dogma indicated His real presence, and yet Jesus was hiding from His priests. Oh, how much more concrete was the SS man assisting at the altar with a hat on his head and a cigarette in his scornfully pursed lips, peering into the celebrant's chalice with a sneer, and sniffing this bit of wine, which was becoming the Most Precious Blood!

"*Hoc est enim Corpus meum,*" the celebrant in striped clothing whispers the words of the Consecration, bringing God to the bloodstained altar through the power given to priests.

"Hurry up, hurry up, dog," the SS man with the cigarette urges him. "It's almost time for the roll-call signal."

Eucharistic Jesus rises for a moment over the head of the prisoner celebrant, lifted up in his grimy hands, which an hour from now will clean the SS men's toilets. Hundreds of heads are bowed in silent adoration, but in the hearts and souls of the prisoner priests, stretched out for months on the debased wood of the cross, trodden in most brutal fashion by the boots of hatred, in their souls and hearts there is night, night! Jesus is hiding. Suffering. No feelings. No consolation. Nothing. Hearts turned to stone and some vestiges of will, dragging over this burial ground of all values. One thing remains most constantly real: *death*.

"*Domine, non sum dignus...* I am not worthy, Lord..."

Due to lack of time (extremely limited for holy Mass by camp regulations), we receive a small piece of the Host in the hand. In a hand that's grimy, cracked, on which a louse just crawled.

"May the Body of our Lord Jesus Christ preserve my soul..."

Is it you, oh Lord? Really You? You with divinity, with omnipotence, with majesty? King of kings in the form of a wafer fragment? In this place where Satan reigns? Is it you?

"I feel like a man who's fallen off a cart; the horses are bolting, and I'm holding on with all my strength and running, but I feel that I'm growing weak, that any moment now I'll fall, that everything will end. I'm losing my faith!" Marian whispers breathlessly into my ear. "It's enough to drive you crazy."

"Console yourself that one day someone will come along who'll sit at a desk in a comfortable easy chair, light a good cigar, and pour out onto paper the most wonderful recollections of heroic martyrdom, unshakable endurance, steadfast faith. Hundreds of casual preachers will talk nonsense about..."

"Zdzich!"

He waves his hand in resignation, while delousing himself.

And so we have a chapel! We have "freedom to practice religion!" Since the daily camp schedule must be observed, however, we have to get up an hour earlier than everyone else in order to fit in daily Mass. Getting up in camp is already early, so they wake us soon after midnight. Obviously, even greater harassment now falls to those ready for uncustomary religious practices. If straightening up the barracks in the morning was previously an occasion for harassment (as it was, anyway, in all other blocks), it now became for us a torment difficult to bear.

"You want to go to church for your hocus-pocus? I'll give you church! I'll give it to you," thunders Fritz. And he delivers: now with his fist, now with his boot, now with a club.

And then — rush for the kettles of coffee. And then — rush to distribute it. And then — put things in order again. And finally roll call. Count off! Again the kicking and beating and the march in tight formation to the chapel. Fritz doesn't go inside. Waiting already at the altar is the SS man on duty, with a hat on his head and a cigarette between his teeth.

"Go to it! Go to it, dogs!"

"*Introibo ad altare Dei* (I will go in unto the altar of God)," begins the celebrant in wooden shoes.

"To God who giveth joy to my youth," responds a choir of prisoners smelling of perspiration and bitten by lice.

It's good if the SS man on duty allows the Holy Sacrifice to be completed. It's worse when, bored, he interrupts the liturgy with a whistle, arguing that it's already time to form units for roll call and encouraging our departure with kicks. The poor celebrant, Fr. Paweł Prabucki, gets it hardest and most often from the SS man. He also gets it from the block leader when, as the last to run out of the barracks-chapel, he often must catch up with a unit that's already marching.

"You dog! You shaveling!"

This was his, and also our, "joyful" thanksgiving following the loving meeting with our Master at the table of Love.

"Jesus! I might be going mad!"

"Church history hasn't known such a mystery of evil."

"Before your eyes, Lord, we place our sins..."

In the meantime, transports arrive at the camp nonstop. Each one brings a larger or smaller number of priests from Poland. Some depart, new ones arrive. The crowding in our priestly Block 56 is so great that we sleep packed to the hilt.

Finally, one August day, they move us to Blocks 16 and 17. Both barracks are equipped with three-decker wooden bunks with straw mattresses. This is a luxury for us, guaranteeing several hours of sleep in acceptable conditions. It doesn't matter that tidying up these "bunks" — in comparison to the straw mats — demands more effort and is a cause for renewed harassment and punishment.

Things are worse with regard to both block leaders. In Block 16, the duties are carried out by the communist Erich; in our Block 17, it's the recidivist criminal Karl, with a green triangle. Both of these camp potentates (senior prisoners with established friendships and

21. A Chapel in the Death Camp

The only moments of rest and relative peace were nights spent in lice-infested bunk beds.

influence) are feuding with each other. The criminal Karl looks hatefully at the political prisoner Erich, while Erich regards the recidivist Karl with disdainful superiority. They both agree on one thing: their passionate hatred for us priests.

The communist Erich cannot forgive us because "Over the years we've gotten drunk on the blood and sweat of poor working people," while the murderer Karl cannot forget that in front of him are those who remind people of God's commandment: "Thou shalt not kill!" Under these two, subject to their favor and disfavor, we are to endure until the end of our stay in Sachsenhausen. Nevertheless, though neither one nor the other ever lacks ideas for the most fanciful harassments and torments, these are no longer the days of bloody Hugo, Bertold, or the Cyclops Fritz. Terror on the part of the SS men has also subsided somewhat. The start of the German-Russian war, the first operations on the Eastern Front and, after that, in August, the beginning of the great air battle for England, all this slows the tempo of bloody "activity" by diverting the attention of the camp butchers.

Not for long, however. As German forces move to the east, there are more and more transports of a terrorized populace from Polish regions, and the death mill picks up speed in an ominous way. The zeal of murderers increases in Sachsenhausen, where the satanic anger of fallen man, outwardly expressing agreement to allow God in here, dares even more brutally to trample all His laws.

22

The Stream of Time Was Flowing

During this same period a pale terror traveled through Germany. Horrifying news, repeated in whispers, concerning the activity of a secret enterprise with the mysterious title "Gemeinnützige Transport GmbH," spread in ever-widening circles. For a long time now officials of that organization were appearing at homes for the aged and disabled and at hospitals for the incurably ill. They examined patients and transported them in special buses to Sonnenstein, situated in the Linz area. These transports came from all parts of Germany. (Let us add in parentheses, in order to avoid a misunderstanding, that in this instance, we're talking about ill German citizens.) Soon it stopped being a secret, especially for residents adjoining this locality, that mass murders were being carried out on their own citizens in that "sanitarium." Martin Bormann's "Catechism," written on the basis of Hitler's personal decision, stated that even within one's own nation everything that is weak, infirm and chronically ill, in a word, everything that threatens the purity of the race or is a burden to the country *must die*. This neopagan catechism of Nazi doctrine bore fruit: the Nazi Moloch more and more boldly was devouring his own children!

If the Nazi monster devoured its own brothers in this way, what could we expect from it, we, a second-class people, slaves imprisoned in a tight barbed-wire enclosure, and especially we, priests of the Catholic Church, which was considered a first-class enemy?

And there was no shortage of victims. In transports coming more and more often to Sachsenhausen there was always a larger or smaller group of Polish priests. They filled up the places vacated by those who were murdered. The merciless mill kept grinding up new beings. Smoke rose from the crematorium both day and night...

---

29 August 1940. They didn't send us off today for "voluntary" work. We're marching in tight formations on the street between the clerical blocks.

"A new transport has arrived. Bigger than any other."

Signals are sounded in the main camp. The block leaders know what this means. They're needed at the take-over of the transport. Erich and Karl give orders to the hall leaders.

"But behave well, you dogs, or..."

Each time one of the larger transports arrived, our day would be easier. The SS men, the block leaders, and the entire pack of camp thugs would rush at top speed to the new arrivals. Of course. Every transport carried lots of goods of all kinds. The SS men would fill their pockets; the block leaders would fill their pockets. Encircling the new arrivals like a pack of hungry hounds, they would leave us in peace.

And it's like that today. The hall leaders who have taken command of the units aren't concerned with us; they're looking for any pretext just to get near the square, where the plundering of new arrivals is taking place. Something always comes in for them, too.

"Apparently there are a whole lot of priests in this group," says someone who is more or less informed.

"Oh well."

We feel the August heat; sweat is streaming down. The hall leaders, not having much desire to conduct exercises, finally make a decision: "Sit down and ... delouse!"

Fine. We sit down in the street in rows, take off our patched shirts, and "hunt."

It's nauseating to look at these skeletons, these sickly bodies covered with ulcers. Swarms of flies, attracted by the smell of pus that seeps from hideous phlegmons, hover insistently above the naked group.

"Don't shoo them away," someone admonishes. "Let them breed maggots. When they eat the rot out of the wound, no doctor can perform a better cleansing procedure."

"Well, you see, formerly every year, in order to restore our failing health, we had only to go to Polish spas, to Ciechocinek, to Szczawnica, to Krynica, to..."

"Stop it! Why do you hurt others and yourself?"

"Myself, too?" the other speaker is surprised. "No. I never had time for trips to health resorts. I had a residential quarter in my parish with so much poverty in it that..."

"Look! Take a look! 'War' is raging again!"

Through the wire fence of the quarantine, looking toward the square where they're receiving the transport, you can see a group of several hundred new arrivals surrounded by SS men and camp thugs. What scenes are taking place there! The Silesian nicknamed "War," a bully like few others even here in the camp, is really "reveling" today. The SS men roar in amusement. It's not for nothing they've made him leader of the disciplinary block. It's not for nothing that coffins stand at the entrance to this place. If near the end of the day War sees that one of the coffins is empty, he gets into a nasty mood. The poor guy couldn't sleep if someone in the morning were to discover such negligence... Oh no! Each morning the coffins in front of War's block are full! They're filled with the "fruits" of his criminal acts. Oh, now he's showing off in front of the SS men and the new arrivals. This War is terrible!

"Wait a minute," says one of the priests. "Is he a Pole?"

"Who knows? He does speak Polish, though in dialect. But he does speak it. Maybe..."

Someone on the side interrupts: "Yesterday in front of the kitchen one of the Jews was telling us that the German air offensive against England is apparently in full swing now."

For a moment there's silence. We're killing lice. Thoughts race through our heads. Although we all have similar thoughts, we don't have the courage to express them out loud...

It's true. The air battle for England was raging full force at this time. We didn't know, however, that at precisely the same time Lucy, the last of the children from Fatima and already 33 years old, was pleading with Pope Pius XII to carry out the Mother of God's

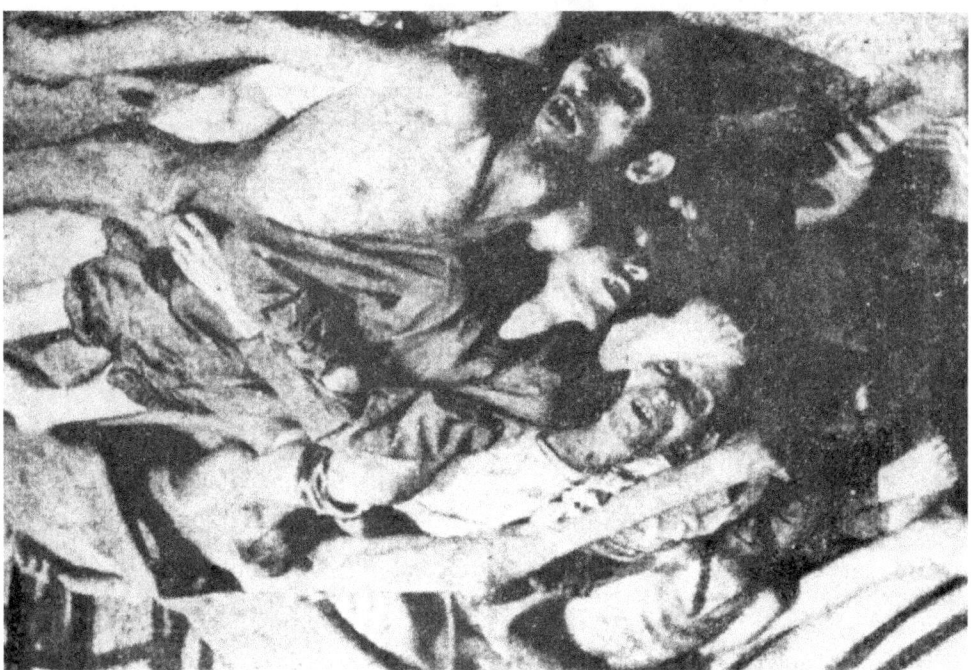

Lying in front of each barracks every day were the bodies of those who died the night before.

wish by consecrating the world to Her Immaculate Heart![1] Besides — let's be honest — how much did we know about the appearances in Fatima then, almost a quarter of a century later, or about Lucy's mission, or the promise of Heaven's Immaculate Ambassador? "Power status" and a fixation on human efforts veiled the "other power" from us.

The sun is at its zenith, beating down relentlessly. Someone is lying stretched out in the street, covered with black gravel dust. Is he resting? Dying? Is he dead? This is of interest only to his closest neighbors. The rest of us? ... What about it? You're not allowed to leave the ranks. You can't help him anyway. Thirst burns your insides. Faucets with cool water are nearby, in the barracks washroom, but who dares to ask the hall leader for permission to go there? It isn't allowed and that's that. Only during the dinner break will there be a chance.

It's already well toward evening of this memorable day, 29 August 1940, when they bring over two hundred newly arrived priests into our street. God! How many acquaintances! Most are priests from the Gniezno Diocese. There's the Rev. Canon Formanowicz; there's the father confessor of the seminary, Fr. Tadrzyński; there are Curia personnel Fr. Ziółkowski and Fr. Palewodziński; there's the Rev. Pastor Gałęzewski; there are the pastors Chilomer, Zieliński, Piszczygłowa, Figas from the Września area and Fr. Głuszek, the former prefect from Nakło; there's dear Fr. Franciszek Nowak, and Józio Pućka, and the Rev. Dr. Małecki, an American by birth; there are Fr. Bronek Pluciński and Fr. Winczewski, sentenced to death, and Fr. Feliks Nowaczewski; there are priests from the Włocławek Diocese with the Rev. Prof. Mączyński and seminarian Kazio Majdański. One priest of special interest to me in that group is Fr. Jasio Januszewski, to whom I'm practically related. We come from the same parish; we've been friends since our youth; we attended the same high-school in Nakło and the same seminary in that diocese...

For the time being we're allowed only to glance at them, to see them standing fearfully in tight ranks. Until the block leader "gives them proper instructions," until an assignment is made as to halls, sleeping space, tins, spoons ... quite a bit of time will still go by. In the meantime, therefore, they stand at attention, with their arms tightly pressed against the seams of their patched pants, and we observe one another. They with horror, and we? ... Probably with dull depression and a torrent of thoughts in our heads.

We meet only after evening roll call.

"Attention, priests! We don't kiss by way of greeting. They"—a movement of the head toward the block leaders—"don't understand this and immediately suspect something different."

The greeting...

"Jasio!"

"My grandparents died in Warsaw," Jasio is saying. "They shot my father, uncle, brother-in-law, and several distant relatives. My aunt, you know Płaczkowa from Sadki, was executed with a group that also included Fr. Leon Kaja."

"And Antoś?" I pick up the conversation since for the moment there was an awkward silence. "Do you know anything about him?" (Antoś, Jasio's younger brother, was also a priest.)

"Antoś ... Antoś," Jasio slowly draws out the words, staring straight ahead. "I looked for him; I asked about him. He disappeared. The last news was that he'd been executed in the Grudziądz fortifications."

"Were you by any chance in Sadki?" I'm dying of curiosity.

"No, I wasn't. You can't imagine how dangerous it was to move around. Any time you stuck your head outside of Wronowa, it would arouse suspicion. But I did have news from there. Almost all the men were shot and killed."

"*Shot and killed.* Good Lord." Another moment of silence. "And Fr. Kaczmarkiewicz, is he alive?"

"He's alive. He's tending cows on some German's estate. But you probably know they executed Fr. Zenon Niziółkiewicz and Fr. Leoś Nowak from Ino?"

"They were executed?"

"And many others. My head's simply spinning. You lose track of who's alive and who's gone."

"Inside the barracks!" The block leader's shout ends this first meeting.

"See you tomorrow, Jasio."

"See you tomorrow."

It came and went — that tomorrow... The days go by... The weeks go by... New transports arrive again and again; there's not one without new priests, and with them comes fresh news.

"These are already their last death pangs!" they whisper with flushed faces. "Just one more month or two and they'll finish themselves off. A lady was saying that her brother-in-law's brother..."

Brrr ... A lady saying! "A.L.S." is the name of that news agency.

"How naïve they are," the pessimists flare up.

"How much faith they have," the optimists express admiration.

"*Antreten*!" The roar of our block leader interrupts the controversy, which arises so easily now on subjects such as faith, lifting one's spirits, the apostolate of good news, not hiding one's light under a bushel...

"*Antreten*! Hurry, you damned, rabid dogs!" Kicks. (No order is given without them in Sachsenhausen.)

"We need two hundred *volunteers* to carry bricks!" the block leader screams, glancing derisively at the arriving work foreman. "You've heard that the privileges accorded you clearly stipulate that, even though you've been excused from the normal camp work program, if one of you voluntarily asks for work to pass the time, the camp command graciously accedes to his request. Therefore, speak up! Two hundred volunteers!"

The foreman, who has just arrived, is already counting off from the front of the unit.

"Hey, hey, not all at once," jeers the "Green" Karl. "Someone has to stay in the barracks."

They rush us off. "Sentenced" by our privileges to a release from work, we had to give all of our more serviceable shoes and clothing to those who were working. In exchange, they gave us old, misshapen Dutch clogs made of wood and tattered uniforms. For "the nonworking" even that was overly generous.

"In step! Keep in step!" seethes the foreman leading the unit. We enter into the assembly square. "If you 'attract attention,' after work this evening you'll get *sport*. Left, two, three, four! Your left! Your left!"

God! How can you maintain a marching step in these wooden clogs that fall off your feet?

"Oh, you rabid dogs!" screams the SS man in the gateway. "Is this how you march! Wait until this evening! We'll teach you how to march!"

And ... after a full day of drudgery, after a full day of running, of being beaten and kicked, when the painful clogs had already made our feet bloody, we had an evening of *sport*!

That's what "clerical privileges" looked like! That's how "volunteer" work looked when it was done for ... recreation!

Every so often the camp's work foremen come to us in the barracks, taking "volunteers" and stimulating our "willingness" with clubs.

"Two hundred shavelings request permission to unload vehicles voluntarily," reports the foreman at the gate of the command building.

"All of you are asking?" the SS duty officer poses the question, striking the top of his boot with his club.

"Yes, sir!" a resounding response from the group. (Woe to us if we hadn't responded!)

"Ha! It's difficult to refuse, when you're asking so earnestly." The SS man spreads his arms in a gesture of feigned helplessness. "It's difficult to refuse. Therefore, in step march, maaaarch!"

And so, driven by clubs, the group of priest volunteers rushes off like a herd of frightened horses.

They use us for various jobs. Of course, it's always "voluntary." Sometimes to carry bricks or haul heavy construction materials; other times to move dirt or clean up around the SS barracks; wherever needed — as volunteers — just do the whole job and do it on the double. Then we carry firewood or haul coal again, and on a day when there are no jobs, we ask, also "as volunteers," to have sport!

We're first-class "volunteers." We start the day an hour earlier than others, and we work on the double, for "recreation," right down to a death sweat...

The days grow colder and colder. Because we're not workers, they've taken away not just our uniforms, leaving only those that were in tatters, but also hats and socks. We feel the cold especially during morning roll calls, which are conducted while it's still dark. The biting cold penetrates to the bone.

"We're not going to survive the winter," someone predicts.

"So you've got something to worry about! Live for the moment."

"Sufficient unto the day is the evil thereof," someone else retorts, citing Holy Scriptures.

People are extremely irritated, upset, ready to quarrel and pick a fight. The "other one," the base one, the animal-like one that lives in each person, more and more often is gaining a voice.

"A psychologist could do an interesting study," Zdzich reveals his thoughts out loud. "How altogether differently phenomena are assessed in theory, on the basis of time-honored principles of unshakable doctrine, with reference to the greatness of eternal philosophical thought, but how differently the whole thing comes out in practice."

"Well, you see, my friend, the setting in which we live today, it's something no one anticipated, no one guessed, no one."

"Right. *Such* a setting for human existence hasn't been seen by anyone in history up to now. Psychologists could declare many time-honored principles bankrupt."

"Only psychologists? And not moralists?"

"Well, yes."

The end of October has arrived. Days are getting increasingly short, increasingly cold, and tear-stained with the rains. We're freezing. During summer the sweltering heat finishes us off; now the cold torments us.

They have been taking us as "volunteers" to carry sod from a meadow located several kilometers from the camp. The rain doesn't let up. So far, we haven't been given anything warmer to cover our hide, nor any socks or hats. Each of us has to carry two sheets of sod that measure about 50 by 50 centimeters. We carry them on our heads. The good side is that this covers us from the rain, but the bad is that mud streaming from the sod trickles over our faces, runs down our backs, gets into our eyes, our ears, our mouths.

"I'm grinding my teeth from this dirt like one of the damned," says Zdzich.

"Let's go! Faster!" urges the foreman.

Our feet, scraped by the wooden clogs, burn and ache.

"Meditate that you're following Jesus on the Way of the Cross. You'll find it easier to endure," encourages Józek.

That dear Józek. Quiet, modest, never complaining, always trying to show a cheerful face. We look at him as though we were looking upon a condemned man for whom we know it won't be long now... Poor fellow, he's walking with his last remaining strength!

"Józek, do you always..."

"I'm trying, I'm trying," he interrupts, as though fearing the rest of the sentence. "This gives me strength and also a lot of quiet happiness, a lot."

"This lad has understood the Gospel," Zdzich judges.

I've been watching for some time how Zdzich tries to help Józek.

"Zdzich!"

A pair of gray vulture's eyes look at me. The bushy eyebrows make a menacing impression.

"What?"

"You know, when I see you trying to help dear Józek and you're barely dragging yourself..."

"You're a fool!" he fires back emphatically.

I understand. The more moved he is, the more he pretends to be harsh.

The SS men have been so furious lately that they give the impression of lunatics. Harassment is increasing. Schubert visits us often now. After we've spent a whole day in untold drudgery, he continues to assign us hours of murderous sport. But it's still worse in the Jews' barracks: screams of terror, moans, stifled cries for help, pleas for mercy! Truly Dantesque scenes must be unfolding there...

"You rotten Jews!" Schubert screams one day. "It's your fault that damned England..." He didn't finish. He realized he had already said too much.

Only after a few days do we learn from news going around in a whisper that the Germans lost the air offensive, that Hitler fell into a real rage, that...

Well, then, it's quite understandable why his servants are raging.

During the first days of November they executed Fr. Figat from our group (along with fifty men from Warsaw). The unfortunate ones stood all day in front of the gate to the commandant's building, their foreheads painted with tar; then during evening roll call shots came from the infamous "Valley of Jehoshaphat." Together with the coming of November, under the influence of the cold, our lack of strength, and these bloody new incidents, an ever deeper despair seeps into our hearts, an ever greater apathy comes over us. The faint glimmer of hope, which had smoldered somewhere at the end of a dark tunnel, now barely flickers. At night more and more prisoners go onto the wires...

To sleep! To sleep! Sleeping is the only escape from horrible "today." Fall asleep and perhaps merciful God will grant that... that there will no longer be a tomorrow full of this same suffering.

What? Is it shameful that we're experiencing a terrible night of the soul? Didn't the saints experience it?

And it was our Lord leading us through the "sea of night." Will we get to see the saving shore, as did the chosen people crossing the Red Sea?

23

Roll Call

Heavy rain clouds hang low over the camp. A cold wind is blowing from the pine forest.

"Will it blow away, or will it start pouring?"

"Let's hope we don't get soaked during roll call."

"Let's hope so!" And we shrink at the very thought of it. We're in a tight column, passing through the camp gates.

"Unit of shavelings from 'volunteer' work," our foreman reports to the SS duty officer.

The assembly square. In front of us dozens of units are already forming; behind us others are returning, like us, from work outside the camp.

We're hungry and frozen to the bone.

"Look at you, devils!" we're greeted by Karl, our block leader, who's already waiting on the square with the rest of our colleagues.

Indeed, we look like a pack of the damned. After a whole day of carrying sod on our heads, so much black mud has dripped over our faces and pants that we resemble Negroes.

"Line up! Line up! Left flank forward!" Karl, who's calling us to order, uses kicking as an aid, like the other block leaders.

Finally the ranks are straight. We wait, shivering from cold. We'll really look great if it starts raining soon... A sudden movement at the gates. SS man Nowacki, the reports director, walks into the square surrounded by a retinue.

"Entire camp — atteeention!"

Over 16,000 prisoners stand motionless. SS men run along unit lines, counting. One step behind them are the block leaders, their hats at the side of their pants.

An icy wind whips up from the forest; above us are layers of clouds. Our teeth chatter, shivers run through our bodies. Hungry stomachs cry out for a meal.

Why does roll call last so long today? It's true that roll calls in Sachsenhausen always last long, but today something is hanging in the air. Worried, we crane our necks. Jasio, who's a head taller than I am, is standing right behind me.

"Jasio, what do you see there?"

Silence.

"Jasio! Do you see anything?

"Wait, wai ... Aha! The leader of Block 72 is walking over. He's stopping in front of the reports director ... Nowacki's furious ... SS men are surrounding the block guy ... It seems that..."

"Shut your mouth, you beanpole!" Karl's boots remind us that our "master" is watching.

After a while they summon all the block leaders. The hall leaders take charge of the units. We wait, but in each head there is the same terrifying thought: probably one of the prisoners has run away! God! ... And this freezing wind that's getting stronger, and these threatening black clouds! Could it be...

The block leaders are running back to their units. Karl stops in front of us. Rage burns in the small piercing eyes of this recidivist murderer when he calls to us:

"One of the Poles has escaped! As punishment we're going to stand on the square until they find him dead or alive." We stand at attention. "No one dare move! If anyone even twitches, I'll have him..." Saliva fills his throat, his face turns blue, and he looks like he's choking.

The iron gate closes with a hollow clang behind the last SS man leaving the square. Silence ... Sixteen thousand prisoners, standing at attention, have frozen in fear!

"What a swine! What a filthy Polish swine!" Karl mutters through clenched teeth. A sleepless night awaits him, too, as it does all the camp potentates. Except that they're dressed warmly, they're well-fed and even fat. What does it matter to them?

A flurry of hushed comments goes through the ranks.

"Where is this fellow's conscience?" whispers someone nearby. "He knows the whole camp has to suffer because of him; dozens will die this night because..."

"It's good that he escaped," someone else interrupts sharply.

"Be quiet. You know yourself it's a crime. There's no moral principle defending..."

"Shut your traps, or I'll shut them for you!" Karl is furious.

In the illuminated windows of the commandant's building you can see figures of the SS men. One of them is looking at the standing units. Karl notices this.

"Stand at attention so we don't get an even worse punishment," he warns. In the voice of the murderer there's now almost a note of kindness. But how can you stand here at attention, God knows how long, in the piercing cold wind, under a heavy cover of clouds, from which streams of rain can pour down at any moment?

The minute hand on the huge face of the tower clock nears seven. So we've already been standing here an hour. In twelve hours it will be seven in the morning. In twelve hours! Will they catch him by then? Will they cart him back shot dead or lead him back alive?

"It would be better if they shot him."

"Why?"

"That would spare him the torment of the underground cell. He'll die anyway."

"You're a pagan. You don't take into consideration that as he suffers, he'll have time to settle his relationship with God."

"Don't annoy me."

"I'm annoying you with that?"

It's starting to rain. It gets darker and increasingly colder. A freezing rain stings our shaved heads, the emaciated scruff of our necks, our bent backs covered only with thin denim.

"These pajamas aren't protecting us at all," someone says mockingly.

Silence is the only answer. What good is it talking to someone like that? He's only waiting to pick a quarrel.

Water streams over our bodies. It chills. The darkness is so deep and the storm-driven sheets of rain obscure our view so much that the commandant's building disappears before our eyes. Slowly we move closer and closer to each other.

"Put your caps on your heads," mutters Karl.

Astonishment. This murderer does have a heart after all. Emboldened by this concession, we huddle into a tight group. I feel Jasio's warm body against my back. It occurs to me that he's completely without cover himself, that the icy wind with its pelting rain still strikes his back.

"Later we'll change places, Jasio."

"Okay."

The clock's illuminated face on the tower is barely visible through the downpour. It's almost eight o'clock. Only eight? This last hour has seemed a century. How many more like it will there be?

"If they keep us in this freezing rain and wind until morning, half of us will die."

"Well, yes. It will be the end at last. Enough of this suffering."

Enough of this suffering? The will defends itself desperately when faced with the question: Why are things this way? The frightening, painful awareness and desperate certainty of the answer are a torture! All this because ... because we couldn't put into practice the greatest of His commandments, the commandment of love. It's because we felt satisfied by *words* pronounced with preacher's bombast, but we didn't manage to go into the trenches of the fight begun for justice, for mercy, for the practice of love. The Mother of God wept in 1846 at La Salette when she appeared to the orphans Maximin and Mélanie, children whose "house" was a barn and who, at the age of almost fifteen, didn't know their prayers, didn't know Jesus, had not been to the Table of Love! She wept foretelling upcoming punishments. And the punishments came and moved like a flame across all Europe. And in the Polish land, prayers of supplication arose in "the dust of fraternal blood," "with the smoke of fires..." Why didn't we draw any conclusions from this painful lesson? Why didn't the world draw any conclusions? ... At that time, blood-smeared Szela* walked with a band of poor and deluded peasants, while today "they" are walking! The scourges of God. The scourges of God are flogging the world! They're flogging us especially, God's students, who had the sacred responsibility of being the first to challenge the obsolete and materialistic world in the name of the One who came to light a fire on this earth!

But why do you flog us right at this moment, oh Lord, when our tormented souls and crucified, emaciated bodies stand at the edge of despair? Why now?

The tunnel filled with night of the soul is as dark as the November night surrounding us. The hand of the clock is probably not moving at all...

Confusion in my head, confusion in my soul, confusion in my weary heart. Jesus! Have mercy!

Why are we so nearsighted? Why do we climb again and again onto altars of self-pity instead of falling at their base with a terrified and humble confiteor?! Why do we try to call something *martyrdom* when it is God's punishment?

"Could you take my place for a while?" Jasio's voice comes to me through the chattering of his teeth.

We change places. Jasio squeezes himself deep into the ranks. I stand at the edge of the unit. The rain whips straight against my back. Shivers begin to shake my thoroughly frozen body.

Oh, Jesus! May this shred of weary life be a drop in the chalice of suffering that was offered You by generations of our forebears. May ... Something in my heart hisses that this is just a delusion, that all is in vain, that God will not hear my prayers anyway, that... And suddenly a horrible wound tears my heart: there is no God!

"Why are you moving around like that?" Jasio's question reaches me.

---

*Translator's note: In 1846, Jakub Szela led a peasant rebellion in Galicia.

23. Roll Call

"I'll turn round and put my back against yours. Okay?"

The torrential rain is whipping me straight in the face. In front of me and inside me is the gloom of unleashed darkness. "There is no God!" something screams within me. My exhausted will defends itself with what strength remains.

"Saint Thérèse!" whisper trembling lips. "Oh, little saint! Save me!"

"Jasio, what's the time?"

"It's almost nine."

"Only nine? God! How these minutes drag."

The rain pours down nonstop. We're already standing up to our ankles in water. The muffled whistle of a locomotive can be heard in the distance. So the world hasn't ended? And there, beyond the walls, people are living?

What are the people closest to me doing this night? My father, mother, brothers? In July we had an opportunity to send our first letter. No matter that it "could include" just a few words. What's important is that this was the first sign of life after so many months of uncertainty.

I'm still standing propped against Jasio's back. We warm each other like animals. Karl is moving around the group. He doesn't object to our being huddled in a mass. Once again I find that there's a human being in him after all.

Trembling lips whisper prayers. Rosary after Rosary. Minutes go by slowly. Hundreds of minutes, each of them like an eternity. After an hour, Jasio and I trade places again. Squeezed into the group, I feel warmth surrounding me.

"Jasio! Better to press your back against mine. You won't feel the cold as much."

And again one Rosary after another... "You're prattling without thinking, like a Chinese prayer-mill," cackles someone inside me. "If the Mother of God..." Dismay: am I already in such a bad way?

Out of the darkness, in the direction of the nearest unit, comes a moan and the sound of muffled beating.

"You dog!" a block leader is furious. "I'll let you sit down!" The dull sound of kicking, the victim's cry.

Many of us, too, are already sitting on the drenched ground. Our numb legs cannot hold out. And water in the square keeps growing because the rain pours and pours...

It's almost twelve. The clock's hand is just indicating midnight when — as though by the wave of a magic wand — the huge square is flooded in light as bright as day! Spotlights from all the towers turn on simultaneously. Packed into tight groups, units are moving around in confusion. Ranks are being formed in panic. Too late: through the open gates marches the camp commandant himself.

"For not following orders, the entire camp will crouch!"

"Crouch! Crouch!" the block leaders' commands roll like an echo.

A flock of crows, awakened by the lights and the yelling, takes off, cawing as they circle over the pines. An apocalyptic night.

We crouch, touching water that reaches above our ankles. The rain again whips our uncovered heads. The huge square has a nightmarish look: filled with streams of light, with thousands of people crouching, arms raised high above their heads.

Only now can you see how many are lying unconscious on the ground.

"Lucky ones!" whispers someone nearby.

The commandant disappears with his SS retinue inside the command building, but the spotlights continue to blind us. This is how it stays until morning...

An hour later, the entire camp is sitting on the ground, paying no attention to the water splashing all around. It doesn't matter. Let them punish us! Let them shoot! Let them kill! The sooner the better! Make it quick! Now and then someone falls over as he loses consciousness.

"It would be better if they shot us dead!" we hear another whisper.

"Olek! Good Lord!" someone nearby admonishes. "Olek! Hang on there. Just a while longer!"

"No, I'm just too tired..."

"For our offenses and those of our fathers..."

"Hours of suffering in the Roman arenas didn't last this long..."

Toward morning, the wind dies down a bit, but it's still raining. My body no longer feels the cold. It has grown numb, deadened... It's even surprising that my spirit still lingers in it. Hundreds of bodies lie on the ground. A new day is dawning beyond the forest. The gate to the commandant's building is still closed. In the faint light of dawn, the camp looks like a horrible battlefield. It's a terrible scene that's hard to describe. At the entrance to the barracks stand kettles with yesterday's untouched supper (while our insides are being torn by beastly hunger). The figures of the sitting prisoners, soaked to the skin, appear somehow small, shriveled, dwarfed; there's dullness and apathy in their sullen faces, dementia cowers in their sunken eyes.

A drizzly day is beginning, without any hope of sunshine. If only the sun would shine just for a few minutes, for a moment, to warm our chilled bodies and throw a ray of light into our eyes...

And once again we wait minutes, quarter-hours, hours... It's quiet in the commandant's building as if everything had died out.

If they would just let us go to work! Even if we're famished, by moving around we at least would warm up a bit.

They won't let us. The law of Nazi concentration camps is terrible, but in matters dealing with an escape, it's simply monstrous. The entire camp must stay on the assembly square until they catch the escapee! In other camps they put ten innocent prisoners to death.

"Entire camp — Atteeention!"

We jump up! Oh, what pain it is to straighten your knees!

"Straighten ranks! Straighten ranks!" Even the block leaders' commands are less vehement.

We stand again in tight units, with the exception of the several hundred who lie on the ground in puddles of water. They'll never stand up again. They no longer care at all about commands.

In the windows of the commandant's building appear the faces of SS men. Smiling faces.

What do such non-humans in high-ranking officers' uniforms think as they look at these tormented thousands of human wretches, who resemble trampled earth? What thoughts occur to them? Do "such people" think at all?

What do the thousands of German prisoners think, those who are tortured with us by their own brothers? Is there hate or forgiveness in their hearts?

It's getting lighter, it's almost day... The gate to the commandant's building is still closed... And it's drizzling. Bodies consumed by fever shiver uncontrollably.

Merciful Jesus! How much longer will this torment last?

On such a gray dawn on Good Friday, after hours of suffering in the Garden of Olives, after hours at night spent in the hands of drunken executioners, the Lord walked to the tribunal at the palace of governor Pilate...

Not until about eleven in the morning do we hear the drone of automobile engines behind the commandant's building. There's activity at the gate. Running around. Some yelling, laughter...

After minutes of tense waiting, the iron gate opens. You can see groups of SS men, and a moment later the unfortunate escapee enters through the gate into the square. (As we learn later, he was a student from the Warsaw Polytechnic.) Small, bent over, he's surrounded by a happy band of SS men.

May God not hold it against him! Let the hundreds who, because of him, passed to the other world in painful death that terrible night not accuse him before the throne of God.

Shortly after twelve noon, nearly twenty hours later, we finally leave the assembly square, thanking God we didn't stand there for several days. An hour later, soaked to the skin, chilled, and staggering on our feet, we go "as volunteers" to carry sod.

"On the double, march! March, you damned dogs! You wasted so many valuable hours, you've got to make them up now!"

So we make them up until late evening, trembling at the thought that some madman could again be tempted by freedom and, on his account, we could again spend a night in the square.

24

The Last Days

November 1940 is nearing an end. From the Eastern Front comes news that is almost incredible. Italy has occupied Greece. Regarding Poland, we only know that terror is increasing there. Our days in camp are indeed shorter now, but at the same time they're colder. We work outside the walls less frequently, and even tasks inside the camp have decreased. We spend more time inside our blocks. Based on our experience of the past months, we sit quietly, afraid of arousing the block leader's anger lest he dash us off for hours of sport in the rain and bad weather. We're finally given some socks and warmer shirts. We freeze less during the long roll calls.

In the first days of December someone brings news that they've decided to move us to another place, where — through the efforts of the Holy See — they're supposed to integrate all Catholic priests. "Rumor" has it that we'll have better conditions there.

"Better conditions?"

Such announcements arouse only fear in us now since they usually prove to be smoke screens veiling a painful and completely opposite reality.

And yet that day came. On 12 December they herd all priests into the assembly square; they give each of us not new but acceptable wooden shoes and a piece of hard bread, announcing that in a while we'll leave for the railroad station. A transport.

It's cold. The snow crunches under our wooden clogs. About noon we leave the assembly square, walking through the famous gate onto the snow-covered road. After an hour of marching we reach the railroad station, or rather the sidetrack adjacent to it. They load us — good heavens! — into coach cars that are warmly heated. The SS men don't kick us or beat us.

Could they really be moving us to better conditions?

Two hours later the train starts. We're on our way. Not one of us knows where. (A prisoner of Nazi concentration camps never knew the direction of his travel or his new destination. That was one of the psychological torments they devised.) The train doesn't stop at any of the stations we pass. It seems to us we're traveling toward the south of Germany.

"But maybe, maybe..." and the voice of the speaker suddenly sticks in his throat.

"Maybe what?"

"Maybe they're ... after so many efforts by the Holy See ... Maybe they're moving us to Rome, under care of the Vatican?"

What a surprise! Contrary to what the speaker had feared, no one laughs, no one scoffs at this suggestion.

"You know, perhaps your hunch is right. After the chapel, after those sad privileges, after the news alluding to some special conditions, it's possible, it's possible..."

An early December evening sets in. We're tired. Our eyelids are heavy. We're overcome by sleep.

24. The Last Days

(We didn't know then that on this very day Lucy of Fatima sent Pope Pius XII, for the second time, a letter reminding him about requests of the Mother of God during her appearances, and insisting on his offering the world to her Immaculate Heart.)[1]

During a dark December night in 1940, a frost-covered train races across the territory of Germany, carrying into the unknown several hundred Polish priests, survivors of Stutthof, Grenzdorf, and Sachsenhausen. We know that only we are unaware of our destination and direction. This new road is known to God and has been ordained for us by Him.

25

A Holy Shipment

The puffing train, covered with frost, crawls like a silver caterpillar into some little station.

"Ready to get off!" the SS men order.

We don't have any bundles, and the bread given us for the trip was eaten a long time ago. We just button our shirts, take our caps and — we're ready. Our hearts are pounding, which is natural. Where have they taken us? ... The train slows down even more.

"What station is this?"

A while ago those near the windows blew "holes" with their warm breath in the thick layer of frost covering the windowpane. They're observing...

"It's some little station. There's no sign," they tell us.

The train stops.

"Get off!" Although the orders come down as usual in military fashion, no one pushes, no one kicks or beats us. This surprises us and, at the same time, keeps alive yesterday's hopes that maybe, after all, they're taking us to better conditions.

As we get off, we're struck by the terrible cold. It must be well below zero. On the opposite platform stands an SS unit with weapons ready to fire. Schubert, who's in charge of the transport, goes up to an SS officer standing at the head of the unit. Heels click, right hands extend smartly.

"Heil Hitler!" they greet each other with a handshake.

"So this is the 'holy shipment' we were told about!" says the officer receiving the transport.

"Yes, sir," confirms Schubert with a smile. "This is the 'holy shipment.'"

"Attention!"

We stand erect in ranks. The officer receiving us is conducting a review. A non-commissioned officer, running after him, is counting.

"It tallies."

On the opposite platform sits a train full of passengers. Almost all of them are dressed in sports clothes and have skis. Therefore, we must be somewhere in a piedmont area. But where? And those in the train look at us as though — it seems to me — they're sad, lost in thought, almost expressing kindness. There's no laughing, no grimacing, no mean faces. We're struck by this and at the same time captivated. We're struck because we're used to other expressions; we're captivated because this seems to confirm that they've brought us to a different and better environment. In addition, there's the derisive, but also somewhat "different" remark: "a holy shipment!"

The officer and Schubert are whispering something on the side. The SS men are stamping, warming their cold feet. It's obvious that, were it not for the rifles, they would gladly beat their hands together for warmth. We're freezing. Suddenly, a nervous whisper runs through the ranks:

"Look! Look! Over there, under the roof of the station building."

I look, and my heart sinks. On a white board written in black letters is the word: Dachau!

"Dachau? Jesus!"

At once, all our hopes fade. Blood rushes to my head!

"Dachau? The infamous convict prison, the mother of concentration camps? They've brought us here? Is this why they're so eagerly looking forward to a 'holy shipment'"?

But the officer is already extending his hand to Schubert to say good-bye, and then another click of the heels:

"Heil Hitler!"

Smiling, Schubert returns to his unit. The officer gives orders to the SS men.

They surround us. Rifles ready to fire are lowered. Only a few faces look out now from windows of the other train. The rest are withdrawing by way of demonstration into the car's interior. This gesture is significant and eloquent. It pleases us.

"Left face! In step, forward march!"

We set off. Our wooden shoes clatter.

"Left, two, three, four. Your left! Your left!"

"Sing!" the command suddenly comes down. "*Heimat Lied.*"

"Left, your left, two, three, four!"

> "To my fatherland I return
> On a wonderful morning.

The railroad station in the town of Dachau.

> There, in a quiet valley is a cottage,
> And in it are those dear to me, among them my mother.
> O, Heimat Land, mein Heimat Land..."

flow the sentimental words of the soldier's song taught to us in Sachsenhausen. Did the SS man choose this particular song about one's homeland as harassment?

We march through empty streets of the little town of Dachau. Not a living soul! Could the residents have hidden on purpose? It's a possibility. After all, people in the railcars were looking at us with some empathy, and later, as we were leaving, almost all of them withdrew into the car's interior. An interesting phenomenon.

"This is Catholic Bavaria," Zdzich, who's walking next to me, explains during a break between stanzas.

"Catholic Bavaria, but still it was right here that Hitler..."

"Mussolini initiated his gangster movement not in Catholic Bavaria, but at the very heart of Catholicism, in Rome, beneath windows of the Holy See."

We enter a section of widely scattered houses on the outskirts of town. A cold wind is blowing from snow-covered fields.

"Attention! On the double, march!"

We start off. The road is covered with snow. The sticky snow adheres to our clogs, forming a build-up under them of several centimeters. How can you possibly run? The dance begins! There are no witnesses here! Here only God himself can see! Therefore: "On the double! On the double! You damned Roman dogs! You wanted to come to Dachau? You'll have your fill of it. On the double!

Feeling cold, the young SS men "warm up" in their own way: kicking, tripping, striking with clubs.

"On the double!"

There's only one remedy, to take off these shoes. A moment later we're running in our socks.

"On the double!"

There are no longer older priests among us. They "dropped out" in Sachsenhausen. We're all young, along with a few who are middle-aged. And yet — these several kilometers of running exhaust us terribly. And they? Like the possessed! They're driving, beating, grinding us down.

"Damned 'holy shipment'! On the double, you dogs!"

We enter the street of SS residences. Smiling women's faces are looking out the windows. These people are different from those on the train or residents in the town of Dachau. The SS men show off even more "wholeheartedly" in front of their ladies...

We run across the bridge over the Amper River. We enter Eikeplatz and there in front of us is an open gate leading to an enormous yard of SS barracks. (Located next to the Dachau camp was the biggest center for SS training in all of Germany.)

We run through some small streets and squares, pass huge buildings and warehouses, and finally stop at another gate, this one forged of iron. On it we see (also forged in iron) the inscription: "*Arbeit macht frei*" (Work makes you free).

"Holy shipment of shavelings from Sachsenhausen!" our unit leader reports to the SS duty officer.

Holy shipment?

So these are the "better conditions" we had anticipated: Dachau!

The camp itself — the commandant's building, farm buildings, barracks, guard towers, all this, in comparison to the camp in Sachsenhausen—gives the impression that it's old, neglected, and rather dirty.

Finally, after submitting reports in the commandant's building, they lead us inside the camp. Several hours are spent in changing uniforms, registration, obtaining new numbers, and other initial formalities. We know all of this. We're already "schooled" in adjusting to any "circumstance." We don't get a thrashing like the usual new arrivals. We're struck by the fact that the camp "leaders" carrying out these formalities don't hit, don't kick, and are somehow more humane...

"Look," whispers Zdzich. "There's not one Green [felon] among them."

"That's because Dachau is a political camp. Whereas Sachsenhausen has the reputation of being a Green camp," explains someone who's already knowledgeable. "No Green here has any say. Only 'Reds' [political prisoners] are in charge."

Twelve noon approaches. Suddenly, a loud whistle pierces the air. Files of "kettle bearers" come out of the barracks and walk toward the kitchen.

"They're going to get dinner."

"It's strange they're walking at a normal pace. In general, take a look, no one runs here!"

"You're right. It is odd." (In Sachsenhausen, we were accustomed to the fact that if a prisoner left his barracks, for whatever reason, he always had to run, and if that rule was violated, the punishment was severe.)

Here, in Dachau, no one runs! No one is in a hurry! Prisoners walk "like human beings!" Dachau or not, maybe it really will be better for us here? Perhaps we really will have "better conditions"?

It's Saturday, 14 December 1940. Changed into striped Dachau uniforms, with new numbers, we walk to our assigned block.

We're "citizens" of Dachau.

On that second Saturday of December of 1940, Pope Pius XII read the second letter from Lucy of Fatima begging him to consecrate the world to the Immaculate Heart of the Blessed Mother...

26

The Sanitarium in Dachau

The little Bavarian town of Dachau, located about 15 kilometers northwest of Munich, lies in an unhealthy malarial area of the so-called "Dachau Swamp," which until recently was regarded as a place for mining peat. Wonderful sunsets, caused by special atmospheric conditions here, are a town attraction known in the art world; therefore, students of the Munich Academy of Art were, perhaps, the only "lovers" of this area. (Dachau was also known to our Polish painters studying in Munich. Among others, the painter Chmielowski, who later founded the Albertine monastic order, sat at his easel here.)

After Hitler came to power, the Nazis established a concentration camp on these very swamps as early as 1933. In the next few years, it swallowed up thousands of ideological enemies of Nazism and, especially, following the famous burning of the Reichstag, thousands of German communists. The prisoners were tortured by murderous work draining the swamps and peatbogs, and this was carried out in a most sophisticated and cruel manner. Such monstrous things were done here that they even aroused disgust and provoked armed reactions by the more benign segment of the first "party" members. It was only when they, too, shared the fate of those they were defending that the Dachau camp could operate unhampered.

Some things were known about Dachau in Europe in the years prior to the war. Despite being a prototype of the torture chambers called concentration camps, it was regarded at that time as a model criminal-justice institution based on principles of behavioral training. It drew quite a few of those who were curious and who "studied these issues," (and let us state this clearly — the future commandants of similar death shops. Sadly, there was also no shortage of Poles taking part in that "training." Our deplorable Bereza Kartuska prison camp is nothing more than a bastard of the Dachau camp). How far the world allowed the wool to be pulled over its eyes is evidenced in articles from the European prewar press (including our *Catholic Guide* from 1938), which elaborated on the "wonderful training method" that Nazi Germany had introduced for its criminals, putting the "most modern pedagogical and psychological" findings into practice.

When we arrived at the Dachau camp on 14 December 1940, we found still living there a small group of German communists and also "Social Democrats" that had survived since 1933. Several months later, when we had been recognized as "senior prisoners," we could discreetly learn from them what it used to be like in "former" days! What was it like during those famous "Besuche" (visits, tours) of the camp by journalists and "interested personnages." The same hypocritical farce that was repeated in our time was already playing then; this topic will be treated again later on.

"Heinrich!" says Ernst Hecht, a native of the Rhine area, an extremely kind man of crystal-clear character, a Social Democrat (and, thus, an enemy hated by Nazism). "Look at the canal that flows along the camp wall and the deep moat surrounding the entire camp like some fortress from the Middle Ages. When we came here, none of this was here. We were the ones who built it all. Do you know how many thousands of prisoners died excavating these moats and this canal, setting up barbed wire fences, installing high-voltage electrical lines, building these walls and barracks, draining swamps and planting the grounds? Heinrich! There's not an inch of ground in this area as far as the eye can see that hasn't been soaked with human blood!"

"After they had murdered thousands of communists, our members, and other political enemies, tens of thousands of Jews started to pour in! Heinrich! Heinrich! Even today, when I recall the crimes committed here, the hair on my head stands up! This cannot be described in speech or writing. Don't forget, this was a time when war was still far off. SS men preparing for future "assignments" got their training here. For example, the great Commandant Piorkowsky [future commandant of Dachau], or Hoffman [future commandant of Auschwitz] entered the SS ranks as eighteen-year-old kids. And where did they demonstrate exceptional qualifications for those lofty and independent positions? Here, on us, Heinrich! By torturing thousands of their countrymen, they proved what they could do... One can never forget those days! Now, since the war has started and you began arriving, conditions have changed a hundred percent for the better. But then..."

Conditions have changed a hundred percent "for the better."

They certainly changed a lot from the moment the war started and with more frequent arrivals of foreigners. When we arrived at Dachau, we already found Austrians, Czechs and Slovaks here, in addition to several thousand Germans, that is, the more valuable but politically dangerous element from nations that fell before Poland.

The camp, which had been designed for 8,000 prisoners, already had tens of thousands in December 1940. It seemed crowded to us, and it really was crowded, although we would find out that it could hold up to 50,000 prisoners! But that was to occur only during the last years of the war, especially during the months of Nazi collapse when thousands of survivors taken from other camps were herded into Dachau in advance of the Allies.

When referring to Dachau, one has to distinguish between the town of that name and the huge SS training center with its barracks, warehouses, factories and other large SS plants in which they used cheap prison labor, drawing enormous profits from those factories and plants. The German people didn't have the slightest idea of the enormous incomes generated by these centers, which at the same time served for "grinding down" thousands of prisoner-slaves who worked in them.

Only in third place — when we talk about Dachau — is the concentration camp itself.

The area it encompasses is not large: a rectangle of land,

Road sign, indicating the road to Camp Dachau.

600 meters in length and maybe 300 meters in width, surrounded by a high wall, along the top of which runs a line of wires. In front of the wall, from the interior side, there's a wide path for SS men who serve as guards at the towers, and inside the path is a tall fence with high-voltage electrical wires. All along this fence is a band of barbed wire several meters wide. A final security measure is a deep moat of concrete. These are the obstacles a prisoner would have to overcome if he were tempted to escape. Faced with such great security, escape from Dachau was completely out of the question. Even here, however, there was no shortage of those "going onto the wires out of despair," although they were fewer than in Sachsenhausen.

A public road runs along the northern wall. Along the southern wall is a canal, and along the canal, lined with poplar trees and leading to the crematorium, is the road the prisoners call "Death Road." At the west end of the camp quadrangle is located the so-called "garden," and at the east end is the assembly square, enclosed by a complex of farm buildings and a kitchen. Behind them is an "execution yard" with the so-called "honor bunker" where prominent personnages are imprisoned. It is also the place where they carry out executions and the most horrendous crimes, witnessed only by the executioners and God. The narrow "execution yard," surrounded on all sides by the high walls of buildings and the "honor bunker," is paved with stone pavers in which special openings can be found for erecting scaffolds.

The housing area of the camp is located, therefore, in the center, between the gardening area and the assembly square. A wide camp street runs down the middle with poplars planted along each side, and from it, to the north and south, run small side streets lined with prisoners' barracks, which, as in all other camps, are called blocks.

The camp has 34 blocks. The first two, on the left side of the camp street, house the camp administration offices, a canteen, a library, and other useful "institutions" of camp life. The first two blocks on the right side of the street are the camp hospital, known in prison jargon as the "sick room." Blocks 15 and 17, separated from the camp street by a high barbed-wire fence, house the "penal company." The black boxes (camp coffins) standing at the entrance to the enclosure speak all too eloquently of the "spirit" that reigns in these "death cells."

For purposes of clarification, we should explain that the blocks on the left side of the street have even numbers, from 2 to 30, while those on the right side have odd numbers. The right side of the camp, which includes the above-mentioned "sick room" as well as the penal company, was regarded during the years we spent in Dachau as a kind of quarantine. Toward the end of the camp's existence, the right side was strictly isolated from the rest of the camp since all kinds of "stations" for experiments carried out on prisoners were located there, as well as places for the execution of Jews, then later Russian officers, and finally people from the Warsaw uprising.

The blocks on the left side of the street, with even numbers, house working prisoners. To be precise, it should be mentioned that Blocks 2, 4, and 6 are occupied only by German prisoners, almost exclusively the camp "aristocracy:" office and administrative workers, work foremen, the so-called "capos." Among them are many Austrians, mostly people from the world of politics. It is understandable that these three blocks are the best equipped, kept the cleanest, and contain no more than the planned number of residents. (For example, in the last year of the camp's existence, when two thousand priests were squeezed into our clerical block, the number of residents in the above-mentioned blocks never exceeded two hundred people). That's why whenever a commission, a delegation, or investigators of "crime scenes" who need to submit a report before "some international tribunal" appear at the camp, the SS men always lead them right to those three blocks. After seeing that the housing is, in fact, set up in exemplary fashion, and without suspecting that the worst misery is cooped up in blocks further along, the visitors drive off with the best possible impression. (A beloved author gushed about it even in the columns of our weekly *Catholic Guide* from Poznań in 1938).

Blocks 8, 10, and 12 house an international "brotherhood": Czechs, Slovaks, and others.

Blocks 14, 16, and 18 are occupied by Poles, including a large number of high-school youth, mostly from Łódź.

In Block 22 live the so-called "asocial" prisoners, condemned to the camp for shirking work. They are mostly Gypsies, itinerant musicians, circus performers, gigolos, and others. In short, all those whom Nazism has labeled as "social pests." In contrast to political prisoners, they wear black triangles on their shirts, which is why they're called "Blacks" in prison jargon.

Block 24 was for the Greens, that is, for professional criminals. Whereas in Sachsenhausen they enjoyed great superiority, controlled the entire camp through a layer of "camp aristocracy" derived from their number, and hated political prisoners, who were a minority, in Dachau it's just the opposite. In this markedly political camp, the Greens are a tiny minority and (in revenge) are treated with hatred by the Reds, that is, the political prisoners.

In Block 26 is located a storehouse of straw mattresses and other furnishings.

View of part of the Dachau camp from the guardhouse roof. The two barracks in the distant corner of barracks (marked "+") are barracks 28 and 30, where Polish priests were housed. The arrow above the trees to the left (a) points to the crematorium, which is surrounded by spruce trees On the left below poplar trees runs the canal (b). From the canal (looking left to right) are (c) the path for SS guards, (d) an electrified fence, (e) a barrier of coiled barbed wire, and (f) the moat. The arrow at the lower right points to (g) the assembly square.

Descending in this way down steps of the camp ladder, from blocks of the prominent through blocks for all kinds of undesirables, to Poles, then to asocials and Green criminals, we finally arrive at blocks 28 and 30, both occupied by priests.

We have one thing closer to us than to all the other residents, namely, the *crematorium*, which is located at an angle just across from us, to the south of both gables of our blocks, blowing right into the windows of our "apartments" and irritating our throats with the smell of burning flesh. It also constantly reminds us: *Memento, homo, quia pulvis es...*

Nevertheless — in spite of everything — the first hours of our stay in Dachau make a rather positive impression on us. While the camp does not have that exterior "elegance," cleanliness, order, and appearance of its cousin in Sachsenhausen, it has instead what could be described as a more "familial" environment. (If one can use this description at all when referring to a concentration camp.) The most important thing is that you don't have to be in constant fear of the SS men and Green block leaders. The Sachsenhausen camp in this respect was exactingly sadistic.

Moreover, even the living conditions in Dachau are more tolerable. The blocks are more appealing with huge window areas, the washrooms are more accessible, and the wooden bunk beds more comfortable. Whereas the camp in Sachsenhausen gave an almost charming impression on the outside and the barracks inside looked like dark and dirty hovels, the camp in Dachau is just the opposite. The outside is neglected, but the block barracks have interiors that are clean, light, and comfortable, with huge tile stoves, with painted and waxed floors that we're afraid to step on while wearing the socks we wore on our trip from the station.

In the same way, there's a pleasant surprise in the bunkroom. Everyone is assigned his "own" bunk, with his own blanket and underwear!?!

A *sanitarium*?

We're beginning to like it in this famous Dachau!

The block leader is a "Red," that is, a political. The leaders of the four halls are the same. True, they yell just as much as barracks personnel in Sachsenhausen, but they don't beat us as did the others, who would murder at any chance they got.

Besides, we're no longer camp novices, we know how to "behave," we have behind us over a year of camp and prison training, and this means a lot; indeed, it can often save your life! In time, every old prisoner acquires a sixth sense which a person living in freedom doesn't have, namely, an instinct for self-preservation! It consists of having the same carefully searching eyes in the back of your head as in the front, of hearing things that others might not hear, of sensing dangers before they occur, of knowing intuitively when and whom you "absolutely must" look in the eye and when and whom you "absolutely never should" under threat of drawing attention to yourself and all that goes with it: kicks, beatings, and worse punishments. Many newcomers unfortunately exposed themselves to the most terrible punishments and harassments, and even caused their own premature death, because they lacked this sixth sense!

Finding ourselves in "our" block, Number 28 (which was to shelter us for years), we settle in, alert to the instructions of our "master," the hall leader, a young communist.

It's three o'clock in the afternoon. A bright December sun sets slowly behind the reddish spruce trees that surround the crematorium. After arranging our bunks and assigned lockers, we sit quietly at the tables, grateful to the hall leader for leaving us in peace. We sit in silence, praying... The doors open slightly. Somebody's voice is whispering my last name.

"They're calling you," the whisper goes from table to table in my direction.

I move quietly along a small passage by the lockers, in order not to "attract the attention" of the hall leader. With foresight, I've tucked my shoes into my belt and hidden them under my shirt, because it's not good to lose your shoes, or any other part of your clothing, during the confusion of the first few days; it could cost you not only a few kicks, but also something more. The "sixth sense" is cautious!

At last I'm in the vestibule. Here you can put your shoes on. I'm curious who would be so eager to see me. I go out on the steps of the barracks. At the wall stand three "Mussulmans." (*Muselmann* was a camp term applied to the most haggard prisoners who were covered with ulcers, wrapped in rags, and emaciated like Bedouins.) They're dressed in old patched military coats, caps pulled down over their ears, their noses blue with cold sticking out from emaciated faces, hands tucked inside frayed sleeves, backs bent and heads tucked between their shoulders, the characteristic posture of a prisoner who is cold. The three Mussulmans are standing in front of the block looking at me in silence.

Still wondering who called me out, I glance down the small street from the steps, over the heads of the trio standing there, and seeing that it's empty, I take a more careful look at them. They bare their teeth at me, and a kind of a grimace appears on their sallow and terribly emaciated faces. Are these supposed to be smiles? Something strikes me in these faces, something which I cannot at the moment understand clearly. My memory feverishly searches to find a place for these faces. So many thousands of similar faces have passed before my eyes in the past year... Suddenly: Jesus! Is it possible?... Those huge blue eyes! The expression in them! ... Heniek?! Heniek Lisiecki?

"Henryk!"

"Heniek!"

"And this is Radoch Fibak, and Stefcio Smaruj."

"Oh my God! My God!" I feel that I'm hugging not "people" but skeletons dressed in patched coats. I can't hold back my tears. They well up in my eyes.

"Why are you blubbering?" Radoch has not lost any of his former beloved brusqueness, which usually masks emotion. "Why are you blubbering?"

"And why are you?"

"Me?" He acts surprised.

We go into the vestibule. With difficulty Heniek drags his foot, which is wrapped in dirty rags. Radoch and Stef enter holding on to the walls. I can't see the threshold through my tears. They streamed from my eyes the same way once when — as a young student — I saw a man being run over by a train. We stop in the cold vestibule. We aren't allowed to go inside.

"It's warmer here," says Stef.

"Warmer?" I'm surprised but, at the same time, I realize how terribly these skeletons, lacking any life-blood and body warmth, must be feeling the cold. Their narrative unfolds... They arrived as survivors from the quarry in Gusen.[1] They went through hell there! A few more days and they would have remained there like many, many others.

"Which of us, besides you..." I don't finish.

"Those who came back with us are the brothers Szczerkowski, Stefan Tomczak, Jasio Wolniak, Eda Stawecki, Leoś Stępniak, and Henio Sych..."

"Henio Sych is alive?"

"Oh, he's 'alive.' Like the rest of us. You can see for yourself. Ruins, not people."

I see! I see! I seeee! screams something inside of me. I don't have the courage, however, to admit it. So I ask: "Is there anyone else, acquaintances or colleagues?"

"Oh, there's also Maryś Piotr, Leoś Kijewski, Zygmunt Pituła, Stach Podemski, Zyga Ogrodowski and Gerard Mizgalski, there's Józek Metler..."

"And Sylwek Marciniak and Bernaś Woltman and Teoś Kubisz and both Majchrzycki priests and ... You know, my head's spinning. You forget who's still alive and who's dead."

"You were lucky to be spared from the camp in Gusen. It's a terrible slaughterhouse."

"It's true. I was lucky." I think back about Neufahrwasser, Stutthof, the quarries at Grenzdorf ... But is this really fitting right now? ... One doesn't put suffering up for auction! "Oh yes, it's true, I was lucky," I repeat, looking into faces that are emaciated to the utmost, covered with impetigo, dull, and sallow. Oh! Those bones sticking out below their skin! Is this then our beloved Radoch, always rather chubby? Is this our beloved Stefcio, whom I remember as a ball rolling down the seminary corridors? Is this Heniek, Heniek, friend and companion during six years of studies, with whom I shared a room for so many years and sat next to in the chapel, in auditoriums ... Terrible! What hunger, work, cold, disease, and lice can make of a human being. The little St. Thérèse admitted on her deathbed that her greatest suffering in the Carmel convent was from *cold*. "I'm dying of cold," whispered the little martyr.

And these three? ... And all of us?

In the evening, as I lie in my place on the bunk, I can't fall asleep for a long time. I keep seeing before my eyes the faces of Heniek, Radoch, Henio Sych, and all those, so close, so dear, and yet today ... so inhumanely changed. We didn't look any better ourselves in Stutthof, in Grenzdorf, in the quarantine at Sachsenhausen. These poor souls have no idea how many of us didn't survive or that those of us who arrived from Sachsenhausen are just a small part — the survivors — of the many hundreds of priests from other camps. I don't know why I'm overcome with shame. I can't erase their faces and eyes from my memory...

First night in Dachau. At the beginning, I constantly taste smoke in my throat from the crematorium. Then everything is erased from my memory. I only know that it's already a new day, that it's the third Sunday in Advent.

"Henio! The bell! It's time to go to the Cathedral. See what a nice day it is today. Groups of the faithful are filing across Chrobry Bridge. Henio! Hurry up!"

We're on our way. Our cassocks flutter against our feet. Heniek carries his beautiful surplice on his forearm. Let all Chwaliszewo see it, let all Śródka look at it! Only little Zosia can make such lace, and there's no other sister like her in all of Poznań!

"Hurry up! We'll be late for choir. Cardinal Hlond himself is celebrating today." Suddenly, I remember that the liturgy coordinator, Maryś Kowalewski, assigned me to assist! How could I have forgotten that! I'm terror-stricken! "Heniek! But I'm..."

Without waiting, I start to run. To the Cathedral! Suddenly ... What's the meaning of this? My legs refuse to move. It's as if they were made of wood. I look around at Heniek with despair. But he stands there, looks at me, and ... he laughs. Yes, laughs! But who can stand that laughter? He's wearing his beautiful surplice, his hands are hidden in it, and with a kind of terrible grimace he bares his teeth. God! And in his face ... it's the mask of a skeleton! Run! But my legs refuse. Scream for help! How can you scream when your voice sticks in your throat? You have to try again: Heniek! Heniek!

"Why are you screaming?" I hear a voice nearby. "You'll wake up the block leader. He's liable to run over here with a club."

Only after a while do I realize that it's the voice of Zdzich, who's lying on the next bunk, that it was only a dream, that I'm not in Poznań, but in Dachau. Good Lord! And still it's only the middle of the night... How high into the sky rises smoke from the crematorium!

Explanation of the Drawing

The drawing, or diagram, on page 156, representing the Dachau camp as it was in the year 1940,* is not intended to be a precise work of cartography. It is recreated as faithfully as possible, of course, but its basic purpose is *to illustrate* the setting in which will play out, on the following pages of this memoir, the nearly four-year history of a group of Polish priests, survivors of many other camps who were integrated into Dachau "to provide them with *better conditions*," which were being sought by the Holy See.

The approximate length of the entire camp was about 600 meters. Its width — about 300 meters. The length of each barracks (block) was 90 meters.

The black line on the diagram that encloses the camp is a high wall with barbed wire on top. As the diagram shows, the wall surrounds the camp on three sides. On the fourth side (at the left side of the diagram), instead of a wall, there was a rather deep canal with moving current...

The small squares, marked on the diagram with the letter "W," which break the line of the wall, are high guardhouse towers, manned day and night by SS men and equipped with powerful floodlights as well as heavy machine guns.

The wide white belt that runs alongside the wall — inside the camp — is the path of the SS guards.

The broken line (dots and dashes) on the diagram represents tall wire fencing charged with high-voltage electricity.

Running parallel to it and indicated on the diagram as an interlaced tangle of lines is a wide band of coiled barbed wire secured with iron bars set in concrete.

The last belt, a line marked with the letters "v," represents a concrete moat, 3 meters deep and 5 meters wide.

Let's again list the "security belts" surrounding the camp. This time we'll count in the other direction, from the center of the camp toward its outer edge; we'll count as though we were planning an escape from the camp.

The first obstacle we would have to overcome is the moat; the second is the wide band of coiled barbed wire that runs behind it; the third — the tall wire fencing on concrete posts, charged with high-voltage electricity.

After penetrating these three obstacles, the escapee would find himself on the "SS guard path," and only then could he attempt to climb over the high camp wall.

The priests' barracks lie at the very back of the block complex on the left and are marked with the numbers 30, 28, and 26. The last hall in Block 26 toward the main camp street (indicated on the diagram with a black arrow) was later turned into a chapel.

The white marks on the roofs of Barracks 5 and 7 show the location of research stations where experiments were conducted on prisoners.

The first two blocks on the right, marked on the diagram with the letters "RR," are the camp hospital. In the right wing of the first hospital block (marked on the diagram with an arrow) is the camp mortuary. That is where the body of Rev. Bishop Michał Kozal was laid along with others. Each day they transported bodies from there to the crematorium, passing through the assembly square to the camp gate (marked with a dotted line), from there along Death Road and then left to the crematorium. (See diagram). That was the final road of a dead prisoner. Hundreds of Polish priests "departed" along it! Death Road was

---

* *Tranlator's footnote:* The cross indicated on the Assembly Square was erected later, on May 2, 1945.

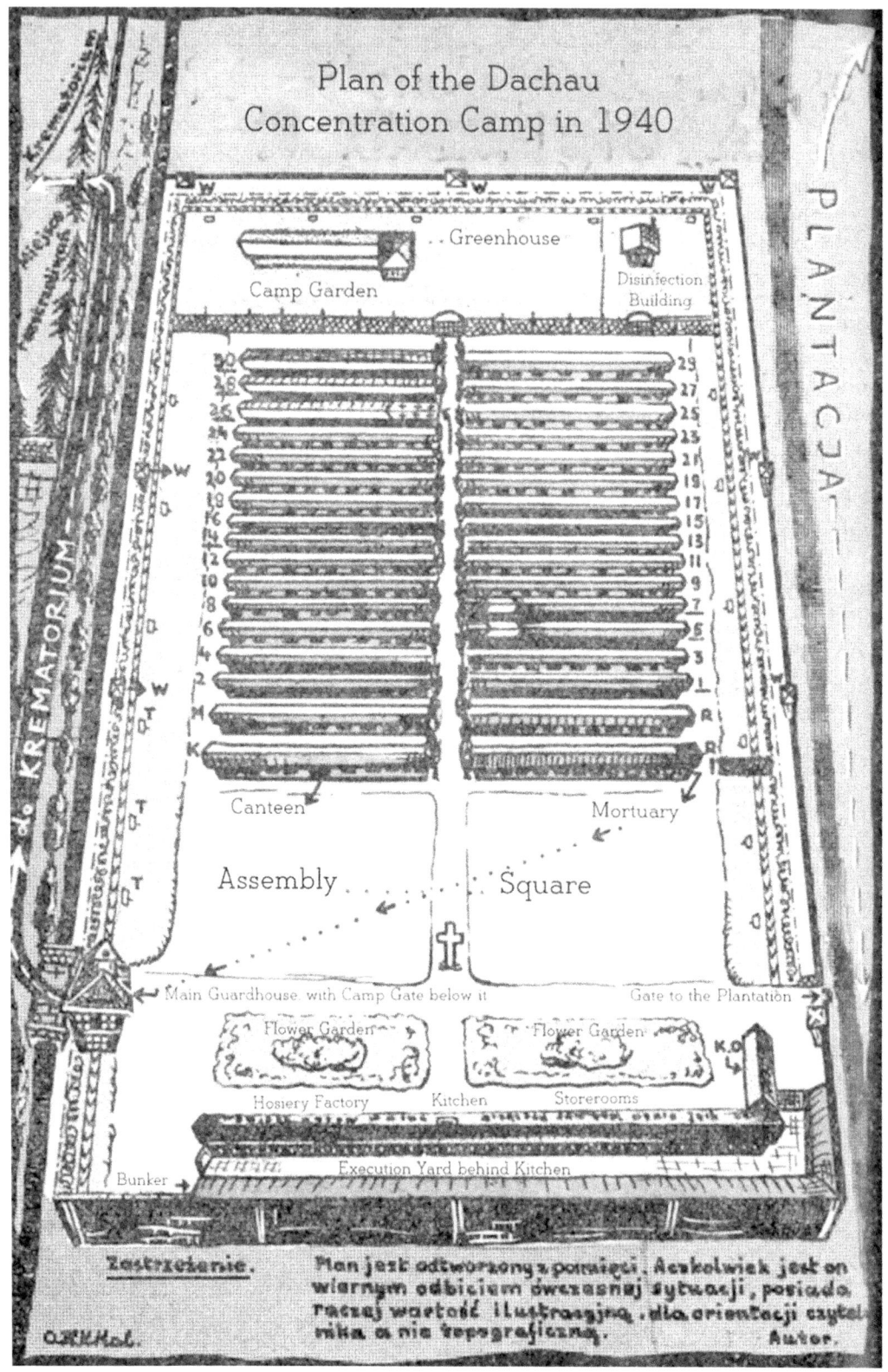

Plan of the Dachau Concentration Camp in 1940 (drawing by the author).

lined with tall, slender poplars. Since the camp was not closed off by a wall on that side, only by the above-mentioned "obstacles" and the canal, you could clearly see whether it was wagons with corpses or units of people sentenced to death that were being taken to the crematorium. (Especially unforgettable were scenes of poor Jews being herded there and, also, toward the end of the war, units of Russian officers.)

The camp gate was located below the main guardhouse. (See diagram.) Emerging from it, a retinue of SS men would stride onto the assembly square in order to take roll call. Individual units were positioned facing the kitchen. Over the gate, at the top of the guardhouse, was a tower with a huge clock. Visible on the roof of the kitchen was a distinctive sign, which is discussed in the text.

Behind the storerooms, kitchen, and hosiery factory, there was a narrow "Execution Yard." Inside the yard, backing against the outer wall, was a notorious bunker. It was there they kept the more prominent political prisoners, who were isolated from the rest of the camp.

To the right of the camp — along the wall — probably over an area of a thousand acres, extended the "Plantation." It was turned from swamp into dry land by German communists, Social Democrats, and Jews. Thousands of them died there! Polish priests, too, were dying there.

To the left of the camp, beyond the canal and Death Road, lay the enormous courtyards of SS barracks, offices, warehouses, and many industrial plants that were in SS hands; thousands of "professional" prisoners worked here (e.g., priest "carpenters" or "masons," and others).

The letters "K.O." indicate the storeroom where a prisoner would run for clothing.

The letter "T" marks where signs were placed along camp fences, cautioning that guards in the towers would open fire — without warning — at anyone who crosses that line!

27

Snow

Who among us doesn't like a winter sparkling with snow, especially when you can admire it from the window of a warm room? Who isn't drawn to winter scenery, a skating rink, skis, and even the heavy frost that traces flowers on the windows? And the crunching of the snow underfoot? All this remains with us as a charming memory from times when we lacked nothing, when we were well fed and warmly dressed.

You look at winter differently in a concentration camp. Although the winter of 1940–41 was not as harsh as the previous winter spent in Górna Grupa and Stutthof, still it was felt by us intensely in the hilly climate of Dachau, located practically at the foot of the Alps and in the very damp air of the Dachau swamps.

When we arrived in Dachau on 14 December from Sachsenhausen, we already found colleagues transported on 8 December from extermination camps in Gusen and Buchenwald, those who had arrived on 12 December from Auschwitz, and a handful of survivors from the Mauthausen death camp and other smaller camps. Our transport from Sachsenhausen was almost the last transport of priests coming at that time to Dachau.

We were surprised that all priests were so suddenly and unexpectedly pulled right off their jobs... Different people offered different explanations. (Not one of us knew then that consolidating all priests into one camp was the result of long and arduous negotiations by the Holy See with the Nazi government. We'll return to that subject a little later.)

In our two blocks, 28 and 30, there were then about a thousand people, including about eight hundred Catholic priests, while the rest were seminarians, minor seminary students, Protestant pastors, and ministers of other faiths. There were also those who raised real questions — later shown to be completely valid — about whether they belonged to any religion at all.

Our transport from Sachsenhausen, however, arrived in the best physical state. Those who looked somewhat worse were from Buchenwald. The transports from Gusen and Mauthausen presented a real picture of human misery! Both Gusen and Mauthausen, known among the prisoners as the greatest slaughterhouses, were located near quarries, like Grenzdorf. Thus, our colleagues from those camps are so horribly emaciated, sick, and weak that they look like shadows, not people. Going to or from roll call, they walk in whole rows holding each other under the arm; they drag their feet with great effort, proceeding that way step by step, like a nightmarish procession of some sort of corpses that have risen from the dead. It's a terrible scene! (Only prisoners in infamous Stutthof looked like that at the end of 1939 and early 1940.) And yet — there's not an old man among them! The old had already fallen. These are all priests between the ages of twenty-seven and forty or so; still, looking at these bent-over skeletons, at legs swollen to the size of logs, at those sallow and emaciated faces covered with ulcers and impetigo, in which deeply sunken eyes shine with

Due to long and arduous diplomatic negotiations by the Vatican, Hitler agreed to gather all priest-prisoners into one camp. Dachau was chosen. In the first half of December 1940, this camp witnessed the unloading of emaciated survivors from hundreds of groups that had been decimated at other camps. Arriving in the most deplorable state were transports of priests from the quarry camps at Gusen and Mauthausen. This is a typical picture of priests in Dachau during those days (drawing by the author).

an unhealthy luster, it's hard to hold back the tears! What did months of labor in the quarries do to these young people, who not so long ago were bursting with health!

They are a picture of such terrible misery that not even the block leaders have the heart to rush or drive them on, which is part of the daily agenda for us residents of Block 28 who arrived from Sachsenhausen. On the day after our arrival we're already convinced that Red block leaders and hall leaders — all German communists — can beat just as well as Green ones, the professional criminals in Sachsenhausen!

Due to their state of physical exhaustion, the mortality among our colleagues in Block 30 is enormous. Each day the "gravediggers" take several, and sometimes even a dozen or so, to the crematorium! If this continues much longer, Block 30 will soon be empty.

Fr. Kazio Mulczyński was with me at the seminary in Poznań. He was in the class behind me. He was a giant with a dove's heart, a wonderful priestly soul! We find him near the block. He's lying in the street, on the frozen ground, with his face covered in blood. When he fell, he struck his face against the edge of the sidewalk. Poor fellow! He's so weak that in spite of all efforts he can't lift himself up. We pick him up and carry him to the block...

"Kazio! Kazio!..."

He died! The next day, when the crematorium chimney emitted smoke, the prayer was repeated anew: "Dear Jesus, our Lord, grant eternal rest..."

Others, too, died in similar circumstances. Not just a single modest volume entitled *Shavelings*, but dozens of volumes written by various other prisoner priests are needed to describe the experiences and events of those days.

Christmas is coming. The second one in slavery. In this hilly locality it snows almost every day. Sometimes such large amounts are dumped at night that it becomes difficult in the darkness of early morning to work one's way to the kitchen to get the kettles of coffee. What makes it even harder is that they didn't give us footwear with laces, leaving us with shoes that cover only the front of the foot. The sticky snow gets packed under them into high "heel wedges." How can you walk in shoes like that? How can you carry the heavy kettles? It's not surprising that people often fall, spraining ankles or even breaking bones, and some get burned by the hot coffee!

> "The powdery bridal train of snow
> Has spread its charms afar,
> Bells ring gaily on the sleighs..."

That's how it happens in a sentimental song, but how differently it was "happening" in Dachau! Since all lay prisoners who are healthy march every morning to roll call and then to work while we priests are the only ones "not working," we are forced to clear the entire camp area of snow. They divide us into three units. The first, armed with huge shovels, pushes the snow into mounds and piles; the second, with smaller shovels, loads it into wheelbarrows; the third unit — and this one is in the worst situation — carries or hauls the snow through the camp gate to the outside, dumping it into the canal that runs along the southern side of the camp.

The job of clearing the snow itself would not be difficult or unpleasant (under normal conditions, in freedom, it's considered rather a source of enjoyment and a type of winter sport). Let's remember, however, that this clearing is taking place in a *concentration camp*, where all work is geared toward the *extermination* of people.

The work director is an Austrian named Stirlitz, a major in the military. He's a man of mild and refined disposition, who gives us the impression that he understands our situation. (It should be noted here that wherever there were Austrians in charge of camp work, the prisoner groups under them always felt good. Besides, practically all Austrians in Dachau at this time were either officers of the Austrian army, distinguished politicians, or people in high positions. I emphasize this so much because it was a common and psychologically understandable phenomenon that wherever a camp position was held by a person with education, with spiritual values, there, in general, humane relations prevailed between him, as head of the given work, and the prisoners doing the work. So much the worse if an uncultivated man had the foreman's job. We could understand that the foreman was less influenced by ill-will than by his limitations, but whatever the justification, work under him would most often become a true hell!)

Major Stirlitz's deputy is a simpleton named Groo, an army deserter, a youngster with a bird brain. He's very hard on us! Since it turned out that capo Groo is considered by the camp operations office to be a foreman for "special duties" and we priests, who still have no specific assignment, form precisely a "special duty" unit, we are, therefore, subordinate to the scoundrel. This embitters our already difficult life for many months.

In addition to clearing snow, our other daily "special assignment" is to carry kettles from the camp kitchen and distribute them three times a day to the respective blocks.

Each of these iron kettles, whether filled with coffee or with soup at dinner, weighs about 150 pounds. Due to the fact that most of the people in our group are terribly weak, it's up to those who are "strong and healthy" to make the run twice. For two people to carry this weight when physically exhausted is an enormous effort. What makes it worse is that we're not wearing normal shoes but wooden "slides," which cause us to slip on the ice. (Snow sometimes builds up under them as much as several inches.) So we get up half an hour earlier than other prisoner-colleagues and have to dress quickly because our "friend" is already whistling in front of our block. It's block leader Willi, known throughout the camp, the leader of Block 14 and one of the most horrible people around. He's about 30 years old, tall, thin, handsome, perfectly nourished (since he is charged with transporting the kettles every day from the camp kitchen, and the kitchen knows how to reward him for this service!). It is he who rushes us three times a day to fetch the kettles, three times a day to carry full kettles to each of the blocks, three times a day to carry empty kettles back to the kitchen! I look at this man, observe him, listen to his words, analyze his conduct, and ... I can't understand him.

"What an *animal*!" Zdzich tersely concludes.

"You can't mean that literally. After all, this is a human being! And so there must be a soul in him; that is, the way he behaves must be the result of certain mental processes..."

Such a statement is applied to many of us concentration camp inmates. "He's a former concentration camp prisoner, and it's generally known that each of them got a little smack on the ear!" That's how they used to talk about us and still do to this day. But communist Willi has been in Dachau since 1933! His conduct toward us can only be explained by the fact that the years of camp "gave him a powerful smack." (Let us add here that following liberation of the camp, he was sentenced by a court and died on the gallows! He died a prisoner, himself tormented for 12 long years; he died together with his tormentors, a group of SS men. But he was accused before the court not by the liberated priests, but by lay prisoners! If he had gotten under their skin to such a degree, it's not difficult to imagine how hard he was on us, the shavelings he hated!)

While searching for psychological motives for his conduct, I come across this one, which is the most certain: communist Willi *hated* us with his whole heart! In hating, he did *everything* to vent his feeling. And he vented it! He vented it several times a day each time the kettles were carried — whether full or empty! I don't know what charges were filed before the court, but one thing is certain: in addition to those charges, we can add that he sent several dozen Polish priests into the next world!

Besides block leader Willi and capo Groo, our blocks are invaded from morning to night by various other foremen. (In camp jargon, they are known as "capo," and from now on we will call all work foremen by this name. It has its origin in the Italian word "capo" or "head," with the extended meanings: first, leading, directing.)

So we move camp furnishings; fit out whole blocks for arriving transports; carry heavy iron beds and straw mattresses; distribute clothing and underwear from the laundry and storage room; take the old clothing back there; take blankets and soiled, lice-infested uniforms to be disinfected; empty some things out of SS warehouses; fill them the next day with other things; clean yards by the SS barracks; clean the squares, streets, and public roads around the camp. In short, during these days and weeks, there's not a single "special task" that we priests are not picked to carry out, including moving gallows to the execution yard.

In sum, we work throughout the day, getting up earlier than all the others and rushing with heavy kettles at a time when our prisoner colleagues have brief moments of rest after work. Since they do "regular" work, they get an extra food ration; we who work our fingers to the bone all day not only do not get this supplement, but "super-friendly" Willi (who makes decisions regarding the allocation of kettles to particular blocks), even cuts our rations since, allegedly, we are not working. And it often happens that — whether due to a big snow fall, the ice, or even because those carrying the kettles are weak — one or several kettles turn over, spilling their contents. Oh Lord! Of course, this is always the fault of those lazy shavelings! The empty kettles must be replaced by full ones. The "others" have to have their meal. The shavelings, after all, don't do any work, and so — they don't need to eat!

Hungry, we carry our own kettles to the "others."

Tired, out of breath, barely dragging our feet, we return to our block, realizing that today — instead of a whole liter of soup — there will be only half! Yet that liter of dinner soup was really the main meal of the day.

Christmas 1940 arrived. Somehow other blocks are relatively quiet. We priests, however, the hated shavelings (maybe this is not nice form, but it's accepted in daily speech), spend the entire day clearing snow in the camp. And because there cannot be work without a foreman, capo Groo, who would rather be in his block this day with friends, is exercising his authority over us. And since we are carrying the snow outside the camp, the guards must also watch us. Who among them would not rather sit in a warm room and sing "Stille Nacht"? Therefore, we get it from them also because we have "spoiled" their holiday!

Finally darkness falls. Evening assembly... It's over. We can relax. The evening awaits us, hopefully in peace and quiet! We're hungry because today Willi came up with a new harassment. Allegedly our colleagues, one of the pairs carrying kettles, attempted to steal an entire kettle. It was difficult to find "these thieves," however. Yet as punishment they not only took away one kettle that was due us (despite the fact that no kettle had disappeared, Willi himself yelling that the theft was only "attempted"!), but — to prevent similar "theft" in the future — they also took away several others. We had to be satisfied with half a daily ration. And this just on the feast day of Christmas!

We're sitting quietly in the hall, afraid of doing anything that might expose us to some new type of painful torture on this quiet holy evening. We sit in silence, praying and reminiscing, our hearts running freely outside the camp wire.

"Attention!" the hall leader's voice is brusque as usual. "Whoever wants to can go to his bunk earlier than usual today!"

We can go to sleep earlier?... What joy!

In the next few minutes the bunkroom is full. The hall becomes completely empty.

"Why all of them today?..." the hall leader wonders.

After a while, intrigued by the silence in the bunkroom, he enters, stops, and looks around. Seeing that most prisoners are lying down with blankets over their heads, he walks over to the first one at the end, lifts the blanket and — drops it just as fast. He stands with his mouth open and looks over the rest of those lying down and, not seeing any faces, he turns around, disconcerted, and moves toward the door. He is just about to step over the threshold when he slowly turns back; once again glancing over the bunks, he clears his throat, swallows, and blurts out:

"So guys ... because today is your holiday ... so ... " His mind is searching for expressions that he hasn't used in years. "So I wish you a happy holiday!" He looks over the bunks and sighs in relief. "Ja, guys! ... Ja! ... Good night, then!"

"Good night, Ignac!"

He turns out the light and leaves, closing the door quietly behind him.

We had never seen our hall leader like this before.

"Something has stirred in that numbed soul," someone whispers.

"Don't you remember the popular saying that on Christmas Day even cattle in the barns talk?" Zdzich drawls ironically.

"Fratres," someone's voice is heard in the darkness. "Fratres! Today, on this holy Christmas night, when the Eternal Word left the Immaculate Virgin's womb, manifesting God-made-Man to the world, today when our thoughts race..."

"What's the reason for this moaning pathos?" whispers Zdzich.

"Fratres," the voice in the darkness continues, "Oremus..."

Outside the windows the evening is full of darkness. Frost embroiders traceries on the panes...

"Fratres! *Christus natus est nobis: venite, adoremus.*"

"*Venite, adoremus,*" flows a whisper of voices.

Heavy snow clouds hang over the camp. Will it snow during the night? Will they herd us out early in the morning with wheelbarrows?

"*Venite, adoremus!*"

Even the black chimney of the crematorium is not emitting smoke on this holy evening. The pile of corpses can wait until tomorrow.

"*Christus natus est nobis: venite, adoremus,*" the monotonous murmur floats out. Behind the wall you can hear the quiet sound of a harmonica. It's the hall leader playing...

In the sky, covered with heavy clouds, there's not a single star...

28

The Year 1941 Approaches

And again a day passes. One of the last in the year 1940. Evening falls. We stand in tight formation on the assembly square, facing a complex of buildings, including the kitchen, warehouses, laundry and hose factory. A strong, icy wind is blowing from the north, tossing drifts of light snow around. We're freezing cold, but roll call again drags on. Roll calls in Sachsenhausen lasted a long time but were not as long as in Dachau. Somehow everything proceeded more efficiently there, more in the Prussian manner, more energetically. Here in Bavaria people are different, and the SS men, too, are somehow different. (Although the Dachau SS training center drew SS men from all of Germany, it was mostly local Bavarians who were in camp administrative positions.)

The number of our neighbors from Block 30 is dwindling before our eyes. Many have left in the last few days, passing on to eternity. As we look at these emaciated human shapes, we become aware that many more will follow both this night and tomorrow and in the days to come.

We stand here, whispering prayers within our hearts. You cannot betray that you're saying prayers by even the slightest movement of your lips. The block and hall leaders pay special attention to this. They're less interested in a prisoner's posture "at attention" (although there are kicks for any deviation in this regard) than in our silent prayers. With truly sadistic persistence they seek out "lip whisperers" in the ranks. There's no end to the beatings for this! Moreover—finding a Rosary, a small cross, or any sort of devotional item could even mean death!

Therefore, we whisper prayers "in our hearts." While reciting the Rosary—to avoid mistakes in the number of Hail Marys—we use our fingers instead of Rosary beads.

"I count the Hail Marys of the Rosary using the sign that's on the roof," Zdzich confided one day.

"The sign on the roof?"

"That's right. Count. There are ten nouns in it. I stop at each one, whispering one Hail Mary."

His words come to mind just now while we're standing frozen in the square, waiting for evening roll call. In the glare of floodlights shining from far off onto the huge roof of the kitchen, which is right in front of the units assembled for roll call, there are enormous letters that spell out the following maxim:

> "**Es gibt einen Weg zur Freiheit** [There is only one road to freedom].
> **Seine Meilensteine heissen** [Its milestones are called]:
> **Gehorsam** [Obedience],
> **Fleiss** [Diligence],
> **Ehrlichkeit** [Honesty],

Ordnung [Love of Order],
Sauberkeit [Cleanliness],
Nüchternheit [Sobriety],
Wahrhaftigheit [Truthfulness],
Opfersinn [Readiness to Sacrifice],
Liebe—
Zum Vaterland [Love of Fatherland]."

"You know," Zdzich then added, "although this is a stretch of sorts, each of these words can be connected in content with figures from meditations of the Rosary."

"Oh?" I'm surprised.

"Take the first mystery, for example: the Annunciation. The Holy Virgin is the central figure in it. Apply these ten words on the roof in front of us to her. The Holy Virgin is *obedient* to the decrees of Heaven, *diligent* in giving her "fiat," *honest* toward St. Joseph, while still hiding her great holy secret from him. And so, counting Hail Marys on these ten words, I also have in their contents an aid in meditating the mysteries."

In general, under the circumstances, the Rosary is the easiest and, at the same time, our most beloved prayer. We recite it almost continuously. At work, in periods of rest, during breaks, lying on bunks in the evening, marching out for the kettles in the early morning while it's still dark, and when returning them...

"*Achtung*!" the shout of the camp senior, the infamous Kapp (let's distinguish this name from "capo," the title given to work foremen), resounds from the front of the units. Several thousand prisoners freeze motionless.

"Caps off!"

Caps hit the sides of pants like the flutter of an enormous banner in the wind. (Woe if they didn't hit at the same time! Then a punishment could fall to us, namely, many hours of drilling on how to take our caps off and put them back on. In any case, it falls to us often.)

We stand erect at attention, with caps and hands against the seams of our pants. The cold wind blusters about our shaved heads, blows snow inside our collars, whips our faces...

SS men, "guardians" of specific blocks (one young guard is assigned to each block), run through the ranks counting and then rush to the guardhouse with reports on the status of personnel in "their" block. Over at a table brought out for this purpose, the report director counts up the numbers. This sometimes lasts quite a long time, sometimes not so long; sometimes it ends with harassment for all prisoners on the square, sometimes for one of the units or a particular block.

"At eeeease!" we hear Kapp shout.

Thousands breathe a sigh of relief. It appears that today there won't be any unpleasant surprises. We'll spend the evening in a more or less quiet barracks.

"Blocks of shavelings remain in place!" Kapp's command is suddenly given. "The rest march off in columns!"

We remain on the square. Our block leader, whose name is Baecher, is furious. This mood spreads immediately to the hall leaders. They move around the unit looking for a chance to kick, beat, or bully us in other ways.

"Stay put, you dogs!" screams Baecher from the front. The leader of Block 30 is calmer. He's a former communist deputy in the German parliament whose name is Wagner. Although a communist, he's a man of totally spotless integrity! I emphasize this knowingly, and this opinion will be confirmed by hundreds of my colleague-priests, grateful because he gave us better treatment and, especially, because he saved lives. If the leader of Block 30 had been another man, such as any average leader of other blocks, less than half the priests in that block would have survived! What the Holy See did not gain from the Nazi government in Berlin through negotiations was attained by Providence itself through such instruments as this communist deputy. For example, block leader Wagner, nurse Hein, and several others who will be discussed later are communists, yet how many priests they saved from death!

"As long as we are prisoners, as long as the same misery strikes us, so long must we support each other, helping each other to survive. When we become free men, then we can continue our ideological war!" This opinion of Wagner's was known to us priests. Here was a human being.

While our block leader — whom we call "Buffalo" — is raging, thereby encouraging the hall leaders to acts of frenzy, quiet prevails in Block 30 next to us. Only here and there block leader Wagner notices something, pointing to someone who's unsteady:

"Take him between you. Hold him up. Let's try not to draw attention to ourselves."

The square is becoming empty. With a song on their lips, the units disappear from the camp street, heading toward their warm and cozy barracks.

"Attention! Attention!" a whisper runs from the front as it's relayed from one rank to another. "Kapp is coming! Kapp is coming!"

Kapp, the camp senior, a mason by trade, was also a long-time communist prisoner. What qualified him for the position of camp senior? His thirst for blood! Short, with long arms that reach to the knees, with wide shoulders and chest, stocky like the trunk of a beech tree, he arouses fear just by his appearance. He's the proverbial ape man. Behind him limps his deputy, whose last name is Szaferski. (Yes, he has a Polish name. It's hard to determine, however, whether anything Polish is still in him). Szaferski is also short, but smaller boned and more corpulent; with his tummy stuck out in front, he totters on short legs behind his fierce superior.

Our block leader Baecher is already stiffening at attention in front of the unit. Baecher was once a high-ranking SS officer. Sentenced to the concentration camp for some kind of Party offense, he hates both us and his fellow communist prisoners. Baecher, however, is a sybarite of the most extreme type. To retain his position as block leader, he's ready to murder the entire unit! We know from what older prisoners have told us how many Jews he slaughtered when he was block leader of the penal company.

"For the shavelings' laziness in clearing snow today, an hour of sport on the square!" Kapp announces audibly.

"Yes, sir!" Buffalo confirms that he got the order.

Seeing that block leader Wagner is not hurrying toward him, Kapp yells at the top of his voice: "Waaagner!"

Walking slowly, with his head tucked between his shoulders, Wagner approaches Kapp.

"Did you hear what I said?"

"I heard." Wagner's voice becomes calmer as the other grows more agitated.

They look each other straight in the eye. Two communists: the former mason and the former deputy. Both followers of the same ideology, yet how radically different! Kapp's tiny rat-like eyes are getting bloodshot. Wagner's deep-set eyes, with wrinkled eyelids, are staring with cold calm into them, and … they are winning. Swearing under his breath, Kapp walks away, swaying on his short legs. Szaferski withdraws behind him.

"Right turn!" comes Buffalo's command.

"Left turn!" Wagner gives the command to his block.

Buffalo leads us to the right side of the assembly square, toward the guardhouse and the gate. Wagner leads his men to the shaded side, toward the wall that separates the camp from the plantation. Zealous Buffalo, seeing that the SS men are observing from the guardhouse windows, pushes us to utter exhaustion. Wagner, after positioning his unit against the wall, thereby shielding it from the blizzard blowing in from the plantation, "trains" his men from time to time ... on how to take off their caps! And when he sees that his men are freezing, he orders them to stomp their feet in place, hit each other on the back, and beat their hands to stay warm.

"As long as the same misery strikes us, so long all battle between us must cease. Someday, when we're free..."

After an hour, we head toward the barracks.

"Left! Left! One! Two! Three! Four! ... Left, left!" roars Buffalo (he got this nickname precisely because of his constant roaring, real buffalo-like roaring. Besides, even his whole powerful shape reminds us of a buffalo). "Sing!"

The snowstorm beats against our eyes. We trudge through snowdrifts heaped across the camp street. No matter. We sing.

Block 30 marches slowly, supporting one another by the arm. Block leader Wagner himself guides them, supporting the two weakest men. A strange scene! A communist sentenced to death in a concentration camp playing the Gospel role of good Samaritan!

"I'm forming a clearer 'dogma of humanity,'" comments Zdzich. "You see, in order to measure how much of that element remains in a person, you must strip him of all that constitutes his outer hide, lock him up in such beastly conditions as ours, and only then will it be revealed in whom there is true humanity and how much of it."

"Attention!" Buffalo orders as we enter the block street.

We press our hands against our pant legs and try to click our clogs together.

"Unit halt! Right turn! At ease!"

Buffalo is getting ready to give his "training" speech.

Good Lord, we already know these hour-long speeches of his. The former SS officer cannot let any chance go by without pouring into our souls the drivel of his small mind.

"So! Attention! If tomorrow you are again as lazy as today, then it won't be the camp senior Kapp, but I myself who will submit a disciplinary report to the guardhouse, and then I'll let the devil off his leash! (That is Buffalo's favorite expression. Besides, he often really does 'let the devil off his leash'! Then he's merciless! Horrible! His striped prisoner's uniform hasn't killed the SS spirit in him). Therefore..."

After at least half an hour, as we enter the barracks, frozen to the bone, we can see through the windows of Block 30 that our colleagues there are already lying on their bunks.

We start to take our supper.

Behind the windowpane sits Wagner, a crooked pipe between his teeth, reading a paper, while at the same time our Buffalo rages: hitting, kicking, spilling coffee from tins! Wagner's conduct is clearly for show! Why isn't this man afraid that Buffalo — who, after all, has the respect of the young SS men who come through the blocks — might denounce him?

It's only after months in Dachau, when they've begun to think of us as "their people," that is, as real Dachau men, that Social Democrat Ernst Hecht explains this to me:

"Heinrich! Denounce Wagner to the officials? Do you know what a silent power the communists are in Dachau? There's just a handful of us Social Democrats here; but Buffalo, as a former SS officer, is completely alone. Before some SS man could hear the end of his denunciation, a secret report about this would already be rushed to potentates of the communist camp administration. Tomorrow, the next day, in a few days at the latest, Buffalo would "succumb" to some kind of sudden illness, some kind of accident, would be forced to the sick-room, and there? There, they would already be waiting for him... You know how easy it is to give some type of "less suitable" injection, and ... that would be the end of Buffalo. The matter is even more dangerous for him since it has to do with Wagner! For us he's an extremely kind man, but for the camp communists he's their party's "sacred figure." Let just a hair fall off his head! They've saved him through these awful years and even rescued him from the SS men, who very much wanted him to die. You see, Heinrich, there's a big gang of them, communists, in Dachau; but they themselves are aware that what's easy to find among them are just "strong muscles and hate-filled hearts." There are only a few brains. The strongest intellect among them is Wagner. In case the war effort collapses and there's a radical change (they still count on this), who from the masses will follow some unknown? The masses will follow Wagner!"

"To your bunks!" sounds the hall leader's order.

We rush to the bedroom. A few minutes later, we're already lying on the bunks.

"Fratres," as with every day, a quiet voice flows out of the darkness. "Oremus..."

It's also dark in the bedroom of Block 30, but a light still shines in the block leader's room. Against the frosted window pane you can see the sitting figure with a crooked pipe between his teeth...

"Because, you see," whispers Zdzich. "God has different "plans" than we people have. I'm not sure whether the communist Wagner knows the Gospel, but one thing is certain, he puts its principles into practice."

"May You punish enemies of the Church," the precentor continues.

"Hear us, oh Lord," echoes forth the response.

"Overthrow enemies of the Church mercifully with Your grace," whispers Zdzich. "So that by getting to know You, who are Eternal Love, they will shake off hatred and lovingly cling to You with their errant hearts."

"Amen."

29

When on Candlemas Day All Was Covered with Snow

Jan Domagała, an official interpreter at Dachau and one of the oldest Polish prisoners in that camp, who was very close to official sources and camp archives, writes the following on page 40 of his work entitled *Those Who Went Through Dachau*:

"The life of a prisoner ... not assigned to work was not envied in the camp. Because during the entire time of his stay in the camp he was at the mercy of the block leader and room supervisor. The block leader used prisoners of this type for various jobs in the block, as well as for cleaning rooms or streets, removing stones from the road, cleaning washrooms and toilets... Prisoners remaining in the block trembled before visits of the Blockführer because that sort of SS man was never satisfied with their work, and if at the first glance he didn't notice anything in particular that he could criticize, he would take a pin and look for dust in the floor cracks. Block leaders did not allow prisoners to remain in the rooms, but chased them out into the street, and woe to anyone who..."

At the end of these explanations, we read: "In the evening, the non-working prisoner was more tired than the working one and, what's more, he didn't receive the additional ration given to those working. During the hard winter, especially in the years 1940–1941 when enormous amounts of snow fell in Dachau, those assigned to clear it were, in particular, Catholic priest-prisoners who were not employed in permanent groups. Horrible scenes took place at this work!..."[1]

Indeed, at "this" work by "non-working priests" truly horrible scenes did take place!

The New Year has brought us such a mass of new snow that they push us from early morning, and then we have to carry kettles with coffee and dinner for the entire camp (in regard to carrying these kettles, the above-mentioned author writes that "this was one of the hardest jobs in the Dachau camp!"),[2] and later we're again compelled to clear snow until the evening meal, and again we're with the kettles and again we return them, and, in addition, we clean up and put away the tools and equipment used in clearing snow. And after that we run to our places for roll call! "So, you damned, lazy shavelings, just as you did nothing when you had your freedom, so even today you smell of idleness!" roars Buffalo, taking the opportunity to beat and kick us. "But I'll show you after roll call, you crazy, smelly Roman swine! You..."

The evening roll call passes exceptionally "smoothly." Of course, it's the New Year! The SS men are in a hurry to attend a festive New Year's party. To compensate, Buffalo keeps his promise! He *does* show us! While in the other blocks there's relative quiet (relative, since there's no shortage of wild lunatics like Buffalo among block leaders in other barracks), in ours it's hell! And when lights go on in the bedrooms of other barracks, a sign that they're preparing to rest, we're just starting to get our supper. And how much harassment comes with it!

Finally, we too go to bed. Quickly and efficiently we slide into our places on the bunks so that by some chance we don't "attract attention" again. The lights go off. Thank God. The pains of this first day of 1941 are ending.

"Fratres," flows a voice out of the darkness, as it does every day. "Oremus... "

Suddenly, steps can be heard in the adjoining room. We recognize them. It's Buffalo's heavy step. A silence falls, full of dread. The door opens. They're turning on the lamps.

"Feet inspection!"

Already trained in this matter, we all sit up on the edges of our bunks, sticking our feet out in front of us. Buffalo walks from one to the other, and as he advances, more and more must hurry barefoot to the washroom to ... wash their feet.

It's pure harassment! That is how Buffalo is, and he'll never be different. Later, after finishing the inspection, he stands with his legs wide apart and goes into a long "training" sermon.

"Your shanks are filthy like cattle in a barn! But why am I surprised? You Poles always were a nation of dirty pigs! *Pölnische Wirtschaft*!* But we're going to teach you order!" He stops those returning from the washroom, inspecting the soles of their feet. He makes many of them rush back there again, not sparing beatings, and he screams without stopping: "You dirty pigs!"

In the entire world it would probably be hard to find another man so perverse. He torments us not only physically, but also mentally, and in terrible ways. A former SS officer, trained in an SS school and fed on "those" doctrines, he knows which psychological tortures to use in tormenting his victims. But unlike most of the block leaders, he hates us chiefly as Poles. This trait is especially characteristic of him.

Finally, after mistreating the last of those returning from the washroom and showering us with insults as a goodnight, he leaves. We breathe a sigh of relief.

"Fratres! Oremus... Let us pray on behalf of our block leader..."

And the following day, from early morning, the possessed Buffalo is frothing worse than ever. We came quite seriously to the conclusion that he's possessed.

That is how the days of January 1941 go by... Difficult days, horrible ones. Days of constant coercion to do the hardest jobs, constantly clearing snow from the entire camp and hauling heavy kettles, days of constant torment by bloody Buffalo and four of his hall coworkers, who imitate him.

"Do you know how many died in this camp during the month of January?" Zdzich asks.

"I have no idea. I only know there were many."

"Four hundred fifty-five."³

"But not all were priests."

---

* Translator's note: Literally "Polish housekeeping," this German term means colloquially "an awful mess."

"That's right, not all, but most of them."

Under these "better conditions" provided to us by Nazism as a result of efforts from the Holy See, our numbers *shrink* from day to day.

Although they released the Rev. Dr. Salamucha, the Jagiellonian University professor who arrived with us from Sachsenhausen, he was the only one who went free. But how many who died in just this month of January will never see freedom? Or rather: How many went to the only true freedom?

Among better known priests who died were young Fr. Antoś Schwarz, the Rev. Dean Obarski, Fr. Paszkowiak, Fr. Ed. Kasior, and Fr. Michałowicz, prefect from Wągrowiec. Fr. Matuszewski from Lipnica, Fr. Sommer, Fr. Lach, Fr. Fiutak also perished... All young colleagues, alas, victims of terrible days in Gusen and Mauthausen. The very elderly Rev. Dean Jan Szlachta, former confessor of Primate Cardinal Hlond and his quiet spiritual director, also died; he was a saintly priest and a marvelous person.

We lose track of who's still living and who has passed away.

"Three Kings at the crèche, the days grow longer by a hen's foot," goes an old saying. In southern Bavaria, days grow longer by two hens' feet, and, by the same token, our day, the day of the "non-working," grows longer!

The Feast of Candlemas falls this year on a Sunday.

"I fear that day," someone whispers Saturday night. "On each feast day of the Mother of God the most painful experiences befall us."

"Pagan," says Zdzich. "He doesn't understand that love for the Immaculate is not based on 'taking from Her,' but on 'giving to Her.'"

And, indeed, at the earliest rays of dawn on Candlemas Day all hell breaks loose! At night there was such a heavy snowfall that, as we walk in darkness to the kitchen for the kettles of coffee, we make our way through snow that practically comes up to our knees. Lord! But the road with full kettles is a true Calvary! Tucking our shoes under our belts, we dig through the mounds in stocking feet. We bump against high snow with the kettles; the brew splashes on our bare, frozen hands; people fall down; coffee spills out; and Willi goes berserk, cursing, kicking, and beating us in his rage. This only increases our panic and leads to further stumbling.

"Didn't I tell you?" Zdzich whispers, catching his breath.

"Tell me what?"

"That Candlemas would reach out to us again?"

"Well, yes."

The distance from the kitchen threshold to the last block is 600 meters. 600 meters...

"Olek, Olek," a plaintive voice offers comfort, "Just a bit more, another minute, ... we'll be there soon..."

A man is only human, and so is a priest; it's not without envy, therefore, that we look into the illuminated block windows, where you see our colleagues, the lay prisoners, just getting up. While they're only now starting their day, we're already worn out from work. Moreover, since today is Sunday, the blocks of working prisoners will have a day off. And we? Since we're "not working," we'll spend all Sunday clearing snow!

"You know what hurts the most?"

"What?"

"When one of our Poles, under pressure from 'them,' thoughtlessly blurts out the often repeated phrase: 'Oh, you lazy shavelings!'"

"Secret self-love!" says Zdzich.

"Self-love? What do you mean?"

"Well, just this. You'd like, at least from your own people, some sympathy, understanding, comfort, whereas they're really... They're really instruments in God's hands, cleansing us completely of ourselves. You'll suffer in this regard until you learn simply to draw joy from it."

"Joy?"

That exclamation must have been rather loud because it drew Willi's attention.

"You dogs, you!" He kicks, beats with his fist, kicks again. He runs at someone else.

"Zdzich! Zdzich!" I'm trying to help him get up.

"I'm all right," he mutters. "The snow is so soft that... Only ... that scoundrel has heavily reinforced boots, and..." He rubs the painful area and then suddenly says: "Well, it's so. You'll struggle and you'll suffer until you learn to draw joy for yourself from their behavior!"

But there's so much snow that they're making the entire camp start to clear it. Including those who are working.

An extraordinary scene. It must have looked like this during the time of the Egyptian Pharaohs when thousands of slaves were building the pyramids. Thousands of prisoners scurry about in fear. Some push wheelbarrows, others — in groups of four — carry the snow on table tops taken from the barracks, still others clear the snow with shovels or pile it up, and over this human swarm comes the shouting, the uproar, the cursing of SS men, block leaders, capos, and all the rest of the camp slave drivers.

We carry and haul the snow outside the guardhouse gate, and just beyond that we dump it into the canal. SS men stand along the route. They're all teenagers. For them, this is a good chance for fun, tricks and jokes. To amuse themselves to the utmost, they're constantly making up new torments.

"Run! Run!" They prod us with rifle butts and kick us...

Only priests and Jews are at the wheelbarrows.

In the narrow opening of the gate — when talking about the gate, we must remember it's a tunnel that passes under the entire guardhouse building — thus, in the narrow tunnel of the gate there's a veritable hell. Wheelbarrow after wheelbarrow, one group of four after another carrying mounds of snow on table tops. The SS men standing along both sides of the tunnel push especially hard here. This results in prisoners falling down and snow falling out. Every few minutes there are traffic-jams, which increase the beating and kicking. Whoever can't endure all this and loses consciousness is thrown out of the tunnel and tossed by the wall of the guardhouse. And in the tunnel the mayhem continues. Screams! Curses! Moans of the tortured! Squeals of those suffocating! Faces express terror and frantic madness. Open mouths gasp for air.

"Run! Faster! Run, you dogs!"

Just beyond the gate is a stone bridge that leads across the canal. Even more horrible scenes are being played out there. High-spirited SS men are throwing prisoners into the water through the stone railing of the bridge. They're dunking them. They're drowning them! If one of the wretches manages to reach the steep cement bank, they push him back; SS boots crush his fingers, break his hands. It's better not to look at the faces of those being drowned because there's so much savage despair and inhuman terror in them...

"Throw it on them!"

Heaps of snow are dumped onto the heads of the unfortunate.

"Throw it!"

The canal is not very deep. In the center of it stands a young Jew, immersed up to his chest in the freezing water. Covering his face with emaciated hands, he stands immobile like a statue, not reacting to either the mounds of snow being thrown from the bridge railing or the brutal shouts of the SS men. He's waiting for merciful death to deliver him finally from tortures that exceed human endurance.

Along this Death Walk, entire mountains of snow are forming since, with such a mass of people hauling and carrying, it's impossible to throw everything at once from the bridge into the canal. So a group of SS men is amusing itself there in a different manner. They're searching with bayonets for those who were buried in the snow... A blood-stained bayonet is proof that the thrust has struck its target. And how heartily they laugh while doing this, how they chortle, how much fun they have!

(Today's reader may consider this narrative to be a literary fantasy. Even so, at the Last Judgment, in accordance with dogma, God will reveal everything. At that time, it will finally be shown how incompetent a human pen was in re-creating these horrible crimes; at that time all their ghastliness will be revealed. But also revealed at that time will be "God's plan," according to which God *allowed* such outbreaks of satanic evil.)

Lying stretched out on top of one pile of snow is a very tall Jew. Teenage SS men are stomping on him as if he were an inanimate object. Finally, one of them (maybe through pity?) steps on his throat. He choked him. (As we learned later, this was one of the better known Jewish literary men.)

And "operating" on the assembly square, the camp street, and the block streets is a gang of camp capos, block leaders, and other slave drivers. They're doing all they can to match the SS men in brutality.

Finally, at eleven o'clock the whistle comes. It's the signal to carry the dinner kettles. Although there were usually no volunteers among our lay colleagues for this difficult job, today half the camp moves toward the kitchen. Some cunning ones abandon their wheelbarrows and drop their work tools just so they can get away and, under the guise of carrying kettles, get back to their blocks.

The life-saving dinner is here. It's quiet in the camp. We also take our rations. Suddenly, from the camp street we hear the call:

"Capo Hentschel! Capo Hentschel!" It's Kapp, the camp senior, calling for the main capo of the camp.

"Capo Hentschel! Capo Hentschel!" the call runs from barracks to barracks. (This was one way of summoning someone in the camp. It was enough for one of the officials to call out from the assembly square the name of the one being summoned, or give an order that had to be executed, and each prisoner, wherever he may be at that time, was obliged to forward the call further. That's how news traveled from one block to another.)

"Capo Hentschel!"

Our hall leader, who was just then serving dinner, stands motionless. The ladle in his hand remains suspended.

"Capo Hentschel!"

A pang of anxiety seizes us. We know that capo Hentschel is in charge of all jobs in the camp. Today's ordeal with the snow is, to a great extent, also in his hands. Or could there again be something else?

The long-legged capo Hentschel is already running toward the assembly square where camp senior Kapp, the ape-man, stands waiting with legs astride.

"Hentschel," roars Kapp, "What is the meaning of these tools abandoned on the square?! These wheelbarrows? This mess?"

Capo Hentschel is not much afraid of Kapp.

"Capo Groo is responsible for the equipment and tools," he calmly informs him.

"So! Capo Groo then," mumbles ape-man Kapp, and already a new summons goes out along the camp street:

"Capo Groo! Capo Groo!"

Running out of the delousing building, located behind Block 29, comes capo Groo. He rushes toward the assembly square.

"You dog!" Kapp greets him. "Is this how you leave your equipment and tools? You..."

"It's those damned shavelings who left them!" capo Groo defends himself.

"Shavelings?" Sparks flare up in the small eyes of the camp senior. "Shavelings! Those damned dogs!"

"*Alle Pfaffen antreten*! All shavelings assemble!"

Mayhem ensued inside our block. It also caused an uproar in Block 30. What a piece of good luck for Buffalo and his helpers! To interrupt the shavelings' dinner, to beat them a hundred times, and send them out for new torments!

A minute later we're standing on the block street in a tight formation. Ape-man Kapp, with capo Groo next to him, is already waiting at the end of the street. At the sight of his superior, Buffalo increases his beatings. After all, each strike with his boot or fist enforces his position...

Capo Groo runs some of us to the square to get the equipment and tools. It doesn't matter that all the prisoners had abandoned them. Only we are "guilty" of it.

"They're taking it out on the shavelings again," you can hear it said around camp.

"Serves them right, the sluggards!"

'As long as you don't learn to draw joy from such occasions, you'll suffer constantly,' Zdzich's words echo in my ears.

Out of the rest — that is, the several hundred remaining priests — a procession is formed. On Kapp's order, each fills his cap with snow and, holding it out in front of himself, sings the words as commanded: "We will not shirk our work... We will not shirk our work ... We will not..."

After gathering the equipment with his unit and running with it to the delousing building, capo Groo integrates us into the ranks of those with the caps. Thus, we walk together singing:

"We will not shirk our work ... We will not shirk..."

The camp heaves a sigh of relief. It continues eating the interrupted dinner. Kapp has already found a victim, and so the rest will have peace.

"Well, because these shavelings are, after all, such..."

An SS man, the report director, stands by the gate opening.

"And what is this bunch up to now?" he's surprised.

"These are shavelings. For laziness at work," reports Kapp.

"Shavelings?"

29. When on Candlemas Day All Was Covered with Snow

"Yes, sir!"

"Ah, the lazy dogs! Keep them amused like this until evening!"

"Yes, sir!"

And ... they *keep us amused* ... They *amuse* themselves with us ... until *evening*...

Such was the Candlemas feast day of the Mother of God in the year 1941. But was it unique? All the feast days of the Mother of God were like this for us priests! There wasn't one when we did not face special harassment! Sometimes it would be some less known feast day of Mary. The torments would start from morning. It would be only in the evening that someone would remember:

"Do you know why they were in such a rage today?"

"Why?"

"Because it's a feast day of the Mother of God!"

"Aha. Of course. A feast day of the Mother of God."

"I'm curious," murmurs Zdzich, "how those of us who survive this hell will talk to the faithful about Mary. During services in May, will sentimental readings continue to pour forth about wonders, about how Mary never disappoints, how she always descends with miracles, how..."

"Oh, you blasphemer!" one of the priests interrupts him.

"I'm as much a blasphemer as you are a pagan!" retorts Zdzich. "Remember how the little St. Thérèse complained about priests? When telling people about Mary, they present Her in such a way that sighs burst forth from the listeners' mouths: 'Oh! ... Ah! ... Oh! ...' This brings on tears, emotion, sentiment, and, in general, a pagan or primitive approach to the Queen of Martyrs! 'If I were a priest,' the little Saint exclaims, 'I would talk about Mary...'"

"Stop it, you heretic!"

A wave of the hand. More and more often now, colleagues distance themselves from him, and he increasingly shies away from them.

"You see," he says at times when the two of us are in a corner alone, "our whole religious practice was so shallow, spread with an icing of sentiment, that I'm even ashamed to recall it. Shallowness, shallowness, and once again shallowness! No depth whatsoever. No digestion. No understanding of the real sense of the teaching of Jesus. Just look at the masses of our lay colleagues: you have the fruits of such religious upbringing. Perhaps God has driven us on purpose to the camps so that we might finally come to understand this? After the war, after this turmoil, there must arise a new generation of priests who will educate the faithful masses differently. Remember what our Żychliński used to say..."

And again it is evening. Again the same fear of what tomorrow will bring. Again the same troubling thoughts...

They have moved a group of Polish Protestant pastors into the block with us. These are mostly young people of our age, our equals. They have been with us since Sachsenhausen, and some since Stutthof. Priests of the older generation hold themselves aloof. We, the young, are somewhat closer. Besides, common experiences, a common roof, a common table and food kettle, all this unites and binds us. Among them there is, for example, a young pastor, Henio Wegner, the last of a family of Warsaw pastors, and Bursche, a very likable and pleasant man, a true friend. There's a young pastor from Łódź, Alfred Hauptman, filled with good will and always ready to help; there's pastor Waldemar Preiss from Bydgoszcz, who's been with us since the terrible days in Stutthof, and there are others. We've become a team with them, and friendships have united us. Zdzich has become especially close to them. And here, just today, before retiring for the night, an unpleasant misunderstanding arose. One of the more opinionated among "us" saw Zdzich in the group of pastors, and so it started...

"You see," he continues in a low voice when we're already lying in our bunks after evening prayers. "After all, they love the same Jesus that we do. If you talk with them, you'll find out how many among them love the Mother of God! This is what one of them told me when talk turned to the feast of Candelmas: 'We pastors living in such a highly Marian environment as our Polish one'—he said verbatim 'as our Polish one'—we cannot simply ignore the Mother of God! Our Polish history is too closely tied to Her. True, we don't walk with you Catholics to Jasna Góra,* but perhaps many of us have a better theological understanding of the Mother of God than you might suspect.' Besides," Zdzich continues, "who gave us a better example of what our attitude should be toward different religions than the great Doctor of the Church and missionary to the Calvinists, St. Francis de Sales? He was the first to find in them not enemies, but brothers that have strayed. He was the first to practice love toward them instead of hate. The time is coming when both we and they will have to reexamine our attitudes towards each other. Let's not be obstinate like inquisitors in the Middle Ages. Not everything that is "ours" is immediately a dogma and the only thing valid; not everything that is "theirs," Protestant, immediately merits condemnation. Only close contacts full of love and friendship, only mutual expressions of opinion, but without the stubborn attitude that we alone are one hundred percent right, only these can lead to understanding and to..."

He breaks off. There's a moment of silence. My head is spinning.

"Are you asleep?" I hear a whisper in the darkness.

"No, I'm not asleep. I'm thinking. My head's spinning."

"Let it spin. Let it. Just so you arrive at the right conclusions. You see, each time I hear a communist like Wagner preaching that 'common misery must bind us,' I think of our pastor brothers. After all, we're united to them by ideals better by far than those of the communist Wagner. And yet? Can Wagner perhaps know how to rise higher than many of us?"

"Can you stop whispering?" says someone irritated. "It's hard to sleep."

"Good night, Zdzich."

Translator's note: The Jasna Góra Monastery in Częstochowa is the holiest shrine to the Virgin Mary in Poland and the country's greatest place of pilgrimage.

30

Allow Us to Work

Our situation in the block gets worse every day. Buffalo is being aided by four well-chosen thugs, known as hall leaders (one for each hall), who are creatures worthy of their boss. In the first hall is a Wehrmacht man who was sentenced for some kind of army offense; in the second is the infamous murderer Ignac; in the third is the best of the four, but, on the other hand, in the fourth hall there's a real monster. We call him "Cretin." He's constantly planning new torments and ways to bully his people. There is in him some strange mixture of innate dullness with conscious and intentional meanness.

The unofficial jobs of the shavelings continue: carrying kettles, clearing snow, all services in the camp; and if there are not enough jobs for all, the rest of the block residents (and it's the same in Block 30) must practice sport in the block street from morning to night. Hungry, cold, ill, wearing tattered clothing and shoes that are so worn that with each step water and mud slushes in them (because the snow is beginning to thaw as the February sun starts to get increasingly warmer), we march, run, practice sit-ups and jumps, we fall and run again, while the above-mentioned hall leaders beat us at random, kick us again and again, and trip us up.

The murderer Ignac beats Fr. Gołąb so badly that the poor fellow loses his mind. During a fit of rage, Ignac is terrible, but Cretin of the fourth is always merciless. Once he has turned against someone, that man has to die.

Many from our group pass at this time into eternity. Among those who lose their lives are Fr. Kaczorowski, Fr. Skórnicki, and the saintly Rev. Dir. Gałdyński, our confessor from seminary days with a wonderful priestly heart; also Fr. Wasielewski, and young Fr. Sibilski, and many others, all from Poznań. We have the hardest time reconciling ourselves to the death of Fr. Mieczysław Strehl. He had been with us from the day of our arrest in Inowrocław. Fr. Mirek Ziarniak, the closest friend of the deceased, is inconsolable. This death depresses us, survivors of the Inowrocław group.

The young missionary Fr. Bederski from Górka Klasztorna, near Łobżenica, also dies. I sense this loss even more since we have known each other from seminary days. Sadki, Wysoka, Łobżenica... How many experiences we shared! How many memories...

"We're crumbling, crumbling," laments Romek Budniak. "Now only a few of us from the old guard are still alive."

"You're right, Romek."

"And if they don't let us do some type of assigned work, but keep us in these conditions for several months, they'll finish us all off. Oh, if only there were a chance to get some kind of command!" (A "command" in camp jargon was an assignment to a permanent job, with the added ration of a piece of bread and other privileges for those officially working.)

"If only we could!" we sigh. "If only."

One day, camp capo Hentschel appears in our block. Buffalo orders everyone to a meeting in front of the block.

We line up.

Capo Hentschel, standing on the steps leading to the block, is speaking. He begins — as is his custom — with abuses, with highly indecent jokes on sexual topics, then moves on to jeering religion, God, the Mother of God, not sparing the most disgusting blasphemies, and, finally, he explains the purpose of his visit.

"We need several dozen volunteers to work in a special command. This group will be repairing roads in the camp."

"Are there volunteers to a permanent command?"

A huge group of us steps forward! Because finally there's a chance to break out of the block for hours at a time!

"I need only seventy," Hentschel reminds us with a smile.

There are, however, about two hundred volunteering — real volunteers this time. Hentschel himself conducts a review, choosing those who look youngest and strongest. It's done.

"Make me a list of this command," Hentschel orders over his shoulder to the block clerk. "Tomorrow, following morning roll call, when the order is given to form work units, form on the left flank as the 'Hentschel Command.'"

The next morning following roll call we line up as ordered. Capo Hentschel approaches and with him comes — horrors! — deputy capo Groo, already too well known to us!

"You are my special unit. Leading you will be my deputy capo Groo. You are to obey him as if you were obeying me. Understand?"

"Yes, sir!" resounds from the ranks, but there's fear in our hearts…

"Command, in step, forward march!"

We move along the main camp street in the direction of the delousing building, located on a large square in the northeastern corner of the camp, behind Block 29. (See diagram.)

This square reminds us of the Valley of Jehoshaphat in Sachsenhausen. It's the camp refuse heap, where all used equipment is dumped. There are stacks of barrels, boxes, metal dishes, tin cans, stove tops, boards, pieces of wood. Standing out in the center of the debris is a small brick building with a high chimney. That is the delousing building.

After bringing us here, capo Groo explains to us what our job will be, adding that "we already know him well" and that as soon as he detects laziness, then … and that he, as the right hand of capo Hentschel,…"

Groo assigns twelve from our group to an enormous steel roller with a long shaft, which measures about 120 centimeters high and weighs at least a ton. Those people are taken to the assembly square where they will do the rolling under the SS men's watchful eyes. (Let us add parenthetically that the work of pulling the roller was considered up to that time one of the harshest punishments.)

It was murderous work.

"They'll finish us off in a few days," Romek Budniak says in the evening after the first day of pulling this instrument of murder.

We, that is, the rest of the volunteers, armed with wheelbarrows, picks, shovels, and other smaller tools, are pressed by capo Groo to clear and level the area around the delousing

One of the most murderous jobs in Dachau was hauling a huge roller. For a long time this work was done by Polish priests, driven by the infamous capo Groo. Capo Groo assigned twelve of us to the heavy roller, which up to that time had been manned only by prisoners from the penal company (drawing by Władysław Krawiec).

building. The work itself wouldn't have been hard if it weren't for Groo. And so we gather beams, boards, barrels, sheet metal, and all kinds of other debris; we stack them up, fill holes with dirt, and level mounds. We're in separate groups spread over the entire square, so Groo, who wants to oversee everything, must constantly move from group to group. Meanwhile, we soon learn the principle of all work in Dachau, namely, that the real trick is to "work with your eyes," which means to work when Groo is nearby and to pretend to be working when he moves away.

In the evening following that first day of official work in the command, we return tired but happy that we've escaped day-long harassment in the block, being chased by the block and hall leaders, unexpected visits by SS men, being subjected to improvised demands by this or that slave driver for duties which never counted, even if they were the hardest. We're happy that it's behind us, that whole status of so-called "non-workers," which led us to be treated like slaves who should never be spared any beatings or work. Just some bread. Exactly. That slice of bread, after all, the supplement for those working, has enormous significance. It's hard to deny it. And does it matter that it's not more than two centimeters thick? But it's there! So lightly regarded in freedom, here it's worth chasing after all day long with a wheelbarrow, expending your utmost energy, even by pushing a roller that's heavy beyond human strength. Just so you can get it.

Are we imagining this or is it true that Buffalo and the hall leaders are beginning to treat us a little better because we're *working* prisoners?

A few days later they take a second group of priests, this time for jobs on the plantation. Their work is not as hard as ours, but it's more unpleasant since, working in the open field early in the year, they're exposed to cold winds whipping them with rain mixed with snow. But they also receive an additional slice of bread! That being so, what does it matter if cold and rain soak you to the skin? A slice of bread!

One day, we're busy filling in an enormous hole which was dug right under the vegetable garden fence. At a certain point, one of the Poles working there throws several slightly rotten turnips across the fence to us. For us these are first-class morsels!

None of those kneeling around the turnips notices as they divide them up that the first deputy to the chief commandant of the camp, an SS captain named Zill, is approaching on his bicycle. It's too late for a warning. The SS officer is already standing over them. Capo Groo runs by leaps and bounds toward him with his cap by his trouser leg and, standing at attention, reports...

It's amazing that Zill is satisfied with several kicks, with curses, and with trampling the wretched turnips into the ground.

"Take down their numbers! Submit a report! An hour on the stake!" he decides.

"Yes, sir!" the capo stiffens.

The SS man leaves. While writing down the numbers, Groo says with malice: "You won't escape the stake, you won't escape it, you'll get a taste of it. Get to work!" he roars, seeing us standing around.

But that day bad luck plagues us! During the afternoon, they're paying each individual prisoner several Germans marks, either from cash which prisoners had brought with them to camp and which was kept in the camp "storehouse," or from money that families had sent.

We're going, too. Happiness. This is our first such occasion — namely, as working prisoners! In the camp canteen from time to time you can buy a few cigarettes, occasionally marinated snails, pickled beets, and slightly spoiled fruit.

We're already inside the disbursement building. Watched by capo Groo, we wait in long rows, moving slowly toward the little windows behind which SS men are working.

Five o'clock approaches; work ends in an hour. Will they have time to pay us? Could we possibly leave with nothing?

Suddenly there's a shrill whistle on assembly square. We know what it is. It's the signal, well-known to us, to carry the kettles. But that's no longer our duty. We're in a command and have a permanent work assignment.

The minutes go by. Slowly we approach the little windows. We'll make it on time! Suddenly there's a commotion at the entrance. Willi enters in a rage.

"Are the shavelings here?" his steel vulture's eyes inspect the ranks. After a while in camp, each prisoner has acquired proficiency in learning a lot from the number we had to wear on our clothing, on the left side of the chest. The camp's old fox Willi is more knowledgeable about the numbers than all of us. When he sees numbers from 22,000 and up, he knows immediately that he has the hated shavelings before him. He's already at our side. He's already kicking and beating us with the club that he always carries.

"Oh, you damned shavelings! All day you lie dilly-dallying in the block and now, when it's time to carry the kettles for your working colleagues, you dogs run after money?"

Capo Groo tries to explain. It's no use. He's lucky he isn't catching heat himself. Willi is foaming at the mouth as if possessed. What is a capo without an armband, namely Groo, against the potentate Willi? Driven, terrified, we race to the kitchen, where the SS men and cooks are already waiting for us! Here, too, we get new beatings.

"Why so late, you dogs?"

It falls to us to take kettles for the last blocks. We have before us, therefore, a run of 600 meters with a load and with the fear that if we tip a kettle and food spills out, they'll take our rations away...

That's not where it ends, however. The delayed delivery of kettles attracts Kapp's attention.

"And what's with these dogs?"

"They deserted the kettles," accuses Willi.

"After they return the kettles, don't let them go to their block, but take them to the square."

Willi eagerly carries out the ape-man's order. We barely put down the kettles when he makes us run to the assembly square. Kapp and Szaferski are already waiting there with some other slave drivers. The punitive *sport* commences!

"At a run, march!"

Well, so we run. We run. It goes at a lively clip. After all, we're all volunteers; moreover, we were carefully selected by capo Hentschel himself. We run, we turn around, we fall, we crawl! And again we run! And then the murderous "leapfrog." Jumps. And again: "At a run, march! Fall down! Get up! Crawl! Run! Fall down!"

After half an hour, sweat is pouring off us in torrents. Kapp orders those who've already fallen to be dumped into snow piles that remain on the square. He orders the others to stomp on them. "Stomp! You dogs! Let them rot! I'll teach you not to be lazy!"

Finally, the buzzer sounds, a signal to everyone in camp that it's time to get ready for evening roll call. We sigh with relief. Soon they'll start coming from the blocks to gather on the assembly square. Our sport has to be over. But ... oh, heavens! What is Kapp doing? He's leading us in tight formation through the gate! We realize what this means!

"Haaalt!" We stop.

"Caps off!"

A window opens in the guardhouse. Captain Zill leans out.

"What is the meaning of this comedy?"

"I brought the shavelings! They refused to carry the kettles!" reports Kapp.

"Shavelings, you say? Well then, if they didn't want to deliver the food kettles, take away their entire food ration and take them to the sick room."

"Yes, sir!"

"Further, keep them standing after roll call until the last buzzer," adds Zill.

"Yes, sir!"

We stand at attention, our heads uncovered. Behind us the assembly square is filling up. SS men come out of the guardhouse. Some heap words of abuse on us. Some kick us.

Finally it's six o'clock and roll call starts. We don't dare look behind us. That could mean death. There's no worse situation in the camp than to lay oneself open to the SS men.

They take our roll call by the gate.

Finally, the end. The blocks are marching back to the barracks, singing. The square becomes empty. The SS men disappear inside the guardhouse. The gate closes with a dull clang. The clock indicates 30 minutes past six. The last buzzer (the camp siren signal for rest) won't come before nine o'clock. Therefore, two and a half hours of standing in the growing cold await us. A freezing wind blows from the plantation. Our bodies, sweaty from the earlier sport and poorly covered, are becoming numb. Our shaved heads ache from the cold. A huge moon emerges from behind the poplars, flooding the square and camp with streams of silver light. From the crematorium chimney looming dark in the distance a flame shoots up into the deep blue sky. The barking of SS men's dogs comes from a kennel in the park next to the crematorium. (They use these dogs to guard us.) In the tower above the guardhouse, just over our heads, a young SS guard hums a song about love. The hands on the illuminated face of the tower clock move at a snail's pace.

We stand erect at attention, with arms along the seams of our trousers. Our fingers grow stiff in the cold; our emaciated bodies shake uncontrollably.

What a black day! First that unexpected encounter with Captain Zill, then an hour of hanging on the stake, then being chased by capo Groo, then the loss of pay, then those wretched kettles, and again a chase, then that sport, after that standing by the gate and having our meal taken away... If only that would end it. If only monster Buffalo doesn't come up with another harassment. We stand there, inwardly whispering prayers...

St. John of the Cross was locked up by fellow brothers in the monastery prison; they starved him and beat him until he bled... No one in the literature of Catholic mysticism has described the "night of the soul" more marvelously than he. How would St. John describe such nights if he were experiencing with us our days of torture?

"How good not to be a priest now!" those around us say.

It's truly difficult to be a priest in Nazi prison camps!

"No! I'm not asking, Lord, why all this must happen, because I understand why. But let us know, clearly and concretely, how you want us to improve and change our lives."

I recall the unforgettable figure of our teacher, the Rev. Prof. Żychliński. What a beautiful priestly soul! "Dearrrest ones," he would say, drawing out the letter *r*. "Critical times are coming which will demand a new generation of priests. Priests in accord with the Heart of the Master. Dearest ones! Are you ready for..."

Dear "Żych" foresaw these times. In foreseeing them he was preparing us for difficult experiences. Did he realize they would be so monstrous?

"I can't feel my feet anymore," someone nearby whispers.

"Try to move your toes at least," another quietly advises.

All is quiet. The freezing wind blows ever more strongly. The moon rises ever higher, and only the hands of the clock seem to have stopped in place.

Finally, at nine o'clock, the anticipated buzzer. The signal for rest.

"Right turn! Forward march!"

We move quietly across the assembly square, which is flooded with the silver glow of the moon. We walk in silence because after the last buzzer the camp must observe "silentium," a silence more than religious. We enter the camp street. Tall poplars cast their long striped shadows.

"Attention ... atteeention," a quiet whisper flies back from the front, "Kapp!"

We pull ourselves erect. We keep in step. In the shadow of the poplars, at the top of Block 2, stands ape-man Kapp.

"Get out of my sight fast! Run!"

We run. Our wooden shoes tap on the frozen ground... Somehow Buffalo leaves us in peace. We get undressed and quickly — without supper — throw ourselves down on our bunks.

"Fratres," a voice begins in the darkness. "Ore..."

"Father, could you leave them in peace today!" a voice interrupts. "Didn't they pray enough throughout the day? Didn't they follow the Way of the Cross enough? Didn't they freeze enough on that Golgotha by the guardhouse? Father, don't you have a heart?"

Hissing drowns him out. Nervous hissing. Comments: "Some sort of heretic! Pagan!"

"Oremus, fratres..."

I hear Zdzich sobbing, his head under the blanket.

Zdzich is crying?

―――

It's still dark night outside the windows when roaring can be heard near our block: "Hentschel command! Assembly!"

A moment later, Buffalo bursts into the bunkroom holding a board in his huge paw.

"Hentschel command! Assembly!" and he beats both the guilty and the innocent.

We run out, buttoning our uniforms on the way. The cold is biting. Snow crunches under our wooden clogs. In front of us stands capo Groo, fuming.

"Oh, you damned dogs! You ran off yesterday, leaving equipment and tools out all night. I'll fix you! I'm going to... Get ready and march!"

We march in quick time toward the delousing station. The SS guards, concerned about this early intrusion, are leaning out of the windowed tower. One of them points a machine gun in our direction, another casts the blinding beam of a spotlight.

"Hentschel command for work!" reports capo Groo from a distance.

"Weiter machen!" Permission is granted.

We're in an area near the delousing building. The moon has set. It's dark all around. Only from the walls and fences surrounding the camp, through the barbed wire and across the moat, a bit of light trickles from far away.

"Pick up the tools!" capo Groo orders.

We grope around, searching for the wheelbarrows, shovels, and pick-axes that we left yesterday when we went to get the money, thinking we'd pick them up when we returned. In the meantime, we know what happened then...

Groo is counting the equipment we bring in. Two pick-axes are missing. Stretched out in a long row, we move on our knees, feeling each foot of ground with our hands. We crawl like reptiles, one next to another...

"Let my lips begin to praise the Holy Virgin,
Begin to tell her marvelous honor."

"Hurry up, you dogs! The buzzer will soon sound for roll call!"

"Hasten to our aid, merciful Lady,
And defend us from all enemies..."

"I have it!" a joyful yell resounds. We don't ask what he "has." We know. He has finally found the last pick-axe.

"You were lucky!" capo Groo ends this expedition. "Assemble for roll call!"

An hour later, we're again at the delousing area. Since yesterday's miserly plate of watery soup for dinner, we've had nothing in our mouths. Supper was lost, breakfast was lost. To be sure, usually the only one eating breakfast is someone who, despite pangs of hunger, has managed to save until morning a few morsels of bread from the small piece he gets in the evening. That's an almost impossible thing. But it would be nice if you could drink even that coffee from acorns to warm up a bit...

"Get your tools, and go to work!" Groo orders.

The twelve "draught-horses" are going to their enormous roller. Several get pick-axes and shovels with an order to dig holes in the frozen ground for posts used in the fencing that is going to go up here. Capo Groo is rushing some of our men to get the concrete posts for this enclosure. We're hauling them to the delousing area. The entire place is already level and clear, since a rabbit pen is to be set up here.

As we return to the block at noon, we're barely dragging our feet. Pushing us, however, is the hope that a plate of warm watery soup is finally waiting for us.

What a terrible disappointment! The hall leader Ignac has taken away our tin plates. It seems they were dirty. As punishment, we *will not get* any dinner!

Again, the noon assembly... And again the heavy concrete posts... And again harassment from the well-fed and fat capo Groo... Oh, how slowly, how very slowly the sun rambles across the sky... We carry the posts over the moat. Beyond it are coiled barbed-wire fences, beyond them the fence with wires in which death waits... You only need to jump into the moat! The warning signs posted near it remind you that "anyone who crosses this line will be met with a round of shots from the guardhouse tower."

"Jump!" calls a voice of temptation. "So what's the use of this suffering? What's the sense in all of this?"

"Jesus!"

"There's no God!" I hear a jeering cry within. "All that is a delusion! Jump! Jump! End this suffering!"

"Little Saint Thérèse, save me!" consciousness desperately defends itself with all its might. "You know I've always been most anxious to fix my eyes on the path by which you walked toward Jesus. You know how rarely I seek the 'shower of miracles' that you promised to send upon the earth, but you see that now, that ... this may be the end of my strength!"

"Do you still believe?" the voice inside me seems surprised. "Ha, ha!" it chuckles. "Thérèse herself is a delusion, like everything else. Jump into the moat! Run onto the wires! That alone makes sense."

"What do you think?" The sudden question brings me out of my depression. "Will they give us supper today?"

"Shut your mouth!" yells Groo, threatening with a stick. "Work! All the posts must be in place by evening. If they're not, you'll come back to carry them after roll call!"

30. Allow Us to Work

And afterwards — we build the rabbit pen... When that work is almost completed, we begin repairing roads in the camp, which exposes us to the constant risk of being harassed by passing SS men, capos, and other taskmasters. These jobs in the fields are difficult and we're becoming increasingly weaker, and yet we would rather do them than remain in the block, where we risk harassment from SS men visiting the barracks, harassment from block personnel, recruitment by any old capo for all kinds of jobs...

"They'll finish you off with this hard work in the fields," our colleagues, the older priests, tell us when they see how we look as we return to the block.

"Well, maybe that would be better..."

31

The Second Freiland

Big, soft flakes of wet snow are falling on the thawing ground, on the diggers, on their emaciated backs and red hands swollen from the cold and barely able to grip the spades. Although there's no frost, only unpleasant dampness, we shiver constantly because our clothing is already soaking wet. Stretched out in long rows, we're digging the meadow to further extend the huge plantation, the so-called "Freiland zwei," which is to supplement the "first Freiland," as well as a parcel consisting of many greenhouses and cold frames that occupy a large area closer to the camp.

Several years ago, groups of communists and Jews had prepared the first Freiland. Now our turn has come, the Polish priests' turn. We are to leave behind us here an "historical monument," just like thousands of those who were killed on the marshes of the first Freiland.

During the early days of March, we are suddenly dismissed from the "Hentschel command," and all priests, without exception, are assigned to work only on the plantation. We had to leave the delousing station, where at least we had been protected by a wall and where, in case of heavy downpours, we had a chance to seek shelter under the eaves of a roof. But now what? Here we have an open field, far from camp, and as far as the eye can see, meadow and swamp, swamp and meadow, and that bluish ribbon of forest, and those clusters of dwarf willows, and that gray, tearful sky above us where spring winds chase rain and snow clouds.

A small group of priests has already been working on the plantation for weeks. They had jobs on the first Freiland, and some worked at greenhouses and cold frames where, in any case, it was easier to find shelter. But an order is an order: the shavelings must all work together, along with the Jews, and only on the second Freiland! Those other priests, therefore, were also pulled out.

There are about a thousand of us priests. There are also about a thousand Jews who work at digging the same meadow, but at a distance from us.

It's not an easy job to get a new piece of land under cultivation. For the first time since nature had formed a coating of peat covered with a thick tangle of roots on this abysmal swamp, a spade guided by human hands is to cut this coating into pieces, turn the layer of peat upside down, condemn the grass to decay, rake and till the soil, so that in one, two, or three months the grower's hands can sow the first seeds here.

It is truly hard labor. The roots of the grasses are so intertwined that you have to pull each chunk with effort to tear it off from the whole, turn it over, chop it up, and level it. A capo circulates behind us with a club and administers punishment for the smallest imperfection.

The main building on the plantation. Behind it were others, and around them were hundreds of acres of land. Bishop Kozal also worked here.

It is generally believed that concentration camps were created by Henrich Himmler, their future general commandant. Few know, however, that the real designer and creator of the first camps was Marshal Hermann Göring himself. It was in the evening of 27 February 1933 when flames shot out of the Reichstag building in Berlin. Hitler, Göring and the limping Goebbels stood on a balcony, plunged in the blood-red glow of the fire, which they had feloniously started themselves.[1] Raising his arms high, Hitler called out pompously: "From now on there will be no mercy! Anyone who stands in our way will fall dead! Every communist official, wherever he may be, will be shot by a firing squad! There will be no protection for any enemy."[2]

This took place two weeks prior to the March elections. The act was played out very well. The arrow of hate was superbly aimed. That very night thousands tramp into prisons![3] The chief opponents are eliminated from play. Hitler has an open road to victory. The German people did not know of this satanic sham. They were lured by the criminals' cunning schemes.

Since the prisons could not hold thousands of opponents, who had to be put out of action at any cost prior to the elections, it was the trusted Hermann Göring who came up with the idea of creating the first concentration camps.

"We will lock up the communists in concentration camps to teach them about work. Human animals who will not allow themselves to be trained must be neutralized forever."[4]

From the direction of the forest comes a victim's cry; it makes your blood run cold. Bloody capo Knoll is murdering another Jew. This is the second one since the start of work today! How many will he murder by evening? ... Yet capo Knoll is one of the German communists who were sent to Dachau immediately after the Reichstag burning. He is one of the thousands of political opponents neutralized by Hitler. "Knoll!" you want to scream, "Good Lord, man, don't you see that..."

"There's as much ideological communist in Knoll as there is God's servant in a church sexton who steals offerings of the faithful from the poor-box," says Zdzich. "You see, there are communists and "communists." Take, for example, Wagner and others like him, and then take Knoll, Willi, Zier, Kapp, Szaferski, our Cretin and others. These are not communists. These are bandits taking advantage of the ideological mantle of communism. You can cover a beast with a banner full of honorary insignia, but by doing so, you will not change it into a human being. A beast will always remain a beast!"

It turns out that in 1933 on these same swamps surrounding Dachau, they murdered communists who were turning the bogs into plantations, and today the communists are murdering us here.

"Do you associate these events of 1933, Hitler's bloody rise to power, with the fact that precisely at that time the Mother of God appeared in Belgium as the Lady with a Golden Heart, first in the town of Beauraing, and later in Banneux?"

"It's strange."

"You're right, it is strange, isn't it? In Berlin, the Reichstag is burning, set on fire by the Nazis, raising a blood-red glow over Europe, like the omen of an upcoming cataclysm; at the same time in little Belgium, on the border of bloody Hitler's future 'world power,' and also in the dark of night, Heaven's Envoy comes down time and time again to assure humanity that in the end She will convert all sinners! She will achieve victory."[5]

"Hey! You dog! Can you stop yapping?" the menacing voice of the capo reaches us through the foul weather.

We interrupt our conversation. We tear the sod with spades. The increasing cold chills us to the bone. Snow mixed with rain keeps falling and falling. The wet peat sticks to our wooden clogs.

"Dig! Dig, you Roman dogs!" So we dig, spread out in long rows.

It's the fourth Sunday of Lent, 23 March 1941. From a distance, beyond the forest, you can hear the sound of a village church bell. Of course. This is, after all, Catholic Bavaria. People are hurrying to go to holy Mass.

"*Introibo ad altare Dei*" Zdzich suddenly whispers.

"*Ad Deum, qui laetificat juventutem meam*," I answer with the words of the altar-boy.

"*Judica me, Deus*... And distinguish my cause from the nation that is not holy; deliver me from the unjust and deceitful man," Zdzich continues in a whisper, laying aside, one after another, chunks of peat torn off the sod.

"*Quia tu es, Deus*... For Thou, O God, art my strength: why hast Thou cast me off? And why do I go sorrowful whilst the enemy afflicts me?"

In a whisper, we recite all the Prayers at the Foot of the Altar ... and the Confiteor. After that: "*Aufer a nobis*... Take away from us our iniquities, O Lord..." Then alternately the "*Kyrie*... Lord, have mercy on us! ..."

The snow stings, driven by gusts of a cold northern wind, and it dances in swirling funnels, pelts our eyes in billows, strikes our backs, hands, and faces, which are growing numb. The capo who's overseeing us has covered his head with a sack and stands turned with his back to us, so he can't hear us through the howling of the storm.

"Today's Gospel reading talks about how Jesus miraculously multiplies loaves of bread, how he feeds the hungry crowd of thousands, how he announces through this miracle the institution of the Most Holy Eucharist," Zdzich continues. "Since we can't be at the Table of Love to unite ourselves with our Master, let's awaken an ardent desire to receive Him spiritually."

Silence falls... We continue to dig in the cold, but in our thoughts and hearts something is thawing. Jesus is with us! Just as when, looking at the hungry crowd and filled with sincere human compassion, He called out, "I feel pity for the people!" so today, too, He's looking at a thousand of his priests who are digging a meadow on Sunday morning... Yes, Jesus is with us!

Not far from us, one of the young Protestant ministers is digging. I observe him out of the corner of my eye.

"You know," he tells me later when I steer the conversation to this very subject, "perhaps it's precisely here, in the camp, that we see and understand even more who unites us: Jesus!" Then, after a short silence, he adds: "But now you should understand even better what a blessing your priestly celibacy is."

"Oh?" I look at him with surprise.

"Do you realize what I'm going through, thinking constantly about my wife and three small children?"

There is so much pain in Alfred's blue eyes... Yes, of course I understand him.

The plantations, those famous Dachau plantations, are an SS enterprise, planned on an enormous scale. Do I know how many acres they encompass? Maybe a thousand? Maybe more? They stretch from the eastern wall of the camp as far as the eye can see. Located closer to the camp, on the first Freiland, are the administration buildings, offices, experimental stations, factories, various workshops, drying houses for herbs and warehouses for them, a grinding mill, greenhouses, cold frames, storage for equipment and tools, and all of this stretches along attractive concrete streets, lined in the summer with strips of lawn and flower beds. It's like a small town unto itself. Working here throughout the summer season are over two thousand prisoners of various qualifications, starting with learned biologists (conducting experiments), chemists, engineers, painters (who do illustrations of plantation plant specimens), artisans of various trades, trained gardeners, and ending with the gray mass of farm or agricultural workers. This is a plantation with rare medicinal herbs, probably the largest not only in Germany but all of Europe, and maybe even the largest in the world. The particular varieties of herbs, planted at an assigned time, "fed" with special chemically processed fertilizers, individually cultivated according to special "recipes," are also harvested at a special time, some dried in the sun, others in the shade, and still others in drying houses, depending on the requirements of each variety.

It would be possible to write a whole brochure about the further chemical processing of particular herbs. An entire staff of specialists works in that department.

Under normal circumstances, work on such a plantation would be enjoyable, but not in Dachau, where it was recognized by the SS as a tested "grinding mill" for despised ideological enemies. At the camp in Dachau there were various work departments, but none swallowed up as many victims as that very plantation! While the group of specialists there was getting along splendidly, and the group of professional gardeners working in greenhouses and cold frames was not doing badly, those hundreds of acres of soil, the famous first and second Freilands, were a real deathtrap for average prisoners, whose only recognized value was their physical strength. There are no horses or tractors on the plantation. All work, even the heaviest, falls here to a human being staggering from hunger. This also includes pulling plows, harrows, seeders, rollers, and other farm machinery. Pulling these things in boggy soil quickly finishes off even the strongest. There still remains, moreover, bringing in manure, carrying heavy metal pails of soil to lower levels, digging, raking, putting in drain-pipes, and other exhausting agricultural jobs.

The greatest bullies and murderers are always assigned to the plantation as capos. There are two noted for their cruelty: Rogler and Rasch. Enormously tall fellows, about fifty years old, both sullen and repulsive, they are a terror for the workers. Under their command are a few "well-chosen" helpers. Of course, there are also several decent deputy capos. They are ours, Silesians, but in 1941 when nothing in Dachau was yet restraining "the devil let loose from his chain," they could do little to help. (Later, when camp conditions improve, many priests will be grateful to these dear Silesians for saving their lives and rescuing them from death, but in March 1941 death constantly stalks them as well.)

Literally a monster in human flesh, that's the infamous capo Knoll, who "takes care of" the poor Jews. He himself admits he has murdered eighty-eight of them up to now but intends soon to reach an even hundred![6] (I don't know how many of these poor souls he had on his conscience when — sentenced by an American court after our liberation — he was hanged on the gallows. Unfortunately, I believe it was a lot more than a hundred!)

Listen, again just now you can hear the dreadful cry of some tortured Jew coming from the forest area.

"Oh, that murderer Knoll!"

The criminal often organizes a game for himself by tearing the cap off a Jew's head as he works, throwing it beyond the guard line, and then giving him the order to go and fetch it. If the Jew does not carry out the order, Knoll will torture him to death for "insubordination." If the poor fellow runs for his cap, the SS man will shoot him to death for crossing the guard line. In either case, death awaits him. It's horrible. Monstrous!

Sometimes we meet for a moment with the Jews as we turn in our work tools.

"Well, Reverend," says a Jew from Żyrardów or Łódź or some other city. "What will become of us? They will murder us! Reverend, do you have a piece of bread?"

His eyes, crusted with pus, are so imploring!

Bread? Good Lord! We ourselves eat everything we can find as we dig the meadow so early in the season: small roots, earth-worms, some kind of white worms...

As long as we worked on "Hentschel's command," we received — like all workers — an additional slice of bread, but when they brought us to the plantation, they took that away, too. We're hungry. Constantly hungry! We and the Jews. The two most hated kinds of people!

"You stuffed yourselves with all kinds of goodies when you were free; now starve!" the capos jeer. "The poor people were dying of hunger while you could afford anything. Now it's your turn!"

"Don't tell me these jeers don't have an element of truth!" Zdzich snaps through clenched teeth. There's so much provocation in his clear blue eyes that I prefer not to pick up the gauntlet.

"Well?" Zdzich is waiting.

I'm silent. There's a marvelous priestly soul in the man, but … it's somewhat inflexible.

"Inflexible?" my colleagues are shocked. "He's an extreme radical!"

"Attention!" comes the warning. "Doggie behind you!"

A young SS man, whose first or last name we don't know, who always walks with a huge German shepherd, which is why we call him "Doggie," is our terror at this time.

He's coming toward us from the forest. The Jews will rest a bit now. It's our turn! Our hearts start to pound; our spades plunge deeper into the sod.

Doggie is almost here. Young, athletic, tall, and terribly handsome. See, he's already managed to kick someone. The poor priest falls, face down into the peatbog. The powerful German shepherd is already sitting on his bony back, tearing at his collar with its teeth. The SS man laughs, satisfied. It's a wonderful chance to train his beloved dog.

Backs bend over the sod! Spades swing briskly. Just so he doesn't notice something! Just not to get into trouble!

Lucky for us, but unlucky for our colleagues on the right flank, Doggie walks toward them. He takes aside several at the end of the row. They're already taking off their uniforms. A search! … They stand naked in this cold. Doggie inspects their clothing… And the snow mixed with rain falls on their naked bodies.

Edek Palewodziński was unlucky. It seems a pinch of tobacco dust was found in his pocket.

"An hour on the stake!"

Doggie shuffles to the next group. Our capo is running a step behind him. We can now relax a bit at work, but we have to move: first, because he could notice, and second, because it's snowing, it's wet, it's cold and we need to warm ourselves…

"In the name of the Father, and of the Son, and of the Holy Spirit!" someone begins. "In the first Joyful Mystery we meditate on how the Archangel Gabriel announced to the Virgin Mary…"

"Holy Mary, Mother of God, pray for us sinners…" the whisper of many voices breaks through the storm. After the Rosary, a litany… After the litany, Lenten Lamentations…

"Quiet! Doggie's coming back!"

But when he reaches the road, he turns toward the plantation buildings. However, our capo does come back.

"Clean the tools!"

We squat over the tools. We clean with whatever we have so they'll shine like silver; otherwise we get a beating when they're turned in. After that, soaked to the skin, muddy, our teeth chattering from the cold, we drag ourselves along the muddy, slippery road to the tool storage. It's quieter and warmer on the street, between buildings.

Standing in long rows with uncovered heads, we turn in the spades. This is what the regulation says. Even so, there are kicks and jabs. They will always find something.

Finally we form into groups of a hundred. Many hundreds, since our number includes both us, the Jews, and workers from the first Freiland. Fellow prisoners—professionals, office and administration workers—are looking at us through the windows of their warm quarters. Why should they go out earlier, before that "black mass" falls into line? The old plantation hands know local customs. The SS men overlook this practice. It's enough if they run outside at the last minute. They'll make it on time.

"Aristocracy!" one of our people whispers with a scoff.

"You used to gaze out like that from the window of your warm rectory on the human…" Zdzich starts to respond, but doesn't have time to finish his sentence.

"Hold me because I'm going to slug him!" rages the one who was provoked.

"Fathers! Fathers!" someone else calms them. "Is this proper now, in these circumstances? ..."

"Attention!" comes thundering from the front. "Everyone in step, forward march!"

We try to keep in step while marching. When we were summoned to work on the plantation, they gave us specially shod shoes that fit like ordinary shoes, but instead of having a leather sole, they have a board plated with metal.

It is, perhaps, 1500 meters to the camp gate. Our shoes clatter on the stone pavement; wheelbarrows follow the last group of a hundred men, carrying those who today have already passed on forever, but who still must be present with us, the living, at their last roll call here.

Inside the plantation gate, which is located across from the main gate (see diagram), a group of SS men is waiting for us.

A search?

Fortunately not! They're only bringing poor Jews to the front of the guardhouse. They'll stand hungry, without supper, until the last buzzer sounds at nine o'clock, and they'll go to sleep, so that tomorrow...

We ourselves stand in our usual place before roll call. We wait. It's beginning to snow more heavily. The north wind blows harder.

"Maybe someone has escaped?"

"No. We're waiting for the butchers' unit."

Finally they arrive. Roll call is almost finished.

"March to your blocks in units!"

We sigh with relief.

We, too, are already marching. We turn off the square into the camp street. Under the eaves of his block stands Kapp with legs astride.

"*Ein Lied*!"

"Wir lagen vor Madagaskar," we sing on command. Our numb feet are trying to keep time.

Suddenly Kapp yells something. What? And who could hear it during the singing? That one moment was enough: the ranks begin to collapse, our step becomes uneven! Buffalo, trying to salvage the situation, gives us the step, but it's altogether wrong. This creates total confusion in the unit.

"Right turn! Shavelings will remain on the square!"

Punitive exercises last until dark. People are falling! Well, is it any wonder? At the same time, the hall leaders vent their fury on us because we've spoiled their Sunday evening.

Standing in front of the guardhouse gate are the units of poor, hungry Jews. Lying in the wheelbarrows are the corpses of those who've been murdered. A game is being played on the vast assembly square: they're chasing Polish priests, chasing them till the sweat runs freely. In the rain, in the snow, in the mud.

Finally, an end. We're leaving the square. The Jews drag along behind us. The New and the Old Testament! Two chosen people. In Nazi concentration camps, both are the most hated and most tortured.

A "sermon" from Buffalo still awaits us in front of the barracks. We learn for the thousandth time that we are not only an accursed band of Polish scum, but also Roman sloths and overeaters and exploiters, that we have stopped being human beings and have become the ultimate cretins, that he, the block master, will give it to us, that from now on after every evening roll call, there will be penalty exercises, and now, in conclusion, since today

A punishment often applied in Dachau was "hanging on the stake." The most lenient term was hanging for one hour. Hundreds of Polish priests were subjected to this torture. On one Good Friday over 200 were hanged on the stake. Wrists were chained so that blood could flow only partially to the hands. After an hour of such hanging, a prisoner could not use his hands for several days, and he often lost either an entire hand or his fingers due to gangrene that developed (drawing by the author).

is officially haircut day: "You will not get supper until you get that wool off your stupid blockheads! And before you go to bed, I will personally examine your clothes and feet!"

It's easy to imagine what happens next! For two halls there is one shared washroom with several faucets, and there are in all (from both halls) about three hundred of us. Woe to us if we bring mud into the washroom! And where can you get rid of it? The hall leader stands at the entrance with a stick in his paw! ... Woe to anyone with muddy socks who leaves tracks on the shiny floor! The wooden clogs must be sparkling clean! Only then do they have the right to be placed on a special rack.

We're finally in the hall. In front of the barber stands a long line that winds along the cupboards. There is one set of hand clippers for a hundred and fifty of us! Our wet clothing is drying on our backs. And if it doesn't dry? Then what? We'll be shivering again tomorrow morning.

"Lice inspection!" screams the hall leader.

We have to strip naked and stand there holding our underwear. Here's the line to the barber! There's the line for lice inspection! Ignac throws some of us out into the street for having dirty socks; others he pummels for having muddy clogs!

Only now, as we stand naked for lice inspection, can you see the full monstrosity of our physical emaciation. These are skeletons covered with withered, ulcerated skin! Boils, carbuncles, festering sores, impetigo, eczema! In a word, human misery the likes of which you'll never see anywhere...

The barber cuts and cuts. A long row of skeletons passes in front of those inspecting for lice... Stragglers return from the street and washroom, solemnly carrying their washed clogs... An old alarm clock calmly ticks on top of the hall leader's table...

Finally, Ignac orders:

"Get the tea!"

Once again we stand in a row, with a tin cup in one hand and a small piece of hard bread in the other.

A ladle dips rhythmically in the leafy brew that is called "tea."

One ... two ... three ... and next ... and next. Order must be observed. And may God help him who let's a drop fall on the shiny floor! The floor in Dachau is a sacred thing. It's an altar at which one "celebrates" every morning on one's knees, bringing it to a magnificent shine. This has claimed many victims. People are killed for staining the floor, for carelessly soiling it or dulling its shiny brilliance. This is not a literary exaggeration or figure of speech. Hundreds of my fellow priests will attest to this.

"One ... two ... three ... next! ... next! ... As he pours the brew into our tin cups, Ignac watches to see whether by chance anyone spills a drop from his cup...

Suddenly, the doors open and Buffalo runs in with a stick.

"What?! So you damned dogs are still not in your bunks? And maybe I'll have to put up with reprimands for you? That won't happen! Now! ... "

Judgment day in the hall! Confusion! A hundred fifty people run to the cupboards, crowding together, overturning and spilling the brew upon Ignac's "sacred" floor.

An animal roar bursts out of Ignac's throat! Buffalo pummels with his club at one end of the hall, Ignac with the ladle at the other, hitting out at random. On shaved heads, on bony backs, on limbs that stick out...

"Jesus!"

"I'll give you Jesssus!" roars Buffalo, beating more fanatically. "I'll give you Jesssus!" Blood spurts... The victim moans.

31. The Second Freiland

You can't moan! Buffalo doesn't like it. He very much doesn't like it. Most often he "silences" the person moaning with a single blow ... forever.

A minute later the hall is empty, but it looks like a battle scene. Tables are overturned! Tin cups and priceless little pieces of bread, the coveted daily bread, are trampled, scattered on the floor, drenched with brew, crushed, marred... God! Never mind that last morsel of bread, but what awaits us tomorrow morning for this floor?

And Ignac in the meantime not only curses but picks up the tin cups that were dropped and puts them into the cupboard. As punishment, their owners won't get any morning coffee or dinner tomorrow. He picks up lost pieces of bread, and look! Look, he throws *bread* into the stove!

"Let these dogs rot!" he mumbles.

Then he calls out from the bunkroom door:

"Block service!"

Several men jump off the bunks. They run toward the hall door at break-neck speed. Ignac is not to be trifled with.

The cleaning begins. Ignac spreads out on his bed. He's feeling tired. Suddenly, steps are heard in the vestibule, and in one leap he's already on his feet, prepared to report. Instead of the SS man he expected, however, the block secretary comes in.

"Are the letters ready?" he asks from the door.

(Once every two weeks we're allowed to write a short letter to our family on a form provided by the secretary. If a prisoner doesn't take advantage of this at the given time, he

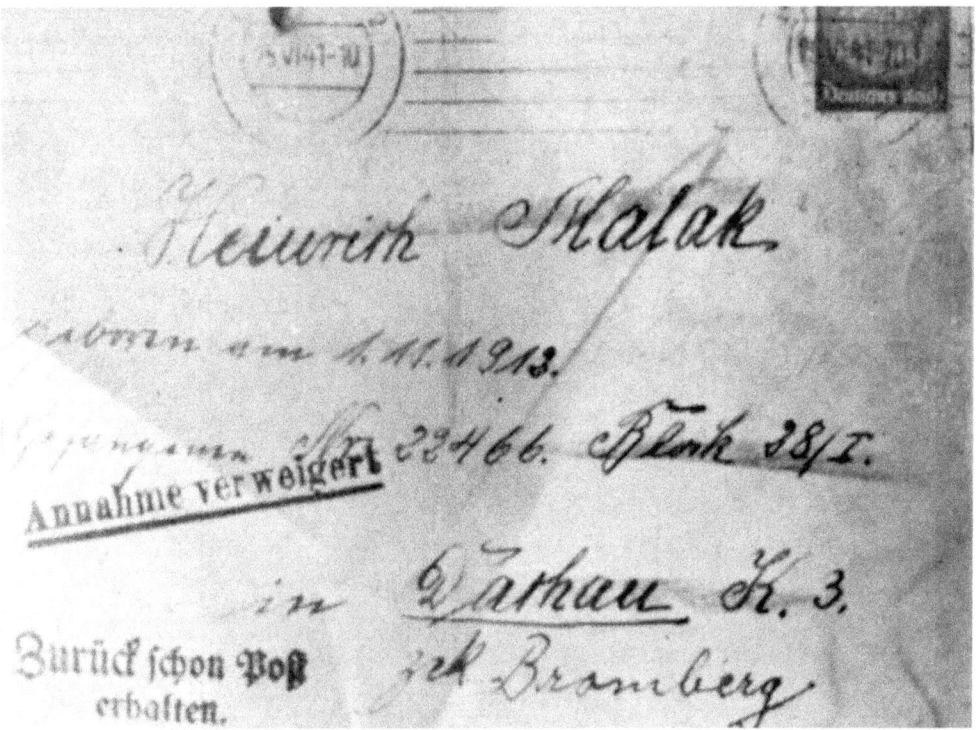

After this "unsuitable letter" arrived in Dachau from Bydgoszcz, it was returned with stamped notifications: *Annahme verweigert* (Acceptance refused)! ... *Zurück, schon Post erhalten* (Returned, since mail has already been received.) Meanwhile, the prisoner waits months for it with longing and worry.

has to wait another two weeks for another chance. Our Sunday for writing letters was just today. And when did we have time for it?)

"Are the letters ready?" the secretary repeats from the door.

"Ready?" Ignac purses his lips. "Did these dogs write? They're lazy cattle!"

"Well," murmurs the secretary. "It will be two weeks before they can write again. Good night, Ignac!"

The door shuts behind him, but at that moment it opens again. Buffalo enters once more.

"Did they wash their feet?"

Ignac is already opening the door to the bunkroom.

"It stinks like a barn!" states Buffalo. "Open all the windows wide! Feet inspection!"

And again the same story... Buffalo goes from bunk to bunk checking, and every now and then another skinny fellow rushes in a scanty shirt to the washroom...

"Block leader! Block leader!" a cry is suddenly heard.

A messenger from the office runs in.

"A transport has arrived! We need forty hands to fill out forms. The camp commandant is waiting."

"The commandant?" Buffalo clicks his heels. "The commandant himself!" He turns suddenly toward the bunks: "Forty record keepers!"

Thus passes the fourth Sunday of Lent, in the priests' Block 28, camp Dachau, in the year 1941. Previous days and the days following were like these — occasionally a little calmer, more often just the same, and not infrequently much worse.

"*Ja, meine Herren.* Yes, gentlemen! *This is* Dachau!"

"We know..."

32

"Joyful Privileges"

We finish digging the meadow. In front of us here lie dozens of acres of tilled peat soil. The Jews near the forest still have quite a patch to complete. How many of them are yet to die there before they finish? Besides, is there any limit to their suffering? Once the tortures associated with digging end, other places of torment will be found for them. In any case, bloody capo Knoll will be with them everywhere!

We're lucky. Our capo bully has become ill. Replacing him is a deputy capo, the Silesian Jaroszka, a good man. It's true that he stands in front of us with a stick, but that stick, a sign of "authority" in Dachau, is only a symbol in his hands. He stands there with a smile on his swarthy face and tells us in his dialect:

"So, you devils, look the part so that something doesn't happen to you! Work with your eyes. But when some devil saunters by, then move like the dickens, quickly, so you won't get noticed and me, too."

Leaning on the stick, he keeps talking like this, but he's looking around carefully.

"Don't work too hard, guys. Not a single devil here."

We dig to keep warm, however.

"And have you heard the latest rumor?"

We prick up our ears.

"You haven't heard, so listen. It's being said that beginning next Monday, you won't be working on the plantation.

"We're not going to work here?"

"Right. That's what I heard."

"And what will we be doing, Jaroszka?"

"So, devil, you're going to worry about what you'll be doing? They'll think of something." Suddenly he says loudly: "Move it, guys! Mooove! Kulas is coming!"

Kulas is the SS "Komandoführer," the supervisor of workers on the plantation. Jaroszka, waving his stick and yelling loudly, is already moving along the ranks of diggers.

"Get going, you devils! Move it! The old man's behind us!"

But Kulas moves on without even looking at us.

"There's some truth in what Jaroszka says," someone breaks the silence. "Such rumors have been going around the camp for several days."

Indeed. The news has filtered out from the storehouse that apparently two crates of breviaries have arrived.

"Breviaries? Here? To Dachau? Amazing!"

The painters hint about painting a chapel, the cooks about better food, and now Jaroszka...

"Hey! Keep moving, you devils! Move! I think Kulas is coming back."

Part of the main camp street, called the Lagerstrasse. The barracks of the Polish priests are indicated with arrows (beyond the trees at left). The photograph was taken in 1948, when camp Dachau was turned into a village for German refugees.

Just like Dachau! Everything is possible. Returning from the plantation one day, muddy and tired, we find in front of Blocks 26, 28, and 30 fellow prisoners from the carpentry unit, who are installing a tall wire fence that separates our clergy barracks and Block 26 from the camp street.

"What are you up to?"

"We're building you a *rectory*!"

"*Isolation* awaits us," whisper colleagues whom we find in the block.

"*Isolation?*"

It seems they're granting us privileges of some kind.

Each barracks consists of four separate "halls." Each has a room proper, with tables, stools and cupboards, plus a sleeping room with bunks. The room located closest to the main camp street is number one, the next is number two, then there's three, and the one located the farthest from the street, at the end of the block, is number four.

This system is in effect in all blocks, both those that are on the left as well as the right side of the street, whether in blocks that house the workers, in quarantine, or even the camp hospital. (See the diagram of camp barracks in Dachau.)

The first room of Block 26, which up to now has served as a kind of storage area for straw mattresses, beds, and other odds and ends, is being configured into one big room by removing an internal wall that up to now had separated the room proper from the bunkroom. The carpenters are building a podium and an altar, the painters are painting

32. "Joyful Privileges"

A view of barracks 28. For a very long time this was "home" for the group of 2,000 Polish priests. Here, in room no. 1, lived the Reverend Bishop Michał Kozal. Beyond the barracks, in the background, behind the fence, moat, coiled barbed wire and canal, runs the Death Road leading to the crematorium. That is why we were usually witnesses to "events" happening on that road.

the walls and covering over the windows with paint... The chapel in camp Dachau is becoming a reality.

On the Feast of the Annunciation, 25 March 1941, Fr. Paweł Prabucki, the same one who alone had the right to celebrate Mass in Sachsenhausen, celebrates the first Mass.

"See? We always fear each feast day of the Mother of God, and here you have a present from Her! The first Mass in Dachau is right on Her feast day!"

"Maybe it's a "downpayment" on Her part for..."

"For more painful experiences?"

"Well, yes."

"Hmm ... Maybe ... maybe ... "

We keep on going to work. We get up an hour earlier than the rest of our fellow prisoners, run to get the kettles, and then — perspiring and out of breath — run to holy Mass, and after that we go quickly to morning roll call and ... to work.

"If it continues this way, they'll finish us off with this routine in no time!"

"That's true."

There is increasingly open talk, however, that we are to stop working.

On 4 April, the feast of Our Lady of Sorrows, as we return from the plantation, muddy up to our waists, they tell us that tomorrow we're not going to work, that from now on we are to remain in isolation, that all contact with fellow prisoners in other blocks is strictly prohibited, that all violations of the prohibition will be severely punished, that we are getting breviaries, that we will receive better food...

That is how the famous period of clergy "privileges" began in Dachau; they were to become for us the cause of much new harassment and suffering, driving between the priests in Dachau and the groups of lay prisoners a real wedge of ill will, which went as far as jealousy and sometimes even quiet hate.

Our daily program now looks like this: we continue to get up an hour earlier than the other prisoners, we run to the kitchen for the kettles and carry them to the whole camp, then we go quickly to holy Mass and afterwards to the square for morning roll call. Following roll call, we don't go to work anymore as does the rest of the camp, but return in tight formations to our isolation and devote ourselves to "block" jobs. These consist of continually making bunks "perfectly," polishing aluminum utensils until they glisten like mirrors, keeping floors shining, cleaning the washroom and toilets, and maintaining the block streets. Our supervisors, moreover, "don't have the heart" to refuse us also the "enjoyment" (?!?) of *sport* in the narrow streets between blocks of the "rectory."

At 11 o'clock, our "friend" Willi rushes us to pick up kettles for the entire camp, and since he now has in front of him "the privileged," there is occasion for even more heartfelt contempt:

"Hurry it up! Hurry, you privileged dogs! All day long you do nothing, so at least carry the kettles for your colleagues who are hard at work instead of you and for you."

"Hey! Shavelings!" prisoners greet us in blocks where we haul the heavy loads: "How's the food at the rectory?"

"Have a good dinner!" they add.

"Will something drop down for us from your plentiful table?"

"Hey! Priests of Jesus! Is the wine tasty?"

"Loafers!"

"Camp parasites!"

"Shavelings!"

"Will you be getting housekeepers in the blocks soon?"

"Ha, ha, ha, ha!"

"You know, if the Vatican had realized how much distress it would cause by obtaining 'privileges' for its priests, it wouldn't have sought them at all."

"You're right."

"You see," Zdzich continues the thought, "if it is the will of God, which it certainly is, that we should suffer, then all human intervention seeking to soften this sentence of God is in vain. Every attempt at this can only increase the suffering. It's the same for us as for a soul whom God, in his goodness, is leading closer to Himself through spiritual cleansing. Whoever wants to bring the soul relief through human means only increases its suffering since, if he were to succeed in providing this relief, he would be running counter to God's plan for that soul. The same is happening with us. God wants to cleanse us. The Pope wants to bring us relief through human means. For months there have been efforts and interventions, and diplomatic negotiations with the Nazi government have taken place, and finally they have succeeded in getting 'privileges' for the group of priests. They didn't realize, however, that this would contribute to greater torment for us."

And that's how it is in reality with our "privileges." They free us from official forced labor, but don't free us from the "joyful" distribution of kettles to several thousand prisoners, a job prisoners consider to be one of the hardest in camp. And our "friend" Willi knows how to make this sixfold chase to the kitchen for kettles and back with empty kettles suitably "*enjoyable*" for us.

Ostensibly the privileges release us from forced labor, but who at the Vatican can complain that, having been released from work, priests are cleaning their own blocks and utensils, making bunks, and *engaging in sport* for health! But it is precisely these innocent-sounding assignments that cause distress, so that, while carrying them out, the prisoner is yearning to do heavy "regular" work.

We're supposed to get better food! This was stipulated in diplomatic agreements with the Nazi government in Berlin. And ... the agreements were satisfied, but only on paper. In practice it works like this: when the entire camp has white cabbage with water for dinner, we — for a change — get cabbage that's red. When the camp has red cabbage, we get the white. Water as a "seasoning" is always the same. And if the Vatican delegate were personally to visit the camp kitchen, he would have to write in his report that, in fact, priests are "favored," receiving "better" food than the rest of the camp since the kettle in which our meals are cooked contains different food.

"Better nourishment!" That certainly must have meant adding fat or maybe meat, but even if a cardinal were to stand in the kitchen during the daily preparation of meals, he wouldn't be able to discern how this directive was being carried out in practice. It was not difficult for kitchen personnel, old camp stagers and sly foxes, to fool any such inspection.

The best way to understand how our "better nourishment" turned out can be shown by the following fact. Our block personnel, which consisted of lay prisoners — that is, the block leader and four hall leaders, the barber, the secretary, and the canteen manager, the whole bunch — were happy they would benefit by eating better food from our kettles. After taking a look at what this improvement in food amounts to, they raise an uproar:

"Give us normal food, the kind all the other prisoners have! We're not privileged clergy! Why are we punished by having to eat what they're eating?!"

The kitchen management acknowledges the complete validity of this request. Of course. How did block and hall leaders and the rest of the personnel in Blocks 26, 28, and 30 merit the clergyman's "better nourishment" as "a punishment"?

From now on — together with our kettles — we bring kettles with a big sign marked in chalk: "For the personnel of Blocks 26, 28, and 30."

"Finally, *decent* food," murmurs the hall leader, sitting down to his mess-tin with dinner for the "non-privileged."

"Get your dinner!" he yells. "Oh *privileged* one!" he adds with a sneer and a mean smile.

The camp canteen, the "wonderful canteen" shown to committees visiting the camp, which includes various "delicacies" on its lists of articles, although greatly misrepresented, nevertheless sometimes gives us a chance to buy slightly spoiled fruit — which no one on the outside wants to buy, but which the prisoner eats, licking his fingers — or some pickles, beets, snails, or bread that's becoming moldy: this canteen is now closed to us. The privileged clergy already have plenty of food!

Oh, how we long for normal treatment, for normal camp food! But what can you do if you've been sentenced to "privileges"?

We still don't know whose idea it was, while negotiating with the Nazi government about improving the living conditions of priests in concentration camps, to include wine among the other privileges. Some day, perhaps, when the documents of those negotiations are revealed, that point will be clarified. But just having it included in the privileges indicates how misinformed those people were who attempted to improve our lives. It smacks of scoffing! Dying of hunger, eating earthworms, grass, and insects caught on the plantation, ready to run up to any trash heap to appease our terrible hunger even with rotting leftovers, we receive for those hungry stomachs — wine! Every other day they deliver bottles of it to our blocks, open them up in the presence of an SS man, pour the wine into tins and order us to drink! Afterward, to comply with inspection, we raise the empty tins turned upside down above our heads, so the supervising SS man can state that everyone drank and no one had any left.

What bitter irony! Each of us would have given a tin of the finest burgundy for one rotting potato! But, then, those who requested the privileges were thinking about *wine* and forgetting about potatoes, not to mention the small piece of daily bread. This was painful and humorous at the same time.

"Here's proof," grumbles Zdzich, "of the ideas that people out in the world have regarding our living conditions. We're rotting to death, but we rot with a breviary in one mangy paw and a cup of wine in the other."

"Zdzich!"

"Well? Maybe you'll say it's not so? That you're in rags, that you're walking around barefooted without socks, that you don't have a shirt: all that wasn't on the mind of those requesting the privileges! Take a look! Isn't this a parody? Look at that skeleton. The rags on him are like those on the worst beggar! Barefoot. Skinny like a ghost brought back from the dead, but ... with a gilt-edged breviary and a tin from which rises, as from a censer at a catafalque, the fragrance of wine that has just been drunk. We know how to pray splendidly, even without breviaries. To say the Rosary we need only our fingers, swollen from hunger and from carrying heavy kettles. Diplomacy has obtained for us breviaries and wine..."

"Zdzich! For God's sake! You're starting to blaspheme!"

"I don't care! It's always been like this, that all human diplomacy wreaks its vengeance on..."

I put my hand over his mouth. I'm appalled.

"Forgive me," he says after a while in a choking voice, rubbing his emaciated hand over his pale forehead. "It's hunger depriving me of reason. Hunger and that suffering, the suffering from looking every day at the dying, at those twisted skeletons, whom the SS man addresses derisively: 'To your health!'"

And how much acrimony there is over this stupid bit of wine, which "privileges" have brought to priests dying of hunger! How much venom, how much resentment, how many blows and ill-treatment! The camp is filled with malicious talk on this subject.

"Why are you so surprised?" one prisoner tells another sarcastically, but in a way that we, who are carrying the kettles, can hear. "Why are you surprised? Their entire life was spent in taking sips, so it's not surprising that when privileges were sought for them, one of the most important was again wine!"

"And our pastor," says another loudly, again so we can hear him clearly, "when he tugged at the bottle, sir, then oh brother..."

We put down the kettles as quickly as possible and escape so we won't hear, so these bitterly spoken words won't cause pain.

The wretched wine is often a topic of discussion, especially among the younger generation of priests.

"The more I think about it," says one, "the more I'm convinced that by giving us this wine, the Nazis have played an excellent trick. There's no way they could arouse more jealousy and hatred toward us than by these damned bottles."

"And what if it's not the Nazis giving them but those who sought to alleviate our fate?"

"I doubt it. That would indicate they don't have the slightest idea of our tragedy."

In general, the older prisoners, that is, those with more years spent in Dachau, such as butchers, bakers, block personnel, hospital personnel, cooks, capos, and many others who have their "connections," are not badly fed. What do they lack? Just something special. Among these special things, many of them feel a craving for alcohol. However, they haven't seen any for years, and if they do get some somewhere surreptitiously, then it's a very small amount, and they're risking great punishment. But here — the hated priests get alcohol regularly, openly, and what's worse, under such supervision that not a drop falls to others.

Is this not a cause for resentment, envy, even hatred?

A certain advantage of the wretched privileges is an afternoon nap. To be sure, it compensates for that hour of earlier rising, but ... even that nap is once again truly Dachau-style!

How many of those who have written their memoirs from camps emphasize the hardship connected with the so-called "making of a bunk"! It had to be made with such precision, and the straw, which was reduced to chaff, had to be so fluffed up that the straw mattress became level like a billiard table; all edges had to be tightened until they had the proverbial "sharpness of a knife." In a word, in all aptness they describe how, once he has made such a fine "altar," the prisoner would have preferred lying down on the bare floor and spending the night there than once again, the next day, having to relive the "making of the bunk," having again to tremble lest the SS man or block leader find some kind of flaw in it and assign an hour of hanging on the stake.

Along with the torment of making our bunks in the morning, the privileges added the torment of making them again in the afternoon. How much harassment takes place at that time, how many punishments are meted out, how much beating and kicking!

Obviously because of this, the block leader and his four aides are seething with anger, being doubly hard on us. Well, why not? When they, deserving senior prisoners, must keep vigil, the shavelings are taking a nap!

And what a terrible impression the sight of our unmade bunks makes, at a time when the rest of our brother prisoners are going to work, barely dragging their sore feet clad in heavy clogs! (The bunkrooms have enormous windows through which you can see everything.)

"Quiet!" many of the marchers sneer as they go by. "Don't wake up our beloved priests. They have to rest!"

That afternoon nap, a most horrible parody in this sea of misery — these priests resting on order and forced with clubs to their bunks while in the street and on the square the lay prisoners, our former and future parishioners, are dying of weakness — that was a satanic trick, which undermined the faith of souls that till then had been most devoted to us.

I said "forced with clubs to their bunks." This was so. Privileges were granted by the commandant's office as "orders" to be carried out. Whoever refused to drink wine or take an afternoon nap would get reported for insubordination, which meant an hour of hanging on the stake!

"It seems to me," again grumbles Zdzich, "that those who so *diplomatically* sought these wretched privileges for us had spent too little time in prayer, and that's why it turned out this way."

Every day we have an opportunity to participate in the Most Holy Sacrifice. The chapel — despite the fact that an internal wall had been cut out — is so cramped that it doesn't hold even half of us. The packed crowd stands at the windows, behind doors, along the outside walls. The presence of SS men during holy Mass is not as frequent as in Sachsenhausen. Our block or hall leaders don't have access to it, either. During this time, however, they don't spare us painful harassment, just as in the other camp.

And our laymen fellow prisoners? ... Since the chapel is one of the hated centers of privileges, they look askance at us.

Warmer days are approaching.

"You know, I simply don't know how to pray in that stuffy, cramped space," I tell Zdzich.

"Now you'll better understand our faithful, who crowded into churches this way. If you return and God gives you a sheepfold, remember, be understanding, and demand from your flock only what you yourself can give to God under these conditions."

And Jesus comes down every day onto the altar in Dachau. He is present on it every day with his true humanity hidden under the appearance of the small Host. But do we appreciate this sufficiently? Do we know how to make use of this daily miracle the way He wants us to?

Due to a lack of documented sources, it's difficult today to judge whether isolating us priests from the masses of our fellow prisoners was also one of the points of privilege or, rather, a decision made by camp officials. We can assume it was the latter because, for sure, this hammered a huge wedge between us priests and our fellow prisoners, making any apostolic work among them, even the most unobtrusive, completely impossible.

"Why do you complain so much? Didn't rectories during our days of freedom become somewhat similar places of isolation? Did our faithful have access to us at any time of the day? What we created then now becomes our portion in the extreme. The SS men have forgotten only one detail."

"What's that?"

"On the isolation gate they should have hung a sign giving 'clergy office hours.'"

"You're horrible!"

"I know I am. If you get released, you'll take away from this experience in camp one valuable detail that we've overlooked till now."

"A detail?"

"Right. You'll have a bell and a sign with 'clergy office hours' because how can you destroy long-held traditions? Don't forget, based on their example — he moves his head in the direction of the guardhouse — enclose the door to your house with barbed wire! Then you'll be certain that none of the faithful will wake you from your well-deserved nap..."

I run from him, but I can't run from myself! There's a young French priest among us. We talk often. He's a kind of enthusiast. Colleagues call him a radical. Zdzich and he are best friends. Anyway, in his statements he's constantly citing Cardinal Suhard of Paris.[1] They caught him in a German factory where he worked as a laborer with hundreds of his countrymen, conducting a secret ministry among them. He tells us that hundreds of young French priests, dressed as workers, were deported into slave labor together with masses of French laborers. They are secretly ministering among them in Germany. Why didn't we also, at the start of the war, hide ourselves among our faithful and go into the underground ministry? Why did we continue at the time-honored "strongholds" of the rectories, not noticing the birth of new times?

They, the young "radicals," are ministering at this moment in factories, dirty and ragged, taken for slave laborers. And we? We're 2,000 priests, awarded "privileges," while every day outside the wires that isolate us dozens of our colleagues are dying, and there's no one to give them the last words of comfort on their way to eternity!

"Jesus! Why this suffering?"

"Again you ask *why*? You know, of course."

"I know, oh Lord!"

A frenzy begins to seize my soul. Instead of Jesus, we carry *kettles* to them!

33

The Reverend Bishop

A terror of the clergy's "isolation" during these months is SS man Munderlein. He's no longer a young man; he must be over forty, short, lean, bent over, with a pale and wasted face, from which peer a couple of pale, almost colorless eyes. When he comes to our blocks, he's always drunk, something rather rare among SS men on duty. Munderlein is an exception. A peculiar exception. In his hate for us, he reminds us of Schubert from Sachsenhausen. He's terribly friendly with Buffalo. Who knows what unites them? Maybe it's an acquaintance from Buffalo's days of freedom and service in SS ranks?

What Munderlein perpetrates in our isolated blocks is difficult to describe. His every appearance ends with a real Sodom and Gomorrah! The contents of cupboards are strewn about the floor, bedding is wrecked, tables and stools are overturned, we're sweating from sport, and many are bloodied from beatings.

So yesterday, for example, after first tearing cupboards apart and throwing everything out of them, he gives the order: "Fall down!" And then: "Roll!" How can you do this with a hundred and fifty men in a small room, especially between turned-over tables and stools? But an order is an order. It has to be carried out. We fall on top of each other, we suffocate each other, we roll like swarms of insects, which Munderlein tramples, which Buffalo tramples, and both beat us at random on heads, emaciated backs, on boils that burst open.

And then, when we already have the appearance of a single mass, sticky from sweat, the next order comes:

"Up on the cupboards, march!"

The cupboards, which stand along the walls around the entire room, are a good two meters high. Who among us can climb on top of them? In addition, they're narrow. When an edge is grasped, the cupboard tips over, crushing with its weight whoever is trying to climb on top of it.

When the interior of the barracks is already a scene of despair, Munderlein throws us out into the street in front of the barracks, and there he begins sport.

Today is 25 April 1941, feast day of the Gospel writer Mark. Munderlein raged the entire morning again, more drunk than ever. We're just sitting at dinner when the camp messenger enters the room, bringing several newcomers with him. They stand in short, badly buttoned pants and shirts. A normal scene, which repeats itself every few days and doesn't interrupt starving people from eating because, although there's only a bowl of steamed nettle, it is after all a bit of warm food... Suddenly, a name spoken by someone in a whisper electrifies everyone in the room:

"Reverend Bishop Kozal!"

"Reverend Bishop Kozal?"

The spoon carrying a mouthful of disgusting "green forage" to my lips stops midway. Now the eyes of everyone eating are directed toward the new arrivals, where attention is focused on a tall, slightly bent and lean figure, with head held high, a pale swarthy face, a well-defined and handsomely delineated nose, eyes covered by eyelids. In one hand is a prison cap, in the other worn clogs, and one of his heels is puffy and swollen, practically violet in color ... Yes! Reverend Bishop Kozal!

The hall leader finishes serving dinner. There are still several liters of the watery soup in the kettle. Hans lifts his puffy, rosy face from above the kettle:

"Seconds!"

No one moves. Hans looks amazed. He doesn't understand this silence. Any other day there would already be a long line of those waiting for seconds, but today there are no candidates at all?

His excellency Bishop Michał Kozal.

"Seconds!" he screams, and seeing that no one is hurrying to get any, he throws the ladle into the kettle, moves it over with a bang and murmurs: "Don't want it, then leave it! What's the matter with them today?"

Hans doesn't lack perception, however. He notices that it's the tall prisoner who's making such a strange impression on us. Sitting down with his bowl and eating, he doesn't take his eyes off the new arrivals.

Our block secretary allows them into his presence only after he has finished dinner and smoked his customary cigarette.

"Come closer!" he calls and reaches for the file box. "Don't lean on the table!" he roars at one of the men in the group. "This isn't a tavern! Your name?"

"Michał Kozal."

"Mi ... chał ... Ko ... zal," he repeats in syllables, writing the information on a card.

"Occupation?"

"Clergyman."

"So you were a bishop?" (Our secretary is a Pole and knows very well who the prisoner is that stands before him. Alas! Years of camp and its bad influence have left their mark even on this Polish teacher.)

"Yes, I am a bishop" the prisoner confirms.

"You are, you are," our secretary is impatient. "Here you are prisoner number 24544! Do you understand? Here there are no bishops!"

Finally, the formalities are completed.

"You can leave."

A group of priests surrounds the Reverend Bishop. Greetings. Memories...

"Hey! You!" the hall leader calls from his corner.

"The hall leader is calling you, Reverend Bishop," we whisper.

Bishop Kozal stands in front of young Hans, who's sprawled on a bunk.

"Why are they kissing your hand?"

The Bishop doesn't answer. He stands there, raising his head in a manner so characteristic for him, with his eyes even now cast down.

Hans is turning purple. (He's wildly impulsive.) He jumps up and sits on the edge of the bunk, holding a board in his hands. But already one of our men hurries with an explanation:

"Hans, this is our Bishop."

"Bishop?" Hans probably doesn't know too well what that means.

"Then you have to kiss his hand?"

"That's customary," the other explains.

"Well, well!" Hans is surprised. "No matter, I don't care about this at all, but I advise you not to let anyone kiss your hands because you could get into trouble over it. Move off!"

Such was the welcome for Reverend Bishop Kozal in the first hall of Block 28, to which he was assigned.

The Reverend Bishop looks terribly exhausted. He's limping on his swollen foot. We find out — not from him because he never talks about himself, but from his fellow prisoners — what he had experienced at the hands of the Gestapo in Inowrocław and also later in Berlin...

For us, a small group of alumni from the Gniezno seminary, meetings with him have a different meaning than for the others, evoking a special feeling. For all others he is the Reverend Bishop, but for us he is our unforgettable priest rector and educator. He recognizes us all. We're happy that he hasn't forgotten our names.

"And, you see, which of us expected then, during our years of study, that the rector would meet his students under such circumstances?"

Each of us brings him some kind of "treasure," something extremely necessary in camp life: a pair of leather shoe laces, a piece of string for tying pants legs, a pin for fastening. The Reverend Bishop thanks us, he's moved by these tokens of friendship, but ... he doesn't accept anything.

"It's of more use to you than to me, an old man."

"Old man? But, Reverend Bishop, you're only 47 years old."

He smiles with the broad smile that's so characteristic of him, revealing a row of white, even teeth.

"What's happened to Fr. Leon Kaja?" he asks when we're alone. (Rev. Prof. Leon Kaja was a close friend of Bishop Kozal and later became the pastor of the parish in Sadki; each year they spent part of their vacation in the country. At that time I was an altar boy and used to serve him at holy Mass.)

"Fr. Kaja was shot."

"Shot?" Tears well up in the Reverend Bishop's clear eyes. "Poor, dear Leoś. Poor, dear Leoś," he repeats. "Were you present at his death?"

"No. I was in Inowrocław at that time. I heard the news from my family."

"Poor Leoś ... We won't forget his beautiful soul. He was a great priest, a great one... And godly," he adds after a while, staring in front of him.

From then on, Reverend Bishop Kozal shares days of ordinary camp life with us. He doesn't agree to special treatment from us; he doesn't accept any help. Indeed, he's the first

33. The Reverend Bishop

to offer all kinds of help. He goes with us for the kettles, takes part in exhausting sports, dragging his ailing foot, experiences with us the hell of SS man Munderlein's visits, and when the latter finds out from Buffalo that he has in front of him a Catholic bishop, he persecutes him more than anyone! We witness him being slapped in the face, kicked, and beaten! Moreover, Buffalo himself doesn't spare the Bishop special harassment, often screaming at him:

"You're their Bishop! You're responsible for them!"

And the unfortunate Reverend Bishop catches it for us!

They bring some in, others leave. On 29 April the unforgettable Fr. Olek Tokłowicz from Września dies, a victim of emaciation in the Gusen quarries; others who die are Fr. Ed. Kundegórski, Fr. Czesio Jerzewski, a fellow student, Fr. Kazimierz Nowak, Fr. Stepczyński, dear Fr. Bronek Herut, Fr. Piotruś Musiał, Fr. Sterczewski, the young Fr. Olek Wilamowski from the Chełmno Diocese; those who follow him from that same diocese are Fr. Józef Wilemski and Fr. Józek Borzyszkowski, who had been with us since Stutthof.

At the same time, more and more depressing news comes to us. Hitler attacks Greece and Yugoslavia, and soon prisoners of both nationalities arrive in Dachau. They're also transporting Jews from those countries.

Hitler enters into a pact of friendship with Turkey!

"This move has a meaning," comment the "experts" on political issues.

They're right this time: on 22 June news spreads through the camp that Hitler has attacked Russia! The camp communists gossip quietly. Their cheeks are flushed; their eyes reveal agitation...

There's excitement among the SS men, which manifests itself in increased harassment of the prisoners. Living conditions become noticeably worse.

In July there are many transports of Jews. Some of them are brought into the camp and placed in isolated blocks like ours. Through the wire fencing we can see many small children among them! But in many cases when a transport of Jews arrives, we see guards lead these unfortunate ones in whole groups right to the crematorium, and only a few minutes later you hear the bursts of machine guns...

It's being whispered that Göring has ordered a complete roundup of Jews from all over Europe.[1]

From the time the war with Russia started, every few days large transports of "certain" people arrive whom they don't bring into the camp, but — if the group is small — they shoot them in a park by the crematorium, across from our clergy barracks; or — as male attendants from the camp hospital whisper — if the group consists of several thousand, they lead them to the rifle range where they're shot by a unit of young SS men, who "are practicing" to fight the Russians. The attendants, who are called over there to take off clothing or pull out gold teeth, recount that they wade in blood up to their ankles and that those who are shot are mainly Russians or people from war areas, which means there is no shortage of Poles among them.[2,3]

The crematorium puffs out smoke night and day! It's as though they can't keep pace in burning bodies. The smell of the burning chokes us at night.

A grim mood prevails throughout the camp as never before. The SS men are raging. They have only hatred in their eyes. Our block personnel vent all their anger upon us.

There's no end to the harassment. Willi, who leads us to the kitchen for kettles, is acting like someone possessed!

Our Reverend Bishop suffers together with us, but he suffers more than we do because the slave drivers' anger is concentrated especially on him.

And they're transporting more of our own to the camp. Recently they brought in Fr. Nazim and Fr. Cieślak, Franciscans from Niepokalanów.

The prisoners brought from Auschwitz are telling us about the death of Fr. Maksymilian Kolbe, who volunteered to change places with one of the prisoners condemned to death. He apparently died on 14 August of this year.

Those coming in on transports talk about the growing terror in other camps. Everywhere crematoriums emit smoke day and night, and in Auschwitz they're already burning whole piles of bodies on the squares, like trash. Satan's handiwork is expanding.

"What will become of us in Dachau?"

Fr. Maksymilian Kolbe (drawing by the author).

34

September 15, 1941

On 15 September 1941, when they suddenly threw us out of the barracks and put us into the block streets (and they threw out only us, the Polish priests), we didn't understand the connection between what happened to us that day and the great events playing out at that time in the world.

On 13 September, that is, two days prior to the events in Dachau, which will be the topic of this chapter, the Nazis issue "Order No. 246 — *Über religiöse Vereinigungen und Religionsgesellschaften* — which decrees that the corporate body of the Catholic Church which had existed in the area of the Warta River basin up to 1 September 1939 (the day war broke out) is currently being replaced by a "religious association," the so-called "Römisch-katholische Kirche deutscher Nationalität im Reichsgau Wartheland" (the Roman Catholic Church of German Nationality in the Warta Region).[1]

This official order completely erased the Catholic Church from Poland's western territories, which were "once and for all" incorporated into the Reich. It was there that Hitlerism wanted initially to introduce the religious administration that was being projected for the future in all of Germany and all other plundered lands.

Thus, the Catholic Church was replaced with some freak "Roman Catholic Church of German Nationality," which later would be so much easier to rename "Church of Old-Germanic Religion" in the formulation of the Nazi "pope," Alfred Rosenberg!

In the wake of this order, the Apostolic Nuncio in Berlin issued a note of protest to the Nazi government on 14 September, demanding freedom for the Church in Poland's western territories and taking the occasion to call to mind his prior note of protest dated 2 September of that year.[2]

And here then on 15 September our senior block leader, the infamous Buffalo, informs us that, effective today, all Polish priests lose the privileges they have enjoyed up to now! "The rest," he says, "will be announced to you by the camp commandant himself after dinner."

During the afternoon (awaited with trembling), we stand in long ranks in the block street. Nearby is Block 30.

What's going to happen? ... What do they want from us? ... Why only Polish priests? ... What will happen to the Germans, French, Czechs, Slovaks, Italians, Lithuanians, Hungarians, Romanians, Swiss, Norwegians, and others? Because they're also clergymen.

On the sidewalk in front of the barracks, several tables have been set up with stools behind them.

"What on earth for? Will there be some kind of a new list? Maybe a transport?"

The anxiety is spreading also to our hall leaders, the secretary, the canteen manager. They move around ... as though they were being stung by bees.

After a while, several dozen prisoner clerks from the political section enter our isolation unit. Each one is carrying a records case under his arm. Several are carrying typewriters.

Suddenly the camp senior, ape-man Kapp, runs in swaying on his short, gnarly legs. Behind him limps Szaferski. Both pay no attention to us as if we weren't there. They disappear into the barracks...

"What does all this mean?"

"Looks like before an execution," someone whispers.

"Drop that talk. What a comparison!"

Soon after, Kapp, Szaferski, and Buffalo come out of the barracks and stand at the isolation gate, nervously looking down the street.

Through the window we can see the block secretary gesturing as he says something excitedly to the hall leaders gathered around him.

"If only we could hear what he's saying..."

"Be patient. You'll find out soon."

There's movement at the isolation gate. Kapp and Szaferski run outside. Taking off his cap and stretching his long arms tightly against his pants legs, Buffalo stands at attention.

"They're coming ... they're coming," a whisper runs through the motionless ranks.

Captain Zill stops at the isolation gate with his inseparable dog; behind him is a large retinue of non-commissioned officers and regular SS men.

"*Aaaachtung!*"

Heels click. We stiffen at attention.

"Caps off!"

One clap!

Buffalo reports: "Block 28 in force..."

Zill isn't listening to the report. He's already in front of us. One of the hall leaders puts down a stool, and Zill steps up onto it. His ever-present dog sits down by his master's shining boots.

The commandant of the entire complex of camps that belong to Dachau is SS Major Piorkowsky. The commandant of camp Dachau itself is Captain Zill. The entire camp trembles before this small inconspicuous figure. Apparently, he's a baker by trade, but as an SS officer he tries to let no one surpass him in matters of "strict discipline." His specialty is the merciless punishment of prisoners![3]

He stands before us dressed in a perfectly tailored uniform, moving his hawkish glance over the group of 2,000 Polish priests. On both sides, along the barrack walls, stands a large SS retinue. Right next to Zill is an official camp interpreter, Ryszard Knosala, the brother-in-law of Fr. Styp-Rekowski; this is a man devoted heart and soul to us and to Poles in general. He's standing with his head uncovered, his face turned downward. Poor fellow! How many horrible commands, how many sentences he had to translate from "SS language" into Polish and other languages...

The group of clerks sitting at the tables have already put sheets of paper on the typewriter rollers; others are already holding pens in their hands.

"Attention!"

Zill's sharp voice pierces the deadly silence, and our hearts stop as we await the sentence.

"All German priests step forward!"

Buffalo, with his cap at the side of his pants, explains that all German priests and other nationalities have already been reassigned and are located in Block 26.

34. September 15, 1941

"In that case," further commands Zill, "all priests who are German citizens step forward!"

Knosala interprets in a trembling voice.

Two step forward, standing in front of the tables.

"No others?" Zill's hawkish eyes move from rank to rank.

Silence.

"All who have any ancestors of German nationality step forward!"

Silence in the ranks. No one budges!

Again, Zill repeats:

"All who have any ancestors of German nationality step forward!"

Ryszard interprets in a breaking, trembling voice:

"All who have had any kind of relatives or kinsmen of German nationality step forward!"

Dead silence in the ranks. The SS men shift nervously ... Zill's eyes pierce into the motionless ranks. Ryszard Knosala's face is ashen white.

"And now," Zill slowly drawls the words through his clenched teeth: "And now all those who feel a spiritual kinship with the German nation step forward."

Silence.

Knosala interprets ... He's speaking in a wooden, dead-pan voice ... Zill looks around at the motionless ranks. Kapp, Szaferski, and Buffalo also give us piercing looks ... A breeze rustles the sheets of paper resting on the tables... The terrier sitting at the SS man's feet looks faithfully into his eyes, wagging its little tail.

"Attention!" Zill raises his voice even more. Rage is brewing inside of him. "Who among you would like to become German and move to your colleagues in Block 26, to better living conditions?"

Silence ... Troublesome, pregnant silence. Pregnant because we feel that this entire game is coming to an end, that any moment now will come the "something" before which we tremble with fear.

"Who among you would like to become German," repeats Zill in a stifled voice, "and move to your colleagues in Block 26, to better living conditions?"

Silence.

"No one?" Zill's eyes move from face to face. "There ... is ... no one ... who ... would like to?"

Silence.

"Then listen, *ihr pölnische Schweine-Pfaffen*!" Zill is choking! His narrow face is beginning to take on the appearance of a hawk's bill. "From this moment all current privileges will be taken away from you! You are prohibited, under the most severe penalties, from all practice of religion and from possessing any items of religious devotion. German priests and all other nationalities will live in Block 26, and they are keeping the chapel, but any contact between you and them is forbidden under severe penalties! From now on, you are no longer clergymen! You are now regular prisoners! You will be treated like all those criminals! Beginning tomorrow, you go to work!"

Zill jumps off the stool and, without even glancing at us, walks toward the isolation gate. The retinue runs behind him, and behind the retinue the ape-man sways, and Szaferski limps. Buffalo, with his cap at his side, escorts the officials into the camp street. The clerks walk behind all of them, their typewriters and files under their arms; on their faces you see something that looks like joy...

We continue to stand at attention, awaiting the first effects of what took place here just a moment ago. The hall leaders are behaving rather strangely...

"Buffalo is coming back! ... Buffalo is coming back," the quiet warning is whispered.

But even Buffalo behaves somehow differently. Not looking at us, he says:

"Those two, you know, the ones related to the German people, can gather up their bundles. They will go right now to Block 26. The rest of you: dismissed!"

Only now are tongues loosened. Talk ... comments ... remarks...

"Now they'll teach us a lesson!" someone predicts.

"But maybe not."

Each of us, regardless of his assessment of the whole event, realizes that today a sentence has come down upon us, the Polish priests.

"Something special must have happened to urge them to apply this repression precisely against us Poles."

"But who knows what their reasons are."

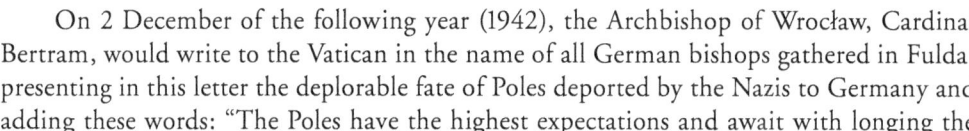

On 2 December of the following year (1942), the Archbishop of Wrocław, Cardinal Bertram, would write to the Vatican in the name of all German bishops gathered in Fulda, presenting in this letter the deplorable fate of Poles deported by the Nazis to Germany and adding these words: "The Poles have the highest expectations and await with longing the revival and restoration of the Polish nation. That is why the German government considers them *all, without exception*, enemies of the German nation."[4]

These words fully explain why Hitler retained privileges for priests of all other nations and withdrew them only from Polish priests! Since we have already mentioned the letter by Cardinal Bertram, let us also add an explanation found in it precisely on the topic of privileges:

> In regard to concentration camps, we have managed to gather very little information up to now since we know very little about the reasons for the deportation of individual prisoners, about the way they are treated, about their lot, their state of health and their needs... At the request of priests kept in Dachau, I sent them 120 Roman breviaries on 25 February 1941... One should not, however, expect the government or party to agree to the departure of imprisoned priests to America or neutral countries; in view of their distrust, they will be afraid that the priests, once they have gone to foreign countries, might tell stories unfavorable to the government and party. With deepest regards... Card. A. Bertram, Archbishop of Wrocław.[5]

If the German Episcopate knew so little about the treatment or life of priests in Dachau in December 1942, as it officially reports in this letter to the Holy See, if that is so, what did it know in 1941?

And if the German Episcopate knew so little when informing the Vatican, how much did the Holy See know about the situation of thousands of priests in Dachau and other camps?

We give Cardinal Bertram's breviaries, therefore, back to the German priests and those of other nationalities in Block 26; we get rid of all devotional items since we realize that frequent inspections await us now in search of just these objects; we remove from our two blocks everything that could endanger us, and ... strengthening more fervently in our tormented hearts the belief that God will not desert us, we await tomorrow. That declared tomorrow, when along with thousands of our colleagues (according to Zill — criminals!) we will go to work.

And this was a memorable day for us, 15 September, the feast of the Seven Sorrows of the Mother of God, in the year 1941.

35

The Fence Fell and with It the Privileges

Early on the following day they began removing the fences and gates surrounding Blocks 28 and 30. The isolation now includes only Block 26, which houses German priests and those of other nationalities. Also remaining in isolation is One Special Prisoner — Jesus in the tabernacle! This last fact is especially painful for us. We will no longer have the Most Holy Sacrifice; there will be no meetings with the Master at the Table of Love. However ... time would reveal that this was exactly what was needed so Jesus would become even closer to our group of priests; this separation was needed so that He, through us, might find himself among the many thousands of his prisoner friends who, until now, have been alone.

Meanwhile, however, it's hard for us to resign ourselves to the way isolation was lifted and the way we were integrated into teams of lay "criminals."

"Look! They've even painted over the windows in Block 26 so that we can't look into the chapel!"

"It's not enough for them to paint over the windows," another adds. "They've also nailed them shut on the inside to prevent any contacts."

From now on two different groups of priests will live side by side: Polish priests, judged by camp officials to be people of inferior rank and unworthy of clerical privileges and, for that reason, excluded from the general community of clergy; and the clergy of other nationalities, who are given a higher classification.

"This is what bothers me most," someone whispers. "That they've ... they've..." He can't find the words. "It's understandable that they've shown partiality to German priests. After all, many of them have brothers and other family members who are soldiers on the front lines. What is especially annoying is that they've extended this favored treatment to all other priests — Belgians, Dutch, French, Hungarians, Czechs, Slovaks, Lithuanians, Ukrainians, to everyone except us, the Poles..."

"Know what's behind what you're saying?"

"What?"

"National pride offended to the core, and self-love!"

"Oh, you always have to bring everything up to higher levels, to..."

"Can you, as a priest, look differently at all that's happening to us?"

Silence.

"In other words," someone adds, "such treatment of us Polish priests is really a distinction."

"Could you possibly doubt it?"

35. The Fence Fell and with It the Privileges

When the gate fell and the barbed-wire isolation fencing was torn down, our Polish clerical blocks again become, as Zill forewarned, an area for lawless pranks by all manner of tyrannical camp officials. Every few minutes there's some capo, some deputy capo, or some deputy to a deputy capo, who chases us with his club to this or that work.

"Get going, go on, you rested, privileged shavelings! You haven't worked for so many months, you gathered strength; now get back to work!"

And ... they drive us! They hurry us! They prod us on!

We continue to carry kettles with coffee and food several times each day, but now we also carry them to our colleagues in Block 26, whose privileges were "increased" by no longer having to carry kettles, among other things. We fix roads. We move bunks, mattresses, and other barracks furniture from one block to another. In a word, we again become "the guys for all camp services"! Anyone who so desires can use us since they believe we've "fallen from the good graces" of the commandant and, therefore, all harassment against us not only escapes punishment, but on the contrary, is viewed favorably "there, at the top."

"If only they were willing to assign us soon to official work!" we sigh.

But it's already almost fall, and summer work is ending. Many of the lay prisoners are losing their assignments for work in one command or another during this period of labor cutbacks. So it's not easy to get work and that extra piece of bread.

Ignac, leader of the second hall in Block 28, becomes a capo of gardeners who travel every day to work in Munich. His place is taken by a young communist, Emil Joas. He's probably about 26 years old. Lean, maybe even skinny, with a birdlike face and shining eyes, he greets us at the outset:

"The camp officials have appointed me as leader of your hall. I'm a proletarian, you are representatives of the bourgeoisie. Between us there's a gulf! I've been sitting in Dachau since 1936. I got to know you well enough when I was free. Cheats, you prattled to the unenlightened about supernatural things of some kind. I believe only in what I can see, touch, and devour! You won't be able to catch me with your phony pitch! At one time you had power, today I have it over you! My school will be hard..."

Up to then, not one of the hall leaders or capos we came across had ever declared their feelings toward us so clearly. Not even any SS men had defined their attitude toward us this clearly. Emil Joas, the young German communist, captured in 1936, immediately following his training in Moscow — as he proudly emphasizes so often — recites word for word what had been instilled in him during those years of Moscow "studies."

In the experience of the Polish priests in Dachau, probably the bloodiest memories are of Emil. Few of the block leaders, and probably none of the hall leaders, murdered so many of us as he did.

In the first days of his "supervision" over the second hall of Block 28 his first victims already fall, killed before our very eyes! When Emil sees blood, he becomes terrible! Watching Emil's behavior, Buffalo only smiles. He has found an excellent helpmate. Emil's best friend is the freak Cretin, leader of the fourth hall. These two non-humans were well matched!

Once a month — as I've mentioned previously — cash payments are made in camp from money the prisoner holds in the camp cashier's office, money he either brought with him from outside or received by mail from his family. A custom generally accepted in Dachau was that following every disbursement at least half the money goes quietly — as a sum "for block needs" — into the block leader's pocket. Since there are about a thousand of us priests in the barracks and each must hand over several German marks, the total comes then to several thousand. What our Buffalo does with it, what he secretly buys with it, how many SS men he bribes, all that remains his secret.

For several weeks, there hasn't been a disbursement. Buffalo walks around looking glum.

"I need money for 'organization'!"

Where can he get it?

Buffalo is furious.

Parenthetically, we should explain that the expression "organization" can describe many things in the camp — a great variety of activities, plans, achievements, facts. For example, one never says that someone is stealing something! Every theft is a proverbial "organization"! It also includes every secret swindle, the acquisition of anything in the most illegal way, smuggling through the guard line, getting through the guard gate into the camp, etc. "Organization" is the word most used in the camp, the most "succinct" word, the one saying the most, explaining everything and ... nothing.

"Atteeention!" yells someone from the door. (According to orders, whoever first notices an SS man entering the block must yell at the top of his lungs: Attention! Then "every living thing" throws everything he has in his hands onto the floor, jumps up, stands at attention, and ... holds still like a rock!)

The SS man enters, guardian of our clerical barracks, a man well-known to us: Munderlein. His purplish face indicates that today he is more drunk than ever.

He starts the cupboard inspection.

"Trash! Dirt! Slovenliness!" he yells, as everything goes falling to the floor: spoons, tins, towels, soap, and all that a prisoner's cupboard contains. The obliging Buffalo walks behind him and removes the rest. (How far did the "organizational" (!) relationship between Buffalo and Munderlein reach? There were various opinions about this.)

"I can no longer deal with this damned gang," Buffalo remarks.

"You can't deal with it?" a smile plays on the SS man's swollen face.

"But their Bishop is here," adds Buffalo. "He has influence over them."

"Bishop?" Munderlein is blinking with his puffy, red eyelids. "Bishop ... Get me that Bishop!"

"Kocal! Kocal!" yells Buffalo. "Kocal, *komm hier*!"

The tall, wasted, and slightly bent figure stands in front of the drunken SS man. Skinny legs in the striped camp uniform poke out from trousers that are somewhat short.

"So you are a Bishop?" The drunk's cloudy eyes assess the man standing before him.

"Yes, sir. I'm a Bishop" confirms the prisoner standing at attention. His clear gray eyes look calmly at the SS man. They size up one another for a moment.

"So it's you who incites these shavelings of yours?" The SS man's face turns even more purple.

"I don't incite anyone," Bishop Kozal states calmly.

"What? You also dare to lie?" And a strong blow falls on the prisoner's face.

The Bishop loses his balance, but doesn't fall. A mark from the blow turns pink on his pale, thin face.

"Will you continue to incite them? Well?" screams the drunken torturer.

"I haven't incited anyone, and I'll continue not inciting."

Another strong blow. And then another!

"Run, you dog! Run, or I'll..." A powerful kick with his shod boot.

"You ... you damned dog! You ... Everyone into the street!" he screams at the rest of us.

The hall becomes a bedlam. Frantic, the group takes off in fear toward the exit. Crush! Push! Heavy stools are flying at heads. Here and there blood is gushing. And near the wall, the motionless silhouette of Reverend Bishop Kozal.

"You, too, into the street!" screams Buffalo, pushing the battered man.

A murderous *sport* commences... Sport is bloodier today than ever before.

"Run! Run! ... " We're out of breath! "Fall down! *Roooollen*! Roll!" The boots of the SS man, Buffalo, and the hall leaders trample over those lying on the ground, but hall leader Emil stomps and kicks with special zeal!

"Get up! On the double, march!" And again we rush, while in our midst Bishop Kozal is dragging his swollen leg with painful effort.

"Faster! Faster, you dog!" and the SS man's club bloodies the unfortunate victim.

The Bishop falls! New blows! ... Merciful Jesus! These devils will kill him!

"Leapfrog! One, two, three ... One, two, three ... " We jump, and there's stinging pain in our tired muscles, overwhelming pain, and pounding in our hearts; hoarse sounds come from our parched throats, we gasp for air ... and clubs beat our backs, our heads...

"On the double, march!" And we run again... Many of our group already lie on the ground unconscious. We have to trample on them. That's an order! And even if you wanted to spare these unfortunate ones, would it even be possible in this terrible crush? "Run! Run, you dogs!"

Behind the paint-covered windows of the chapel in Block 26, Jesus is in the tabernacle...

"My sons! I endured the same thing that terrible night in prison... I endured the same thing on the Way of the Cross... All this will be revealed in its full horror at the Last Judgment... There, too, I will reveal your suffering..."

Yes, for no word can recount this, nor pen describe it, nor brush ever paint it...

During a free moment following supper, a group of us, his former students, gathers around our beloved teacher.

"Reverend Bishop, you were badly beaten..."

He interrupts with a smile. On his pale face there is so much peace.

"Do you remember our Friday Stations of the Cross at the seminary?"

"Of course."

"You see, over there I presided during the Stations in a cassock, surplice, and stole; here, it's in a striped camp uniform. That's the only difference. Fathers, we must suffer all of this. God has special plans. In fullfilling His will lies both our penance and our reward, and a down payment toward the future glory of a renewed Church in our country, and a down payment as well toward our glory in eternity."

The longer we live with our Reverend Bishop, the greater is our admiration for him. Only a special grace from God can give a human being as much saintly composure as he possesses in this hell. As seminarians we thought of him as a pious priest, but today we regard him as a saint.

Even Zdzich, who during his studies often had difficulty with the demanding Rev. Rector Kozal, often laughing at his comments, today cannot find words to express his admiration.

"You know, that's a *great man*! That's a *priest*! You know I'm not inclined toward mawkish exaltation, and yet, observing him, you have to admit that only a saint could look like that!"

"Saint Bishop!" is whispered more and more often.

And he? The more often he's subjected to special attacks and harassment, the more he maintains his dignity as a bishop, the greater his composure, you might even say his *majesty*!

Buffalo takes his bad moods out on him in particular! The Bishop is blamed for everything! The Bishop is responsible for everything! The Bishop gets it for everybody!

The more Buffalo, the hall leaders, and SS man Munderlein become upset and the more they seethe, the more self-control, peace, and cheerfulness there is in him. Yet we see in his pale face how much he's suffering! He falters on his injured leg more and more often! The smile never disappears from his lips, however. That inner peace of his, that cheerfulness, and that smile are precisely what drive his executioners crazy.

A dozen or so of our priests have finally been taken to work on the plantation, with the understanding, however, that there will be no additional piece of bread. They went eagerly, nevertheless, in order to escape harassment in the barracks.

Several days later, the wagon capos appear in our block.

"We need several dozen of you to serve as 'horses' for the wagons!"

Several dozen volunteers come forward. Romek Budniak and Aloś Gotowicz are among them. A dozen of them are assigned to one huge flatbed. The job of pulling the flatbed wagon is one of the hardest in the camp, which is why there are no volunteers for it among our lay colleagues. Our own men, however, are satisfied because they get a piece of bread as a supplement!

The most murderous wagon is the one from the "Praezifix" factory. All day they haul machines on it to the train station and all sorts of scrap iron from the station. Even more unfair for its crew is the fact that ... they can't bite on the iron. With other wagons, there's sometimes a chance of finding something with which you can deceive an empty stomach.

Best is the trash wagon, which carries out waste from the camp as well as the SS men's barracks. There you can always find something fit to eat.

Several of our men get into the workshop where wooden spoons and clogs are made. The capo of that command is a very kind Social Democrat named Hecht, a friend of the labor office director, the Austrian Brenner. The men in the workshop are happy because the work isn't hard, it's under a roof, and they get an extra piece of bread. Kapp finds out about them, however, and chases them out.

"That work is too easy for you, shavelings!"

The following week a larger group of us goes to the plantation, but again — without the bread supplement. We work, however, at hothouses where you can always find some kind of half-rotten potato, a cabbage core, or a discarded turnip... We're satisfied. First, because of these rotten vegetables and, second, because we're escaping harassment in the block.

This does not excuse us from carrying kettles for the entire camp in the morning. We continue to haul them. One day, when the camp street is slippery with mud after a heavy rain, Fr. Czesio Koczorowski, who's carrying one in front of us, trips; the heavy kettle falls on him and breaks his leg. We sit the poor man down under a poplar tree.

"Wait here; we'll deliver our kettle quickly and come back for you."

Romek and I run, carrying our kettle to Block 20; we put it down and return for Czesio.

"How do you feel?"

"My leg is broken for sure," moans Czesio. "Try somehow to get me to the camp hospital."

We each grab an arm and carry him, worrying terribly whether we'll find anyone there at such an early hour.

We find the hospital chief himself, senior capo Heiden. They say that he's a blacksmith by trade. He's the terror of all the sick.

"What's the matter?" Heiden has already noticed two details that tell him "everything" about us! The number 22,000 reveals that we belong to the "caste" of the despised shavelings, and the letter "P" on a red triangle designates, in addition, that we are Poles.

"Sir oberkapo," we prisoners stutter to our "fellow" prisoner. "Sir oberkapo, our colleague has broken his leg while carrying kettles. We request that you..."

"Get lost, while you're still in one piece!" hisses Heiden to the one sitting on the ground.

At that moment there appears a Polish male nurse, young student R, who, unfortunately, is regarded in camp as "notorious." (He was later sentenced to death by officials in Poland.) Heiden, who considers him as his right-hand man, transfers Czesio to his "care."

"Come with me," he says to Czesio.

"Nurse," asks the priest with the broken leg, sitting on the floor. "Maybe my colleagues can help me, because I can't by myself..."

"Don't fake it! Don't fake it!" bursts out the Polish student to the priest. "Get moving, move! You shavelings only know how to pretend and complain. Go ahead!" He brutally pushes Czesio who's standing on one leg.

And Fr. Czesio hobbles on one leg, holding on to the wall; the nurse, who's following him, instead of helping, only pushes him.

"Don't curse!" Zdzich chides me as I tell him about this morning's incident. "You still don't understand that we need to experience precisely all of this, especially from those at whose hands we should be fully entitled to expect compassion! As long as you fail to understand this..."

"I won't find happiness in suffering, which is our portion," I finish his thought for him.

"That's right!" he nods. "Our Lord and Master assured us of it. You see, the priesthood is a great privilege, and as with every privilege, the greater it is, the greater responsibility it imposes. Not in vain did the Lord say, "Whoever wishes to be my disciple..."

I hurry off! I know! Zdzich is right! But...

In the evenings, when autumn darkness is already descending but there's still free time, many of our men stand by the paint-covered windows of the chapel...

"See? It's like Jews at the ruins of the Temple, at the Wailing Wall."

The Wailing Wall... Those paint-covered windows of the chapel in which resides the Lord...

However, from this time forward we have holy Masses every Sunday. Instead of the one official Mass, formerly in the chapel, we now have one in each hall!

A ghastly terror was moving through the Polish land! The last churches were closed! The last priests were arrested! Thousands upon thousands were forced to leave their ancestral homes (drawing by Władysław Krawiec).

"If you don't want me to throw you out into the street, sit quietly!" warns the hall leader from his corner, fenced off with cupboards from the rest of the hall.

That's all we need! So we sit quietly at tables, and at the center table, hidden behind the stove, one of us sitting there celebrates the Most Holy Sacrifice in a metal cup.

Where did the materials for it come from?

You can always get one host and a bit of wine from colleagues in Block 26. How many devoted friends we have there!

The Eucharistic Jesus is therefore with us. What is even more joyful is that slowly, very slowly and secretly, our colleagues from the lay blocks are filtering into our Sunday "High Masses." The Dachau "catacombs" are gathering ever larger crowds...

But the autumn days grow shorter, the evenings longer... October passes slowly, the month of our Lady of the Rosary...

Who among us knew then that during this very period the greatest persecution of faith and Polish nationality was on the move through our native regions? ... that hundreds more churches had been closed ... that there came another wave of arrests, even the last priests of that land! ... that in the Bojanowo concentration camp hundreds of nuns were imprisoned under terrible conditions ... that in Poznań only four priests remained in freedom for a quarter million of the faithful! ... that when the Holy See protests these outrages, it receives on 10 October a "note verbale" from the Hitler government, its official and final response, announcing that "...according to the understanding of the Reich government, canon law is purely internal Church law" (*dass nach der Auffassung der Reichsregierung das Kanonische Recht rein innerkirchliches Recht ist*) "and, therefore, in these matters, one needs to apply German law exclusively."[1]

36

A Memorable Transport

On the last day of October 1941 five hundred new prisoners are herded into the assembly square, most of them Polish priests!

"*An ... tre ... ten!*" Buffalo's cry runs through the barracks. "*Antreten!*"

We run outside! We form ranks. With Buffalo you don't fool around.

"Attention! A new transport of shavelings has arrived! They will be assigned to our Block 28. Five hundred of you must move to Block 30. *Achtung*! Count off from the right side!"

"*Eins, zwei, drei...*"

"Enough!" Buffalo determines, stopping the count at five hundred. "Gather your lice-infested rags and march immediately to Block 30. Understand?"

"Yes, sir!"

Good Lord! Block 30 is already overcrowded. It already has several times more residents than the lay blocks. How awfully cramped it will be in there!

Bishop Kozal is among those being transferred. They assign him to the fourth hall. The prisoners welcome him with open hearts, but what kind of life will they have if three hundred people are cooped up in an area intended for forty-five?

We meet the newcomers toward evening as we return in a small group from work. The great majority are priests from the Poznań Diocese; there are also a handful from the Gniezno Diocese and many from the Łódź Diocese. So many colleagues from seminary days, so many acquaintances!

"Your uncle, Fr. Ćwiejkowski, is also with us," Stefcio Pabiszczak tells me happily.

Well, that's Stef... He's lost none of his good nature.

In a few minutes I find my mother's brother. He's assigned to the third hall, which isn't too bad. The hall leader is a decent person. After greeting my uncle, I try to explain this to him, but I see he doesn't understand at all what I'm telling him.

"Eh!" he waves his hand in disdain. "He's just a kid!"

"Uncle! The hall leader is a lord of life and death!"

"What are you saying? You know," he changes the topic of conversation, "I like it here. These beautiful surroundings, this air — it's a real sanitarium, isn't it? The fact they pushed one or two of us around a bit during the welcome can't discourage old soldiers. Well, yes (again an indulgent gesture of the hand), after all, you remember the first World War? You were a tiny child then. When I was with Fr. Leoś Kaja and Fr. Blericqui in the trenches..."

"Where did they take you from, Uncle?" I quickly ask, interrupting memories heard many times before.

"Where did they take me from? Well, where else but right from the rectory in Nowy Tomyśl? What amazes me is that they just came, took us without any justification, and..."

"Uncle, that's their method. It was the same for us..."

"For you, for you," he interrupts with a hint of impatience. "Two years ago when they arrested you, just after military operations ended, then..."

"Then what, Uncle?"

"Eh, you see, it was different then, and it's different now, too."

"So, Uncle, you think we had something on our conscience that warranted our arrest?"

"No, no, I'm not saying that; only think about it: after two years matters had stabilized, relationships were beginning to normalize, and it appeared that..."

Following this welcome talk with my mother's brother, I somehow couldn't fall asleep for a long time. I was confused.

"Do you know what Krzych told me?" Zdzich whispers to me. "He told me he doesn't understand why they moved them to Dachau and locked them up together with us?"

"Has he gone crazy?"

"No! He was completely serious when he said it. And he wasn't the only one..."

"My boy," says my uncle the next day, "after being locked up for two years, you've all become some kind of pessimists; you've lost your faith in... My boy! These are already their death throes! They've entered so deep inside Russia that they'll be destroyed there like Napoleon. What's more, they're so scattered all over Europe that when — at any time now — there's a move against them, they'll be squashed like bedbugs."

I'm going back again to my hall, my head filled with thoughts and doubts! They — the newcomers — are all such optimists! Amazing.

"Zdzich!"

Silence. I touch his shoulder.

"Don't touch me. What do you want?" In his voice there is some kind of unfamiliar and hard tone. I've never heard him like this before.

"Nothing, Zdzich. Good night."

Silence...

Those crazy optimists, they might as well be singing "Wojenko, wojenko"* at the open doors of the crematorium furnace. And Zdzich here has been stung by something because he's angry as a wasp. My head, meanwhile, is spinning.

The first days of instruction, information, and training have begun... For the recent arrivals everything is new... Meanwhile, in free moments, we recognize and greet each other; we recall old times, people, events...

There is elderly Rev. Canon Greinert from Gniezno, the Rev. Msgr. Łagoda from Miłosław, and the Rev. Canon Kunka, chancellor of the Włocławek Curia, as well as the Rev. Canon Jedwabski, chancellor of the Curia in Poznań; there is the mitred Rev. Msgr. Styczyński from Gniezno, and the Rev. Colonel Wilkans, dean of troops from Poznań, or — in a word — those of our dignitaries who had still been living in freedom. The professors

---

*Translator's note: a patriotic Polish military song.

36. A Memorable Transport

and pastors whom I meet are: Fr. S. Szymański, Fr. Kazimierz Rakowski, Fr. S. Poczta, Fr. Piotrowski, elderly Fr. Jan Wojciechowski (known soon to almost the entire camp as "Dear Uncle"), surrounded by his relatives Staszek and Stefan Wojciechowski. There is also the Rev. Dr. Kornel Wierzbicki and the Rev. Dr. Koperski, the Rev. Dr. Dziasek, Fr. Teodor Korcz, Fr. Sylwester Konieczny, Fr. Marian Kaszewski, the Rev. Prof. Antoś Majchrzak from Bydgoszcz, and Fr. Werbiński from Gniezno; there is huge Fr. Miecio Januszczak, the pastor of Polonia in France, and Fr. Maryś Bogacki from Szamotuły. There are young priests from the Łódź Diocese: Fr. Siekiera, Edmund Chard and Piotruś Beściak, and Wacek Tokarek, as well as Eugeniusz Przychodzeń. There are my colleagues from the seminary years: Stefek Pabiszczak, Maryś Walorek, Bronek Stachowski, Henio Kaliszan, Staś Jezierski, Milan Kwiatkowski, Władzio Kasprowicz, Wacek Krauze, and Józek Woźniak and Miecio Ratajski, and Alfons Viola, and... But who can name them all? There are also Capuchins, young and likeable; there is Fr. Gorgoniusz Nędza of the Order of the Reformati as well. Although quite some time has already passed since the transport arrived, we continue to meet acquaintances and friends for the first time, people we haven't seen for years.

And in the meantime November, one of the most treacherous months in Dachau, forges ahead, its icy winds already blowing, its cold mornings already biting. There are clouds during the day and in the evenings most often a fine, persistent drizzle.

The newcomers haven't been given either caps or socks or anything warmer under their tattered coveralls. They walk to the assembly square three times a day in bare feet, with uncovered heads, wearing flimsy, striped summer uniforms. Even if one of us senior prisoners secretly brings them some old socks, a cap, or a piece of rag to be worn under the shirt (since up to now no official issue for the newcomers has taken place), all these items are considered "stolen" goods, and each carries a punishment! Buffalo and the hall supervisor don't skimp on inspections. They often conduct them several times a day. Therefore, the poor fellows are subjected to punishments that only Buffalo can invent, and his hall servants carry these out with great precision.

From morning to night, the street in front of Block 28 is full of people squatting and engaging in deadly sport... There's no end to the harassments devised in all this.

You notice a curious phenomenon in practically every old prisoner (old not as to age but years in camp). Whereas he shows a certain friendly and understanding partiality toward a young colleague, he conveys — for unknown reasons — more ill-will toward a colleague who is old, weak, or ill. We observe the same phenomenon among SS men. Could this already be the influence of Nazi training? Perhaps it's only some little-known law of the primitive human psyche finding expression under these exceptional, abnormal conditions...

Whereas all other transports of priests to Dachau (as already mentioned earlier), having lost their elderly inmates in other camps, had a component that was mostly emaciated but young and capable of recovery when given the chance even under camp conditions, the last transport, having arrived straight from freedom, includes mostly priests who are older, weak, ill, or even completely handicapped. With what singular sadism, difficult to explain, Buffalo and the hall elders murder them!

We know from two years' experience that any time a transport arrives at camp from outside in late spring, summer, or early fall, the newcomers' chances of survival are always better. But the opposite is also true. Each time new arrivals come in late fall, harsh winter, or early spring, when the transition is too great from warm underwear and clothing to thin denim, as well as from warm housing to a freezing assembly square, it is then that victims multiply.

Thus it is with the latest transport of priests. Many of them arrived in Dachau in furs, the rest in warm coats, and all in warm underwear. Then suddenly they're clothed in very thin "pajamas" and forced to remain for hours barefooted, with uncovered heads, in snowstorms, rain, and freezing wind. And so large numbers of victims fall. Many priests from that transport die as quickly as the older and weaker priests died in Stutthof, in the quarantine at Sachsenhausen, as well as in Gusen, Mauthausen, Auschwitz, and hundreds of similar death camps.[1]

In hundreds? Isn't that an exaggeration? someone may ask. No, unfortunately, it isn't an exaggeration. It is only a quotation from the German document "*Liste der Lager, Kommandos und Gefängnisse, die zur Inhaftierung gedient haben,*" which cites *four hundred* such places of torture.[2]

I'm part of a group of colleagues working on the plantation. Exhausted from work, covered with mud, we return very late to our block. Today I managed to slip a half-rotten carrot under my shirt by fastening it with the belt to my pants. Following roll call, I return to the third hall. I find my uncle lying on his bunk. Oh, with what shining eyes he grasps the carrot, warmed by my body.

"God bless you, my boy, God bless," and he starts munching. "But," he says between one bite and the next, "have you heard the latest news?"

"News?" Already the worm of weariness is gnawing me. I know what this will be again, some kind of preposterous camp rumor. And it's just as I thought.

"It seems that somewhere in the odd-numbered blocks across the camp street (a vague gesture of the hand in the opposite direction, toward the crematorium), they're already making a list of those who want to move to 'better living conditions.'" He's looking at me with a questioning expression on his emaciated face.

God, how he resembles my grandmother and mother...

"Well, what? Is it true?" He grasps me by the wrist. "You have such rough hands," he whispers.

"I don't know, Uncle, whether it's true. I don't know; let's wait."

Should I tell this dear human being what I've absorbed over the years from the constant smell of crematorium smoke, from the stink of rotten corpses, from devouring the worms caught in compost piles on the plantation? Should I kill the tiny flame of hope in him that's still smoldering, that...

"Because you know, my boy, as I told you several days ago, if it's going badly for them in Russia, if they've scattered like bedbugs all over Europe, if..."

He's talking, talking... His blues eyes are shining... He has my mother's eyes, the same eyes... And I see behind him, against the background of a fogged window pane, the smoking chimney of the crematorium...

"My boy!" The thin hand touches mine. "I'm talking and talking, but you're not listening to me at all."

"I'm listening to you, Uncle."

"Listen. I'll tell you something in confidence. When I last met with Bishop Dymek and our conversation turned to the topic of Cardinal Hlond, he told me a secret. That is, my boy..."

"Toooo the baaaaracks!" comes a cry from the street.

I jump up.

"Wait a minute." A look of helplessness appears on his face. (Perhaps it's fear of being left alone?)

"Uncle, I have to go! Our hall leader Emil won't excuse me. Good night, uncle!"

"Good night, my boy."

He goes back to chewing the rest of the carrot. Noticing that I turn around at the door to look back at him, he waves his hand. "Be of good cheer!"

In the foyer of the first and second hall they've already managed to lay down several bodies. This pile will grow overnight... It will grow... It's better not to think about how high it will have grown when morning comes again.

37

Zdzich's Hanka

Zdzich has been walking around for several days as if depressed. There's a certain obstinacy in his face, a dark fire in his eyes. He's silent. Stubbornly silent! I know he's suffering terribly.

"Zdzich, what's wrong with you?"

"Don't ask!" he replies curtly, in an unfamiliar, harsh voice that I hadn't heard him use before.

So I don't bother him for several days, but his suffering distresses me all the more.

Then, finally... And this occurs on one of the first days of December. We're sitting in gloomy darkness on the floor by the cabinets, quietly whispering prayers while waiting for evening roll call. We had been driven mercilessly all day until we were completely exhausted! The day was a hard one! Capo Hentschel drove us before noon and after him the awful Groo; Willi chased us with a stick while we distributed the kettles, then Kapp, and finally our Buffalo! And what still awaits us during roll call or even afterwards?

Glancing at Zdzich who was sitting by my side with his fingers over his face, I see that he's crying.

"Zdzich! Zdzich! What's wrong?"

He couldn't hold back. The pain he stifled inside for so many days erupts. It's good that it does.

"They've wasted her! Trampled! Defiled her! Devils! Devils!" The words escape through tightly compressed lips.

"Zdzich, for God's sake! What are you saying? Who are you talking about?"

At last I find out what's been burning this soul for so many days. Zdzich has only one sister. I remember her: Hanka, a beautiful girl, with flaxen hair and eyes as blue as cornflowers, still a child with the soul of an angel, an angel who seemed surprised she had been sentenced to walk here below. When the war started, she was barely sixteen years old.

"And today she's at her mother's, with an out-of-wedlock child!" the cry bursts out of Zdzich's tormented heart.

"Oh, God!"

"They took her by force from the house! Tore her away from her widowed mother! Locked her up in a soldiers' brothel! Took away her virginity! Everything for the might of the SS soldier, marching 'through joy to strength'! Monsters! Then some officer took her for himself... He left her when she was several months pregnant... The Satan!"

"Zdzich!" I want to put my arms around him, but I'm afraid, knowing he doesn't like such signs of friendship. "Zdzich..."

"The letters from home had worried me for a while," he continues. "There was something in them I didn't like, but ... you know yourself how those letters look, both theirs and ours, when written under the dictate of fear. I attributed unexplained things in them to that fear. Then suddenly..."

"How do you know about ... about this..." I can't find the words to describe it.

"The news was brought by arrivals on the last transport. Kazio is from my area. He was at my mother's, he talked with Hanka, he..."

There is a moment of painful silence...

How do I respond to all this? How can I calm him when I can't find any words of comfort? How can one bear such a thing? His beloved only sister... Oh God, God! There are no words of comfort for this...

"*Antreten!*" Buffalo interrupts this difficult moment.

"*Antreten! Antreten!*" cries in the street resound like an echo.

We get up without saying a word.

Sloshing through the mud of the soggy street, we march toward the assembly square. Zdzich is walking next to me. I notice that he's out of step.

"Get into step," someone behind us hisses.

I turn around with a look that tells him to leave Zdzich alone. I don't know whether he understood, but he said no more.

The roll call drags on. A fine, freezing rain starts to fall. Streams of light flow from the guardhouse windows. Silhouettes of SS men flash from behind the window panes.

"Dress the ranks!" yells Buffalo, kicking the first person in our rank.

I move Zdzich about a quarter of a foot toward the front. He looks like a wooden puppet.

"What's wrong with him?" whispers the guy standing to the left.

"Don't ask."

"*Aaaachtung!*" Kapp's voice roars out.

The camp comes to a standstill.

"Caaaps off!"

Luckily, Buffalo didn't notice Zdzich's delay.

"Hold on, friend."

"March off by block!"

Block by block we leave the square.

"*Ein Lied!* A song!" Buffalo throws out the order.

"Lore!"

"Left! Two! Three! Four!"

So we sing on command about a lovely girl named Lore... Poor Zdzich! Mud pushed down by our wooden clogs splashes all around; the freezing wind lashes our faces with a sharp drizzle; dead leaves rustle in the poplar trees, and one block after another moves toward the barracks, each with a different melody.

There are many more cases like this, many more! News of this kind arrives with each transport, news that causes the soul to moan.

One had his daughter violated! Another his wife!

"I will liberate humanity from the filthy, demeaning, poisonous madness they call morality and conscience!"[1] This outcry of the Führer absolved his "fighters" of everything! Just as a German girl proudly wore a patch on her sleeve with the letters "I.B.B.," that is,

"I am impregnated," so a Polish girl was to consider it the greatest honor if an SS man chose to rape her. A man of irreproachable blood — was taking her, a slave!

It's dark outside. We've finished our supper.

"Get ready for sleep!"

It's only now that I notice Zdzich's absence. In vain I look for him in the bunkroom, the washroom, the bathroom... No one has seen him since we returned from roll call.

I step out into the block street. Darkness. A cold rain comes down harder and harder. Streaks of dim light filter out from the hall windows. In that faint light I barely see someone kneeling by the paint-covered windows of the chapel. Zdzich?

Yes, of course, it's Zdzich! Bent over, soaked to the skin, with his face hidden in his hands, he's kneeling in the mud, his trembling body crouched against the frigid wall of the barracks.

"Zdzich!" He doesn't resist. He allows me to lead him like a child. Convulsive sobbing overwhelms him. And like a child he repeats helplessly:

"My Jesus! Why? ... Why? ..."[2]

38

Now You'll Rot in Dachau!

The only daily permitted by camp officials is the Nazi propaganda rag *Völkischer Beobachter*, an organ of Joseph Goebbels. Each hall receives its own copy. Camp officials know why they allow this propaganda paper! Not for nothing is it run by Joseph Goebbels.

Shortly after the last big transport of priests arrives in Dachau, the paper carries the banner headline:

"INVINCIBLE GERMAN ARMY AT THE GATES OF MOSCOW!"

The depressing impression created by that news had barely faded when one heading after another recounts the successes of General Rommel's invincible army in Africa!

To be sure, November brings news of a Red Army counteroffensive, but master of propaganda Joseph Goebbels knows how to present the situation: when you take into account a "tactical withdrawal of German troops to positions chosen in advance," the Russian army is still losing. (?!)

On the feast day of the Immaculate Conception, which we experience painfully anyway, as is the case with all other feasts of the Blessed Mother, the newspaper treats us to titles about the victory of the Japanese air force at Pearl Harbor.

After that news, *Völkischer Beobachter* goes on to the next item: Japan has declared war against the United States!

On the feast of Our Lady of Loretto we receive news about tremendous successes of the Japanese in the Philippines.

The next day a real bomb is dropped: *Völkischer Beobachter* announces in enormous letters that Germany and Italy have declared war against the United States!

For a moment, the camp is struck dumb! The SS men rage as though possessed by the devil.

"Now, after we defeat America," Munderlein foams, "you'll all rot in Dachau! You'll rot! Understand?"

"Yes, sir!" the ranks reply in unison.

"Therefore ... Fall down! You dogs!" and the SS man's steel-reinforced boots trample, crush, tread down! The drunkard was raving mad with hate. We had never seen him like this before.

"Well, you see, it's in the nature of things; the stronger and more victorious one is, the more bloodthirsty."

Edek Francuskiewicz is one of the Polish high school students working in the camp sickroom as a nurse. A wonderful boyish soul. How much good he does for his countrymen, how much for us, the priests! Now, since they've lifted the isolation, he's often a guest in our barracks. He's also one of the "faithful" who comes to our quiet catacomb-like Sunday "High Masses."

He comes this evening, also. We sit in a corner on the floor.

"Only, for God's sake, don't betray me because you know it could cost me my life. Well, then this priest ... this priest—I can't remember his last name. Well, you know, the one who had those pains after he took a beating from the hall leader... Well, you know, they brought him to the sickroom on Thursday..."

"Reverend Canon Wojsa?"

"Yes, that's it. Wojsa. For sure. So Heiden himself took him into the operating room, ordered that he be fastened to the operating table, and, without giving him any anesthetic, while he was conscious, sawed through his skull and then picked at his brain."

"Picked at his brain?"

"That's right. It seems he wanted to discover the cause of his illness."

"Dear Jesus!"

"If only you heard how the poor guy screamed! Although they had taped his mouth, a real roar came out of his throat. Can you imagine his suffering?"

"And what did they do with him?"

"Just this..." Edek makes a gesture that imitates giving an injection. "After just a few minutes he was gone. Only, for God's sake, if you betray me!"

And was the Rev. Canon Wojsa from Lublin the only victim of such bloody experiments on the part of the smithy Heiden?

At that same time, notes from the Apostolic Nuncio were sent to the government in Berlin on behalf of Bishop Kozal, on behalf of bishops "tortured to death" in the camps—Nowowiejski and his suffragan Wetmański from Płock—and on behalf of Bishop Goral.

In regard to Bishop Michał Kozal, the government in Berlin gave a reply on November 18, 1941, announcing that "this bishop was transferred from Ląd to Dachau" and that "for reasons of *public security* he cannot be freed at this time." And when the Nunciature kept insisting and demanded in a letter of December 12, 1941, that reasons for the arrest be given, a note from the government in Berlin tersely explained that "the monsignor had carried on political activity in a spirit hostile to Germany." And at its end the note states again that "for police and security reasons (*aus praeventiv polizeilichen Gruenden*), releasing him is not possible."

In the face of further pressure from the Nunciature on this matter, the government in Berlin fell silent; no response was given.[1] A judgment had come down on Bishop Kozal!

"Go on! Go! Go, you dog!" screams the capo, covering the back of the distinguished prisoner with blows from his stick. "You think that just because you're a bishop you don't have to work? Go on, you dog! Get going!"

And the Bishop pushes wheelbarrows day after day together with us. He falls down doing this, lifts himself up again, staggers, but won't allow anyone to take his place.

"Thank you. No! I'll manage somehow."

Anyway, would they let someone take his place? They keep watch over him especially! It's easier for any of us to get lost in the crowd of workers than for him. The eyes of the capos, the foremen, Buffalo, and the others rest constantly on him...

38. Now You'll Rot in Dachau!

Oh, how hard it was to be a *bishop* in Dachau!

But the cost of *wanting* to be a bishop was sky-high!

And Bishop Michał Kozal not only *wanted* to be a bishop with his whole heroic heart, he truly *was* one! I don't know when or where he was greater: was it during the most solemn pontifical celebration in the cathedral or when, stripped of everything, emaciated like a skeleton and covered with the rags of his striped prison uniform, he pushed wheelbarrows in Dachau?

We're removing snow again from the entire camp. Again our first worry upon awakening is summarized in the question: "Did it snow today?"

"It snowed," answer those lying by the windows.

"And how!" someone adds.

"God! Again we'll have the daylong nightmare of beatings, kicking, drudgery! Why did You wake me today? Why didn't You take me quietly this night? Why must I fall under the clubs of these torturers?"

"*Antreten*! It's kettle time!"

And again...

Every day several of "those freed forever" depart; every few days several new prisoners are brought in. Recently they brought in Fr. Leitgeber from the Września area, where he had been imprisoned for quite some time. He has some news from old Września about Fr. Kinastowski, about the vicars, about our acquaintances...

Christmas goes by in gloom. This year, too, we spend the day working on snow removal. In the course of this work we face newly invented harassments. After all, it's the year 1941, the year of great victories, and — according to Joseph Goebbels — it's the year that will bring final victory for the Germans!

While for us?

39

The Mountain Girl with Little Thérèse's Face

"Heinrich, Heinrich," says capo Georg Wilhelm, a stocking weaver, tapping me on the back so that I have to stop working. "You're lucky, very lucky that you're not with them." He points through a fogged-up windowpane toward the assembly square where just now they're escorting one hundred twenty prisoners: the old, the weak, the handicapped, and those who volunteered to leave "for better living conditions."

But before continuing further about the group of priests in Dachau, I need to provide some explanations. Admittedly, they will be of a personal nature, but they are important for showing the authenticity of information chronicled in this book. In 1947 and 1948, following the first edition of *Shavelings,* there was a flurry of friendly critical comments, amendments, and corrections. I was and am sincerely grateful for them because they reinforce the credibility of this memoir. If I have any reason to complain, it is only that these frank critical comments from living colleagues with whom I experienced the described events were too few in number, too brief, and not specific enough.

Today, fifteen years since my release from Dachau, when the second edition of *Shavelings* goes out into the world, there remain alive only a handful of us who went through Inowrocław, Świecie, Górna Grupa, Stutthof, and Sachsenhausen. Of course, there is quite a group of former Dachau inmates still alive, but even they are disappearing with each passing year. How much invaluable historical material has gone to rest in graves together with colleagues who have passed away during the last fifteen years! And which of us will live another fifteen years? Perhaps none? ... That is why I turn here with a sincere request to my living colleagues who obtain this second edition of *Shavelings* that they be kind enough to send me their critical comments regarding the dates, circumstances, events, facts, and first and last names presented in the current edition. If the writer of these words can no longer make use of them, then they can be used by someone else who in turn takes over this effort, someone better suited for compiling a strictly historical work.

Today, of course, fifteen years later, when we already have access to a great deal of historical source material, it would not be difficult to write a strictly historical account; nevertheless, I am avoiding that approach on purpose. My book about "shavelings," in both the first and the current editions, is meant to retain the authentic nature of a *chronicle* about the experiences of only a single group of priests, and in this way it will be only one small brick found among others in the historical monument that will someday "be erected" by someone especially called to the task.

In recent years I have been questioned many times by officials regarding the sources of my information. I am obliged to provide explanations that were not given in the first edition.

Providence so strangely directed that in Dachau I might find my way into a camp area that included the best informed group, and because of this, many issues or events not well understood by my priest colleagues were much clearer to me.

I include this comment only to emphasize the historical authenticity of the facts that my book contains. I bring myself to provide this explanation only now in the second edition due to the fact that *Shavelings*, a small unpretentious volume in the first edition, has gained documentary value over the years for German courts that are investigating cases of my colleagues, former prisoners. That is why the above explanation indicating other sources even more firmly supports the authenticity of facts provided, both for the German courts and perhaps even for a German history of this period.

After these explanations, I return to Dachau, to the days following Christmas 1941, so that (compelled to make these personal revelations) I can trace the path that led me to the sources mentioned above.

One evening, after I've returned from work on the plantation, colleagues greet me with these words:

"It's too bad you weren't here because after morning roll call they were looking for candidates for the woodcarving shop. We mentioned you, but because you were on a job outside the camp and..."

I became interested in this bit of news.

"Then what?" I ask.

"You're too late. It seems that several dozen laymen have already volunteered, and they've been taking part in a competition since this morning."

"Who could help me in this?"

"Only the block secretary."

After eating a meager supper, I run to our secretary.

"Sir! They were supposedly looking for a woodcarver. Well, I..."

He interrupts me with a wave of his hand, and continuing to read the *Völkischer Beobachter*, he mumbles:

"There's no use talking. That's right, they were looking, but that was this morning. There are already several dozen candidates. It's too late."

"But perhaps if... If you would be so kind..." I stutter timidly, having resolved to make an attempt, prompted by the firm realization that a life raft is passing by and I must grab hold of it.

"Don't bother me!"

The end!

"Well, what?" Zdzich asks when I return to my bunk.

"Eh," I answer, discouraged and bitter. "He didn't want to talk to me."

"Well, good night then!"

"Good night, Zdzich."

I can't fall asleep. The idea of the woodcarving shop haunts me. I already feel the thick linden block under my crooked fingers; my nostrils are already filled with the fragrance of honey!

Is that Buffalo coming? Frightened, I pull the blanket over my head. I wait... The footsteps come closer and closer. Someone stops next to me. Oh, God! Someone takes the blanket off my face and suddenly: No! I don't believe my own eyes! In front of me stands a nun of short stature; she smiles, smiles so sincerely and says something I don't understand.

"Who ... who are you?"

There is no answer.

Aha! For a moment I thought it was Sister Albana![1] But no, it's not; it's someone else. Someone also very familiar... And suddenly I recognize her: it's little Thérèse, the Carmelite!

"Saint Thérèse! Saint Thér..."

"Oh! And what are you doing?"

I feel someone tugging at my arm. I open my eyes. The bunk room is flooded with light; my colleagues are already "celebrating at the holy beds," skillfully making them.

"Get up! Get up!" Zdzich urges me. "You've overslept. What were you mumbling about in your sleep?"

I jump down from the bunk and start making my bed according to the sacred formula, but I still see before me the smiling face of the little Carmelite. (I had a special devotion to her as a seminarian and also later during my years as a priest.)

"Tooo the ke-e-ettles!" comes the cry from the street.

In an instant we're running toward the kitchen. The snow crunches loudly under our clogs. We can see puffs of breath coming out of our mouths. It's freezing! Above us is a sparkling sky.

"Faster! Get going! You lazy dogs!" Willi "encourages" us either with curses or with his club.

Running into the kitchen in formation — and you have to be careful not to trip on the wet and slippery floor — we grab the kettle assigned to us, and we're already running toward the exit after earning a kick from the SS man who keeps count at the door. This "form" of counting is most appealing to the youngster.

"Where are we supposed to carry it today?"

"Wait a minute, I couldn't see, my glasses got so fogged up... To number thirty."

"Thirty? Ugh! That's a long way."

"That will warm us up."

Kettles are carried in the following way (after such a long time, you become a specialist, like movers of heavy pianos): you pick it up, run with it several dozen steps, then put it down, resting a moment, catching your breath and ... once more:

"Ready! Grab it. Up!" and again several dozen quick, short steps.

It's good if the brew doesn't spill out of the kettle. It's not so good if the cover doesn't fit tightly or if it's bent and the brew spills on your hands. But we have a trick even for that. You wrap the handle with a cap and ... somehow you get protection and, in addition, the kettle's sharp handle doesn't cut into your fingers as much.

We finally get to the thirtieth block. We put our load down at the end of the block street, and we're about to run back to our block when someone's voice is heard in the darkness:

"It's cold today."

"Cold, indeed," I answer, and at that moment something flashes in my dulled brain. Why that's Kurt, the secretary for Block 30. To be sure, he's a communist, but he's a man with a good heart.

"Go to him!"
Who's whispering this? The smiling little Carmelite?
"Go to him!"
Some kind of force practically grabs me by the hand.
How on earth is this possible? He's not the secretary for our block! He's a stranger, a German, and a communist.
"Go to him!"
"Ku ... Kurt."
"Ja?" mutters the German, puffing on his crooked pipe. I explain my case to him briefly (in Dachau, as in America, everyone's in a hurry and doesn't have time for much talk). "Ja, Hein," answers Kurt. "Yesterday I myself nominated our seminarian over there; his name is Sarnyk.[2] He told me last night they've already started working. I can't help you. If you had come yesterday..."
"Kurt. I'm at the plantation..."
"Ach so. Plantage ... Ja, that's even worse because you have a command and..."
Thérèse! If it was you who put this notion into my head, then...
"Wait!" says Kurt suddenly. "I have to see capo Hein anyway." He thinks for a moment and then, with animation, he says, "Know what I advise you to do? After morning roll call, when the order is given to form work units, instead of joining your unit, run to the rear of our block. I'll slip you through somehow."
"An ... tre ... ten ...! *Zum Appellll*!"
There's no time to get a sip of coffee. When I run into the street of our block, my colleagues are already standing in formation.
"Where were you?" Zdzich greets me.
In a whispered answer I tell him about Kurt's advice.
"If you manage to get in there, even I will believe in this Thérèse, who sends showers of roses down from heaven."
"You're a character."
"No, not a character. You know me. But I don't like it when a person's entire devoutness hangs on the garment of some little nun Thérèse, or on the rope girding St. Anthony's habit. Faith and devoutness, Henryk, they're..."
"*Achtung*! In step, forward march!"
We go...
St. Thérèse! You know very well I've never sought and am not now seeking any small miracles from you. You know that if I was close to you it was for the sake of the "path" you took to Jesus, but today... And furthermore, today it's not just about me, about this woodcarving shop, but about "conversion" of that very dear pagan, Zdzich. Thérèse, if today you...
Roll call is the same as every day. The cold is terrible. We're freezing to death. A cold fog descends. We feel it on us.
Finally we hear the order eagerly awaited but, at the same time, awaited with fear:
"*Arbeitskommando formieren!*"
The square is abuzz. Several thousand prisoners, standing motionless until now, are suddenly stirring, moving, running! Some in one direction, others to another part of the square. The yelling of capos, the cries of block leaders, the clatter of hundreds of wooden clogs on the ground.
"Run," Zdzich prods me, "and ... may your Thérèse..."

After making the sign of the cross, I run off, pushing against those in my path while others whose path I block push me.

"Hein," Kurt suddenly yells, trying to show that he's nearby. A few steps and I'm next to him. "Let's go," he says simply.

To my surprise, instead of leading me to the barracks that house the carving workshop, Kurt leads me straight to the entrance of the main camp street. Two policemen block our way. (Camp police posts are also manned by prisoners.)

"Where to?" A policeman's hand, covered in a heavy glove, stops us.

"Secretary of Block 30 with a prisoner summoned by the Arbeitseinsatz."

"*Rein!*" he lets us into the street.

"First, we'll go and eat something, and then we'll see."

I'm lucky that Buffalo doesn't see me as we pass our barracks... Kurt offers me a cup of coffee, breaking off a piece of his bread...

And then — to Hein. My heart is pounding. Thérèse...

After entering the workshop, Kurt leaves me standing by the door while he goes inside and talks for a long time with capo Hein...

They finally make their way toward me, continuing their conversation. I strain my ears, but, to my dismay, I don't hear Kurt say anything about my case.

"I'll be seeing you, Hein," Kurt says and stops in front of me. It's only then that he remembers why he brought me here. He turns around and calls:

"Hein, one more thing!"

Capo Hein looks at us inquiringly.

"I have a guy here who wants to enter the competition."

"The competition?" The grimace on capo Hein's face does not augur well. Little Thérèse! "Oh, there are already twelve of them. They started yesterday morning. Tomorrow evening will be the end. Too late." Hein eyes me up and down. He apparently doesn't much like my ragged pants and patched, stained clothing (shavelings were not given anything better for work on the plantation).

"Hein," Kurt slaps him on the back. "Give him a chance. He's such a skinny devil."

"He can stay."

"Danke!" A strong slap on the back, and then he turns to me: "Good luck, Heinrich!" And the door closes behind him.

"Hey, Burek," the capo shouts in the direction of one of the carvers. Take care of this one." And then he's back at his desk, which is covered with some drawings.

"Come," the broad-shouldered man says and leads me straight into the workshop. "Since yesterday we have twelve like these. Look," he points to the men bent over the workbenches. "You're number thirteen, and what's more, you're late by a whole day. Here's your wood. But plan well because you won't get another. Also, we don't have any more tool kits. Borrow from the others. Sit down and work. But hurry," he adds,"if you want to show anything. You don't have much time."

I'm in a soaking sweat. First, because it's really warm in the workshop; everyone is working in undershirts without a jacket. Moreover... Good Lord! "Take this, sit down, borrow some tools, and work! Hurry, because you don't have much time!"

I know. I realize that time is really short. I take off my jacket. I'm appalled by my torn undershirt. In order to put the jacket on a hangar, I have to walk to a distant corner of the workshop. The reinforced clogs make a terrible racket. I feel like a beggar who suddenly finds himself in an elegant living room. Capo Hein, roused out of his thoughts by the tapping of my wretched clogs, looks at me over his glasses and points to a corner by the door. When I look over there, I see pairs of shoes lined up in a row. I understand. I take off my clogs and carry them now, walking in my socks.

"Burek," capo Hein calls from his desk.

I see out of the corner of my eye that he's handing him a book and that Burek is coming over to me...

"Here's an album with photographs of works of art. You can choose whatever you want."

I look through it. Only masterpieces, from Phidias through Michelangelo, to pearls of the late Gothic and Baroque periods, and finally moving on to native Tyrolean art. The longer I look, the deeper my fear grows.

"Don't take anything from this!"

"Why not, Little One?"

"Because these are the very pearls of the masters. Can you imitate them? ... Oh, take a look at these twelve competitors. Each has a similar album in front of him. Stand behind them and observe their work... When you compare their work with examples in the album, you'll see how strikingly incompetent these imitations are. Submit your own composition. Stimulate the imagination of those who'll be looking at it. That will appeal to them more than comparison with an illustration from the album."

"You're clever."

"You need to be clever, too. Only such people attain heaven."

"Did you attain it like that?"

Instead of an answer, a smile. "In any case," she adds, "I didn't like the ready-made examples from the albums of sainthood."

"Burek, do you have a piece of paper, sir?"

"For what?"

"For a sketch."

"You're not taking anything from the album?"

"No..." I stammer. "I'd like to ... myself ... by myself..."

He goes over to the desk of the capo, who looks at me over his glasses, but hands me the desired pencil and paper.

Sitting on a wooden storage box (there was no longer room at the "inn" of contestants for a thirteenth straggler) and unfolding the paper on a small board, I hold my pencil in a paw swollen from the pitch-fork and ... and nothing. My mind is blank as never before.

"Little One! My mind is totally blank. Help me! After all, you painted in the Carmel. You had so many interesting ideas. Help!"

I follow some white snowflakes with my eyes as they land on the huge windowpanes. Zdzich and my other colleagues must be taking care of compost on the plantation, and our group in the barracks is looking out with dread because there's snow again, while my poor uncle waits for a carrot, but today, unfortunately, he won't have one, because Henryk...

I rouse myself. Yes, Henryk is entering the competition. Instead of whining, sketch! But what? An idea, give me an idea!

"Remember the Carpathian Mountain Girl?"

"The Mountain Girl?" As a seminarian at the Poznań seminary, I started working one day with clay. My imagination ran wild and I formed — wretchedly — a Mountain Girl in a tight vest, with her scarf flying in the wind and a wide wind-blown skirt, holding two poles in hands covered with mittens. She was leaning forward, coming downhill fast on skis. My colleagues thought I had outdone Wit Stwosz, no less; our dear Sister Cecilia, however, a Sister of Charity and the seminary housekeeper, was of an entirely different opinion. "If this were St. Cecilia with her head cut off, then I would like it," she declared, "but this?! ..." One day the Mountain Girl, an object of my colleagues' admiration but a scandal for Sister Maria Cecilia (due to the supposedly too prominent bust in the tight-fitting vest), disappeared from my cell. There were many searches and even more inquiries; the dean of the course initiated a formal investigation, but everything was in vain. To this day I don't know whether my Mountain Girl fell victim to one of my colleagues who "fell in love" with her, or whether (one has a tendency to be suspicious) she burned in the oven of the seminary kitchen, thrown there by the small inquisitorial hand of dear Mama Cecilia.

"What's this going to be?" capo Hein's shrill voice rings out right behind my back.

I stand up at attention although it wasn't necessary, but a prisoner gets so many blows for shortcomings that he begins to "overcompensate."

"Sit down, stupid! What's this going to be?"

I explain...

"Have you studied painting?"

"Yes, I have."

"Mm ... And do you do woodcarving, too?"

"A little."

"What do you mean, a little?"

"Just a little."

At ten o'clock when they bring a breakfast supplement into the workshop and capo Hein orders a break, my Mountain Girl is already taking shape in the block of linden wood. And in the sketch attached to the board, above the vest wrapped in fur and the scarf blowing in a wind fragrant with the resin of mountain forests, you can see smiling ... the face from my nighttime apparition ... that same... Little Thérèse!

"So, so," murmurs capo Hein, who — with his extra portion of bread in hand — is reviewing contestants' work. "So, so. Nicht schlecht. Not bad. Burek, give him a place next to one of the workbenches. And here, take this," he breaks his bread in half, "and eat!"

Following the breakfast break, I have at my disposition both a workbench and a most beautiful chisel from master Burek himself!

"So you're a priest?" he's surprised. "Where from?"

"From Sadki, Bydgoszcz, Gniezno, Poznań, Września, Inowrocław," I recite. "You can choose one, sir, because those are places in the stages of my life."

"Do you know Tumska Street in Gniezno?"

"How could I not know it? After all, as a seminarian..." and suddenly it becomes clear! "Could it be, sir, that you're one of the Burek woodcarvers who in Gniezno on Tumska Street..."

"Indeed, the very same. Franciszek Burek, master woodcarver, specialist in church woodcarvings, servicing almost all churches in the entire Gniezno Diocese and..."

"Good Lord! So you, sir, also in Sadki at Fr. Kaja's, that marvelous baroque altar..."

"So Father remembers?" (Master Burek now calls me "Father.")

Past events are revived, those who were murdered are resurrected ... but during this whole joyful conversation, beneath my fingers the Mountain Girl starts to come alive ... with the face of St. Thérèse.

"They'll chase You out of Heaven."

"For what?"

"For posing as a model."

She becomes serious. Her smile fades like the sun momentarily covered by a cloud; but then, with dignity, which doesn't suit her face at all, she says:

"I hope you'll take me always and everywhere as your 'model.'"

"You mean spiritual modeling?

"You know."

"I'm trying, aren't I?"

"Not much!" She looks deeply into my soul; then after a moment: "But right now, do your project!"

And, again, that same smile, that same jocular flash in her eyes.

"Hurry, because you don't have much time."

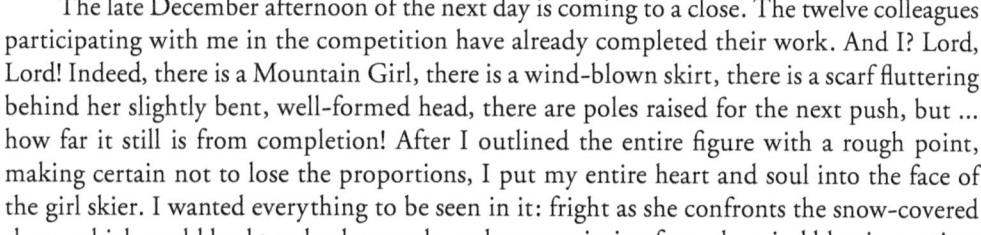

The late December afternoon of the next day is coming to a close. The twelve colleagues participating with me in the competition have already completed their work. And I? Lord, Lord! Indeed, there is a Mountain Girl, there is a wind-blown skirt, there is a scarf fluttering behind her slightly bent, well-formed head, there are poles raised for the next push, but ... how far it still is from completion! After I outlined the entire figure with a rough point, making certain not to lose the proportions, I put my entire heart and soul into the face of the girl skier. I wanted everything to be seen in it: fright as she confronts the snow-covered slope, which could lead to a broken neck, and eyes squinting from the wind blowing against her, and her stubborn will to make the run, and that joyful smile of some deep-seated happiness, and...

"Father, where did you get this face from, this smile?" asks Burek, looking over my work with the critical eye of an old master. "This is ... It reminds me of something from an altar, something..."

I smile. I guard my secret. What should I tell him now? That I see this face before me, that last night... He'd probably think I've gone crazy.

"*Achtung*!"

We jump up and stand at attention, throwing down our tools. Several SS officers come into the workshop. Capo Hein reports.

"Weiter machen." And they're already going around the workbenches. I wait nervously. I realize that at any moment the die will be cast, that a decision will be made not only about my work in this warm shop, but about *life itself*, about surviving Dachau, about whether someday...

They're behind me at this moment. I don't stop working.

Capo Hein explains that I came a day late and for that reason I'm behind, that...

"Where's the album with the image?" asks a high-ranking officer.

In order to answer an SS man's question, you definitely must stand at attention. I jump up according to regulation, throwing down my chisel and mallet.

"I'm not copying from the album."

"From what then?"

"From my own sketch."

"Show it to me."

I turn the board over. He takes it into his hands. The whole group examines it. Capo Hein glares at me over his glasses. Why is he glaring again?

"Did you make this yourself?"

"Yes, sir."

"Yes, sir," seconds capo Hein. "He started the sketch yesterday morning."

"Whom does this represent?"

I explain what I know about the mountain people ... about the Tatras ... about skis...

"It's something like our Tyrol," adds one of the younger officers.

"So, so," the most senior officer nods his head. "And could you produce a Tyrolese man, a Tyrolese woman?"

"I could."

"Have you studied?"

"I've studied," I answer, but to myself I add: theology! After all, he didn't ask me specifically about woodcarving.

"Finish and prepare for roll call," orders capo Hein. "A decision will be announced tomorrow morning. One of you will be accepted for a special assignment..."

The next day, we report back to the workshop. Our painstaking work has disappeared.

"The work director himself will come and announce who has won the competition," capo Hein informs us."Meanwhile, sit down and get busy with something. Oh, several of you can clean the workshop!"

The work director, a high-ranking SS man whose last name is Welter, appears only after breakfast. Upon arriving, he takes a small parcel out of his briefcase, places it on the capo's desk, and announces that the one who produced this work has been accepted, while the rest are to get back to their barracks.

Capo Hein opens the parcel and ... blood rushes to my head. On the desk stands my Mountain Girl with the smiling face of St. Thérèse!

"Take down his personal data," orders Welter.

And right here it starts! At the very first question I get a kick such as I'd rarely gotten before.

"Number?" asks capo Hein.

"22466."

As if on command they all give me a look!

"So you're a damned shaveling?" cries Welter.

"Yes, sir."

And so in that very place I was "regaled."

"What's to be done now?" Welter asks the capo.

"I don't know," Hein answers, but ... if I'm not mistaken, he does so with a slight smile while looking down at the questionnaire. "As a professional," he says, "I only know that this fellow understands the work, and of the thirteen — despite starting a day late — he turned something out good enough to get the decision from the commandant's office."

"Na, ja, ja," Welter rubs his forehead, probably trying to remember at whose order he was sent and with what decision. "Damned business!" He curses, as only a native Bavarian can curse, by all that's holy, by heaven, hell, and Lucifer! "What do you suggest?" he turns to the capo.

"I suggest taking the guy as he is. He understands his work," he emphasizes once again, knowing how highly the SS men value his opinion as an expert and one of the best woodcarvers.

"Well, it's too bad," sighs Welter. "In that case, finish his personal data and let's go, because I have to take him to supply, so they can give him some decent clothes. After all, such a ragman can't work for..." He suddenly breaks off. "Do you have lice?" he asks me, although less harshly now.

After dinner, I report again to the workshop, but now I'm in a new striped uniform, with a clean undershirt on my back, wearing shoes, holding a brand new cap in my hand, and washed with "R.I.F." soap. (This is allegedly an abbreviation for "Reines Juden Fett," translated as "from pure Jewish fat"!)

"Have you taken care of all formalities at the labor office?" asks capo Hein.

"I have."

I have in my pocket a special pass — for the camp police — which states that prisoner number 22466 is at the special disposition of the "Arbeitseinsatz," whereas confidentially they told me that I'll be producing woodcarvings for some high-ranking personage and that I'm directly subordinate to Brenner himself, chief of the above "Arbeitseinsatz." But I must "keep my mouth shut" if I don't want to get fifty on my rear end, and capo Hein will explain the rest to me.

"Well, then," and capo Hein begins with his questions: Where did I learn to draw, where did I learn to carve, what was the standing of the Poznań School of Decorative Arts, and what about the Zakopane movement? I'm surprised how well-informed Hein himself is about this.

"When we worked on our Tyrolean woodcarving in Munich, we watched with interest the development of Zakopane art in your country, and you'd be surprised to know how much your art influenced our creativity..."

It's late afternoon when Hein finally tells me: "Ja, Heinrich, returning to the point: you'll belong to me, but you must work separately."

"How is that?"

"Your work must be hidden. You don't understand everything now. Later, more will become clear to you. Our official woodcarving workshop is under constant fire from various visits, commissions, reviews. We're setting up your workshop, therefore, in — don't be surprised — in the hose-weaving shop. That's right!" he emphasizes, seeing my surprise. "There you'll have your well-hidden corner, and there you'll chisel. You'll get all material and tools from us. Brenner himself or Welter will give you the assignments. Be careful with the latter one because he's a devil. You experienced that yourself today." He smiles.

Thus, I found myself in the hose-weaving shop, as prisoner number 22466, assigned to the special disposition of the "Arbeitseinsatz," with the assignment of quietly making woodcarvings for a very high-ranking dignitary. And he was — as they later told me in confidence — none other than Hermann Göring, who at this time was furnishing for himself a special little hunting lodge in the Alps. Along with fashionable furniture, the lodge needed many carvings in the old Germanic style! From now on, I work on patterns and sketches provided me either by Brenner himself or Welter, or sometimes by a high-ranking officer who gives me special explanations for the sketches.

That is how, with a special pass in my pocket — a pass respected not only by the camp police, but by capos of all ranks and by work foremen as well, a pass that provides an "explanation" to all SS men who come into the hose-weaving shop — that is how without any conscious effort I get inside a place where even the highest-ranking SS men hide their secret interests and right where the clever camp "aristocracy," taking advantage of the fact that this block is secured by the authorities, establishes a secret center for its own interests and schemes.

"Guard this pass," quietly advises the Austrian Brenner. "Use it only when absolutely necessary. Don't flaunt it. The more quietly you sit and the less conspicuous you are, the better it will be for you, but also," he adds, lowering his voice, "for our cause."

What is this "our cause"? That question bothers me. I was to get an answer to it in the weeks that followed, either from my own observation, or from Brenner's statements, or — finally — from his friends. (Gathered around Brenner, a former Austrian envoy and a practicing Catholic, is a core group of Social Democrats, in opposition to the group of communists, who were the strongest group in the camp.)

I am providing the explanations contained in the foregoing chapter especially for German justice officials, to underscore even further the credibility of many facts presented in this work. In order to reach this goal, I am forced to make personal revelations that could give the impression of an author's boastfulness (which I tried expressly to avoid by leaving these details out of the first edition of *Shavelings*), and for this, Dear Reader, I most sincerely ask your forgiveness.

Each time I think about the experiences described above, the same question arises: Whether, where and at whom — after Göring — is she smiling today, that Mountain Girl skier with the face of St. Thérèse, my first work done by chisel in Dachau? Perhaps she's standing on the desk of an American G.I., a conqueror from those days? ... Perhaps the woodcarving has turned into ashes, like the man for whom it was carved by an imprisoned Polish priest? ...

One thing is certain: she lives in my memories just as real as she was then.

But — my Heavenly Model knows this and more...

40

The Dismal Beginning of 1942

"Oh, Heinrich, Heinrich," capo Wilhelm is tapping me on the back. "You're really lucky not to be with those fellows over there!" Through a fogged-up windowpane he points at the assembly square, where a group of the ill, the weak, the handicapped, and the candidates "for better living conditions" are dragging along.

Capo Wilhelm is director of the hose-weaving workshop, which has two hundred prisoners tasked with darning socks and gloves and making other minor repairs of prison clothing. Wilhelm is a friend of "Arbeitseinsatz" director Brenner, as well as a "confidant" of many SS men, including high-ranking officers. And what SS wife during these war years doesn't need yarn, ready-made socks, needles, thimbles, and other odds and ends so hard to get now?

"I have them all in my pocket," Wilhelm tells me in confidence, and he often tells me the biggest secrets, knowing that I'm close to his friend — Brenner.

"Wilhelm," I ask as we watch the procession of human degradation dragging through the square. "Why do you say I'm lucky not to be among them? After all, they're happy. Just look at their faces! They know they're going to better living conditions. There are rumors it will be to some nursing home or even a convent."

"Heinrich!" Wilhelm says through clenched teeth, moving a stool over and sitting down near me. "What I'm going to tell you, keep it a secret, because spilling it could cost you dearly, and me and others as well. Do you know where they're heading? Do you know?" The gray eyes of the capo are fiery. Bringing his lips close to my ear, he whispers: "They're going ... to ... the gas chamber! For extermination!" Backing up, he observes what impact this information has on me.

"Wilhelm?!"

"Yes, yes," he nods with a tragic expression on his face. "Only, for God's sake!" It seems that his eyes are going to pop out of their sockets. "Heinrich! Don't say a word to anyone about this! After a while everyone will know about it anyway."

In Poland it was often said, "If you want the latest gossip, stop by the tailor's or the shoemaker's. Favored occupations, but ... only for spreading gossip."

That's the prevalent opinion of the hose-weaving shop in Dachau!

"Ah, probably from the hose-weaving shop?" colleagues jeer. "Agency of the holey sock!" others correct.

Indeed, the hose-weaving shop in Dachau is a hatchery of the wildest "rumors." Perhaps that's because the workers have a lot of time to think, talk, and discuss, but also because mainly senior prisoners sit there and it is an assemblage of all different nationalities (in Dachau there are thirty-seven, not counting those without a country); in addition, they represent all possible professions and public services. Thus, the hose-weaving shop has parliamentary deputies, consuls, generals, colonels, monsignors, medical doctors, lawyers, professors, engineers, artists, journalists, poets, painters; it also has craftsmen and laborers. A veritable tower of Babel.

No wonder they "know everything" there, can explain everything, can assess everything, can read between the lines. Generals and colonels gathered from dozens of nations, that is, an allied staff the likes of which the world has probably never seen before! If the Americans and Russians knew what geniuses of strategy the Nazis were wasting in Dachau by making them darn socks, they would certainly have sought to steal them away instead of the "fathers" of the atom bomb, which was being developed at this time! Just as allied staffs never imagined the existence of this strategic Dachau treasure, so, too, the Vatican didn't realize how many "secret advisers" it had right in that same hose-weaving shop among dear elders, monsignors, canons, holders of doctorates, and venerable clergy of lower ranks who were darning smelly socks.

It was, therefore, a "source" of all news, plans, and projects, and it was a source that never ran dry!

Part of the hose-weaving shop is partitioned with cabinets. And there, behind them, is where you find the true camp "information center." It's there, at "dad" Wilhelm's, that capos, block leaders, secretaries — in a word, the camp aristocracy — get together for chats. It's there (at times well-chosen by Wilhelm) that SS men come in to spend long quarter hours in "confidential" talks. It's there — and this source is the most authentic — where Brenner himself, a former deputy from Vienna and a devout Catholic, comes in for a moment of rest. Brenner, who knows that no one is going to search him, comes in one day and — looking around to see whether anyone can hear him — makes a request:

"Herr Pfarrer (Brenner never addresses me in private in any other way than with complete respect, using my priestly title): Father, could you please bless this Rosary for me?" Of course I blessed it, and not just that one...

In the same barracks, behind the wall, is a shop where they make spoons and wooden clogs. The capo there is a Rhine-area native named Hecht, mentioned earlier, Brenner's and Wilhelm's friend. Next to that shop is a small shoemaker's shop. Several dozen Poles work there, specialists in that trade. The capo is Richard Seitz. This small team works for some firm in Munich, from which shoes are brought twice a week for repairs and taken back after they're fixed. It's so easy to smuggle out something small in the hundreds of pairs of shoes... After a while, Wilhelm himself initiates me into "this contact" with the outside world.

"You have something in you," he justifies himself, "that makes me tell you everything."

Oh, no. Wilhelm can keep a secret, especially those for which he could answer with his head, but since he sees Brenner with me every day, as well as others from the camp aristocracy, he begins to consider me one of the trusted.

In a word, the entire barracks, which looks so inconspicuous on the ouside, is nevertheless one big proverbial "milking cow" for the SS men who are stealing and "organizing," and that is why in that place, well guarded against an unannounced visit of some committee, they also hid a woodcarver working "privately" for some high-ranking big shot. At the same time, this very barracks, but especially Wilhelm's little corner in the hose-weaving shop, is a real center for all information, not only whatever is brought there by SS men and various "quite knowledgeable" camp personnel, but also whatever comes from the outside world through ... messages smuggled in shoes!

"Listen, Wilhelm," one day I question the credibility of a certain piece of news. "How can that SS man have so much trust in capo Richard that he tells him such things?"

"Well, you see, Heinrich!" He looks around to make sure that no one is listening:

40. The Dismal Beginning of 1942

"Richard's sister is the fiancée of this SS man. Understand? After all, they're future brothers-in-law! He's the one that brings Richard, under his unifor..." He breaks off, realizing he's said a little too much.

I knew that communist prisoners were gathering weapons in secret — grenades and other necessary equipment — to make a move as soon as the Russian army came closer.

It was there, in my corner of the hose-weaving shop, after receiving my first order — for a chess set consisting entirely of carved figures (15 centimeters in height) from the period of the Thirty Years' War, knights on one side, peasants on the other — that I was to spend many months of the memorable year 1942.

I fully realize that the entire previous chapter and the above section of this chapter are very personal in nature, but I emphasize once again that I've decided to include them, publishing first and last names of personnel known in the camp from the world of camp "aristocracy," in order to indicate what was, after all, a rather important source from which I drew much information that was not as well known or was completely unknown to the rest of my colleagues. In any case, during the course of writing about later events, there are going to be names of lay colleagues, who are still alive, and who will corroborate the authenticity of the given facts. (An especially valuable witness — still living — is a merchant from Inowrocław, Stefan Pracki, who was at that time capo Wilhelm's right-hand man.)

The confidential information from capo Wilhelm's mouth that a transport of men who believe they're headed for better conditions is going to the gas chamber gives me no peace. I carve the chess figures, but my thoughts are always with them...

Good Lord! After all, a large group of those eager to live in better conditions has also volunteered from our clerical blocks! What can be done? What can be done?

In the evening, I tell Zdzich in a whisper about this.

"I'm certain that this fate and no other will befall those poor people. This is something unmistakable, even without capo Wilhelm's assertions. How can one be so naïve and believe in SS assurances about better conditions? Indeed, you'd have to be a naïve child. Tomorrow we'll start discreetly talking about this to the people concerned."

"But, Zdzich..."

"No, don't be afraid. We can't divulge the source of the information under any circumstance. Good night. Sleep."

Hours go by, but sleep escapes me. From the guardhouse comes the distant cry of commands, from the crematorium fence every now and then the barking of dogs, or a tarred roof cracks in the frost; there's rhythmic breathing all around, only at times the sound of bare feet on the floor breaks the silence...

Tomorrow I must warn my uncle. He's such an optimist that he may volunteer; the same is true of my pastor Fr. Handke, Fr. Wróblewski, and others.

On 2 January 1942, i.e., the day when representatives of twenty-two nations were in far-off America, in Washington, signing the Atlantic Charter, which guaranteed four freedoms, and among them — freedom from the fear of terror, on that very day, the first transport of the handicapped departs Dachau for extermination.

All of January 1942 was one big hell in Dachau! Suffice it to say that in this one month eleven such transports, a total of 1,200 colleagues, left "for better conditions." That gives you some idea of the terrifying atmosphere in which the entire camp lived! And when letters from families arrived in mid–January with references to the death of those who had been taken away, it was no longer secret for anyone what these "better conditions" meant. The notorious committee of murderers, "Gemeinnützige Transport Gmb. H.," had reached Dachau! The commandment in the "cathechism" by Martin Bormann "Du sollst töten!" (You must kill!) was being incorporated ever more widely into life. In Dachau, a new term was adopted:

"DEATH TRANSPORT"![1]

On January 9 in the park next to the crematorium they hanged the Salesian Fr. Wojciech Michałowicz, a school director from Kielce, and the Rev. Msgr. Dr. Józef Pawłowski, pastor of the Kielce cathedral!

Although we're used to daily murders, both executions make a deep impression on us. In the evening when I bring several pieces of bread that I've saved, even my optimist uncle, the poor wretch now already emaciated like a skeleton, shakes his head and whispers: "My boy, they really are devils!"

"Did you know that dear Rev. Msgr. Schönborn has died?" Mirek Ziarniak asks me.

"Died?"

"I'm afraid so. Yesterday." (That was January 14.)

"Mirek! How many of us from the Inowrocław prison remain?"

"I don't know, but looking at the large group already gone, it's certainly only a handful. But you'll survive," he adds. (I believe and know he says this with no particular malice.)

"You'll survive… You have it good… You're lucky." I face these statements more and more often now.

I know there's no desire to hurt; whoever says these things only senses and fears he might not have a chance to survive, just like all those who, staggering from hunger, must perform each arduous job and endure each torment.

"You know, Zdzich, sometimes I'm such a nervous wreck that I'm ready to quit the work there."

"Are you crazy? Don't pay any attention to those remarks. Try to understand them. Everyone has a right to take such work if he's given a chance. You're doing honest work; you're not doing anything that could be a moral burden. Eh, in general, it's not worth talking about. Besides," he adds with a smile, "did you get this from praying to your little St. Thérèse or not?"

"Little Thérèse!" At the very recollection it's hard for me to suppress a smile.

"Have you forgotten you've already converted one person."

"Converted?" I suddenly remember his words. "Aha, you pagan! I still have one big request of her."

"What's that?"

I'm slow to answer.

"What?" he asks with growing interest.

"It won't offend you?"

"I promise that even if it does, I won't show it."

"I ask her constantly that you might bring yourself to … to…"

"To do what?" he frowns.

"To write a letter to Hanka."

The huge old fir tree standing next to the crematorium, with its enormous bough, most often had the "function" of a gallows. In the background, behind the tree, a concrete wall is visible; beneath it, firing-squad executions took place.

Silence. Only the twitching in his jaws shows me how hard it is for him. Finally, without looking at me, he says, "Maybe that 'miracle' is closer than you think?"

Two weeks later, when our block has its turn to write letters, Zdzich wrote a letter to poor Hanka.

"Alfred Skowroński is no longer alive!" Again, one from our group of "seniors." At the time of death he was 32 years old.

How many were taken in the course of those difficult days...

Four hundred of our men go every day to "school."

Capo Wagner, a communist, but — as I've often emphasized — a man with a great heart, upon seeing the ill-treatment of Polish priests, gets permission (probably after a long argument) to allow two hundred of the younger priests to be trained as carpenters and two hundred as masons. In addition, after securing for these four hundred the "school" roof over their heads and a warm room for the winter, he convinces officials that if the camp is to get service from these "trainees" in the spring, they will need to be nourished by giving them the bread supplement that other workers get.[2]

Imagine! The supplement is approved! Four hundred priests receive truly better conditions. They'll survive several terrible winter months, get fed a bit, get warm, and when spring comes? "The higher the sun, the closer our release!" goes a saying in Dachau. When the time comes, we'll manage.

At this time, also, our men are slowly, discreetly slipping into other commands. Our blocks become increasingly empty during the day. Buffalo and the hall leaders are less irritated, which gives those sitting in the block a little more peace, and somehow life goes on. Just make it to spring!

Bishop Kozal is sickly. It would be best for him if he could get into some quieter command, but the "stigma" of episcopal consecration places a barrier everywhere!

"I'd take him," says capo Wilhelm many times. "You know, however, what a sensation that would cause. Kapp would come down on me, the Bishop would be thrown out, and I would catch hell. Even Brenner himself, while very much devoted to you, cannot help here. You see, a Bishop in Dachau is like a raisin that has found its way into a loaf of wholewheat bread. It attracts everyone's attention."

And the poor Bishop continues to suffer harassments in his block.

In the tailors' command behind the wall, Rudolf Mueller, the longtime representative of a big German trade firm in Italy, has been the block secretary for several days now. He was imprisoned because of suspicions regarding contacts with the Allies. He fears that he may already have been sentenced to death in absentia. He speaks Italian fluently. He has some secret contacts with Italians in the camp. I don't dare ask him about it, and he doesn't disclose anything himself. One day, Rudolf runs in with an expression indicating he has some important news.

"This will make you happy," he whispers. "That is, a Polish army is being formed in Russia. Yesterday Roosevelt addressed the Poles on radio. It appears that Stalin strongly supports you... Because of this, you've gained an advantage among local communists. That's good. It will help many of you to survive because, as you know, they're in charge of everything here. Even someone like Brenner must reckon with them."

In the meantime, the death transports continue. They started up again on February 16, and they go out almost every day. The poor souls now know very well where they're being taken. Oh, that hopeless despair in their faces, that look of terror mixed with silent pleading in their sunken eyes! At least half of these poor creatures are people who are just exhausted and not handicapped. They volunteered at one time in the hope of really being sent to some more tolerable place, but they're going straight to their death. So many heart-rending goodbyes! So many tears...

And our men continue to be driven at the wheelbarrows! It breaks my heart to watch them from the warm room in the workshop where I work with no one goading me, where — on the contrary — I find oblivion and lose the sense of painful reality. While the others are driven! beaten! kicked! mauled! They're also pelted by rain mixed with snow. And among them is our poor Bishop. But how will it help them if I quit my job and go into the square?

I'm calmed a bit by the fact that several hundred of our men are already in similar conditions; still ... such shame often grips me! The shame that I, a young and relatively strong man, am sitting in a warm place, under a roof, with an extra piece of bread, while over there are the ill, the old, the deserving ... Jesus!

While in the first weeks I was happy about my work, which I still like very much, now each chisel cut reminds me of their suffering. It's a good thing I'm doing ornamental carvings now because if I were carving figures, I would probably evoke in each face the suffering of those men.

Fr. Cegiełka, a Pallotine priest, has been brought here from Paris. He talks a lot about the situation in France. The optimists have gained a new member. But, perhaps, it's for the better? Perhaps if there were no such optimism, many of our men wouldn't have the strength to push those wheelbarrows across the square?

Some acquaintances have died recently: the Rev. Mitred Msgr. Styczyński, the Rev. Counselor Suszczyński, the Rev. Canon Greinert, all three from Gniezno. In addition, Fr. Ogrodowski from Krotoszyn, which is especially painful for his nephew Zygmunt. I look at my uncle. After all, he's only 49 years old, he's been in the camp only a few months, but he's already a total wreck! I need to lift his spirits often now since he has given up so completely. The only thing that animates him are those two morsels of bread I can share with him. Is it possible, though, to save a man with that?

On March 13, after several large death transports had once again driven off, they hanged Fr. Henio Szotek of Sandomierz. He lived only 33 years, but looked even younger. What was he sentenced for? "God alone knows and ... the Gestapo," answers Brenner.

Yesterday, on March 20, capo Wilhelm brings news that they're setting up some kind of new experimental station in Block 5. Once again there will be victims.

In the evening, Romek startles me with word that the Reverend Bishop has become much weaker.

Today Zdzich is in an unusually good mood: he has received a letter from Hanka.

"I'll give it to you to read, but not until tomorrow. I've got to enjoy it fully myself. I read it over and over again and can't get enough..." He stops short, noticing he has departed from his usual mood. "Well, don't rush to the conclusion that I'm falling apart," he defends himself. And then, after a while: "Good night. And tell that 'Little One' of yours, you know, little Thérèse, that, that ... Eh, good night! Sleep well!"

"Sleep well, Zdzich." I quietly make the sign of the cross over him.

The fragrance of spring pours in from every side through open windows. In the park around the crematorium, in darkening fir trees, a golden oriole sings plaintively.

To think the bird chose this gloomy place for its love songs...

41

Holy Week 1942

The fact that I have chisel cuts on my hands is a trivial matter. After all, I haven't held such metal in my hands for so many years that I'm out of practice, and it's no wonder that with any movement the cutting edge jumps. What worries me, however, is what has happened in the last few days in the camp, especially in our clerical barracks.

On Saturday before Palm Sunday, March 28, on the feastday of St. John Capistrano, I'm returning at noon to our barracks for dinner. Four hundred colleagues, the masonry and carpentry trainees, are walking in front of me. As we approach the street to our barracks, I see a traffic jam.

"Put away the stools," screams the camp senior Kapp, "and fall into ranks!" (Colleagues participating in masonry and carpentry training take their stools with them from the block and bring them back when they return to the barracks.)

Everyone knows that wherever Kapp is, that's where you find the proverbial unleashed devil.

We file into ranks. Kapp and Buffalo are in a rage! How they kick! How they beat!

"It's bad," whispers Aloś Gotowicz, standing next to me after just returning with Romek from the wagon detail.

"Do you know what this is all about?"

With a movement of his head he calls my attention to our barracks. Good heavens! It's as though a horde of Tatars had gone through it! The interior itself is completely empty. All of our men have been led out. And in the vacated rooms? Cupboards, tables, stools, mattresses, bunk beds, utensils — everything has been heaped into disorderly piles. An eerie scene!

"But what does it mean?"

"How should I know?"

"*Achtung*!" roars Buffalo. "Unit, in step, forward march!"

We set out. Kapp and Buffalo are running around the ranks, kicking, pushing, breaking the rhythm of our step.

They're leading us into the isolation area of Block 21, located on the opposite side of the camp street. Entering the side street to the block, we already have a clue. Our men are standing naked, and folded in front of each is his clothing and underwear.

A search! But provoked by what?

They make us stand there in the street and order us to get undressed. We don't delay for a moment, knowing what each second of hesitation will bring. The SS men and block leaders from the neighboring barracks carry out a scrupulous search of each piece of clothing and underwear. Of course, this cannot be done without beating, kicking, and harassment. The Bishop, too, stands stark naked. The red marks on his cheeks betray the fact that they've already mistreated him.

41. Holy Week 1942

Despite the fact they took away our privileges, many of our men secretly kept Rosaries, medals, and other devotional items. Now all of these things are being found by those conducting the search. The devotional articles that are found fall to the ground, trampled with hatred under the SS men's boots. Their owners are being dealt with!

"What's the sense of keeping these things," whispers Zdzich, who is standing nearby. "Couldn't one just pray using his fingers? After all, each of us knows what awaits the entire barracks when they're found."

"Be quiet!"

"Ugh! Be quiet! Be quiet! It makes you want to scream at such stupidity. It's a good thing no one has a stole under his shirt as an indispensable symbol of the priesthood."

We stand, shivering in the cold although it's March. And already they're getting closer to us.

"Oh," Zdzich nudges me. "Look, take a look at the hero now, treading the medal into the ground himself!"

"Zdzich!"

"Well, what? Isn't that some kind of paganism? Someone like that thinks if he doesn't have a medal or a Rosary on him, he's no longer a priest. Paganism!"

And after a minute: "Look, look now! They're beating the Bishop! For what? Because a few foolish people wanted to keep their devotional items, knowing they're risking not only their own health and life but also that of their colleagues!"

Anyway, similar expressions of indignation can be heard all around. Zdzich is not alone in these remarks.

They're already next to us... Now we begin to feel the heat.

"Attention!" yells Kapp, standing on the block steps after the search. "On one of you we found some dollars! We suspect you have more of them. You will practice *sport* until you give them all up! *Achtung*! Attention! Right turn! In step, march!"

They lead us into the assembly square, divide us into groups of a hundred, each group headed by an SS man, a block leader, or a hall leader, and ... the bloody sport begins!

Why bother with a description? Even so it's difficult to believe what hatred is capable of inventing!

That torture continues until it's time to carry the evening kettles. We're forced to run with them under the clubs of Willi and others, then a roll call, and after that another sport. When they finally allow us to return to the barracks, another painful surprise awaits us.

"You'll get supper only after you've completely cleaned up the entire barracks!" Buffalo announces.

But inside it's as though there's been a conflagration! Several hours won't be enough to put the place in order, and we have half an hour for it. That's because when they suddenly took all our men to be searched (even before my return), Kapp ushered some Blacks and Greens into our barracks so they could have a good time. And did they ever have a good time! Everything that could be eaten disappeared. The rest was smashed!

Just outside the barracks lie those beaten to death or unconscious, carried back from the square... Inside the barracks, a real hell... Buffalo and the hall leaders do all they can to keep us from cleaning up in time... Consequently, we go to sleep without supper, after delivering kettles of food to the barracks of those very same Blacks and Greens.

It's only after we're already in our bunks that the precentor, who leads our prayers every evening, explains what a deplorable incident had occurred: they found a dollar bill on one of the priests, and...

"A dollar bill? By what miracle?"

"Well, yes. When privileges were put into effect, they allowed distribution of breviaries kept in the storeroom. This priest had a dollar glued inside the cover of his breviary. When privileges were ended and all prayer books had to be returned, the priest kept the dollar bill and..."

Voices of indignation! Terrible indignation! The bedroom seethes in the darkness.

"Fratres! Fratres," the precentor tries to restore calm. "I ask you to be quiet. The hall leader or Buffalo himself could come running in, and then there will be even more trouble. Fratres! Oremus... Let us pray for our colleague W., who was tortured to death."

"For dollars," someone hisses in the darkness.

"Oremus..."

He died. But in effect ... he was tortured to death. Already he has rid himself of everything, but both clerical barracks? Two thousand exhausted colleagues? ... And the poor old ones who've survived since the October transport? ... And the ailing Bishop...

"*Ten days* of continuous sport!" the penalty came down.

Ten days of sport? ... Good Lord! Who can endure that?

So they "exercise" us without pity from morning till night. In addition, twice a day Kapp lets a gang of Blacks and Greens into our blocks to revel! Three times a day we clean the interior! They take our food at every opportunity! They beat! They pummel! They murder! Over and over, the weaker among us fall in the assembly square!

What's worse, Buffalo Baecher and hall and block leaders from the other barracks spread veritable legends in the camp about dollars found, about sums of foreign currency, about...

The camp is in an uproar! Aspersions, calumnies, slanders, verbal abuse, malicious remarks, and jeers pour down in a torrent on the ill-treated priests!

"It serves them right! All their lives they chased money, robbed the poor, provided no ministry without a payment, and their greed showed up even here in camp! It serves them right!"

This spiritual suffering is a thousand times greater and more painful than the tortures during sport in the square! Even those most loyal and friendly toward us are starting to change.

I shun Zdzich because sarcasm and bitterness pour out of him. It's hard to deny that he's right, but still ... I don't have the energy to listen to his painful remarks. He's become bitter to the core, and he's so weak he can barely drag his feet.

How many fall each day of sport? It's hard to say! Some die from heart attacks, others only lose consciousness. But who can endure it any longer?

And in this tormented group is our Bishop. He runs limping with his swollen foot, complete exhaustion evident on his pale face. He falls, picks himself up, and runs some more. Can he keep this up for ten days? Will he have the strength?

"One day they'll write that Bishop Kozal was tortured to death in the camp," murmurs someone, not Zdzich this time. "Just so they don't forget that in some degree we caused this suffering ourselves."

We're irritated like wasps whose nest has been ripped open by the blade of a plow. People are ready to sting each other! The horrible exhaustion, starvation, and spiritual depression have, as it seems, taken away our reason. Only God can grasp and fully understand this state!

How slowly, how very slowly these terrible days go by...

We're not granted the feast day of the Resurrection! Sport continues on from morning.

And again at noon we clean the room interiors, and in the afternoon back again to the square, sport again until the evening rush with kettles; after that roll call, then sport once again, then another cleaning of rooms, and ... we go to sleep hungry because on this day, too, Buffalo has found an opportunity to take away our food.

"Happy Easter!" someone whispers through tears.

It was only on Monday, April 6, that they released us from the square. The ten-day torture had finally ended. If you estimate that we averaged 50 kilometers a day of marching, running, jumping, and falling, and then running again, we covered in those ten days about 500 kilometers, equivalent to the distance covered on foot by later evacuation transports during which scores of people fell. No fewer fell in our ranks during those days.

Three commands are currently being planned especially for priests: the plantation, the SS farm known as Liebhof, and the "SS Gaertnerei." All three have only heavy farm work, consisting of pulling farm equipment — such as plows, harrows or seeders — digging, raking, hauling manure, and bringing in clay to cover wet areas, and all this work — without the additional coveted piece of bread! Our lay colleagues, of course, receive the supplement, but priests are excluded from this norm.

In these three commands, moreover, there exists a special campaign against priests. Punishment and harassments are continually meted out. Trying to save the situation at Liebhof is the secretary of that command, a druggist named Płotkowiak from Września, an extremely kindhearted man, who for this humane attitude is punished several times by flogging. But even with the best intentions, can he help everyone?

Capos Rasch and Rogler, a pair of bloody scoundrels, are raging on the plantation.

"My boy," complains my uncle, "they drive our group from morning until evening as we carry pails full of heavy clay, which we dump into the low places. I can't go on any more, my boy, I can't! These are my last days."

For the first time I see tears in my uncle's eyes.

"Brenner," I ask the next day. "I have an uncle on the plantation. Would it be possible to..."

"Herr Pfarrer," he interrupts me, distressed. "An instruction came to Arbeitseinsatz that all Polish priests must work in commands specially designated for them unless they have training in occupations important for arms production. Those are the only ones who can be transferred to commands working in factories. I'm very sorry, but at this time I can't help you at all. Maybe later."

Therefore, priests are dying on the plantation, they're dying on the fields of Liebhof, they're dying while they cultivate vegetables. Every day colleagues carry on their shoulders or bring in wheelbarrows those fallen that day from exhaustion or under the capos' clubs.

The special campaign against these priests now finds expression in a veritable flood of punishments! No Saturday afternoon goes by (when punishments are meted out in the washroom) without several priests hanging "on stakes" or getting flogged.

One day, they bring Fr. Alojzy Liguda from the plantation. Capo Rasch had beaten him so mercilessly that the giant man cannot stand up without help. He is assigned to Block 27, the so-called "handicap isolation." If God doesn't deliver him out of there by a miracle, he'll go on a death transport. (Fr. Liguda was Father Superior of the monastery in Górna Grupa.)

Hunger is increasing among the clergy. People are simply swelling up! Those on the plantation and at Liebhof poison themselves with grass, snails, worms — in a word, with all kinds of nastiness found in the fields, which are still mostly bare at this time of year. Unfortunately, reason becomes silent in the face of hunger.

"I managed to get out of pulling that damned Praezifix-factory wagon," says Romek Budniak. "I'm going to the plantation. It's easier over there. Maybe I'll be able to get something to eat!"

Oh, Romek! Good Lord! He's so swollen that if you touched his distended skin with a pin, water would squirt out as though from a puffed-up blister. Instead of eyes, there are only two small slits in his face.

"Priest carpenters will go tomorrow to the W.B.!"

W.B. are the initial letters of the noun "Wirtschaftsbetriebe" (Industrial Enterprises). These are enormous SS carpentry workshops where more than two thousand prisoners work. They produce big orders for the army: all kinds of barracks equipment such as wardrobes, beds, tables and stools; also hundreds of thousands of ammunition cases and other things, including the chassis of heavy transport vehicles painted in light sandy colors, intended for Rommel's army in Africa.

The work there is hard, but since it is considered especially important for armaments, it provides a food supplement. Moreover, workers at those shops enjoy the sure protection of officials as well the "respect" of the camp taskmasters. Therefore, the mood among the two hundred of our men assigned there is optimistic. Having completed carpentry training, they have "gained status" and significance as prisoner specialists.

"What will they do with us?" worry the priest masons.

The answer arrives the following day in the form of an order:

"The priest masons will start tomorrow digging foundations for 'Barracks X.'"

"'Barracks X'? What kind of animal is that?"

None of us has any idea. But this will probably become clear soon. The important thing is that they'll be working under the supervision of capo Wagner, the same person who initiated the training of priests as carpenters and masons during the winter.

"It won't be bad under him!"

"Herr Pfarrer," the Arbeitseinsatz director turns to me the following day. "Many changes are taking place in the camp. Captain Zill is leaving. For now, Jarolin is taking his place. There is talk, however, that even greater changes will take place in the next few months. The hose-weaving shop is going to be moved shortly to the building next to the execution yard. The Hecht command is being moved to the W.B. plant. We need to conduct purges in the camp."

Surprised, I wonder where this talk is heading.

"Father, you will also move to the W.B."

"Me?"

"That's right. Please come this evening after roll call to the Arbeitseinsatz office. You'll find out specifically what and how and where."

"Heinrich," Wilhelm whispers confidentially after Brenner leaves. "Something fishy's going on in the camp!" His raised eyebrows indicate that Wilhelm knows more. "There's talk about a new commandant coming, about a turnover of the entire SS staff, about how Dachau has been designated as a camp "important for armaments.""

In the evening I meet capo Hein in the Arbeitseinsatz office.

"Heinrich," he tells me quietly when we stand aside. "My woodcarving workshop must be moved to the W.B. The painters' shop has already been transferred to the "pigsty" command. You're moving with us."

"It's too bad I didn't know this earlier. I've started…"

"It doesn't matter. Our move won't take place either tomorrow or even in a week. And our shop has unfinished orders. They need to be completed before the move. That will take at least a month. So you have enough time. Be aware of this, however, and plan your work so you'll be ready in about a month."

"Did you know I'm going to the vehicle shop?" Zdzich greets me in the barracks.

"You?" I can't hide my surprise. "How did that happen?"

"They sorted us out today at the plantation command. They were moving all skilled metal workers out of there, and as you can see," he adds, "I've become a privileged prisoner 'important for armaments.'"

"Are you going to be the only priest?"

"No. Fr. Henio Zimny is working there already as an upholsterer and Fr. Henryk Maciejewski as a watchmaker, and it's likely several others of us have a chance of getting in there as well."

So a different wind is beginning to blow in the camp. We don't understand much of this, but we know for sure that these hirings for privileged jobs could save us from extermination. Each of us, if only he meets two conditions—enough physical energy and an understanding of some kind of trade—now has a chance to get into a tolerable command, where there's a roof over your head, where there's a food supplement, and where the work is not just inane running around, exposed to maltreatment. Time after time someone returns to the block with excitement on his face and news on his lips:

"I have a command!"

We didn't know then, of course, that on March 21, 1942, Fritz Sauckel received an order from Berlin to mobilize all possible forces to procure hands for work, not only by supplying hundreds of thousands more Poles, who were being deported for slave labor into Germany, but also by using every prisoner of war, every prisoner who could strengthen Germany's armaments potential.

Several years later, Fritz Sauckel stood in front of the tribunal in Nuremburg charged with the slavery deportation of five million people, and he was sentenced to death by hanging for crimes committed. But for us, his orders (although we didn't realize then that they were from him) became a deliverance. Because even many young and strong priests would not have endured to the end, and the registry of priests' deaths would have numbered hundreds more if not for these "secured" jobs in "militarily important" commands. (Of course, even if someone wanted to, he could not avoid such work.)

Forced by extreme hunger and exhaustion to think of work that was "militarily important" to our oppressors as a life-saving raft, we were so struck during the first days by the improved conditions on those jobs that we were quite ready for optimistic assumptions: Well, maybe the terror will subside? Maybe they'll treat everyone in more humane ways? Reality soon stripped us of our delusions.

"Tomorrow 'applications' for the handicap transports continue for all volunteers wishing to leave for 'better conditions,'" hall leaders announce in late April in both clerical halls.

In the halls there's a deadly silence… "So starting tomorrow morning, new sign-ups for the death transports!"

"Fratres! Oremus…"

The voice of the precentor trembles like the voice of the oriole warbling in the crematorium park.

Black clouds of smoke obscure the stars over the camp.

42

Polish Priests Build a Crematorium

Odilo Globocnik, an SS general, is driving Obersturmführer Kurt Gerstein, an inspector sent from Berlin, around concentration camps set up by the Nazis in Poland. The year is 1942. This verbatim description of that visit is taken from documents of the Nuremburg trials:

"...This entire matter is the Reich's greatest secret," General Globocnik explains. "As you can see, sir, the crematoriums in Auschwitz are already working at full speed, and to date we can show about 2.5 million incinerated. The Belżec camp (in the Tomaszów administrative district) unfortunately has the capacity to burn only 15,000 bodies a day. The camp in Treblinka near Warsaw burns 25,000 bodies a day. The camp in Sobibór, near Włodawa, burns 20,000 a day... Currently, our greatest shortcoming is that our gas chambers are operated by Diesel engines. Your assignment as inspector, sir, is to present our needs in Berlin and seek modernization of our work methods... The day before yesterday Hitler was here with Himmler, and the Führer was not much pleased."

"He was not pleased?" Gerstein says with surprise.

"Unfortunately, no. According to him, this entire action is proceeding too slowly. 'Faster! Faster!' he shouted."[1]

At the same time in Dachau... Hoffman (soon transferred out of here and named commandant at Auschwitz), one of the bloodiest butchers in Dachau before whom the whole camp trembles, accompanied by Jarolin, another torturer similarly lacking all human feelings, is visiting a work site started in the crematorium park.

"So, so," murmurs Hoffman, grimacing with dissatisfaction on his bloated face. "So this is where 'Barracks X' will stand." With a critical eye he measures the enormous dimensions of the excavation where future foundations will be located. "Don't you think, sir," he turns to Jarolin, "that this whole construction will be too small?"

"Too small?" Jarolin says with surprise. "The plans went to Berlin; they were looked over, corrections were made, and everything was approved."

"Na, ja," murmurs Hoffman. "Yes, but they didn't take into account that this is not some kind of Auschwitz or Treblinka or Majdanek. This is Dachau! Da ... chau!" he repeats with emphasis. "This is Da ... chau, Mr. Reports Director! ... We cannot let others outdo us!" And then, looking through the slits of his squinting eyes at the two hundred priest-masons who are dumping soil from the excavation, he shouts to capo Wagner: "Hey! Wagner!

Make sure these dogs move faster! They're being lazy! Lazy! On Saturday I want to see on my desk a packet of penalty reports!"

"Yes, sir!" answers Wagner, with a barely noticeable grin around his clenched mouth. He knows that on Saturday he will not submit even one single report! Because that is precisely what Wagner is like.

"Hurry up with the work! Hurry up!" threatens Hoffman, shaking his fist. "Faster! Faster!"

Hitler is not pleased as he looks at the "work" of the crematoriums in Poland; bloody Hoffman is not pleased as he sees how slowly work is going on the new crematorium in Dachau, raised by the hands of two hundred Polish priests.

The camp soon managed to find an answer to the puzzle as to what the secret "Barracks X" is supposed to be. The SS men gave it away themselves. After all, they didn't see any reason to hide it any longer.

And two hundred Polish priests bend their skinny backs, dumping masses of soil, pouring concrete into foundations, raising the huge walls of a future "death factory," where four modern furnaces operated by electricity will stand, where there will be completely modern gas chambers, where there will be all modern equipment, so that SS men visiting this new crematorium will come away convinced that Dachau, the mother of concentration camps, is the leader in this respect, too.

The days grow warmer. The priest-masons sweat as they do the hard work. Capo Wagner — contrary to camp regulations, which state that prisoners must work in full uniforms — allows them to take off their jackets and even their shirts. One can see only now, in all its horror, the emaciation of these poor wretches. What strikes Wagner even more, however, are the marks from beatings on many of them.

"Who has beaten you like that?" he asks one of them.

"Our hall leader."

"What hall do you live in?"

"The second."

"Is Emil Joas your hall leader?"

"Emil."

"And you, who fixed you like that?" he asks another, looking at the black and blue marks on his back.

"And you're from hall two, also?" he turns to another priest, looking at the dry clotted blood.

"Yes."

"And you're also from the second? ... And you? ... And you, too?"

"Yes. From the second."

In the evening, following roll call and supper, when it's almost time to retire for the night, capo Wagner walks into the second hall of Block 28.

Hall leader Emil Joas greets him with unsuppressed delight. Everybody knows that Wagner is an important person in the camp, and even more important within the circle of camp communists.

They sit down in the hall leader's corner, which is separated from the hall only on one side by a cupboard. After a while, the smile disappears from Emil's face. Leaning toward him, Wagner is speaking calmly but firmly. Snatches of his emphatic remarks reach us.

"It's really a dirty shame how you treat your people! I would have more reasons to beat them. The work is not moving fast, the SS men rush me and make threats. These 'Mussulmans' barely drag, I know. I've risked my neck for them, but still ... ask them whether I've ever hit any of them. And you?"

"Wagner!" interrupts Emil with a note of hate in his voice. "After all, these are shavelings! Our enemies! Representatives of the bourgeoisie."

"That's true, but now when they bear a common burden with us, when SS men are killing them the way they used to murder us and are ready to go on murdering, the shavelings are our friends. We have a common enemy, Emil." Wagner raises his eyebrows high and says emphatically: "We still don't know, but the shavelings may stand with us, shoulder to shoulder, when the time comes..." He breaks off, makes a move with his head in the direction of the SS barracks. "You know what I'm thinking."

From that day on, Emil changes to the extent that when he beats someone, he looks to see whether that person is from capo Wagner's command or from another one. He tries to avoid Wagner's people. On the other hand, he beats with hatred those from other brigades! (When he himself is dying in the camp clinic some months later, roars of fear escape from his throat: "I don't want to die!" But for now he is the sole lord of life and death and inflicts death without hesitation or pity.)

And the mysterious "Barracks X," the new crematorium, is growing. Thick walls are rising, mysterious windowless chambers are expanding.

And yet, what with changes occurring in the camp and the fact that more and more of us are getting work under a roof, it seems to us that somehow things are getting better. In particular, the dear, incorrigible optimists are exalting!

"You see how they're getting softer! What's going on now was predictable. As things get rougher on the front and as their domestic situation becomes more and more difficult, they're beginning to make concessions. Just a bit longer and we'll witness wonders. They'll curry our favor so as to have support when faced with the victorious Allies."

Oh, these optimists!

Neither they nor the pessimists who suspect Nazi deceit everywhere and in everything, none of us knows that in Berlin, at the highest level of Nazi planning, it has been determined at this time that the Germans *have a shortage of hands for arms production*!

Thus, a decision is made, the content of which is best expressed in a sentence taken from documents of the Nuremburg trials that precisely pertains to our fate:

"*Some are being condemned for extermination through work* and for that reason are temporarily allowed to live, but for the rest" (those sufficiently wasted by years of hunger, by work beyond their strength and by inhumane treatment — author's comment), "there remains only a second path, namely: *the path to the gas chambers!*"[2]

That is why, in accordance with the above decision made in Berlin, two hundred Polish priest-carpenters are working in the W.B. and several hundred are plowing and cultivating soil on the plantation, at the Liebhof and in SS gardens; that is why Polish priests instead of horses are pulling several camp wagons; that is also why two hundred of our men are bending their emaciated backs in construction of a new crematorium!

Those hundreds "are still allowed *to go on living*"! But which of us knew then that this was just another method of putting us to death, in compliance with a sentence already passed against each of us when we became prisoners in the camp? Which of us knew that the work we found, even the most necessary work, was set up in such a way that extreme exertion would turn us very quickly into invalids, that is, candidates for Barracks X?

One of four furnaces at the new crematorium in Dachau (drawing by the author).

Hence the haste in construction. That is why officer Hoffman is so dissatisfied with the slow growth of this huge building! After all, it will be needed so very much!

Will be?

It's already needed now! There's an urgent need for the gas chambers and four huge furnaces. After all, the plan outlined in Berlin that provides for those who can still work to continue working — extermination through work — has sentenced the rest to a quicker end, in gas chambers...

In view of this, what do those in Berlin think of Dachau and its management since it still doesn't have its own chambers (the old crematorium burns with such awkward slowness) and since it must send transports of prisoners unsuitable for work all the way to Linz or Hadamar?

That is why Hoffman is in such a rush!

"*Faster! Faster!* You Roman dogs!"

43

Three Hundred Polish Priests to the Gas Chambers

Toward the end of 1941, when authorities in Dachau started to make lists of the handicapped, the weak, the old, the ill, and those who volunteered to leave for "better conditions"—but before anyone suspected that behind this entire action stood the horrible "Gemeinnützige Transport Gmb. H." (created by order of Hitler himself for the purpose of "freeing" the nation from the physically weaker element, considered "unnecessary" deadwood)—at that time, among those who signed up voluntarily, in addition to hundreds of lay prisoners, there was no shortage of volunteers from the ranks of the clergy.

Let us note objectively that there was, after all, a rather large group of priests who were older, ill, or weak, who in good faith and not suspecting a hellish trick hiding in these lists, signed up voluntarily on the "handicapped" lists.

It was only in January 1942, when the news spread and was then painfully confirmed that these transports were going to the gas chambers, only then did the priests who had signed up on the handicapped lists find out what fate awaited them — that they had signed up for death in a gas chamber. Any intervention aimed at crossing them off the list was fruitless. Lists of names, once they were placed on the desks of those who put a stamp on them for the death sentence, could not be amended.

In the meantime, the leaders of both our clerical blocks get instructions to continue making new lists!

While the leader of Block 30 undertakes to carry out this order decently, our Buffalo displays increased zeal toward the enrollments. You would like to avoid any kind of latent feelings of animosity or hatred toward the SS men; how can you ignore, however, the fact that while the leader of Block 30, *a communist* and, therefore, an ideological opponent of the clerical group, does all he can to protect his enemies from extermination, former high-ranking SS officer Baecher does just the opposite: he tries very hard to have as many priests as possible sent to a terrifying death!

That very fact, a horrible fact, was one of the main reasons why he was later sentenced to death.

It is precisely he, Buffalo Baecher, who makes the selection for a transport, takes care of lists, makes life and death decisions! He receives outstanding help in this horrible operation from hall leader Emil Joas, as well as Cretin from hall four. It's hard to establish how many of the three hundred Polish priests asphyxiated in gas chambers were sent to their death at that time by Buffalo himself. On the basis of personal observations, however, as well as my colleagues' opinions, it can be said that about half of them were directly the victims of former SS officer Fritz Baecher, a Bavarian and, therefore, a Catholic by birth!

On May 4, 1942, our block secretary, a Pole, reads from a list the names of the first colleagues who are to be sent away today on a transport of the handicapped. Knowing what he is about to do at this time, he reads with an expressionless voice, just like his voice every day when he calls us to clear snow or to some other camp duty.

"Jan Bączek!"

"Yes, sir!" Rev. Msgr. Dr. Bączek, chapter canon in Łódź, cries out with a trembling voice.

"Stand on the left side, old man! Farther! Get moving!" Buffalo hastens the old man's departure from the ranks with a kick.

"Jan Bąk," the secretary continues to read with an even more expressionless voice.

"Yes, sir!"

"To the left side!"

And Fr. Bąk, pastor from Smolice, shuffles to the left, dragging his shoes behind him.

There is deadly silence in the ranks. After all, they're pronouncing death sentences! Pale, trembling lips imperceptibly whisper prayers.

And they walk over, one after another, to the left side. Each time a name is read, there's a short moment of dead silence, and then only that shuffling of the clogs on their bare feet... They go: artist-painter Fr. Dziadzia from the Gniezno Diocese and Fr. Jan Dziegiecki from the Poznań Diocese; after him Fr. Wiktor Falkowski from Prusiece and Fr. Stach Fengler from Iwonicz and Fr. Drelowiec from the Podlaska Diocese, who's barely 36 years old, and Fr. Walek Dwornicki from Poznań; after him Fr. Jan Dybizbański from Nowe Miasto, who's not yet 50; Fr. Paweł Białas from Ruchocice goes next and the Rev. Dean Bombicki from Wolsztyn; after him, dragging his clogs, is skinny Brother Broczuk from the order of Brother Albert in Kraków and the very young Pallotine Franek Bryja, who had survived torture in the Pawiak prison; after him the young Orionist from Rajsko, Fr. Ignacy Brzezik, and the Rev. Msgr. Chabrowski from the Włocławek Diocese; after him the Rev. Msgr. Chabowski from the Płock Diocese and the Rev. Dean Chwiłowicz, Aurelian from Pajęczno; after him Fr. Marian Chwilowicz from the Włocławek Diocese and young Fr. Marian Czajkowski from Dzierzbin and the Rev. Msgr. Dean Józef Czempiel from the Katowice Diocese and Fr. Dahlke from Gniezno and the Rev. Dean Jan Brucki from Osie, who has been with us since Górna Grupa. He's very pale, and in his eyes there's so much fear, so much entreaty and grievance...

Merciful Jesus! Will the reading of this list never end? We stand helpless; only tears fall onto the gravel of the street...

It's still a long way to the end of the alphabet!

How many of them left that terrible day? It's hard to count when your blood runs cold and tears fill your eyes...

The end.

"*Achtung!*" Buffalo's shout makes the "chosen ones" jump to attention. "In step, march!"

In Dachau you must keep in step even going to your death!

They left.

"You know they also took Rev. Canon Formanowicz?" Henio Lisiecki whispers to me with fear in his eyes.

"Canon Formanowicz? On the transport? But yesterday he was operated on for a double hernia!"

"Exactly. That casts additional light on the entire transport. They brought him naked on a stretcher straight from the "clinic," dumped him into the vehicle, right under the feet of those standing, and that was it."

"Good Lord! It's just so hard to comprehend, that a day after such major surgery..."

They're taken from barracks to transports of the handicapped, people are taken from work, they're taken at night from their bunks, they're taken from the clinic with no concern that stitches are breaking right after major surgery, that viscera stick out from insides torn open... SS men aspiring to be physicians, seeing such "convenient occasions" to practice, operate quickly and furiously. In several hours the crematorium will swallow up the victims anyway, and who will learn about the botched jobs! "If you only saw what they're doing!" whispers attendant Edek Francuskiewicz.

On May 6, the next transport leaves... Again it consists almost exclusively of Polish priests. Included in this group is our seminary professor from Poznań, the Rev. Dr. Jan Kiciński, editor of the noted "Preacher's Library," who was barely 50 years old. There's also Fr. Kiszkurno, brother of the Polish master marksman; there's the Rev. Envoy Downar, a warmhearted priest, and Fr. Czesław Gmerek from the Poznań Diocese, the Rev. Msgr. Gmochowski from the Włocławek Diocese, the Rev. Canon Jan Golędzinowski from Warsaw, Fr. Edmund Grocholski from Czerlejno, Fr. Franciszek Grzesiek from Przygodzice, Fr. Jan Guder from Poznań, Fr. Jan Jarczewski from Gogolewo and young Fr. Jan Karbowiak from Donabory and young Fr. Franek Gliszczyński from the Chełmno Diocese and the even younger Jesuit seminarian Bronek Gładysz from Białobrzegi and Fr. Tadeusz Gronwald ... and many, many others.

In the evening, as I bring my uncle a piece of bread, I find him in such a state of nervous agitation that it leaves me at a loss. My uncle's friend, the Rev. Dr. Jarogniew Preiss, who is at the bunk where my uncle is lying, motions for me to leave him in peace.

"These handicap transports are so depressing for him," he whispers to me after we go out into the street. "But it's not surprising. So many of his contemporaries and colleagues are leaving. It depresses him."

"But he, too, is on his last legs."

"What can we do about it?" He opens his hands in a gesture of helplessness.

And death is cutting us down during these months as never before. Mainly young priests are dying, exhausted from work and hunger. The seminarian Pilchniewski dies; after him goes the young Jesuit Felczak; after them 32-year-old Fr. Tadek Pawlak, director of Caritas in Gniezno, and the young Carmelite Leoś Koza and Stach Kowalczyk from Wojcin and Fr. Buchwald from Magnuszewice and Fr. Kazimierz Schulert from Pobiedzisko... It's not possible to mention them all here.

To be sure, intensive air raids by the Allied air forces are taking place at this time, one after another, turning German cities into ruins. Admittedly, this news raises hopes in Dachau that perhaps everything will change soon, but since all our attention is riveted on the death transports, we can't shake off the state of terrible depression. Up to now we were afraid of the feast days of Our Lady, knowing in advance they would bring us new suffering, but this month of Mary has exceeded all our worst expectations...

On May 18 they finish lists in Dachau for a new transport of Polish priests destined for the gas chambers. After their names are read off in the morning by the block secretary, they have some time until one o'clock in the afternoon. They can still say goodbye.

Among them now are both the old and the young and the very young, including seminarians. Among the condemned are monsignors, doctors of theology, canons, people of science and erudition, holy priests with big apostolic hearts; there are distinguished activists in the field of Catholic social ministry and professors; there are pastors and vicars who had just begun their priestly ministry. Among them is saintly Rev. Dean Noak from Łekno, a priest with a great heart; kindly Rev. Dean Napierała from Gniezno; the Rev. Pastor Felicjan Nowicki from Polędzie; Fr. Kownacki from Wąbrzeźno and Fr. Kroplewski from Krzemieniewo. Also with them are vicar general of the Włocławek Diocese the Rev. Dean Canon Stefan Kuliński, an associate of Bishop Kozal; Fr. Leon Kutzner from Poladowo; the Rev. Dr. Franciszek Lewandowski, administrator for Primate Hlond and director of papal "Work for the Propagation of the Faith;" Fr. Józef Ludwik from Ostrów Wielkopolski, and many others. There's probably no one among us who won't be saying goodbye to someone especially close in that group. How close to us, for example, are Józio Mueller from Bydgoszcz, with whom we have traveled together from the prison in Inowrocław, and young Fr. Stach Marusarz from Strzałkowo, a friend of Fr. Mirek Ziarniak, and the unforgettable Fr. Antoni Ludwiczak, university director from Dalekie, who has been with us since our days as prisoners in Inowrocław, and the silver-haired old man with the face of a child, the Rev. Canon Kubski, pastor of St. Mary's Church in Inowrocław, who — as the first priest arrested in that city several weeks before us — survived terrible days of Gestapo interrogation...

A lovely afternoon unfolds on this day in May. In half an hour, they must stand in the assembly square, which is already lined with camp police. We surround them in a tight circle. Lay colleagues are also there with us. Zygmunt Stylo and Stefan Pracki, both from Inowrocław, have come to say goodbye to Rev. Canon Kubski. Last words are spoken. They are barely audible, for something is holding us by the throat.

"Greet my family in Bydgoszcz," asks Józek Mueller. I squeeze his hand for the last time. It's cold, clammy. A death sweat, I think with horror.

Romek Budniak and Aloś Gotowicz are saying goodbye to their pastor. They themselves are standing on their last legs. They're really walking skeletons. Tears stream from the slits of their swollen eyes.

"Grześ," Rev. Canon Kubski turns with complete composure toward my pastor. "You'll return and most likely take my place at St. Mary's Church. Don't forget, the wall fell in because of wasteful exploitation by the salt works. If you don't want the church to collapse, urge them, press them, so that the Mining Department somehow settles the matter. Romek will show you where we hid the monstrance and the chalices. Greet the parishioners for me... Take care of them and the church... I had hoped to do so much more... God intends otherwise. This is how it must be since He wants it so. May His will be done."

"Father canon, please take this piece of bread for the road!" Zygmunt Stylo places the slice in the old man's hand.

"What's this?" Fr. Kubski is upset. "I won't be needing it any more, but you'll need this piece of bread that you're sacrificing. You have a wife and children. You must live for them."

The Rev. Director Ludwiczak's jaw twitches nervously.

"Go with God, my friends! And don't forget that Poland must extend to the Oder. No, don't blubber, don't blubber. It's time for me, an old man. You keep going. Don't break down."

"I'm a bit afraid of this moment," whispers the reverend canon with a pale smile, "but I trust that God will give me strength. Pray that I may have strength."

From the assembly square comes the hoarse sound of a siren.

"It's time for us... Time..."

And again the final squeezing of hands, the final priestly embraces...

They move away... They're going on their last journey...

Tears obscure our vision... Those stupid tears...

"Go with God!"

"May God be with you!"

Someone is sobbing loudly just behind me.

Leaning on a corner of the barracks, my uncle cries uncontrollably.

"*An ... tre ... ten!* Assemble for work!" Buffalo's yell runs through the street. Life must go on.

But is this really life?

From the assembly square we hear vehicle motors starting up...

On May 20 a new transport of the handicapped leaves Dachau, most of them Polish priests. They go with pale faces, with fear in their tear-filled eyes... There is a certain one in this group. Just as he once walked — tall, straight, poised — through the streets of Poznań, so, too, he walks now. A great mind and a great priest! Unforgettable Rev. Msgr. Prądzyński!

A fifth transport of Polish priests leaves two days later, destined for death in a gas chamber. Among them this time is kindhearted Rev. Msgr. Flaczyński from the Płock Diocese, who has been with us since the terrible days in Stutthof and later in Sachsenhausen. There to say goodbye to him are his diocesan colleagues: the brothers Franek and Stach Sokołowski, Leszek and Stach Grabowski, Fr. Hubert Kamiński, Fr. Kazio Krzyżanowski, Fr. Stef Zielonka, and others.

Going to their death with the Rev. Msgr. Flaczyński are Fr. Skórnicki, Fr. Staniszewski, Fr. Sulek, the Rev. Dean Szymański, Fr. Leoś Tomczak, Fr. Warmiński — all from the Poznań Diocese; along with them are Fr. Szymczak from the Włocławek Diocese and young Fr. Stach Stefaniak, pastor of the port of Gdynia, a wonderful priestly soul, and others ... and others ... and others...

That same day, May 22, Nazi newspapers carry news from Prague of an assassination attempt on Heydrich, the bloody "wieszatier"* and butcher of Czechs! SS men in the camp are biting like mad dogs! Additional penalties come down on prisoners of Czech nationality.

"We'll show you!"

We, too, are trembling. Of course. No matter who gets punished, the hated shavelings always get punished as well.

The death transports continue... And it will be that way the entire year, for us the bloodiest year in Dachau, the year of our greatest losses, and the year of our greatest mental depression.

---

*Translator's note: The word "wieszatier," probably taken from the verb "to hang," was a nickname given to Mikhail Nikolayevich Muravyov (1796–1866), the so-called "hangman of Vilnius," for his brutal suppression in Lithuania of the January Uprising, 21 January 1863.

"My boy," my uncle whispers in the evening, "this is the end for me."
"Uncle!"
"No, don't try to deceive me," he interrupts. "It's the end for me. Oh, if I could just return again into the world, to the priesthood and apostolic work, but" he stops, out of breath, "in returning, *start life anew! ... Another life!*"

Through the windows you can hear crickets chirping in the crematorium park.

"You'll get out," uncle whispers again. "You will ... get out... Remember, my boy, that this will be an exceptional gift for you ... a gift from Mary... Don't forget, however... Don't forget, and lead your life as She would want ... because it will no longer belong to you."

―――∞∞∞―――

In documents of the Nuremburg trials, in a section on crimes committed on the basis of the horrible euthanasia decree, we read that when children in the little town of Hadamar saw the death vehicles with their paint-covered windows approaching, they would call out: "*Da kommt wieder die Mordkiste!*" (The murder box is coming again!)[1]

In just such "murder boxes" they transported thousands of weakened prisoners from Dachau, including three hundred Polish priests, moving them on to "better conditions." (?!?)

From depositions given by SS personnel on trial, it would be possible to cite a description of how the poor victims were gassed. But what for? No one can take back their suffering! No one can pay for the tears of their families!

But ... these same documents of the Nuremburg trials provide another small detail, which is that the children of Hadamar — knowing full well what was happening inside the secret plant to which thousands of people were being transported — would call out when they wanted to scare each other:

"*Du kommst nach Hadamar in den Backofen!*" (You'll go to Hadamar, into the bread oven!)[2]

"You'll go on the handicap transport, you Roman dog!" Buffalo often threatens us.

44

Guinea Pigs

Capo Wilhelm's right-hand man, the intermediary between him and the two hundred hose weavers, the one who distributes the work and collects it after it's done, is the son of a merchant from Inowrocław, Stefan Pracki from St. Nicholas parish.

Since we're both from the same town and have much in common, Stefan spends much time in my workshop after he distributes the work. He's handicapped: his right hand is maimed.

"Wilhelm saved me," he states. "If it were not for him, I would have been on one of the first handicap transports. I'm not the only one who owes my life to him. If you only knew how many hose weavers here would have met the same fate as those over there (he points toward the gate) if Wilhelm had not warned them, if it were not for his intervention..."

(Here I need to underscore — if only in parentheses because there's no room for a wider discussion — that many Polish priests owe their lives to this communist, Georg Wilhelm, a screamer, who for the sake of appearances would shout at prisoners so loudly you could hear him all along the camp street and would later secretly bring a piece of bread to the person at whom he had shouted. Clearly, he could not restrain his tears at the sight of torment and suffering! For example, when he found unfortunate young Fr. Władzio Gawinek from the Kielce Diocese, who had been roughed up by one of the capos and left in a deplorable state lying in the street, he managed to keep him for days hidden behind bags of old socks, feeding him with his own bread supplement. There were similar cases with Fr. Miecio Januszczak from the Poznań Diocese and with many others.)

Wilhelm had been gone from the hose workshop for over an hour.

"The old guy is poking around, looking for news," whispers Stefan. "It seems things are going extrordinarily well in Africa and also in Russia. Hey!" he yells at a talkative bunch of hose weavers. "Be quiet! If Kapp hears you, he'll come in and make us do sport; then we'll be sorry!"

"Wilhelm's coming back!" someone next to a window yells suddenly.

"Wilhelm is coming back! Capo is coming! Quiet down!"

Wilhelm returns, lost in thought. He comes up to Stefan's table.

"Ah, I see that instead of supervising the job, you're talking for hours with Heinrich." Then he takes a small package out of his pocket and, throwing it on the table, explains:

"They gave me a piece of raw hide. It's supposed to be from a pig. Take care of it, Stefan!"

I bend over my chisels and concentrate on my work because in a few days I'm supposed to move to the W.B. I pay no attention to Stefan's comings and goings until, after quite some time, he says:

"Listen! Do you know anything about hides?"

"Well, maybe just a little. Why?"

"Take a look! Is this a hide from a pig?"

Stretched out on Stefan's table is a piece of fresh hide in the shape of a diamond, the color of flesh, like a real piece of hide taken off a pig.

"Just look at it carefully," Stefan urges. "Pay attention to the complete absence of hair on the entire piece, and then look right over here, on the very edge!"

I had seen quite a few hides from wild pigs, which were numerous in my part of the country. Indeed, this piece doesn't resemble the hide of that animal at all. Its surface is smooth, and the skin itself gives the impression of being very delicate. And only on the edge, where the diamond is the narrowest, can I see a thin band of light golden hair. And suddenly a terrifying thought comes into my head: This is a piece of skin from the back of a human being! That fragment of hair is the beginning of hair on a head. Struck by this discovery, I lift my head up. Standing a bit to one side, Stefan nods his head meaningfully, whispering:

"Yes, Henryk, this is skin from a human being!"

"Oh, God!"

After a while capo Wilhelm is also at the table. At our summons capo Richard soon appears; he's the most expert among us. Block secretary Rudolf Mueller stands nearby with eyes wide-open in horror.

"This is skin from a human being!" declares capo Richard. "You can believe me, an old shoemaker, who in his lifetime has handled many types of skins."

Capo Wilhelm hits upon an idea. Cutting off a scrap from the section with hair, he wraps it in some paper, puts it in a pocket, and makes his decision:

"I'll run to the laboratory in the camp hospital. I know someone over there. Let him test it. You, Stefan, keep order. "Hey!" he yells at the hose weavers, "Are you going to be quiet, or do I have to throw you into the street and arrange sport?!"

We sit as if on hot coals, waiting for Wilhelm's return. In the meantime, Stefan relates that at one time here in the camp interesting tatoos and skulls were supposedly prepared, whereas this...

After a long time, Wilhelm returns. Judging by his pale face, we can guess what news he's bringing. He comes toward the table, leans toward us, and whispers with horror in his eyes:

"This really is the skin of a human being! They took a sample under a microscope in the camp hospital and confirmed it without any doubt. Stefan," he turns to Pracki, who's sitting dumbfounded, "Wrap this up well, and I'll take it right back." Tfui! He spits vehemently. "What dirty dogs these SS men are! What dogs!" He shakes with rage.

Documents of the Nuremburg trials provide a lot of material gathered under oath which proves irrefutably that in the camps they prepared scientific specimens of human skulls, that they mummified entire heads of "non–Aryan types," that they produced lamp shades from tatoos cut from prisoners' skins, that they prepared specimens of the more interesting and representative dentitions, that they made ashtrays from sawed-off skulls and paper-weights from other skulls, that they prepared specimens of entire human skeletons, that from burned bodies they produced fertilizers, that they attempted to manufacture soap from human fat.[1] There were numerous attempts at tanning human skin in Dachau. I cite in my book this one incident as an example. My sworn statement in this matter was corroborated in the presence of witnesses who are still living.

It was an autumn day in October 1941. In the marble chamber of the German legation in Rome three men sat eating a hearty dinner. The German envoy at the Quirinal, Baron von Mackensen, is hosting the event. Two of his guests are Dr. Leonard Conti, Director of the Department of Health at the Ministry of Internal Affairs, and Dr. Schilling, specialist on tropical diseases, professor at the University of Munich, and a former student of the noted scientist Dr. Koch. The discussion shifts to subjects of scientific research and experiments undertaken by the above-mentioned professor... Dr. Conti notes that concentration camps are a veritable mine of experimental subjects; he then turns to Professor Schilling, asking him in the name of science and the good of humanity to take an interest in that very issue, adding that he himself will do all he can to promote this matter with the people in charge. [From Nuremburg documents.]

Not long after that conversation, Professor Schilling has in his pocket permission to establish an experimental malaria station at the Dachau camp. Himmler himself, having a "deep understanding" of the importance of this matter precisely for the "good of humanity," grants him an unlimited right to use human material for experimental purposes!

The station is ready at the beginning of 1942, and they're taking the first prisoners for experiments on malaria. Initially they take Greens, that is, the professional criminals; when it appears there are too few of them, however, camp officials find an unlimited source of experimental human material right in the two blocks of Polish priests!

What are still rather strong and relatively healthy human subjects in clerical Blocks 28 and 30 are to be used in experiments. They choose the names in sequence according to Herr Secretary's card file. The only exceptions are priest-carpenters employed at the W.B. and those in some other jobs that are important for armaments.

Various methods are used to infect subjects with malaria. Some simply get an injection; others have a small mesh "cage" with mosquitoes attached to their naked bodies; still others get special injections into specific organs. Several hundred Polish priests pass through the experimental station of Professor Schilling.

In the meantime, another experimental station is established in Dachau, namely one whose goal is to do research on phlegmon. For these experiments they take forty priests, only the young subjects and, as far as camp conditions go, the healthiest and strongest. They get a shot of pus drawn from the phlegmon of an ill person and have to wait. After a few days or sometimes about a dozen, horrible purulent abscesses erupt in the formerly healthy organism, causing terrible pain, and it is only then that the "subjects are ripe" for testing!

Some are treated with certain kinds of pills, others with injections, still others have whole parts of their body cut away, and painful drainages are made through which the built-up pus oozes out. They excise the diseased flesh of some; they leave others without any aid (for the sake of the experiment), observing whether the organism itself can deal with the horrible infection.

The male nurse at that station is a young communist, Heinrich Spiess, a man with the heart of a St.Vincent de Paul. At night, when he knows he's not being supervised, Spiess takes all possible measures to provide aid to the unfortunate victims and applies helpful treatments on his own. The SS physicians who come in the following day stand in amazement regarding the effectiveness of "their" experiments and send enthusiastic reports about them. And not one of them knows the results were based on false data!

Unfortunately, despite the solicitous treatments of nurse Heinrich, most of those taken for these experiments die. The remaining ones, such as Rev. Msgr. Biłko, Fr. Henryk Kaliszan, Fr. Feliks Kamiński, Fr. Wolak, Fr. Bączyk, as well as several others, leave the station following many months of painful treatment seriously injured, with scars you can place both hands into at once!

Feldkommandostelle, 24 October 1942.
Reichsführer SS.
Nr. 1397. 42. Geheime Reichssache. (State Secret subject).
Dr. Sigmund Rascher
Muenchen.
Trogerstr. 56.

Lieber Rascher!

I confirm the receipt of letters dated 9 October and 16 October 1942. I have read with great interest your report regarding experiments on restoring consciousness to the frozen. SS Obersturmbannführer Sievers should provide you possibilities for conducting these experiments in institutes subordinate to us. I personally consider as *traitors* to the fatherland those people who even today oppose doing experiments on human beings, unconcerned about brave German soldiers who without these experiments fall as victims of freezing!... I thereby authorize you, Sir, to denounce people like that to the most senior officials. In November, I will invite you, Sir, to meet me for a discussion... I am extremely curious regarding the results of your research employing animal warmth in these tests... In the meantime, please inform me in writing about everything, and we will meet in November to discuss the rest in person. Heil Hitler! Devoted H. Himmler.[2]

An "institute" (?!?) subordinate to the SS and located very close to Munich was the camp in Dachau. Despite complaints by Dr. Rascher — as Himmler's letter indicates — that there are still individuals who oppose carrying out experiments on human beings, the camp in Dachau gets its third experimental station. In this case, two problems are addressed.

The first concerns research on resuscitating pilots and sailors who, after falling into the ocean in winter, lose consciousness due to exhaustion and a drop in body temperature.

The second has to do with experiments on the body's endurance, especially the lungs of a pilot who, without a mask or with one that is damaged, is forced to fly at a high altitude where the atmospheric pressure is inadequate.

Both of these stations are set up in Block 5. For experiments on freezing, concrete pools are built, surrounded by the required measurement devices, and for "pilot" experiments a large, specially equipped truck is brought in, parked on the street by Block 5, and closed off by a high, secure wooden gate.

In addition to Professor Schilling — a bent-over, sullen old man who appears every day in the camp — military doctors and high-ranking officers come to Block 5 to assist with the experiments conducted by Dr. Rascher.

Mysterious Block 5, isolated by the high, secure gate, becomes a source of terror for prisoners. We pass it in fear. Various stories circulate about it in the camp, but who among us knows the whole truth?

"I fear for myself," says Fr. Leoś Michałowski, a prefect from Świecie, who has been with us since Górna Grupa, that is, since 1939. "I'm afraid because my heart is so weak that if they take me for malaria experiments and give me an injection, it will be the end of me."

Several days later, Buffalo sends precisely Fr. Leoś with a group of others to the malaria station for experiments. However — what a surprise! They test him longer than the others, write down his personal information in greater detail, and finally order him to return to his block.

"You see," he gestures with his hand in disgust. "Didn't I tell you? The state of my health is such that I'm not even fit for malaria experiments."

Soon, however, they summon Fr. Leoś to the camp clinic. It appears that during initial tests given prior to a malaria injection, they found him to be in exceptional health, especially his heart, and decided to use him in freezing experiments. That is, as we say in the camp, "They took him for pilot experiments!"

Fr. Leoś Michałowski comes out of them after many days with the strictest order not to discuss what he experienced there. However, Fr. Leoś doesn't keep any secrets from me.

"I'm afraid they'll finish me off anyway as an inconvenient witness, and that is why I'll tell you everything in detail so that someday, if you get out…"

I let him speak for himself, therefore, citing here his own account:

They dress me in a pilot's suit, button me up securely; well, they dress me just as every pilot dresses for a flight. Wires of some kind, connected to lots of different equipment and timing devices, are attached to my wrists and ankles. Then they throw me into a tank and immerse me up to my neck in cold water. Physicians and specialists at the devices write some sort of notes. The suit immediately becomes soaking wet. I start feeling colder and colder. I'm shivering from the cold, but they start putting blocks of ice into the pool to lower the temperature further. I realize this is probably the end for me. Shivering from the penetrating cold, I recite the Rosary continuously, preparing myself for death. Slowly I begin to lose my sensitivity to the cold, although the temperature must have dropped below zero since I was covered completely with ice. After an hour, I no longer feel anything. My body is a dead log.

During the entire time the physicians and officers asked me all kinds of questions, probably conducting tests that showed the effect of freezing on my mental and psychological state in general. They also asked me to solve various problems, writing down my every answer, checking the reaction on their equipment. After some time I noticed that logical thinking was becoming more difficult for me. What is curious is that they didn't address me by the familiar "you" used in the camp, but called me "Sie Herr Pfarrer" (Father). Which means the physicians and officers knew I was a priest!

Among various tests of my body's reactions to physical stimuli, they gave me, for example, a lit cigarette, then a glass of alcohol, and during every such activity they carefully checked their equipment.

I had to tell them what physical and mental feelings I was experiencing.

After almost two hours, I became increasingly tired and sleepy. I could no longer move either my fingers or my toes. They had become stiff. I felt my heart beating more and more slowly, more and more weakly; my body felt more and more as though it was no longer my own, as though it was somebody else's, far away, wooden; before my eyes everything grew darker and darker...

I was aware of one thing, however:

Here ... comes ... death...

I awoke in the camp clinic.

(I am free now to testify to something that, at the request of the late Fr. Leoś Michałowski, I had to keep secret in the earlier edition of *Shavelings*: he was very likely the first of the guinea pigs brought back to life by means of "animal warmth," in which Himmler expressed such great interest in his letter to Dr. Rascher. That "animal warmth" was provided by two poor women prisoners, brought in especially for this purpose from the women's camp in Ravensbrueck, and they provided it with their naked bodies! Everyone who knew the saintly soul of the late Leoś Michałowski and his exemplary priestly life will not only not regard this "event" as a shadow on his beautiful character, but, on the contrary, will deem it as one of the many painful thorns driven into the soul and suffering heart of this holy priest!)[3]

"You know," Fr. Leoś often whispers following his return to the block. "I'm afraid, I'm so afraid that one day they will take me to the camp clinic and give me a deadly injection so they can be rid of an inconvenient witness to these terrible things."

Poor Fr. Leoś didn't know that he was under constant observation, that his life was, in fact, further proof that Dr. Rascher's "marvelous" experiment had been a success, that the medical world was enriched and was priding itself on its new achievement, that this would bring a new wave of fame!

And Himmler, delighted in the extreme, sends a telegram of congratulations to Dr. Rascher![4]

The terrifying rumor regarding achievements in Block 5 becomes so well known that in 1943 Dr. Rascher turns to Himmler requesting permission to transfer the station to Auschwitz ... since those taken for experiments let out screams when they're freezing to death in the pools."[5]

Himmler, meanwhile, is apparently not too worried about the "screaming" of those poor souls taken for experiments because he doesn't grant the request, and the station remains in Dachau. That is unfortunate since, from then on, they start taking prisoners more aggressively for experiments in the truck mentioned above. Locking a prisoner inside of it, they slowly pump air out of the vehicle, gradually lowering the pressure to a point at which blood starts to seep not only from the prisoner's mouth, nose, ears, and eyes, but even from the pores of his skin! The person condemned to such suffering literally sweats blood. Only a few come out of this experiment alive. Most perish!

Both blocks of Polish priests in Dachau were thought of by camp officials at that time only as an assembly of cheap guinea pigs. Real rabbits had a different price. They were raised in rabbit pens built with our hands. The select "angora" species received tender care.

And although there were five thousand of them, if even one died, the prisoner in charge could pay with his life.

A rabbit is considered by the SS men more valuable than a human being!

And then one day, when they summoned a new group of priests for new phlegmon experiments, Fr. Stach Szczypiński, a young priest from the Chełmno Diocese, stood firm, refusing to go!

It took away the block leader's breath! It took our breath away, too, from the shock! This had never happened in Dachau — a place where not just an order but a mere desire could bring a death sentence — that a prisoner, and what's more a hated shaveling, was resisting legitimate authority! ...

"Stach, for God's sake!"

"What do you want of me? So what if they kill me for resisting? Whether I die here or during the experiments, it's all the same."

But Fr. Szczypiński did not die. He took his "just desserts," he suffered, but he remained stubborn.

"I never prayed as much in my life as during those critical days," he later admits.

With great indignation, the clinic capo and prison officials reported the entire incident to the guardhouse, expecting repressive measures in return. We trembled as we waited because we feared that punishments again this time would come down on both clerical blocks, in accordance with the SS system for practicing collective responsibility.

Meanwhile, time passes, and the guardhouse is silent. Slowly the matter is forgotten. From that time on, they stopped taking Polish priests for experiments.

Besides, throughout Germany, throughout Europe and Africa, and really throughout the entire world, great events were taking place, so great that possibly under their influence the repressive measures were postponed to a more suitable time.

45

At the Turning Point of 1942

"Every day we look into the sky with fear and trembling, wondering whether we might finally see weather that alternates between blessed rain and warm sunshine. We are truly a poor nation, and if we are to continue existing as a people..." writes Goebbels, knowing full well that the heat waves and dry spells, which came after a long, severe winter, do not raise high hopes for the harvest. He consoles himself, however, that they will take all they can out of Ukraine, that granary of eastern Europe, but ... and here is a new worry to keep him awake at night: Russian and Polish partisans are in such control that there's not a train going to or from the area that isn't threatened by them. Under such circumstances how can you have hope that Ukrainian or Polish harvests will reach Germany? In addition, a new difficulty has arisen, that is, an ever growing shortage of rolling stock, which is being destroyed more and more often at the fronts and in recently intensified attacks on German cities by squadrons of Allied aircraft. The domestic situation, especially with respect to food, is just alarming! Moreover, what is probably worst of all (and Goebbels understands this well), letters from wives and mothers that report all these shortages to husbands and sons fighting on the front lines are lowering troop morale.

It isn't surprising that a sigh escapes even from Goebbels on the pages of his diary, one that sounds so strange especially on his lips: "Every day we look into the sky with fear and trembling..."[1]

The only things that console him at this time are defeats of U.S. forces on the Japanese front and the British army's desperate situation in Africa. Then — following the capture of 150,000 Russian soldiers on the Kerch Peninsula — when Crimea appears to be finally and completely conquered, a cry full of joy and relief bursts from him on pages of the diary: "Finally, our first victory over the Russians this year! We take a breath, therefore, and I believe our nation will take one, too."[2]

And ... the nation "was taking a breath," a breath inflated by Minister Goebbels' propaganda. Hungry and fearful every night under Allied bombing, it willingly accepted consolation and promises.

Oh yes, Minister Goebbels knew how to do that!

And we in Dachau also gaze into the sky with fear and trembling during those days, into that monotonous, intensely hot, mercilessly burning sky... Increasing numbers of Polish priests, hundreds upon hundreds, are assigned to work on the plantation, to Liebhof, and to grow vegetables for the SS. There's a constant need of hands for work.

For a long time now, Bishop Kozal has been working on the plantation, where whole groups of older priests also work. The handicap transports have caused so much fear that even priests who are barely holding up because of exhaustion decide to drag themselves with their last strength to work or to some task, just so they can get away from the block, just to demonstrate they're "still" capable of doing something and can be productive.

As a result, they fall from sunstroke while still in the camp street! They fall in the assembly square! They fall on the way to the workplace! They fall during work in the fields from great exertion, or under the capo's club or boot.

And the heat is merciless. It's hard to endure it without caps and in such a state of emaciation. Besides, people are swelling from hunger; they swell from drinking water in excess and from poisoning by weeds with which they try to quell their hunger. All the lay prisoners, however, have that small but somehow always significant supplement of a piece of bread, and only the Polish priests have to work without it.

In Block 26, priests of all other nationalities take an afternoon nap.

"Don't talk like that! It's envy that's talking through you," Zdzich grumbles.

Hunger is increasing in the camp. It's not surprising when we consider that during this period even Goebbels is gazing at the sky with trembling and that, after all, a large part of the German nation is close to starving, and we won't even mention the millions dying of starvation in Russia, the malnutrition of the population in Poland, which even blood-thirsty Governor Frank notices and emphasizes on the pages of his journal.

"I am completely indifferent as to how Russians or Czechs are living," Himmler shouts to his SS generals. "The fact that other nations are living in comfort or starving to death interests me only if we need them as slaves to build our culture. And the fact that ten thousand Russian women fall from exhaustion while digging defensive ramparts and trenches interests me only in one respect, whether that anti-tank trench will be ready for Germany."[3]

"Production! Production! More military production!" Goebbels cries out in his diary.

"More production!" the echo reaches SS ranks.

"More production!" the shouts thunder over millions of foreign slaves, worn out from work, hunger, and vile treatment.

In Dachau we notice through tears the painful results of this new Nazi slogan!

Meanwhile, two hundred Polish priests are already completing the new crematorium. Its brand new chimney reaches high into a blazing sky.

"More production!" screams an SS man, the "director" of that factory for grinding down human bodies.

Every day a platform-hearse moves toward the crematorium, bringing piles of corpses, and almost every day they lead groups of the condemned along the Road of Death. No one bids them goodbye... Only the poplar trees rustle for them on this most sorrowful road.

"And yet," says Stach through parched, cracked lips, "and yet this is the longed-for road."

"Longed-for?!"

"What about poor Fr. Władek Młynarczyk?"

A deep sigh. Fr. Władek Młynarczyk, taken to the camp clinic, left it during the night ... and in the morning they found him riddled with bullets in the wires! We knew that the poor fellow was completely exhausted both physically and mentally. And he was such a model and holy priest! He went through the death camp in Działdowo, he went with us through the horrible months in Sachsenhausen, and now only a bloody scrap of him remained.[4]

"He's not the last one," whispers Stach.

At the beginning of June a new order is issued, stating that in addition to the normal

Every day the "hearse platform" took out piles of the dead, moving them along the Road of Death to the crematorium. That is how they moved thousands of dead Polish civilians, how they moved hundreds of Polish priests, how they moved the Reverend Bishop Michał Kozal, who was tortured to death.

"short" haircuts, each prisoner must have his hair shaved even shorter across the middle of the head.

From now on we begin to resemble zebras.

This order, as well as the order to collect all hair cut from prisoners and to cut the hair off dead women whose bodies are burned in the crematorium — all this is dictated by a military requirement...[5] In the disinfection courtyard, they're raising several thousand angora rabbits, whose hair is diligently combed out to be used in the production of clothing for pilots. And in the camp itself, they're "raising" several thousand prisoners, whose hair is needed in the production of felt. The hair of St. Thérèse was saved for relics. When relics of a Polish priest-martyr from Dachau are needed, it will be enough to search in some museum for the felt boot of a Nazi pilot...

The Rev. Dr. Antoni Zawistowski, professor of theology at the Catholic University of Lublin, is on his deathbed. One of the oldest prisoners, arrested in November 1939, he was then with us in Sachsenhausen; he survived that, but now... What a priestly soul this was! Quiet, always collected, always prayerful. Another one is leaving from the group of admirable Lublin men whom we met in Sachsenhausen, where they had already been imprisoned for several months: the Rev. Dr. Zdzich Ochalski, curia chancellor; the Rev. Dr. Wojciech Olech, curia notary; the Rev. Dr. Stach Krynicki, auditor of the episcopal tribunal; the Rev. Dr. Franek Zawisza, the walking embodiment of Salesian goodness and cheerfulness; the Rev. Dr. Franek Trochonowicz, spiritual complement of the former; Fr. Dominik Maj, a mystical soul; Fr. Tadek Malec; Fr. Władzio Kłos, Wacek Staniszewski, Maryś Bardel, and many others... They say goodbye to Fr. Zawistowski.

45. At the Turning Point of 1942

They will soon say goodbye to many who are here today. The Rev. Dr. Ochalski can barely stand up... But is he the only one?

On June 5 a transport arrives from Auschwitz, and it includes a large group of priests. There are Fr. Adolf Zagrodzki and Fr. Antoś Kwarta and Fr. Konrad Szweda and the Rev. Dr. Paweł Kajka, the seminary professor from Janów, and Adaś Zięba from Kraków and the Rev. Dean Rewera from the Sandomierz Diocese and Fr. Jacek Tylżanowski and Fr. Władzio Święs and several Franciscan brothers, pupils of Fr. Maksymilian Kolbe from Niepokalanów... There is fresh news, the latest rumors. Our optimists reach the most far-fetched conclusion, that this is "it"! Our pessimists put on a new pair of dark glasses. Fr. Konrad Szweda brings a lot of information regarding Fr. Maksymilian Kolbe's last moments...

We barely had time to recover from the shock of many priests' deaths, including Fr. Józek Pawlak from Czerlejno and Fr. Kazimierz Skoczylas, the seminary professor in Łódź, when we hear about the horrible murder in Lidice of all men and boys over 16 years of age, while the women and children of that village were deported: the women to Ravensbrueck and the children separately to one of the camps in Poland.

The following day a new death transport leaves Dachau, and in it is the young seminarian Popławski, whom camp leader Kapp dragged out of bed in Block 30 during the night. With him go the Rev. Msgr. Paweł Załuska, Fr. Julian Wolniewicz from the Poznań Diocese, and Brother Cyprian Zbytniewski, a colleague of Fr. Maksymilian Kolbe from Niepokalanów.

Lidice... Death transport... Desperate attempts by the poor seminarian Popławski to have his name removed from the transport list because he feels completely strong and healthy; after all, he's working! ... Attempts by capo Wilhelm and Brenner to have him crossed off the list, their futility and the poor fellow's despair, all of this shakes us! And then, on June 17, a new wave of fear! On that day they shoot to death young Fr. Stefcio Kozak from the Podlaska Diocese!

"They knocked Stefcio's brains out, did you know?"
"Bronek Drewniak has died!"
"Aloś Góranowicz is dead!"
"Fr. Józef Echaust from Skoki has died!"

All were young priests, between 30 and 40 years old, and all had been in concentration camps for a long time! Fr. Aloś Góranowicz from Przechowo had been with us from the earliest days. What a wonderful priestly soul! Bronek Drewniak? ... Even one's own brother could not have been closer. A fellow seminarian at whom you looked as though at a saint. For he was indeed a holy seminarian, a saintly priest, and if the seminary in Poznań were looking for a patron, it could not find a more worthy one. The son of a poor widow who understood human poverty and misery, he had only one desire: to bring to this human misery the Eucharistic Bread, Jesus, but also the daily bread from the Our Father.

"Fr. Bronek's dead?" The Bishop, who accepts everything with such calmness, is totally devastated. "Our dear, dear Fr. Bronek." (Fr. Bronek was Bishop Kozal's pupil, whom he entrusted with the position of Dean of Curriculum at the Gniezno seminary.)

Tears stream down our faces as the "gravediggers" throw Bronek's small body, shriveled to a skeleton, onto the platform.

"Lord, that poor, overworked mother of his," whispers Fr. Wolniak, the dead man's friend.

The next day, Włocławek men bid goodbye to the remains of the Rev. Dr. Potempa, author of works on pastoral ministry. He survived Sachsenhausen with us; he survived such a long time in Dachau...

And now a group from the Poznań seminary, ordained three months before the war, is saying goodbye to a colleague from Antoś Hądzlik's course.

The victorious armies of General Rommel, "the desert fox," as the Allied press calls him, having conquered Tobruk, press forward in an unhindered wave toward the border of Egypt.

The Japanese gain new victories in the Pacific. Australia is threatened!

The Germans are preparing for a final offensive against Russia! "This winter our troops will not be in the field! This winter they will be in Moscow! In Leningrad! In Stalingrad! In Rostov!"

General Jodl signs Hitler's order to the German armies that under no circumstances should they accept the surrender of either Moscow or Leningrad since these cities must be completely destroyed, wiped off the face of the earth, erased from the map of Europe! "New" cities will rise there! Cities of the "new world order!"[6]

German armies occupy the entire Crimean Peninsula! German armies stand at the Don! The invincible German armies prepare for their final victory!

Running day and night from France, Belgium, and Holland are trains filled with thousands of unfortunate Jews. Where to? ... *Auschwitz!* Waiting there are new crematoriums equipped in accordance with the latest specifications.

On July 7 they bring a transport of Polish Army chaplains to Dachau from the Buchenwald concentration camp. In keeping with international law and all conventions, they were released from prisoner-of-war camps, provided with civilian clothing, even given a few German marks for a ticket, but waiting for them at the railroad stations, at the ticket counters, was ... the Gestapo!

Can the world have any grounds whatsoever for complaint? After all, they arrested those who were "already" civilians and, what's more, "dangerous" ones, pursuing the same "hostile, anti–Nazi policy" as Bishop Kozal and thousands of other Polish priests.

"It isn't the old bishops who are most dangerous for us!" Goebbels explains to Hitler. "These young clergymen who serve as chaplains in armies at the front, even when they wear on their chests meritorious crosses of the highest order, these are the most dangerous ones for us, these are the aggressive types, and in addition — they know how to express themselves because they have recourse to their experiences from the front."[7]

And Goebbels adds: "The Führer shares my opinion."

The Nazi doctrine was in "its own way" logically conceived and ... consistent.

Polish chaplains, arrested in a treacherous manner as civilians and locked up in Buchenwald, must even there have been considered dangerous if they were transferred to Dachau! Here the "Nazi mill," driven by Minister Goebbels' satanic propaganda, apparently grinds "better" and ... faster. We shudder in fear that both blocks of Polish priests might soon be emptied...

The Dachau grist mill would also grind up a high percentage of those chaplains.

46

My Mother's Brother

At the very time when Poles released from gulags and exile stream in throngs from the farthest corners of Russia to join the ranks of a Polish Army being created in the U.S.S.R., so as to get out of Russia with that army and salvage what is left of their lives, at that same time Poles in Dachau experience something just the opposite. On August 10 a new death transport leaves! After that one, another leaves on August 12. Both claim many new victims from our ranks. So many of our men have departed during the past several months, so many are dying in the camp clinic and handicap blocks, so many are on future transport lists, so many can barely drag their feet, and it is quietly said about so many that these are now their last days; so many that you completely lose your awareness of who is still alive, and who has "already departed."

The better known priests from those two transports include kind and saintly Fr. Detkens, Doctor of Divinity (D.D.) from Warsaw, rector and pastor of the academic "parish;" with him our unforgettable first "block" leader from Stutthof, the Rev. Dean Bolesław Piechowski, a seminary attorney from Poznań; Fr. Kornel Wierzbicki, D.D., prefect of the Polish high-school from Kwidzyń; Fr. Stanisław Zuske, D.D., probably the most senior prisoner of all since he was arrested even prior to the start of the war; another who leaves is Fr. Boleś Prabucki, who has been fading before our eyes for three weeks since the death of his brother Alojzy Prabucki. One cannot describe the pain with which the Rev. Dean Paweł Prabucki, our celebrant from the Sachsenhausen chapel, bids goodbye to his youngest brother, who's being taken away to the gas chamber. There's a twenty-year difference in age between them. The Rev. Dean Paweł always treated Boleś as if he were his own son.

"Go with God, Boleś ... go with G..." Tears choke the old artillery captain. He traces the sign of the cross on his youngest brother's forehead. "Ov ... over there ... (tear-filled eyes are raised to Heaven) greet mom, and dad and Aloś ... and tell them..." He wipes away tears with the dirty sleeve of his striped uniform. "Tell them, Boleś, I'll soon follow you there." (Eighteen days after this goodbye, the Rev. Dean Paweł Prabucki died. "What's left in the world for me?" he whispered before his death. "They've killed Aloś; they've asphyxiated Boleś in the gas chamber; they've murdered the rest of my brothers in Poland; what's left in the world for me? ..." He died with a smile on his emaciated face. His death closed the pages of history on the admirable Prabucki brothers from Iwiczno near Starogard.)

Leaving on those same two death transports were several more unforgettable priests from the Pomorze Diocese: Fr. Leoś Dzienisz from Toruń, Fr. Teoś Falkowski of that same city, Fr. Konrad Klin from Pączewo, and none of them was older than forty. Since 1939 we had passed together through Stutthof, Grenzdorf, Sachsenhausen, and the Dachau years... The Chełmno Diocese, which had lost half of its priests right after the start of the war and then many in the camps of Stutthof, Sachsenhausen, and others, is now about to give up to death half of those who survived until Dachau. Right after the departure of the transports, Fr. Leon Pryba, D.D., an old friend from Stutthof, dies, and he's followed by young Romek Galikowski, also a Stutthof survivor...

The Poznań Diocese loses more of its priests. Those who died were Fr. Młotek from Gołańcz, young Fr. Witold Stachowiak from Wągrowiec, Fr. Kazimierz Andrzejewski from Grodzisko, Fr. Jan Bąk from Lubosz, Fr. Bolesław Ciszak from Bukownica, Fr. Leoś Maciejewski from Murowana Goślina, Fr. Leoś Czwojdziński, the prefect from Poznań, Fr. Antoś Tomiński, and Fr. Grzegorz Kucharski...

Gniezno Province loses its men: The dead are Fr. Władysław Adamski from Ludzisko, Fr. Aleksander Sobaszek from Siedlemin, the very young and unforgettable Fr. Jasio Mądry; Fr. Leoś Kurkowski from Biechowo also passes away; Fr. Mieczysław Potocki from Skarboszewo, a Września neighbor; Fr. Władzio Mączkowski, a dear colleague from the seminary; after him Fr. Maryś Lapis from Orchowo departs; Fr. Marian Jezierski, a Bydgoszcz native; Fr. Maksymilian Scherwentke, a neighbor and colleague from our Września days and the administrator of Żydowo, about whom we vicars would say that if he dies in his Żydowo, he will probably be the first Catholic priest to be buried in a "Jewish"* cemetery. Sadly, that didn't happen. The wind scattered his ashes over the fields of Bavaria, as a fertilizer!

Young Fr. Edmund Schreiber also dies, a former vicar from Sadki, under whose influence my vocation had matured.

The new crematorium in Dachau, built by the hands of Polish priest "masons."

*Translator's note: The Polish adjective "żydowski," referring to the town of Żydowo, also means "Jewish."

46. My Mother's Brother

"If you get out, and you stop by Sadki, greet its residents and tell them I often thought of them and prayed for them in Dachau…"

Romcio Budniak walks around as though not of this world, grief has so affected him after the death of his friend Aloś Gotowicz. Together during days of their vicarage at St. Mary's, together in adversity during days of war, and then together from the prison in Inowrocław through Świecie, Górna Grupa, Nowy Port, Stutthof, Grenzdorf, Sachsen…

It's the evening of September 23. We're returning in groups by block from the assembly square. Buffalo is barking as usual. His powerful voice rises above the tapping of the wooden clogs.

I have only one thought: to eat this small piece of bread and sleep! Sleep!

Following supper, however, someone's voice calls me out into the street. I go out. Standing there is Fr. Jarogniew Preiss, D.D., bent over, emaciated, with a gaunt but still handsome face.

"Your uncle has died," he says. "If you want to see him again, come. I'll take you."

We walk along the dark street to Block 21, where they had taken him from the plantation.

"They brought him at noon. I had no time or chance to inform you," he explains in a labored, broken whisper. "After returning from work, before roll call, I went to see him. He was no longer alive. But," he whispers, pausing and taking something from a fold in his shirt. "Your uncle gave me this for you."

Surprised, I take in my hand some kind of trinket wrapped in a small piece of rag. Jarogniew explains.

"Those are gold crowns from his teeth. He told me yesterday: 'Give them to Henryk. Maybe he can use them to get bread. Hug him for me.'"

"No, he's no longer in the room," a neighbor informs us as we stand by the bunk on which Jarogniew found the deceased before roll call. "As soon as they drew his rations, they carried him right out," the neighbor finishes.

"You don't know where?"

"Where else but to the privy."

By the wall in the bathroom lay bodies. On top of that heap, with his head hanging down toward the smelly toilet, with mouth wide open, are the remains of my mother's brother. A skeleton covered with mangy skin. While I always saw in his face a great resemblance to my grandmother and mother, now there was no trace of it. The bare skull and the bones sticking out from bluish skin bore no resemblance to the living.

This is how my grandmother must have looked two weeks after being laid to rest in her grave; it is how my mother will look; it is how I will look. When? Maybe soon…

"You'll get out. Don't forget, my boy, to start your life anew, but a life…" It seems to me I hear those last words of his.

"*To start life anew!*"

The tapping sound of reinforced clogs comes from the entryway. The latrine door squeaks.

"Move to the side," a voice grumbles. "We're bringing another one in here."

Two hall aides carry a newly deceased by the legs and arms. Swinging the body to gain momentum, they throw it on the heap…

From under the body just thrown, my deceased uncle's head and part of his chest are sticking out.

"Maybe we should leave," whispers Jarogniew.

"All right." I move closer in order to say goodbye, if only by a touch of the hand, to the one my mother took care of when he was a child. Marked with indelible ink on his emaciated chest you can see the number 28253. Across his high forehead rambles a louse...

This is all that's left of my mother's brother.

Oh, no! Still remaining are his last words: "Return to life and begin it anew!"

It's already very late. Jarogniew has dragged himself off to his hall. (Fr. Jarogniew Preiss, D.D., died on the 27th of that month. He survived my uncle by only five days.)[1]

There's activity in the halls. It's a sign the order has been given: To bed! The camp siren will sound now, and we'll have to go into the barracks. My head is spinning: my dead uncle ... my mother ... my family... The tiny packet in my hand burns: my uncle's gold teeth.

"Give these to Henryk. Maybe he can use them to get bread!" I remember his words.

Several gold teeth are a fortune in Dachau. A fortune, or ... a death!

The siren sounds from the assembly square.

"Everyone into the barracks!" the cries fly like an echo along block streets.

A few steps and I'm near the wire fence. A second of hesitation and ... the tiny package flies through the darkness over the camp wall. I sigh in relief. If some poor soul finds it, may it help him. If a scoundrel finds it, he'll use it badly. I won't risk my life or that of my colleagues. For me, uncle, a single pearl will be enough for my whole priestly life! It's what you said: "Return to life and begin it anew!"

I will begin! I will begin it anew, if...

"Hey, you! You don't plan to go into the barracks? You want the SS man to serve you a bullet from the tower?"

"Fratres, Oremus..."

With wooden lips I dutifully repeat the prayers, but my thoughts... Outside the window the night is black. A flame flares up from the crematorium chimney.

Tomorrow that's where they'll burn the body of my mother's brother...

47

They Would Have Survived...

The two official translators in camp Dachau are Poles: Jan Domagała, a teacher, and Ryszard Knosala, brother-in-law of Fr. Józef Styp-Rekowski, the unofficial "minister" of religious denominations in the territory of the Reich. Domagała is an older, more serious person; besides, there was no opportunity to get close to him. But I developed a real friendship with Ryszard, who often dropped by Wilhelm's hose-weaving shop and spent quite a bit of time at my workbench.

"I'll let you in on something," he whispers one day in October, "but on one condition: for the time being, don't spread it around!"

I strain my ears.

"We'll soon be receiving food packages."

"Food packages?!" I can't hide my emotion.

He nods, placing a finger on his lips as a sign not to tell anyone.

"Next Sunday when we're scheduled to write letters, each of us will be allowed to let our families know about this privilege."

"That's hard to believe. Ryszard, is it possible you may have heard some rumor about this and..."

"No. It's very reliable information. The office already has a specific order on it. Besides," he continues, "don't you see changes taking place in the camp?"

And the conversation continues on the subject of the new camp commandant, Sturmbannführer Weiss, who recently replaced Commandant Piorkowsky, and Weiss's new assistant commanding officers, Captains Redwitz and Lippman. We talk about the fact that the new commandant — contrary to his predecessor, who showed absolutely no interest in the camp — personally examines the smallest details, controls his officers and non-commissioned officers, supervises the kitchen and warehouses himself, and has abolished the post and the floggings...

"A different wind is blowing in the camp," Ryszard concludes. "See how Kapp and Szaferski and the other bullies behind them have become less important! Commandant Weiss is keeping them on a shorter leash than regular prisoners. He warned them that for arbitrary beatings and harassment they would face prosecution."

"It's true, something's going on, something's happening, but how do you explain it all?"

"Personally, I don't know. Maybe it's the influence of America, which is entering more and more decisively into the war. Have you heard about the exchange of American and German journalists who were imprisoned up till now?"

"Aha."

"Well, you see then! So what we're observing here in camp, maybe those are moves along the same line? The Germans are keeping us in camps; Americans have millions of Germans in their country who could be locked up. But I'm saying — maybe. Someday we'll get at the truth. It's time for me to go now." As he gets up from the workbench, he reaches into his deep pockets. "Before the packages arrive, here are a few potatoes, and take care! I'll stop by when I have a chance. And greet Styp," he adds from the door.

In fact, the following Sunday we put in our letters the news that, from now on, our families can send us a limited number of food packages!

Joy simply bursts from the barracks!

And several weeks later the eagerly awaited, lifesaving packages begin to arrive.

"We'll make it then!" whisper toothless mouths.

"We'll make it," lisps someone ill with scurvy.

"We'll make it," thousands standing at the brink of the grave are bolstered in their belief.

The mortality rate begins to drop. Skeletons slowly begin to acquire flesh. Within nourished outer bodies, the spirit also grows stronger. Eyes begin to shine.

A package will not just feed you; treasures included in it are an excellent means of payment, whether at the supply room to get a warmer piece of clothing for the coming winter or at the clinic to get some medication; and "buying" a capo or SS man on duty can't be excluded.

For several months there have been more and more deployments to the front of young SS men. They're replaced by reserves, which are made up of older people, sometimes really old, and although they're dressed in menacing SS uniforms, they remember other times and don't have the Nazi ideological training; on the contrary, they're often frankly hostile to the Party and the entire system. Goebbels complains and rends his garments in columns of his diary about growing dissatisfaction among officers of the regular army. If he had seen the old SS men at Dachau toward the end of 1942 and in the following years, he would have wailed in despair.

"You know," you hear more and more often, "these old men dressed in uniforms and tied to revolvers (this expression characterized the physical state of our new guards. It wasn't the revolver that was tied to them but they who were tied to the revolver!), they're ready to sell the entire camp for a piece of bacon or a pack of cigarettes."

The aforementioned deputy assistant to the commandant, Captain Redwitz, apparently with a "von" before his surname since he was supposed to be descended from old gentry, soon gets a "papa" before his name. Always quite tipsy, he has a great tendency to talk. He talks every chance he gets. He talks during roll calls. Although he makes it longer this way, he creates a phenomenon not seen or heard in Dachau until now, namely, laughter from thousands of prisoners on the assembly square!

We stand. The counting off is done. It's far different from the former full "drill" and fear before the block leader or Kapp. We're straining our necks to see what's going on at the guardhouse because assembly is taking such a long time, when we suddenly hear from the first blocks some sort of strange buzz, which quickly turns into laughter and then becomes a truly universal roar.

"Papa Redwitz is telling jokes!" the word goes from unit to unit.

"Jokes? Papa Redwitz?" We wait... When the first unit starts to laugh, the neighboring blocks pick it up, and several seconds later several thousand prisoners are already choking with laughter, howling, tapping their feet, yelling, although only a handful of those standing closest to the guardhouse know what it's all about.

Some unpleasant situations, however, also arise from this. Sometimes it happens that Papa Redwitz comes out in the evening in a sour mood and, at the first opportunity, starts to get angry. The closest blocks, adapting to his mood, now join him in echoing the alleged indignation. The next blocks, however, thinking this is the usual signal to laugh, begin to howl with laughter! Papa Redwitz grows silent, opens his mouth to speak, but noticing that the laughter doesn't stop and believing that they're making fun of him, he naturally goes into a rage.

"Shut your mouths!" scream the block leaders. "Just shut your mouths!"

Slowly the camp becomes proficient in this, too. Those standing in the first ranks, with an unrestricted view right to the gate, send a signal to blocks in the rear.

"Laugh!"

And the camp howls!

"Indignation!"

And the entire camp feels indignant together with Papa Redwitz.

One day, standing with legs far apart so as not to lose his balance, Papa Redwitz calls out: "Next Sunday I'd like to see a soccer game on this square!"

"A soccer game?" Our astonishment has no limits.

And the next Sunday there is a soccer game. Of course! Soon a league of teams is created: block leaders, cooks, shoemakers, carpenters, plantation workers, and even (oh, good heavens!) a clerical team! That's right!

Papa Redwitz is in his element!

"Look! Look!" he chuckles. "See how these priests can play!" Suddenly he opens his mouth, stares ahead and yells out: "And don't German priests and those of other nationalities have their own teams? Next Sunday I want to see a game between them and the Polish priests!"

Next Sunday there is a game: the team of Polish priests against a combined team of priests from all other nationalities. Redwitz roars with laughter!

After the soccer games, when snow already covers the ground, there are orchestral concerts, choir concerts, film showings, variety theater...

Finally, Commandant Weiss orders that there won't be any more evening assemblies! From now on, instead of marching into the square and standing for hours in the cold, wind, rain, or snow, we step out for several minutes into the block street; an old SS man rolls in on an even older bicycle, rides along the ranks pretending to count off, takes a report from the block leader in his hand and puts a piece of sausage (from a package, of course) into his pocket, and ... rides off satisfied, while we — even happier — return to our barracks, where the stove burns brightly from coal "bought" with ... packages.

"You know," someone declares out loud: "Very soon they'll be taking roll call in the bunkroom!"

Laughter! Certainly! Those packages are a marvelous "medicine." How people have revived during these past several weeks, and how different the mood is, and ... in general.

Only Zdzich is still the same. He doesn't get any packages because his elderly mother herself is barely getting by, and that's why he hasn't even informed her that parcels are now allowed. But because others who get packages sometimes don't eat the camp's bread and cabbage supper, Zdzich can take as much as he wants from the kettle.

"No, thanks!" He pushes it away politely when someone offers him something. "I'm not hungry. What I have is enough for me."

"An eccentric! I swear, he's a rare character."

"Leave him alone," others advise.

He doesn't attend soccer games, doesn't go to concerts or films, and only takes advantage of one thing. Since they've made the camp library accessible, he borrows one book after another there and reads avidly, devoting every free moment to it. And since we return from work early thanks to the early onset of darkness, he reads hour after hour until bedtime.

"You should start reading, too," he advises me now and then.

"I'd do it gladly, Zdzich, but my German, you know…"

"You're lazy, that's what it is," he snorts. "If only you wanted to, you could learn that language. Look," he adds, "if you want to write about them sometime, you have to get to know them very well. You won't learn about them or their history or culture or ideology without knowing their language."

The very next Sunday, he brings me Ludwig Ganghofer's *Die Martinsklause*.

"Read!"

I read. I finish the first page. Yes, I understood a few dozen expressions, but that's all. The Bavarian-Tyrolean dialect and the style itself make it even harder for me to understand. I read it once again. And again.

"And so?"

"I don't understand anything."

"Because you don't ask about the meaning of words. Ask."

Zdzich got his way. After a short time, I'm already devouring novel after novel. One day he brings me *Mein Kampf*.

"And I'm supposed to read this trash?"

He raises his eyebrows in surprise.

"I thought you wanted to get to know them. What makes you think that it's trash?"

"Everyone says so."

"Fools! They repeat everything like parrots without troubling to make a thorough study. Oh, look there," he points at one of the tables. "Bridge goes on all Sunday afternoon. There's time for that. Take the time *and read*," he says emphatically.

I read, and the more I get into it, the more this reading captivates me.

"Do you know Nietzsche?"

"Of course. From lectures on the history of philosophy."

"Kindergarten!" he states. "In this library you have his entire work. Read it."

"And the Church Index?"

"You can ask after leaving the camp. Besides, here you have the Reverend Bishop, the professors, theologians, and all kinds of authorized people; request permission if you're so scrupulous. Nota bene, on this subject: do you have a dispensation from fasting? Do you have jurisdiction to hear the confession of those ill with typhus? Oh, I see that you've fallen not into just one but a lot of Church censorships. I'm giving you a dispensation to read Nietzsche. Read it!"

By the time of my release, that is, over the next two years of my stay in Dachau, I was already able to "have a debate" with him on the topic of National Socialism. The camp library was, of course, very well supplied in that area.

"See how grateful we should be to Goebbels since, with propaganda in mind, he filled the library precisely with these works!"

It's easier for us now in Dachau under the greatly changed conditions. That doesn't mean, however, that death no longer cuts us down, though the mortality rate has dropped. Camp officials have come up with the idea that we transport kettles to and from the kitchen by flatbed truck, thus eliminating both the heavy lifting and the opportunity for harassment. Packages probably contribute most to the general improvement in conditions. But years of ruthless terror and starvation have taken their toll. Those years are inside of us, our entire organism, like poison. And we have to keep working, and the work isn't easy.

Masses are being celebrated in the halls more and more boldly, and no longer just on Sundays. Holy Communion is distributed more openly in the morning before breakfast and roll call.

"*Achtung!*" the call makes us freeze during distribution of Holy Communion. A young SS man stands in the doorway. Young! Where did he come from? We're petrified.

"Priests," he begins as he stands in the middle of the room. "I'm the newly assigned director of your barracks. I was curious to see you, so I came earlier to the camp. For the past several minutes I've been observing you through the windows. Priests," he speaks now in a lowered voice: "There are only priests here. I trust you. I'm a practicing Catholic. Many of us are trying hard to get into the camps in SS uniforms because we want to help you. But dear priests! Take care. What if instead of me, a real SS man had seen you at this moment?"[1]

From now on we try to be more careful. On the other hand, the words of the young SS man strengthen hopes awakening in us.

Each evening a loud prayer of the Rosary resounds in the halls, while at entrances to the block street our hidden guards are now posted.

Unfortunately, as though heaven wanted to remind us that this isn't the end of suffering, a new handicap transport leaves on October 12 for the gas chamber! It seems even Commandant Weiss himself could not call it off. Once lists were sent to Berlin and signed as death sentences for all who were on them, the sentences had to be carried out!

The Rev. Professor Henryk Brzuski, D.D., deputy rector of the seminary in Włocławek, is among those listed. Bidding him goodbye are Bishop Kozal, with tears in his eyes, as well as priests from the Włocławek Diocese, the second largest group of priests in Dachau after the Poznań group. From a total of 223 unfortunate Włocławek men, only 74 were to come out of Dachau alive, including a dozen or so young seminarians. Percentage-wise, no other diocese had so many victims in Dachau as the Włocławek Diocese! And now — they're again saying goodbye to their own. In addition to the Bishop, those saying goodbye to them include Fr. Korszyński, D.D., seminary rector; the Curia chancellor Fr. Bolesław Kunka, D.D., as well as colleagues and professors of that seminary, Fr. Biskupski, D.D., and Fr. Mączyński, D.D., and former students who are now already priests. There is also a group of seminarians. The condemned man is 45 years old. He's in his prime. But what does it matter since no one will cancel the sentence! Those going to death from the Poznań Diocese include Fr. Stanisław Ciążyński and Fr. Józef Gorgolewski, a Poznań pastor, and Fr. Witold Klimkiewicz, national deputy of the Catholic Youth Association and professor at the Catholic University of Lublin... Others, too, are leaving for extermination...

Another death transport leaves on October 14. The thirteenth day of this month of Mary is thus caught within the painful framework of those two terrible moments. This time we priests and graduates of the Poznań seminary bid goodbye to the Rev. Professor Karol Mazurkiewicz, D.D., member of the Knights of Malta Council, assistant professor at the University in Lwów, instructor at the University of Poznań, author of many works, and one of the most eminent experts in the area of pedagogy in Poland. Saying goodbye to him with heavy hearts are his relatives, Fr. Handke and the Rev. Professor Wróblewski. The death transport also takes another distinguished scholar and professor at the University of Warsaw, Fr. Franciszek Rosłaniec, D.D., one of the first prisoners to be arrested.

After them go others, not as many as in preceding months, but they go. Among those sent to their death are Fr. Józef Panek and Fr. Stach Kubiński from Kwieciszewo and Fr. Józef Banaszak and Stach Płaczek and Fr. Józef Krzywoszyński. And when, on Saturday, October 31, all of Portugal falls to its knees at the feet of its Lady, when in the capital, Lisbon, the Patriarch Cardinal — leading the entire Episcopate, with the head of state and government officials in attendance — renews the consecration of the homeland to Her Immaculate Heart, giving thanks for saving the country again from the deluge of the terrible war, on that very day in Dachau a brilliant priest dies, the former rector of the Polish Mission in France, the Rev. Msgr. Dean Leon Łagoda.

The solemn words renewing the covenant between the Portuguese nation and Mary had barely been spoken when hundreds of thousands of radio speakers echoed them throughout the country. The Vicar of Christ, Pope Pius XII, joyfully acceding to requests expressed by the Mother of God in Fatima, publicly makes the solemn act of dedication of all the world and all humanity to Her Immaculate Heart![2]

The first condition brought to the world by the Ambassador of Heaven when She came down to Fatima for negotiations with humanity has been fulfilled.

How will Heaven keep the agreement?

After all, assurance had been given: from that moment the war will start coming to an end...

An autumn evening in late October descends over Dachau. In halls of the clerical blocks you can hear murmured prayers of the Rosary.

48

Autumn of 1942

The W.B. carpentry workshops employ us (over 2,000 prisoners) as "skilled workers" in the lumber industry. Workshop buildings form a veritable labyrinth. They are huge and divided into various sections, each of which is then subordinate to an SS master specialist, who has several skilled SS workers assisting him in supervising individual subunits; and all this is under the supervision of the chief director, Nazi officer Deiner. The latter is a carpenter by trade. He's a bully if there ever was one! Born in Bavaria, he weighs at least 300 lbs, has broad, well-developed shoulders, fists as big as loaves of bread, and is the terror of our group of two thousand.

Attached to one side of the buildings is the so-called "lumber yard" or depot. Standing in it are enormous piles, probably hundreds of freight cars loaded with boards, logs and, in a word, every variety of partially processed material brought in from sawmills. Some of the piles are marked with seals indicating that this one came from France, that one from Holland, another from Poland, Yugoslavia, Hungary, or other annexed countries. This is the booty flowing into the SS storehouse for all of Germany, which is at Dachau.

Work here in the yard is difficult, especially during the winter since we spend all day outdoors. This is where they've assigned many of our priest-carpenters. Young Fr. Miecio Filipowicz is among them.

Lumber of all kinds is transported from the yard to the workshops through the so-called "porch." A huge machine stands there—a saw that cuts two sides simultaneously. The saw foreman is Carmelite Fr. Maryś Nowakowski from Kraków. Through his hands must pass the whole enormous supply of material for these huge workshops, material that provides work for hundreds of prisoners employed in them.

It's true that Fr. Maryś is young, that he's only 28 years old, that he's physically strong, and that he has the help of three lay assistants. Even for the young and strong, however, that post is still one of the most demanding and, in addition, one of the most unhealthy. Because the wind blows unmercifully through gates that are open to let in freight cars loaded with lumber, there's a constant draft on the porch, and during the winter snow drifts in.

But even so, Fr. Maryś is satisfied; he keeps going and works at a feverish pace.

The machine he operates wails like a band of the possessed.

"You know," says Maryś, "one good thing is that even when SS men are yelling at me, I don't hear anything."

The wood that's been roughly processed moves into the machine room behind him.

That's an enormous hall containing over two hundred machines of various types, which perform all kinds of work: planing machines that shave all four sides at once and howl like damned souls, circular saws of all sizes, band saws with belts ranging in width from as much as two inches to those as thin as threads, drills, boring machines, lathes, whistling drill bits (there are some that rotate 36,000 times per minute), disk, belt, and drum sanders. At every step here you find a Polish priest.

Fr. Dziasek, D.D., stands at a band saw; close by is Fr. Koperski, D.D., at a milling machine; there, too, are Fr. Kazio Głogowski and Fr. Leoś Kijewski; there are Fr. Józio Eggert and Fr. Grzesiek, Fr. Kaczorowski, Fr. Marciniak, and Fr. Stawecki... Who can spot them all in this tumult of speeding and roaring machines, in this clatter of falling boards, in this whirl of cars moving at full speed with hundreds of prisoners running around. Hundreds, since some machines need to be serviced by several people.

The work is hard because of a 10-hour workday. Of course, there's a bread supplement and a roof overhead, and yet there's not strength enough. There is no lack of tragic accidents, which occur especially toward evening when hungry and exhausted prisoners fall asleep at machines that are still running.

Behind the machine room is another, just as large in its dimensions, where hundreds of carpentry workbenches stand in rows. Here the number of priests is very small since the work requires real skill in carpentry. Working here are Fr. Stefcio Smaruj and Jaś Skowronek, an SVD seminarian from Rybnik.

Stefcio, who as a young boy had worked in his father's carpentry shop in Września, is a master, and soon they give him as helpers two young Russian boys, whom he's training.

Some of our men have gotten into the smaller departments: the mill, the paint shop where Stefcio Zielonka is the master; Fr. Matura works in a textile materials dye house that is next to the workshops; Fr. Stach Grabowski, of the Order of Christ from Potulice, together with Staszek Kucharzak from the Włocławek Diocese, are doing all sorts of masonry work in the workshops since they received training in masonry courses. The Rev. Rector Antoś Banaszak has the sweeper's job and is also a mace bearer at the Hitler Jugend school located near the workshops. The Rev. Professor Antoś Majchrzak works in the "toy shop," which in advance of the Christmas season takes on several dozen additional priests.

It's there, to the W.B., that the carving shop of capo Hein — and with it my messy workbench — finally moves from the hose-weaving shop.

The professional woodcarvers are as follows: Franciszek Burek from Gniezno, an old experienced master of the chisel; two Belgians and the German teacher Breznik. The rest are Polish students who, although young men of talent, are just serving as apprentices. There's Henio Dubiel, who's very talented and even more conscientious and hardworking; there's Staszek Stawiński, who's far advanced in his work; there's Tadek Czernicki and several others. And stopping in to see us often are colleagues from the department of artist-painters, where Władek Kowalski of the Warsaw Society of St. Luke and Professor Idźkiewicz work on SS orders for portraits and other paintings, alongside an old professor from the Vienna Academy of Fine Arts.

In our woodcarving shop all kinds of work is being done, depending on what is ordered, but mainly we recreate beautiful, enormous models of old sailing ships, which go to museums.

Most important for us priests, something closely linked to work in these colossal workshops, is our transfer from the clerical blocks to Blocks 8 and 10, where W.B. workers are housed.

Therefore, as in Stutthof, we now live side-by-side with our lay colleagues and, moreover, with the international element. We Poles are in the majority, mostly high-school and college students, mainly from Łódź; the rest include many Czechs, Slovaks, Belgians, Dutch, Germans, and no shortage, also, of young Russians.

During the first days, we priests feel somewhat ill at ease in this lay group. We realize that from early morning when we jump out of the bunk until evening when we lie down on it to sleep, we are the constant "object" of dozens of curious eyes, especially those of young high-school and college students.

On one side and the other there is a discreet reserve and ... waiting.

Slowly, however, a thaw occurs. Our lay colleagues, who up to now had heard so many negative stories about us shavelings, gradually begin to be persuaded that these "fararz" (taken from the Czech for "priest") are not as black as camp propaganda has painted them.

Most of our priests are also young men, not even thirty years old, so there's little difference in age; moreover, with head shaved bald, with a striped uniform that makes everyone equal, at the same kettle, with the same kind of bunk and the same work, differences fade quickly, and a sincere fellowship, even friendships, are formed.

On the other hand, our contact with colleagues in the clerical blocks must now be limited to Sunday attendance at holy Mass whenever the W.B. doesn't operate on Sunday mornings, which happens more and more often, and to "dropping in" on them from time to time in the evening.

Soon there's another change, however, which limits our contact even further. With a constant increase in orders and pressure from Berlin to accelerate production, the W.B. workshops begin working in three shifts. The enterprise benefits since it now operates 24 hours; while for us, working now eight hours under a roof and with a ration supplement and packages received from families, conditions are not bad. Especially meaningful for us is the fact that, while working on three shifts, we're largely independent of the daily camp schedule. It's this very circumstance, the chance to avoid running into camp SS men, that makes most of us apply for the night shift, so we can sleep during the day, not attend roll calls, and not be subject to other events in the daily camp routine. Thus, while we live in the camp, it's as though we form an oasis that isn't visited even by the SS men, who are restrained by their awareness that these two blocks house prisoners "important" to the arms effort. (That was the official description of W.B. workers and those of several other commands.)

From now on, we have a chance to visit the clerical blocks only on some Sundays, and celebrating Mass in Blocks 8 and 10 is out of the question not only because of the national and religious diversity among us, but from concern about block personnel who, while not persecuting us priests and, indeed, treating us like all others, at the same time discreetly observe us.

The secretaries in both W.B. worker blocks are Poles. In ours, it's Walter Cieślik; in Block 8 it's Marcinkowski. Cieślik is a student. I don't know what Marcinkowski is by trade but, in any case, he's an educated person. Both are of exceptional character, helpful, truly devoted. They can live in harmony with the "top;" they can get anything for us, anything they're able to wheedle and do, including the risky matter of keeping people in blocks during working hours, sheltering the ill, obtaining medications from the camp clinic, and getting periodic work releases for the weak.

The senior in our group of priests in those blocks is rector of the seminary in Gniezno, the Rev. Msgr. Antoni Banaszak. Although he's only forty years old, he's the oldest among us and, therefore, the senior. He's the one who maintains most contacts with the "elders" of our clerical blocks; he's the link between them and us, bringing news from them and informing us of the hour for Sunday Mass.

What is quite a privilege for those of us living in the W.B. blocks is that we live far more comfortably here. While our colleagues in the clerical blocks must be cooped up with four hundred in one hall, less than a hundred reside here. There's so much less irritation in the washroom, in the toilets, in the bunkrooms, in the very halls! In addition, we're obviously never all in the block at once because a third of our men are always at work. Therefore, there's plenty of room in our blocks, which are quiet, unconstrained, and clean. Since all of us are treated as "important" for the arms effort, we don't even have to clean up either our own blocks or the streets adjacent to them. This is done by the hall leaders themselves with the help of several young Russian boys who are "paid" for this work with a bowl of dinner soup. In a word, the W.B. workers are very privileged gentlemen, and this group includes two hundred Polish priests. I emphasize this especially so as to admit that, after all, during this period we had much better conditions than our colleagues in the clerical blocks, who continued to face harassment.

There is one drawback for me. During this period I very seldom see Zdzich. Sometimes we can't meet each Sunday because he's at work or I'm on the day shift. The thread that binds us together even now is the reading of German books from the camp library. (Polish books circulate among the prisoners, passed hand to hand, after being plucked somewhere out of a pile of "banned equipment" destined for burning. They had been taken from people in the various transports. They're so rare that a hundred people wait for each one.) Zdzich makes sure that I learn the German language well and get to know the source literature of National Socialist policy. In this field (as I've already mentioned), the Dachau library is very well endowed. There is everything by Hegel and Nietzsche and Spengler and others; there are also all the writings of living Nazi advocates; in a word, there's opportunity for studies in this field. After eight hours of work and eight hours of sleep, I'm left each day with several hours for quiet reading. It's quiet, taking into consideration the suitable conditions in our current blocks and protection against the intrusions of SS men and other slave drivers.

It must be clearly stated here that Blocks 8 and 10 were like an oasis of calm in the camp. They had simply exceptional conditions, and in no way can you judge from them what life was like at that time in the whole camp. Of course, from the time of changes in command, and in particular from the time old reservists become guards, and above all thanks to the packages, the place is no longer the same deathtrap. In general, life is easier, but that doesn't at all mean Dachau stopped being a Nazi concentration camp! The changes taking place now vividly reveal a line dividing the prisoners: on one side, a group that can and must be exploited to the fullest at work, even at the price of some relief and moderation; on the other side, a group from whom nothing more can be squeezed and who are thereby sentenced to prompt extermination. Thus, handicap transports continue and executions multiply. And though people seek salvation in assignments to various jobs beyond their limits without considering age or lack of strength, there, too, death quickly catches up with them.

"What's happening with the Bishop?" I ask Romek one Sunday.

"He's still working on the plantation, but the difference now is that he's gotten into a warehouse, under a roof. Władek Rybak, you know, that deputy capo, the dear Silesian, is doing what he can to help him, and Lieutenant Władzio Parzonko looks after him at work. Our boys take care of him, but his health keeps getting worse."

Many older priests get into capo Wilhelm's hose-weaving workshop, others into capo Hecht's, where they carve spoons and clogs; many have taken places at other jobs, and because there are packages, you don't need to rely on a bread supplement, just so you've found some kind of work.

At this time, also, both blocks of Polish priests organize an unofficial Caritas. Each month 500 loaves of bread are donated to blocks of the handicapped; every Saturday 250 go to other blocks, and every day dozens of kettles of dinner soup are given, not to mention friendly help offered individually, most often secretly, mainly for the purpose of saving young boys, including Russians, and young people in general.

When malicious gossip was still being spread in camps that were already liberated — gossip about the stinginess of priests, about their receiving great quantities of packages, about how the packages were getting moldy — I included in the first edition of *Shavelings* quite a few comments precisely on that subject. Today, after so many years, when "that talk" has already died down and now exists only in the first publications printed about Dachau, revisiting this subject seems to me unnecessary.

Let's just note this, that such malicious gossip did exist and that even those who wrote about life in Dachau succumbed to it.[1]

Of course, we must admit that both blocks of Polish priests were receiving the largest number of packages. Families made sure of that, as did parishioners. We shouldn't forget, however, that both clerical blocks had a total of over 2,000 recipients. So taking into account the number of our fellow prisoners in other blocks, the same number of parcels would have to be distributed to at least four blocks. But let's not dwell on this question. Envy has always had big eyes. It had them also in Dachau.

In Blocks 8 and 10 we had about a hundred Czech intelligentsia. There you could really see what it meant "to receive a huge number of packages." And what packages, too! The Czechs received many more of them and much better ones, but ... these were Czechs and not ... shavelings.

"Henryk," says Jasio Januszewski, "I've come to say goodbye."

"To say goodbye? What do you mean, goodbye?"

"We're leaving."

"Where are you going?"

"To Feldafing, as masons. We'll be building new barracks there."

"Feldafing? Where's that? I've never heard of it."

"In upper Bavaria, a little to the West of Lake Starnberg."

"That's practically in the Alps."

"Almost. In any case, at the altitude of Zakopane."

"Are many of you going?"

"Several dozen. Tadek Etter[2] and Jaś Kujawa from the Poznań Diocese, Fr. Franczewski from Łódź, Fr. Józef Brzeziński from the Płock Diocese, Fr. Walek Liberski, the Franciscan Fr. Albin Białogłowski, the Jesuit seminarian Zieliński, and the Albertine Brother Chwedorowicz, but it seems others will also be added. Well, goodbye and stay well! God willing, we'll meet again. But if not, then when you return… Greet my family, and tell them that…"

He moves away, his heavy clogs clattering down the street … Jasio… We were born in the same parish, so many long years at the same school desk, then years together at the seminary… Again another chapter ends… He didn't look back even once, but I know his sensitive heart too well. The deeper he's moved, the more he tries to hide it… I watch as he walks away, slightly bent over… Lord, how thin he's become! … He could have looked around just one more time … I know: Jasio's crying!

49

Goebbels and the Catholic Nuns

"At St. Hedwig's Hospital (in Berlin — author's note) I had an opportunity to make additional observations regarding the splendid order and management in such a religious hospital," writes Goebbels when, suffering an attack of kidney stones, he ignores hospitals run by Nazi "brown sisters" and orders that he be taken to the above-mentioned Catholic hospital. And afterwards he adds, "I'm very happy I issued an order forbidding the closing of religious hospitals in Berlin because they appear to be terribly important. We should allow the nuns to practice nursing since they cannot do any harm in this area; on the contrary, they are true benefactors of suffering humanity."[1]

At the same time, however, Polish nuns are being deported to labor camps and concentration camps, while others are being sent back to their families and forbidden to wear habits. A special camp for nuns was established in Bojanowo and is beginning to become more and more crowded.

A sick Goebbels receives beneficial care from Catholic nuns, while in Dachau Nazi male nurses kill prisoners with injections. Every day piles of bodies are taken out of the camp hospital, horrible experiments are conducted on people, and some from the ranks of Polish Catholic priests also fall victim...

Young Fr. Czesio Sibilski dies, followed by the Rev. Canon Narcyz Putz, provost of St. Wojciech's — the Poznań Skałka — who was a former prisoner at Pawiak and the Gusen quarries.* On the same day, 5 December, the body of the Rev. Msgr. Julian Wilkans, a colonel and dean in the Polish Armed Forces, falls upon the pile of corpses. After him young Fr. Józef Krych from Sarnowa passes away. Just on the Feast of the Immaculate Conception they take Fr. Alojzy Liguda from the handicap barracks. He was rector of the Society of the Divine Word in Górna Grupa and had survived with us since 1939. "If I don't come back," he confides to Fr. Michał Z. at the last minute," you'll know they murdered me." Several days later the news is spread in a whisper that they hanged him.[2]

On 9 December the unforgettable Fr. Bronek Stachowski from Poznań, a former classmate of mine, died. Thirteen of us in Dachau came from a group that was ordained one year before the war started: Fr. Maryś Balcerek, Fr. Edzio Jęczkowski, Fr. Henio Kaliszan, Fr. Stach Krzyżanowski, Fr. Henio Lisiecki, Fr. Radek Fibak, Fr. Stef Pabiszczak, Fr. Maryś Piotr, Fr. Maryś Walorek, Fr. Szczepcio Weber, Fr. Feliks Woźniczak. And there was the late Fr. Bronek Stachowski.

---

* *Translator's note*: "St. Wojciech's — the Poznań Skałka." In 1079 Bishop Stanisław was beheaded at Skałka in Kraków, site of the Basilica of St. Michał and St. Stanisław. In 997, the year after Poland received Christianity, Bishop Wojciech was slain by the Prussians he was trying to convert. Before leaving for Prussia, he is said to have preached at the site of the current Church of St. Wojciech in Poznań. "Pawiak" was a prison in Warsaw run by the Gestapo.

My colleague Gronostaj was shot to death in Poznań. Others? Who knows what happened to them. And now Bronek has passed away. Bronek, our group's ray of sunshine, a man with the heart of an angel. Phlegmon experiments finished him off. He was not, of course, the first victim of that horrible experimental station! Before him others had paid with their lives, and more came after him in the days that followed: the young Jesuit seminarian Staś Bukowy and Fr. Tomek Lis from the Łódź Diocese, 29 years old, and Fr. Ludwik Leśniewicz from Bukowiec, and others. All were young priests and relatively strong. They were, after all, chosen for the experiments precisely because they were the strongest. At the point of death for the same reason is Fr. Maryś Konopiński, whose days are already numbered (he died on 1 January 1943); Fr. Henio Kaliszan, from our group, is battling against death...

There are recurrent cases of typhus. The sick, admittedly, are isolated in blocks specially vacated for this purpose, but in spite of that the typhus continues to spread. Overcrowding in the barracks, lack of hygiene, less frequent changes of underwear — all these things bring about a sudden recurrence of lice infestation and pose the threat of an epidemic. We've already lived through epidemics in Dachau twice. They took a heavy toll. That's why there's talk now about paratyphus, that is, a relapsing typhus fever.

"It's horrible, the way they're treating those sick people!" relates Czesio Golimowski, who surreptitiously looks inside the isolation blocks when he delivers bread there. "It's the same as it was during the notorious scabies epidemic. Everything is set up to finish off those unfortunate people as quickly as possible. The SS men and nursing personnel consider 'that' to be the most effective way of fighting an epidemic."

The scabies epidemic... Who among the old prisoners in Dachau doesn't remember those terrible days! Transports coming in from other camps brought this illness to Dachau. Under normal conditions it wouldn't be anything dangerous; in our situation, however... Finding favorable conditions on the mangy skin of thousands of emaciated people, the scabies began suddenly to spread. Camp management, in coordination with personnel of the camp clinic, struck upon a unique treatment. Following a health inspection of all prisoners, they separated those suspected of having scabies and packed them into isolation quarters, which included several barracks. It was winter, a severe Alpine winter. According to the SS "prescription," the scabies germ dies most quickly from ...*freezing cold*. Therefore, they completely undressed those two thousand unfortunate men, took away all their blankets, opened all the windows in their sleeping areas and ... froze the germs. The fact that each day several dozen prisoners who had frozen to death were dragged from the barracks did not, of course, play a role. In order to destroy the epidemic more effectively, these unfortunate people weren't given any food for a dozen days or so. Every morning they were driven in groups, naked in the biting cold, to baths, where the sickness was "scraped off" their bodies with stiff scrubbing brushes. Boiling-hot water was poured over them at intervals, which made their skin peel; they were then doused with freezing-cold water. Whoever didn't die of a heart attack would be killed off by the cold and starvation. After several weeks, when a report was sent to Berlin: "The scabies epidemic in Dachau has been stamped out," the last of the "patients" were being moved to the crematorium!

"Now they're 'treating' those poor typhus patients the same way," Czesio tells us with horror in his eyes.

One of the last Jewish crews in the Dachau crematorium goes to the furnace! Currently only Jews are assigned to operate this death furnace. These crews are housed separately, having no contact with other prisoners; they're better fed and get special supplements — even alcohol — especially on days when mass executions take place (basically to deaden their nerves), and then, after several weeks of work at the furnaces, in order to get rid of inconvenient witnesses, they themselves are sent to the gas chamber and ... into the furnace! Other Jews take their place!

We know about this. We sympathize with these unfortunates, but how can we help? The following question begins to worry us: Whom will they take for this job after the Jews since there are fewer and fewer of them in the camp? ... Perhaps us priests? ... Maybe, because Jews and Catholic priests, especially Polish priests, are the categories of people most hated by SS men.

While writing about the constant, uncompromising, and rigorous extermination of the poor Jews, Goebbels advances the need to reach a decision regarding future work crews in Dachau. Polish priests are completing the new crematorium. Are we also going to have the "honor" of operating its four new furnaces? This might indeed happen, but that would be before the world finds out, before it can bring itself to exchange diplomatic notes, to protest... Would the world, in fact, bring itself to do so? ... Goebbels continues to promise "a final resolution" of the Church issue following the victorious war! "Re ... so ... lu ... tion...!" We know what he has in mind... Maybe then a plaque will be put in the crematorium saying it was built and operated by Polish priests, the parasites, from whom National Socialism has saved humanity...

"The situation of our army in Stalingrad is hopeless," Goebbels notes further. "The situation of our troops in Africa is also terrible. Our military power diminishes with each month... The constantly growing partisan movement in annexed territories is a great danger for us... Oh, how exhausting is this terrible war of nerves that the Allies are imposing upon us... The extent to which weather favors our enemies seems truly grotesque ... as if the devil himself had put his hand to it..."[3]

What a terrifying reversal of concepts! Goebbels, although raised in a Catholic family and even by devout parents, didn't notice the work of Satan in all of Hitler's crimes, but when that horrible work begins to topple, he discerns Satan's hand in it... With blind belief in the genius of Hitler, he is nevertheless aware of the situation, and despite all his arrogance, he writes on 20 December: "...We're doing everything possible, but we're encountering elements that exceed our strength."[4] And the intriguing thing is that, even brought down by illness and surrounded with the care of Catholic nuns, he appears never to return in his recollections to the years when his mother talked to him about God, about the Blessed Mother, and about the Supreme Power that decides the fate of the world...

Thus, starting with the act of consecration of the world to the Immaculate Heart (made by Pius XII at the end of a ceremony marking the silver anniversary of the appearances in Fatima and solemnly repeated on 8 December at St. Peter's Basilica), the war begins to come to an end. It is as our Lady of Fatima promised.

Locked in behind wires, isolated from the world, fed solely with the trash of Nazi propaganda, we don't notice this pivotal moment, and what's more, we're paying God back with additional expiatory victims.

Christmas of that watershed year 1942 approaches. How different it is from Christmases past. There's even a package from home, packed by my mother's solicitous hand; there's an *opłatek*, on which tears have fallen, and yet we know that the road before us is still a hard one...

50

The Year 1943

"The war must end with our final victory!" With these words Hitler greets the start of 1943, attempting in his speech to give the German masses a new anesthetizing injection.[1]

"Twenty-two divisions of select Nazi troops with all their costly equipment, together with their leader, Marshal Paulus, and several dozen generals and several thousand officers, are breathing their last in Stalingrad!" radio Moscow broadcasts to the whole world.

"Realizing the terrible loss from Russian imprisonment of 3,000 of his select troops, Hitler flies into a rage and chews on a rug in his fury," according to camp "rumors."

In Fatima, a pleading whisper flows from hundreds of thousands of people to the Immaculate Heart.

At the convent of the Sisters of St. Dorothy in Villa Nova de Gaia, near Porto, Sister Maria Dolores, formerly Fatima visionary Lucy, lies prostrated in the form of a cross, begging for God's mercy on a world in flames...

Roosevelt and Churchill arrange a meeting in Casablanca...

In Dachau, heavy snow is falling, a source of distress for the group of Polish priests, especially those who have not found assignments to jobs needed by the military or those dismissed from such jobs for the winter.

"The Reverend Bishop is growing weaker," we hear every day.

"And the French bishop has ordained Leisner to the priesthood."

"That's right. He ordained him."

"You know, what really hurts and stings is that because he's a Frenchman, he lives in a safe environment in Block 26, while our bishop hauls snow in wheelbarrows as if he were the worst criminal."

"It does hurt. Well, what can you do about it? It's fate. They consider us Poles a lower class of people, that's why."

Typhus is spreading at an alaming rate. Isolation blocks are already overcrowded. The crematorium is smoking day and night. In the barracks of working prisoners there are more and more who are sick. They have to stay where they are because there's no room in either the clinic or the isolation. What will happen next?

In mid–January a quarantine is announced for the entire camp due to the typhus. Just a handful of plantation workers has been released to service the hothouse and do the jobs needed inside; a small group of people has also been released to do other vital jobs. Those men will live outside the camp perimeter. The rest of us remain... To prevent spread of the illness, an order has been issued forbidding any contact with other barracks. Each barracks becomes an isolated corner during this quarantine. From now on, we don't go out for any roll calls. Kettles from the kitchen are delivered by a special wagon pulled by prisoners who take the place of horses at this job. Our contact with the blocks of our priest-colleagues also ends now. The sole contact is the wagon that delivers bread every morning. Doing that work are Fr. Józek Woźniak and Fr. Alfons Kropidłowski. Whenever our hall leader calls out in the morning for volunteers to pick up the bread, we priests run forward just for a chance to get some news. The SS man supervising bread delivery usually stands at a certain distance for fear of catching the disease, and at that time Józek or Alfons tells us in a whisper any news from the clerical barracks.

"Well, people are sick. The more serious cases were taken to the camp clinic, but other than that, we somehow manage."

The quarantine also has some advantages, especially in our W.B. workers' barracks. Some of our colleagues had time to bring tools and pieces of wood into the block, and they're carving marvelous objects here. Professor Idźkiewicz is painting his splendid illustrations for fairy tales, which he hopes to take back to his beloved grandchildren. Professor Stachowicz sketches, planning his future woodcarving works. Fr. Miecio Januszczak rehearses his amateur vocal quartet for days on end. Many have made packs of cards or chess sets or other games and play them all day long.

Fortunately, I had taken books from the library, and since others also have some, we'll be able to exchange them, and that will be enough reading material for weeks. The more thoroughly I investigate the ideological principles of Nazism, the better I understand current events, but I also see more clearly what still lies ahead of us.

The day is 26 January, the Tuesday following the third Sunday after Epiphany. It's a morning that sparkles with frost and snow.

"Volunteers to pick up bread!" calls the hall leader.

Although it's terribly cold, we're motivated to go because there could be some news, which is even more in demand since our Reverend Bishop was recently taken to the camp clinic. We run. The snow crunches under our clogs. The frozen SS man stops today right at the head of the barracks. The wagon with the bread is already moving into the block street. It will be hard to communicate. Fr. Józek is in the wagon. He throws the loaves into our outstretched hands:

"Two! … Four! … Six!"

One of the loaves falls into the snow.

"Oh, you oaf!" the hall leader says in anger. The SS man blows his nose loudly.

"Eight… The Reverend Bishop has died! … Ten…"

Two loaves of bread again land in the snow.

"What are you doing today?" the hall leader mutters. "Have your paws frozen or your eyes frosted over? Hey," he turns to the next in line, "take his place!"

The Reverend Bishop has died… The Reverend Bishop no longer lives… If we could only get some details, but the wagon is already starting to move.

"Maybe tomorrow there'll be more about this," whispers Józek.

"Until tomorrow."

The Reverend Bishop had been sick in bed for a dozen days or so in the fourth hall of Block 30. Typhus? A cold? … It's difficult to say. In addition, those terrible earaches! Maybe there was an abscess inside?

50. The Year 1943

All efforts to get him into the camp clinic were unsuccessful. Capo Zimmerman, the horrible butcher and camp terror, turned down the sick man. And so the days passed.

When the sick man, consumed by high fever, lost consciousness, the priests carried him to the camp clinic, and he was finally admitted, but only so that he could end it there.

"Did they give him an injection?"

"Many rumors on the subject are going around. The murderer won't admit it, and where are you going to find witnesses?"

"I've offered my life to God so that you can leave this place and work for souls." Those were his last words while still in the barracks before he lost consciousness.

Steps were taken to claim his body. All in vain. No one saw the body after death. It was thrown on a pile with the other dead and burned in the crematorium.

Maybe it's just as well. The tortured Polish Bishop shared to the end the fate of hundreds of his priests and thousands of his fellow citizens. A great and saintly priest passed away! He passed away in the prime of life, at the age of 49.

The sad news moves quickly from one barracks to another — despite the quarantine.

"The Reverend Bishop Kozal is dead!"

"It's over for him. They'll no longer push him around or beat him; they won't summon him 'for show' in front of the gate," concludes the kindly Rogalski, a senior carpenter from the W.B.

Right after the Bishop's death, his former pupil Fr. Franek Marciniak dies, and then others follow. Death in Dachau is an everyday occurrence. The wave of forgetfulness covers names of even the greatest. Corpses carted out daily in piles now have only numbers marked with indelible pencil on their naked chests, for verification at the crematorium, and the ashes thrown in a heap now have only the value of fertilizer... Nowhere did the naked truth of the words "Remember, man, that you are dust" come across more forcibly than right here, in the concentration camp.

Days and weeks pass... The climate here has this characteristic feature: it possesses two springs. The first awakens as soon as early February, but weeks of new frosts and snowstorms driven by winds from the Alps quickly chase it away. Only then does the second spring set in, and that one isn't far off now... The quarantine continues.

In the meantime, major events are being played out in the world! From week to week, the military power of the Allies grows... The Russians finally take the powerful German army prisoner at Stalingrad — capturing them along that entire front. Tragic troop withdrawals by the Germans begin elsewhere. Goebbels announces national "all-out war!" ... Himmler issues an order for liquidation of the Warsaw ghetto! ... Stalin increasingly pressures England and America to create a second front... On 13 March at a location in Russia there's a failed assassination attempt on Hitler by his officers! There's an alert in the Dachau camp, and ... two days later the quarantine is canceled; the commands start back to work.

"Production! Production! The army needs arms! Tanks! Equipment!"

All-out war...

Goebbels closes over 100,000 restaurants! Gigolos and other types considered asocial move into the camp. Hitler announces that he won't hesitate to take workers by force from the annexed nations! That provides a signal for horrible new excesses. From Poland come additional thousands of people, taken away for slave labor. Goebbels, writing in his diary about taking food from the Lublin area and emphasizing that it is, after all, the granary of Poland, also touches on the question of "recruiting" workers: "Fifty thousand Poles were to be evacuated; our police, however, succeeded in catching only 25,000, while the rest fled to the partisans."² The little doctor is terribly worried about this, especially because, as he writes: "Currently we're supposed to evacuate another 190,000, but in the meantime it isn't known whether they, too, can be 'caught.' But this matter has been turned over to the Warsaw governor, Fischer, and he certainly can make it happen."

On 20 March Fr. Jan Trzaskowa from the Płock Diocese dies; he had been a prisoner in the Polish concentration camp in Bereza Kartuska.

"You know," says Zdzich, "our beloved Fr. Trzaskowa ought to be the patron saint of all concentration camp priests. He started his 'career' during the days of a free Poland, he was with us through Sachsenhausen, and now he dies in Dachau."

In general, however, the mortality rate among us is decreasing. Packages from home and work in commands, along with the improved conditions in camp life, have had an impact. People have been nourished and become stronger, so even if the work is very hard and exhausting, it stops killing, especially since — after departure of the handicap transports — only the young remain, the healthiest and the hardiest.

On 13 April, German radio brings news regarding the discovery of graves in Katyń. During the following days, the press is full of details and commentaries on the subject. Nazi propaganda exploits this moment to the fullest. The German communists scowl at us. A wall of ominous silence comes down between us. We feel that they're waiting for our reaction.

Our situation at work in the commands, where the capos are mainly communists, becomes even worse when, a few days later, news comes to camp that the Moscow government has broken off diplomatic relations with the Polish government-in-exile in London. The capos don't have any doubts as to our views on that matter. Here and there harassments on their part begin anew, although not to the same degree as in years past. They realize that, given current attitudes and the weight attached to an element needed for work, they could get into trouble themselves with camp officials. Besides, faced with increasingly more frequent and forceful attacks by Allied air squadrons on German cities, everything else seems less important. Although newspapers allowed into camp contain only very moderate references to this subject, we supplement them with information coming in now and then from outside, especially with the transports of new prisoners.

Goebbels refers in his diary to Allied retaliatory air activity as "cut-throat attacks" (apparently forgetting about Luftwaffe crimes in this war), but the prisoners walk about as though in a fever of excitement, one induced by the joyous hopes those air strikes stir in them. At the same time, the communists are ecstatic due to the successes of Bolshevik troops.

And these successes become greater and greater. To be sure, the Nazi press constantly announces that German troops have strategically withdrawn from "previously selected positions," and another time that "by design" they carried out "a successful front reduction," but we already know how to read between the lines; in any case, we're certainly less affected by Minister Goebbels' deceitful propaganda than the German people. The Russian avalanche — after the fall of Stalingrad — had begun a powerful offensive on the segment between Voronezh and the Caucasus. Since March, the Nazi press is full of names: Murmansk, Lake Lagoda, Leningrad, Velikiye Luki, Kirov, Sumy, Belgorod, Novorossiysk. Capo Hein of the carpentry shop has a map of these areas drawn on a piece of plywood, and every day he hammers several new nails into it.

"Look! Look!" he says happily: "In a week or two they'll already be inside the borders of Poland."

50. The Year 1943

Germany, deploying part of its forces from France and the Balkans, prepares a fresh offensive in April near Belgorod, in the direction of Kursk. The first strikes are successful. The Nazi press is triumphant! A new spirit stirs among the camp SS men, and only the old, the ones with mustaches, dismiss the news with an unambiguous wave of the hand. Goebbels, however, worries on the pages of his diary (emphasizing that the same worry also tugs at the Führer's heart) because the Russians still have such huge reserves of troops and armaments.

The division between the Wehrmacht, namely the regular army, and SS units widens more and more. We see this ourselves in officers who visit the camp; we hear it from German prisoners who have brothers or relatives in the regular army; we sense it in press releases; and we take note of it after the executions of soldiers, which are carried out in an enclosure by the crematorium.

The horrible Nazi doctrine is devouring children of its own nation!

On 7 April a conference lasting several days between Hitler and Mussolini begins in Berchtesgaden. Goebbels writes that Mussolini arrived at the conference as a gray-haired, bitter old man, but left—following a boost in morale received from the Führer—with a brightened face. "The final victory must be on our side!"

"More production!" a telegram from Berlin exhorts the commandant's office in the Dachau camp.

"More production!" scream the SS bosses to the commands.

"More production?" drawl the communist capos through their teeth, and in response there's an increase in well-concealed, hard-to-detect, yet relentlessly constant sabotage! It's hard for SS bosses to detect this, but we prisoners see instances of it and take part in them more or less knowingly.

Besides, even the SS men have utterly lost heart. They certainly know much less than Minister Goebbels, but ... they know, they see, they feel. The old men, the ones with mustaches, have already given up and take no interest in either the prisoners or their work, and sometimes they even have the courage to whisper: "The war is ending!" The younger ones, who enjoy every day saved from the danger of the front, drag out their work, contrive hundreds of adjustments and problems, and steal like proverbial ravens. Because the war is ending anyway; whoever's smart, let him seize the opportunity to save what he can and as much as he can for himself. At every type of job within commands so-called "organization" is practiced on a large scale with the participation of prisoners, because without them the SS men couldn't manage to smuggle stolen goods or carry out unauthorized work. Corruption is in full swing, which results in familiarity between prisoners and SS men, quiet collusion, and a division of the loot.

The optimists are predicting that the war will end at any moment. They're supported in this conviction by recently arrested prisoners who tell us about the public mood in the world.

The pessimists—lying low and bristling—still go on maintaining their silent mistrust.

"These Satans shouldn't be believed. It's not for nothing that Hitler declares in *Mein Kampf* that before his nation perishes, millions of slaves will first die."

Oh, those pessimists!

In Dachau—it's as if you weren't in Dachau. Commandant Weiss works hard for continuous variety, entertainment, and provides further improvements. Prisoners arriving in transports from other camps bring similar news on this subject. Those from Auschwitz admire Commandant Hoffman, the same person who in Dachau was one of the bloodiest butchers!

"Hey, buddy," lisps a mangy new arrival from Auschwitz, "if you had seen what a man he is, what a man ... an angel! The former commandants were Satans. This one changed everything for the better. The prisoners were ready to dote on him!"

"Heinrich," whispers capo Hecht. "Don't trust these scoundrels. You see, Weiss was also an ordinary SS guard during my years in Dachau prior to the war. He murdered like all the others. He returned to us after all these years and today is as sweet as licorice. It's the same with Hoffman and the others. You see, in plain words, from the time camps were recognized as necessary for armaments, commandants have been transferred from one camp to another, so as to erase any memory of their cruelties; but don't believe that what they are today is their true face. Any day when a different wind blows, new orders will come from Berlin, and those who today hide from us behind a humanitarian mask will be the first to shoot at us..."

Among various benefits, privileges, and entertainments, the camp in Dachau at this time gets ... a house of ill repute. They located this shrine of debauchery in the disinfection enclosure, behind Barracks 29, the place where two years ago we endured terrible days under capo Groo.

"The residents of that 'house' are female political prisoners brought from the camp in Ravensbrueck!" The secret news travels from barracks to barracks.

"Let no Pole dare stop by that place!"

And the Poles didn't go there. The Austrians, almost all from the intelligentsia, didn't go. But there was no shortage of candidates from among the thousands of other prisoners.

Horrible! Nazism, which presented the Germans a "dogma" about purity of race and which was supposedly fighting prostitution with such zeal, which punishes contacts between foreigners and German women by death, introduces bawdy houses into concentration camps, filling them with ... female political prisoners of other nationalities.

"The Jews have started an uprising in Warsaw!"

That piece of news electrifies the entire camp.

In the crematorium they killed off the last Jewish work team.

Whom will they take now? Us priests?

They took young Russian boys.

And from the Vatican at just this time a call goes out to all bishops in the entire Catholic world to consecrate their dioceses in the upcoming month to the Immaculate Heart of the Mother of God![3]

51

At the Turning Point of 1943

A beautiful May evening descends over Dachau. The main street is deserted; the small streets between blocks are beginning to empty. We lie on our bunks inhaling the fragrance of spring that enters through open windows. Our bunkroom is full of chatter. So typical of the young!

There is no end to the most preposterous rumors, jokes abound, gibes are fired off. The hall leader knocks on the partition from time to time to indicate there should already be silence, but who's afraid of the hall leader these days? A year ago it was different. The door to the room creaks. The kindhearted Silesian Wala walks in.

"Listen here! Listen!" he yells, trying to drown out the talkers. "The hall leader orders that the chatterboxes cut it out because if they don't, he'll shove them into the washroom."

Laughter is the only answer.

"Eh, Wala, say it again," one of the young students teases the old man, trying to imitate his dialect.

"Eh, son-of-a-gun, watch out or I'll teach ya," someone else adds in a mocking tone.

"Wala, tell the hall leader he has to teach the chatterboxes himself and..."

At this moment the siren sounds.

"Air raid warning!" someone calls with joy in his voice.

"An air raid? At this hour?"

For several months we've had a number of air strikes on neighboring Munich, which is located a mere 17 kilometers from Dachau, but these were made under the cover of darkness. This is the first time one comes at such an early hour, just at dusk.

"You're surprised?" explains Jurek, an expert on military issues. "They're much closer now, flying from Africa."

"Across the Alps?" someone asks.

"What are the Alps for them? ... "

Right after the first siren, others follow, both those located nearby in the barracks area next to the camp and more distant ones in the town of Dachau and near Munich.

"Can you imagine the panic now in Munich?" asks Henio Dubiel in a whisper. "I wouldn't want to be in their place right now."

And in the distance you can already hear the sound of the engines. Many engines.

"There must be a lot of them today."

"Well, the more the better."

The young minds of the Łódź high-school students begin making fanciful conjectures. Sleep is out of the question. Every living thing has jumped over to the windows. Only Professor Idźkiewicz remains on his bunk.

"Professor, aren't you curious to know how they..."

"Ehhh," he mumbles. "they'll teach the Nazis a lesson without me." And turning onto his other side, he settles down to sleep.

And in the fading blue sky of the May evening hundreds of engines drone.

"They're headed right at us!" comes a sharp whisper from the window.

"At us?!"

Several steel birds are in fact heading right toward the camp.

"Good Lord!"

"*Ja sakra*!" whispers one of the Czechs. "I think they..."

But before he can finish his sentence, something drops from the first aircraft, something shining in the rays of the setting sun. It drops more and more slowly, finally hovers at a height of about 2000 meters, sways for a while, and suddenly fans out into a sheaf of colored sparks.

"They're hanging 'Christmas trees,'" explains Zyga Zieliński.

"Ah, 'Christmas trees.'" We sigh with relief.

During night strikes on Munich, Allied aircraft would suspend some sort of lights over the camp, at its four corners, which would usually glow for about an hour or more. We already knew this was a signal to the next squadrons that the area enclosed within the square of hanging lights should be spared. Never before, however, had we seen the actual process of dropping these light signals down. Until just now...

The first squadron is followed by others in succession. A second, third, fourth, fifteenth, with each consisting of several dozen aircraft. All around they flit to and fro, like swarms of mosquitoes, small nimble fighters providing cover for the bombers.

"It's the twenty-sixth," someone near the window who is counting meticulously informs us.

"So how many of them are flying today?" someone asks, surprised.

"Several hundred, at least."

The anti-aircraft artillery deployed around the camp and barracks is firing like mad. The noise of exploding shells shakes the barracks. But the squadrons move slowly, majestically, as though scoffing at the helplessness of those firing.

Goebbels, observing similar air strikes in Berlin and other cities, writes in exasperation: "Our Luftwaffe is totally disappointing, and the artillery falls short. Who imagined that these gangsters would bomb so accurately from an altitude of 10,000 meters?"

After some time, the sound of distant explosions reaches us.

"They're pouring it on Munich," someone whispers.

"And how!"

Explosions heard from one moment to the next follow one another so closely that they resemble the distant sound of a machine gun.

"They're laying down a carpet."

"Uh-huh. Carpet bombing."

Suddenly the barracks shake. Metal utensils and spoons clang in the cupboards. It seems that the powerful blast will bring down the walls. Those of us more easily frightened jump back from the windows.

"Don't be afraid of anything," Zygmunt assures us. "Those are aerial mines."

"Mines?"

"Right. That kind of colossus weighs several thousand pounds and explodes just over the ground, blowing away whole areas of a city."

"Good Lord!"

"Why are you wailing? Maybe you're ready to whisper 'Eternal rest' for those bastards."

"But those are people, too."

"People? Sakra!" one of the Czechs swears. "They're the same as cattle, those SS men! Don't talk such nonsense. It serves them right."

"Only a few SS men are over there. Most are women, children, the elderly, the sick in hospitals..."

"They wanted a total war, they've got it."

And the explosions continue, as do the blasts of aerial mines. It has to be a judgment day over there. Hundreds of aircraft have flown over us. If each carries several dozen bombs, thousands of them are falling on the heads of city residents. And there are also small incendiary bombs, several thousand of which are carried by a single bomber. And the terrible phosphorus bombs... True, it's against our enemies, and yet... How much blood is flowing at this time, how many tears, how much terror in sinking hearts, how many cries of innocent little children...

"Apocalyptic times," whispers Rev. Rector Banaszak. "Apocalyptic times."

"Terrible. Horrible," adds Fr. Antoś Majchrzak.

"Eh, you parish priests, you have soft hearts," says one of the Czechs.

Time passes. Overhead the sky is a deep navy blue. "Christmas trees" continue to shine at corners of the camp, throwing off stars. The bloody glow of fire rises over Munich. Silhouettes of SS men loom dark in the guard towers. What does a young SS man think about at this moment when he sees what's going on? After all, many of them have someone close over there. Maybe even a mother and father, maybe brothers and sisters. What is he thinking at this moment?

And the next day they bring to Dachau small groups of Munich residents, mostly women, via Death Road along the camp's wire fencing toward the crematorium. These are people whose nerves could not stand it during the air strikes and who made some sort of "disloyal comments" against the Führer or the SS. It wasn't in vain that Goebbels had sought a "suitable reform" of the law, which was to conform to "the requirements and needs of the time..." He got his reform. Whoever preached defeatism or cast aspersions against the Führer or the party must go against the wall!

Behind the wall that surrounds the crematorium a machine gun is firing. It's been going on for some time now. We know full well that unfortunate people are falling dead over there: women, the aged, the handicapped. After a while, single shots from a revolver can be heard. That's officer Jung and report director Boetger finishing off those who are still alive. In all likelihood, Jung regrets that the condemned weren't delivered on the previous day. It's no secret in the camp that this barbaric SS officer first rapes hapless condemned women and then personally shoots them.[1] Jung doesn't pick and choose. It doesn't matter that it's a German woman, a daughter of the same nation, since "legally" (?!?) she's been excluded from that nation.

"Hey, Russki!" calls the SS commander of the crematorium, pointing to the pile of women just shot: "Don't forget to cut off their hair!"

The day after every air strike on Munich a larger or smaller group of "grumblers" was brought to Dachau to be shot. Sometimes, too, a special execution team would leave the camp; this happened when it was necessary "to provide a warning" to the population that

Nazism knows how to punish all signs of insubordination to the rule of total war. At the head of the team was SS man Bach, Director of the Political Office, whom we prisoners knew only too well and too painfully from times of investigation and interrogation. To help out, he usually took along both camp seniors, Kapp and Szaferski.[2]

The chapel continues to be officially off-limits for us, although we now celebrate Mass more boldly in the halls of both clerical blocks. In addition, more and more lay colleagues are attending these services. And when at last — by order of the camp commandant — the clerical blocks get their own personnel, when priests become leaders of their barracks and respective halls, religious life comes fully out into the open, and the old SS men, "bought" with supplies from packages, are even willing to perform church functions...

Transports coming from other camps also include Polish priests. Recently they brought in Fr. Romek Siwa from the Gniezno Diocese, Fr. Jan Niedojadło from Stary Sącz, Fr. Józef Brudz, father confessor at the seminary in Tarnów; while Fr. Karol Radzięta and Redemptorist Fr. Wacław Pilarczyk arrive in a transport from Sachsenhausen.

As the SS men lose heart, the spirits of the prisoners rise. The ultra-optimistic mood even produces such fine ideas as the secret formation of a ... future Polish government, complete with a forecast of the primate and military bishop... That's *people* for you!

Zdzich, whom I have seen only rarely in the past months, describes our optimists bluntly, in his own fashion: madmen!

"Have you heard?"

"Yes, I have."

"Heard what?" The optimist is somewhat confused. After all, he ran especially to our barracks so he could change the pessimist into a pillar of salt, and then, unexpectedly, the other fellow already knows. But he asks again: "Heard what?"

"That a transport of starving prisoners has arrived from Flossenburg, and it included Fr. Franek Wajda."

"Nah," the other waves his hand with impatience. "That's nothing new!" And then, lowering his voice he smugly whispers up close: "Our boss, you know, the one with the mustache, the one who would sell us Hitler himself, he brought the news early last evening that radio London had announced a ten-day non-stop bombing of Germany." Moving away at arms length, he checks the effect. "Well? What do you say to that?"

"We'll see."

"Bah, you disgusting pessimist! Don't you realize that an avalanche has moved against the scoundrels!! The Russian front is a complete flop! Africa is done with, and the Allies are about to land in Italy at any moment. German submarines are kaput! Now ten days of continuous bombing... Sikorski's at the head of the Polish army..."

And two days later ... not only radio London, but German radio is blaring loudly: "General Sikorski has died in an air crash at Gibraltar, together with his daughter, while returning from the East!" Then, a minute later: "*Achtung*! *Achtung*! A special report from the main headquarters of the Führer: The victorious German army is deploying today for a huge offensive on the Orel-Kursk-Belgorod line!"

Goebbels and the faithful leaders are rubbing their hands. Their faith in the genius of Hitler has not disappointed them! "Victory will be ours!"

At the same time, in the distant United States, a modest vicar, Fr. Peyton, seeing the bloody struggles in Europe and remembering the promises of the Heavenly Ambassador who came to Fatima, organizes the "Family Rosary Crusade." This young priest, who started with a small group of altar boys and young school girls, soon wins over several million Catholic families to this crusade of prayer. Evening prayers are heard on the radio from the Atlantic to the Pacific. Over four hundred film artists, many leading politicians and social activists help to spread the Crusade. Fr. Peyton didn't forget to reach even into the ranks of the American army. "Prayer — it is America's most effective secret weapon!" This slogan goes from skyscrapers to farms tucked away on the prairies. "This is our path to peace! We will gain it through prayer!"[3]

That was an optimism mindful of the Lord's words: "Without me you can do nothing!"

But arrogant players at the world's bloody chessboard were still under the impression that it was they who were playing out the game.

The dear optimists were right; the Allies do indeed bomb German cities without ceasing, day and night, from 3 to 13 July. The sirens in Germany wail for ten days! During the ten days thousands of engines drone up in the sky! During the ten days millions of people live in mortal fear.

On 10 July, the Allies land in Sicily. Pope Pius XII walks over the rubble following the first bombing of Rome. Hitler and Mussolini have a new "friendly" meeting. Russian troops, having broken the German offensive, begin their own victorious offensive!

"Immediately issue the strictest orders for readiness," the Führer addresses Himmler.

That day in Dachau, SS men in the guard towers take the covers off their machine guns. The crematorium director worries whether he'll have enough "cyclone" gas.

Even the mustachioed old SS man walks in a steel helmet.

"I'd like to take it to my house after the war," he says. "My woman would have something in which to set hens for laying eggs."

"But perhaps Mr. Blockführer would like some scrambled eggs?"

"Scram..bled.. eggs?" The old man swallows hard. "*Mensch*! Man! Scrambled eggs, you say? Real scrambled eggs, from real eggs?"

"With bacon," adds the hall leader.

After a time, the old man takes the belt from his uniform and puts it with his revolver on a nearby stool. "Man! Real scrambled eggs!" he murmurs.

At airports in England and Africa fresh crews are climbing into bombers. The residents of German cities don't want to take their clothes off at night anymore because that night, too, will certainly not end without a terrible air strike. In Dachau precentors are starting prayers in the halls. The mustachioed old SS man dreams about his next portion of scrambled eggs. Crematoriums are burning in Auschwitz, Majdanek, Stutthoff, Dachau, and four hundred other concentration camps. The unforgettable curate from Września, Fr. Bernaś Pawlicki, lies dying.

Guard towers were positioned around the camp. The barrels of machine guns protruded from windows on the top level.

In the distant United States, Fr. Peyton's prayer of the Rosary streams from thousands of radios...

"Holy Mary, Mother of God, pray for us sinners," the human pleading runs through the expansive American land, from ocean to ocean, and moves across the borders of Canada...

In the convent of the Sisters of St. Dorothy, Sister Maria Dolores lies in front of the tabernacle with arms outstretched in the form of a cross...

"Our Lady of Fatima, intercede for us."

52

Autumn of 1943

For the past several days at the W.B. we've had a young SS man, a trainee or visitor. He could be about 30 years old. Tall, redheaded, curious, smiling, he goes around all the workshops, looks in all the corners, stops at every machine, asks about its operation and about output of the produced material.

"Well, yes, the machine can produce so much, but how much can you produce in a day?"

The only answer is a disconcerted smile from the prisoner and a shrug of the shoulders.

"I understand," blinks the smiling young SS man, "I understand. Of course, we're not working for ourselves," he adds with an enigmatic look and a wink.

"That's right," the prisoner agrees and, won over by the SS man's friendliness, confides...

The redhead, poking around the workshops, finds even the most cleverly disguised hiding-places for taking a break and smoking cigarettes.

After several days, he becomes a daily visitor. We become accustomed to him. Bungling and crooked deals continue with abandon. The redhead sees it. He smiles and gives an understanding wink.

One day he didn't come to the workshops. We forgot about him. Then one morning as we enter the W.B. in groups, he's standing at the gate, but look at him! He's in the uniform of a high-ranking officer, with epaulettes, wearing a high cap with a wide silver border around it and above the border a skull and crossbones!

"People! What kind of a masquerade is this?"

"Did you see what he has on the cuffs of his sleeves?"

"I didn't notice."

"He has a black band, and embroidered on it is the inscription 'Hitler Leibstandarte.'"

"No way!"

"Trust me. My eyes didn't deceive me. This is a very high-ranking Party member."

That day he addresses us. He refers to the fact that he has been here, that he has seen and found out everything, and that from now on, "meine Herren," there will be no more of it! "Starting today, I'm taking over all the plants. Starting today, we begin working! *Work*, my dear sirs! I will punish most severely all acts of sabotage! And what that assurance means, you will soon come to know..."

And we did come to know: several SS bosses who were the biggest receivers of illegal work were discharged; many capos in various departments were changed, and good capo Hein was dismissed from our carvers command. Lucky for us — though of concern in the future for our new redheaded plant director Schultz — an even better man came, a Rhineland native well-known to us, the democrat Ernst Hecht.

52. Autumn of 1943

Only several days later does the information reach us — from mustachioed SS bosses, whispering confidentially: the damned redheaded dog had been specially sent from Berlin as a spy; he smelled out everything and returned with the greatest powers. "It will be hard," they sigh. He ordered young SS men to be sent immediately to the Russian front.

A similar "reorganization" was conducted at this time in many other commands. Berlin was striving more and more for *production*.

Capo Hecht received notice from a court, obviously through official channels from the commandant's office, that because he's been sitting in the camp for 10 years, his wife has filed for divorce. The court hearing is to take place at a courthouse in Munich on such and such a day.

Our hearts break when we see tears running down the face of the gray-haired Rhineland native.

"Heinrich, you're a priest, so you understand me best. After so many years ... after so many years ... I have one daughter. She's 14 now. The desire to return to her, to my wife, used to hold me up. Now they're stealing my last hope. What do I have to live for..."

The next day, Burek carves a walnut plate. He carves it using beautiful designs, and around the rim he puts the inscription: "To my most beloved child — your unhappy father."

"I'll smuggle this to the court hearing and give it to my daughter as a last memento."

After several days of surreptitious, intermittent work, the plate is done. It's truly beautiful. Homesick himself, Burek put the full depth of his feelings into it. The capo placed the plate carelessly on a table by the window. Schultz, who was poking around the plants, notices it. In a moment he's already in the workshop.

"Whose plate is this?"

"It's mine," answers capo Hecht.

"For whom was it made?" (Schultz thinks it's probably for one of the SS bosses. He'll send another SS man to the front, cleaning up the plants — he thinks to himself.)

"For my daughter," capo Hecht's answer lets him down.

"Don't talk nonsense, you dog!" screams the redhead. "Where's your daughter? How can you give it to her? Don't lie! Tell me, who is it for?"

Hecht explains about his upcoming divorce proceedings.

And surprise! The redhead not only doesn't beat him, doesn't kick him, doesn't scream, but speaks with a strange calmness in his voice:

"Why didn't you come to me and tell me about this matter?"

"Because I knew I wouldn't get permission for this work anyway."

"How's that? Why are you so sure?"

And here words were uttered which the workers on Hecht's command would not forget as long as they lived:

"I knew, sir, you would refuse me because you SS men don't understand a father's pain. You're ... you're heartless!"

We're paralyzed with fear! Bending over our workbenches, we hold our breath, awaiting judgment day. Meanwhile, at the capo's table there's silence. Silence...

Sitting somewhat to the side, I sneak a curious glance...

Hecht is standing at attention with his gray-haired head held high, tears streaming down his cheeks.

"I'm taking this for now," the redheaded director's voice breaks the silence. "Before you leave for the proceedings, come and see me. I'll give it to you with a letter stating that you received it from me, so that you might know even SS men have a heart."

Heels click, doors bang as they close. In an instant we surround Hecht.

"Ernst! Ernst!" We don't know what to say.

"You know that I'm a Protestant," he tells me later, leaning against my workbench. "But from now on, I believe that Mary, whom you Catholics venerate so much, does after all perform miracles."

"That's right, Ernst, that's right…"

One Monday, we come into the workshop in the morning and … suddenly blood rushes to my head. On the workbench where I work together with high-school student Henio Dubiel, all of our "illegal" jobs are standing in a row, uncovered from all the hiding places that only a longtime prisoner can "devise." In front of them is a card with handwritten instructions not to touch anything and wait.

We stand in silence, helpless, with the entire command at the workbench.

"There's no time to waste," Hecht urges us. "Every one of you has the same stuff. Take these things immediately and hide them in more secure places."

There's feverish activity in the workplace. Fitful sentences.

The plant director appears only after a two-hour wait. It could be that he had been busy with other jobs, or it could be that he kept us under stress on purpose…

Capo Hecht submits the regulation report regarding the state of the command.

"You, there," the SS man points toward the table at the window.

"Don't interrupt and tell me that even those odd jobs are for your daughter."

An interrogation begins, which soon turns into a burst of rage on the part of the redhead. He hits us in the face, kicks us over and over again…

"This is sabotage! The only thing for this is a bullet in the head! You dogs! You damned dogs!"

The whole incident ends with an order for both Henio and me to be transferred immediately to the camp and included in the transport for Auschwitz being organized just then in the washroom.

We know too well that we'll be going to our death.

An armed guard escorts us to the camp. From the gate other guards hurry us to a washroom.

Stripped naked, we sit in a large group of those similarly "condemned to death." Hours go by in silence. What is there to talk about at such moments?

The transport is supposed to leave at night. Oh, how slowly the time passes! About three o'clock in the afternoon the secretary of the work office comes into the washroom. He's Brenner's right-hand man, a communist named Julius, who is well-known to us (known for his good side).

"Number 22466!" he yells to the gloomy, silent group.

"Here!"

"Over here, on the double!" yells Julius even louder. "You dog! So, despite the fact you're on the list of skilled workers for repair workshops, you sit here and feel like going on a transport?" A slap on the face closes my mouth, which was just opening with an explanation.

"Hurry up! Hurry up, dog!" he pushes me violently toward the door. "Hey, capo Karl!" he yells in the direction of the washroom, "just give him some rags to cover his back!"

"Heinrich," he says warmly when we're already crossing through the assembly square to the work office. "Don't have it in for me for the screams or the slaps. They were needed to erase this whole stupid matter."

52. Autumn of 1943

I look at kind Julius, not understanding much.

"You see," he explains. "When the carvers command returned to the camp for dinner, Hecht ran in to see us, telling us the whole story. You know that if someone's number is provided to the commandant's office and it's placed on the transport list there, it's not easy to remove it. If you only knew what lengths Brenner has gone to on this matter!"

"Na, Herr Pfarrer, Herr Pfarrer." The kindhearted Austrian Brenner has tears in his big blue eyes when we meet in the work office. "Na ja, na ja, no need to thank me, no need. Today I help you, Father; maybe tomorrow Father will help me."

Brenner looks perplexed when I present him Henio Dubiel's case.

"Father, you know that you don't need to ask me twice, but I can't help this boy at all. It's too bad. The transport leaves in a few hours. The lists of names are already done."

"Heinrich," interrupts Julius, who's standing nearby. Do you know anyone among the camp clinic personnel?"

"Hm ... Why yes. I could find someone there. But why?"

"Listen! All of them will still be checked by an SS doctor. That's the latest order of Commandant Weiss. If this Dubiel had, for example, a high fever during his physical exam, then..." Julius smiles knowingly and winks. "Understand?"

A few minutes later, I'm rushing to nurse Edek Francuskiewicz, who knows Dubiel rather well anyway, and then to Dr. Fiałkowski, who was already working at the clinic at that time...

"Oh, dear me, dear me," grumbles the kind doctor, scratching his shaved head. "You two crazy ones want to stuff me into a penal transport. To bring on a high fever is no problem, but how can I get to him? The vigilant capo Karl is on guard in the washroom."

"Wait," Edek cries out. "I have an idea. My friend from Block 14 knows the Block 4 secretary, who is friends with capo Karl. That German will do anything for a piece of sausage or a package of cigarettes."

Half an hour later, the plan has been talked over and worked out to the smallest detail.

"You're crazy," the doctor feigns anger, "but what can I do? Here are three pills. Have him take two right away and the third one during roll call, after which the physical will take place. If the boy doesn't have a temperature of 42 degrees, then you can have me..."

It still took us many steps before we got a supply of sausage, a piece of bacon, and two packages of cigarettes, but ... following the evening roll call, they drag Henio to the clinic.

"Look," the clinic capo says surprised, showing Dr. Fiałkowski the thermometer. "This is probably typhus, or what?"

"Could be, could be," assents Dr. Fiałkowski gravely, with an expression of concern on his face.

"I thought I'd burst out laughing" says Edek, telling the story later in the evening.

"But Edek," I worry, "What if tomorrow his fever goes down, then..."

"Don't worry about that. If we got him into the clinic, and that was the most difficult thing, it's up to us to keep him under observation for several days, suspected of typhus. Then we'll find other symptoms, and the weeks will go by; they'll forget, and..."

"Hey, Heinrich!" a joyful call suddenly rings out nearby.

Before us stands capo Hecht. He's looking at me with a smile.

"Heinrich, Heinrich, you're a lucky guy."

"Ernst. If not for you, if not for Brenner..."

"Eh," he just waves his hand, "No use talking. But you know what I can tell you?"

I look at the smiling man with anticipation.

"Today I can tell you for the second time that your Mother of God performs real miracles."

"That's what I keep telling you, you kindhearted pagan."

"However, I've come here on business, friend. Tomorrow morning you'll be with the 'repair workshops' command.

"Repair workshops?" I hear a cry from the usually sedate Zdzich. "But that's my command!"

"You work there?" asks Hecht. "So much the better. Take him with you. Everything's been arranged at the job office. No one is permitted to be taken from there to any transport. Over there, capo Erich will meet you. He's a *Spanienkämpfer*,* a communist, but a decent guy. He's been briefed on everything. He'll show you around as needed."

"But wait a minute! What will I do there? I know as much about trucks and tanks as about stars and..."

"Don't be afraid. You won't be in the workshops."

"Not in the workshops?"

"You'll be carving for Col. Stirll, director of that plant."

In Dachau, work surges ahead at full speed. Frightened by the airstrikes, SS men are moving the more essential operations, especially precision skills related to airforce and artillery, into the camp's interior, convinced that they won't be subject to destruction there. After all, the Allies won't be bombing the camp itself. Within the barracks area they've started to build a huge air-defense shelter. Our priest-masons bring us information that the ceiling alone will contain four meters of steel-reinforced concrete. This is understandable, after all, because the main SS disbursement office for all of Germany is in Dachau, and located here are archives and other valuable SS treasures, including silver bells with Polish inscriptions, stolen from...

Suddenly, an extrordinary piece of news starts circulating around the camp: longtime communist prisoners are being given a chance to enlist voluntarily in the army, so they can show gratitude to their "beloved" homeland and repay their debt (!?!).

"What debt?"

"For ten years or more of sitting in Dachau," blurts out Julius from the jobs office.

"They're looking for madmen," say the young Spanish "fighters for the freedom of the Spanish people," whom Hitler locked up in camps following the defeat inflicted by General Franco. "Not even one communist should volunteer!" they declare.

Oh! Not even one? The hunger for freedom is stronger. They volunteer, they volunteer. Not only Buffalo and Knoll, former SS men, but even ideological communists. Those who volunteer include the camp leader Kapp, capo Wilhelm of the hose-weaving shop, the shoemakers' capo Seitz, and others, and several days later they're dressed in SS uniforms, given steel helmets, and — obviously for propaganda purposes — sent out for exercises on the assembly square.

The volunteers go with the hope that as soldiers (albeit in hated SS uniforms) they're leaving for freedom. They don't know they're being inducted into the "Sonderkommando 1005," a force created by Himmler after the defeat at Stalingrad, which has orders to obliterate

---

Translator's note: A "*Spanienkämpfer*" was someone who fought in the Spanish Civil War.

traces of SS crimes committed in the East and to conduct bloody executions of the population in that region. Nor do they know that they'll suffer the full vengeance of the partisans, none of whom will realize, of course, that hidden under the SS uniform is a former long-term prisoner who has been tormented by those very SS men.

The first volunteers left with a soldier's song on their lips, equipped to the last button. After them went others. The hunger for freedom was great. The illusions that sick fantasy painted were even greater. The example of those who've gone ahead draws them. The strong, numerous, and until now cohesive group of camp communists shrinks with every week. It shrinks even more when many of them — mainly from top positions in the camp, that is, block leaders, capos, block secretaries, and clerks, including Szaferski, a deputy of the camp senior — are suddenly placed on a transport, allegedly to Auschwitz! The SS men, apparently well informed concerning the power held by communist prisoners in the camp, are slowly but effectively "cracking" this problem. They're cracking it with even greater zeal because, with the Eastern Front breaking up and the growing threat of a domestic revolution, they want to rid the camp of an element so dangerous to them.

Only the *Spanienkämpfers* remain. They already know the smell and taste of a war in which partisans play an important role.

After months, information arrives that so-and-so of the former volunteers has been killed in action...

They didn't enjoy even that relative freedom very long. The SS men, after arming the former prisoners — their ideological enemies — and making sure they didn't go over to the Russian side, pushed them into situations where they didn't want to deploy regular SS soldiers and where there was only one way out: stubborn defense to the last bullet and... death! How much tragedy there is in this: to die in a hated SS uniform at the hands of those with whom you professed the same ideology. To be sent to the communists for a deadly payment after years of imprisonment for communism...

On 8 September 1943 Munich experiences a monstrous daytime airstrike![1] Above the Dachau camp are hundreds of Allied bombers; the barracks shake under the blasts of exploding aerial bombs... Anti-aircraft artillery deployed around the SS barracks and factories surrounding them is active. A state of readiness is in effect at our plants during every airstrike. It consists of this: all the SS take their place in the small shelters that encircle the factory, but we're chased out of the factory into the adjoining paved streets. We lie on our backs under rays of the still warm sun, and shielding our eyes with our hands, our gaze fixed on the blue sky, we count the squadrons passing over the camp. The steel four-engined birds shine like silver. SS men observe us through loop-hole slits of the shelters. Talk is forbidden. The daring "fighters for the freedom of the Spanish people," a large number of whom are in our command, nevertheless whisper a comment from time to time...

The next day a great many Munich residents are again led toward the crematorium, and again the crematorium sends up its smoke all night long...

On that same day a new piece of news hits the camp! Joyful news! Italy has capitulated! The government has resigned!

"An end of the war in Italy?"

Dachau is in a state of high readiness. SS men are armed to the teeth. They wear steel helmets from morning until night.

"Something's wrong."
"Well, the end is near for them!"
Oh, those incorrigible optimists!

"Hitler is speaking!"

The entire German nation is frozen in nervous anticipation! Washington, London, Moscow turn on their radio speakers; neutral countries listen attentively, including the Portuguese nation...

"The Führer is speaking!" There's an uneasiness among Dachau SS men. This time they don't send us into the assembly square beneath the loudspeakers, where we usually had to stand at attention for hours with uncovered heads. They're not making us go now because, after all, the situation is unclear. Who knows what the Führer will say? It's better if these thousands of prisoners aren't informed at the outset.

"Tomorrow morning I'll tell you anyway," whispers a mustachioed old SS man, adjusting the steel helmet on his bald head, the future nest for his laying hens.

And the following morning?

"Our rapid deployments in Italy, especially the occupation of Rome, and the Führer's speech yesterday have affected the people like champagne," notes the lame Propaganda Minister.

"Phooey," the mustachioed SS man purses his lips. "Like always!" And he waves a hand scornfully.

New masses of the arrested are packed into prisons and concentration camps. These are German people and also foreigners who were deported for slave labor, with Italians in the forefront; in the last days of the Italo-German crisis they had started to talk too openly about the upcoming end. There's no shortage among them of people from a world hated by the Nazis: the German aristocracy and intelligentsia. There's even no shortage of high-level Party people who had the misfortune of allowing their faith in the Führer to falter for a moment. Foolish ones! Why didn't they wait for the "intoxicating champagne of his speech"?[2]

In Dachau wild "rumors" are circulating. They come both at the sight of new rank-and-file prisoners and at each arrival of large shipments in long trains with all kinds of goods from Italy.

"The Italians are accusing us of theft," complains "poor" Goebbels.

And trains to Dachau arrive day and night. No longer just a single command but several hundred prisoners work at unloading them.

"If only you could see what they're bringing in! Railcars full of the most beautiful Italian fabrics, linens, shoes, silks, all kinds of equipment. Wealth, so much wealth, you stand there awestruck just looking at it..."

One evening during those memorable days a messenger from the jobs office arrives at the clerical barracks:

"We're looking for several wine-tasting specialists. It's a matter of classifying various qualities."

"Wine specialists? What kind of joke is this?"

"Well, you priests are known for it, so..." Laughter! Proposals. Names are dropped. Few sense the irony in the messenger's voice.

"Would you like to know what our work consists of?" asks one of those accepted as a "specialist." "Well, they bring us various kinds of wines and ask us to evaluate them. After each sip we take a bite of dark bread and then another sip..."

And, thus, a new command started up in Dachau: judges of wine that now comes in shipment after shipment from Italy.

"How much? I don't know. It's hard to say," someone from the new command reports. "Maybe millions of bottles since they're bringing in whole trainfuls of it and stacking it in the SS cellars."

Since that time, it's rumored, officer Jung can hardly wait for new groups to be shot, and as for papa Redwitz, he walks around lush from early morning. Some say he never sobers up at all.

And in the camp itself? The price of all underwear, sweaters, and shoes drops. If the SS men conducted body searches in Dachau as often as they did formerly, they would notice that the prisoners are wearing the most stylish Italian officer underwear, that some who are more particular even wear silks, and that the splendid shoes of Italian Alpine units are being worn every day to work. It's easy to cover this up now since camp headquarters has given permission to receive shoes and underwear from families.

"The Germans have spirited away Mussolini!"

"No way!"

Nevertheless, it's a fact. This rumor is confirmed by Nazi newspapers and radio.

Mussolini sets up his temporary headquarters in the capital of Bavaria, and over the roofs of the camp barracks in Dachau can be heard his fervent appeal to Italian fascists as he calls on them to continue being faithful to their devoted Nazi friends.[3]

Following Mussolini's speech in Munich, throngs of fascists sneak across from southern Italy, which has been occupied by the Allies, into northern Italy or even into Germany, hoping they can join the ranks of a fascist army that is being created anew.

The poor Italians, duped by deceitful Nazi propaganda, sneak across so they can stand in defense of their country, making their way by the tens of thousands to German factories. And thousands of them land in concentration camps, including Dachau, because an imprisoned worker is, after all, a hundred times cheaper and causes less trouble. But if needed, scaffolds and firing squads are always in readiness, and a new crematorium awaits with its four modern ovens.

"*Padre! Un pezzo di pane*," beg starving Italians in front of the clerical barracks in Dachau. "Father, a piece of bread!" In their dark, tormented eyes, often filled with tears, there's so much pain.

"These are accursed fascists who along with the Nazis murdered..."

"Man! Aren't you put to shame sometimes by communist capo Wagner, communist nurse Hein from the clinic, communist capo Wilhelm, Julius from the jobs office, and many others who showed us Catholic priests so much kindness, despite the fact that ideologically we're mutual enemies? True, these people here are former fascists, but right now they're beggars dying of hunger, just as we were only a year ago."

"*Tante grazie! Tante grazie!*" and the skeleton runs off with a blessed chunk of bread, upon which flow joyful tears of gratitude.

Besides Italians, there are Croats, Slovenes, Jugoslavs, and other nationalities arriving in increased numbers from the endangered Balkans, where partisans have become a real disaster for Nazi units. Among the arrivals, there's no shortage of Greeks. Within these groups are a lot of children who have been in transit to Dachau for many days without a bite of food, who are so hungry they no longer have strength to ask like the others, and only those large dark eyes typical of southerners are begging: "Father ... bread!"

This period is one of the most beautiful chapters of our clerical experiences in Dachau because it gives us a chance to render aid to our neighbors. God knew why he allowed them to revoke our privileges, free us from isolation and leave us among many thousands of lay colleagues. We have many more opportunities to show mercy in W.B. blocks, to which the destitute have easier access. No one writes about these acts of priestly hearts, no one until now. Those who have written about Dachau so far haven't noticed it. On the contrary, a spittle of envy, bias, and malice directed at Polish priests has dribbled out. No matter. For the night of the soul, which Polish clergy experienced in concentration camps, that, too, was needed. What is important is what the Almighty and only fair Judge will reveal from heavenly "chronicles" on the day of Final Judgment.

While Goebbels again complains that Italians are doing the Nazis harm by continuing to claim that "we Germans are now plundering Italy,"[4] the Dachau Italians, forced to unload trains with treasures brought to Dachau from their poor homeland, work with tears in their eyes as they think about their families dying of hunger and cold in the country they left...

"Have you heard?" discreetly whispers capo Erich, the *Spanienkämpfer* and my current supervisor. "'The Free Committee of German Officers' gives a talk on the radio from Moscow every evening, calling on all soldiers to throw down their arms and telling people to commit sabotage? Heinrich, dear shaveling, do you know what this means for us? ... Don't forget! They're calling for *sabotage*," he repeats with emphasis. "But in what way can you commit sabotage?" he reflects as he looks at the huge size of the oak frame that I'm working on now. "Perhaps you can put fewer oak leaves or acorns on it, or those old Germanic emblems? In any case, may your God in whom you still believe keep you from working with too much haste. But be careful: don't breathe a word about this! Not to anyone!" he ends with a flash in his steely eyes.

"Henryk," says Zdzich, who's currently working as a welder in the workshops producing bodies for armored vehicles and smaller tanks at the front. "If you only saw how those "Spanioles" (that's what we called German communists who had fought in the Spanish revolution against General Franco), how those Spanioles are sabotaging. Outwardly you can't tell, such a vehicle might even make it to the front, but..."

October approaches. The prayer of the Rosary resounds now not only in clerical barracks, but here and there in lay barracks. These emaciated Italians have indeed brought much spirituality into the lay ranks. We admire their faith. Maybe it's based only on feelings, sometimes primitive ones, but we admire its dynamism in these poor wretches.

On the 13th of that month of the Rosary, on the very anniversary of the final appearances of Our Lady of Fatima, a bombshell drops: Italy has declared war against Germany!

"*Evviva Badoglio! Evviva Italia!*"

These Italians, they're lovable madmen.

That's not the only disaster for the Germans: Portugal, the country of Our Lady of Fatima, which has been neutral until now, agrees to provide the Allies with bases and airports.

And bombs keep dropping on German cities day and night! "We won't be able to endure this horrible loss of people much longer," Goebbels despairs. "In addition, if we take into account that the Eastern Front alone has cost us three million deaths up to now, no one can deny that we're paying an immense price..."[5]

On 8 November, Hitler gives a speech in Munich. An entire clique of Nazi leaders is gathered around him. It includes the famous Professor Schilling and Dr. Rascher, from the Dachau experimental stations. The Führer is speaking! The Führer is giving the nation a new injection. Victory will finally be ours!

"Heil! Sieg! Heil!" scream SS men in the hall.

In city streets that are buried under rubble there is silence... Only enormous rats prowl in the darkness, feeding on corpses covered with debris.

But in a Löwenbrau Bierkeller a drunken group of madmen is "finding solace."

"I promise you soon some wonderful new weapons! New aircraft! Terrifying new and deadly bombs!" the Führer shouts.

"Heil! Sieg! Heil! Heil!"

"Victory must be ours!"

"Heil! Heil! Heil!"

"I promise you that following the war I will quickly rebuild our cities!"[6]

While Hitler's words are still ringing out in Munich, a deadly hail of bombs falls on dozens of German cities! The blood-red glow of fires leaps high into the dark sky; bloody scraps of torn human flesh splatter across the ruins; a nation's moan resounds...

"Sieg! Heil! Hail victory!" howls a gang of crazed SS men, intoxicated by alcohol and the Führer's words.

At the experimental station in Dachau, victims of experiments are dying. Communist nurse Hein puts his cool hands on the foreheads of people burning with fever, so as to bring them some relief...

"Orate, fratres," a prayerful whisper passes through the clerical halls...

The wind rustles in the leaves that cover the camp street.

53

The Nazi Nero

We had barely entered the workshop in the morning when Col. Stirll himself shows up. Walking up to my woodcarving corner and taking a look at the job I started, he says:

"You'll take (Stirll uses the polite form, never the familiar "you," when speaking to me) your tools, a few pieces of wood, some stain and lacquer, and you'll go for the whole day to Munich, to my residence. There are some repairs to be made and a few scratches on furniture to be removed. Anyway," he adds, "my wife herself will show you what's needed."

An hour later, I'm already sitting with an SS guard in an official compartment of the train going from Dachau to Munich. The SS man knows I'm a priest and touches upon this in our conversation. It appears that he himself is a Catholic from the Sudeten and that — as he claims — the SS uniform has not changed his beliefs at all.

I listen, saying little myself. What if he wants to catch me on something? One can never be too careful in such situations.

Finally, after an hour's ride, Munich. Many of my colleagues come here frequently, delivering or picking up something, or as workers brought from the camp to remove rubble, or even as helpers in bomb disposal. They tell us that this is a city of a million residents, the capital of Catholic Bavaria, and the place where the Nazi movement had its beginnings; at present it looks like one huge pile of rubble. I have an opportunity to see this in person. The destruction is terrible. Only here and there an entire house stands — to my amazement — in the midst of ruins. As far as the eye can see, there's only rubble all around. Sticking out of the rubble are bare, blackened chimneys; here and there you can see the arch of a gate or the remains of a wall. A trolley crawls along gullies of streets lined on either side by the high mounds of rubble. Stuck in the mounds are the street numbers of houses that used to be in that place and cards with information from those who indeed survived but had to seek some other shelter. The card provides information about the new address. This will help in locating families lost during the airstrikes and make it possible to deliver a letter.

The trolley is packed to the hilt, but in spite of that, an empty circle begins to form around me, a prisoner in striped uniform holding a sack of tools. People are afraid to touch me. At one of the stops, a group of waiting passengers again starts to board. Backing up to make room, I step on the paw of a huge German shepherd that is just behind me. The dog yelps horribly. A young civilian standing nearby starts calling me names, screaming something about the mangy, lice-infested felons who should be dragged on ropes behind the trolley, which is intended for people, not criminals, and that he would like to...

The mustachioed SS man escorting me interrupts him, explaining that he brought me onto the trolley, that I'm not a felon, but a political prisoner, who for the duration of the war...

The young civilian opens the lapel of his coat and shows the SS man some kind of pin. The SS man stiffens to attention:

"Heil Hitler!"

"Heil Hitler. Your service I.D. card, please."

The mustachioed SS man, slow to respond, murmurs something under his nose...

"Hand me your I.D.!"

With a trembling hand, the mustachioed man opens the breast pocket of his uniform, takes out his I.D., and hands it over. The other man compares the photograph with the SS man's face, takes a notebook, writes something in it, gives the I.D. back to the SS man, and gets off at the next stop.

"*Sauhund*! (swine dog!)," an older man next to me calls after him with scorn.

Aside from that, there's silence in the trolley, but you can see from the downcast faces that there's an uneasiness in these hearts, that anger is choking them, and if not for a paralyzing fear...

The trolley makes a stop. Again it's packed. An older lady, squeezing by me, searches out my hand and presses a small packet into it. Through the paper I can feel two pieces of bread. I'd like to thank her with a smile, but she never turns around.

There are situations where not a single word is uttered but you learn more than from a flood of words. That's how it is at this moment. I feel that the sympathies of the passengers are on my side and on the side of the SS man who defended me. People are careful, however. They know from experience what results from an outward manifestation of true beliefs and feelings. Aren't enough Munich residents dying already in the enclosure of the Dachau crematorium?

The trolley continues to drag through the gullies of ruins, swaying abruptly at numerous turns, bouncing on the irregular surface of bomb craters where temporary rails have been laid. Slowly, however, we manage to reach a suburb where there's less damage, and finally we're in a district where not a single bomb has yet landed.

"So ein Hund," spits the mustachioed SS man, as we get off in front of the colonel's house.

"It wasn't the dog's fault," I come to its defense. "It was me; I didn't know that..."

"Not the one on four paws!" the SS man says irritated. "The civilian, he's a damn dog! You know?" he adds after a moment: "That was a Gestapo agent!" He spits.

For the first time in years I find myself in a "decent" home. I feel ill at ease. The shiny floors, the rugs, mirrors, white tablecloths — all so familiar, yet so distant. The colonel's wife greets us with a friendly smile. Judging by her behavior and words, I conclude that my mustachioed SS guard is well known here and comes often.

"I bring one of the prisoners here every few days," he explains to me later. "Sometimes it's to clean up the garden, sometimes to tidy up the house or fix something, and that's why they know me here. Go ahead and take care of your repairs. I'll take a nap."

There are just a few repairs: a carved piece has come unglued from a library bookcase; a table rim has also become detached; a touch-up is needed on a scratched piano top; and a chair leg needs to be glued — all minor things. Around ten o'clock the colonel's wife herself brings a chunk of bread and a small pot of coffee.

"Take some refreshment, Father."

So she has learned from her husband, or maybe from the mustachioed guard, that I'm a priest. Sincere kindness flows from her whole demeanor. The dinner, while wartime in nature, is nonetheless copious. We eat together: the colonel's wife, two daughters who have returned from an office, my SS guardian, and I. It's a strange sight: a hated SS uniform, a striped prison uniform, the wife of a high-ranking SS officer, and two offsprings in BDM* uniforms at one table! What is even more curious is that all of us cross ourselves, bow our heads, and quietly whisper a prayer before and after the meal.

My head spins from thoughts, reflections, impressions, conclusions...

The hours pass quickly. About three in the afternoon, sirens begin to sound. First one, then another, and after a while dozens.

"Air raid warning!" the mustachioed SS man's face turns pale with fear.

"We're going to the shelter," the colonel's wife says calmly, as she comes in with her purse and a fur on her arm.

Without any haste, we go to the most distant corner of the garden where, under a gazebo covered with hops, there's an entryway to a small concrete shelter. Upon entering, I stand amazed: the interior is furnished as comfortably as the colonel's own residence. The colonel's wife, noticing my surprise, explains:

"You see, Herr Pfarrer, lately we spend more nights in the shelter than in the house, and that's why..." she gestures.

There are comfortable sofas, two upholstered easy chairs, a small kerosene stove, a thick rug on the floor, and suitcases standing against the walls...

The sound of explosions can be heard in the distance.

"They're bombing somewhere very far away," the colonel's wife says.

The mustachioed SS man stands at the entryway. I go out and stand beside him.

"A small airstrike," he says with relief, pointing to several shining points in the distance. "They're finishing off the city center. There's just rubble over there anyway!"

I'm happy the airstrike is minor. I wouldn't want to experience the kind that usually take place in this city.

An hour later, lavished with chunks of bread (and the old SS man is more eager for his than the prisoner), we leave for the railroad station. We ride the trolley again through the pitiful remains of streets. It's impossible, however, to look with indifference at the piles of ruins and the passengers' faces, on which no smile can be seen.

At the railroad station we come across two SS men escorting several of my prisoner colleagues to camp. Like me, they were doing work in Munich. Among them is the old poacher Anton, a Tyrolean, who was locked up in camp for killing a deer that forest wardens had chosen as a target for Göring himself (at least that's what he says). On his shirt Anton wears a black triangle, the symbol given to all so-called asocial prisoners. We stand in a line along a wall, with the SS men close at hand. A small group of passengers gathers in front of us. Observing us, they whisper among themselves, curious regarding some detail. Finally, one of the older women comes closer and whispers to Anton, who's standing at the end:

"Why do those fellows over there," she moves her head in our direction, "have red triangles, while you have a black one?"

"They're communists," answers Anton in a whisper.

"Communists?" Fear appears on the face of the old woman. "And you?"

"*Geistlicher* ... a clergyman," explains Anton, lowering his eyes bashfully.

"*Geistlicher*? A clergyman? *Mein Gott!*" sighs the old woman. She goes back to her group and whispers something to them. After a while, purses are opened... The old woman collects something, then approaches the SS men and shows them gathered pieces of bread...

---

*Translator's note: "BDM" is the German abbreviation for "League of German Girls."

The SS man with a mustache nods his head in approval. The woman moves quickly over to us and hands the gifts… to Anton!

"That's for you, Father."

When the SS men inside the railcar learn all about the incident, they burst out laughing with us. Oh, that old tippler Anton!

And the old Alpine poacher smiles with his toothless mouth.

"Ha, ha, I've pulled off even better tricks. When Göring's deer…" But here he realizes that, after all, SS men are listening to him; he breaks off, feigns a cough, chokes…

"Hey, you old drunkard!" the mustachioed one gestures menacingly. "You drunkard!"

It's only when we get closer to the camp that the SS men become reserved, as befits guards.

Looking at the camp with fresh eyes, as it were, after my short excursion to the outside, I see even more clearly the changes that have recently taken place. While even now thousands of prisoners must put forth their last strength in hard slave labor, it's now without harassment, without beating, without kicks, without standing for hours on end in the assembly square in freezing cold, without penalty nights outside in the open. There's none of that now. But the harsh memory stays with us. We sometimes tell new prisoners about those days, but it's difficult for them to believe those terrible things; they simply can't conceive of what we went through.

Transports arrive, and in them from time to time is a small group of priests, either directly from outside or from another camp. They bring with them extraordinary news: about fronts that are suddenly breaking up, about a rising spirit of resistance, about the growing partisan movement, about the hopeless domestic situation in Germany, about the terrible destruction of cities from bombing. In our blocks, spirits are up, rumors abound, and since we're slowly approaching Christmas and packages arrive in abundance, the mood becomes increasingly optimistic, increasingly rosy…

In the meantime, Allied airstrikes on German cities continue without pause. "A person could almost go crazy," Goebbels writes, "seeing with what defiance they attack us, and we are helpless! Our production effort is dropping to a minimum. The only place where work is still done securely is in factories located right next to concentration camps. The Allies are still sparing these and not bombing them."[1]

"You know," says Fr. Aloś Klinkosz, who rides around the whole camp area in a fumigation vehicle. "Over there, behind the west wall, they're putting up new barracks. Supposedly they're intended for an aviation training school with the most modern equipment. That's what prisoners working there have told me."

These stories are being repeated. SS officials are "nestling" some new head office against the walls of the secure camp. Moreover, in the very heart of the camp they've already taken over two barracks to make room for precision-tool workshops that are shrouded in secrecy.

"If they continue this way, the time will come when all of us prisoners will be living outside the camp and our barracks will be turned into factories, so as to shelter them from the bombings," one of our men grumbles.

"It would be even more appropriate," another adds, "if each of us were given a valuable machine to put under our bunk."

And the Allied airstrikes go on. They don't just go on; they get stronger from one week to the next. From the time the Allies take half of Italy, squadrons of bombers numbering in the hundreds, frequently more than a thousand, deploy from there.

"Why are they pounding Munich so hard?" someone asks with surprise. After all, it's just one rubble heap over there…"

"The suburbs still stand untouched."

"Uh-huh."

"The situation of our cities, defenseless and exposed to constant airstrikes, is hopeless!" Goebbels writes in his diary. "Lately especially the Allies are bombing Berlin itself with great intensity. The airstrikes are so frequent and cause such destruction that you can't even wash or shave yourself!"[2]

The airstrikes on Berlin don't let up. "Today several hundred of them came flying over, burying the city in a sea of fire. It's horrible! And we're helpless!" admits Goebbels.

Berlin is burning. Of all the high-ranking Nazi big shots, only Goebbels remains in the capital. Hitler sits in East Prussia, in his bunkered main headquarters, giving more and more horrible orders. Göring is hunting in the Alps! Himmler goes from camp to camp, continuing to sow terror.

Berlin is on fire, the remnants of German cities are on fire, but Goebbels still wants to believe in Hitler's words. "After all," he consoles himself, "after all, the Führer has promised that final victory will be ours!"

Terrified crowds for whom there is no shelter rush about in the streets of Berlin. Bombs fall out of the sky by the thousands; a rain of phosphorus pours down. "Both the Führer's and my own private residence" complains Goebbels, "are dismal sights! ... It seems as though all elements of nature have conspired against us! I simply can't look at this!" And after a while, he adds: "The sky over Berlin is all blood red, all a dark red of unspeakable beauty!" Like Nero, the arsonist, watching from the terrace of his palace as Rome burns...

But what was the fire of old Rome compared to the disasters of Berlin, Warsaw, Hamburg, Munich, and other European capitals?

Goebbels, with eyes fixed upon dying Berlin, cries out: "The next generation not only will worship us, they will envy us because it was our fate to live in the torrent of these great events."[3]

And thousands of people are dying on streets of the capital! Thousands die every day in other cities! Thousands die every day at the front!

Of what value to bloody Goebbels are thousands of prisoners from nations thought of as inferior, thought of as slaves?

Of what value to terrible Nazism are we, those of us in Dachau?

Only as slaves, who for now are given a chance to work, to shore up a staggering armed power, and who after the war will be whipped into clearing away the ruins from which the colossus of a Nazi "new order" is to arise.

54

Spring of 1944

Christmas of 1943 has passed, my fifth in slavery, yet how different it was from those before it! On the assembly square opposite the kitchen, they set up an enormous fir tree trimmed with hundreds of electric lights; holiday melodies flowed from a radio loudspeaker throughout the holiday; there was calm in the guardhouse, silence in the guard towers; there was a better dinner and even a movie in the evening; in short, we never had such holiday atmosphere in the camp before.

Holiday packages and optimistic "rumors" rounded out the picture. In all the halls of the clerical barracks Christmas Eve Masses were held, and "solemn" high Masses were celebrated on Christmas day. Right now, there's not a single SS man in the camp itself. Only in the distance, beyond the wires, one of them moves from time to time, and then it's deserted again.

"Following the holidays, a transport will leave for Auschwitz," Edek Francuskiewicz brings the news. "Henio Dubiel is still on the list. He hasn't been forgotten after all. They're inquiring at the camp clinic about his health."

"They're asking about him? After such a long time?"

"That's right. There's only one thing that can save him."

"Which is?"

"Like this: if he agrees to move to the airforce experimental station as one of the personnel. I've already gotten some information. They need a carpenter there. Henio could fill that place."

When the scheduled transport to Auschwitz leaves several days later, Henio Dubiel, the young high-school student from Łódź, has already been drafted as an "indispensable skilled carpenter" at Dr. Rascher's airforce experimental station. This is one aspect of Dachau life, which is full of paradoxes. Even in places where some have been murdered, you could hide others securely, saving their lives!

The New Year came and went in an atmosphere similar to that at Christmas. Although we know that right after the holiday the next transports of the handicapped are supposed to leave for the gas chambers, they have stopped being dangerous for the clerical barracks. The weaker element among us has already been moved out on earlier transports, and even if there are still some among us who are older and weaker, food packages and recent shipments of warmer underwear have been of great help. Those blessed packages bring with them well-smuggled medications! If the commandant's office had allowed them earlier, it would have saved the lives of several hundred more priests.

Even the Nazi press, which is allowed in the camp, carries news making us more aware that the end is near. The line dividing optimists from pessimists among us becomes increasingly more distinct. There's even a third faction, the "self-described" realists, but for all intents and purposes that group belongs to the pessimists.

Such a division may seem to be childishness, and yet in those days it was real, powerful, divisive, creating two groups mutually at odds. The optimists have already ended the war very early, unwavering in their belief that at any moment the Allies will drop paratroops into the camp and liberate it, whereas that kind of prattle irritates the pessimists. They burst out angrily at the absurdity of it, asserting that at any moment the Nazis could liquidate us to a man. The realists, supposedly evaluating the situation in the most objective way, certainly agree in principle with the pessimists' predictions, but basing their opinion on the great demand for laborers, they believe liquidation can occur only during the final moments, when everything starts to fall apart and we're no longer needed as a work force.

During this period, huge transports arrive at the camp with the clothing and underwear of those who were gassed in Auschwitz. Hundreds of freightcars deliver it all. Everything that's warmer, such as furs and coats, goes toward a "military fund" for the soldiers; the rest is for us prisoners. From that time on, almost all striped prison uniforms disappear in the camp. We change into civilian clothing on the back of which they paint big red crosses, using oil paint. Such is the regulation, meant to provide officials a safeguard against making escape easier for prisoners by handing them civilian clothing.

On Saturday afternoons, when we don't go to the factories, and on Sundays as well, they make hundreds of prisoners sort out this bloody booty. All kinds of things are there! Clothing of the best quality, made from the most expensive English or Belgian textiles, the most fashionable silk underwear, the most expensive lace sets. Of course. The deported Jews, for the most part wealthy people, financial tycoons from all of Europe, took for this final trip the most expensive, most durable and best clothing they had. The Nuremberg trials established that from camps on Polish territory forty million kilograms of clothing from murdered Jews were sent to Germany; this required sixty freight trains, each with a hundred boxcars.

These shipments, sent to concentration and labor camps, were labeled as "gifts" from the German nation to foreigners who needed clothing! That action, described as *Spinnstoffsammlung*,* which was robbery committed on millions of victims, but which was dressed by Minister Goebbels in a gown of philanthropy, became once again a source of great income for the SS men and a fresh opportunity for abuses. Because soon after, a new "dry goods market" was opened for the prisoners in Dachau. Thousands of silk stockings, thousands of pieces of silk underwear disappeared in hiding places known only to prisoners and then landed in the bottomless pockets and bags of SS men. When camp officials noticed that great quantities of the shipped goods were disappearing and started to conduct body searches of prisoners who were charged with sorting the clothing, extraordinary ideas for hiding these treasures began to multiply. Silk stockings, after a seam in the toe was carefully slit open, were very easily rolled up together with the sleeves of a shirt. What SS man would suspect that the prisoner being searched is carrying several pairs of them right in his sleeves or that he has silk underwear or other valuable items tucked in the cuffs of his rolled-up trouser legs?

Sorting clothing and underwear became the occupation of many unemployed Polish priests as well during the long winter months.

"Well, it does smell bad," the 'sorters' say, "but the work is done sitting down under a roof, and it's easier and better there than in our block, where they force us to do hard camp work."

**Translator's note*: textile materials collection.

54. Spring of 1944

In Barracks 28 for senior priests lives the unforgettable Fr. Jan Wojciechowski, a pastor from Kozielsko, who is already over 70 years old. Physically strong, full of optimism and always cheerful, he has managed to avoid the terrible transports of the handicapped. We all call him Uncle Wojciechowski.

Uncle is holding up bravely, but he has just one weak spot, namely, cold ears!

"Hey, you," he repeatedly turns to the clothing sorters, "bring me some earmuffs. My ears are so cold!"

Unfortunately, there's no such item in the piles of clothing and underwear. Uncle doesn't much believe that.

"You don't want to bring them!" he grumbles, disappointed.

At last, one of the young jokers gets an idea. After finding a black, rather small padded bra, he brings it to the block and gives it to Uncle, who looks it over with surprise and mumbles:

"How strange these earmuffs are, how strange, a kind I've never seen before..."

"Well you see, Uncle, these come from Jews in Amsterdam, and style there is a bit different than in Poland..."

That day, dear Uncle Wojciechowski parades to evening roll call with a bra on his ears that once belonged to some poor Jewish girl who was murdered.

"You know, those Dutch understand what's good," he compliments them. "These earmuffs are warm and practical, though a bit strange..."

These days in January 1944 are, after all, full of exhilarating hopes, so it's not hard to joke. Even though we clear snow and must perform difficult work, we do it now without a club over our heads, with rather good food and in warm clothing. The Dachau winter, which we always dreaded so, has become less threatening. At times now it even has some charm...

Airstrikes are increasing on Munich and smaller neighboring towns, and especially on the airfield located beyond the woods. The frozen ground carries the shock of the explosions. More and more SS bosses leave for the front, and more often their places are taken by old people.

The shops where I work have recently been directed to put armor plate on civilian vehicles. I feel like laughing when I see an old, dilapidated 1930 Ford with a puffing, sputtering engine get an armored body. A grandpa that's been used until now for delivering vegetables is supposed to go to the front!

"It's the same with our SS guards," laughs Zdzich, as he solders steel plates. "If only you knew how we join these plates; it's easy to find places where the quality control boss can't detect anything! This is going to fall apart before it reaches the front."

"Oh, it won't fall apart; it'll get there because the front is no longer that far away."

"That's right. The Russians are already crossing the borders of Poland."

"In Italy it keeps getting worse."

"If only those Allies would decide to invade soon!"

Many Russian officers are now being moved to the camp. They are locked up and heavily guarded in special isolation quarters for fear they might come into contact with other prisoners. There are several thousand young Russians in Dachau who were taken from civilian jobs, but, strangely, they shun their arriving countrymen. We can't understand why until one day young Ivan, who works as an apprentice at Fr. Stefcio Smaruj's workbench, explains it to us.

"These young fellows taken from their jobs are mainly volunteers who signed up to come to Germany." Ivan looks around to make sure no one can overhear and continues in a whisper: "Because, you see, we thought that Hitler was coming to free us, to..." he waves his hand meaningfully. "At that time many, many of our people fled to the Germans. Then when we saw what kind of devils they are, we regretted it... But what can you do? You're born only once. It's done. And now these officers of ours are looking at us as though we're traitors..."

"So that's it!"

On 22 February there's some commotion in the Soviet officers' isolation quarters. Out of nowhere appear young SS men in helmets, in combat readiness, with submachine guns ready to fire.

They lead out several dozen officers, moving the unit toward the crematorium. After a while we hear shots. We know what that means. An execution!

From this time on, the shooting of Russian soldiers is repeated often, considerably increasing the number of shocking experiences in Dachau.

Male nurses in the camp clinic, called upon to undress the condemned, whisper in horror that the SS is executing Russians en masse at the rifle range. The poor souls are pushed into a trench, and young boys drafted into the SS ranks train by shooting them with heavy machine guns.

"Then we wade up to our ankles in blood! The very sight makes us sick... Bodies of the executed lie piled high in layers, so it's hard to pull them apart when we have to load them onto trucks."

The February sun warms us more each day.

"Soon we'll start soccer league matches," announces drunken Captain Redwitz.

In the distant rifle range, machine guns are firing...

"I tell you they're barely, just barely alive, and I can imagine your surprise, you awful pessimist, when early one morning you wake up and see the sky dotted with parachutes of the Allies coming to free us..."

"Out of 5 million foreigners working in Germany, there aren't even 200,000 who came here of their own free will," states Fritz Sauckel on 1 March 1944.[1]

"Why are you crying, Michałek?"

"Tomorrow I have a court hearing in Munich," he answers, wiping tears with his sleeve.

"What about?"

"They've charged me with having sexual relations with the daughter of a German farmer, but, Father, I never... Only I don't know German, and I couldn't defend myself, so..."

Michałek never returned from Munich. Ryszard Knosala, who was at the trial as an interpreter, reported back that the young man was sentenced to death!

More often now they're bringing others like Michałek into the camp, people deported from Poland as children and now charged with some real or imaginary crime.

Many of them, especially those charged with "polluting pure German blood," are sentenced to death.

And from Poland ever sadder news arrives about acts of terror, about starvation, about a terrible wave of the flu that carries off great numbers of the living.

Unexpected news about the death of my father shakes me to the core... When his funeral is already over, I receive a letter he wrote two days before his death... It's true that this is a personal experience, which has no right to be on the pages of *Shavelings*, but since there's probably no one in our group of priests who hasn't mourned the death of someone close to him, such moments are also part of "our mutual memories from the death camps." Still more curious is an event that I can't explain myself and that not one of my colleagues has explained to me, which is that my late father—*appeared* to me in Dachau…

55

The Fruitful Summer of 1944

May in Dachau has always been one of the capricious months, one day displaying all the charms of an Alpine spring and another day blowing a blizzard right from snow-covered Alpine peaks, but May of 1944 is capricious as never before.

No wonder that even Minister Goebbels complains about the nasty weather, considering it to be the reason for disasters on the Eastern Front, where the Russian army makes greater and greater advances. He also complains, of course, about the Allies, who with the help of modern equipment unceasingly bomb German cities, forcing hundreds of thousands of city dwellers to spend cold and rainy nights in the open air.

Almost every day we witness airstrikes on Munich and its environs. On the plantation they've set up two more batteries of heavy anti-aircraft artillery, operated by young girls (according to Fr. Romek Budniak, who works on the plantation).

"If only you could see how quick those kids are during the airstrike! It's just amazing."

"Kids?"

"That's right. Probably not one of them is over eighteen."

The plantation command doesn't return to camp during airstrikes, but seeks shelter in dugouts located near the job site, which is why Romek can observe them in action.

A series of heavy anti-aircraft guns has been positioned not just on the plantation, but generally around the entire camp, so whenever squadrons of Allied aircraft fly over us toward Munich, the artillery begins to raise real hell! Hundreds of shells explode over the camp. A rain of fragments falls on barracks roofs.

"They've manned the entire camp so diligently for fear the Allies could be tempted by all these industrial plants that were recently set up all around, even inside camp barracks," Zdzich speculates.

"Bloody battles in central Italy!" the Nazi press announces.

"The Polish Second Corps bleeds on the slopes of Monte Cassino!"

It is hard to describe the impression these news items make on the thousands of Poles locked up in Dachau. The optimists exult!

"See! Didn't we tell you!"

They would really have exulted had they known that at this time Minister Goebbels, seeing disaster on the Eastern Front, was thinking more and more seriously about initiating peace treaties with America and England, with the aim of mounting a joint front against Russia...

"Monte Cassino has fallen!"

55. The Fruitful Summer of 1944

Excitement in Dachau! It's because the Polish Second Corps is so very close to us! Just across the Alps! In a week or two, not later than a month, they could be here.

"Nonsense!"

"Pessimist!"

There's an infernal din inside the hall of the repair shops. Hundreds of hammers are tapping, three power hammers are pounding, riveting machines are making a racket, grinding machines are rasping, oxygen equipment is hissing. I have to go through this hall several times a day because the bathroom is located far over on the opposite side. Usually I stop for a while to talk to Zdzich. But where can he be today? I don't see him in his usual place.

As I pass an armored box on wheels, I hear the sounds of a Kujawiak melody coming from within, and through the hiss of the soldering flame, the words are audible: "Geese beyond the water, ducks beyond the wa..." The song breaks off when the blowtorch flame goes out. The oxygen tank is standing on the outside, so I turn the knob off and listen ... I hear grumbling coming from inside the armored body... After a moment, a mask perched on a forehead appears, and beneath it is Zdzich's lean, surprised face. He catches on right away.

"You want to play jokes," he murmurs, wiping off sweat with his soiled hand. "You want to play jokes, you aristocrat in a white collar! ("White-collar aristocracy" is a term workers in the machine shop use for prisoners from offices, from the administration, or from the "planning" department, where I have my woodcarving corner.)

"Did you know that yesterday they knocked down the old guy's house in Munich?"

"They bombed Stirll's villa?"

"That's right. The colonel's wife also died in the airstrike."

"The colonel's wife?!" I can't hide my emotion.

"That's why the old guy didn't come to the factory today, and Lili went to console him. She was the least concerned of anyone. And the old guy probably not much, either."

"Hey, drop it; don't jeer even at your enemy in misfortune."

"Maybe the old guy will invite you to the funeral? You worked for him at his house. You knew his old lady. His daughters are left..."

Mrs. Stirll is no longer alive. This woman was a stranger, moreover the wife of a high-ranking SS officer, and yet this news has cut me to the quick. I see in my mind's eye an elderly gray-haired lady with an intense expression on her face, making the sign of the cross before a meal...

That night we witness another huge airstrike. The glow from the fire is so great that it covers half the sky and is reflected with blood-red rays in windows of the Dachau barracks.

"Man, they're really hitting them today!"

Metal bowls clatter in the cupboards. From time to time the walls of the barracks shake.

"They're dropping mines," someone whispers.

If the airstrikes were something of a curiosity for us several months ago, today we've grown indifferent, and most of my colleagues are resting in their bunks, not even bothering to go to the windows. Many don't even hear them, having fallen into a deep sleep.

"How much shrieking over there, how much moaning, how much fear!"

"Eh, your imagination again!" rebukes Zdzich. "Don't think about it. Sleep."

Toward the end of May and the beginning of June, literally not one day or night goes by without increasingly intense airstrikes and bombing. It could be they're hitting so hard because they see that the end is near.

At this time an incident took place in Block 28 that dampened the spirits of the optimists for a few days. During one of the evening airstrikes, while the "optimists society" sat in a darkened room to discuss the situation, no one noticed that an SS man had slipped into the room. Since he understood Polish, he listened to what the prisoners were saying and then... Then all of a sudden came investigations, inquiries, interrogations... We remembered we were still in Dachau and that "they" hadn't forgotten at all about methods of punishment, about beatings, about harassments... The whole affair ended with elderly Fr. Józef Biały and the young Jesuit seminarian, Jurek Musiał, being sent in a penal transport to the camp in Mauthausen.[1]

"For *extermination*!"

"Well, it was their own fault."

From then on the optimists "planned the end of the war" less boldly and were less open in setting a date for the final defeat of Nazism.

During these days several priests have been brought in, including the Salesian Fr. Jan Kasprzyk. The priests have a lot of news we knew nothing about, which once again rouses the optimists... But Fr. Kasprzyk himself didn't altogether share the optimistic assumptions they were making prematurely.

"It's falling apart for the Germans, that's true, but one has to understand the obstinacy of the Nazis. They're ready to annihilate us before they meet the end themselves..."

"Orate, fratres," the preceptor's voice is heard... "And for the souls of those who on the slopes of Monte Cassino..."

"The Allies have launched an invasion in France!" the joyful news spreads in whispers throughout the camp... "They've landed on the shores of Normandy. It seems they attacked with such force and pulled it off so suddenly that the Germans withdrew in panic and are retreating in disorganized packs."

Invasion!

In the following days even the Nazi press has to confirm this, adding, however, that: "Our troops have withdrawn as planned to positions chosen beforehand."

Dachau is humming with "rumors," news items, and speculation... This spreads even to the SS men. Only our gray-haired colonel Stirll continues to walk around dejected. His wife's death and the bombing of his house have depressed him terribly.

"The old guy wasn't much interested in the factory and the work," says capo Erich, "but now he doesn't care about anything."

"And Miss Lili?" asks Zdzich teasing.

"Not even about her. She also sits with reddened eyes."

"Wait. They'll get even redder."

Today is an exceptionally beautiful and sunny day. What day is it? Ah, yes, 13 June. Our building, which is almost entirely glass, shines in the sun as if enchanted. The siren sounds the signal for the midday dinner break. Our command doesn't go back to camp for the meal because they bring us dinner in trucks. After eating a bowl of turnip and munching on a piece of bread from a package, we lie down on the grassy lawn surrounding the workshops, when suddenly the afternoon silence is broken by the ear-splitting blast of an anti-aircraft siren. Then another, a third, and others repeat it.

"An airstrike at high noon! That hasn't ever happened before."

"Excellent. The dinner break will be extended."

Since the sun is beating down mercilessly, I lie in the shade right next to the foundation of the factory's glass wall and try to doze off. My colleagues, lying in an open area, are counting the squadrons.

"Fifth... ninth..."

"Each one has thirteen four-engine bombers," a colleague points out.

"Hey," another one says. "The old guy is sauntering around the hall. If one of those bombs hits our factory, that would do it for the colonel."

"It would be too bad. They'd give us some young fool, like the one in the W.B., and he'd just grind us down."

"Twelfth," someone counts, "thirteenth," but before the next number comes up, he quickly adds: "Oh! Look! Look! They're flying right at us!"

I open my eyes. It's true. A squadron of thirteen enormous bombers, veering from the course they've been following, is headed right for us!

"They're coming down!"

"Jesus!"

Shrill whistling pierces the air! Screams of terror escape from hundreds of onlookers, and suddenly: the ground moves under us ... pieces of glass rain down ... the walls crumble ... powerful explosions fill the air!

A strong blast throws me somewhere straight into a cloud of dust or smoke; something stings my back; it burns; hammers pound in my temples...

When I come to, clouds of dust and smoke still obscure my view. I don't know how long I've been unconscious. Maybe only seconds? Maybe minutes? I can hear the bombers somewhere in the distance. Someone next to me is moaning, someone's crying, wailing, someone's cursing...

"*Alles antreten!*"

I recognize the colonel's aging voice, screaming.

"Everyone fall in!"

Footsteps of SS men resound through the cloud of smoke and dust; their shouts ring out.

I try to get up, but my legs refuse to obey. I check them over. Nothing hurts. My bones are intact. It's probably just nerves, out of fear.

"You're bleeding, too," someone tells me as I take a place in the ranks being formed.

Fortunately, the wounds are only from splinters of glass. My back, however, is burning.

"What do I have there?"

"What do you have? Your whole shirt is torn. The skin is scraped off."

"Ah, I see. The explosion blew me across a rough cement walk."

After a midday breeze has dissipated the clouds of dust and smoke, we face an eerie scene. Only a steel skeleton remains of the huge building that was our factory. Nothing more. A heavy bomb fell right by the wall on the other side and blew out all the glass.

"Are there any casualties?"

"Several dozen! Many are seriously injured. Those who were on the other side of the factory were unlucky."

The Allies dropped thirteen heavy bombs on the SS barracks, factories, plants, and warehouses that surround the camp. Half of the main SS disbursement building was wiped out. Over forty prisoners were allegedly killed there as well. There are victims in other commands, too. In the ensuing confusion it's hard to count all the killed and injured. Afraid that many of us—taking advantage of the confusion—might escape, the SS men herd us all into the camp.

At the guardhouse gate they separate the healthy from the injured. Although I don't have any serious wounds, I'm covered with so much blood that the physician directs me to the camp clinic along with others who were injured. For the time being I feel fine. It's only at night that my temperature goes way up... That memorable bombing of 13 June by the thirteenth squadron, consisting of thirteen bombers, each one dropping a thousand-kilogram bomb, making a total, therefore, of thirteen bombs, gave me the gift of a three-month stay in the clinic. During this period, the camp ceases to exist for me.

"Edek," one day I express my anxiety to nurse Francuskiewicz. "Are they ready to sign me up for a handicap transport?"

"No," he reassures me, "don't be afraid. All of you who were directed to the camp clinic from bombed-out factories have special protection as prisoners needed for arms production. You don't face transport, only a return to the factory, which they're rushing to put back into working order now at all costs."

"Monsters! Monsters!" Dr. Fiałkowski, who visits me often in the sickroom, repeats through clenched teeth. "Do you know what these beasts have done?"

"What?"

"They shot to death everyone in the village of Oradour, in France! The entire village! Understand? And they commit this crime when everything is falling apart for them in France, when the Allies are starting to drive them back with full force..."

"But when their marvelous new V-1 weapon flies day and night against London!" adds Fr. Stef Zielonka, who stops by my bunk unnoticed.

"What marvelous weapon?"

"Doctor, didn't you read about it in the press? New rockets, reportedly with tremendous destructive power. And Hitler, of course, announced in his last address that he'll give the nation several such weapons, which will assure the Germans final victory."

"Damn it all!" and the doctor rushes off, banging the door behind him.

"I slipped out of the factory because they're predicting another airstrike," explains Stef as he sits down on the edge of my bunk. (Fr. Stefan is a secretary in the painters command and has a pass that allows him to walk freely through the guardhouse gate.) "Oh, can you hear them? The sirens are screaming already."

Our conversation falters. Since 13 June, when they bombed factories around the camp, we've become aware that the Allies, wanting to completely destroy all centers of German industry, cannot take into consideration the lives of even several hundred prisoners. After bombing centers around the camp, they're likely to try to destroy barracks—turned into shops for airforce precision instruments—within the camp itself. In any case, we have information that this is exactly the way they bombed several barracks at the Buchenwald camp. We're very mindful of the fact that in the course of such an operation many of us could die. That's why the conversation is going nowhere. Stef, uneasy, walks up to the window.

"They're flying over us."

Anti-aircraft artillery, batteries of which have been doubled since that memorable airstrike, fire like crazy! Blasts from the firing shake the barracks. Hundreds of shells burst in the blue July sky, generously raining down fragments on the roofs.

"All patients from third-floor bunks seek shelter immediately on the lowest level!" the order comes down from a senior nurse.

55. The Fruitful Summer of 1944

There's commotion, made worse by the firing of shells. Explosions are heard not very far away.

"They're bombing the airfield in Schleisheim, behind the plantations," one of the bolder observers explains from the window.

Suddenly, there's a horrible noise, as though thousands of birds with powerful wings were flying over us.

"Jesus of Nazareth," screams the old Czech Hlowa. "It's coming at us!"

We can't breathe, there's not a single thought in our heads! Our hearts stop beating for a moment...

"It passed," someone whispers in the midst of the deadly silence.

"What was that?"

None of us knows.

"Maybe an aircraft fell? Maybe bombs came down?"

"If it was bombs, we'd have heard the explosions."

After the airstrike we find out what caused that terrible noise. An Allied bomber that was struck, wanting to get rid of ballast, threw out a great many pyrotechnic candles, and it turned out, unluckily, to be just over the camp. Fortunately, the candles, being carried by momentum, sailed diagonally just over the barracks, showering a parcel of field on the plantation right behind the camp wall. Only a few fell inside the camp, killing one of the SS men. A unit of prisoners, sent to gather these pyrotechnic bombs, counted over 2,000 of them.

"If they had dropped just 200 meters closer, the entire horrible load would have hit the very center of the camp barracks."

Was this really a necessary drop? Or maybe a pilot error? Or maybe the Allies did it on purpose ... to deny the Nazis thousands of workers? ... We made a lot of different conjectures. One thing was certain: the bomber that was allegedly struck didn't go down, but flew away!

That evening, Romcio Budniak steals into the sickroom.

"I've brought you something from a package."

Judging by his appearance, I see that Rom is distressed about something.

"What's on your mind? Tell me!"

"Oh, nothing," he waves his hand. "I was shocked when I saw how they bombed that new anti-aircraft battery I was telling you about."

"They bombed it?"

"Horribly! ... Our shelter," recounts Romcio," is dug into the ground, and it's located about two hundred meters from that battery installation. The shelter exit, in fact, is directly across from it. When the airstrike began, knowing they wouldn't bomb us in our dugout, I stood by the exit watching. I was interested in how that group of girls would operate the guns. They fired into the sky like old soldiers at the front. Suddenly, I saw a bomber break away from one of the squadrons and with a skillful sideslip drop down right toward the battery. I could clearly see an entire cluster of bombs spill out of the fuselage and rush with an awful hiss toward the ground. I fell down in terror. Everything started to whirl beneath us! It felt as though I were lying on a cover and boiling water was bubbling underneath. When I got up, there was literally nothing at the site of the battery! The guns had disappeared, the wall that surrounded the site was gone, all the girls were gone. After the airstrike, when we ran over to that spot, a huge crater was already filling with water, and by evening a still pond was looking up at the gray sky."

We grow silent. Heavy breathing of the sick comes from the bunks.

"You know," Rom resumes quietly, "through one of those same girls we made contact with the pastor from the town of Dachau. She was delivering wine and hosts to us for holy Mass."

"Ah."

Silence. We sit immersed in thought.

"Did you know a huge Russian offensive has begun?"

"No, I didn't. It's begun, you say?"

"They're pushing back the Germans. Bolshevik troops have already entered Latvia and crossed the Polish border."

"Into Poland, too?"

"And they're pushing them like the devil in France! The same in Italy. You know how careful I am in assessing the situation, but now everything indicates the end is near."

The airstrikes continue. Air-raid warnings, which earlier lasted an hour or sometimes a little longer, drag on now for several hours. Allied aircraft are active in the area literally without interruption.

On 20 July Dachau is at high readiness. Uneasy SS men walk around all day in helmets, fully armed. Guard duties have been doubled at the towers. Covers have been removed from machine guns pointed at the camp. All this must mean something.

It's only the following day that the news explodes in the camp like a bomb: yesterday afternoon there was an attempt to assassinate Hitler with a bomb at his main headquarters! The attempt was not successful. Several people in his entourage were killed, but he came out unscathed himself, with only minor injuries. An hour later, he received Mussolini, who had just arrived for a visit.

Hitler himself gives Mussolini a tour of the place where the attempt was made.

"I was standing right here," he explains, pointing to a heavy table where he was looking over plans with his entourage. "The bomb went off right by my feet. Isn't it significant that nothing happened to me? Undoubtedly Fate has decreed that I continue on my way and bring my task to completion. What happened here today is a climactic turning point! ... I am more than ever convinced that the great cause I serve reached a critical point today, so as to proceed from this time to a fruitful conclusion."

Listening to these words, looking at the demolished interior, at the huge crater made in the floor by the bomb, at Hitler alive, Mussolini can't control the thoughts racing through his head:

"Our situation is indeed bad, one might almost say desperate," he whispers, fixing his eyes on Hitler in admiration, "but what has happened here today, in this place, gives me new strength. After this obvious miracle, it is inconceivable that our cause could end in failure."[2]

At five o'clock in the afternoon, comforted by the "miracle" he has seen with his own eyes, il Duce boards a train that takes him from distant Rastenburg, near Królewiec, across Polish lands to sunny Italy.

At one o'clock in the morning, the Führer delivers an address to the nation from a radio station in Królewiec! "...My first reason for speaking to you today is that I want you to hear my voice and know that I'm not injured, that, on the contrary, I feel fine; and the second — that you might know about a crime unparalleled in German history. A small clique of ambitious, irresponsible, senseless, and stupid officers concocted a plot to eliminate me, and with me..."

The Führer gives the distressed nation a new injection!

"This gang, this criminal element, must be crushed without mercy! I therefore have given an order..."[3]

When news came from Królewiec about the order for merciless extermination of the "criminal element," Goebbels, in Berlin, suppresses the revolt with deadly force. Going against the wall that very evening are the attacker, Count Col. Stauffenberg, and with him the generals: Olbricht, Hoeper, Beck, and a few of lower rank. That very night the Nazis make numerous arrests. It suffices to say that the number of shot or hanged leaders from the "criminal element" stigmatized by Hitler reached about 8,000! In order to bring joy to his beloved Führer, Goebbels gives an order to film the horrible scenes as sentences are carried out. Evenings, the Führer watches them with pleasure...[4]

Hideous scenes of choking mortal enemies — generals and high-ranking officers, members of the German aristocracy and leading figures of political and cultural life, who were hanged on piano strings (!?!) — provide the monster a sadistic satisfaction![5] The "director" of this dark film, Goebbels himself, when given a preview showing of it, covered his eyes with his hands, horrified at the agony of the condemned.[6]

And in Dachau at this time?

In Dachau the main effort is directed toward putting bombed factories and shops back in order. Thousands of prisoners are involved in this task. Other "duties" continue as before. Stations for inhumane experiments continue to operate; new groups from the "criminal element" make their way to the crematorium to be shot; Russian officers, those still alive for the time being, continue to starve; and every day the death platform hauls away piles of corpses. And only optimistic "rumors" go up like flares looking for a host of parachutes to drop at any minute from the Dachau sky in a rush to save "invaluable treasure," which for the Allies unquestionably must be the prisoners in Dachau, no less!

Hitler, Goebbels and the galaxy of bloodthirsty butchers know only too well that on 20 July the attacker, Count Col. Stauffenberg — before he got into the airplane that was to take him to the Führer's main headquarters with a bomb hidden between documents in his briefcase — had spent a lot of time that morning in church. In a Catholic church! Had he been to confession prior to the attack? ... And if so, did he receive absolution? ... These questions are to this day an issue of interest to historians. For the Nazis, the important thing was that the attackers emerged mainly from Catholic circles!

Minister Goebbels makes a new entry in his diary, declaring that after the victorious war it is imperative to "deal" with the reactionary Catholic Church! (If only he knew that after the war this hated Catholic Church would appoint a few dozen bishops precisely from among former prisoners in Dachau, whose lives at that moment Goebbels held in his hands!)

"We wanted to do something great," are the last words of General Henning von Tresckow, who was the heart and soul of the conspiracy against the tyrant among officers on the Eastern Front. "Hitler is not only the archenemy of Germany, he is the archenemy of the whole world. In a few hours I will stand before God and will have to give an account of my deeds, my failures and imperfections. I trust I will be able, with complete serenity, to uphold before Him all that I have done in the fight against Hitler."[7]

56

The Nun Barbara

"Here's your doctor's note, signed by the chief of the camp clinic himself, stating that upon leaving you must have lighter work for many weeks and, if possible, in fresh air."

"And if the colonel in the repair workshops demands..."

"Don't worry about what he can do. This note will protect you for the next few weeks, and in the meantime there might be some changes that could make the old guy forget about you. Well, so long, old friend! And drop by the clinic sometimes for a chat."

After Dr. Fiałkowski bids me goodbye, I leave the clinic after three months with a doctor's note in hand and a bundle under my arm, returning to my regular block. I'm quite happy about that doctor's note. It keeps me from going to the shops where I worked up to the day of the bombing. I'm not eager to return there, especially since Zdzich has gone off to the plantation in the meantime.

The plantation, separation from the camp, the prospect of quietly surviving airstrikes—that's my dream at this time. Something from the moment of that bombing remains in my psyche. Shock—as Dr. Fiałkowski describes it. Possibly. Since that day the sound of an air-raid alarm causes unpleasant nervous feelings inside me, even manifesting themselves in uncontrollable shaking throughout my entire body along with stomach contractions. Let's just tell it as it is: I now have a deadly fear of airplanes and bombs!

In the meantime, instead of the desired plantation, I land the next day at the clothing storehouse! That's because when I present myself, bundle under my arm, to the secretary of our block, he just happens to have a requirement for a worker in the storehouse.

"The work there isn't hard, and it's under a roof; you can loaf around as much as you like," he consoles me.

Indeed, the job isn't hard and is even rather pleasant. It consists of sorting clothes, giving them out, counting, making lists of new things needed, and sending used clothing to the tailor shop, laundry, or disinfection unit. Working next to me in the underwear storeroom is Fr. Mirek Ziarniak; a bit farther away is Fr. Czesio Koczorowski; and the Protestant ministers Alfred Hauptman and Henio Wegner work where "personal effects" are stored. In a word, more and more often clergymen are given positions that require unfailing trustworthiness.

After several days, I begin to like this work, especially because you can do a great deal of good for the camp unfortunates who come in for a change of clothing. The clothing exchange takes place only in the evening when the commands return from their jobs. All the storeroom personnel then stand at a counter, and our fellow prisoners come up in rows, one after the other, presenting their needs. Good Lord, what abject poverty! We "well-supplied" senior prisoners who have "our connections" have forgotten what it means to be a "Neuzugang" in the camp, namely a new arrival, chased like a dog, pushed, driven away naked and cold.

In Dachau even today there is no shortage of that element. Not a day goes by without new prisoners being brought in, either straight from the outside or in transports from other camps. How much extreme poverty there is among these haggard-faced, mistreated people; how much fear in their every look and every move! Their hands tremble when they show their torn pants or tattered shirt because, of course, you never know when someone may decide to call it sabotage, and you can never foresee what may cause someone to start beatings or verbal abuse...

What a joy it is to be able to do some good for these poor people!

And right there in the clothing storeroom you have constant opportunity for this. A dear wretch, shaking, begs for "any kind" of shirt, but now ... not only does he get a warm hooded cloak, but a sweater tucked into it and warm socks inside a sleeve and a friendly wink with a smile and — in addition — the question: "You're not changing those pants?"

A mouth opens in surprise: "They're ... they're still fine," he stutters in amazement.

"Take them off quickly; here are some warm ones. Put them on and run! But keep quiet, and don't tell anyone!"

Lord! My heart jumps with joy when I see in the recipient's eyes something you can't buy for money and can't obtain even with riches...

There's plenty to give away because the storeroom has been stacked to the ceiling with thousands of the most expensive items once worn by unfortunate Jews who were gassed. If these were normal striped uniforms, we'd have to keep detailed "books," but since this is a matter of civilian clothing, for which the SS men don't have any kind of numerical accounting, we can give and give, just so the capo doesn't see — but even he has a good heart.

"Poor devils. Go on giving, provided it doesn't result in shortages," he tells us when he's in a good mood. Besides, he usually sits in his office and seldom drops into the storeroom.

After a few days, others working in the storeroom notice that the line at my counter is always the longest.

"Why are they so drawn to you?"

There are several of us Poles in the storeroom. Slowly I "enlighten" them ... I notice with joy that soon the dear guys are competing with each other in "giving"! Goodness is contagious.

The work in giving out supplies sometimes continues late into the evening. On the other hand, we have a lot of free time during the day. I'm happy that, after months in the clinic, where I could devote whole days to reading, here again I have time to read. We're more busy only in the morning when we prepare clothing for outside commands, which send somebody around to pick it up.

One day the capo gives me an order that dumbfounds me. He orders a search for several dozen pairs of women's stockings, sweaters, and other items of women's apparel.

"Who's this for?" I ask, taken by surprise and amazed.

"Tomorrow women prisoners are coming from an Aussenkommando. So put in a bit more than what's on the list."

At least half of the clothing shipments to Dachau (from Auschwitz) included women's clothes. Much of that had disappeared, smuggled by prisoners doing the sorting, but despite that, the storeroom shelves were stacked with all types of women's apparel. There's plenty to choose from. Moreover, since the capo is encouraging me to pile it on, I really *pile it on*, stuffing the bags with as much as possible and with whatever is the best and warmest, because autumn is just around the corner, and who knows whether there will be another opportunity before winter.

On the following day, a pretty young SS woman comes into the storeroom with three women prisoners.

"Take the order," she turns to them, "and wait until I return."

"She ran off to the clinic," explains the capo, who has known her for years. "She's in love with Dr. Binderfeld. She won't be back soon. No need to hurry."

"Are any of you Polish?" I ask in a whisper after the door shuts behind the capo.

"Are you Polish, sir?" I hear a question instead of an answer. Joy flashes in the woman prisoner's eyes. "I'm Polish, that one is Hungarian, and the little one is a Jewess from France," she explains. The conversation begins.

"It seems there are many Polish priests in the camp?" she asks timidly at one point.

"Yes, there are," I answer.

"Are there any from Poznań?"

"Of course, right from Poznań and from surrounding areas. Do you know someone from there?"

"Oh, many!" she answers, her haggard face flushing. "Sir, are you Catholic?" she suddenly asks, afraid.

"Catholic," I affirm, stuffing sweaters into the bag.

"So you won't betray me. Please greet those priests on behalf of Sister Barbara from the hospital..."

"Sister Barbara?" I open my mouth wide. "Then ... then perhaps you're a nun?"

"Quiet," she whispers terrified. "Someone could overhear!" She notices my glance toward the two women prisoners, who are helping in the packing. She has understood. "No, I'm not afraid of them. They know who I am."

As long as I live I won't forget the astonishment that appeared on her emaciated face when I told her that I'm a priest, that I studied in Poznań, that as a seminarian I was at St. Elizabeth's Hospital, that Sister Albana was my friend from school, that...

Big tears stream down the prisoner-nun's face...

"Heinrich!" the capo's voice breaks in so suddenly that I turn in fright. "Here! Give them this, too." He hands me several pieces of bread.

Several minutes later there's a commotion in our storeroom. We bring whatever we have in the way of food. The capo himself pours coffee into some cups. "Watch carefully there," he admonishes a fellow posted by the window, "so the shrew doesn't break in on us unexpectedly!" (He means the SS woman.)

Whereas here in the men's camp conditions have changed greatly for the better, largely because rabid young SS men have been called up to the front, in the women's camp, apparently, not only is nothing better, it's very much the opposite. The young SS women guards on duty are becoming more and more hateful. Especially after the attempt on the Führer...

"She's coming!" a warning from the window interrupts our conversation. In no time the cups disappear.

"Among the clothes, in this bag, Sister, you'll find some food."

"God bless ... God bless," the nun's trembling lips whisper. "God willing, we'll soon return to..."

"*Achtung!*"

We stand at attention before the SS woman.

"Ready?"

"Yes, ma'm!"

...Several minutes later all the storeroom personnel are standing at the barred windows...

Carrying the bags with clothing, bent under their weight, three prisoners walk toward the guardhouse. Behind them is the slim, shapely SS woman, wearing elegant boots.

If only she knew that Barbara is a Bride of Jesus!...

There are over seventy smaller affiliates that belong to Dachau. During the time I worked in the storeroom, I had a chance to become acquainted with many people who were sent for clothing. Despite inquiries, however, I never heard anything more about prisoner Barbara, the Sister from Poznań, Order of St. Elizabeth.

"Herr Pfarrer!"

The appearance of old Brenner is a surprise for me.

"Morgen, Brenner. I'm happy to see you, sir. How's your health? So much time has passed since our last meeting."

Unfortunately, the foreboding I felt when I saw him entering the storeroom was justified.

"Ja, ja, Herr Pfarrer. Col. Stirll is showering us with questions about you, Father, about when you'll return to the workshops. It's hard for us to equivocate. You'll have to..."

"Herr Brenner," I interrupt, worried but full of hope, "I have a note from the chief doctor at the clinic that..."

"So, so," chats the kindhearted Brenner, reading. "So, so. 'Leichte Arbeit im Freiem,' Therefore, Father, you should disappear, slip away as fast as possible to the plantation."

Two days later I'm marching in the "plantage" units. I miss the storeroom a little; I miss the work done there and the colleagues I've come to know, but ... maybe now the war really won't last long?

Suddenly I catch myself in that crazy thought and laugh inwardly. If only one of the optimists could hear it, wouldn't he be elated!

"*Ein Lied!*" the head capo shouts out a command.

"*Gruene Heide!*"

Singing, the column heads toward the plantation, which is already turning drab with autumn colors. Gossamer threads spin through the blue sky...

I don't know why, but at this moment the thought of Sister Barbara comes to mind.

Our fate is not to be envied, but the fate of unfortunate imprisoned women is a hundred times worse. How many spiritual torments must a nun suffer, torn from the seclusion of a convent and thrust into an environment of hatred and the vilest instincts it unleashes — the environment of a concentration camp...

57

A Diary

"Write a diary, write, make notes, examine yourself," an unforgettable professor, Wincenty Birkenmajer, would encourage me during my high-school years. "If you want to find yourself, you need to look at yourself on the pages of a diary."

Professor Birkenmajer was killed, but he "did not die entirely." His words have remained, and among others, the words quoted above.

Fr. Sylwester Konieczny, the leader in our hall (from the time we've had our own staff in the clerical barracks, colleagues are leaders in both blocks and in individual halls), had thrown out a thick notebook, which was left by the bully Emil Joas. I picked it up and behold ... I begin a diary. I'll be keeping it hidden in the carpenter's shop at the plantation, where it's less likely to be found, and maybe I'll manage to conceal it until the days of freedom...

Today is 2 September 1944. Saturday. The carpentry shop capo, a decent Silesian named Franciszek Wilhelm, has ordered the shop to be straightened up. I have a small niche—again for wood carving—in the very corner of the carpentry shop between two windows and screened with two pieces of plywood, so I don't need much time to clean it, and since it's still a while until roll call, I sit down and write.

The head capo of the plantation command, an Austrian officer and Brenner's friend, who had been informed by Brenner about my previous job, assigned me—after several days of work in the greenhouses—to the carpenter's shop, with the following order: "You'll carve for the director of the plantation, officer Vogt."

So again I've been carving for several days. I'm even happier to do this because this SS officer Vogt is reportedly an extremely kind and decent man. We hear constantly that when the Allies arrive, all the prisoners who work under his supervision at the plantation will submit a petition for leniency toward him.[1]

The camp is full of the most preposterous "rumors," according to which the war is supposed to end tomorrow. In the meantime, more prisoner transports arrive from the outside as well as from other camps, and the Nazi press boasts about new gains.

I've noticed a strange memory loss. I often catch myself, for example, in the following: while talking to one of my friends whom I've known for years, I can't remember his first name. Even worse, it's the same with the names of my closest relatives. This phenomenon is apparently rather common and is caused by a lack of vitamins and being undernourished. Will this ever get better?

5 September 1944

I still can't forget yesterday's execution of twenty Russian officers. They shot them by the crematorium. They walked in a tight formation like a flock of sheep! And yet barely twelve SS men were escorting them... If they had jumped them, they might have disarmed them in a second. Horrible treatment of war prisoners! These Nazis don't respect any law, any international conventions. News keeps coming about the shooting of American and British pilots.

I'm interested in the phenomenon that when a condemned person is going to his death, he's overcome by some kind of mental and physical inertia. Why does a man who's drowning or going through some kind of disaster desperately fight for his life to the very last moment, driven by a horrible animal fear and a desire to save himself, but the condemned man goes ... like a meek sheep. A psychologist could make an interesting study of this.

7 September, Thursday

The German press admits there was an uprising in Warsaw, but they present it in such a biased way that...

The several thousand Poles in the camp are exuberant. Of course, rumormongers have obtained new grist for their mill.

Feast of the birth of the Mother of God, 8 September

Today we survived a long airstrike. This time the squadrons didn't head for Munich, but scattered to bomb surrounding regions. They dropped a number of bombs at the Schleisheim airfield, just beyond the woods. The plantation is the best "insurance" today against bombs. Nevertheless, we have an order to leave the buildings and seek shelter in dugouts, which individual work units have built for themselves in various parts of the extensive plantation.

Our carpenters' dugout is located at the very end of "Freiland II."

"Why so far away?" I ask capo Franek.

"So we can take a stroll," he answers with a smile. We really do have a good stroll since the path to the dugout takes about fifteen minutes, and the return is just as long.

Knowing that they're not going to bomb these far-reaching fields, I stood outside because there was water up to our ankles in the dugout, and it was terribly cold, but the fallout from shell fragments is so extensive that there's a real need to have some kind of shelter overhead.

16 September

The news from the front is extremely favorable for us. The Allies have launched a second invasion, this time in the south of France. Our Second Corps is pushing ahead in Italy. The Russians have pushed the Germans completely out of their country. Unfortunate Polish land! Once again the steamroller of war rumbles across it. What will remain?

The death rate in the camp is rising again. There are fewer and fewer packages from Poland. If the front line continues to move at the current rate, in a few weeks the packages will stop arriving completely, and a wave of hunger will follow. Romek Budniak — that lovable far-sighted pessimist — advises us to organize a small pantry, so as to have something in reserve for the hard days.

3 October 1944

I haven't been to work for several days. I became sick again. At first I thought it was probably typhus because I had such a high temperature, and my fear had some basis. Radek

Fibak was showering me with all kinds of pills that he got at the clinic. Fr. Konieczny, the hall leader, sneaked me into a third-level bunk as a sick person. Formerly, that was altogether out of the question, but today one can permit oneself such things.

From the plantation's drying room capo Franek brought some kind of herbs that were supposedly recommended by Dr. Skowroński. The capo brewed them on the small hot plate used to heat carpenter's glue. I'm sipping the brew. It's acceptable to cook and brew tea in the carpenter's shop and in all other plantation units. Even a year ago, if someone got caught doing this, it could cost him his life. Today one can do a lot.

And the airstrikes continue. We have them every day. We freeze in the dugouts several hours each day. And with this going on, what can our work be like? But that's how it is in all the commands. Only at the W.B.—as our men report—hot-headed director Schultz, the same man who ordered me and Dubiel to go on the transport to Auschwitz, won't allow any work breaks.

"If they bomb the plants," he says, "to hell with you, too! I don't care about it!"

Today is St. Thérèse's day... How would she have practised her "little way of childhood" in Dachau?

8 October 1944

Yesterday was Rosary Sunday. They made us sort a whole lot of apparel that was dumped again in huge piles in front of the storeroom on the assembly square. A fine rain was drizzling. I feel like crying when I see these piles of "evidence" of Nazi crimes. Mixed in with the clothing of men and women, there's no shortage of children's apparel; there are little boys' outfits and little girls' dresses. Company labels indicate that the garments come from all over Europe, namely, from France, Belgium, Holland, Denmark, Hungary, Czechoslovakia, and even Greece. The clothing, piled in stacks and treated this way for months, is already partly damaged, moldy, and decayed. We take the better items to the storeroom; the rest goes to be burned. As we sort, we pray the Rosary. The day after tomorrow is the feast of the Motherhood of the Most Blessed Virgin Mary. What will that feast day bring us?

Plantation in Dachau on All Saints' Day 1944

Today is my 32nd birthday, and tomorrow is the fifth anniversary of my arrest. Thirty-two years of life, including six years in the priesthood, and of these barely one year of work in the Lord's vineyard; the rest spent in a concentration camp. Would I still be able to celebrate holy Mass without making mistakes? I doubt it. So many years away from the altar.

I have written practically nothing for three weeks because we were afraid of a possible inspection on the plantation. There was talk in the camp that Vogt is spoiling the prisoners too much, that he's giving us too much freedom. On several evenings in a row they searched us at the camp gate, finding many kinds of things, especially food produce from the plantation, and supposedly the entire command was under threat of a surprise visit, but somehow this passed, and up to now no one has come. So I've taken my diary out of its hiding place, and I write.

The plantation on 2 November, All Souls' Day

Our arrest was five years ago. It's been five years from that day. They took us in a large group, but how many of us are still alive? The Rev. Pastor Handke, the Rev. Professor Wróblewski, Romek Budniak, and I. What a small handful of survivors! Each year in our churches there were memorial services for our dead. In how few churches will mournful hymns be heard this year! And yet there is so much deep mourning in millions of hearts...

There is hopeful news coming from the front. Several days ago the Allies occupied their first German city, Aachen. For the first time during this war the Germans have to defend their own land now that Allied troops are crossing their borders. There is even happier news from the Eastern Front. I've expressed myself poorly by writing "happy." Welcome, of course, but at the same time tragic, since once again Polish land is bleeding. The Warsaw uprising has collapsed! The capital is in ruins! Transports of Warsaw underground fighters are coming to Dachau. I found among them a friend from my high-school days, Leoś Piotrowski. A skeleton. Those transport prisoners are only made to change into prison uniforms and are then moved elsewhere. They say they're going west to build fortified trenches that are supposed to stop (!?!) the advancing American and British forces! How many of them will die there?

The plantation in Dachau on 13 November 1944

The weather is terrible. Well, typical of Dachau. Airstrikes every day. Sometimes they last several hours. On the other hand, we are somewhat concerned that the Germans are testing a new type of aircraft, the so-called jet. The test flights are often conducted right over the plantations. What tremendous speed they have! This is probably one of the new "wonderful" weapons that Hitler has been talking about for a long time now, predicting that they'll bring final victory for the Germans. The German press is full of news about the destructive impact of German V-1 rockets, which have been dropped on London and, in general, on England.

The death rate in the camp is going up again. Last month about five hundred prisoners died. This month the number of dead will certainly be even greater. Packages are arriving less frequently. Hunger is getting worse. Food rations are shrinking with each week. Evacuation transports are coming in from the west with prisoners who are in a state of complete debilitation. The mortality rate among them is especially high.

With each day, the news from Poland is worse. Hitler has ordered the total destruction of Warsaw! "Warschau noch waehrend des Krieges dem Erdboden gleich zu machen!"[2]

There is much discussion about the horrible treatment of war prisoners. It seems Hitler has issued an order to have them all murdered without exception.[3]

The Warsaw underground fighters have brought news that Fr. Salamucha, D.D., professor at the Jagiellonian University, was killed in the uprising. We had met him in the Sachsenhausen camp; he came with us to Dachau, but was released in 1941, and now he has shared the fate of thousands who fell on the streets of Warsaw.

20 November 1944 — Monday

Yesterday we again sorted stacks of clothes, from a new transport that was dumped on the assembly square in front of the storeroom. The wet, moldy, partially rotten clothing gives off such a terrible stench that it takes your breath away. Lying in piles on the square and getting wet (and there's no shortage of rain in November), it deteriorates completely. We sort it, every day a special command sorts it, but there are such large stacks that we can't keep up. Most of these things will go to waste.

It's been pouring since morning. Heavy clouds hang low over the ground, but despite that, we had an airstrike. We freeze in the dugouts, where there's more and more water, which oozes from the bottom and comes in with the rain.

The mood in our block is unpleasant. Perhaps the terrible weather has contributed to this? People are moving at a snail's pace. We begin to feel hunger. There are fewer and fewer packages. There is little news from the front. Somehow the action has all but stopped in the west. We had expected that by Christmas they would push deep across the Rhine, but it looks like the Allied troops intend to winter over in warmer France. Is it possible the Germans were still so strong that the Allies, who entered the war only recently and did so, moreover, with a large arms potential still intact, can't manage to deal with them? Hitler has called up the last reserves of a national mobilization. In the neighboring SS barracks we see kids dressed in SS uniforms.

28 November

Inclement weather goes on and on. Snow fell a few times, but then it melted. There's mud everywhere. Returning to camp, we can barely drag our heavy clogs covered with black gook. Small groups of young people from Poland are being brought to the camp. They tell us wild things about mass roundups for slave labor. Sometimes all passersby are rounded up on a street that they close off with a heavy police cordon. Sometimes on Sunday they take all the men and young boys from the churches. These are decent fellows, those who get here to Dachau, and yet they're somehow different. One can see that in the past five years a generation has grown up that we don't understand very well! It's no wonder. Over there, in real life, under new conditions, young personalities are being formed differently from those of us who are locked inside the "jars" of concentration camps, having no contact with the outside world and living solely with the memory of what we left five years ago. Simply put, it appears that if we were released now to return to life, it would be hard for us to get our bearings and adapt to new conditions. Is it possible we're losing spiritual contact with our people who live outside the barbed wires?

The plantation in Dachau on 2 December, Saturday, 1944

Yesterday a transport arrived with prisoners from Mauthausen, and — what a surprise! Returning in it were Fr. Biały and the seminarian Jurek Musiał, who had been moved to that camp in May as punishment. They say terrible things about conditions over there. Practically nothing has changed there! The same discipline as in past years. The same hard work. Both came back terribly emaciated, tired, and weak. It's too bad they're arriving at a time when it's already hard to get packages, but still something will be found for both half-starved men. They also brought Fr. Edward Lubowiecki, Secretary General of Catholic Action in Kraków . There's new information in our barracks. Fr. Biały and Jurek Musiał, however, are very discreet today when they relate it.

Immaculate Conception of the Blessed Virgin Mary, 8 December 1944

Today is Friday, but for us it's the great feastday of the Immaculate Lady. We spent many hours in dugouts due to a lengthy airstrike. Allied aircraft now fly less often over Munich, where everything is probably already in ruins; instead, they fly around the region, bombing the more important buildings. The frozen ground carries vibrations and shocks caused by the explosions. One small, maneuverable aircraft was repeatedly firing at the plantation. We found a few shells. They're made of steel and half the size of a man's thumb. Brrr ... to be hit by one of them...

Only six of us work in the plantation carpenter's shop, and all are Poles, practicing Catholics; we pray the Rosary aloud together during work. How deep the faith of those dear carpenters! But — perhaps it's because these are already somewhat older men. The spirit of our young men, brought to camp during their childhood and growing up here for five years separated from normal conditions, is not as good. It's not their fault. And yet in every one of these young souls one can find a spark of goodness. Fanned, it slowly begins to smoulder, to catch fire, and to consume the young heart. One thing is certain, that in postwar years traditional methods of our priestly work will need to be thoroughly reassessed and modernized.

18 December 1944

Today I met Fr. Andrzej Czeluśniak, of the La Salette Order. They brought him here a few days ago from Mauthausen. He's such a quiet, calm, and deep soul. He stayed a long time in Hungary, where he organized Polish education; he was picked up there at a time when the Nazis' situation had already started to go bad. He's rather introverted, somehow distrustful. One has to pull words out of him. I tried to win him over because I wanted to find out as much as possible about the appearances of the Weeping Mother on the hill in La Salette in 1846. After all, they were loaded with predictions that were fulfilled in later years. Apparently the Mother of God had said some harsh words against priests of those days. Another prisoner, Fr. Joseph Kentenich, a saintly German priest and a great thinker, had discussed this subject when we visited him recently. Zdzich, also interested in the appearances in La Salette, spends a lot of time with Fr. Czesluśniak. I believe Zdzich will gain his trust. Their personalities are somewhat alike. That will bring them closer.

They also brought a group of priests from Sachsenhausen and Gusen. Among them are Fr. Maryś Samoliński and Fr. Brunon Halla. Just recently they brought Fr. Konrad Scheffler from the Chełmno Diocese. Because he spent a long time during 1943 at Stutthof, that is, at the camp we 200 helped to build and organize in 1939 and the beginning of 1940, we're interested in knowing what kind of conditions they have there now. From what he tells us, Stutthof developed from a primitive state into one of the most modern camps, comparable in its operating systems to Dachau.

It's a curious psychological phenomenon. We experienced so many days of torment there, and yet something remains that draws you to that old dump, and you'd like so much to look around there again. Could these possibly be signs of a psychological abnormality?

A few days ago kindly Fr. Józio Kałuża passed away, a longtime prisoner who had survived with us so many interminable years. He was 38 years old at the time of his death. Lately I haven't made any notes regarding the deaths of my colleagues; you simply lose track of their number. I was much closer to Józek.

Overall, 997 or almost a thousand of my fellow-prisoners died this past month, that is, in November! That indicates we're again heading toward days of hardship. Growing hunger, worsening health conditions, and the terrible weather, too, are taking their toll. Winter in Dachau has always decimated prisoners. It's doing so now as well.

The plantation, 29 December 1944

Prior to the holidays they brought in Fr. Paweł Pękacki from Kcynia, and from Auschwitz Fr. Marcel Pasiecznik and Fr. Stefan Hanas, a pastor from Belgium. In general, the prisoners bring information that we already know, namely, that the Nazis' situation is extremely difficult, that everything is falling apart, that their final defeat must come by spring of next year.

And for us? ... It may be that I'm a pessimist (although I've never been one) and that I see the days ahead of us as too grim, but I can't get rid of the thought that if "they" begin to die, they'll do everything in their power to take as many victims with them as possible!

As the holidays themselves passed, we felt various emotions. On the whole, however, one can detect a great psychological weariness, and that is so — even among the optimists. All this has lasted just too long.

Discouraging news comes from the German press, which screams about successes of an offensive initiated by the Germans in the Ardennes. Again they're driving back the Allies, and the latter are like helpless novices! It's hard for us to understand how the Germans, exhausted after so many years of war and having not even a tenth of the weapons with which they attacked Poland in 1939, would still have strength to defeat Allied troops in such a way... Maybe Goebbels is altogether justified when he writes that if the Allies had come into contact with the German military five years ago, they would have been given a real thrashing. Lately there have been quiet rumors — and this appears to be information from SS men — that the German offensive has just been stopped, but how much truth is there in this?

The airstrikes continue. We spend several hours each day in the dugouts. We've carried wood shavings from the carpentry shop into our dugout; we've furnished it with boards for a floor and with bags to sit on. We're not as cold, therefore, but we're still cold. After each airstrike, we return to the workshop frozen to the bone, and work is out of the question. My hands are so stiff that I can't hold a chisel.

Sunday is New Year's Eve. The last day of the year. What will the new year, 1945, bring? ... Freedom? ... Or perhaps...? The crematorium keeps puffing out smoke.

58

At the Dawn of 1945

2 January 1945

Henio Dubiel tore himself away for a short time from the airforce experimental station and ran in for a visit. He doesn't look too bad, although psychologically he's depressed. He has serious misgivings about what will happen to workers at that station. Although he works as a carpenter and doesn't have any contact with experiments conducted there, he still worries constantly that, as inconvenient witnesses, they could all be liquidated one day. It was he who brought the information from the hospital secretary that 1,915 prisoners had died in the camp in December! The death rate not only isn't going down; on the contrary, it goes up every day! The camp clinic estimates that if this continues, January will bring about a thousand more deaths. There are quiet rumors that this is a new wave of typhus, that hospital doctors and the commandant's office are well aware of the problem, but ... since Berlin is pushing for production, they don't have the courage to defy it and shut the camp for weeks, or maybe even months, for another quarantine. Besides, maybe they see in this a "providential" hand in bringing about our slow and inconspicuous liquidation?

13 January 1945

There was another heavy snowfall. Because tomorrow is Sunday, they will surely make the entire camp clear it. While these are not the days of old, forcing us to clear this white camp plague is always combined with harassments. News comes from Poland that a powerful Russian offensive is underway, and the Germans are fleeing in panic. Today Jesuit Fr. Podoleński, a former prisoner from Auschwitz and other camps, has died, and in the camp clinic the Rev. Pastor Józef Palmowski from Parkowo lies dying. Lord! How that dear man suffered through each airstrike! In any case — he's not the only one. After all, we're all more or less emotionally exhausted from constantly running to shelters. I'm especially affected during those times. When an airstrike occurs while we're at work on the plantation, I don't feel too bad, but if it catches us in the confinement of crowded barracks, I simply feel as though I'm suffocating! I'm terrified by the horrible lack of space, the rain of fragments falling on the roofs... And the Allies are bombing closer and closer to the camp. Every day we expect them to drop bombs on barracks that have been converted to workshops within the camp itself. And then...

19 January, my namesday

I feel touched to be remembered by our good carpenters! I found my workbench decorated with a few fir branches, some little bits of paper, and (what's important) a loaf of rationed bread as a present.

"Today you're not doing anything," decides capo Franek, "and the rest of you, work with your eyes" (which in camp jargon means don't do anything, but be careful they don't catch you!).

Unfortunately, we were surprised by another lengthy airstrike. Today Romek Budniak paid a visit to our dugout.

"I've brought you a bowl of cooked beans."

Oh, that Romek!

As we eat the cold beans, which we all take by the handful since this is a namesday party, we talk and talk unceasingly while anti-aircraft artillery shells burst over us, and a hail of fragments falls on the dugout turf. Suddenly, there's a shrill whizzing sound! We press close to the ground in fear. We wait. Something falls, slamming into the frozen field nearby.

A bomb?

After a while, someone who's more daring sticks out his head.

"You know what fell? It's probably the rear disk of a shell." He runs outside and after a while comes back with a steel disk weighing several pounds.

"That's right," confirms capo Franek. "That's the back of a shell that didn't break up when it exploded."

The airstrike drags on. The bombing sometimes moves closer, sometimes farther away. Romek and I reminisce... We count those who have passed and the few from our group who remain; we recall our student days at the Poznań seminary; we recall our days as vicars in Inowrocław. Time passes, but the sirens don't cancel the alarm...

26 January 1945

Joy! After many weeks, a letter from my mother... In a few days it will be the first anniversary of my father's death... Why do I have such a stupid, impressionable and sensitive heart? ... So much suffering...

Yesterday Fr. Antoś Świadek from Bydgoszcz died, barely three years older than I am. He was such a terrific person! Such a wonderful priestly soul! How hard it must be to die on the eve of approaching freedom! The Russians are pushing the Germans out of East Prussia. Fleeing must be terrible when the winter is so harsh! Stutthof will soon fall into their hands. Undoubtedly, the Nazis will be evacuating prisoners. But maybe they'll shoot them all in the nearby woods where there are already thousands of graves...

Dachau, 6 February 1945

As Zdzich and I return from Block 10, where we had gone to visit colleagues still working at the W.B., we meet Fr. Styp-Rekowski in the dark street. We exchange greetings.

"Did you know my brother-in-law Knosala has died?"

"Ryszard has died?" The news surprises us.

"Yes. Today. I took steps to get his remains. It was futile. The body had just been transported to the crematorium. I only succeeded in getting this: they'll cremate his remains separately and hide an urn with the ashes. I'll take them someday to the family. May he rest in the family cemetery."

It's so hard to find words in such situations... Sometimes a conventional expression of sympathy will simply stir up disgust. We walk together to our barracks in silence, and it's only in our heads that thoughts are drumming... Ryszard is dead! It was he, if anyone, who had a chance to survive. Rather, we should have feared that SS men might want to get rid of him as a witness who knew too much. For many long years he was an official translator at the commandant's office and, as such, was privy to many matters that he didn't disclose for personal safety reasons, but promised to reveal sometime in the future. Thus, one of the invaluable witnesses to the Polish tragedy in Dachau has passed away. Only one other translator remains here now, Jan Domagała. If only he can manage to survive! He was a good soul, our Ryszard of blessed memory... God had other intentions for him. His death touched me even more since we used to make plans for working together if a time came when we could publish our experiences in the camps. Oh, well, it wasn't to be as we had planned.

Dachau, the plantation on 9 February 1945

In January almost three thousand prisoners died in the camp![1] Therefore, about a hundred die each day. A military company! The camp clinic predicts that unless special safety measures are taken, the number will double during this month. No one makes a secret of it anymore, and there is official talk — about another epidemic of typhus.

Since transports continuously arrive at the camp with prisoners being evacuated from the west, which is under threat from an Allied advance, the terrible overcrowding becomes even worse. They've liquidated clerical Barracks 30, moving all its residents to our barracks. Currently there are about four hundred of us living in one room. The crush is just incredible! What's worse, lice are again multiplying in a frightening way, and they, of course, are carriers of typhus germs.

The new crematorium cannot keep up with the burning of corpses, so they've set up a cemetery at the edge of the woods. Brother Franciszek Przewłoka, a quiet Albertine from Kraków, became its capo. Every day piles of those they were unable to burn are moved out there.

And hunger in the camp is getting worse! Those of us on the plantation, where it's easier to get some dried vegetables, fruits, beans, or peas from the warehouses, find extra food when we can, but the poor guys working in other commands or the unfortunate people brought here in evacuation transports are dying like flies in autumn!

14 February — Ash Wednesday

A real *Ash Wednesday*: in front of the crematorium there are piles of bones! Due to time constraints and a need for very frugal use of fuel, bodies are not totally burned to ashes, but piles of incompletely burned bones are thrown on top of ash piles.

Brother Przewłoka complains that if this continues, he and his command won't be able to keep up with burying the dead near the woods. Corpses lie in the streets, between the barracks, everywhere, since the gravediggers command cannot keep pace moving them out.

We're fighting lice! But what kind of battle is this when there are no measures we can take against them? Formerly, there were changes of underwear, disinfection was operating, they took us to baths, but now, with the camp overcrowded and the baths constantly swamped by new arrivals, all these measures are no longer available. The scourge of lice reigns supreme, and with it the epidemic is spreading dangerously.

16 February 1945

Today an announcement was made in the camp that they're looking for volunteers to be staff personnel in the isolation barracks, where typhus is rampant. Formerly, when a position as barracks or hall leader was a paying "occupation," the camp communists filled all those posts. Today, when there's an epidemic in the isolation barracks, there are no longer any volunteers among them. On the other hand, more than forty Polish priests volunteered.

All the priests are young, enthusiastic, self-sacrificing. This is not just a sentimental legend. This is a fact, which cannot be denied by any of those writing maliciously about Polish priests in Dachau.

Going into the typhus barracks as staff, they realize that they're walking into great danger and that many of them will not come out of isolation. After making their confessions and saying goodbye, they leave...

19 February, Monday

There are few changes in the camp. Evacuation transports continue to arrive, every day over a hundred dead are moved out, and yet the number of those brought into the camp is higher than the number of those who "leave." We're more and more crowded. The barracks, which were intended for two hundred residents, now hold about two thousand. It's somewhat less crowded inside blocks of the camp's prominent prisoners. They are able somehow to defend themselves. It's worse inside our clerical barracks, and it's utter desperation inside the barracks for isolated wretches infected with typhus!

Minor air raids continue. We have them day after day, and sometimes they come twice a day with a third one at night. The SS men, even those old, mustachioed ones, walk around looking somewhat sullen... They have a strange expression on their faces. After all, which one of them isn't concerned about his family and which one doesn't worry about what will happen when ... when the Allies catch him unawares in an SS uniform?

24 February, Saturday

Fr. Stef Frelichowski of the Chełmno Diocese died yesterday. He was young, a year younger than I. A lovable daredevil! He'd been with us since Stutthof; he went through Sachsenhausen, through hard years in Dachau, and then he catches typhus while hearing the confessions of poor wretches inside isolation Block 30. Unforgettable Stef! The first victim from the latest group of volunteers! How many will follow him?

They're suddenly filling in all the anti-aircraft trenches in the camp that we had dug the previous year. In addition, around the camp they're building several dozen strong cement bunkers with loop-holes facing the barracks. It looks as though the SS men fear a prisoner riot, or ... they're preparing our extermination!

3 March 1945

Information reaches us from the camp clinic (from secretary Henio Wronka) that 3,977 prisoners, that is, almost four thousand, died in February![2] If the death rate continues at this pace, then by the time the Allies arrive the camp could be ... *empty*! Camp optimists didn't foresee such a possibility. But somehow we don't see the anticipated Allied parachute drop, "rushing" to free us from Dachau. Am I bitter? Perhaps. What irritates me terribly, though, is the childish, uncritical talk.

15 March 1945

There are no packages or letters from Poland. Once in a while a delayed straggler-type package turns up, but it's so moldy and damaged that it only stirs a memory of what someone's loving hands put into it. We can no longer count on any aid from that source. Camp food, moreover, gets worse and worse. Again, as in 1940, instead of the announced dinner soup, there's warm water with a parboiled cabbage leaf floating in it. Formerly, we were given a loaf of bread for four; now it's for eight; that is, we get a small piece of something clay-like, something still called bread, but there are more potatoes and sawdust in it than flour. Hunger intensifies. Typhus is spreading at an alarming rate. Death swings its scythe, and survivors of evacuation transports keep pouring into the camp.

18 March 1945

Brother Przewłoka, the cemetery capo, died yesterday. The poor man buried others with such reverence and rendered the last service to thousands, that quiet, humble little brother of the great Brother Albert. But here today they hauled his body out very early in the morning, and no one even knows whether they took him to be burned in the crematorium or to the cemetery that he managed.

For some time now, they've stopped all newspapers. They don't allow any in the camp. They're afraid the prisoners might get to know too much. But we know anyway. Here and there an SS man or one of the lay workers in factory offices whispers a piece of news, and on the plantation, in particular, our people know a lot: that's where contacts with the laity are easy; where the SS men, headed by Vogt, are friendlier; and, yes, that's where it's easier to conceal a radio. Who will find it in the enormous warehouses, hidden in stacks of herbs or other dried crops?

23 March

There's excitement in the camp. They say the Americans have crossed the Rhine! The Russians are moving quickly over Polish territory. Airstrikes continue... How can these Germans still defend themselves? And won't this nation rebel against Nazi tyranny?

26 March

We haven't had any air raids for two days. A meaningful silence! When bombs are dropping, we're afraid; but now, when we haven't heard them exploding for several days, we're disappointed. Typhus holds sway over everything! It's rumored in the hospital that there's no way it can be overcome. There are no measures to fight the epidemic.

27 March

Carmelite Fr. Paweł Januszewski, one of the volunteers in the isolation barracks, died yesterday. A new victim of love for one's neighbor! He was young, only 38 years old.

In all the commotion, I found out only yesterday evening about the death of unforgettable Fr. Stef Zielonka, from the Płock Diocese. He used to visit me in the camp hospital every time the radio announced that enemy squadrons were approaching. "I'm so terribly afraid of the bombs," he would admit with a pale face.

Poor Stef ran from the W.B. to avoid bombs, but he couldn't run from one small louse that brought him the typhus germ. An unforgettable person! Among the thousands of prisoners, there was probably not a single one who didn't like this young priest, he was such an engaging man...

30 March, Good Friday

Yesterday evening Henio Dubiel showed up in our barracks.

"I came to say goodbye. Tomorrow morning they're moving out the entire airforce experimental station."

"Where to?" The news takes my breath away. Little Henryk and I had become close over all these years.

"I don't know. They're mumbling something about the Alps, that it's quite close to the Swiss border. You see, Henryk," he explains, "I don't have a choice. If I go back to the barracks from the station, they can still pack me off on a transport for Auschwitz because, although everything's falling apart, you know how they can blindly follow orders. That's why I'd rather leave. Besides, I'm not going alone. Alfons Majchrzak will be with me, you know, the relative of Reverend Rector Banaszak and Fr. Antoś. Maybe over there we'll have a chance to bolt when the Allies get closer. Maybe..."

He left. Another chapter was closed. At this time, as I write these words, they're already on their way, and with them the horrible airforce experimental station leaves Dachau. Fr. Leoś Michałowski breathes a sign of relief.

Two more days until Easter. It will pass under a sign of death since every day more people die.

Good Friday ... There's a holiday mood on the plantation. Of course. Because this is the biggest Protestant holiday, and even though the SS men don't observe it, the tradition still continues. We didn't have an air raid today. The Allies, too, have respected the day on which our Lord was dying on the Cross.

59

The Last Month

The plantation, 2 April 1945

Yesterday was the feast of Easter! In our barracks there are holy Masses, joy, greetings, because these are certainly the last holidays in slavery, so that...

I'm probably mentally ill. I can't stand such displays of emotion! I run away. I want to be alone with my thoughts. I feel best in my corner of the carpentry shop, separated from the world by planks of plywood... I carve, I think, I pray the Rosary ten times in a row, and I think some more. The words of my dying uncle keep coming back to me: "Go back once again to life and begin it anew..."

Critical days for us are approaching. Everything is falling apart around us! The fronts are breaking up! There's panic in the nation! But — let's not be deceived — horrible Nazism, which condemns its own nation to death, will not spare us whom it has placed at the top of its agenda for destruction!

In the past month, that is, in March, 3,668 colleagues have died in the camp.[1] Since the New Year, more than 11,000 have died in all. For three months, the number is terribly high! How many will pass this month? How many in the following month if the "liberators" don't hurry? Jurek Musiał has died. He had just come back from Mauthausen, the death camp. Among his first words following his return were: "Now I know I'll survive. Mauthausen would have finished me off."

Jurek didn't know, however, that God had decreed otherwise.

The feast of Easter itself passed under the sign of hunger. That's why we willingly rush to work on the plantation, where we can always find some potatoes or a handful of peas. Now I appreciate Romek's advice to set up some kind of a small pantry here. We should have done it then ... but who would have thought? Besides, how do you store reserves when so many new arrivals are dying of hunger?

6 April — first Friday of the month

Currently we have unofficial but unrestricted access to the chapel. The German priests are now less afraid of letting us in. I attended the morning holy Mass. In the evening there will be another one, in the hall. I noticed that my carving of St. Joseph has been placed on a small side altar. (An older German Benedictine, Fr. Gustav Spitzig of Wuerzburg had come to our workshop as a volunteer. Well, a so-so "whittler," as they used to say. "Father, would you like to do a carving of St. Joseph for our chapel?" he asks me one day. After he arranged the whole business of this unofficial task with the capo, a St. Joseph "began to be born" under my crooked fingers. Now for the first time I saw it at the altar.)

What made a special impression on us, however, is the fact that suddenly during the night SS men ran into the barracks, wearing helmets, armed with submachine guns ready to fire, with grenades at their belts.

"*Antreten*! Assembly in the street!"

It's not hard to image what's happening in a hall where four hundred agitated people suddenly start to get dressed in a big hurry! Even in hell there can't be worse crowding! I grab my bundle under my arm, clogs in the other hand, and try to squeeze through into the entryway. When I manage to do this, I see that even here it's already packed. We get dressed while being pushed to one side and then the other, rolling with the wave of the tightly packed human throng.

"*Antreten*!"

How threatening the shining black SS helmets look! We're surprised that they're black this time. Only the SS men in Stutthof wore the black ones. In Sachsenhausen and Dachau they always wore the same green-colored uniforms and helmets as the regular military. We're even more surprised that they've sprung suddenly out of nowhere, all of them young. There's not one mustachioed granddad. We thought all these young ones were already at the front, but suddenly there are so many of them here and they somehow look so fierce, staring sullenly from under their helmets, that it makes us really afraid.

After getting dressed, I go out cautiously in front of the barracks. I'm curious to see what's happening on the main camp street, so I walk in that direction.

"Halt!" comes a roar in the darkness from the roof eaves of the barracks. "*Zuruck*!" (Turn back!)

I quickly withdraw. What if he takes a notion to fire at me with the submachine gun? I meet Fr. Staszek Sokołowski.

"What does all this mean?"

"I don't know."

"It's strange that they ordered us to take everything with us. They usually do that when they're taking..."

"For execution," finishes Stach. "I thought of that, too."

"*Antreten*! Assembly!" the cries are heard from neighboring barracks.

A swarm of clerics pours out of the halls into the darkness of the night. Due to fears of Allied aircraft, no lights are turned on outside. The darkness is so thick that we bump into each other. And only the flame from the crematorium chimney flares up into the black sky.

Finally, we fall into line. We count off.

Voices in the darkness of this April night quaver somehow strangely. But it was only an evacuation practice. We stood there for a while, and then they let us go back to the barracks.

We have a foretaste, however, of what they can do to us in a matter of minutes. A sudden nighttime execution of the entire camp could look the same. Good Lord! Where on earth did they suddenly get such a number of young SS men? That reality is a surprise even for the pessimists.

10 April, Tuesday

They've started releasing German priests. The first group left today. Rumor has it that they'll release all of us. Other rumors, however, say that the Red Cross will take charge of all prisoners.

11 April

There's growing disorganization in the camp. We hardly see any SS men. It is said that Commandant Weiss has left, taking the post of inspector of camps, and was replaced by Ruppert. The information is not trivial, but we don't dwell on it thanks to news from the front. They say the Russians are bombing Berlin, and the Americans have surrounded 250,000 German troops in the Ruhr Basin and are pushing into the interior of Germany. They say that in Italy the Allies, together with our Second Corps, are already reaching the Alps. Our release then is just a matter of days! But how many surprises can happen during these few days?

12 April

The German radio is trumpeting today about the death of President Roosevelt! Do the Nazis expect any changes advantageous for them as a result of this event?

All work has already stopped in many commands due to a shortage of materials. Here at the plantation there is plenty of work, but who thinks about it? Moreover, the SS men aren't pushing us anymore. Prisoners saunter from department to department, visit each other, organize meetings. Today I finally made use of the opportunity and "returned the visit" to Gustaw Morcinek, who works in the plantation bookbindery. With him are the teacher Bruca, Bronek Neiniger, and other acquaintances.

Morcinek, who visited me several times in the carpentry shop, got an idea for original figures after seeing a carved set of chessmen, but for now he doesn't want to disclose the project. I like to talk to him. Besides, I admit feeling like a schoolboy when I'm with this famous author and writer. I'm happy I have a chance to talk with him and exchange views on many issues. In general, I see that he has a great influence on young people around him. Naturally. An authority.

13 April, Friday

It's been raining since morning. Well, that's April in Dachau... We had several hours of anxiety due to Allied aircraft, without any major bombardment. There is hunger in the camp! The food keeps getting worse and the servings more miserly. Lately we get only a small loaf of bread for ten! Those who don't have a chance to get a bite of something at work will soon become weak. The wretches who arrive as survivors of evacuation transports relate terrible things. Several thousand of them were shipped out, but barely hundreds made it to their destination, to Dachau. They either died on the way from exhaustion or were shot by SS men! En route they marched continually for many days without a bite to eat. The rain has been coming down since morning, and thousands of these poor guys lie side by side on the assembly square because the barracks are so full that you couldn't even stick a pin into them. So they lie in the rain, in the bad weather, in the cold, and it's hard to tell which of them are still alive, and which are dead. Every day the gravediggers command gathers several platforms of corpses, taking them to the crematorium and the cemetery.

14 April, Saturday

We had just come back to work from dinner when capo Franek announced that the entire afternoon would be dedicated to thoroughly cleaning the workshop, when suddenly the sirens blared. Air raid!

We trudge along in single file on the narrow path to our dugout, without hurrying, when suddenly the first squadrons appear over the horizon. The artillery begins its usual concert. We pick up our pace. As we run into our dugout, shells are already bursting over our heads and a shower of shrapnel comes down.

Today's airstrike was as powerful as any we had seen up to now! Maybe hundreds of bombers passed over us. Most of them headed straight for Munich; others flew about in the vicinity. Schleisheim and Allach were hit hard. Today for the first time we saw as many as three bombers shot down. One of them was struck so squarely that it broke into pieces. We couldn't see any of the crew with a parachute. The entire crew was killed. The two other planes kept flying a bit farther and fell somewhere beyond the woods, but ballooning parachutes remained in the sky, falling slowly toward the ground. SS men rushed in their direction with weapons ready to fire. The Komandoführer raced down the road in front of us with his Mauser in hand. The sight of them running as though to an attack amused us. We didn't hear any shots. Maybe the airmen weren't killed...

It was just today that I realized how really dangerous these airstrikes on Germany are. How many pilots have been killed and are being killed, like the crew of that first bomber? How many of them drop in parachutes and find death immediately at German hands? How many, in the best of cases, land in captivity? The residents' rage against Allied "pirates," as Minister Goebbels calls them in his propaganda reports, is enormous. Mob trials are not uncommon.

16 April

Yesterday, Sunday, we were filling in the rest of the anti-aircraft trenches in the camp area, and outside the fence they're hastily completing concrete bunkers. Either they're afraid

Part of camp "security" seen up close. Any escape from the camp itself was completely out of the question. Toward the end of the war, as if such "security" were not enough, they built concrete bunkers all around with loop-holes directed toward the camp. One of them is indicated here with a "+" and an arrow (lower right side of photo).

of us, or they're getting ready to finish us off... And typhus continues to rage, each day taking about two hundred colleagues! Minor airstrikes continue almost without interruption. The assembly square becomes more and more cluttered with all kinds of trash and rags, with scattered corpses, but also with some who are still alive. Today the kitchen didn't serve any dinner. They say there was a shortage of water.

18 April, Feast of St. Joseph the Protector

Solemn services in the chapel. All priests, joined by many of our lay colleagues, vowed to St. Joseph that if he saved them, then ... These prayers to St. Joseph have already been going on since 19 March, but because today is again his feastday...

I personally didn't make this vow. I already offered my entire stay in camp to the Immaculate Heart of the Mother of God back in 1939, and I'm abiding by it. I'm a bit afraid, like a superstitious aborigine, that St. Joseph could... but that is really just a tribesman's fear. The Immaculate Heart made such great promises to those who completely trust in her that whatever happens to me, even death, will turn out for my good. Yes, even death, since in my offering I gave Heaven no conditions, surrendering myself completely to the will of God. I very much dislike piety that attaches conditions: "If You give, then I'll do this!" I prefer the principle: "Here, take! If You know this is for my good, You will grant it!"

In the streets between the barracks lie stacks of corpses. The crematorium has stopped operating due to a lack of fuel. They say there's a shortage of SS men to supervise the gravediggers command at the cemetery. We're lucky that the days are still cool and these bodies are not decomposing. They smell bad, it's true, but you can get used to that. Typhus is taking more and more victims. Emil Joas, that terrible murderer who used to kill when he was a hall leader in our barracks, has died in the camp hospital. Colleagues who saw him before he died say that in addition to typhus some dreadful illness had so contorted his arms and legs that he lay horribly twisted, like a block of wood with roots. They say he howled in pain, begging for help. It's so easy to conclude that this was God's punishment on that criminal, who with those very feet crushed so many priests and choked so many to death with those hands; even so, his death in "that way" is shocking! Perhaps it was a punishment. He was a terrible murderer of priests!

Zdzich prayed for him.

"After all, there was an immortal soul in him, too."

"But this was a murderer!"

"If there wasn't enough grace for murderer Emil, would Jesus come again into the world to go to death for him alone?"

"He would."

"Well, you see! And how do we understand this teaching of the Master?"

---

19 April 1945

I cleaned up my little corner, tied the most useful chisels into a bundle, and chose several of the best pieces of linden wood; I'll take them to the barracks because I've decided not to return again to the plantation. This cannot continue much longer and must end any day now. I'd rather live to see that moment in the barracks near the chapel in the company of my colleague priests than over here. I'm also taking my diary with me. Recently I've been secretly carving a small Crucifix, part by part. I already have a decent, nearly finished corpus inside the mattress, in the barracks. I'm taking along the little hands today. I'd like to take Him with me from the camp as the only memento of the many pieces that I've done. Romek and I picked some peas, string beans and kidney beans, and we've hidden them in the barracks at the bottom of the mattress; that should last us for a few days. And then? Either we won't need anything more because the Americans will liberate us, or ... we won't need anything at all!

Evening of the same day, 19 April, already in the barracks

The hall is hunting for lice. After inspecting my dirty underwear (because it hadn't been washed for weeks), I lie down in my bunk and write. The crowding and stuffiness in the room is unbearable. The most preposterous rumors fly from mouth to mouth. Sounds of howling come from the isolation blocks. They say that again they're murdering capos. Who? Those who were evacuated from other camps. Standing on the brink of the grave, they "mete out justice" to those who were killing them. Terrible scenes are being played out at these mob trials; no one can help, no one can stop the enraged mob that burns with a desire for bloody revenge. It is Hell! Fleas are biting hellishly because we have millions of them, but the experts maintain that it's precisely fleas that defend us against the lice. This could be so, since we really do have few lice, and maybe that's why the typhus epidemic takes so few victims from our barracks. Radek, who works in the storeroom, brings some naphthalene and sprinkes it into our bunks. This nasty stuff stings the skin a lot, especially when your body is wet with perspiration, but it protects against insects.

No one should get the impression that the conditions in which we live dispose us to prayer and spiritual life. On the contrary. Everything simply deters us from our spiritual life, everything makes it difficult. The one thing sustaining it is the realization that prayer under such conditions — demanding great effort, grown stiff, burned out, and preoccupied with chasing fleas — is all the more meritorious, provided it has been brightened by loving intentions. When you think of all those good hermits who ran away from life, from the tumult, from people, turmoil, rushing and crowding, you don't see the greatness of their sacrifice. Only imagine one of them finding himself in our little hell, where four of us are squeezed together on a single rotten mattress, crowding each other, breathing in the smell of sweaty bodies...

20 April, Friday, the namesday of Fr. Teoś Korcz, leader of our barracks

We know how to "celebrate" it even under these conditions: holy Mass in his intention, after that a breakfast consisting of a black brew from dried acorns, called coffee, and ... a piece of bread from those who heroically saved it from their small portion yesterday. As I had already decided, I didn't go to work today. Even so, I kept going there a long time. Most of our men had long ago "unharnessed" themselves. Following roll call, we returned to the barracks. Today the weather is fine, and the sun has come out for the first time in a good while. Romek solemnly announced beans for dinner. He intends to invite colleagues from our group because — is it possible? — this could be our last "paschal" supper together before the "exodus" awaiting us.

"They brought in a transport of Frenchmen," says Fr. Karol Radzięta, catching his breath; he belongs to a command that cleans the camp and has closest access to the commandant's office. "There were several priests in the group. They took one of them immediately to the crematorium and shot him dead!"[2]

"They shot him?"

"Right. We saw him. His colleagues from the transport were whispering that it was probably for taking part in the resistance."

In general, although we don't see SS men anywhere in the camp itself, quite a lot of them move around in the area of their barracks, beyond the fence and river. From time to time they lead small groups of lay prisoners to the crematorium, and a few days ago an entire SS company herded a group there (said to be a mix of Hungarians, Ukrainians, Bulgarians, and others) and shot them to death for stirring up insurrection at the front.

"Black" is on a rampage! (Black is one of the asocial prisoners who wear black triangles on their shirts. His name is Wernike.) We all know he's an informer for the SS political department and heads a small group of undercover informers and helpers, but for now we can't do anything about it. One word from him could mean a death sentence. We need to wait and see what the next days will bring. Another such despised person is the current camp leader, a Georgian named Meansarian. He especially hates Russians. He harasses them every step of the way, punishes and torments them. They'll pay him back one day! The greater the commotion in the camp, the more one needs to be careful because such huge numbers have come in, so many thousands of strangers, that we can't be sure there aren't SS men among them in disguise. And this suspicion is not without basis.

Sunday, 22 April 1945

Today several holy Masses were celebrated in the chapel. We know that no one is watching now, so the order that only one priest be specially authorized to celebrate no longer holds. A few lay colleagues also show up in the chapel, and following the Masses we gather in small groups to discuss the situation. Until now, pressed by our daily jobs, we've maintained little contact with each other, although we lived together in the same or neighboring barracks. We were glad when after work we could drop into a bunk to do some reading, thinking, and praying on our own.

No matter which group you join, it's the same everywhere: rumors! rumors! rumors!

What irritates me is the gullibility, the lack of criticism, the simply childish attitude. Because it makes it seem that the Allies don't care about matters of universal importance, that their sole concern is prisoners locked up in camps—especially those of us in Dachau!

I still have some books from the library; I run off to a third-level bunk, retire into our corner, which has been sprinkled with naphthalene by Radek, and read... This takes me away from reality, calms me, and suggests other thoughts.

24 April, Tuesday

Worsening hunger in the camp! Today no bread whatsoever was given out, and the soup was so thin it was just plain water. We still have some reserves in our bodies from the time we got packages, but those poor wretches who arrived in decimated transports are dying like flies! It's no wonder that typhus takes hold so easily in those weakened organisms.

It's hard to die at the dawn of approaching freedom...

25 April

Quietly whispered news is going around that injections against typhus, recently given in the camp hospital, are causing these numerous deaths. Could there possibly be some truth to it? What's intriguing is that following the injections, besides those most debilitated, death is taking the camp's so-called prominent people who first volunteered for them, hoping to save themselves on the eve of liberation.

Radek believes in naphthalene. He brings bags full of it from the storeroom and sprinkles and sprinkles it; then during the night it bites us worse than a thousand lice, but that's precisely why we don't have them.

I had always thought I was ready to die at any moment, and there were some long periods when every evening I asked God to take me. Now that our stay in the camp is counted in days, however, I want very much to live and see the moment of liberation! To be sure, I don't specifically ask for life, and every day I renew the act of offering myself completely to the Immaculate Heart, but Jesus knows how unpleasant it would be for me to die now. I want so very much to meet with my family once again...

I found a can with a lid that screws on. My little diary will fit into it. It's too bad the can isn't any bigger because it could also hold the small Crucifix, taken apart in pieces. If something were to happen to us... I'll throw the can into the canal, and maybe someone will fish it out somewhere and give it to my mother.

After I wrote those words, the thought occurred to me that I'm getting somewhat sentimental. I'm in a bad way. I'm trying to remain calm, and on the outside, at least, I feign calmness, but inside of me everything's trembling, everything's shaking...

There's a terrible scene on the assembly square! I suppose the Valley of Jehoshaphat must have looked like this.

Air raids occur so often that we don't even go inside the barracks. First, because aircraft don't pass over the camp now, so anti-aircraft artillery doesn't fire above us and no shrapnel falls; second, to sit in small barracks that are horribly crowded, amid all that general irritation, produces strange apprehension. I'd rather be outside to see the sky overhead, people still alive, trees just turning green ... I somehow feel more cheerful then. Artillery surrounding the camp keeps pounding, while bombs fall so close to us and the blasts are so strong that the barracks shake.

In late afternoon of this same day, there's talk about an evacuation of the whole camp! Where will they make us go if Allied troops have encircled the entire district? Maybe into the woods, to be shot?

The chapel is constantly packed with people praying. Due to a lack of room, many stay there throughout the night, lying side by side on the floor.

Dachau, 26 April 1945

Someone mislaid the can I used for storing my diary. I have to find another one. Since this morning, there's a terrible excitement in the camp. A group of German priests has again been released, and it's rumored that Czech priests and those of other nationalities will go next, and maybe after them it will be our turn?

No concrete information reaches us any longer from the outside. Besides, our impression is that even the Germans themselves are completely confused. Outside the camp fence we can see a large SS unit, but we hardly believe our eyes! Instead of vehicles, small Russian horses, most likely originating from Poland's eastern border area, are hitched to peasant carts! Where's the motorized Nazi army that forced its way into Poland with such arrogance in 1939?

To kill time, I begin to carve, if this whittling can be called carving. Since there's very little space in the hall and there's such crowding, moving from the door to a shelf by the windows takes several minutes of hard effort as I push my way through. After finally getting there, I take out the chisels and, squeezed into a corner, I whittle my Christ.

Suddenly someone runs in and yells from the door:

"Camp evacuation! By twelve o'clock, everyone has to be on the assembly square!"

Agitated turmoil in the human swarm! *Evacuation?*

We realize with fear this means that we're to go from a quiet, sheltered corner of the camp right into the rushing current of wartime events! All around, in nearby and more distant areas, we hear the rumbling of constant bombardment, the blast of explosions, the rattling of machine guns... But in reality, we fear what we'll encounter on the outside after more than five years of separation from life. It's some kind of peculiar phobia, the mental illness of a longtime prisoner who thinks fearfully about life outside the bars. Our fear is even greater since we're to leave the camp still prisoners and go into life as it is in these catastrophic, critical days.

Just a while ago they called all block leaders to a briefing. Our Fr. Korcz also ran over there. I wonder what this will bring...

Announcement: "The Dachau camp must be evacuated! All who are healthy and capable of walking will leave. The weak, the handicapped, and the ill will remain in place."

As the barracks leader, Fr. Korcz organizes a meeting. Several hundred of us attend it, each holding a blanket in one arm and a bundle of modest possessions in the other. I have the chisels with me. I had worked with them so many years, they saved my life, so I'm taking them with the unfinished corpus of Christ, taken apart in pieces. Maybe I'll be lucky to get it out... Maybe sometime I'll finish it... We're staying together: Zdzich, Romek Budniak, Jasio Januszewski — who returned several days ago from a command in Feldafing — Józio Pućka, Fr. Szczepek Weber, Fr. Henio Sych, Fr. Józek Woźniak; behind us stand the Rev. Pastor Handke with his constant companion Fr. Zygmunt Kaczmarek, and with them the Rev. Professor Wróblewski, Fr. Szczepan Misiak, Fr. Ludwik Sobieszczyk, Fr. Leon Mencel; joining us are colleagues from the W.B., including Fr. Stef Smaruj with the seminarian Skowronek. The Rev. Rector Banaszak stays close to the Rev. Professor Antoś Majchrzak. In further ranks are the Rev. Canon Jedwabski, the Rev. Professor Tadrzyński, the Rev. Professor Gałęzewski, the Rev. Professor Tadeusz Zieliński, the Rev. Dr. Romek Zientarski, the Curia notary Fr. Jasio Ziółkowski with Fr. Edem Palewodziński, the Rev. Dean Zenker with Fr. Bronek Pluciński and the Rev. Dr. Małecki... In short, we gather in groups of close friends, we cling to our own kind... Maybe underlying this is a subconscious belief in the possibility of help, just in case... Maybe this expresses a trust in people with whom you have gone through so many difficult years, sharing with each other a last piece of bread...

Fr. Bernaś Czapliński, who never loses his self-control, calm, poise, or cheerfulness,

As the front lines grew closer, the Nazis evacuated the camps, driving thousands of prisoners into the interior of Germany. Whoever grew weak on the way was felled by an SS man's bullet. Thousands and thousands of those who were shot littered the transport routes.

gathers around him young Pomeranians. Poznań natives stick to their group. It's the same with those from Płock, Włocławek, and others. The monks keep to their own groups. From various parts all are drawn at this time to their own.

We start out without "keeping step." We walk slowly in a group of hundreds, leaving the barracks where we had spent so many years behind us and in them a handful of those who decided to stay...

Several colleagues join us on the way to the square. Among them are Fr. Radek Fibak, Fr. Edek Skowroński, Fr. Zygmunt Pituła, Fr. Antoś Musiał, Fr. Miecio Siudziński, Fr. Kazio Głogowski with Stach Kucharzak and Stach Grabowski...

We stand on the right side of the assembly square. The left side is completely swamped with thousands who are wandering around in the open; it resembles an Eastern market except that, instead of the proverbial afternoon sun beating down, the day is dark and gloomy, heavy clouds hang over the camp, a rather strong, cold wind is blowing from the north, and a cold drizzle is starting to fall. In front of us, closer to the kitchen, there are a few armed SS men and some officers, and in their midst is Commandant Ruppert.

Attention, they're calling out Germans, Russians, Bulgarians, and Romanians. They place them in units at intervals... Many, instead of heading to the formed units, make an about-face and go either into the ranks of foreign blocks or right into the barracks. The camp police, trying to maintain order, are helpless. The louder the SS men scream, the more commotion there is in the ranks and the more prisoners flee from the square. Our men are also walking away! They leave individually and in whole groups.

"Romek? Do we stay?"

"Let's wait a bit," advises Fr. Antoś Majchrzak. "We'll see what happens."

We stand. We wait. The drizzling rain becomes unpleasant. There's increasing commotion in the units. The nomads on the left side of the square are agitated like a bunch of vermin in rotting trash. The wind carries a stench of decomposing corpses.

Commandant Ruppert stands with his legs astride, hands on his hips, and calmly observes the few SS men who are rushing around.

"You know," Romek interrupts the silence, "it looks as though they didn't care at all about conducting this evacuation. If they had wanted to terrorize us, they only needed to spray some rounds of machine-gun fire over our heads from the towers, and we'd become docile like sheep."

"Romek!" Antoś Majchrzak says in a humorous tone, "if I were Hitler, I wouldn't look for a new Himmler. You surpass him."

"In wit," Romek defends himself.

"*Achtung*!" Zdzich's whisper, sharp and loud, suddenly interrupts the conversation. "Whoever doesn't want to get soaked to the skin, come with me! Without keeping step, march after me!" And, pulling me by the sleeve, he pushes his way through the ranks toward the camp street. Romek and a few close friends are behind us.

"Hey! You Gniezno guys," Staszek Sokołowski's voice reaches us. "Where are you headed?"

"To the barracks!"

"To the barracks? Not a bad idea. Hey! Płock company! Follow me, no hesitation!" Stach always has a sense of humor. Pulling his learned brother Franciszek, he tramps along after us with a group of colleagues. Behind them come others.

"Ja, sakra?! And where are you priests going?" comes from a group of Czechs.

"To the barracks! Good Czechs…"

"Are we any worse? Hey, you Hessian lads! After me!" and the Czech group turns toward the street.

The camp police have been scuffling for quite a while with people leaving, but seeing a new and much larger wave approach, they give up any further defense and step aside. A few minutes later we're in the barracks, which, surprisingly, is already very crowded.

"We're not going! Going out in such miserable weather means sickness and torment anyway, and death! So whatever they plan to do to us, let it happen right here, in this place! We need to be united! All to a man! Everyone who goes…"

"The people's tribune!" murmurs Zdzich, taking off his soaking wet shirt. "And to think the poor Catholic Church hasn't duly appreciated him and hasn't by now appointed him…"

"Attention! Atteeention! Colleagues!" we suddenly hear Fr. Korcz's voice at the door. "The commandant wants you to know that he grants permission for a temporary stay in the barracks, but we must be ready for any alarm. Evacuation of the camp must be carried out."

There's buzzing as in a beehive… Rain drizzles down outside the windows… The wind whistles through cracks in the roof…

I found another can, and it's even better than the first one because the screw top has a rubber rim that makes it tight-fitting; therefore, the diary won't get wet in it, even if it has to stay there for many months. The rain has stopped. Romek is cooking beans in the block street. I sit down under an old military tarpaulin and write. I can't forgive myself for not having started this diary sooner. It might have been source material for those writing on the subject of Dachau. If I had thought that...

I interrupted my writing because Gustaw Morcinek arrived. He was actually looking for Kazio Michalski, a very close friend of his, but — not finding him, he sat down under the tarpaulin. I'm too small not to enjoy this acquaintance, but "big" enough to admit to this vanity.

"You're not carving? It's good for killing time."

"Well, how can I in this mess?"

"But you'll carve after our release?"

"No. I'd rather write."

"Write?" Gustaw's bushy brows arch up in surprise. "That's not an easy thing and rather thankless," he says slowly, looking straight ahead.

"And do you plan some kind of major work on the subject of camp life?"

He waves his hand. "First I have to catch up on sleep and restore my mental balance. I have such a mess up here," he rubs his hand over his forehead, "that at this time no ideas are springing up. For now, I have only one 'plan.'"

"? ... ? ... ? ..."

"To return to Silesia!"

The sound of voices, like a far-off waterfall, comes from the camp square in the distance.

"Oh, hear it?"

"They're trying to restore order in the units of young Russians," explains Fr. Franek Nowak, who has just come from there.

"They won't be able to, anyway. There are just thousands of them."

"And what will happen to us?"

"God only knows. We have to wait. Each hour can bring remarkable changes. Each is precious and each can decide our life or death."

Outside the camp fencing, beyond the canal, in the little streets between the blocks of barracks, we can see SS men preparing to leave. They're packing their possessions onto the above-mentioned small carts drawn by horses. Could they be fleeing? They're loading in such haste!

The Road of Death is empty. Silence reigns at the crematorium. Since this morning, there hasn't been a single execution. The crematorium chimney isn't emitting smoke because of a fuel shortage. They say that the bodies of the last crew members are lying at the top of the mound of corpses. They didn't have time even to burn them. If the Americans come and find these stacks of corpses, they'll have the best possible evidence of crimes committed. A rumor is going around that one of the officers intended to shoot Commandant Ruppert, but they say he himself died at the hand of the commandant.

The plantation command's head capo and many of his supporters no longer return to the camp at night. They sleep there and wait. The prisoners say openly among themselves that their officer Vogt protects them at this time, and, in turn, they will defend him when the Allies arrive. Many capos have taken off their "official arm bands" with the label "Capo." They're afraid! One capo, Ernst Hecht, still wears it.

"Ernst," I say when we meet today. "All capos are taking off their 'bands,' and you..."

"I had the courage to wear it through the years of captivity; I must have the courage to wear it until the day of liberation." He smiles, "It will either indict me before the liberators, or it will defend me. And with you, Heinrich, I'd still like to talk a lot, quite a lot. You know what about?" He looks straight ahead, into space. "I've received so much from Mary that... I wear Her medal!" he finishes emphatically. (I had given it to him one day after finding it in the storeroom while sorting transport clothes. As a capo, he was much less subject to personal searches.)

Night of 26 to 27 April 1945

Such crowding in the bunks, the naphthalene, too, is annoying, and the fleas are biting so badly that, despite being tired, I can't sleep. So I have made my way through the crowd of sleepers (it's worse in the dark with people lying side by side all over the floor). I sit in the washroom on the basin for washing feet, and I write by the faint light of a night lamp that smolders near the ceiling. The windows are covered with black curtains, and behind them are an equally black night and silence terrifying in its inscrutability. Under the cover of this dark night, beyond the camp wires, great events are taking place...

What will the coming day bring?

I carry the can with the diary constantly; it hangs on the belt loop of my pants. The ball-point pen smears in my sweaty hand. It's terribly hot in the barracks as well as in the washroom. So many hundreds of bodies crammed together! We're not allowed to open any doors or windows due to security concerns. SS men in the towers are ready to fire if they think we're giving signals to Allied aircraft.

Tomorrow — excuse me because it's already today, probably about three in the morning — this morning I will go to...

Eleven o'clock in the morning, on Friday, 27 April

I fell asleep on the basin and woke up when a wave of those awakening began to pour into the washroom. The kitchen isn't in operation! They say there's no water. It's strange that we have it in the washrooms, although the toilets at night were blocked and smell terrible. Apparently there was no water at night. Following holy Mass, attended in the chapel of Barracks 26 (where many of our men now live because as soon as German priests are released, we move into their places), after breakfast with no "coffee" but with a small piece of bread in the hands of those who by some miracle still have a little, we march to the assembly square. To count these thousands, given the current disorganization and shortage of SS men, is completely out of the question. No one knows exactly how many prisoners are currently in the camp. They're not even numbering the arriving transports. Prisoners with numbers from other camps are walking among us. There are even rumors that many SS men (in prisoners' uniforms) are hiding among us! Even that's possible since in this human sea, and with this jumble of over thirty nationalities, no one would ever find out. We stand in units on the assembly square and wait... The guardhouse gate is locked. In the building itself there's silence. Not a living soul.

"Have they run off, or what?"

After an hour, there's movement at the gate. Commandant Ruppert appears there, stands a while, looks in the direction of the packed square, finally waves his hand and disappears inside the guardhouse.

Was this possibly a signal from him to march off?

Most likely, since some units are turning around and marching back toward the barracks. And we follow them...

"What does it all mean?"

"Stop pondering over it," advises Romek. "It's important to find a few pieces of wood so I can cook the beans."

We had barely returned to the barracks, and Romek was still worried where he would get the wood for fuel, when Zdzich is already starting a fire.

"Zdzich! Where did you find it so quickly? ... Oh, you monster!" laughs Romek. "But those are legs from a stool! That's sabotage, you could be hanged for it."

"Formerly could be hanged," answers Zdzich calmly, continuing to kneel and fan the fire. "Formerly could be. Soon not only the stools but all these barracks will go up in smoke."

One o'clock in the afternoon

The kitchen put out kettles with a brew of red currant leaves, called tea. That's all! If not for the dinner prepared by Romek, we would complain of hunger, as thousands, unfortunately, are complaining. To be sure, mixed in with the beans loudly proclaimed by Romek are more oats, wheat, and some other grain that I can't even name, but a few spoonfuls of that food still means something to the stomach.

"Romek! Since we've already eaten, tell us finally what was that? Where did you scrape it up?"

Romek smiles slyly, and finally says: "Remember those bags with feed meant for the chickens?"

"So you..."

"That's right. Every day I put a few handfuls into my rolled-up pants legs, then poured it into the mattress, just in case, and you see that it came in handy."

"Pfui! How many dead fleas and flea eggs were in there?" Zdzich spits.

"Don't get excited. I tried to rinse it thoroughly; I just couldn't pick out all the tiny stones, but they say they're good for the stomach."

"A transport has arrived from Buchenwald!" Fr. Józef Kopczewski brings the news.

The information stirs us all up.

"A transport from Buchenwald?! Such a long distance? On foot?"

"That's why only a few hundred out of several thousand made it."

In the transport is a young seminarian, Piotruś Skarga, from the Vilnius seminary. From him we get the most credible information. Not having enough SS men for deploying thousands of prisoners, they dressed the Greens, prisoners who are professional felons, in SS uniforms; they gave them machine guns and a promise that if they brought the transport safely to Dachau, a reward awaited them in the form of *freedom*. "If you only saw how those devils murdered people along the way!"

We can imagine! Monstrous! It's probably already a final act of the Nazis' "new order!"

Neither the seminarian Piotruś nor any of the survivors from the Buchenwald transport received a Dachau number. Who has the wits in this complete disintegration to think of such things?[3]

"Henryk!"

I turn around. Calling me is Fr. Feliks Kamiński, who is still a hall leader in the isolation block located across from us. I come close to the fence. We talk. Feliks, as always, is very specific when assessing a situation. I like him because of that. Suddenly from his barracks come sounds of screaming, howling, shrieking!

"What's that?" I ask, worried.

"Eh," he waves his hand. "They're tearing apart some capo."

"You don't forbid them to?"

"Forbid them? That mob turned into brutes? Try it. I tried to influence them with words; several times I tried physically; I organized a special guard and you know what happened? During the night they cut the throats of the guards and of the capo they were after!"

"How horrible!"

"If you only saw these madmen running around with bloody claws![4] Yesterday I found a note pinned to the blanket on my bed saying that if I don't want to die also, I should leave the barracks at such times and pretend I don't see anything."

Suddenly, there's a cry:

"The Americans are coming!"

"The Americans?"

Frenzy takes over the crowds in the camp street! A human swarm runs toward the isolation wire fence in the belief—following the screams coming from Fr. Feliks' barracks—that it's over there, on the plantation side...

"The Americans!" the cry runs through the camp!

"The Americans!" it spreads like fire from barracks to barracks.

The SS men in the guard towers feverishly take the covers off their machine guns...

Behind us, on top of the table, stands Romek, stretching and turning his head in the direction of the plantation. His face is flushed with joy!

"It's true! The Americans are coming!"

It turned out that this was a column of German tanks rolling across the plantation toward the woods. It was a blessing and maybe special protection on the part of Providence that the frenzied mob of thousands of prisoners didn't attack the guardhouse at that time or didn't rush toward the walls. The SS men in the towers already had their fingers on the triggers of their heavy machine guns. There would have been an unbelievable massacre! Hundreds would have died, maybe thousands. Antoś Majchrzak and I are going to the chapel to say the Rosary. Many of our men already are on their knees in front of the tabernacle; others are asleep side by side on the floor. These are the men who, due to overcrowding, had to suffer through the whole night someplace.

Three o'clock in the afternoon

They're rounding up the remaining Germans and Russians. They've announced to the Frenchmen that they should gather in the washroom, and from there the Red Cross will take them away!

"Don't believe it. This could be a trap!" warns Zdzich.

Meanwhile — indeed, vehicles with the insignia of the Red Cross do arrive; they stop outside the camp fence at the guardhouse; some uniformed and civilian men get out of them... Could it be that the Red Cross will take over the entire camp?

In our barracks a great many canvas tents were recently finished for the troops. Currently, since the SS men didn't show up to collect them, the stuff is scattered all over the muddy street, and here and there some have used them to build bonfires. In general, a camp that used to be always as clean as the proverbial drinking glass (clean at the expense of prisoner drudgery) is now full of trash, garbage, all kinds of filth, scraps of paper, cartons, cans, and rags; all this, moreover, is soaking wet from the almost constantly drizzling rain and covered with mud; in the midst of it all are stacks of corpses that have not been removed. If this situation continues any longer, in addition to typhus, some other epidemic will break out. Your flesh creeps at the very sight of this hell.

Evening falls. Zdzich has pitched a canvas tent near the wall, thrown down several rolled tarpaulins and made sleeping quarters. He assures us that we'll certainly sleep much better than in the crowded barracks, where you can't find a place anyway.

Saturday, 28 April 1945

I woke up frozen to the bone. The tent over our heads tore off at one of the corners, uncovering us, and the rain at night completely soaked our feet. I slept like a rock, tired from events of the previous days and nights, but now I can barely hold the pencil in my numb fingers. Zdzich, Romek, and Radek went to the assembly square to get some news. I wanted to stay. My stomach is growling. Romek, to be sure, promises two more meals from the feed supplies that he keeps in the mattress, but one is reserved for today's dinner and the second or last one is for tomorrow's dinner. And then?

In the morning we didn't have any water either in the washrooms or the toilets. It's not hard to imagine what this means when there's such congestion in a confined space. It smells so bad that it causes you to gag and feel nauseated. They promise, however, that we'll have water about noon. The boiler-room command is taking care of it by itself. The SS men certainly aren't concerned about it. It's being said that some kind of "international prisoners committee" has been organized in an effort to maintain order in the camp and take care of things. I don't go to the square, and that's why I know very little about what's going on. I spend a lot of time in the chapel, where I also do most of my writing, sitting on the floor against the back wall. I read a bit, but I also nap most of the time. I somehow feel strangely weak. My mind drifts. Zdzich says it isn't a sickness, it's simply due to hunger.

"Romek," I say to him as he returns from the square with information, "Where are you keeping the rest of the grain supplies? Aren't you afraid someone will find them and take them?"

Smiling, he shows me a strange swelling above his muddy clogs. "I tied my pants and poured the stuff here," he smacks his hand over the swollen muddy pants leg. "This is the most secure place. No one will take it from here."

"Oh, that Romek!"

There's nobody on the assembly square. Whereas even yesterday there was activity starting in the morning because they were drawing up units of the Germans, Russians, Bulgarians, Romanians, Italians, and by evening the French, since this morning it has been completely quiet there. In the guardhouse it's as though everything has died out. Not a living soul. The gate is locked. From time to time, an SS man moves outside the fencing and disappears into one of the buildings.

What's going to happen? Even the airstrikes have ended. Such silence…

It's only at about eleven that they summon the rest of the Italians and Jews to the square, those who were brought from somewhere several days ago in an evacuation transport. It's the same old story. Some units enter the square, others come back from it. And the unfortunates are bivouacking there, seeking protection from the rain under stacks of all kinds of rubbish. Here and there, a bonfire smolders with puffs of acrid smoke. It smells like the crematorium…

Coming back from the square, I meet Fr. Franek Nowak, the prefect from Gniezno. We walk along, commenting on events and making conjectures, when suddenly a siren goes off, followed by another, then others…

An alarm?

The sirens blare for a long time, but, surprisingly, without any of the breaks known to us.

"It's the warning signal that an enemy advance guard is approaching," someone feverishly recalls information recently given to us.

"We remember an order that, following such a signal, we're all supposed to be in the barracks."

"Let's go to the chapel," advises Franek.

―――⚬⚬⚬⚬⚬―――

The chapel is mobbed. Everyone's kneeling. Our hearts are moved!

"*Te Deum laudamus!*" intones one of the Italian priests.

"*Te Deum confitemur!*" intones the group of hundreds of priests.

The hymn of thanksgiving continues; tears fill our eyes…

Suddenly another blast from the siren! The alarm is cancelled…

"You could go crazy," whispers Zdzich, who's kneeling next to me.

Resourceful Romek is already pushing through toward the door with the can of not-quite-cooked feed under his arm.

"Look at him," whispers Zdzich. "Isn't he a lovable madman?"

It's difficult — with all the tragic nature of the moment — to keep from smiling even in the chapel.

"Oh, that Romek, that Romek."

"You see," he explains a while later, as we sit squatting next to him around the bonfire, "My whole life I've always followed the principle: 'You don't have people's welfare at heart if you don't first give them bread.' I'm sure God didn't hold it against me because I sang out a joyous "Te Deum" while I had a can of not-quite-cooked dinner under my cloak. Although," he adds with a smile, "that beastly can was really burning me..."

"Is that why you sang so loudly?" laughs Radek.

The dinner was much delayed, and there was a lot of "munching" on grit, but there was a dinner. Romek is beaming. How he loves to make others happy!

"You know," Czesio Koczorowski says with excitement, "German radio reports that some kind of Bavarian government has formed in Munich, that it's calling upon all soldiers to lay down their arms, and it's urging all Poles and other foreigners to cooperate in disabling SS men."

"They've gotten started early!" Zdzich snorts.

"Nonetheless, that's a good sign for us. Maybe Munich residents will rush the SS men and rescue the camp, calculating that they'll find thousands of prisoners willing to..."

"Eat away!"

"Hey now, you always have to be so cynical."

"I'm just dampening your great enthusiasm. Because how can they count on us, realizing that these thousands are in greater need of a hospital than a barracks! Besides, even if you wanted to, where do you get weapons? Will you go with bare hands?"

Toward evening they lead in a transport of about 150 women. Some among them are also from Bydgoszcz. They're starving, swaying on their feet, dirty and full of lice, a picture of destitution and despair! They can barely move their feet. They've moved them into the camp's house of ill repute. Most likely the poor women don't even know about the "reputation" of those barracks. The camp police are guarding the gate to the enclosure.

The guardhouse gate opens from time to time only to allow in another new group of skeletons from evacuation transports. Madness! They've been evacuating our camp since yesterday, and others are coming in! The SS men have lost their heads, and we have, too. We're terribly hungry. Romek promises another "dinner" of chicken feed tomorrow. Again tomorrow. But what will happen if this goes on several days, or several dozen?

The dead are constantly being thrown out into the street. The stacks of skeletons are growing. They say that again pieces of bodies have been cut out. Horrible, but for us so very understandable.

Prisoners from the Buchenwald evacuation transport have murdered five block leaders and capos in the washroom. The leaders were murdering prisoners not long ago; now the prisoners are retaliating. Terrible! Stefcio Pabiszczak, who witnessed one of these scenes, describes it with horror in his eyes. "These are no longer people! It's a gang of madmen."

How does God look at this?

59. The Last Month

The Rev. Dr. Franciszek Przybyła has become deranged. With fear on his face and madness in his eyes he runs from barracks to barracks yelling: "They're already coming! They're already coming! They're already murdering!" At the same time, yelping in a shrill voice, he hides under the bunks, squeezes into the farthest corner, and after being chased out by residents of one barracks, he runs into another, trying to hide there.

Those who were close to him whisper that a reliable SS man had told him that everyone in the camp is to be shot to death and burned with a flame-thrower!

We don't believe this, and yet, and yet ... we're worried to death. Perhaps there's some truth in it?

P.S. It was only hours later that news broke which made us realize how dangerous our situation was precisely during those critical hours!

We fall asleep under Zdzich's canvas tent. Damp cold penetrates from below. A thick fog, creeping into the interior through all the cracks, aggravates my bronchitis. Suddenly in the darkness a cry rings out that makes your blood run cold! I jump up from my sleeping area, listening.

"That's Franek Przybyła," Zdzich comforts me. "Lie down and sleep because maybe tomorrow we'll need all our strength."

60

The Last Sunday

29 April 1945

"Get up! Get up!" Zdzich is shaking me urgently by the arm. Zdzich is that excited? So something very important must have happened... Without asking any questions, I rush as quickly as possible out of the tent, which is damp from fog and dew.

"See?!"

Oh, my God! Is this real or a dream? White flags, signs of surrender, are flying from the tops of the guard towers!

"Run and wake up our men! I'll run to the third and fourth hall!"

"The SS men are surrendering! They're surrendering the camp and us!"

Commotion in the halls! Throngs of awakened prisoners burst forth into the street! People are overcome with emotion. With eyes wide open, they stare and stare, afraid that this might be just another illusion, that it could disappear at any minute...

The joy that comes over the clerical group is impossible to describe. Only now does it become apparent under what tremendous nervous tension we've been living in these last days. Even those who had seemed the strongest, most resilient and supposedly hardest had tears in their eyes. Here and there dry, fitful, nervous sobs can be heard. We realize that in an hour, in two hours, in several at the most, we will be free. Free! ... after almost six years, after so much...

At such a moment who could think about breakfast, about the nagging hunger, about frozen and numb fingers...

"To the chapel!"

"To the chapel! ... to the chapel! ..."

On that Sunday morning, there's one holy Mass after another, now without any fear that SS men, that orders... The Lord is with us. And although He was always near, it was never like today. After all, it's the morning of resurrection!

And the day — in contrast to yesterday — is fine and sunny, and there's so much sun in our worn-out hearts, so much joy... White flags still flutter from the towers in a light spring breeze. In open windows at the top level, where heavy machine guns stand covered over, where formerly there were two or sometimes three SS men every day, now there's only one. He smiles at the prisoners. He throws down some candy. In short, we feel he's standing there only because he has to, because order must be maintained until the Americans arrive, and at this moment our hearts are so indulgent, what does it matter to us anyway after so many, many years if we have to wait these few more hours?

"See how he's ingratiating himself now?" someone comments.

"Hey, stop it. This guy is the least guilty. If he and the other old men have to stay here to the end in order to transfer us to the Americans, it's the least of faults."

60. The Last Sunday

We admit that the speaker is right. We nod in agreement. Everyone knows — if a Pole is pushed, then... But just stroke him, smile at him and you get: "Let's love one another!"

Around noon, a huge black aircraft appears at not too great a distance. Strange, strange how slowly it moves! Moreover, it's moving back and forth over the same area.

"Maybe it's some kind of special reconnaissance plane?" someone guesses.

"Most likely," we agree, continuing to observe the strange size and even stranger speed of the black steel bird.

"You could easily shoot something like that down. When it moves like a turtle, it makes an excellent target," someone else adds. His words were barely spoken when white puffs appeared at a distance from the strange aircraft.

"They're firing at it!"

After a few seconds, explosions are heard.

"Right, they're firing. But look! Look!"

The black steel bird, which up to now had been moving very slowly and giving the impression of a turtle poking along, suddenly takes on tremendous speed, makes turns, climbs high and disappears into a cloud.

"What a rascal! He flew away!"

"Supposedly so sluggish, yet so nimble! How quickly he picked up that terrific speed!"

We hear machine guns starting to fire in the distance.

"Aha! Seems like it's starting!"

But — "it seemed like that" throughout the afternoon! Distant artillery fire, closer bursts from machine guns and, from time to time, single shots from hand weapons, then silence again, and then once again the same music. On the other hand, as the day passes, the weather changes. Heavy clouds move in, covering the sky, and finally about four o'clock a light rain begins to fall. Weary and tired out by restless waiting, people start going back to the barracks.

"Today I'm making *supper*!" announces Radek to the astonishment of our whole group, and especially Romek, who didn't find anything in the mattress except some fine straw.

"Dinner? Out of what?"

"Peas!"

"Peas?!" We open our mouths in wonder.

"And you're going to tend the fire," orders Radek; "Antoś Majchrzak is going to run to the rabbit pen for more fuel. Romek and I are going to sneak quietly into the barracks next door in search of salt."

An order! Coming!

It's almost five o'clock in the afternoon. The drizzle continues stubbornly. Radek, Romek, and Antoś are busy with the preparations. Wrapped in an old military coat, I'm crouching near the barracks watching the treasure, that is, the peas cooking in a can, which sits on three bricks placed in the small street. Our "hearth" is located where we can look directly across the wire fencing that up to now has separated the small street of Block 26 (where we've been living now for several days), across the moat, across the camp wires, across the canal and the Road of Death, straight into the area of the SS barracks. Even yesterday individual SS men were moving around there, but since this morning not a single one is to be seen. There hasn't been any gunfire for a good hour. Silence. An unpleasant silence. They won't come now today for sure. Is the solitary mustachioed SS man in the guard tower "worried" like me? What kinds of thoughts are going through the head today of a hungry man who's watching the treasure of a dinner being cooked? ... All kinds. Especially, however, about members of his family, who haven't had a sign of life from him in months, or who, perhaps, are no longer alive? After all, it's so easy to have an "accident" during bombings. And Bydgoszcz — according to what newspapers were still reporting — had been hit again, and hit hard.

"Hurray, Americans!" I suddenly hear a shout coming from the direction of the guardhouse.

"Has someone gone crazy?"

"Hurray, Americans! Hurray, Americans!" It's no longer a single voice, there are hundreds, thousands of roars rising up to the cloudy sky. I jump up!

"Americans!!!" I don't know myself how that cry bursts out of me: Americans!

People are rushing out of the barracks in streams. Nothing can stop them now! They're rushing right toward the enclosure that blocks entry to the small street.

"Oh, Lord! My peas!"

The frantic mob pushes... In a second the wires go down, together with the huge poles. The first ranks fall under pressure from those who follow. The raging wave moves over them!

"Americans! Americans!"

Two soldiers in gray are moving along a small street between the SS barracks. In front of them is an enormous German shepherd, with his nose pointed downward, sniffing, and behind him a prisoner in a striped uniform.

Could these be soldiers?! Wearing some kind of greenish-gray windbreakers and helmets, or maybe not helmets, on their heads, they somehow look sporty, like hunters stalking an animal; they're probably not soldiers. They don't have any knapsacks or ration kits or bayonets! Only the short rifles in their hands and that stealthy, catlike gait betray that these are, after all, that perhaps they are...

The first soldier, sticking his head out carefully from behind the corner of the barracks toward the Road of Death and looking around quickly, fires a burst of shots from his hip toward the crematorium.

"Jesus!"

The second one signals to us with a hand gesture to drop to the ground. Can you drop down in such a crowd? We stand.

And they fire bursts of shots to one side, then to the other, and signal for the SS man in Tower B (which stands closest to the top of our barracks) to come down. Joyous, emotional shouts resound from the square. A person can express joy about freedom this way only if he has already stood with one foot in the grave...

In Tower B we hear the tapping and thumping of many feet, running down the wooden stairs. The door opens with a bang, and ... the scene takes our breath away: instead of one mustachioed SS man, who was visible throughout the day inside the glass-enclosed section of the tower, several of them run out! Young! Armed to the teeth! Hand grenades on their belts! Steel helmets on their heads! Good Lord!

"Look how much vermin sat hidden in there," whispers Reverend Rector Banaszak, squeezing me impulsively by the elbow. "Thirteen! Fourteen! Fourteen men armed as if for an attack at the front!"

Could it have been a trap? ... Had this been a precautionary reserve "just in case"? ... Was this part of a plan for slaughtering the camp in the evening? ... Who knows?

60. The Last Sunday

Both short Americans (as a rule, these GI's were all short in stature. Perhaps so they would take up less space in tiny reconnoitering tanks?) approach the canal by way of the Road of Death, holding submachine guns on their hips to cover the standing SS men. One gives the SS men a sign to throw down their weapons. With trembling hands, the SS men take off their guns, unbuckle their revolvers and grenades and place them in stacks. That's according to regulations since a soldier is taught to respect his weapon.

In the meantime, while the first American holds the SS men who are disarming at the point of his submachine gun, the second one, also keeping his weapon aimed at those laying down their arms, crosses the canal bridge toward them and, when he gets there, orders them to put up their hands.

"*Hände hoch*!" the "order" comes from our group of prisoners standing by the wall behind the fencing.

The obedient SS men raise their hands over their heads. The American pats down their sides and pockets, in search of weapons and, not finding any, gives a sign with his head to the one standing across the canal. The latter walks toward those standing in line. The first American enters the tower, but suddenly runs out and sprays a burst of shots inside!

After a while, a fifteenth SS man comes out, a young fellow, maybe seventeen years old. He comes out with his hands up over his head and stands at the end of the line with his colleagues. The American searches his sides and pockets, his pants legs, and he's just about to turn around and leave, when suddenly he aims his gun at him, reaches under the fellow's shirt and pulls out a revolver. As he shows it to his buddy, he tells him something in English, throws the revolver into the canal, moves away a few steps, and before we have a chance to realize what's happening, he fires a burst of shots along the line of the SS men, and ... fifteen bodies are kicking the dirt in agony! A few shoves with the foot and they fall into the canal. The current takes away the corpses...

"Horrible," whispers Reverend Rector Banaszak with emotion. "How cheap life is! For one pigheaded boy, fourteen older men, perhaps fathers of families, have lost their lives..."

"He must have been one of those young Hitler kids."

"But what did he hope to gain? He wanted to save the situation with one revolver?"

"The law of war is terrible."

"And didn't he know about it?"

"Hey! Put on a happy expression! Don't you see, they're taking our picture!"

Indeed, both Americans are taking pictures. They're armed only with a small submachine gun and a camera.

"Okay!" one of them calls, smiling from under his helmet.

"What did he say?"

"That he'll take you to Hollywood."

"You're stupid."

Seeing that both Americans are heading along the canal toward the guard tower, the crowd moves in the same direction, stepping on each other, pushing, and again venting their joy by shouting.

"Let's run toward the camp street," advises the Reverend Rector. "We'll get to the assembly square before they do."

Unfortunately, the camp street is so crammed that it's hard to push through.

"Let's go into the side street!"

We enter the assembly square from a street next to the clinic mortuary just at the moment when a dozen or so young Russians lift up rifles aimed at several dozen SS men, who stand with their hands up along the wall separating the assembly square from the plantation.

"Don't shoot, comrade," they call. "We're Russians, too!"

"You're Russian and so's your mother! But you knew how to murder!"

Irregular shots are fired, guided by incompetent hands. Barely five fall at once, those who were struck squarely. Others fall to their knees; one sways leaning against the wall. From the lips of the wounded burst forth screams of despair, entreaties, pleading!

"Forgive us! Mercy!"

The young Russians finish off killing the wounded...

"Let's go! I can't watch this. The Americans shouldn't allow these things to happen. If they're shooting, that's understandable, after all they're soldiers, but to give weapons to these kids, that's already a crime."

Edek Francuskiewicz shows up.

"Edek, why are they shooting them?"

"They're from the tower across from the guardhouse. When the Americans were already coming into the square, one of them started to fire at them."

"But that was their right."

"No! As soon as the white flag went up as a sign of surrender, they didn't have the right to fire. That transgression is considered one of the most punishable violations of the law of war. Look over there: white flags on the towers, and when the other side approaches, they open fire on them..."

The assembly square, covered with piles of trash, the place where poor souls arriving in evacuation transports had camped out, is now packed with thousands of cheering prisoners. Young Russians and Italians, hiding in barracks from the time they were being rounded up for evacuation transports, are now coming out by the thousands. Scenes are being played out that no pen can describe.

From the guardhouse gate, prisoners are carrying a young American soldier. Hoisted over the heads of the shouting human multitude, he gives a sign with his hand and calls out: "Are there any Poles here?!"

"Jesus! It's an American of Polish descent!"

"Of course! There are Poles here! There are several thousand of us!"

"I'm from Cleveland! When I was leaving for the front, my sister gave this to me." He opens his shirt. "She sewed it herself and asked that I give it to the first Poles." He takes out a package, opens it, and ... we stand amazed: over the head of the soldier flutters a small flag with the Polish national colors!

"Poland has not yet perished," someone intones the national anthem.

"As long as we still live!" picks up the crowd of thousands... Tears stream down the sunken, emaciated faces...

Someone with good foresight turned off the electric current from the camp's wire fences. In no time, the group of prisoners rushes toward them. They tear them down! The crowd makes its way to the American soldiers across the canal... In the street leading to the guardhouse stand several small tanks... Inside the guardhouse gate, prisoners are hugging the unit's chaplain. Afterwards, they raise a small, slender soldier up in their arms. What a surprise! His lips are painted red! It turns out this is a young American female reporter!

Someone has stuck a Polish white and red flag on top of the guardhouse tower. Cheers, applause, and shouts of joy come from the crowded square! At the time of liberation, there are thirty-seven different nationalities in the camp, but the biggest group is ours, the Poles, because there are about thirteen thousand of us. Half are farm laborers; then there are about four thousand skilled workers and almost two thousand small farmers. So the majority are simple people, but with hearts that are sound, enthusiastic, and very much subject to emotion.[1]

"Long live Poland!"

"Long may it live! Long may it live! Long may it live!"

The chaplain of the Seventh Army, which liberated the camp, steps out with his associates into a small guardhouse gallery that is just under the enormous clock and lifts his arms up high, as a sign that he'd like to speak.

The crowd of thirty thousand gradually quiets down, and only in places along its periphery the enthusiasm doesn't die out.

"*Brothers!*" the strong words flow into the crowd from on high. "Today, after many years of suffering, you have once again become free men! No one calls you prison slaves any more! You return again to the great family of free people! That's why I call to you with all my heart: *Brothers*! Don't thank us, but thank Almighty God for your rescue! Let each one of you, in his native tongue, say with me a prayer of thanksgiving: Our Father, who art in heaven..."

"Hallowed be thy name! Thy kingdom come! Thy will be done," chant tens of thousands of voices...

One of the soldiers tapes the entire event on a magnetic tape. Next to the chaplain stands the young woman reporter in uniform and several soldiers, and all hold helmets in their hands pressed to their hearts, with heads bowed.

"And forgive us our trespasses as we forgive those who trespass against us, and deliver us from evil. Amen."

"Amen ... men ... men," the echo carries from the square out between the barracks, to the execution yard, to the SS barracks, to the vast plantations, up to the dark line of the forest.

The woman reporter speaks after the chaplain. The wind blows her blond hair, and although we don't understand her words and don't know what she's saying, judging by the girl's flushed cheeks, her trembling painted lips, the gestures of her slender hand (in her other hand she's holding her helmet), we infer that she's saying words that are not just ordinary, that they come from the depths of her heart, that they're full of emotion...

The soldier continues to tape, moving the microphone under the speaker's lips.

When the reporter has finished her talk, someone with a strong voice, trembling with emotion, intones, "O God, who through..." and thirteen thousand voices pick it up, "so many centuries surrounded Poland with the brilliance of power and glory!" The soldier doing the taping holds the microphone toward the square.

"To your altars we bring our prayer: return a free Homeland to us, Lord!"

We choke with emotion. Something is tugging at our hearts. No one is ashamed of tears. The chaplain puts on his hat again, as do the rest of those with him; they wave their hands in a friendly manner for a while, and then disappear inside the tower.

"Long live, America!"

"Long may it live! Long may it live! Long may it live!" The joyous excitement of the huge crowd is reaching its peak.

Suddenly, a dissonance penetrates this chord of joy. Hundreds of young Russians and

Italians surround the guardhouse. They grab hold of the grilles on the lower windows, climb up them from the windows to the ledges, then to the upper windows that have no grilles; you hear windows being broken, and the swarm of locusts climbing the walls pours inside.

After a while typewriters, stacks of documents, books, all kinds of office equipment, and finally furniture fly out through the windows into the square.

"Good Lord! Look at that vandalism," whispers Reverend Rector Banaszak, holding me by the arm. "But these are real barbarians! It's shameful, in front of these soldiers and this chaplain, who just now recited a prayer with us. Let's leave. I can't look at this."

Well, yes. Dachau, the camp of political prisoners, filled up last year with an element that was not always "political." Among thirteen thousand of us Poles, there were about five hundred criminals, who had been sentenced earlier in Poland, and what can be said about those thousands of undisciplined young Russians, Ukrainians, Italians, and others?[2]

Tomorrow and the day after, committees formed to deal with specific and pressing matters pertaining to these thousands will search in vain for typewriters, paper, and ink because today the human barbarians are destroying them!

We push our way through the crowd, moving toward the camp street. It's not so easy to wade through this surging wave! Here, some prisoners crowd around one of the soldiers; over there, they toss another one up in the air, and in still another place, they carry the conqueror in their arms. We notice that the soldiers, while yielding to the crowd's signs of joy, hold onto their submachine guns, keep their helmets on, and continue to be attentive to what's around them. Simply put, we don't realize that freedom has trickled onto this piece of land in only a small stream, that all around the camp mortal danger still lies in wait, that people are dying, that the war has not yet ended. The soldiers are well aware of this, and that's why they're so watchful.

At the crowd's request, the soldiers shot "Black" Wernike and one of his informers. The camp's senior official, the Georgian Meansarian, met the same fate. Just a while ago they were in command; now they lie thrown upon the pile of corpses.

The crowd drags suspects from the barracks and lynches them! Together with freedom being gained, all dams break open! The words of the prayer just recited, "and forgive us our trespasses," have flown off somewhere with the wind!

We leave because maybe we could catch it, too!

From the tops of the barracks fly the national flags of thirty-seven nationalities. What surprises us very much, however, is to see flying next to them many red communist flags with the hammer and sickle! Look! over there on the Russian barracks, on the Yugoslav, the Bulgarian, the Italian, the Czech, and on many others that house mixed nationalities.

"I didn't realize there are so many communists and their sympathizers in the camp."

"There really are a lot of them!"

On the camp street and small streets there is the same joyous frenzy as in the square, with this difference, that on these streets the first moments of freedom are experienced by unfortunates who don't have the strength to walk or drag themselves to the square. Crawling out from the barracks are half-corpses, human skeletons, lice-infested, stinking of pus and feces; bits of inarticulate sound break out of their festering throats. But, after all, is it possibly some kind of speech? Who even knows all the languages spoken today in Dachau? Dragging along, as they hold on for dear life to the walls, are shadows of people, emaciated from bloody diarrhea, typhus, hunger, and fever. Just once to look at the face of freedom and then — so be it, even if one must die! In gaunt faces covered with boils there stirs a joy not seen for a long time. Battered human dignity has roused itself. In front of Block 22, a half-naked "Mussulman" holds a pole with both hands, dancing around it. Tears, mixed with blood, stream from his festering eyes. "Free! Free!" His toothless lips try to smile again. We look at his rotten gums, wasted away by scurvy...

"He's a mathematics professor," whispers Fr. Banaszak.

People who don't know each other, who've been pushed from recently arrived evacuation transports into one or another of the Dachau barracks, throw their arms around each other, hugging, kissing, crying together.

"We're free! Brother! We're free!"

Those who realized sooner than others that even their stomachs should take part in the general merriment are already returning through the plantation gate. They're hauling bags of peas, beans, and potatoes. Here and there, they build camp fires. The starving human throng, which has not had anything in its mouth for so many days, is waiting for a bowl of food. It doesn't matter that there are still stacks of corpses in the block streets; it doesn't matter that the stopped-up toilets stink, that human waste is scattered all around, hunger must be appeased! That is a first desire of the free.

At the guardhouse gate lies the only prisoner shot by the Americans while the camp was being seized: Patalas from Poznań. A tailor by trade. He worked at a plant that serviced the seminary there, so we knew him even during our days of freedom. He was coming back from the W.B. just as the American tanks were approaching the guardhouse. Dressed in clothes that once belonged to Jews, not understanding the language, he didn't stop when they called, and — a burst from a machine gun cut him down. They had mistaken him for an SS man in disguise.

The human swarm is still bubbling over in the assembly square; meanwhile, evening falls.

When we finally reach the chapel, it's almost full. Eucharistic Jesus reigns in the monstrance.

"We praise Thee, O God," flows the melody of the thanksgiving hymn! "We acknowledge Thee to be the Lord!" ... And then — the litany to the Immaculate Mother... "Dear Mother, Protectress of people... Exiles of Eve... Have pity, have pity, don't let us wander homeless!..." Darkness falls outside the windows. The first evening of freedom after so many years!

From the square, the streets, and the neighboring barracks comes the sound of a crowd drunk with freedom; it comes like the distant murmur of a waterfall. For the first time in years all the lights in the camp are turned on. (Due to fear of Allied airstrikes, the camp was under orders to remain dark.) Not one of us thinks about how, at any minute, German aircraft could fly over and... How many bombs are needed to turn this packed crowd into a heap of flesh torn to bits? You need only one aircraft!

They say that about three hundred SS men were taken prisoner at the camp. All the more prominent ones saved themselves by fleeing.

Yesterday, Saturday, the Americans had already attempted to take the Amper River valley; since they encountered considerable resistance, however, (apparently about four hundred of them were killed) they withdrew in order to "prepare" the area by bombing from aircraft on Monday, and only afterward were they to move with armored units. On Sunday afternoon, following morning services (if it's a matter of duty to God, an American, whatever his religion, is very conscientious, even in the front lines), they sent out a motorized patrol to conduct a reconnaissance; it consisted of twenty-four people (including a chaplain and a female reporter). On a railroad siding near the town of Dachau, this patrol came upon a train with over forty closed freight cars. Imagine the horror felt by the American soldiers when, upon opening the cars, they found them loaded with corpses of prisoners who had starved to death! The chaplain, after saying prayers over the victims, gazes at the soldiers' faces as they stand with uncovered heads. There are twenty-two of them, plus a slim young woman in uniform.

Not a word is uttered. Their eyes are speaking... In the distance looms the camp...

"Guys! It's true we don't have an order, but ... if ... Do we go?"

"We go!"

Twenty-two young men from New Jersey, Pennsylvania, Chicago, Buffalo, and Cleveland, from the distant open spaces of Arizona, from sunny California and Louisiana, advance stealthily with rifles toward the SS barracks and the camp. They move like cats, and only their hearts are pounding, while before their half-closed, straining eyes the picture still remains of those thousands starved in railcars... A young, twenty-year-old lieutenant is in the lead. A handful of madmen, deployed only to conduct reconnaissance, makes an attempt to seize the mother of camps and SS headquarters for all of Germany!

Madmen!

And yet — it is precisely this handful of madmen who capture three hundred SS men armed to the teeth. They seize the formidable SS barracks. They free almost forty thousand prisoners!

They alone know what kind of risk they took! That is why, while we're overcome with joy and imagine that nothing now threatens us any longer, they're aware that at any time a stronger SS military unit could arrive, and then...

The SS Viking Division is coming in haste from Munich to burn down the camp!

It's supposed to be defended by a handful of American GI's and a chaplain! A radio message goes out to the rear units: "We have taken the mother of concentration camps, Dachau! With it — SS barracks, warehouses and factories belonging to the complex! Three hundred SS men have been taken prisoner! The Germans don't realize what a small handful they have to deal with. In addition, we're threatened by an approaching division from Munich. Request you provide defensive fire so we can hold out until morning!"

The general swears! The colonel nervously chews gum. The radiotelegraph operator scratches his head.

"Tomorrow, I'm going to, all of them! I'm going to ... lock them up! And that lieutenant will be demoted..."

"Well, general," the colonel has stopped chewing for a moment, "it's not so much the lieutenant as that chaplain... Don't you know him, general? He's a madman!"

At mention of the chaplain, the general's anger subsides. The chaplain ... If each chaplain in the American army is someone who must be especially respected, then this one from the Seventh Army, this madman, enjoys such respect both among the troops and all the officers that even the general himself...

The general paces back and forth for a while, stifling what's left of his anger. Finally he says:

"Okay! It's no use! Provide defensive fire from all guns! Don't spare it! Those twenty-two madmen..."

"Twenty-four," corrects the colonel.

60. The Last Sunday

"What twenty..."

"The chaplain and the reporter."

"Ah! Then we need to save those twenty-two madmen and two super-madmen, the chaplain and that kid Elsie. As soon as it's daybreak, we advance full force! Then we'll show them what it means to ignore the orders of their superiors..."

"But I think we'll need to prepare twenty-four awards."

"Awards?" the general flushes.

The young colonel nods his head and smiles.

We're sitting in the rabbit warren, where Fr. Antoś Majchrzak has invited us for a rabbit supper, when suddenly we freeze in fear. We hear whizzing, howling, and wailing just above us.

"Mother of God! Is it Germans?"

A second passes, and from the fields come powerful, distant explosions. And again: howling, whizzing, wailing just above us and more explosions!

We run outside. Above us is a spider web of fire.

"You know what? That's the Americans providing defensive fire," Reverend Rector Banaszak, the eldest of the terrified group, finally explains. "It will probably go on like this until morning, when their main forces arrive."

And that, indeed, is how it was until dawn. For several hours during the night, hundreds of artillery shells rushed over our heads, exploding several kilometers from the camp, barring access to it by SS units.

The young lieutenant is sleeping, propped against the edge of a table. In the night darkness a dozen American GI's walk around the camp, watching over us, the liberated. The reporter is tapping out an article on a manual typewriter. The chaplain stands at a window without panes, whispering prayers, and looks over at the camp, where a human throng of thousands in dark, lice-infested barracks is experiencing the miracle of a first night of freedom.

If it were not for the chaplain and his twenty-two men, we would all have perished. Heaven sent us this deliverance at the last minute.

In the commandant's office, they found an order from Himmler himself... Its origin is as follows: sometime in mid–April, when the situation at the front had already become hopeless, the camp commandant turned to Himmler with a proposal to transfer the prisoners to the advancing Allies. As an answer, he received an order, dated 14 April, from which I quote an excerpt word for word: *"Die Übergabe kommt nicht in Frage. Das Lager ist sofort zu evakuieren. Kein Häftling darf lebendig in die Hände des Feindes kommen..."*

(—) H. Himmler

```
atek z rozkazu H. Himmlera dla Dachau
  lossenburga w odpowiedzi na propozycję
 endanta obozu wydania obozu aliantom:
14. 4. 45.
" O oddaniu nie może być mowy.
 Obóz należy natychmiast ewakuować.
 aden więzień nie może dostać się
 żywy w ręce nieprzyjaciela. Wię-
 źniowie zachowali się okropnie
 wobec ludności cywilnej w Buchenwaldzie."
             (-) H.Himmler

   iąg ze sprawozdania sSS. Hauuptsturmführ.
   warza, który przedstawiono SS. Obergruppen-
       rohlowi w dniu 24 kwietnia.

    . 45
      ie bergabe kommt nicht in Frage.
           er ist sofort zu ev      eren.
```

A documentary text of Himmler's orders for the immediate evacuation of the Dachau camp, or ... its slaughter, because "No prisoner is to fall into enemy hands alive."

In English translation:

"A transfer" (of the camp to the Allies) "is completely out of the question. The camp must be evacuated immediately. No prisoner is to fall into enemy hands alive..."

Evacuating the camp was not feasible because, although several thousand had been led out, delayed evacuation transports from other camps would arrive in their place, including those forty railcars of corpses on the sidetrack; therefore, what remained was the second part of Himmler's order, contained in the sentence, "No prisoner is to fall into enemy hands alive!"

The Dachau camp was to be burned and all prisoners murdered, precisely on Sunday evening, 29 April! The SS Viking Division was already marching toward Dachau! Twenty-two American boys with their chaplain and a young female reporter beat the SS men by several hours, and now a defensive barrage guards access...

It's already late at night. After eating supper in the rabbit warren, we go to our respective halls. I don't want to sleep this first night. After adoration in the chapel, where the floor continues to be covered with people lying side by side, I sit once again in the washroom on the basin for washing feet, and I write. I've thrown out the can in which I was to hide this diary. I won't need it anymore; I'll take it like this. Zdzich is asleep, sitting on the stone floor, resting his head on my knees. I feel my legs getting numb, but I'm afraid to move because he might wake up. Water drips from the ill-fitting faucets. All around is the heavy breathing of sleeping colleagues. Every now and then there's a hurricane of fire over our heads, and then explosions break the silence. After that the barracks shake, metal dishes jingle in the cupboards, then again for a while there's silence. The sound of gunfire is coming from the plantation! Could there be some kind of skirmish? Maybe the SS men are arriving? ... But then again we hear shelling above us... Each salvo from heavy guns positioned somewhere tens of kilometers from us provides the joyful certainty that over there are people and hearts who are watching with us, thinking about us, defending us...

"What time is it?" asks Zdzich, who suddenly wakes up.

"I have no idea. In any case, it's still far from morning. Get up! You'll catch cold on these cold bricks. Let's go to the chapel. It's crowded there, too, but you'll find a place somewhere."

The little perpetual lamp flickers at the altar. The floor is covered with sleepers. Zdzich sits down at the wall, making room for me. I don't want to sleep! I won't sleep! You don't sleep through a night like this! There, in the tabernacle is God become Man. True God and true Man! Why have we so greatly blurred the dogmatic truth about His Humanity? Why do we meditate on it so little? ... Perhaps that's why Jesus is so distant for us, placed so high, on a throne, in heaven, and is so little seen with eyes of faith on earth. After all, like us, He used to sit down tired; He, too, was thirsty, hungry, humanly worn out; and just as we are today — He was joyful. Man — God ... God become Man! My Jesus! I believe in You, worship You, trust in You, and love You, asking You to forgive all those who don't believe in You, who don't ... (again violent gunfire can be heard coming from the plantation!) ... don't worship, don't trust, and don't love You!

Once again a wave of fire has passed over our heads, howling, whizzing, cackling! ... Seconds of silence and ... again explosions! The red flame of the perpetual lamp flickers. St. Joseph, liberator of the prisoner group, "my St. Joseph," caressed with crooked fingers from a block of birchwood, is smiling... Somewhere in far-off Portugal, Sister Lucy of the Immaculate Heart of Mary is kneeling at the tabernacle, making amends for a sinful world...

Because, Sister Lucy, you weren't with us in Dachau, you don't know what these years were and therefore... But, Sister, please tell your Heavenly Lady that it's not out of disrespect for this holy place that they lie here side by side, sleeping by the tabernacle; please, Sister, say that...

"What are you muttering?" Zdzich's voice brings me back to consciousness.

"Was I asleep?"

"And how! And you mutter so much that nobody can sleep."

Through faded colors of the chapel's painted windows joyful rays of the sun fall within. It's the sun of the first day of freedom!

Epilogue

Shavelings is a chronicle, a historical work, a document without any fictional plot. So let this epilogue of that period on the fate of almost three thousand Polish priests, barely one-fourth of whom survived, continue along the same lines. I turn then to the pages of my diary to provide just a few short notes about the days after liberation.

Dachau on Monday, 30 April 1945

The first morning of freedom! We are intoxicated with that word: Freedom! Free! Liberated! To freedom!

When we finally get up after that first unforgettable night of freedom, we already see racing around outside the coiled barbed wire of the camp some small, fast, maneuverable military vehicles, which — as we learn later — are called jeeps. Farther away, mud-covered tanks are resting after a long journey. All around there's activity; troops are everywhere. This creates a strange impression on us. Accustomed to seeing the European soldier, loaded down like a camel and in a tight uniform buttoned up to the chin, we get the impression as we look at the American soldier that this is rather a type of sportsman or perhaps a hunter, although even that last comparison is not quite suitable. The European hunter goes hunting wearing more of a military outfit than these Americans who come to seize Germany. This surprises us, but as we become more familiar with it, we begin to like it. Those rubber-soled, comfortable shoes in which the feet step quietly like cats' feet, those comfortable uniforms worn with a certain nonchalance typical of Americans, that lack of decorations for some kind of senseless military drill, the friendly saluting by a touch of the hand even to an uncovered head, that mutually friendly relationship between a private and an officer, what's more — even right up to the general himself, that lack of fawning servility: all this jars us at first, but slowly it wins us over, and finally we begin to like it. Democracy!

They brought in some biscuits and other food; they brewed the first real coffee; but these units, chasing the enemy and supplied with only the most basic food rations, cannot treat us more generously.

"Food transports are coming behind us. They'll arrive in a few days," the soldiers comfort us, sharing with us all that they have.

The former prisoners "appropriate" a bit from the warehouses that are, unfortunately, practically empty, as well as from the plantation; but what does that mean for the hundreds of thousands? Hunger continues in the liberated camp! People continue to die! They continue to take the dead out to the existing piles of corpses, turned green and now terribly malodorous.

Around noon trucks come in, bringing thousands of cans of horse meat that was acquired by the Americans on their way to Munich.

Joy in the camp! The first nourishment!

Control over the camp was transferred to an "International Committee," made up of representatives of each nationality. Orders, proclamations, and appeals start to appear.

The Rev. Canon Jedwabski assumes authority over the clerical group. There is talk about checking us out and issuing substitute identity papers. We hope the bishops' curia in Munich can provide us help in this matter.

Like the proverbial cat around a bowl of hot milk, I walk around the person who assigns places on the list for celebrating Mass. I live in the hope of possibly getting a place on the list of names of hundreds of others who are just as eager. After so many years, to stand at the altar, that will be some experience!

"Let's wait until the first rush is over," advises Jasio Januszewski. "We'll get our turn, too."

Taking advantage of the fact that many colleagues spend hours outside the barracks, I catch up on sleep lost in the past nights, although I'm afraid of lice. Typhus is still around. To get it now and die when already liberated would really be a great pity.

Toward evening that same day.

Thousands of young Italians, Russians, and others, including our Polish boys (those the SS men moved here from jobs during recent months, accused of various offenses) started out early this morning for an "appropriation" in the town of Dachau and the surrounding area. They return loaded with everything that caught the fancy of their greed! Some are hauling handcarts, others — how amusing it is, given the total disgust this scene evokes — are pushing baby carriages. They plundered all kinds of things! Of course, they bring things that are needed, such as underwear, clothing, shoes, food; but there are also things that are completely useless, for example, wall clocks, irons, furniture parts. If they "went on a spree" over there as they did yesterday at the guardhouse, then we can expect that tomorrow or the next day this same mob could "go on a spree" in our clerical barracks.

Following evening services, one of our colleagues brings news that the Americans are fixing the camp fences, securing the coiled barbed wire, and posting guards around the camp. At first this surprises us, but when some clarifications are provided about today's "doings" committed by the above whippersnappers, we see the wisdom of such an order.

"There is another reason for this lockup," explains the bearer of this news, "namely, that typhus continues in the camp, and American physicians have ordered a month-long quarantine."

"A quarantine for a month?!"

"On condition that the epidemic dies out. Otherwise, the isolation could last two months or longer."

Dachau, 1 May 1945

Today is a cool and cloudy day. A cold rain is falling. Many barracks, however, are overflowing with greenery, cut from the camp poplars. Dismally drooping from the edges of roofs are dozens of red communist flags. After all, today is their holiday!

One of our colleagues "appropriated" a radio set somewhere, perhaps acquired by one of the youths in yesterday's looting, so we sit listening, engrossed. We're interested in the "Free Europe" radio broadcast. "Poles," the speaker calls with pathos, "you're free! However, our Poland is not free... There the enemy continues to trample Polish fields... You are free! No one is forcing you to return. You have complete freedom of choice! Those who decide to remain in temporary exile will be fully cared for by governments of the western Allies. Poles!..."

"That doesn't pertain to us," someone grumbles. "The western Allies surround us with such friendly care that they've locked us in quarantine and are telling us to die!"

I read and write, and I sleep, and then I read again. I have to get going on completing the small Crucifix. I believe now that I'll be able to take it out of Dachau...

"Friends, do you know how many in the camp died today?" The speaker, who has just arrived, is silent a moment, wishing to make a bigger impression: "*Over two thousand!*"

"More than two thousand?"

"Yes. Twisting of the bowels, caused by that canned horse meat!"

"God!"

"After all, organisms were exhausted and starved for such a long time, and here suddenly the tough canned horse meat!"

Yesterday we were passed over during distribution of the cans. The shavelings have gotten packages and don't need it! — it was decided.

Our luck! How many of us would be among the dead today?

Dachau on 2 May 1945

Again today it's cold, damp, dreary. How this weather influences people's mood! We sit in the barracks. It's hard to stick one's nose outside. It's terribly crowded. More than three hundred of us live in a hall that's 150 square meters in area, that is, barely half a square meter falls to each individual. Many sit in the entryway or in the washroom on brick floors; those suffering from diarrhea (there continues to be no shortage of them) seek a place either in the bathroom or nearby. The stench from clogged toilets reaches even to the hall. We're still hungry. Following the recent death of thousands due to canned food, the American doctors have ordered the camp to be placed on a special diet. They want our stomachs to get used to normal food, and our bowels are growling — from one morning to the next.

The stacks of bodies, which include SS men shot to death, continue to remain within the camp. There are visits from some committees, groups of reporters and officers; they conduct interviews, take hundreds of pictures, shoot a film, and, covering their noses, make their escape, while we continue to live with the cadaverous smell of hundreds of rotting bodies!

A group of Poles, former W.B. workers, received permission to go to the plants and build a cross, which is to be erected tomorrow on the assembly square. They've come to ask me to carve a figure of Christ, but how can I do that in just a few hours? Moreover, the cross is supposed to be 16 meters high, so the figure of Christ would have to be at least life-size.

The "Polish Committee" is preparing feverishly for tomorrow's celebration.

Seminarian Władzio Sarnik from Włocławek is painting an enormous picture of Our Lady of Jasna Góra.

And I'm depressed. I can't contain my bitterness because so far I haven't been able to celebrate holy Mass, although some colleagues have already stood twice at the altar. Jasio tells me not to worry. Zdzich grumbles and, full of bitterness, "threatens" that even if they should now offer him the chance, he won't take it. He'll wait until his release. (That's a peculiar kind of revenge!)

Dachau, 3 May 1945

The weather isn't any better, but the Polish barracks are covered in greenery and national colors... A huge cross was set up on the assembly square, and in front of it a field altar with a picture of Our Lady of Częstochowa.

At 10 o'clock a solemn holy Mass will take place on the square.

5 May 1945

The first Saturday of the month, feast of the Immaculate Heart of Mary. To this day I haven't been successful in getting to celebrate holy Mass. I'm so filled with resentment toward everyone and toward myself as well...

The weather is good today. For the first time in many days it's sunny. The camp, which up to now had a gloomy appearance, is taking on colors and making us more cheerful. Thousands of prisoners are coming out of stuffy barracks into the fresh May air. Radio broadcasts are bringing the latest news every few minutes, but ... when will this horrible war finally end?

I take a book and also come out of the barracks. The small street is packed with people. I walk along the block wall toward the moat that surrounds the camp because no one is there. I'll take a breather. That terrible crowding, that crush, that constant stepping on each other's heels is making all of us nervous, but perhaps me in particular.

The ground is wet, and the cold still rises from it. I sit on a piece of board that's warm from the sun. In front of me is the guard tower from which in either direction run barbed-wire coils that have already been repaired; behind them is an American guard walking slowly back and forth along the Road of Death. What is he waiting for? Is it for us to be finally consumed by the typhus epidemic? After all, we're free people! Why do they continue to treat us like slaves? Like animals at a zoo into which a horrible glanders germ has crept?

The Crucifix that was carved secretly in Dachau by the author and kept hidden until the days of liberation. The loin cloth covering the Lord is the color of the striped prison uniform that was worn by Polish priests, with a number and a red triangle on it. The carving measures 20 inches high and 10 inches across.

Each day hundreds of new curiosity seekers arrive; they stand behind the moat and wires, tell us to "put on a happy face," take pictures, and then throw us bags of some kind of food. Really, just like a cage for monkeys at the zoo.

"Hey!" I hear someone behind me calling. I don't turn around. Well, what for? I open Hamsun's *Die Weiber am Brunnen* in order to read.

Seconds later Zdzich stops in front of me.

"I signed you up on the list of volunteers for celebrating Mass. They've accepted us both. We're leaving in half an hour."

"What do you mean? Are you crazy? Celebrate at this time of day?"

"Over there they celebrate not only throughout the whole day, but also throughout all hours of the night!"

"I don't understand."

"You see," he explains, squatting in front of me. "The Americans have finally become mindful of the thousands of dying wretches. They've more or less fixed up the SS barracks and set up a temporary hospital in them for about fifteen thousand patients. Of course, everything is in short supply, except beds. These they have. However, there's a shortage of personnel. They can provide only two physicians and four nurses at this time."

"For fifteen thousand patients?"

"That's right. Remember that in providing even that much, they're taking personnel away from their own soldiers at the front. After all, the war is still going on, and battles are being fought. Therefore, they've turned to the camp itself, asking for volunteer nurses and…"

"And you volunteered us both."

"That's right. Besides, those who also volunteered are Romek Budniak and Antoś Majchrzak and Józio Woźniak and Fr. Piotrowski from Owińska and Leoś Michałowski and Stefcio Flisiak and Michał Bąkowski and Jasio Przydacz and many others, fifty in all. In a quarter of an hour we're supposed to be in front of the guardhouse ready to go."

The clock on the guard tower shows four o'clock when the familiar iron gate opens in front of us.

"Fifty Polish priests to the hospital as nurses!" the fellow leading us reports to the American guard.

"Okay!" the busy jaws continue chewing gum. The heavy gate closes behind us.

Beyond the little bridge, we make a turn onto the Road of Death. The sun is setting behind the dark tops of fir trees surrounding the crematorium. Its blackened chimney stands out against the dusky blue of the May sky. To the right, beyond the canal and the coiled wire, lie stuffy barracks filled with human wretchedness. Before us is the black, gravel-paved Road of Death. So many thousands walked this way to lose their lives; bringing our whole life as a gift obtained through the pleas of our Lady, we walk here on this her day, the first Saturday. Isn't it fitting that we, who have been so blessed, should bring aid to those who are near death while at the threshold of freedom?

"We're going to celebrate," says Zdzich with a smile.

"That's right, Zdzich … *we're going to celebrate at the altar of love.*"

After almost six years spent behind the barbed wire of a death camp, we enter life again free…

What will it bring us?

Chapter Notes

Chapter 1

1. The Rev. Canon Kazimierz Kinastowski took over as pastor of the parish in Września in 1932, and to this day—the year 1960—he remains in this position.

2. Fr. Henryk Warkoczewski, ordained in 1935, was vicar in Września until June 1939, after which he took over the administration in Rzadkowo, close to the German-Polish border. During the September invasion he went to Warsaw where he took the post of chaplain at a military hospital, and from that time no one knows what became of him. Later inquiries did not yield any results. Most likely, he died during the bombardment of Warsaw in his function as a chaplain of the Polish Forces..

3. Robert Leiber, S.J., "Pius XII," *Stimmen der Zeit*, Nov. 1958.

4. Ibid.

Chapter 2

1. Edmund Jan Osmańczyk, *Dowody prowokacji* (Himmler's unidentified archives), Warsaw, Czytelnik, 1951.

2. Deposition of the Rev. Dr. Prof. Jan Szukalski and the teacher's own deposition.

Chapter 3

1. This was one of the young German women, a Catholic, known to the author by sight. Having secret information about the upcoming arrest of Catholic priests, she wanted to warn us in this manner.

2. In a nearby forest they shot all of the patients from the institution in Świecie. In any case, this followed Hitler's directives regarding the law of euthanasia.

Chapter 4

1. Fr. Leon Michałowski, a professor from Świecie, knew that young German nurse. It was she who informed my parents in Bydgoszcz about where we were staying, and from that time on our families started to visit us, bringing food and clothing.

2. Near the town of Górna Grupa, where the monastery of the Fathers of the Society of the Divine Word (SVD) was located and where we were interned, was Dolna Grupa, an exercise square and Polish Armed Forces barracks. It was there that they held interned Poles, shooting them in nearby woods.

3. Walter Hofer, *Der Nationalsozialismus, Dokumente 1933–1945* (Frankfurt am Main: Fischer Bücherei, 1957) p. 311.

Chapter 5

1. Osmańczyk, *Dowody*.

Chapter 6

1. Following his release from Dachau, Fr. Bernard Czapliński became Auxiliary Bishop of the Chełmno Diocese.

2. Fr. Ignacy Wojewódka and Fr. Wacław Tokarski organized the weekly "Słowo Katolickie" (*Catholic Word*), which was published during the first few weeks after liberation in the Freimann barracks and later in Munich. The publication was later transferred to Paris, where it was integrated with "Polska Wierna" (*Faithful Poland*). Fr. Wojewódka died in 1954 at a journalists' convention in Madrid, Spain. His body was moved to Paris, where it lies at the resting place of meritorious Poles.

Chapter 7

1. In 1958, when German courts were investigating reasons for the arrest of Polish priests, official German representatives charged in correspondence to me that I wrote *Shavelings* less as a priest and more as a Pole. (The correspondence remains in the author's archives.)

2. Taking the above into consideration, I make every effort in the second edition to eliminate this charge. That is why I depend, for the most part,

on German authors and publications, purposely avoiding Polish ones.

Chapter 8

1. The furniture and the entire library of Fr. Górecki, prefect of the Polish high-school in Gdańsk, were confiscated following his arrest and were moved — with a lot of furniture belonging to other Poles, residents of Gdańsk — into warehouses in Nowy Port. From there some articles were transferred to the camp in Stutthof.

Chapter 9

1. As a result of show trials, which Nazism staged against clergy and members of religious orders in Germany, and under the influence of Nazi newspapers that deliberately and falsely magnified these issues, the young SS generation viewed each priest and nun as a criminal or sexual deviate. That was the source of such disgusting provocations and allusions in regard to priests in the camp.

Chapter 10

1. Witnesses to the shooting of the entire so-called "penal company" in camp Stutthof, which consisted almost entirely of Poles from Gdańsk, including the two Polish priests who were mentioned, are all former prisoners of camp Stutthof at that time.

Chapter 11

1. This was an attempt to win over Poles who had German-sounding names, which allegedly were proof of their German ancestry. It misfired in Stutthof. Despite strong pressure, despite enticements and promises and, finally, despite harrassment, not one of the Polish priests who had a German last name presented himself as a *Volksdeutscher*.

Chapter 14

1. Title taken from the German collection of documents: Joe J. Heydecker; Johannes Leeb, *Der Nürnberger Prozess: Bilanz des Tausend Jahre* (Köln-Berlin: Kiepenheuer & Witsch, 1958), p. 321.
2. Ibid.
3. Ibid.
4. Hofer, p. 88.

Chapter 15

1. Hofer, pp. 217, 305.

Chapter 16

1. Hofer, p. 305.

Chapter 17

1. Hofer, p. 88.
2. Ibid., p. 17.
3. Heydecker, p. 338.
4. Ibid., p. 336.
5. Ibid., p. 420.
6. Ibid., p. 134.
7. *Kristall* (magazine), *Die Aussergewöhnliche Illustrierte*, Hamburg, 1959.

Chapter 18

1. Heydecker, p. 165.
2. Jacques Benoist-Méchin, *Der Himmel stürzt ein — Frankreichs Tragödie 1940* (Düsseldorf: Droste Verlag, 1958), p. 23.

Chapter 19

1. Hofer, p. 166.
2. Ibid., p. 108.

Chapter 20

1. Heydecker, p. 337 ff.
2. Hofer, p. 241.

Chapter 22

1. John De Marchi, *The Crusade of Fatima* (New York: P.J. Kennedy & Sons, 1948), p. 157.

Chapter 24

1. De Marchi, p. 157.

Chapter 26

1. Gusen was a camp subordinate to the Mauthausen camp, both located in upper Austria. Camps at quarries were regarded as some of the most horrible. The work and living conditions were much worse than in Dachau. Both Gusen and Mauthausen earned the name "camps of death and extermination." Many Polish priests died in them. Unfortunately, since no German encyclopedias issued after the war include this name, the camp in Gusen has not yet found a writer to provide a narrative about it.

Chapter 29

1. Jan Domagała, *Ci, którzy przeszli przez Dachau [Those Who Passed Through Dachau]* (Warsaw: "Pax," 1957), p. 41.
2. Ibid., p. 42.
3. Ibid., p. 46.

Chapter 31

1. Heydecker, p. 118.
2. Ibid., p. 118.
3. Ibid., p. 122.
4. Ibid., p. 123.
5. Don Sharkey; Joseph Debergh, *Our Lady of Beauraing* (Garden City, NY: Hanover House, 1958); J. B. Lass, *Die Erscheinungen unserer lieben Frau in Banneux*, Innsbruck, Marianischer Verlag, 1956.
6. Domagała, p. 29.

Chapter 32

1. Cardinal E. C. Suhard, "Zmierzch czy rozkwit Kościoła" ("Fall or Rise of the Church") *Słowo Katolickie*, Munich, 1949.

Chapter 33

1. Heydecker, *Der Nürnberger Prozess*, regarding Göring's directive of 31 July 1941, which mandated the arrest of all Jews in Europe.
2. Domagała, p. 45.
3. Heydecker, p. 433.

Chapter 34

1. Note to Minister Ribbentrop from the cardinal who was Secretary of State for His Holiness, dated 2 March 1943, in *The Holy See in Defense of the Rights of Polish Catholics (Stolica św. w obronie praw polskich katolików w Rzeszy i w Polsce pod okupacją niemiecką, dokumenty z lat 1942–1943)* Second edition, Rome, 1946, p. 5.
2. Note of protest from Nuncio Orsenigo in Berlin to the Reich government, ibid., p. 3.
3. Domagała, p. 26.
4. Letter of Cardinal Bertram dated 7 December 1942, describing the difficult conditions of Poles in the Reich: *The Holy See in Defense of the Rights of Polish Catholics*, p. 29.
5. Ibid.

Chapter 35

1. Letter of Cardinal Bertram dated 7 December 1942, p.12.

Chapter 36

1. From that transport, which numbered 500 priests on the day of its arrival (30 October, 1941), only 70 were alive on the day of liberation from Dachau.
2. Eugene Aroneau, *Konzentrationslager-Tatsachenbericht über die an Menscheit begangenen Verbrechen, Dokument F. 321, für den internationalen Militärgerichtshof in Nürnberg* (Concentration Camp Fact Report on the Crimes Committed on Mankind, Document F. 321, for the International Military Tribunal at Nuremburg), provides an alphabetical list of 400 concentration camps as well as their branches, pp. 113–130.

Chapter 37

1. Heydecker, p. 165.
2. The author omits — for obvious reasons — the names of colleagues whose sisters were violated by SS men, but is prepared to provide them to officials if the need arises — after receiving prior permission from those who endured this painful experience.

Chapter 38

1. Note of the nunciature in Berlin regarding Bishop Kozal, *The Holy See in Defense of the Rights of Polish Catholics*, p. 7.

Chapter 39

1. Sister Albana Orłowska of the Order of St. Elizabeth, a native of Sadki in the Wyrzysko District, died on 14 January 1959.
2. Władysław Sarnyk, seminarian from the Wrocław Seminary.

Chapter 40

1. Domagała, p. 45.
2. Since all persons named in *Shavelings* are historical, the Germans and Austrians in this chapter are likewise historical.

Chapter 42

1. Heydecker, pp. 457–459.
2. Ibid., p. 471.

Chapter 43

1. Heydecker, p. 340.
2. Ibid., p. 340.

Chapter 44

1. Heydecker, p. 563.
2. Hofer, pp. 114, 115.
3. Fr. Leon Michałowski endured years in camp Dachau. After he left, he was called to Nuremburg as a witness; he then served several years of pastoral duty in refugee camps in the English zone. In 1951

he emigrated to the United States and settled in Chicago. He served in the parish of St. Francis of Assisi, but the years spent in the camp took their toll and my friend Fr. Leon passed into eternity. He is buried in the Cemetery of St. Wojciech in Chicago.
    4. Heydecker, p. 463.
    5. Ibid., p. 463.

Chapter 45

    1. Joseph Goebbels; Louis Paul Lochner, *The Goebbels Diaries* (Garden City, NY: Doubleday & Co., 1948), p. 224.
    2. Ibid., p. 222.
    3. Heydecker, p. 427.
    4. Domagała, p. 173.
    5. Heydecker, pp. 445 and 562.
    6. Ibid., p. 383.
    7. Goebbels, p. 374.

Chapter 46

    1. Domagała, p. 197.

Chapter 47

    1. Although rather weak for obvious reasons, the spirit of opposition to Nazism spread in Germany, resulting in numerous victims. It reached even to concentration camps here and there. Cf. Leber, Annedore, *Das Gewissen steht auf,* Berlin, Mosaic Verlag, 1954.
    2. Pius XII, "The Act of Holy Consecration to the Immaculate Heart of the Mother of God," *Heilslehre der Kirche*, (Freiburg: Paulusverlag, 1953), p. 326.

Chapter 48

    1. Both Gustaw Morcinek in his *Letters from under the Mulberry* (*Listy spod Morwy*, Paris, Księgarnia Polska, 1945) and Mieczysław Grabiński in his *Diplomacy in Dachau* (*Diplomacja w Dachau*. Dachau: Słowo Polskie, 1946) unfortunately succumbed to propaganda that was being promoted, and they presented this issue nonobjectively and injuriously.
    2. Fr. Tadeusz Etter was consecrated in 1959 as Auxiliary Bishop of Poznań.

Chapter 49

    1. Goebbels, p. 331.
    2. Domagała, p. 158.
    3. Goebbels, pp. 253, 353.
    4. Ibid., p. 252.

Chapter 50

    1. Goebbels, p. 257.
    2. Ibid., pp. 289, 396.
    3. De Marchi, p. 158.

Chapter 51

    1. Domagała, p. 26.
    2. Ibid., p. 45.
    3. Da Fonseca, L. Gonzaga, *Maria spricht zur Welt* (Innsbruck: Marianischer Verlag, 1954), [n.p.].

Chapter 52

    1. Goebbels, p. 424.
    2. Ibid., p. 447.
    3. Ibid., p. 458.
    4. Ibid., p. 463.
    5. Ibid., p. 493.
    6. Ibid., p. 509.

Chapter 53

    1. Goebbels, p. 515.
    2. Ibid., p. 526.
    3. Ibid., p. 535

Chapter 54

    1. Heydecker, p. 438.

Chapter 55

    1. Domogala, pp. 74 and 176.
    2. Shirer, William L., *The Rise and Fall of the Third Reich — a History of Nazi Germany* (New York: Simon & Schuster, 1960), p. 1056.
    3. Ibid., p. 1068.
    4. Ibid., p. 1070.
    5. Ibid., p. 1069.
    6. Ibid., p. 1071.
    7. Ibid., p. 1074.

Chapter 57

    1. The plantation director, SS officer Vogt, due to his kindhearted treatment of prisoners, was defended by them and avoided sentencing by the American court.
    2. Hans Adolf Jacobsen, *1939–1945: Der zweite Weltkrieg in Chronik und Dokumenten* (Darmstadt: Wehr und Wissen Verlagsgesellschaft, 1959), p. 421.
    3. Ibid., p. 422.

Chapter 58

    1. Domagała, p. 46.
    2. Ibid., p. 46.

Chapter 59

1. Domagała, p. 46.
2. Ibid., p. 325.
3. Ibid., p. 213.
4. In those days of confusion and anarchy, the prisoners themselves took a terrible vengeance on the people who had oppressed and beat them. In particular, they lynched the capos and leaders of barracks or halls. Perishing in this way was the notorious deputy leader of camp Dachau, Martin Szaferski, who was murdered by prisoners in a railcar during transport to another camp.

Chapter 60

1. Jan Domagała, in the work already cited, provides the following compilation of Poles in camp Dachau on the day of liberation, 29 April 1945:

clergy	800
physicians	c. 50
lawyers	c. 100
engineers	c. 50
university and high school teachers	15
elementary school teachers	85
white-collar workers	c. 500
career soldiers	c. 200
landowners	c. 100
high school students	400
craftsmen and tradesmen	3,600
farmhands	1,800
blue-collar workers	5,000
criminals, convicted in Poland	500

2. Domagała, p. 22.

Sources

Source Materials

The author's personal experiences and the testimony of fellow prisoners.
Documents taken from the camps.
Letters to relatives.
The author's diary from his final months in Dachau.
Documentary photographs and photostats.

Bibliography

[Amended and corrected by means of the Online Computer Library Center, WorldCat.org]

Aroneau, Eugene. *Konzentrationslager-Tatsachenbericht über die an Menscheit begangenen Verbrechen, Dokument F. 321, für den internationalen Militärgerichtshof in Nürnberg.* Edition of the society "Das Licht," 1946. Cf. Baden-Baden: Arbeitsgemeinschaft "Das Licht," 1947.

Ballmann, Hans. *Im K-Z: ein Tatsachenbericht aus dem Konzentrationslager.* Backnang, Württemberg: Praktikus Verlag, 1945.

Barthas, C. *Fatima ein Wunder des zwanzigsten Jahrhunderts.* Freiburg: Herder, 1958.

Beckert, W. A., and Ernst Busse. *Die Wahrheit über das Konzentrationslager Buchenwald.* n.p., 1945.

Benoist-Méchin, Jacques. *Der Himmel stürzt ein — Frankreichs Tragödie 1940.* Düsseldorf: Droste Verlag, 1958.

Bihlmayer, Karl. *Kirchengeschichte. 3. Die Neuzeit und neueste Zeit.* Paderborn: Schöningh, 1956.

Biskupski, Stefan. *Księża polscy w niemieckich obozach koncentracyjnych.* London: F. Mildner, 1946.

———. *Meczeńskie biskupstwo księdza Michała Kozala.* Włocławek: Drukarnia Diecezjalna, 1946; Warsaw: n.p., 1955.

Blond, Georges. *The Death of Hitler's Germany.* New York: Pyramid Books, 1958.

Bucheim, Hans. *Das Dritte Reich — Grundlagen und politische Entwicklung.* München: Kösel Verlag, 1958.

Burckhardt, Carl Jacob, and Jan Šmarda. *Meine Danziger Mission 1937 bis 1939.* München, Zürich: Fretz & Wasmuth; München: Callwey, 1960.

Bullock, Allan. *Hitler, a Study in Tyranny.* New York: Bantam Books, 1958.

Callaey, Fredegand. *Praelectiones historiae essleciasticae aetatis recentioris et praesentis.* Rome: Apud Athenaeum Pontificium Urbanum de Propaganda Fide, 1955.

Chart, Edmund. *Spis pomordowanych Polaków w obozie koncentracyjnym Dachau.* Munich: "Słowo Polskie," 1946.

Clarke, Comer. *Eichmann: The Man and His Crimes.* New York: Ballantine Books, 1960.

Collier, Richard. *Ten Thousand Eyes.* New York: Pyramid Books, 1959.

Confalonieri, Carlo. *Pius XI.* Aschaffenburg: Paul Patloch Verlag, 1958.

Crankshaw, Edward. *Gestapo.* New York: Pyramid Books, 1956.

Der Grosse Herder, Volumes I–X. Freiburg Herder, [1952?] 1953.

Deuel, Wallace. *People under Hitler.* New York: Brace and Co., 1942.

Domagala, Jan. "Duchowni w Dachau." *Ci, którzy przeszli przez Dachau.* Warsaw: "Pax," 1957.

Donovan, John. *Eichmann, Man of Slaughter.* New York: Avon, 1960.

Ehler, Sidney Z., and John B. Morrall, trans. and eds. *Church and State through the Centuries: A Collection of Historic Documents with Commentaries.* Westminster, Maryland: Newman Press, 1954.

Frank, Anne. *Das Tagebuch.* Frankfurt am Main; Hamburg: Fischer Bücherei, 1957.

Frischauer, Willi. *The Rise and Fall of Hermann Göring.* New York: Houghton Mifflin, 1951.

Fryszkiewicz, Melchior. *W cieniu krematoriów*, Chicago: Drukiem Dziennika Chicagoskiego, 1947.

Geissler, Christian. *Anfrage.* Hamburg: Claassen Verlag, 1960.

Goebbels, Joseph, and Louis Paul Lochner. *The Goebbels Diaries.* Garden City, N.Y.: Doubleday, 1948.

Gonzaga da Fonseca, Luis. *Maria spricht zur Welt.* Innsbruck: Marianischer Verlag, 1954.

Grabiński, Mieczysław. *Diplomacja w Dachau*

(*Diplomacy in Dachau*). Dachau: *Słowo Polskie*, 1946

Hagen, Louis. *Hitler's Secret Service*. New York: Pyramid Books, 1958.

Halecki, Oskar. *Eugeniusz Pacelli: papież pokoju*. London: Hosanium, 1951.

Heydecker, Joe J., and Johannes Leeb. *Der Nürnberger Prozess: Bilanz des Tausend Jahre*. Ko″ln-Berlin: Kiepenheuer & Witsch, 1958.

Hitler, Adolf. *Mein Kampf*, XXXIX Auflage. München: Zentralverlag der NSDAP, Franz Eher Nachf., 1939.

———. *My New Order*. A collection of documents and speeches. New York: Reynal & Hitchock, 1941.

Hlond, August Cardinal. *Na straży sumienia narodu*. Ramsey, NY: Don Bosco, 1951.

Hofer, Walter. *Der Nationalsozialismus, Dokumente 1933–1945*. Frankfurt am Main: Fischer Bücherei, 1957.

Huber, Raphael M. *Our Bishops Speak. National ... conference: 1919–1951*. Milwaukee: Bruce, 1952.

Hunter, Edward. *Brainwashing*. New York: Pyramid Books, 1958.

Hyman, Nat. *Eyes of the War: A Photographic Report of War II*. New York: Tel-Pic Syndicate, Inc., 1945.

Jacobsen, Hans Adolf. *1939–1945: Der zweite Weltkrieg in Chronik und Dokumenten*. Darmstadt: Wehr und Wissen Verlagsgesellschaft, 1959.

Jasiński, Walery. *Ku nowej pięknej Polsce*. Milwaukee: XX Salvatorians, 1941.

Jaspers, Karl. *Vom Ursprung und Ziel der Geschichte*. Frankfurt: Fischer Bücherei, 1957.

Jong, Louis de. *Die deutsche fünfte Kolonne im zweiten Weltkrieg*. Stuttgart: Deutsche Verlags-Anstalt, 1959.

Karweina, Guenter. *Der Grosse Treck (Dokumentarbericht über die Flucht und Austreibung von 14 Millionen Deutschen)*. Stuttgart: E. Wancura Verlag, 1958.

Klaus, Stefan. *So wahr mir Gott helfe*. München: Desch, 1958.

Klukowski, J. *ABC każdego Polaka*. Munich: "Słowo Polskie," 1946.

Kogon, Eugen. *The Theory and Practice of Hell: The German Concentration Camps and the System Behind Them*. New York: Berkeley, 1951.

Kowollik, Paul. *Das war Konzentrationslager Buchenwald*. Waldkirch: Waldkircher Verlag, 1946.

Kramer, F. A. *Vor den Ruinen Deutschlands: Ein Aufruf zur geschichtlichen Selbstbesinnung*. Koblenz: Historisch-politischer Verlag, [1946; 1948].

Krzesiński, Andrzej. *W Obronie Polski*. Chicago: Polish-American Book Co., 1946.

Lasch, Otto. *So fiel Königsberg — Kampf und Untergang von Ostpreussens Hauptstadt*. München: Gräfe und Unzer, 1958.

Leber, Annedore. *Das Gewissen steht auf*. Berlin/Frankfurt a.M.: Mosaik Verlag, 1955.

Leiser, Clara. *Lunacy Becomes Us*. New York: Liveright Publ. Co., 1939.

Lengyel, Olga. *Hitler's Ovens*. New York: Avon Book Div., 1947.

Librowski, Stanisław. *Ofiary zbrodni niemieckich pośród duchowieństwa diecezji włocławskiej*. Włocławek: Księgarnia Powszechna i Drukarnia Diecezjalna, 1947.

Malinowski-Pobóg, Władysław. *Najnowsza historia Polski*. Paris: the author, 1953–1960.

Maurel, Micheline. *An Ordinary Camp*. New York: Balmont Books, 1958.

Montgomery, Bernard Law, the Viscount Montgomery of Alamein. *The Memoirs*. New York: Singer Pub. New American Library, 1958. [Cleveland: World Pub., 1958.]

Morcinek, Gustaw. *Listy spod Morwy (Letters from Under the Mulberry)*. Paris: Księgarnia Polska, 1945.

Neumann, Peter. *The Blacks March*. New York: Bantam Books, 1958.

Nowacki, Józef. *Kościół katedralny w Poznaniu, studium historyczne*. Poznan: Sw. Wojciech, 1959.

Ordega, Adam, and Tymon Terlecki, eds. *Straty kultury polskiej. Praca zbiorowa,* Volumes I-II. Glasgow: Książnica Polska, 1945.

Osmańczyk, Edmund Jan. *Dowody prowokacji* (Himmler's unidentified archive). Warsaw: Czytelnik, 1951.

———. *Niemcy 1945–1950*. Warsaw: "Książka i Wiedza," 1951.

———. *Notatki korespondenta*. Warsaw: Czytelnik, 1951.

Papini, Giovanni. *Weltgericht*. Freiburg/München: Karl Albert Verlag, 1959.

Pepper, Dan, and Max Gareth. *The Enemy General*. Derby, CT: Monarch Books, 1960.

Pfeilschifter, Georg. *Deutsche Kultur, Katholizismus und Weltkrieg*. Freiburg im Breisgau: Herdersche Verl., 1915.

Pius XII, *Papież Pius XII a Polska, Przemówienia i listy papieskie, garść dokumentów z lat 1939–1946*. Second edition, Rome, 1946.

———. *Von der Einheit der Welt*. Freiburg: Herder, 1957.

Podolski, H. *Prawda o Polsce*. Detroit: Tow. Ośw., 1947.

Popp, Georg. *Die Mächtigen der Erde*. Würzburg: Arena Verlag, 1957.

Pospieszalski, K. M. *Documenta occupationis teutonicae*, Volumes I–IV. Poznań: Wydawnictwo Instytutu Zachodniego, 1945–49.

Pross, Harry. *Die Zerstörung der deutschen Politik: Dokumente 1871–1933*. Frankfurt am Mein: Fischer, 1959.

Rogalski, Aleksander. *Katolicyzm w Niemczech po II wojnie światowej*. Warsaw: "Pax," 1952.

Rogalski, Aleksander. *W kregu Nibelungów: studia nad problematyka Niemiec współczesnych*. Poznań: Wydawnictwo Poznańskie, 1958.

Roper-Trevor, H. R. *The Last Days of Hitler*. New York: Berkley, 1947.

Rosenberg, A. *Der Mythus des 20 Jahrhunderts*. München, Hoheneichen-verlag, 1935.

Rothfels, Hans. *Die deutsche Opposition gegen Hitler*. Frankfurt am Main; Hamburg: Fischer Bücherei, 1958.

Russell, Edward Frederick Langley [Lord Russell of Liverpool]. *The Scourge of the Swastika — A Short History of Nazi War Crimes*. New York: Ballantine Books, 1957.

Schnabel, Ernst. *Anne Frank, Spur eines Kindes: ein Bericht*. Frankfurt am Main: Fischer Bücherei, 1958.

Schultz, Sigrid. *Germany Will Try It Again*. New York: Reynal & Hitchcock, 1944.

Shirer, William L. *The Rise and Fall of the Third Reich: A History of Nazi Germany*. New York: Simon & Schuster, 1960.

Smith, Emma Peters. *World History: The Struggle for Civilization*. Boston: Ginn and Co., 1955.

Stark, Johannes. *Nationalsozialismus und Katholische Kirch*. Antwort auf Kundgebungen der deutschen Bischöfe. München: Eher, 1931.

Stolica święta w obronie praw polskich katolików w Rzeszy i w Polsce pod okupacją niemecką. Kilka dokumentów z lat 1942–1943. Second edition, Rome, 1946.

Teresia Renata de Spiritu Sancto. *Edith Stein*. [Freiberg?] Herder, 1958.

Thorwald, Jürgen. *Defeat in the East: Russia Conquers, January to May 1945*. New York: Ballantine Books, 1959.

Uris, Leon. *Exodus*. Toronto: Bantam Books, 1959.

Vollmer, Bernhard. *Volksopposition im Polizeistaat: Gestapo und Regierungsberichte 1934–1936*. Stuttgart: Deutsche Verlags-Anstalt, 1957.

Wasiutyński, Wojciech. *Tysiąc lat polityki polskiej*. Munich: "Słowo Polskie," 1946.

Wassermann, Charles. *Unter pölnischer Verwaltung*. Hamburg: Blüchert Verlag, 1958.

Wedel, Hasso von (colonel on the general staff). *Die Soldaten des Führers im Felde*. München: Raumbild-Verlag, Otto Schönstein. K.-G., 1939.

Winkler, Ernst. *Four Years Nazi Torture*. New York–London: D. Appleton Century Co., 1942.

Wise, Stephen S. *Never Again. Ten Years of Hitler*. New York: Jewish Opinion Publishing Corporation, 1943.

Wojciechowski, Zygmunt. *Studia historyczne*. Warsaw: "Pax," 1955.

Zeiger, Henry A. *The Case Against Adolf Eichmann*. New York: Signet Books, 1960.

Ziemba, Adam, Rev. *Pajda chleba*. Poznań: Pallottinum, 1957.

Articles from Periodicals

Out of several hundred articles gathered from the press in various languages, I provide only a handful of those that are most relevant to topics discussed in *Shavelings* and that are taken exclusively from the German press. [No page numbers are cited.]

"Der Episkopat und die katholische Presse im dritten Reich." *Herder Korrespondenz*, May 1960.

Heydecker, J. H. and J. Leeb. "Kreuz und Hackenkreuz," ein Dokumentarbericht. *Münchener Illustrierte*, 1958.

Hitler, Adolf, as quoted in *Kristall, Die Aussergewöhnliche Illustrierte*, Hamburg, 1959.

Stimmen der Zeit:

Alble, Rolf. "Staatsbürger in Uniform." Oct. 1959.

"Friedensbemühungen des Hl. Stuhles." Aug. 1959.

Leiber, Robert. "Pius XII." Nov. 1958.

Pribilla, Max. "Die Fritsch-Krise 1938 deutsche Schicksalwende." n.d.

Roth, Paul. "Deutschland und Polen." Oct. 1957.

Simmal, Oscar. "Die Stimme Hitlers." May 1960.

Die Zeit:

"Anne Frank rief die Jugend — Bergen Belsen wurde Wallfahrtsort." Hamburg, 21 March 1957.

"Die 'Basis' für den Massenmord." Hamburg, 2 January 1958.

"Die Bestien unter die Besten." Hamburg, 20 May 1960.

"Besuch im Buchenwald." Hamburg, 1 January 1960.

"Dürfen wir vergessen?" Hamburg, n.d.1956.

"Der deutsch-pölnische Krieg findet doch statt." Hamburg, 30 August 1956.

"Eisele und die Hinterbliebenen." Hamburg, 1 August 1956.

"Hände die töteten statt zu heilen." Hamburg, 27 February 1958.

"Himmlers geheime Denkschrift." Hamburg, 4 April 1957.

"Schluss mit den Nazi-Greueln." Hamburg, 7 November 1958.

"Das Verhältnis der Deutschen zu ihrer Geschichte." Hamburg, 1 May 1958.

Katholische Kirchenzeitung:

"Alle Schuld gehört unter das Kreuz." Hildesheim, 26 June 1960.

"Lebt in Deutschland noch der Nationalsozialismus?" Munich, 12 April 1959.

"Sühne für Blutbad." Hildesheim, nr 13, 1957.

"Sühnekirche für KZ in Dachau." Munich, July 1960.

Walterman, Leo. "Hoffnung aus des Brüderlichkeit." Hildesheim, 14 August 1960.

DANA (German News Service) Meldungen, Nov. Dec. 1946:

"Aussagen über Dachau."
"Bestialitäten in Dachau."
"Dachau — Zeugen sagen aus."
"Dann wurde der Priester wieder in das Becken zurückgeworfen."
"Frauen Hinrichtung in Dachau."
"Der Gefangenenmord auf Befehl."
"Menschen als Versuchskaninchen."
"Mord an vier Fliegern — Dachau."
"Priesterleben im Konzentrationslager Dachau." Pfarrer Richard Schneider.
"36 Todesurteile in Dachau."
"Die Todesmühlen."
"Die Verteidigung in Dachau."
"Wissenschaftler als Verbrecher."
"Zeugenaussage in Dachau."

Sources Not Yet Published [as of 1960]

(Property of the legal defender, Władysław Chwiałkowski, Esq., who has represented cases of former prisoners in German courts since 1945.)

Seraphin, Hans-Günther, PhD, Professor at the University of Göttingen (who was tasked by German courts to research the issue whether the Polish clergy was persecuted for religious reasons or only for national ones): "Die Beurteilung der römisch-katholischen Geistlichen pölnischer Nationalität durch die Besatzungbehörden und die Gründe für das Vorgehen gegen sie in den von Deutschland besetzten Gebieten." Type-written copy of 68 pages. This work takes the position that the Polish clergy was persecuted by Nazism solely for national and political reasons.

Broszat, Martin, PhD, "Verfolgung pölnischer katholischer Geistlichen 1939–1945." Typewritten copy, 87 pages, September 1959, Munich. Based on all-source documents, the author arrives at a completely different conclusion from the one cited above, stating that — aside from a few exceptions — the Polish clergy was persecuted by Nazism for ideological and religious reasons.

Stasiewski, Bernard, PhD: "Die Kirchenpolitik der Nationalsozialisten im Warthegau 1939–1945." Special insert in the weekly "Das Parlament," Bonn, 18 February 1959.

I offer my most sincere thanks to Mr. Chwiałkowski for kindly providing me with access to valuable sources and the use of documents from about 150 trials, which he has won up to now in German courts.

Index

Adamski, Fr. Władysław (from Ludzisko) 282
Akold 37, 47
Albana, Sr. 236, 342
Alphonsus, St. 113
Andrzejewski, Fr. Kazimierz (from Grodzisk) 282
Anton, the poacher 324, 325

Bach, SS officer 308
Bączek, Rev. Msgr. Dr. Jan (Łódź) 264
Bączyk, Fr. 272
Badoglio 320
Baecher, Fritz ("Buffalo") 165–170, 174, 177, 178, 180, 182, 183, 192, 194–196, 206, 209, 211–213, 217–219, 220, 223, 225, 228, 229, 232, 236, 238, 250, 252–255, 263, 264, 268, 273, 283, 316
Bąk, Fr. Jan (from Lubosz) 282
Bąk, Fr. Jan (Smolice) 264
Bąkowski, Fr. Michał 394
Baksik, Fr. Sylwester 110
Balcerek, Fr. Marian 296
Banaszak, Rev. Rector Antoni (Gniezno) 292, 293, 307, 356, 365, 378, 379, 382, 383, 385
Banaszak, Fr. Józef 290
Barbara, Sr. 34–343
Bardel, Fr. Marian (Lublin) 278
Beck, SS general 339
Beck, Józef 84
Bederski, Fr., missionary (from Górka Klasztorna) 177
Bertold (Sachsenhausen) 93, 96–101, 128
Bertram, Cardinal 214
Beściak, Fr. Piotr (Łódź Diocese) 225
Białas, Fr. Paweł (from Ruchocice) 264
Białogłowski, Fr. Albin (Franciscan) 294
Biały, Fr. Józef 334, 348
Bielicki, Fr. Franciszek 38, 79, 82
Biłko, Rev. Msgr. 272
Binderfeld, Dr. 342
Biniakowski, Klemens 106
Birkenmajer, Prof. 344
Biskupski, Rev. Dr. (Włocławek Diocese) 289
Bismarck 66

Blericqui, Fr. 223
Boetger 307
Bogacki, Fr. Marian (from Szamotuły) 225
Bolt, Rev. Senator 61
Bombicki, Rev. Dean (Wolsztyn) 264
Bonawentura, Fr. (Lublin Diocese) 107
Borkowski, Captain 38
Bormann, Martin 248
Borowczyk, Fr. Stanisław 104
Borzyszkowski, Fr. Józef (Chełmno Diocese) 209
Brenner 220, 243–246, 250, 251, 255, 256, 279, 315, 343, 344
Breznik 292
Broczuk, Brother, Albertine Order (Kraków) 264
Bruca (a teacher) 359
Brucki, Rev. Dean Jan (from Osie) 264
Brudz, Fr. Józef 308
Bryja, Franciszek, a Pallotine 264
Brząkała, Fr. 96, 98
Brzezik, Fr. Ignacy (from Rajsko) 264
Brzeziński, Fr. Józef 295
Brzuski, Rev. Professor Henryk (Włocławek) 289
Brzuski, Fr. Jan (Pomorze) 28
Buchwald, Fr. (from Magnuszewice) 265
Budniak, Fr. Roman 20, 23, 24, 26, 98, 99, 115, 116, 118, 177, 178, 220, 221, 251, 252, 256, 266, 285, 294, 332, 337, 345, 346, 352, 362, 365–368, 370–374, 377, 394
Bukowy, Stanisław, a Jesuit seminarian 297
Burek, Franciszek 238–241, 292, 313
Bursche, Pastor 175

Cegiełka, Fr., a Pallotine (France) 251
Chabowski, Rev. Msgr. (Płock Diocese) 264
Chabrowski, Rev. Msgr. (Włocławek Diocese) 264
Charczewski, Rev. Canon 100
Chard, Fr. Edmund (Łódź Diocese) 225

Chilomer, Fr. (Gniezno Diocese) 131
Chmiel, Fr. Józef, a Bernardine (Skępe) 38
Chmielowski, Brother Albert, founder of Albertine Order 148
Churchill 121, 299
Chwedorowicz, Brother, Albertine Order 295
Chwiłowicz, Rev. Dean Aurelian (from Pajęczno) 264
Chwiłowicz, Fr. Marian (Włocławek Diocese) 264
Ciążyński, Fr. Stanisław (Poznań Diocese) 289
Ciemniak, Fr. (Inowrocław District) 20, 67, 68
Cieślak, Fr. (from Niepokalanów) 210
Cieślik, Walter 293
Ciszak, Fr. Bolesław (from Bukownica) 282
Cofta (Inowrocław) 20, 22
Conti, Dr. Leon 271
"Cretin" (Dachau) 177, 188, 217, 263
Ćwiejkowski, Fr. (author's uncle) 223, 224, 226, 247, 251, 255, 265, 267, 268, 284
Czajkowski, Fr. Marian (from Dzierzbin) 264
Czaki (Czacki), Rev. Dean (Włocławek Diocese) 35, 46, 100
Czapliński, Fr. Bernard (Toruń) 38, 365
Czeluśniak, Fr. Andrzej, (La Salette Order) 349
Czempiel, Rev. Msgr. Dean Józef (Katowice Diocese) 264
Czernicki, Tadeusz 292
Czwojdziński, Fr. Leon (from Poznań) 282

Dahlke, Fr. (from Gniezno) 264
Dębski, Rev. Professor (Inowrocław) 10, 19, 100, 108, 109
Deiner (Deinert) 291
Detkens, Rev. Professor (Warsaw) 120, 281
"Doggie" (Dachau) 191
Domagała, Jan 169, 285, 353
Downar, Rev. Envoy 35, 46, 265

Index

Drelowiec, Fr. (Podlaska Diocese) 264
Drewniak, Fr. Bronisław 279
Dubiel, Henryk 292, 305, 314, 315, 327, 346, 351, 355
"Duck" (Sachsenhausen) 91, 92
Dwornicki, Fr. Walenty (from Poznań) 264
Dybizbański, Fr. Jan (from Nowe Miasto) 264
Dymek, Rev. Bishop 226
Dziadzia, Fr. (Gniezno Diocese) 264
Dziasek, Rev. Doctor 225, 292
Dziegiecki, Fr. Jan (Poznań Diocese) 264
Dzienisz, Fr. Leon (from Toruń) 281

Echaust, Fr. Józef (from Skoki) 279
Efrem, Fr. Superior (from Lubartów) 107
Eggert, Fr. Józef 292
Erich (Dachau) 316, 320, 334
Erich (Sachsenhausen) 126, 128, 129
Etter, Fr. Tadeusz (Poznań Diocese) 295

Falkowski, Fr. T. (from Toruń) 281
Falkowski, Fr. Wiktor 264
Farulewski, Fr. (Inowrocław District) 20, 94, 99
Fatima, Our Lady of 130, 131, 143, 147, 290, 298, 299, 309, 311, 320
Felczak, Fr., a Jesuit 265
Fengler, Fr. Stanisław (Iwonicz) 264
Fiałkowski, Dr 315, 336, 340
Fibak, Fr. Radoch (Gniezno Diocese) 152, 296, 346, 362–364, 366, 372, 374, 377
Figas, Fr. (Września area) 131
Figat, Fr. 135
Filipowicz, Fr. Mieczysław 104, 291
Fischer 302
Fiutak, Fr. 171
Flaczyński, Rev. Msgr. (Gniezno Diocese) 267
Flisiak, Fr. Stefan 394
Formanowicz, Rev. Canon (Gniezno Diocese) 131, 264
Francis de Sales, St. 176
Franco, General 316, 320
Francuskiewicz, Edward 231, 265, 315, 327, 336, 380
Franczewski, Fr. (from Łódź) 295
Franek (capo for carpenters in Dachau) 345, 346, 351, 352, 359
Frank 277
Frelichowski, Fr. Stefan (from Toruń) 38, 45, 63, 66, 354
"Fritz, One-Eyed" (Sachsenhausen) 92, 108–115, 117, 126, 128

Gajdus, Fr. Wojciech (Pelplin Diocese) 38, 62
Gałdyński, Rev. Director (Gniezno Diocese) 177
Gałecki, Fr. Stanisław (pastor from Szubin) 73
Gałęzewski, Rev. Professor (Gniezno Diocese) 131, 365
Galikowski, Fr. Roman 282
Ganghofer, Ludwig 288
Gański (Gdańsk) 40, 41, 57–59
Gawinek, Fr. Władysław (Kielce Diocese) 269
Gburczyk, Fr. 112
Gerstein, Kurt 259
Gładysz, Bronisław (seminarian from Białobrzegi) 265
Gliszczyński, Fr. Franciszek (Chełmno Diocese) 265
Globocnik, Odilo 259
Głogowski, Fr. Kazimierz 292, 366
Głuszek, Rev. Msgr. (from Nakło) 131
Gmerek, Fr. Czesław (Poznań Diocese) 265
Gmochowski, Rev. Msgr. (Poznań Diocese) 265
Goebbels 187, 231, 233, 276, 277, 280, 286, 288, 296, 298, 300, 301–303, 306, 307, 309, 318, 320, 321, 325, 326, 328, 332, 339, 350, 360
Gołąb, Fr. 100
Gołąb, Fr. (Society of the Divine Word) 177
Goldman 54, 64, 65
Golędzinowski, Rev. Canon Jan (from Warsaw) 265
Golimowski, Czesław 297
Goral, Rev. Bishop Władysław 119, 232
Góranowicz, Fr. Aloś (from Przechowo) 29, 38, 279
Górecki, Rev. Professor M. (Gdańsk) 35, 54, 63–65
Gorgolewski, Rev. Pastor Joseph (Poznań) 289
Göring 187, 209, 243, 244, 324–326
Gotowicz, Fr. Aloś (Inowrocław District) 20, 72, 220, 252, 266, 283
Grabowski, Fr. Leszek (Płock Diocese) 267
Grabowski, Fr. Stanisław (Płock Diocese) 61, 267
Grabowski, Fr. Stanisław (Society of Christ; from Potulice) 38, 292, 366
Greinert, Rev. Canon (Gniezno) 224, 251
Grocholski, Fr. Edmund (from Czerlejno) 265
Gronkowski, Rev. Professor (Gniezno Diocese) 11
Gronostaj, Fr. (Poznań) 297
Gronwald, Fr. Tadeusz 265
Groo (Dachau) 161, 162, 174, 178–184, 228, 304
Grzelak, Fr. Kazimierz 29, 44, 48, 51
Grzesiek, Fr. 292
Grzesiek, Fr. Franciszek (from Przygodice) 265

Guder, Fr. Jan (from Poznań) 265
Gustav ("Iron Gustav," Sachsenhausen) 96, 119
Gustowski (Just) Stutthof 49, 69

Hądzlik, Fr. Antoni (Poznań Diocese) 280
Halla, Fr. Brunon 349
Hanas, Fr. Stefan (Belgium) 349
Handke, Rev. Pastor Grzegorz (Inowrocław) 8, 9, 13, 14, 19, 20, 22, 23, 35, 55, 94, 109, 247, 266, 290, 346, 365
Hans (hall leader, Dachau) 207, 208
Hauptman, Alfred, pastor 175, 340
Hecht, Ernst 148, 168, 220, 246, 256, 294, 304, 312–316, 369
Hegel 294
Heiden (Dachau) 221, 232
Hein (Dachau) 237–243, 256, 292, 302, 312
Hein (nurse) 166, 319, 321
Helmut (Sachsenhausen) 114
Hentschel (Dachau) 173, 174, 178, 181, 183, 186, 228
Herut, Fr. Bronisław 209
Heydrich 267
Himmler 67, 90, 94, 187, 259, 271, 272, 274, 277, 301, 309, 316, 326, 367, 385
Hinc, Fr. Franciszek 112
Hitler (Führer) 6, 11, 18, 45, 48, 66, 82, 94, 99, 100, 104, 106, 114, 121, 138, 146, 148, 159, 187, 188, 209, 214, 222, 229, 259, 260, 263, 280, 298, 299, 301, 303, 307–309, 316, 318, 321, 326, 330, 336, 338, 339, 342, 347, 348
Hlond, Cardinal 154, 171, 226, 266
Hlowa 337
Hoeper, General 339
Hoess (Sachsenhausen) 91
Hoffman 149, 259, 260, 262, 303, 304
Hugo ("Bloody Hugo," Sachsenhausen) 93, 98–103, 110, 128

Idźkiewicz, Professor 292, 300, 305
"Ignac" (Dachau) 163, 177, 184, 194–196, 217

Jakubowski, Fr. Jan (Bydgoszcz) 77
Januszczak, Fr. Mieczysław (France) 225
Januszczak, Fr. Mieczysław (Poznań Diocese) 269, 300
Januszewski, Fr. Antoni 132
Januszewski, Fr. Jan 132, 235, 295, 365, 390, 392
Januszewski, Fr. Paweł (Carmelite) 355
Jarczewski, Fr. Jan (from Gogolewo) 265
Jarolin (Dachau) 256, 259
Jaroszka 197
Jasiński, Fr. Tadeusz (Pomorze Diocese) 61

Index

Jaśkowski, Rev. Canon (Inowrocław District) 20–22
Jęczkowski, Fr. Edward 296
Jedwabski, Rev. Canon (Poznań Curia) 224, 365, 390
Jernajczyk, Rev. Professor (Inowrocław) 5
Jerzewski, Fr. Czesław 209
Jezierski, Fr. Marian (native of Bydgoszcz) 282
Jezierski, Fr. Stanisław 225
Joas, Emil (Dachau) 217, 219, 227, 260, 261, 263, 344, 361
Jodl, General 280
Julius 314–316, 319
Jung (Dachau) 307, 319
Just (see Gustowski) 49, 69

Kaczmarek, Fr. Zygmunt 29, 67, 365
Kaczmarkiewicz, Fr. (Sadki) 132
Kaczorowski, Fr. 292
Kaczorowski, Fr. (Poznań) 177
Kaiser (Sachsenhausen) 96, 111
Kaja, Rev. Prof. Leon 132, 208, 223
Kajka, Rev. Dr. Paweł (professor at seminary in Janów) 279
Kaliszan, Fr. Henryk 225, 272, 296, 297
Kałuża, Fr. Józef 349
Kamiński, Fr. Feliks 272, 371
Kamiński, Fr. Hubert 267
Kapp (Dachau) 165–167, 173, 174, 181, 183, 188, 192, 212, 213, 220, 228, 229, 250, 252–254, 269, 279, 285, 286, 308, 316
Karbowiak, Fr. Jan (from Donabory) 265
Karl (Dachau) 314, 315
Karl (Sachsenhausen) 126, 128, 129, 133, 136, 137, 139
Kasior, Fr. Ed. 171
Kasprowicz, Jan 8
Kasprowicz, Fr. Władysław 225
Kasprzyk, Fr. Jan, a Salesian 334
Kaszewski, Fr. Marian 225
Kentenich, Fr. Joseph 349
Kiciński, Rev. Dr. (Poznań) 265
Kiełbasiewicz (Inowrocław) 18
Kijewski, Fr. Leon 153, 292
Kinastowski, Fr. Kazimierz (Września) 5, 233
Kiszkurno, Rev. Canon 46
Kiszkurno, Fr. 265
Klein, Rev. Pastor 100
Klimkiewicz, Rev. Prof. Dr. Witold (Lublin) 289
Klin, Fr. Konrad (from Pączewo) 281
Klinkosz, Rev. Msgr. Aloś (from Tczew) 38, 63, 325
Kłos, Fr. Władysław (Lublin Diocese) 110, 278
Kmieć, Fr. Franciszek 29
Kneblewski, Rev. Dr. (a Salesian) 28
Knoll (Dachau) 188, 190, 197, 316
Knosala, Ryszard 212, 213, 285, 330, 352

Koch, Professor 271
Koczorowski, Fr. Czesław 29, 102, 220, 340, 374
Kolbe, Fr. Maksymilian 2, 29, 44, 48, 49, 51, 60, 91, 210, 279
Komf, Fr. Janusz, chaplain (from Kutno) 48, 99
Komorowski, Fr. Bronisław 54, 63, 65
Konieczny, Fr. Sylwester 225, 344, 346
Konitzer, Rev. Counselor (from Świecie) 28, 46, 99
Konopiński, Fr. Marian 297
Kopczewski, Fr. Józef 370
Koperski, Rev. Dr. 225, 292
Korcz, Fr. Teodor 225, 362, 365, 367
Korszyński, Rev. Dr. (Włocławek Diocese) 289
Kowalczyk, Fr. Stanisław (from Wojcin) 265
Kowalewski, Fr. M. 154
Kowalska, Sr. Faustyna 124
Kowalski, Władysław 292
Kownacki, Fr. (from Wąbrzeźno) 266
Koza, Leon, a Carmelite 265
Kozak, Fr. Jan (Lublin area) 110
Kozak, Fr. Stefan (Podlaska Diocese) 279
Kozal, Rev. Bishop Michał 157, 187, 199, 206–210, 218, 219, 223, 232, 233, 250, 251, 254, 266, 276, 278, 280, 289, 299–301
Kozłowicz, Fr. (Inowrocław) 16
Kozubek, Fr. (Society of the Divine Word) 67, 100
Krajewski, Fr. Franciszek (from Brodnica) 28
Krasiński, Zygmunt 55
Krauze, Fr. Wacław 225
Krawczak, Fr. Ksawery 20–22
Kropidłowski, Fr. Alfons (Pomorze Diocese) 61, 300
Kroplewski, Fr. (from Krzemieniewo) 266
Krych, Fr. Józef (from Sarnowo) 296
Krynicki, Rev. Dr. Stanisław (Lublin) 116, 278
Krzywoszyński, Fr. Józef 290
Krzyżanowski, Fr. Kazimierz (Płock Diocese) 267
Krzyżanowski, Fr. Stanisław 296
Kubicki, Fr. Telesfor 72
Kubiński, Fr. Stanisław (Kwieciszewo) 290
Kubisz, Fr. T. 153
Kubski, Rev. Canon (Inowrocław) 16, 266
Kucharski, Fr. Grzegorz (Poznań Diocese) 282
Kucharzak, Fr. Stanisław (Włocławek Diocese) 292, 366
Kujawa, Fr. Jan (Poznań Diocese) 295
"Kulas" 197
Kuliński, Rev. Dean Stefan 266

Kundegórski, Fr. Ed 209
Kunka, Fr. Bolesław (Włocławek Curia 224)
Kurkowski, Fr. Leon (from Biechowo) 282
Kurt 236–238
Kurzawa, Józef 53
Kutzner, Fr. Leon (from Poladowo) 266
Kwarta, Fr. Antoni 279
Kwiatkowski, Fr. Milan 225

Lach, Fr. 171
Łagoda, Rev. Msgr. (from Miłosław) 224
Łagoda, Rev. Msgr. Leon (former rector of Polish Mission in France) 290
Lapis, Fr. Marian (from Orchowo) 282
Latos, Jan 106
Laubitz, Rev. Bishop (Gniezno) 18
Leisner, Karol, a deacon 299
Leitgeber, Fr. (Września area) 233
Lenckowski, Fr 96, 114
Leopold III 105
Lesiński, Fr. Jan (Gdynia) 61
Leśniewicz, Fr. Ludwik (from Bukowiec) 297
Lewandowski, Rev. Dr. Franciszek 266
Lewandowski, Fr. Zygmunt (from Kamień) 38
Lewański, Fr 96, 97
Liberski, Fr. Walek 295
Liguda, Alojzy (rector, Society of the Divine Word) 26, 28, 30, 31, 33, 46, 78, 255, 296
Lippman 285
Lis, Fr. Tomasz (Łódź Diocese) 297
Lisiecki, Fr. Henryk 152, 264, 296
Litewski, Fr. Kazimierz 38
Liwerski, Fr. Ludwik 110
Łój, Fr. (Szubin District) 29
Lorkowski, Antoni (Bydgoszcz) 78, 80, 81
Lubowiecki, Fr. Edward (Kraków) 348
Lucy of Fatima (Sr. Maria Dolores) 130, 131, 143, 147, 299, 311, 387
Ludwiczak, Rev. Dr. Antoni (Inowrocław District) 20, 29, 67, 266
Ludwik, Fr. Józef (Ostrów Wielkopolski) 266

Maciejewski, Fr. Henryk 257
Maciejewski, Fr. Leon (from Murowana Goślina) 282
Mackensen, von 271
Mączkowski, Fr. Władysław (Gniezno Diocese) 282
Mączyński, Rev. Prof. (Włocławek Diocese) 132, 289
Mądry, Fr. Jan (Gniezno Diocese) 282
Maj, Fr. Dominik (Lublin Diocese) 110, 278
Majchrzak, Alfons 356

Majchrzak, Rev. Prof. Antoni 225, 292, 307, 356, 365, 367, 372, 377, 385, 394
Majchrzycki brothers, priests 153
Majdański, Kazimierz, seminarian 132
Mąkowski, Fr. (from Gniewkowo) 20, 96, 99
Malec, Fr. Tadeusz 278
Małecki, Rev. Dr. 131
Manikowski, Fr. Stanisław 38
Marciniak, Rev. Prof. Franciszek (from Nakło) 106, 301
Marciniak, Fr. Sylwester 153, 292
Marcinkowski (industrial enterprise blok) 293
Maria Cecilia, Sr. 240
Marusarz, Fr. Stanisław (from Strzałkowo) 266
Mateo, Fr. 62
Mathesius (Stutthof) 40, 44–49, 56, 60, 61, 67, 68
Matura, Fr. 292
Matuszewski, Fr. (from Lipnica) 171
Max (Sachsenhausen) 119, 120
Mazurkiewicz, Rev. Prof. Dr. Karol (Poznań) 289
Meansarian 363, 382
Meger, Fr. (Pomorze) 28, 115
Mencel, Fr. Leon (Inowrocław District) 20, 365
Metler, Fr. Józef 153
Metler, Fr. Marian (from Pomorze) 61
Michałowicz, Rev. Msgr. (Wągrowiec) 171
Michałowicz, Fr. Wojciech, a Salesian (Kielce) 248
Michałowski, Fr. Leon (Świecie) 28, 79, 273, 274, 356, 394
Michalski, Fr. Kazimierz 368
Michnowski, Rev. Pastor (Pomorze) 28, 29
Misiak, Fr. Szczepan 29, 365
Misiaszek, Fr. Stanisław 54
Miszczuk, Fr. 110
Mizgalski, Fr. Gerard 153
Młotek, Fr. (from Gołańcz) 282
Młynarczyk, Fr. Władysław 277
Młynik, Fr. Zbigniew 29, 51
Mojówka, Fr. Viator (Lublin area) 107
Molotov 7, 18
Morcinek, Gustaw 359, 368
Mueller, Fr. Józef (from Bydgoszcz) 64, 266
Mueller, Rudolf (Dachau) 250, 270
Mulczyński, Fr. Kazimierz 160
Munderlein (Dachau) 206, 209, 218, 220, 231
Murat, Fr. Aleksander (Lublin area) 110
Musiał, Fr. Antoni 366
Musiał, Jerzy, a Jesuit seminarian 334, 348, 357
Musiał, Fr. Piotr 209, 366
Mussolini 106, 146, 303, 309, 319, 338

Muzalewski, Fr. Alfons (Gdańsk) 38

Napierała, Rev. Dean (from Gniezno) 266
Napoleon Bonaparte 224
Nazim, Fr. (from Niepokalanów) 210
Nędza, Fr. Gorgoniusz (Order of the Reformati) 225
Neiniger, Bronisław 359
Neubauer — alias Neugebauer (Stutthof) 49, 64, 75
Niedojadło, Fr. Jan (from Stary Sącz) 308
Niemir, Fr. (Inowrocław District) 20, 27, 46, 53, 61
Nietzsche 288, 294
Niziółkiewicz, Fr. Zenon 132
Noak, Rev. Dean (from Łekno) 266
Nowacki (Sachsenhausen) 96, 136
Nowaczewski, Fr. Feliks 132
Nowak, Fr. Franciszek 131, 368, 373
Nowak, Fr. Kazimierz 209
Nowak, Fr. Leon (Inowrocław) 132
Nowak, Fr. Stefan (Płock Diocese) 61
Nowakowski, Fr. Marian (Carmelite, from Kraków) 291
Nowicki, Rev. Pastor (from Barcin) 99
Nowicki, Rev. Pastor Felicjan (from Polędzin) 266
Nowowiejski, Bishop 232

Obarski, Rev. Dean 171
Ochalski, Zdzisław, Rev. Dr. (Lublin) 116, 278, 279
Ogrodowski, Fr. (from Krotoszyn) 251
Ogrodowski, Fr. Zygmunt 153
Olbricht, General 339
Olech, Rev. Dr. Wojciech (Lublin) 116, 278
Orsenigo, Rev. Msgr. Cesare, nuncio 6, 100
Orzeł, Fr. Jan (Lublin Diocese) 110
Osowski, Fr. Jan (from Rybno) 38
Ossi (Sachsenhausen) 93, 96–98, 110

Pabiszczak, Fr. Stefan 223, 225, 296, 374
Palewodziński, Fr. Ed 131, 191, 365
Palmowski, Rev. Pastor Józef (from Parkowo) 351
Panek, Fr. Józef 290
Parzonko, Lt. Władysław 294
Pasiecznik, Fr. Marceli 349
Paszkowiak, Fr. 171
Patalas (from Poznań) 383
Paulus 299
Pawlak, Fr. Józef (from Czerlejno) 279
Pawlak, Fr. Tadeusz (from Gniezno) 265
Pawlicki, Fr. Bern. (Września) 309

Pawłowski, Rev. Msgr. Józef (Kielce, a Salesian) 248
Pękacki, Fr. Paweł (Kcynia) 349
Peyton, Fr. 309, 311
Piechowski, Rev. Dean Bolesław 38, 44, 46, 63, 281
Pilarczyk, Fr. Wacław, a Redemptorist 308
Pilchniewski, a seminarian 265
Piorkowsky (Dachau) 149, 212, 285
Piotr, Fr. Marian 153, 296
Piotrowski, Fr. 225
Piotrowski, Fr. (from Owińska) 394
Piotrowski, Leon 347
Piszczygłowa, Fr. 131
Pituła, Fr. Zygmunt 153, 366
Pius XII 6, 7, 130, 143, 147, 290, 298, 309
Płaczek, Fr. Stanisław 290
Płaczkowa (from Sadki) 132
Płotkowiak (from Września) 255
Płuciński, Fr. Bronisław 131, 365
Poczta, Fr. S. 225
Podemski, Fr. Stanisław 153
Podoleński, Fr., a Jesuit 351
Pohl, Oswald (Stutthof) 48, 67–71
Pomianowski, Fr. (Inowrocław District) 20, 99
Popławski, a seminarian 279
Posadzy, Fr. General 38
Potempa, Rev. Dr. (Włocławek Diocese) 280
Potocki, Fr. Mieczysław (from Skarboszewo) 282
Prabucki, Fr. Alojzy (Chełmno Diocese) 69, 70, 281
Prabucki, Fr. Bolesław (Chełmno Diocese) 69, 70, 281
Prabucki, Fr. Paweł (Chełmno Diocese) 69, 70, 124, 126, 199, 281
Pracki, Stefan (Inowrocław) 247, 266, 269, 270
Prądzyński, Rev. Msgr. 267
Preiss, Rev. Dr. Jarogniew 265, 283, 284
Preiss, Waldemar, pastor 176
Pronobis, Fr. Aleksander 61
Pryba, Rev. Dr. Leon 282
Przekop, Rev. Dr. Józef 104
Przekop, Fr. Walery (of the Society of Christ) 104, 106
Przewłoka, Brother Franciszek, Albertine Order (Kraków) 353, 355
Przybyła, Fr. (Śląsk) 110
Przybyła, Rev. Dr. Franciszek 375
Przychodzeń, Fr. Eugeniusz (Łódź Diocese) 225
Przydacz, Fr. Jan 394
Pućka, Józef (Inowrocław District) 20, 131, 365
Putz, Rev. Canon Narcyz (Poznań) 296

Radzięta, Fr. Karol 308, 363
Rakowski, Fr. Kazimierz 225
Rasch (Dachau) 190, 255
Rascher, Dr. 272, 274, 321

Index

Ratajski, Fr. Mieczysław 225
Redig (Grenzdorf) 75, 76, 78–83
Redwitz (Dachau) 285–287, 319, 330
Rewera, Rev. Dean (Sandomierz Diocese) 279
Ribbentrop 6, 7, 18
Rogalski (from the industrial enterprise) 301
Rogler (Dachau) 190, 255
Roja, General 96
Rolbiecki, Fr. Władysław 115
Rommel 280
Roosevelt 250, 299, 359
Rosenberg 30, 211
Rosiński (Września) 6
Rosłaniec, Rev. Prof. Dr. Franciszek 290
Rowecki, General 119
Równy, Fr. Kazimierz 104
Różycki, Rev. Major 67
Ruppert (Dachau) 359, 366–368, 370
Rutecki, Fr. Aleksander 61
Rybak, Władysław (a Silesian) 294

Salamucha, Rev. Prof. Dr. 116, 171, 347
Samolej, Fr. Jan 110
Samoliński, Fr. Marian 346
Sarnyk (Sarnik), Władysław, seminarian (Włocławek) 237, 392
Sauckel, Fritz 257, 330
Scheffler, Fr. Konrad (Chełmno Diocese) 349
Scherwentke, Fr. Maksymilian (from Żydowo) 282
Schilling, Dr./Professor 271, 272, 321
Schönborn, Rev. Msgr. (from Kruszwica) 20, 67, 120, 248
Schreiber, Fr. Edmund (from Sadki) 282
Schrijvers, Fr. J. (Redemptorist) 54
Schubert (Sachsenhausen) 96, 97, 100, 104, 105, 111–113, 119, 120, 123, 124, 135, 144, 145, 206
Schulert, Fr. Kazimierz (from Pobiedzisko) 265
Schultz (Dachau) 312, 313, 346
Schwarz, Fr. Antoni 171
Seifert (Sachsenhausen) 96, 111
Seitz, Richard 246, 316
Seroka, Rev. Pastor 29
Sibilski, Fr. (Poznań) 177
Sibilski, Fr. Czesław 296
Siekiera, Fr. (Łódź Diocese) 225
Sienkiewicz 89
Sievers 272
Sikorski, General 67, 308
Sikorzak (Inowrocław) 9
Siudziński, Fr. Mieczysław (Inowrocław District) 20, 366
Siwa, Fr. Roman (Gniezno Diocese) 308
Skarga, Piotr, seminarian (Vilnius seminary) 371
Skoblewski, oblate Fr. Mieczysław (Inowrocław) 20, 98, 99

Skoczylas, Rev. Prof. Kazimierz (Łódź seminary) 279
Skórnicki, Fr. Antoni (Poznań Diocese) 177
Skórnicki, Fr. Władysław (Poznań Diocese) 267
Skowron, Fr. (Inowrocław District) 20
Skowronek, Jan, seminarian (from Rybnik) 292, 365
Skowroński, Dr. 346
Skowroński, Fr. Alfred 250
Skowroński, Fr. Edward (Inowrocław District) 20, 114, 366
Śledziński, Fr. 104, 112–114
Smaruj, Fr. Stefan 152, 292, 329, 365
Sobaszek, Fr. Aleksander (from Siedlemin) 282
Sobieszczyk, Fr. Ludwik 20, 365
Sokołowski, Rev. Prof. Franciszek (Płock Diocese) 61, 91, 267
Sokołowski, Fr. Stanisław (Płock Diocese) 61, 79, 267, 358, 367
Sommer, Fr. 171
Sonsała, Fr. (Society of the Divine Word) 99
Spengler 294
Spiess, Heinrich 271
Spitzig, Fr. Gustav 357
Sroka, Rev. Pastor 69
Stablewski, Fr. 5
Stachowiak, Fr. Witold (from Wągrowiec) 282
Stachowicz, Prof. 300
Stachowicz, Fr. Stanisław (Lublin Diocese) 110
Stachowski, Fr. Bronisław (Poznań) 225, 296
Stalin 17, 18, 250, 301
Staniszewski, Fr. (Poznań Diocese) 267
Staniszewski, Rev. Prof. Wacław (Lublin) 110, 278
Staszak, Fr. Feliks (Września) 5
Stauffenberg 339
Stawecki, Fr. Ed. 153, 292
Stawiński, Stanisław 292
Stefaniak, Rev. Pastor Stanisław (Gdynia) 267
Stepczyński, Fr. 209
Stępniak, Fr. Leon 153
Sterczewski, Fr. 209
Stirlitz 160, 161
Stirll, Colonel 316, 322, 333, 334, 343
Stirll's wife 322, 323, 334
Strehl, Fr. Mieczysław (Inowrocław District) 20, 26, 29, 68, 69, 112, 177
Stryszyk, Rev. Major 92
Styczyński, Rev. Msgr. (Gniezno) 224, 251
Stylo, Zygmunt 266
Styp-Rekowski, Fr. Józef 116, 212, 285
Suhard, Cardinal (of Paris) 204
Sulek, Fr. (Poznań Diocese) 267
Suszczyński, Fr. (Gniezno) 251

Świadek, Fr. Antoni (from Bydgoszcz) 352
Święs, Fr. Władysław 279
Sych, Fr. Henryk 153, 365
Szaferski (Dachau) 166, 181, 188, 212, 213, 285, 308, 317
Szczepański, Fr. 115
Szczerkowski brothers, priests 153
Szczypiński, Fr. Stanisław (Chełmno Diocese) 28, 275
Szela, Jakub 138
Szkiłądź, Fr. Bolesław 104
Szlachta, Fr. Jan 171
Szotek, Fr. Henryk (from Sandomierz) 251
Szukalski, Rev. Prof. 17, 46, 112
Szweda, Fr. Konrad 279
Szymański, Fr. Bronisław 28, 54, 72, 83, 85
Szymański, Fr. Bruno (Świecie) 35, 112
Szymański, Rev. Dean (Poznań Diocese) 267
Szymański, Fr. S. 225
Szymaszek, Fr. Jan, a Redemptorist 29, 83
Szymczak, Fr. (Włocławek Diocese) 267

Tadrzyński, Rev. Prof. 131, 365
Thérèse, Saint, a Carmelite 122, 139, 153, 175, 184, 234–244, 248, 251, 278, 346
Tokarek, Fr. Wacław 325
Tokłowicz, Fr. Al. (Września) 209
Tomczak, Fr. Leon (Poznań Diocese) 267
Tomczak, Fr. Stefan 153
Tomiński, Fr. Antoni 282
Trembecki, Jan 71, 76
Tresckow, Henning von 339
Trochonowicz, Rev. Dr. Franciszek 110, 278
Trzaskowa, Fr. Jan (Płock Diocese) 302
Tybor, Fr. Tadeusz 29
Tyczka, Fr. Kazimierz 17
Tylżanowski, Fr. Jacek 279
Tymiński, Fr. Jan 104

Viola, Fr. Alfons 225
Vogt 344, 346, 355, 369

Wagner 165–168, 176, 188, 250, 256, 259–261, 319
Wajda, Fr. Franciszek 308
Wala (a Silesian) 305
Walewski, Fr. (from Tomaszów, a Salesian) 28
Walorek, Fr. Marian 225, 296
"War" (Sachsenhausen) 110, 112, 115, 130
Warkoczewski, Fr. Henryk 5, 6, 16
Warmiński, Fr. (Poznań Diocese) 267
Wasielewski, Fr. (Poznań) 177
Wąsowicz, Fr. (from Brudnia) 27, 29, 67, 94, 96, 97

Weber, Fr. Szczepan (Szubin District) 21, 67, 94, 118, 296, 365
Wedelstaedt, Fr. Konrad 61
Wegner, Pastor Henryk 175, 340
Weiss (Dachau) 285, 287, 289, 303, 304, 315, 359
Weizsaecker 6
Welter 242, 243
Werbiński, Fr. (from Gniezno) 225
Wernike ("Black"), (Dachau) 363, 282
Wetmański, Bishop 232
Wierzbicki, Rev. Dr. Kornel 225, 281
Wierzbicki, Rev. Pastor (from Kościelec) 20, 114
Wilamowski, Fr. Aleksander (Chełmno Diocese) 209
Wilczewski, Fr. Bruno 72
Wilemski, Fr. Józef (Chełmno Diocese) 209
Wilhelm, Franciszek (a Silesian) 344
Wilhelm, Georg 234, 245, 246, 250, 251, 256, 269, 270, 279, 285, 294, 316, 319
Wilkans, Rev. Msgr. Julian, a colonel (Poznań) 224, 296
Willi (Dachau) 161, 162, 171, 180, 181, 188, 200, 210, 228, 236, 253
Winczewski, Fr. 132
Wład, General 48, 100
Włodarczyk, Fr. (Inowrocław Diocese) 20, 67

Wohlfeil, Fr. 100, 112
Wojciechowski, Fr. Jan (from Kozielsko) 225, 329
Wojciechowski, Fr. Stanisław 225
Wojciechowski, Fr. Stefan 225
Wojewódka, Fr. Ignacy 41
Wojnowski, Prof. (Gdańsk) 35
Wojsa, Rev. Canon Stanisław (from Lublin) 232
Wolak, Fr. 272
Wolniak, Fr. Jan 153, 280
Wolniewicz, Fr. Julian (Poznań Diocese) 279
Woltman, Fr. Bernard 153
Woźniak, Fr. Józef 225, 300, 365, 394
Woźniczak, Fr. Feliks 296
Wróblewski, Rev. Prof. (Inowrocław District) 19, 247, 290, 346, 365
Wronka, Henryk 354

Zabłocki, Rev. Dean (Inowrocław) 16
Zagrodzki, Fr. Adolf 279
Załuska, Rev. Msgr. Paweł 279
Zawistowski, Rev. Prof. Dr. Antoni (Lublin) 116, 278
Zawisza, Rev. Dr. (Lublin, a Salesian) 110, 278
Zbytniewski, Brother Cyprian (from Niepokalanów) 279
"Zdzich," a priest 54, 55, 62, 65, 67, 69, 71–74, 83, 88, 93, 96, 99, 102, 103, 105, 113–116, 120–124, 134, 135, 146, 147, 154, 161, 163–165, 167, 168, 170–172, 175, 176, 183, 188–191, 200, 202–204, 219, 221, 224, 228–230, 235–237, 239, 247, 248, 250, 251, 253, 254, 257, 277, 287, 288, 294, 302, 308, 316, 320, 329, 332–334, 340, 349, 352, 361, 365, 367, 370, 372–376, 386, 387, 392, 394
Zenker, Rev. Dean 365
Ziarniak, Fr. Dobromir (Inowrocław District) 20, 117, 177, 248, 266, 340
Zięba, Fr. Adam (from Kraków) 279
Zieliński, Fr. 131
Zieliński, a Jesuit seminarian 295
Zieliński, Rev. Prof. Tadeusz 365
Zieliński, Zygmunt 306
Zielonka, Fr. Stefan (Płock Diocese) 267, 292, 336, 355
Ziemski, Rev. Msgr. (from Toruń) 98
Zientarski, Rev. Dr. Roman 365
Zier (Dachau) 188
Zill (Dachau) 180–182, 212, 213, 215, 217, 256
Zimmerman (Dachau) 301
Zimny, Fr. Henryk 257
Ziółkowski, Fr. Jan 131, 365
Złotożyński, Fr. Antoni 104
Zuske, Rev. Dr. Stanisław 281
Żychliński, Rev. Prof. 62, 175, 182

www.ingramcontent.com/pod-product-compliance
Lightning Source LLC
Chambersburg PA
CBHW081533300426
44116CB00015B/2611